Standard Catalog of®

32nd Edition

UNITED STATES
PAPER MONEY

THE WORLD'S AUTHORITY ON PAPER MONEY

Published by

Krause Publications, a division of F+W Media, Inc.
700 East State Street • Iola, WI 54990-0001
715-445-2214 • 888-457-2873
www.krausebooks.com

To order books or other products call toll-free 1-800-258-0929
or visit us online at www.shopnumismaster.com

Photos courtesy of Stack's, Lyn Knight, and selections from the collections of William Brandimore, Ray Czahor, Chester L. Krause, and the Aubrey and Aideline Beebe Collection at the American Numismatic Association Museum, Colorado Springs, CO

ISSN 1081-5996
ISBN-13: 978-1-4402-3800-0
ISBN-10: 1-4402-3800-6

Cover Design by Jana Tappa
Designed by Sandi Carpenter
Edited by George Cuhaj

Printed in China

Table of Contents

Introduction

Though paper media representing gold or other intrinsic-value stores of wealth has been issued in the United States and its predecessor colonies and territories since 1690, the widespread acceptance of paper currency by the American people is a comparatively recent development and came only grudgingly.

Paper money emissions by the British colonies in New England, the earliest paper currency within the borders of what is now the United States of America, circulated alongside other untraditional exchange media such as Indian wampum shells and musket balls during chronic periods of shortages of "real" - coined - money.

Even though the first issues of an organized central government, the Continental Congress' currency notes, promised to pay the bearer face value in "Spanish milled dollars, or the value thereof in gold or silver," these notes circulated at a heavy discount - if they were accepted at all. The fledgling government's final solution for the Continental Currency problem, accepting them in 1787 at 1% of face value in exchange for interest bearing bonds, did nothing to bolster public confidence in paper money.

Neither did the often larcenous "banking" practices of the various elements of the private sector to whom the note-issuing prerogative fell. With states denied the power to issue money by the Constitution of the United States, and the powers of the Federal Government to do so left unspecified; various private issues of banks, railroads, utilities, and even individual citizens, cropped up, with varying resources to guarantee their value, until the Government halted the practice in 1863.

By the late 19th Century, U.S.-issued paper money had become a viable part of the nation's commerce as people recognized that such notes were, indeed, redeemable on demand for gold or silver. By 1963, paper currency was such an ingrained part of the American economy that the Government was able to remove all specie-redemption quality from its currency issues, raising only minimal objections from strict interpretationists of the Constitution.

Now, ironically, paper money may be on the way out as a circulating medium of exchange. The growth of demand deposits (checking accounts), electronic fund transfers and the arrival of the home computer age may one day soon put an end for the need for physical symbols of wealth to pass from hand to hand.

Scope of this catalog

It is not the intention of this catalog to provide a reference to every type of official and unofficial paper currency which has circulated in the United States. Indeed, such a project between the covers of one volume represents an impossible, though intriguing challenge.

Rather, this catalog will provide a guide to those paper money issues since 1812 of the Government of the United States of America, along with several related currency issues which are traditionally collected by paper money hobbyists in conjunction with the regular issues of the U.S.

Such a scope is intended, therefore, to provide the collector of U.S. paper money with a catalog reflective of the current state of the hobby.

The reader will be provided with sufficient background information to facilitate and illuminate the building of a collection, without being subjected to fiscal, legislative or historical data that would be of interest to only a small minority of readers.

Numbering System

In using this book, you will immediately notice that "KL" and "FR" numbers are used at the beginning of each entry. This catalog system was invented as a shorthand identification system for use in price lists, advertisements and auction catalogs where space is at a premium. Instead of writing a full description of a $1 Legal Tender Note, series 1923, you can write KL-28. Therefore, many more notes can be listed in an ad for the same cost. The two commonly used numbering systems are Friedberg (FR) numbers, invented by pioneer cataloger Robert Friedberg, and Krause-Lemke (KL) numbers created by Chester L. Krause and Robert F. Lemke as an improvement. Both catalog numbers are given for each listing in this book for your convenience.

History of Pre-Federal Paper Money in the U.S.

To better understand the forces which shaped the United States Government's issues of paper currency since 1861, it is necessary to look backward to the many and varied public and private currency issues which preceded them in this country. The use of paper money in the area which would become the United States actually predates its use in many parts of Western Europe and in most of the rest of the world. While paper currencies had been in use in China since the 7th Century, when it was known as "flying money" because of its light weight and ability to circulate widely with ease, it was not until the late 17th Century that the western world began experiments with non-metallic circulating currencies. Surprisingly quickly, the North American continent had its first "paper money" issues in 1685, when the Intendant of New France (Canada) issued promissory notes hand-printed on pieces of playing cards, to circulate as money until the delayed arrival of the paymaster.

The Massachusetts Bay Colony followed suit soon after, issuing in December, 1690, £7,000 worth of the first publicly authorized paper money notes in the western world to pay expenses of a border war with Canada (previous paper money issues in Europe and North America had been either issued by banks, or were emergency measures not authorized by any public body).

Following that precedent, by the turn of the 18th Century, other colonies were emitting paper currencies as needed to run their specie-short economies. By the end of the War for Independence, all 13 colonies had issued some form of paper currency. Beginning in May, 1775, the Congress of the newly unified former colonies began the issue of Continental Currency to finance its fight for freedom.

The Continental Currency was plagued, though, by increasing public distrust. The Continental paper dollar was able to hold its value at par with a specie dollar only until October, 1777, by which time widespread counterfeiting by British, Tories and opportunists conspired with the natural inflation of a printing press economy and increasing uncertainty as to the outcome of the war to push the exchange ratio of the Continental Currency to $11 in paper for $10 in specie.

After that point, the devaluation accelerated. By the next year, October, 1778, the ratio was 4.66 to 1.

The low point was reached in April, 1780, when a dollar in silver or gold was worth $40 Continental. And these were the *official* exchange ratios adopted by the Congress and many of the states, to offset the rampant inflation. In actual commerce, the Continentals were all but worthless. George Washington lamented that it took a wagonful of Continental Currency to purchase a wagonload of supplies for his army. A truer measure of the value of the Government paper currency could be found in the fact that by October, 1787, amid speculation that the Continental Currency might never be redeemable, it was selling at the rate of $250 paper for $1 specie. Eventually, the Government issued 6% interest bearing bonds at the rate of $1 for every $100 of Continental Currency turned in.

Issued current with the Colonial and Continental currencies were numerous privately-sponsored paper monies produced by banks (as early as 1732 in Connecticut), utilities, merchants, individuals and even churches.

These issues continued after the Revolutionary War, and proliferated in the 19th Century. Today, lumped together under the generic, if not altogether correct, label of "broken bank notes," these colorful, historic notes and their collectible adjuncts make up a significant portion of the paper money hobby's interest.

The tens of thousands of privately-issued bank and scrip notes of the 1800s ranged in denomination from one-half cent to several thousand dollars. While today their collector value depends on a combination of rarity, condition and demand; their value when issued was solely dependent on the reputation of the issuing authority - be it bank, railroad or Main Street apothecarian. In those days, when a note might be worth every cent of its face value or might be worth nothing more than the paper on which it was printed, an entire industry sprang up to supply banks and merchants with accurate, timely information about which notes would pass current, which should be accepted only at a discount, and those from an issuer who had gone "broken." In addition, because of the wealth of larcenous talent available for changing broken bank notes into "good" notes through the alteration of a bank or city name, or raising the denomination of a note from $1 to $10 by deft penmanship; those who handled the dizzying variety of paper money in circulation in the mid 19th Century needed books which listed and described the genuine issues of a particular bank. (It is, incidentally, from the common name of these paper money reporting services that the name *Bank Note Reporter* was derived for the monthly paper money newspaper published by the publisher of this catalog.)

The only restraints on the issue of paper money at that time were those which the individual states cared to apply, and such restraints were infrequent and ineffective.

The Federal Government put an effective end to these halcyon days of currency free-for-all in 1863, by imposing a 10% tax on outstanding notes; and later through the 14th Amendment to the Constitution, forbidding the private issue of circulating media of exchange altogether.

The Government of the United States of America has attained a monopoly on the note-issuing function which it has maintained, except in localized emergency situations, to this day.

Paper Money Grading

Introduction

Grading is the most controversial component of paper money collecting. Small differences in grade can mean significant differences in value.

To facilitate communication between sellers and buyers, it is essential that grading terms and their meanings be as standardized and as widely used as possible. The standardization should reflect common usage as much as practicable.

The grades and definitions as set forth below cannot reconcile all the various systems and grading terminology variants. Rather, the attempt is made here to try and diminish the controversy with some common-sense grades and definitions that aim to give more precise meaning to the grading language of paper money.

Grading Guide

Crisp Uncirculated (CU): A perfectly preserved note, never mishandled by the issuing authority, a bank teller, the public or a collector.

Paper is clean and firm, without discoloration. Corners are sharp and square, without any evidence of rounding. (Rounded corners are often a tell-tale sign of a cleaned or "doctored" note.) An uncirculated note will have its original, natural sheen.

About Uncirculated (AU): A virtually perfect note, with some minor handling. May show evidence of bank counting folds at a corner or one light fold through the center, but not both. An AU note cannot be creased, a crease being a hard fold which has usually "broken" the surface of the note.

Paper is clean and bright with original sheen. Corners are not rounded.

Extremely Fine (XF): very attractive note, with light handling. May have a maximum of three light folds or one strong crease.

Paper is clean and bright with original sheen. Corners may show only the slightest evidence of rounding. There may also be the slightest sign of wear where a fold meets the edge.

Very Fine (VF): An attractive note, but with more evidence of handling and wear. May have a number of folds both vertically and horizontally.

Paper may have minimal dirt, or possible color smudging. Paper itself is still relatively crisp and not floppy.

There are no tears into the border area, although the edges do show slight wear. Corners also show wear but not full rounding.

Fine: A note which shows considerable circulation, with many folds, creases and wrinkling. Paper is not excessively dirty but may have some softness.

Edges may show much handling, with minor tears in the border area. Tears may not extend into the design. There will be no center hole because of excessive folding.

Colors are clear but not very bright. A staple hole or two would not be considered unusual wear in a Fine note. Overall appearance is still on the desirable side.

Very Good (VG): A well-used note, abused but still intact.

Corners may have much wear and rounding, tiny nicks, tears may extend into the design, some discoloration may be present, staining may have occurred, and a small hole may be seen at center from excessive folding.

Staple and pinholes are usually present, and the note itself is quite limp but no pieces of the note are missing. A note in VG condition may still have an overall not unattractive appearance. **Good (G):** A well-worn and heavily-used note. Normal damage from prolonged circulation will include strong multiple folds and creases, stains, pinholes and/or staple holes, dirt, discoloration, edge tears, center hole, rounded corners and an overall unattractive appearance. No large pieces of the note may be missing. Graffiti is commonly seen on notes in Good condition.

Fair: A totally limp, dirty, and very well-used note. Large pieces may be half torn off or missing besides the defects mentioned under the Good category. Tears will be larger, obscured portions of the note will be bigger. **Poor:** A "rag" with severe damage because of wear, staining, pieces missing, graffiti, larger holes. May have tape holding pieces of the note together. Trimming may have taken place to remove rough edges.

The above Introduction and Grading Guide is an adaptation work prepared under the guidance of the Grading Committee of the International Bank Note Society.

How To Look At A Banknote

In order to ascertain the grade of a note, it is essential to examine it out of a holder and under a good light. Move the note around so that light bounces off at different angles. Try holding it up obliquely so that the note is almost even with your eye as you look up at the light. Hard-to-see folds or slight creases will show up under such examination.

Cleaning, Washing, Pressing

Cleaning, washing or pressing paper money is generally harmful and reduces both the grade and the value of a note. At the very least, a washed or pressed note may lose its original sheen and its surface may become lifeless and dull. The defects a note has, such as folds and creases, may not necessarily be completely eliminated and their telltale marks can be detected under a good light. Carelessly washed notes may also have white streaks where the folds or creases were (or still are).

Processing of a note will automatically reduce it at least one full grade.

Other Defects

Glue, tape or pencil marks may sometimes be successfully removed. While such removal will leave a cleaned surface, it will improve the overall appearance of the note without concealing any of its defects. Under such circumstances, the grade of that note may also be improved.

The words "pinholes," "staple holes," "trimmed," "writing on face... tape marks," etc., should always be added to the description of a note.

The Term "Uncirculated"

The word "Uncirculated" is used in this grading guide only as a qualitative measurement of the appearance of a note. It has nothing at all to do with whether or not an issuer has actually released the note to circulation. Either a note is uncirculated in condition or it is not, there can be no degrees of uncirculated. Defects in color, centering and the like may be included in a description but the fact that a note is or is not in uncirculated condition should not be a disputable point.

Large Size Currency

For the convenience of the reader, brief and basically historical backgrounds have been provided for each of the major types of U.S. currency. No great amount of fiscal or legislative data has been provided, except where it might serve to clarify some aspects of the notes themselves or their collectibility.

Demand Notes

Despite two issues of interest-bearing Treasury notes in 1860-1861, the opening guns of the Civil War found the United States Government short of the necessary funds to put down the rebellion in a protracted war.

Congress moved swiftly in the national emergency to provide legislation authorizing the issue of $60,000,000 by Acts of July 17, and Aug. 5, 1861.

It is generally believed among numismatists today that the Demand Notes were backed by faith in the Government alone; but this was not entirely the case. By the terms of the authorizing legislation, the Demand Notes were not payable in gold. But, in a circular from the Secretary of the Treasury sent out before the suspension of specie payments on Dec. 21, 1861, they were declared payable in coin, and the Government redeemed them as such in order to sustain its credit. Thus, for a short time in 1861, the Demand Notes were quoted on a par with gold. However, as the war progressed, in most parts of the country the Demand Notes - and all other paper money of the U.S. Government - were acceptable only at a discount, even though they were receivable for all payments to the Government, including duties.

The Demand Notes took their famous "Greenback" nickname from the color of their back designs (back designs in themselves were scarce on paper money in the U.S. prior to the Civil War). The name was subsequently applied to virtually every other form of U.S. currency and remains current today.

Because the United States Government was not prepared to be in the note-printing business in 1861, the work of producing the Demand Notes was contracted to the American Bank Note Company and National Bank Note Company. Working with essentially stock currency elements, the private contractors turned out more than 7.25 million $5, $10 and $20 Demand Notes.

The actual "issuing" of the notes required that they be signed by the Treasurer of the United States (Francis E. Spinner) and the Register of the Treasury (Lucius E. Chittenden), or persons designated by them.

Accordingly, platoons of clerks within the Treasury Department were put to work autographing Demand Notes. However, on the very earliest specimens, the engraved blanks on the face of the notes indicated only the office of the signer, and the clerks were required to pen in the words "for the" on each note as they signed it, a most laborious process that was eliminated with the addition of "for the" on the engraved face plates themselves. The Demand Notes which survive today with the hand-signed "for the" on the face are much scarcer than the engraved version, and command a significant price premium.

Rarity and value of the Demand Notes is also affected by the engraved location on the face of the note indicating where the notes were issued and, therefore, payable.

The obligation on the notes reads: "The United States promises to pay to the bearer five dollars (or ten dollars or twenty dollars) on demand ... payable by the Assistant Treasurer of the United States at..."

One of five cities was then engraved. Those notes payable at New York are far and away the most common among the survivors, with Philadelphia second and Boston third. Specimens which promise redemption in Cincinnati and, especially, St. Louis, are extremely rare and seldom encountered.

United States Notes (Legal Tender Notes)

The longest-lived type of U.S. paper money, the United States Notes (called interchangeably Legal Tender Notes because of the wording of the obligation) was first authorized in 1862 and is still current today, though none have been issued since 1969.

The subject of major Constitutional debate at the time of their issue, the notes did much to pave the way for future issues of U.S. currency backed only by the credit of the Government.

While there are five official "issues" of large size Legal Tender Notes, as well as the small size series, they are generally collected today by type (major design) and, occasionally, by signature combination. The First Issue of United States Notes, dated March 10, 1862, was issued in denominations of $5, $10, $20, $50, $100, $500 and $1,000.

Two different varieties of notes, bearing different obligation wording on the backs, are popularly collected among the First Issue notes.

The earliest First Issues bear what is known as the First Obligation on back, reading: "This note is a legal tender for all debts public and private, except duties on imports and interest on the public debt, and is exchangeable for U.S. six per cent twenty year bonds, redeemable at the pleasure of the United States after five years."

The Second Obligation, much rarer, reads as follows: "This note is a legal tender for all debts, public and private, except duties on imports and interest on the public debt, and is receivable in payment of all loans made to the United States."

These First Issue notes do not carry the large face inscriptions "United States Note" or "Treasury Note," which are found on later Legal Tender issues.

Dated Aug. 1, 1862, and issued only in denominations of $1 and $2, the Second Issue U.S. Notes carry the Second Obligation on back.

The Third Issue U.S. Notes, dated March 10, 1863, were issued in denominations from $5 through $1,000, again using the Second Obligation.

Fourth Issue Legal Tenders were authorized by an Act of Congress dated March 3, 1863, and issued in denomination from $1 through $10,000 in the various Series of 1869, 1874, 1878, 1880, 1907, 1917 and 1923. Those notes in Series 1869 bear the label "Treasury Notes" on face, with all later issues carrying the "United States Notes" designation.

Back obligation on all series is the same: "This note is a legal tender at its face value for all debts public and private, except duties on imports and interest on the public debt."

The Fifth Issue Legal Tenders consisted solely of the Series 1901 $10 note (the popular Bison design), issued under the authority of the Legal Tender Acts of 1862-1863. A new face obligation was introduced: "This note is a legal tender for ten dollars subject to the provisions of Section 3588 R.S.," on back, the obligation reads: "This note is a legal tender at its face value for all debts public and private except duties on imports and interest on the public debt."

Compound Interest Treasury Notes

Circulating currency notes which grew in face value each six-month period they remained in circulation were just one of the innovations to which the Federal Government turned to finance the protracted Civil War.

Authorized by Congressional Acts of March 3, 1863, and June 30, 1864, these notes were intended to circulate for three years, bearing interest at the then-attractive rate of six percent a year, compounded semi-annually. The backs of each note carry a table spelling out the actual interest earned and current face value of the note through maturity. Theoretically, a note that was acquired when issued at face value, could be spent a year later as $10.60; although little is known as to whether this theory worked in practice. It is known, though, that those persons holding the notes at maturity generally took their profit, leaving very few surviving specimens for today's collectors.

Neither should it be assumed that the surviving notes continue to earn interest. The interest payments ended at maturity.

The face of each note bears a surcharge in large gold letters, reading "Compound Interest Treasury Note," along with corresponding numerals of issue value. Unfortunately, the gold ink used for these overprints contributed greatly to the demise of the notes themselves, for it is highly acidic and attacks the rather fragile paper to the point where many examples are found with this surcharge "burned" into and through the paper. Additionally, the $50 and $100 notes, the highest values which could practically be said to have circulated, were extensively counterfeited and the Treasury was forced to withdraw them in the face of such "competition."

In any denomination, the Compound Interest Treasury Notes are scarce in better than Fine condition.

Examples are known with a number of different issue dates on the face. The $10-$50 notes with the June 10 or July 15, 1864, dates are the rarest, with dates from Aug. 15, 1864, through Oct. 16, 1865, being more common; while in the $100 notes, the June 10, 1864, date is most common, followed by the Aug. 15, 1864-Sept. 1, 1865, dates. No July 15, 1864-dated $100 Compound Interest Treasury Notes are known, nor are there any reported survivors among the $500 and $1,000 denominations, though the Treasury reports several examples still officially outstanding.

Interest Bearing Notes

As a group, probably the rarest type of U.S. paper money is the Interest Bearing Note issues of the Civil War era. Like the Compound Interest Treasury Notes and the Refunding Certificates (also interest bearing), they were something of a desperation currency issue by the Federal Government to bolster the Union war chest.

The Interest Bearing Notes were issued in a trio of distinctive types, all of which are very rare, or unknown to have survived.

The first issue was a series of One-Year Notes, issued under authority of the Act of March 3, 1863, and paying interest of five percent for one year. Face designs of the one-year issue were similar to the Compound Interest Treasury Notes, without the gold surcharges. Backs were significantly different, lacking the tabular interest-figuring chart. A face inscription reads: "One year after date the United States will pay to the bearer with five per interest - dollars." On back, the obligation was worded: "This note is a legal tender at its face value, excluding interest, for all debts public and private, except duties on imports and interest on the public debt."

Denominations of the One-Year Notes ranged from $10 through $5,000, with no specimens of the $500, $1,000 or $5,000 known. Each note bears an individually stamped date of issue on the face. One year from that date, the notes were redeemable for face value plus interest.

Two-Year Notes were also authorized by the March 3, 1863 Act of Congress. Issued only in the $50, $100, $500 and $1,000 denominations, and paying five percent interest per year for a two-year term, they are naturally much scarcer because of the high return they offered the holder near the end of the Civil War. Designs were completely different from the One-Year Notes, although the face and back inscriptions are similar.

Like the Interest Bearing Notes themselves, the Three-Year Notes are comprised of three separate issues, due to three different authorizing Acts of Congress; July 17, 1861, June 30, 1864, and March 3,1865. Again issued in the higher denominations, from $50 through $5,000, the notes paid interest at the rate of 7-3/10 percent a year; the highest rate the Government paid on circulating notes. Like the Compound Interest Treasury Notes, the actual amount of interest is spelled out on the notes, though in this case it is expressed in terms of interest per day. Thus, the $50 note expresses a promise to pay interest of one cent per day, while the $5,000 bill paid interest at the rate of $1 per day.

That the notes were not intended to circulate widely is indicated by the fact that they are payable to the order, not to the bearer. That is, there is a blank on the face of every Three-Year Interest Bearing Note for the name of the original holder, and a corresponding blank on back for endorsement at the time of maturity.

Another feature which makes the Three-Year Notes unusual among U.S. paper money issues was the original attachment of five coupons to each note. Each coupon indicated the interest payable for a six-month period, and was removed from the note when that interest was collected semi-annually. The final interest payment was made when the note itself was presented for redemption at the end of the three-year period. This arrangement is spelled out on the face of each note.

As mentioned earlier, these notes are of the greatest rarity, most of them unknown to survive, existing only in proof form or existing in a unique, or nearly so, issued example.

Refunding Certificates

More of a government security than circulating medium of exchange, the Refunding Certificates authorized by Congress in the Act of Feb. 26, 1879, brought these interest bearing instruments within the reach of more Americans in that they were denominated at $10.

The authorizing legislation intended that these notes bear interest of four percent annually in perpetuity. However, in 1907 Congress passed a law stopping interest payments as of July 1, forever fixing the "face" value of these notes at $21.30. Presumably at that time the incentive for the public to hold these notes was removed, and their redemption accelerated.

The $10 Refunding Certificates were issued in two different forms, one type payable to the bearer, the other to the order of the original purchaser. Like the Three-Year Interest Bearing Notes, the Refunding Certificates payable to order had spaces on face and back for the owner and endorser. The "pay to order" type is far rarer than the "pay to bearer" variety.

Rather than being redeemable for specie, per se, these notes, in amounts of $50 or more, were convertible into four percent bonds.

Silver Certificates

Among the most popular of U.S. notes due to their wealth of design excellence and challenging, but not impossible rarity, the Silver Certificates of 1878-1963 comprise five major issues of large size notes, and the various series of small size notes.

Authorizing legislation for all issues were the Congressional Act of Feb. 28, 1878, and Aug. 4, 1886.

The First Issue Silver Certificates consist of Series 1878 and 1880 notes in denominations from $10-$1,000. The notes of 1878, besides bearing the engraved signatures of G.W. Scofield, Register of the Treasury, and James Gilfillan, Treasurer of the U.S., have on their face an engraved or autographed countersignature of the Assistant Treasurers in New York, Washington, D.C., and San Francisco, attesting that the requisite amount of silver dollars had been deposited in their offices to cover the face value of the notes. In addition to the Series 1878 countersigned notes, several $20 Series 1880 Silver Certificates are known bearing the engraved countersignature of T. Hillhouse, Assistant Treasurer at New York.

The silver bills' Second Issue was made up of notes from $1 through $1,000 in the Series of 1886, 1891 and 1908, although not all denominations were issued in all series

The "Educational" notes, $1, $2, and $5 Silver Certificates of Series 1896, are the sole component of the Third Issue.

Similarly, the Fourth Issue Silver Certificates are made up of $1, $2 and $5 notes of the Series of 1899.

The Silver Certificates of the Fifth Issue are the Series 1923 $1 and $5 notes.

The obligation on the First Issue notes reads: "This certifies that I there have been deposited with the Treasurer of the U.S. at Washington, D.C. (or Assistant Treasurers at few York and San Francisco) payable at his office to the bearer on demand silver dollars. This certificate is receivable for customs, taxes and all public dues and when so received may be reissued."

Obligation on the last four issues of silver notes was worded: "This certifies that there have been deposited in the Treasury of the United States silver dollars payable to the bearer on demand. This certificate is receivable for customs, taxes and all public dues and when so received may be issued."

Treasury or Coin Notes

Pushed through Congress by the silver mining industry, the authorizing legislation of July 14, 1890, which created the Treasury Notes carefully did not specify that they be redeemable in silver; only that they be issued to pay for silver bullion purchased by the Treasury and that they be payable "in Coin" (hence the more commonly encountered name Coin Notes). With the cooperation of Treasury officials, silver sellers were able to turn their bullion in at artificially high official prices, receive the Coin Notes in payment, and redeem them immediately for gold coin and a tidy profit.

In denominations of $1, $2, $5, $10, $20, $100 and $1,000, the Coin Notes were issued in Series 1890 and 1891 form, the 1890 issue bearing ornately engraved green back designs that filled the print area. The $50 was issued only in Series of 1891, and the $500 note, which had been designed and a plate prepared with the portrait of Gen. William T. Sherman, was not issued at all. It was felt that even as late as 25 years after the Civil War, the use of Sherman's portrait on a currency note would inflame passions in the South. The 1890 notes are much scarcer and in greater demand than the Series 1891 issue, especially in new condition.

Face and back obligations of the Coin Notes are interesting and unique. They read: "This United States of America will pay to bearer - dollars in coin." And, "This note is a legal tender at its face value in payment of all debts public and private except when otherwise expressly stipulated in the contract

National Gold Bank Notes

Gold and the American West have been inseparably linked as part of this nation's history since the discovery of gold at Sutter's Mill in 1848. The unique, but short-lived National Gold Bank Note (N.G.B.N.) series was a contemporary part of "The Golden West," and today trades on that romantic image - and the inherent rarity of the notes themselves - as one of the most sought-after types of U.S. paper money.

The National Gold Bank Notes were authorized under the provisions of the Currency Act of July 12, 1870, and are very much analogous to the regular National Currency issue.

The principal difference, besides design, is that the National Gold Bank Notes were payable - and prominently said so - in gold coin. This was a concession to the traditional mistrust of Western America in paper currency and the California area's long history of gold use as the principal medium of exchange, whether in the form of gold dust, nuggets, private-issue coinage or genuine coins of the United States Mint.

Under the general provisions of the National Bank Act of 1863, the National Gold Banks had to secure the issue of their currency with the deposit of bonds with the Treasurer of the United States. However, the conditions for the N.G.B.N. issues were a bit more stringent. The Gold Banks could issue notes only to the value of 80% of their deposited bonds, while the other National banks could issue to 90%. Additionally, the Gold Banks were required to have on hand in their vaults gold coinage equal to 25% of the value of their note issue. The responsibility of redeeming these notes *in gold,* lay with the issuing banks, not the Federal Government, which did not resume specie payments until 1879, nearly a decade after the N.G.B.N. issues began. The Treasury would, of course, redeem National Gold Bank Notes for other lawful currency.

This gold redemption property gave the N.G.B.Ns the necessary credibility, and they circulated at par with the precious metal. They circulated so extensively that surviving notes are generally found in conditions which many collectors would find unacceptable in other U.S. currency types. No strictly uncirculated National Gold Bank Note is known today, and the average condition found is Good to Very Good. Examples in Fine or better condition command attractive premiums in the infrequent times when they become available.

Though authorized in denominations from $5-$1,000, National Gold Bank Notes were issued to circulation only as high as $500. The face of each note was similar to corresponding denominations in the First Charter National Bank Note series, while the backs had as their central feature a photo-like engraving of a stack of U.S. gold pieces, representing $211.50 face value in $1 through $20 denominations.

In all, 10 National Gold Banks were chartered, nine in California and The Kidder National Gold Bank in Boston, Mass. Notes were actually printed for the Kidder N.G.B., and delivered, but the bank eventually returned them all for cancellation, never issuing them to circulation. The Kidder was the only National Gold Bank to have $1,000 notes prepared.

Because of the relatively small size of the issue, much can be determined about the issue and survivability of the National Gold Bank Notes.

In the period 1870-1878, exactly 196,849 notes, with a face value of $3,267,420, were issued.

Treasury records indicate a total of 6,639 notes remain outstanding (including four $500 examples, none of which are known to collectors).

Like the other National Bank Notes, National Gold Bank Notes are known in both Original Series and Series of 1875 issues, although all nine California banks did not issue all denominations in both series. Indeed, the Series 1875 notes are somewhat scarcer than the Original notes.

Federal Reserve Bank Notes

Often confused with the Federal Reserve Notes, which are currency issues of the Federal Reserve System itself, Federal Reserve Bank Notes were issued by the 12 individual Federal Reserve Banks, much like the National Bank Notes. Indeed, Federal Reserve Bank Notes, large and small size, carry the "National Currency" inscription. In the large size note-issuing period, the similarity of Federal Reserve Bank Notes to Federal Reserve Notes extended to nearly identical back designs in the $5-$50 denominations. FRBNs were also

issued in $1 and $2 denominations, while the FRNs were issued in value from $5 through $10,000.

Two separate issues of Federal Reserve Bank Notes comprise the large size issue, while there was a single

issue in small size.

The Series 1915 FRBNs were authorized under the terms of the Federal Reserve Act of Dec. 23, 1913. Issued only in denominations of $5-$20, only the banks in Atlanta, Chicago, Kansas City, Dallas and San Francisco participated, with the Frisco bank issuing only $5s.

Like the National Bank Notes, the obligation to pay the bearer on the FRBNs is made by the issuing bank, rather than the Fed system or U.S. Government. The security notice on the 1915 issue reads: "Secured by United States bonds deposited with the Treasurer of the United States."

That obligation was changed for the Series 1918 FRBNs, issued under authority of a Congressional Act of April 23, 1918. The modification reads: "Secured by United States certificates of indebtedness or United States one-year gold notes, deposited with the Treasurer of the United States."

The Series 1918 FRBNs consist of all denominations from $1 through $50, though again, not all 12 banks issued all denominations. For instance, only the Atlanta and St. Louis banks issued $20 Series 1918 FRBNs, while only St. Louis issued $50s.

Spurred initially by demand for the attractive "Battleship" back design of the $2, and the defiant eagle on the $1 (symbols of America's defense posture in World War I), all large size FRBNs are actively collected today, especially in new condition. A wealth of combinations of U.S. Government signatures combined with signatures of the various Governors and Cashiers of the individual issuing banks, creates myriad varieties to keep the series challenging.

Also contributing to the challenge is the sheer scarcity of surviving specimens. Treasury sources indicate just over $2 million worth of FRBNs outstanding, from a total issue of more than $760 million.

Federal Reserve Notes

Authorized by the Federal Reserve Act of Dec. 23, 1913 and first issued in 1914, the Federal Reserve Note is the only type of U.S. paper money which continues in production today.

The large size issues of FRNs are in two series, 1914, in denominations from $5-$100, and 1918, in denominations from $500-$10,000. Additionally two distinctive varieties of 1914 notes exist, those with red Treasury Seal and serial number, and those with the elements in blue. The Red Seal 1914 FRNs are considerably scarcer than the blue.

While they are issued to circulation through the twelve Federal Reserve Banks, the FRNs are an obligation of the United States Government, rather than bank named thereon (unlike the Federal Reserve Bank Notes). Neither are Federal Reserve Notes secured by government bonds, precious metals or other reserves. The obligation on FRNs simply states that: "The United States of America will pay to the bearer on demand - dollars."

On back, the redemption qualities of the large size FRNs was spelled out thus: "This note is receivable by all National and member banks and Federal Reserve Banks and for all taxes, customs and other public dues. It is redeemable in gold on demand at the Treasury Department of the United States in the city of Washington, District of Columbia or in gold or lawful money at any Federal Reserve Bank."

This redeemable-in-gold clause continued in use on the Series 1928 small size FRNs, but was revoked with the passage of the Gold Reserve Act of 1933. The obligation, beginning with the Series 1934 notes, was modified to read: "This note is legal tender for all debts, public and private, and is redeemable in lawful money at the United States Treasury, or at any Federal Reserve Bank."

Beginning with Series 1963, the obligation was changed to its present form: "This note is legal tender for all debts, public and private."

Wide variances in the number of notes printed for each bank in any particular series of a denomination have created many challenging issues within the Federal Reserve Note series, both large and small size.

NOTE: Three interesting, if not altogether popular among collectors, varieties exist within the large size FRNs bearing the White-Mellon Federal signature combination, and two within the Burke-McAdoo combination notes. The variations deal with the size and placement of the numeral-letter combination designating the bank through which the notes were issued, and appearing in the lower left corner of the face. The earliest variety has a large size combination, matching that in the upper right corner of the note. The second variety has the combination greatly reduced (compared to that in the upper right). The third reverts to the larger size, but the combination has been moved higher and more to the left, while the Treasury and Fed Bank Seals on each end of this variety have been moved closer to center. Not all three varieties exist on every bank in every combination. While the second and third varieties command some premium from interested collectors, the demand for them is not such as to greatly influence the market for the type as a whole, and they are, therefore, not cataloged individually.

Gold Certificates

With their bright orange back designs (though some early gold notes are uniface), the large size Gold Certificates issued from 1865 through 1928 are a popular and tangible reminder of the days when U.S. paper currency was "as good as gold."

While many of the earlier Gold Certificate issues were not designed to be used in general circulation, due to their high face value, later types did enter the channels of commerce, circulating alongside the myriad other currency issues of the late 19th and early 20th Centuries.

Nine separate issues of Gold Certificates were created in the large size series, several of which were used almost exclusively in inter-bank channels to transfer and settle gold accounts.

The first issue goldbacks were authorized by the Currency Act of March 3, 1863, and consisted of notes in denominations of $20, $100, $500, $1,000, $5,000 and $10,000. While examples of the two lowest denominations survive, they are extremely rare.

No known examples of the second issue Gold Certificates are known today. Issued pursuant to the same act, and countersigned and dated by hand in the 1870-71 period, they were in denominations of $100-$10,000 only.

Third issue gold notes, bearing the impression "Series of 1875," were also issued in limited denominations: $100, $500, and $1,000. Uniface, the issue is represented today by only a few examples of the $100 note.

With the fourth issue, Gold Certificates entered general circulation, and the type begins to be known by its series designation. Ten-dollar goldbacks were issued in Series 1907 and 1922; $20 in Series 1882, 1905,1906 and 1922; $50 in Series 1882,1913 and 1922; $100 in Series 1882 and 1922; $500 in Series 1882; $1,000 in Series 1882, 1907 and 1922; $5,000 in Series 1882 and 1888; and, $10,000 in Series 1882,1888 and 1900. Naturally, the notes in denominations above $100 are very rare, though not unknown.

To correspond the various issues to the series in these post-1875 notes; the fourth issue consisted of the Series 1882 notes; the fifth issue comprises the 1888 Series, the sixth is the 1900 $10,000 notes; the seventh issue Gold Certificates are the Series 1905, 1906 and 1907 $10 and $20 notes; the eighth is the $1,000 of Series 1907; and, the ninth issue of large size Gold Certificates are the Series 1913 ($50 only) and 1922 goldbacks in $10-$1,000 denominations.

United States Notes
One Dollar

Salmon P. Chase at left.

Numerals "1 2 3" vertically in center.

National Bank Note Co. American Bank Note Co. in lower border.
No ABNCo monogram.

KL#	Fr#	Series	Signatures	Seal	Fine	XF	CH CU (63)	Gem CU (65)
1	17	1862	Chittenden-Spinner	Small red	15,000.	60,000.	Rare	—

National Bank Note Co. American Bank Note Co. in lower border.
ABNCo monogram.

2	17a	1862	Chittenden-Spinner	Small red	450.	1250.	2860.	4250.

National Bank Note Co. twice in lower border. No ABNCo monogram.

3	16	1862	Chittenden-Spinner	Small red	325.	1300.	3250.	6000.

National Bank Note Co. twice in lower border. ABNCo. monogram upper right.

4	16a	1862	Chittenden-Spinner	Small red	675.	2750.	3000.	18,500.

George Washington at center, Columbus' discovery of land at upper left.
Red serial numbers. National Bank Note Co., bottom back.

KL#	Fr#	Series	Signatures	Seal	Fine	XF	CH CU (63)	Gem CU (65)
5	18	1869	Allison-Spinner	Large red	500.	1750.	4000.	10,000.

National Banh Note Co., lower portion back design.
Red serial numbers. Red ornamentation at right, face design.

KL#	Fr#	Series	Signatures	Seal	Fine	XF	CH CU (63)	Gem CU (65)
6	19	1874	Allison-Spinner	Small red	200.	750.	1775.	3750.

Engraved & Printed at the Bureau Engraving & Printing on face at right.
Columbian Bank Note Co., twice near bottom back.

KL#	Fr#	Series	Signatures	Seal	Fine	XF	CH CU (63)	Gem CU (65)
7	20	1875	Allison-New	Small red	255.	600.	1450.	2750.
			Series A in lower right face.					
8	21	1875	Allison-New	Small red	900.	3600.	9000.	11,000.
			Series B in lower right face.					
9	22	1875	Allison-New	Small red	1250.	3000.	15,000.	24,000.
			Series C in lower right face.					
10	23	1875	Allison-New	Small red	1200.	2000.	5250.	8500.
			Series D in lower right face.					
11	24	1875	Allison-New	Small red	1150.	8750.	31,700.	—
			Series E in lower right face.					
12	25	1875	Allison-New	Small red	1875.	5000.	13,000.	18,000.
13	26	1875	Allison-Wyman	Small red	200.	500.	1075.	2000.

Series 1878 at top margin, Printed by Bureau of Engraving & Printing at lower margin on back.

KL#	Fr#	Series	Signatures	Seal	Fine	XF	CH CU (63)	Gem CU (65)
14	27	1878	Allison-Gilfillan	Small red	275.	650.	1250.	3850.

George Washington at center, Columbus' discovery of land at upper left. Plain ONE at right. Blue serial number within an ornate panel.

KL#	Fr#	Series	Signatures	Seal	Fine	XF	CH CU (63)	Gem CU (65)
15	28	1880	Scofield-Gilfillan	Large brown	200.	500.	800.	1875.
16	29	1880	Bruce-Gilfillan	Large brown	200.	600.	1050.	1900.
17	30	1880	Bruce-Wyman	Large brown	190.	600.	975.	1750.
18	31	1880	Rosecrans-Huston	Large red	425.	1400.	3250.	6000.
19	32	1880	Rosecrans-Huston	Large brown	570.	2250.	3500.	5000.
20	33	1880	Rosecrans-Nebeker	Large brown	700.	2000.	5000.	8750.
21	34	1880	Rosecrans-Nebeker	Small red	190.	500.	1100.	1500.

George Washington at center, Columbus' discovery of land at upper left. Plain ONE at right. Blue serial number within an ornate panel.

KL#	Fr#	Series	Signatures	Seal	Fine	XF	CH CU (63)	Gem CU (65)
22	35	1880	Tillman-Morgan	Small red	175.	600.	1050.	1500.

George Washington at center, Columbus' discovery of land at upper left.
No serial number panel.

KL#	Fr#	Series	Signatures	Seal	Fine	XF	CH CU (63)	Gem CU (65)
23	36	1917	Teehee-Burke	Small red	80.00	200.	450.	650
24	37	1917	Elliott-Burke	Small red	80.00	140.	375.	500.
25	37a	1917	Burke-Elliott	Small red	300.	650.	2000.	3000.
26	38	1917	Elliott-White	Small red	55.00	100.	325.	500.
27	39	1917	Speelman-White	Small red	60.00	150.	325.	700.

George Washington at center.

KL#	Fr#	Series	Signatures	Seal	Fine	XF	CH CU (63)	Gem CU (65)
28	40	1923	Speelman-White	Small red	125.	375.	550.	1075.

Silver Certificates

Martha Washington at left. Blue serial number.

KL#	Fr#	Series	Signatures	Seal	Fine	XF	CH CU (63)	Gem CU (65)
29	215	1886	Rosecrans-Jordan	Small red	250.	750.	1750.	3700.
30	216	1886	Rosecrans-Hyatt	Small red	360.	875.	2000.	3450.
31	217	1886	Rosecrans-Hyatt	Large red	325.	1000.	2200.	3500.
32	218	1886	Rosecrans-Huston	Large red	300.	1000.	2700.	4150.
33	219	1886	Rosecrans-Huston	Large brown	400.	1050.	4500.	6275.
34	220	1886	Rosecrans-Nebeker	Large brown	250.	1050.	4250.	5500.
35	221	1886	Rosecrans-Nebeker	Small red	325.	1000.	2850.	5500.

KL#	Fr#	Series	Signatures	Seal	Fine	XF	CH CU (63)	Gem CU (65)
36	222	1891	Rosecrans-Nobeker	Small red	300.	850.	2300.	2600.
37	223	1891	Tillman-Morgan	Small red	200.	800.	1350.	2750.

History instructing youth; Washington D.C. and Constitution at center right. Martha and George Washington on the back.

KL#	Fr#	Series	Signatures	Seal	Fine	XF	CH CU (63)	Gem CU (65)
38	224	1896	Tillman-Morgan	Small red	280.	950.	2750.	3100.
39	225	1896	Bruce-Roberts	Small red	325.	925.	2750.	4200.

Eagle on flag, capitol behind, at center; small portraits of
Lincoln and Grant below. Series date above upper right serial number.

40	226	1899	Lyons-Roberts	Small blue	200.	275.	600.	1375.

Series date below serial number.

KL#	Fr#	Series	Signatures	Seal	Fine	XF	CH CU (63)	Gem CU (65)
41	226a	1899	Lyons-Roberts	Small blue	175.	250.	600.	975.
42	227	1899	Lyons-Treat	Small blue	150.	250.	700.	1000.
43	228	1899	Vernon-Treat	Small blue	100.	250.	550.	750.
44	229	1899	Vernon-McClung	Small blue	160.	325.	550.	900.

Series date vertical at right.

KL#	Fr#	Series	Signatures	Seal	Fine	XF	CH CU (63)	Gem CU (65)
44A	229a	1899	Vernon-McClung	Small blue	500.	2000.	5000.	9000.
45	230	1899	Napier-McClung	Small blue	150.	225.	625.	1000.
46	231	1899	Napier-Thompson	Small blue	400.	1500.	2500.	3250.
47	232	1899	Parker-Burke	Small blue	150.	225.	650.	700.
48	233	1899	Teehee-Burke	Small blue	150.	200.	600.	900.
49	234	1899	Elliott-Burke	Small blue	150.	300.	550.	1150.
50	235	1899	Elliott-White	Small blue	150.	225.	550.	700.
51	236	1899	Speelman-White	Small blue	150.	275.	500.	850.

George Washington at center.

KL#	Fr#	Series	Signatures	Seal	Fine	XF	CH CU (63)	Gem CU (65)
52	237	1923	Speelman-White	Small blue	35.00	70.00	125.	150.
53	238	1923	Woods-White	Small blue	45.00	90.00	125.	200.
54	239	1923	Woods-Tate	Small blue	200.	450.	1000.	1500.

Treasury or Coin Notes

Edwin M. Stanton at left.

KL#	Fr#	Series	Signatures	Seal	Fine	XF	CH CU (63)	Gem CU (65)
55	347	1890	Rosecrans-Huston	Large brown	500.	2500.	5350.	7000.
56	348	1890	Rosecrans-Nebeker	Large brown	450.	2000.	20,000.	25,000.
57	349	1890	Rosecrans-Nebeker	Small red	725.	1750.	5950.	20,000.
58	350	1891	Rosecrans-Nebeker	Small red	210.	700.	1150.	2000.

KL#	Fr#	Series	Signatures	Seal	Fine	XF	CH CU (63)	Gem CU (65)
59	351	1891	Tillman-Morgan	Small red	250.	650.	1250.	1850.
60	352	1891	Bruce-Roberts	Small red	200.	650.	1250.	1675.

Federal Reserve Bank Notes
1918

George Washington at left. Eagle on flag on back.

KL#	Fr#	Bank	Federal Sigs.	Bank Sigs.	Fine	XF	CH CU (63)	Gem CU (65)
61	708	Boston	Teehee-Burke	Bullen-Morss	125.	200.	500.	1100.
62	709	Boston	Teehee-Burke	Willett-Morss	225.	375.	1500.	2000.
63	710	Boston	Elliott-Burke	Willett-Morss	110.	250.	650.	750.
64	711	New York	Teehee-Burke	Sailer-Strong	110.	200.	750.	1050.
65	712	New York	Teehee-Burke	Hendricks-Strong	110.	300.	500.	850.
66	713	New York	Elliott-Burke	Hendricks-Strong	100.	185.	475.	1000.
67	714	Philadelphia	Teehee-Burke	Hardt-Passmore	110.	200.	750.	1000.
68	715	Philadelphia	Teehee-Burke	Dyer-Passmore	125.	300.	500.	1500.
69	716	Philadelphia	Elliott-Burke	Dyer-Passmore	160.	300.	500.	1200.
70	717	Philadelphia	Elliott-Burke	Dyer-Norris	110.	280.	500.	1125.
71	718	Cleveland	Teehee-Burke	Baxter-Fancher	110.	250.	500.	850.
72	719	Cleveland	Teehee-Burke	Davis-Fancher	110.	175.	775.	1000.
73	720	Cleveland	Elliott-Burke	Davis-Fancher	110.	225.	425.	1300.
74	721	Richmond	Teehee-Burke	Keesee-Seay	135.	400.	750.	1200.
75	722	Richmond	Elliott-Burke	Keesee-Seay	110.	275.	750.	1250.
76	723	Atlanta	Teehee-Burke	Pike-McCord	110.	250.	600.	750.
77	724	Atlanta	Teehee-Burke	Bell-McCord	160.	850.	1500.	2000.
78	725	Atlanta	Teehee-Burke	Bell-Wellborn	300.	900.	5000.	12,650.
79	726	Atlanta	Elliott-Burke	Bell-Wellborn	180.	220.	700.	875.
80	727	Chicago	Teehee-Burke	McCloud-McDougal	105.	200.	500.	1000.
81	728	Chicago	Teehee-Burke	Cramer-McDougal	105.	250.	725.	1000.
82	729	Chicago	Elliott-Burke	Cramer-McDougal	105.	225.	600.	825.
83	730	St. Louis	Teehee-Burke	Attebery-Wells	160.	350.	600.	1250.
84	731	St. Louis	Teehee-Burke	Attebery-Biggs	160.	350.	1500.	2500.

KL#	Fr#	Bank	Federal Sigs.	Bank Sigs.	Fine	XF	CH CU (63)	Gem CU (65)
85	732	St. Louis	Elliott-Burke	Attebery-Biggs	400.	900.	725.	1100.
86	733	St. Louis	Elliott-Burke	White-Biggs	110.	225.	625.	1100.
87	734	Minneapolis	Teehee-Burke	Cook-Wold	100.	350.	925.	1750.
88	735	Minneapolis	Teehee-Burke	Cook-Young	475.	2500.	6000.	12,650.
89	736	Minneapolis	Elliott-Burke	Cook-Young	110.	350.	1000.	1500.
90	737	Kansas City	Teehee-Burke	Anderson-Miller	110.	200.	450.	1000.
91	738	Kansas City	Elliott-Burke	Anderson-Miller	110.	250.	425.	1200.
92	739	Kansas City	Elliott-Burke	Helm-Miller	110.	200.	400.	850.
93	740	Dallas	Teehee-Burke	Talley-Van Zandt	80.00	300.	700.	1500.
94	741	Dallas	Elliott-Burke	Talley-Van Zandt	400.	2500.	3750.	—
95	742	Dallas	Elliott-Burke	Lawder-Van Zandt	100.	300.	650.	3750.
96	743	San Francisco	Teehee-Burke	Clerk-Lynch	110.	400.	425.	1500.
97	744	San Francisco	Teehee-Burke	Clerk-Calkins	200.	725.	1500.	3000.
98	745	San Francisco	Elliott-Burke	Clerk-Calkins	110.	800.	3000.	5000.
99	746	San Francisco	Elliott-Burke	Ambrose-Calkins	150.	275.	725.	1500.

United States Notes

Two Dollars

Alexander Hamilton at left center.

Red Numerals "1 2 3" vertically in center. National Bank Note Co. vertically at left; Patented April 23, 1860, National Bank Note Co., in lower border.

KL#	Fr#	Series	Signatures	Seal	Fine	XF	CH CU (63)	Gem CU (65)
100	41	1862	Chittenden-Spinner	Small red	850.	3000.	5500.	21,850.

American Bank Note Co. vertically at left;
Patented April 23, 1860, National Bank Note Co., in lower border.

KL#	Fr#	Series	Signatures	Seal	Fine	XF	CH CU (63)	Gem CU (65)
101	41a	1862	Chittenden-Spinner	Small red	500.	2000.	10,000.	17,500.

Capitol Building at center, Thomas Jefferson at upper left.

Red serial numbers, red seal at right.
Engraved and printed at the Treasury Department, vertically at left;
American Bank Note Co. Bottom left, face design and twice below on back.

KL#	Fr#	Series	Signatures	Seal	Fine	XF	CH CU (63)	Gem CU (65)
102	42	1869	Allison-Spinner	Large red	625.	3000.	8300.	17,500.

Red serial numbers. Red ornamentation at right.

KL#	Fr#	Series	Signatures	Seal	Fine	XF	CH CU (63)	Gem CU (65)
103	43	1874	Allison-Spinner	Small red	460.	1200.	2500.	5250.
104	44	1875	Allison-New	Small red	480.	1100.	2000.	4000.

Series A at lower right of face design.

KL#	Fr#	Series	Signatures	Seal	Fine	XF	CH CU (63)	Gem CU (65)
105	45	1875	Allison-New	Small red	975.	3600.	18,400.	—

Series B at lower right of face design.

KL#	Fr#	Series	Signatures	Seal	Fine	XF	CH CU (63)	Gem CU (65)
106	46	1875	Allison-New	Small red	850.	2400.	6500.	9000.
107	47	1875	Allison-Wyman	Small red	480.	1100.	4000.	8900.
108	48	1878	Allison-Gilfillan	Small red	380.	800.	2000.	4250.
109	49	1878	Scofield-Gilfillan	Small red	5000.	35,000.	Rare	—

Capitol Building at center, Thomas Jefferson at upper left.
Red serial numbers. Ornamentation removed.

KL#	Fr#	Series	Signatures	Seal	Fine	XF	CH CU (63)	Gem CU (65)
110	50	1880	Scofield-Gilfillan	Large brown	250.	600.	2000.	3500.
111	51	1880	Bruce-Gilfillan	Large brown	285.	600.	1500.	3500.
112	52	1880	Bruce-Wyman	Large brown	275.	500.	1100.	2500.

Capitol Building at center, Thomas Jefferson at upper left.
Blue serial numbers.

KL#	Fr#	Series	Signatures	Seal	Fine	XF	CH CU (63)	Gem CU (65)
113	53	1880	Rosecrans-Huston	Large red	1250.	3000.	15,000.	20,000.
114	54	1880	Rosecrans-Huston	Large brown	3500.	13,500.	—	—
115	55	1880	Rosecrans-Nebeker	Small red	200.	900.	2700.	6500.
116	56	1880	Tillman-Morgan	Small red	250.	500.	1000.	1600.

Capitol Building at center, Thomas Jefferson at upper left.
Red serial numbers.

KL#	Fr#	Series	Signatures	Seal	Fine	XF	CH CU (63)	Gem CU (65)
117	57	1917	Teehee-Burke	Small red	100.	225.	800.	1000.
118	58	1917	Elliott-Burke	Small red	140.	225.	425.	750.
119	59	1917	Elliott-White	Small red	100.	200.	500.	800.
120	60	1917	Speelman-White	Small red	75.00	150.	350.	875.

Silver Certificates

General Winfield Scott Hancock at left.

KL#	Fr#	Series	Signatures	Type/Seal	Fine	XF	CH CU (63)	Gem CU (65)
121	240	1886	Rosecrans-Jordan	Small red	650.	1750.	3000.	5000.
122	241	1886	Rosecrans-Hyatt	Small red	600.	1500.	3000.	4000.
123	242	1886	Rosecrans-Hyatt	Large red	500.	1750.	3500.	5325.
124	243	1886	Rosecrans-Huston	Large red	700.	1850.	4000.	5200.
125	244	1886	Rosecrans-Huston	Large brown	700.	2000.	4500.	9500.

William Windom at center.

KL#	Fr#	Series	Signatures	Seal	Fine	XF	CH CU (63)	Gem CU (65)
126	245	1891	Rosecrans-Nebeker	Small red	650.	2750.	6000.	7475.
127	246	1891	Tillman-Morgan	Small red	650.	2200.	3750.	8000.

Science presenting Steam and Electricity to Industry and Commerce.
Robert Fulton and Samuel Morse.

KL#	Fr#	Series	Signatures	Seal	Fine	XF	CH CU (63)	Gem CU (65)
128	247	1896	Tillman-Morgan	Small red	625.	3300.	5500.	9775.
129	248	1896	Bruce-Roberts	Small red	750.	4000.	5500.	9000.

George Washington at center, flanked by Mechanics and Agriculture.

KL#	Fr#	Series	Signatures	Seal	Fine	XF	CH CU (63)	Gem CU (65)
130	249	1899	Lyons-Roberts	Small blue	175.	700.	1050.	1850.
131	250	1899	Lyons-Treat	Small blue	200.	450.	1350.	2300.
132	251	1899	Vernon-Treat	Small blue	250.	550.	1000.	1750.
133	252	1899	Vernon-McClung	Small blue	400.	750.	1400.	2250.
134	253	1899	Napier-McClung	Small blue	250.	550.	1100.	1750.
135	254	1899	Napier-Thompson	Small blue	550.	800.	3500.	5250.
136	255	1899	Parker-Burke	Small blue	250.	500.	1150.	2200.
137	256	1899	Teehee-Burke	Small blue	265.	525.	1000.	2000.
138	257	1899	Elliott-Burke	Small blue	200.	900.	1600.	2000.
139	258	1899	Speelman-White	Small blue	200.	500.	1175.	1950.

Treasury or Coin Notes

General James B. McPherson at right.

KL#	Fr#	Series	Signatures	Seal	Fine	XF	CH CU (63)	Gem CU (65)
140	353	1890	Rosecrans-Huston	Large brown	900.	8500.	20,000.	50,000.
141	354	1890	Rosecrans-Nebeker	Large brown	2000.	7500.	38,000.	44,000.
142	355	1890	Rosecrans-Nebeker	Small red	650.	4000.	15,000.	37,500.
143	356	1891	Rosecrans-Nebeker	Small red	460.	1400.	3750.	4250.
144	357	1891	Tillman-Morgan	Small red	600.	1750.	3250.	4500.
145	358	1891	Bruce-Roberts	Small red	650.	1625.	3000.	4500.

Federal Reserve Bank Notes
1918

Thomas Jefferson at left. Battleship New York.

KL#	Fr#	Bank	Federal Sigs.	Bank Sigs.	Fine	XF	CH CU (63)	Gem CU (65)
146	747	Boston	Teehee-Burke	Bullen-Morss	400.	750.	2450.	3900.
147	748	Boston	Teehee-Burke	Willett-Morss	250.	900.	4000.	4500.
148	749	Boston	Elliott-Burke	Willett-Morss	425.	900.	3225.	4000.
149	750	New York	Teehee-Burke	Sailer-Strong	500.	950.	1775.	3250.
150	751	New York	Teehee-Burke	Hendricks-Strong	450.	1100.	2500.	3500.
151	752	New York	Elliott-Burke	Hendricks-Strong	500.	850.	2000.	3500.
152	753	Philadelphia	Teehee-Burke	Hardt-Passmore	500.	850.	2000.	4500.
153	754	Philadelphia	Teehee-Burke	Dyer-Passmore	500.	1250.	2000.	3000.
154	755	Philadelphia	Elliott-Burke	Dyer-Passmore	500.	2500.	—	—
155	756	Philadelphia	Elliott-Burke	Dyer-Norris	450.	850.	2600.	4500.
156	757	Cleveland	Teehee-Burke	Baxter-Fancher	550.	1300.	2800.	3250.
157	758	Cleveland	Teehee-Burke	Davis-Fancher	320.	1100.	2750.	6400.
158	759	Cleveland	Elliott-Burke	Davis-Fancher	550.	900.	1750.	3200.
159	760	Richmond	Teehee-Burke	Keesee-Seay	420.	1500.	3000.	3750.
160	761	Richmond	Elliott-Burke	Keesee-Seay	400.	1100.	3000.	3250.
161	762	Atlanta	Teehee-Burke	Pike-McCord	450.	1300.	3450.	4400.
162	763	Atlanta	Teehee-Burke	Bell-McCord	1440.	5000.	—	—
163	764	Atlanta	Elliott-Burke	Bell-Wellborn	900.	2000.	6000.	6500.
164	765	Chicago	Teehee-Burke	McCloud-McDougal	400.	850.	2350.	5500.
165	766	Chicago	Teehee-Burke	Cramer-McDougal	550.	1150.	2500.	2650.
166	767	Chicago	Elliott-Burke	Cramer-McDougal	550.	1000.	2000.	3000.
167	768	St. Louis	Teehee-Burke	Attebery-Wells	550.	1050.	5000.	6000.
168	769	St. Louis	Teehee-Burke	Attebery-Biggs	1100.	3500.	8700.	10,000.

KL#	Fr#	Bank	Federal Sigs.	Bank Sigs.	Fine	XF	CH CU (63)	Gem CU (65)
169	770	St. Louis	Elliott-Burke	Attebery-Biggs	1100.	3000.	8700.	10,000.
170	771	St. Louis	Elliott-Burke	White-Biggs	300.	1500.	2700.	4750.
171	772	Minneapolis	Teehee-Burke	Cook-Wold	575.	2000.	2500.	4000.
172	773	Minneapolis	Elliott-Burke	Cook-Young	575.	1600.	2800.	4500.
173	774	Kansas City	Teehee-Burke	Anderson-Miller	350.	1200.	3000.	3500.
174	775	Kansas City	Elliott-Burke	Helm-Miller	450.	850.	3250.	6500.
175	776	Dallas	Teehee-Burke	Talley-Van Zandt	375.	800.	2350.	4000.
176	777	Dallas	Elliott-Burke	Talley-Van Zandt	400.	800.	3550.	6250.
177	778	San Francisco	Teehee-Burke	Clerk-Lynch	500.	1850.	2500.	4500.
178	779	San Francisco	Elliott-Burke	Clerk-Calkins	600.	1400.	—	5500.
179	780	San Francisco	Elliott-Burke	Ambrose-Calkins	575.	2000.	4000.	4500.

Demand Notes

Five Dollars

Statue of Freedom at left, Alexander Hamilton at right.

KL#	Fr#	Payable at:	VG	Fine	VF
180	3-A	Boston	Unique	—	—
181	3	Boston	2500.	3000.	3350.
182	1a	New York	14,000.	35,000.	65,000.
183	1	New York	1600.	2250.	5000.
185	2	Philadelphia	3200.	4500.	6500.
187	5	St. Louis	10,000.	18,000.	38,000.
189	4	Cincinnati	14,000.	Rare	—

United States Notes

Statue of Freedom at left, Alexander Hamilton at right.
Red serial numbers. "Series" on face.
First Obligation inscription (in octolobe at center).

American Bank Note Co. in top border on face.

KL#	Fr#	Series	Signatures	Seal	Fine	XF	CH CU (63)	Gem CU (65)
190	61a	1862	Chittenden-Spinner	Small red	450.	1250.	2600.	8000.

Statue of Freedom at left, Alexander Hamilton at right. Red serial
numbers. Second Obligation inscription (in oval) at center.

American Bank Note Co. in top border on face.

KL#	Fr#	Series	Signatures	Seal	Fine	XF	CH CU (63)	Gem CU (65)
191	62	1862	Chittenden-Spinner	Small red	750.	2000.	5000.	10,000.

American Bank Note Co. and National Bank Note Co. lower border on face.

KL#	Fr#	Series	Signatures	Seal	Fine	XF	CH CU (63)	Gem CU (65)
191A	63	1863	Chittenden-Spinner	Small red	450.	1300.	3000.	4000.

Statue of Freedom at left, Alexander Hamilton at right. One red serial number. Second Obligation inscription (in oval) at center.

American Bank Note Co. twice in lower border on face.

KL#	Fr#	Series	Signatures	Seal	Fine	XF	CH CU (63)	Gem CU (65)
192	63a	1863	Chittenden-Spinner	Small red	550.	1150.	3250.	7000.

Statue of Freedom at left, Alexander Hamilton at right. Two red serial numbers. Second Obligation inscription (in oval) at center.

American Bank Note Co. twice in border on face.

KL#	Fr#	Series	Signatures	Seal	Fine	XF	CH CU (63)	Gem CU (65)
193	63b	1863	Chittenden-Spinner	Small red	500.	1100.	6000.	7500.

The Pioneer at center, Andrew Jackson at lower left.

American Bank Note Co. twice in lower border on face.
Two red serial numbers.

KL#	Fr#	Series	Signatures	Seal	Fine	XF	CH CU (63)	Gem CU (65)
194	64	1869	Allison-Spinner	Large red	600.	1500.	3150.	5000.

Bureau, Engraving & Printing, upper left on face.
American Bank Note Co., upper and lower margin on back.

Red serial numbers. Large "V" in red ornamentation at right.

KL#	Fr#	Series	Signatures	Seal	Fine	XF	CH CU (63)	Gem CU (65)
195	65	1875	Allison-New	Small red	350.	800.	2000.	2500.

Series A in lower right of face design.

KL#	Fr#	Series	Signatures	Seal	Fine	XF	CH CU (63)	Gem CU (65)
196	66	1875	Allison-New		1500.	4000.	15,000.	—

Series B in lower right of face design.

KL#	Fr#	Series	Signatures	Seal	Fine	XF	CH CU (63)	Gem CU (65)
197	67	1875	Allison-New		340.	750.	1525.	2500.
198	68	1875	Allison-Wyman	Small red	320.	775.	1350.	2600.
199	69	1878	Allison-Gilfillan	Small red	250.	800.	1500.	2600.

The Pioneer at center, Andrew Jackson at lower left. Red serial numbers.

KL#	Fr#	Series	Signatures	Seal	Fine	XF	CH CU (63)	Gem CU (65)
200	70	1880	Scofield-Gilfillan	Large brown	650.	1250.	5000.	7500.
201	71	1880	Bruce-Gilfillan	Large brown	440.	600.	1750.	2850.
202	72	1880	Bruce-Wyman	Large brown	300.	750.	1350.	3500.

The Pioneer at center, Andrew Jackson at lower left. Blue serial numbers.

KL#	Fr#	Series	Signatures	Seal	Fine	XF	CH CU (63)	Gem CU (65)
203	73	1880	Bruce-Wyman	Large red	450.	600.	1200.	1850.
204	74	1880	Rosecrans-Jordan	Large red	275.	900.	1300.	1500.
205	75	1880	Rosecrans-Hyatt	Large red	480.	2200.	52,000.	—
206	76	1880	Rosecrans-Huston	Large red	425.	1600.	4000.	4500.

KL#	Fr#	Series	Signatures	Seal	Fine	XF	CH CU (63)	Gem CU (65)
207	77	1880	Rosecrans-Huston	Large brown	450.	1350.	6000.	54,625.
208	78	1880	Rosecrans-Nebeker	Large brown	925.	2000.	7000.	22,000.

KL#	Fr#	Series	Signatures	Seal	Fine	XF	CH CU (63)	Gem CU (65)
209	79	1880	Rosecrans-Nebeker	Small red	250.	400.	775.	1500.
210	80	1880	Tillman-Morgan	Small red	250.	550.	925.	1400.
211	81	1880	Bruce-Roberts	Small red	250.	400.	800.	2500.
212	82	1880	Lyons-Roberts	Small red	300.	550.	2000.	4000.

The Pioneer at center, Andrew Jackson at lower left.
Red serial numbers. Ornamental "V" at left.

KL#	Fr#	Series	Signatures	Seal	Fine	XF	CH CU (63)	Gem CU (65)
213	83	1907	Vernon-Treat	Small red	190.	450.	775.	1500.
214	84	1907	Vernon-McClung	Small red	190.	450.	800.	1325.
215	85	1907	Napier-McClung	Small red	190.	300.	700.	1250.
216	86	1907	Napier-Thompson	Small red	300.	1200.	5000.	6000.
217	87	1907	Parker-Burke	Small red	190.	400.	600.	1250.
218	88	1907	Teehee-Burke	Small red	160.	325.	550.	1250.
219	89	1907	Elliott-Burke	Small red	190.	400.	1250.	2000.
220	90	1907	Elliott-White	Small red	190.	325.	800.	1000.
221	91	1907	Speelman-White	Small red	135.	375.	550.	1150.
222	92	1907	Woods-White	Small red	150.	375.	750.	1200.

National Gold Bank Notes

Columbus in Sight of Land at left,
America Presented to the Old World at right. Various U.S. Gold Coins.

KL#	Fr#	Series	Issuing Bank	Location	Good	Fine	VF
223	1136	Orig.	First Nat'l Gold Bank	San Francisco	1750.	5000.	13,500.
224	1137	Orig.	Nat'l Gold Bank & Trust Co.	San Francisco	4500.	—	17,000.
225	1138	Orig.	Nat'l Gold Bank of D.O. Mills	Sacramento	4000.	6325.	17,250.
226	1139	Orig.	First Nat'l Gold Bank	Stockton	4000.	9200.	—
227	1140	Orig.	First Nat'l Gold Bank	Santa Barbara	7500.	Rare	—
228	1141	Orig.	Farmers' Nat'l Gold Bank	San Jose	2500.	11,500.	—

Silver Certificates

Ulysses S. Grant at right center. Blue serial numbers. Five silver dollars.

KL#	Fr#	Series	Signatures	Seal	Fine	XF	CH CU (63)	Gem CU (65)
229	259	1886	Rosecrans-Jordan	Small red	1500.	4500.	12,500.	27,500.
230	260	1886	Rosecrans-Hyatt	Small red	1200.	4250.	17,500.	22,000.
231	261	1886	Rosecrans-Hyatt	Large red	1100.	4500.	11,000.	27,000.
232	262	1886	Rosecrans-Huston	Large red	1000.	4500.	14,500.	32,000.
233	263	1886	Rosecrans-Huston	Large brown	850.	4750.	10,000.	25,000.
234	264	1886	Rosecrans-Nebeker	Large brown	1250.	9000.	18,000.	22,000.
235	265	1086	Rosecrans-Nebeker	Small red	1250.	8100.	20,125.	27,500.

Ulysses S. Grant at right center.

KL#	Fr#	Series	Signatures	Seal	Fine	XF	CH CU (63)	Gem CU (65)
236	266	1891	Rosecrans-Nebeker	Small red	700.	2000.	6000.	—
237	267	1891	Tillman-Morgan	Small red	500.	1800.	4000.	8000.

Electricity presenting light to the world.
Ulysses S. Grant at left and Philip H. Sheridan at right.

KL#	Fr#	Series	Signatures	Seal	Fine	XF	CH CU (63)	Gem CU (65)
238	268	1896	Tillman-Morgan	Small red	1275.	5000.	11,500.	16,500.
239	269	1896	Bruce-Roberts	Small red	1350.	5000.	9000.	16,500.
240	270	1896	Lyons-Roberts	Small red	900.	5450.	12,000.	20,000.

Chief Tatoka-Inyanka
(Running Antelope) of the Hunkpapa Sioux at center.

KL#	Fr#	Series	Signatures	Seal	Fine	XF	CH CU (63)	Gem CU (65)
241	271	1899	Lyons-Roberts	Small blue	375.	1300.	3250.	7000.
242	272	1899	Lyons-Treal	Small blue	650.	1500.	2850.	5200.
243	273	1899	Vernon-Treat	Small blue	460.	1400.	3500	4750.
244	274	1899	Vernon-McClung	Small blue	500.	1300.	3750.	7000.
245	275	1899	Napier-McClung	Small blue	450.	1300.	3900.	6300.
246	276	1899	Napier-Thompson	Small blue	900.	3220.	8500.	20,000.
247	277	1899	Parker-Burke	Small blue	425.	1500.	2850.	7000.
248	278	1899	Teehee-Burke	Small blue	500.	1400.	3250.	5225.
249	279	1099	Elliott-Burke	Small blue	475.	1350.	2900.	6000.
250	280	1899	Elliott-White	Small blue	450.	1400.	2500.	6000.
251	281	1899	Speelman-Whitc	Small blue	500.	1425.	2750.	3000.

Abraham Lincoln at center.
Obverse of the Great Seal of the United States.

KL#	Fr#	Series	Signatures	Seal	Fine	XF	CH CU (63)	Gem CU (65)
252	282	1923	Speelman-White	Small blue	625.	2250.	4000.	10,000.

Treasury or Coin Notes

General George H. Thomas at center.

KL#	Fr#	Series	Signatures	Seal	Fine	XF	CH CU (63)	Gem CU (65)
253	359	1890	Rosecrans-Huston	Large brown	1500.	4000.	9000.	20,750.
254	360	1890	Rosecrans-Nebeker	Large brown	3000.	57,000.	—	115,000.
255	361	1890	Rosecrans-Nebeker	Small red	800.	3000.	8500.	14,000.

KL#	Fr#	Series	Signatures	Seal	Fine	XF	CH CU (63)	Gem CU (65)
256	362	1891	Rosecrans-Nebeker	Small red	550.	1500.	2500.	3800.
257	363	1891	Tillman-Morgan	Small red	550.	1625.	2800.	3900.
258	364	1891	Bruce-Roberts	Small red	400.	1750.	2750.	4100.
259	365	1891	Lyons-Roberts	Small red	800.	1250.	9000.	12,000.

Federal Reserve Notes
1914

Abraham Lincoln at center. Red Seal.
Columbus discovery of land at left and Landing of the Pilgrims at right.

KL#	Fr#	Bank	Signatures	Fine	XF	CH CU (63)	Gem CU (65)
260	832	Boston	Burke-McAdoo				
			a Plate letter at upper left.	400.	750.	3200.	4000.
			b District # and letter above plate letter at upper left.	350.	800.	1750.	4900.
261	833	New York	Burke-McAdoo				
			a Plate letter at upper left.	300.	650.	1750.	2800.
			b District # and letter above plate letter at upper left.	275.	950.	1750.	2150.
262	834	Philadelphia	Burke-McAdoo				
			a Plate letter at upper left.	325.	700.	1900.	3250.
			b District # and letter above plate letter at upper left.	300.	950.	2300.	2750.
263	835	Cleveland	Burke-McAdoo				
			a Plate letter at upper left.	500.	1200.	2150.	4600.
			b District # and letter above plate letter at upper left.	300.	1000.	3700.	4500.
264	836	Richmond	Burke-McAdoo				
			a Plate letter at upper left.	500.	2350.	3250.	4000.
			b District # and letter above plate letter at upper left.	400.	850.	2500.	10,400.
265	837	Atlanta	Burke-McAdoo				
			a Plate letter at upper left.	500.	875.	3500.	4500.
			b District # and letter above plate letter at upper left.	500.	1150.	2500.	3250.
266	838	Chicago	Burke-McAdoo				
			a Plate letter at upper left.	350.	600.	1750.	4050.
			b District # and letter above plate letter at upper left.	400.	800.	2100.	3650.
267	839	St. Louis	Burke-McAdoo				
			a Plate letter at upper left.	500.	1150.	1750.	3250.
			b District # and letter above plate letter at upper left.	500.	750.	4200.	5000.
268	840	Minneapolis	Burke-McAdoo				
			a Plate letter at upper left.	550.	1100.	6000.	7500.
			b District # and letter above plate letter at upper left.	275.	800.	2250.	6500.
269	841	Kansas City	Burke-McAdoo				
			a Plate letter at upper left.	550.	2250.	4000.	7000.
			b District # and letter above plate letter at upper left.	350.	1300.	3000.	3500.
270	842	Dallas	Burke-McAdoo				
			a Plate letter at upper left.	750.	7500.	9000.	11,500.
			b District # and letter above plate letter at upper left.	375.	950.	4600.	5500.
271	843	San Francisco	Burke-McAdoo				
			a Plate letter upper left.	1000.	3000.	3750.	4000.
			b District # and letter above plate letter at upper left.	600.	2000.	3000.	4000.

Abraham Lincoln at center. Blue seal.
Columbus discovery of land at left and Landing of the Pilgrims at right.

KL#	Fr#	Bank	Signatures	Fine	XF	CH CU (63)	Gem CU (65)
272	844	Boston	Burke-McAdoo	75.00	235.	600.	2000.
273	845	Boston	Burke-Glass	80.00	900.	1300.	1500.
274	846	Boston	Burke-Houston	350.	760.	1350.	1950.
275	847	Boston	White-Mellon				
		a	Upper case district letter in lower left.	80.00	175.	375.	700.
		b	Lower case district letter in lower left.	90.00	185.	550.	1025.
		c	Blue seal to left of district letter.	—	Rare	—	—
276	848	New York	Burke-McAdoo	55.00	200.	400.	1150.
277	849	New York	Burke-Glass	60.00	200.	1450.	2000.
278	850	New York	Burke-Houston	100.	200.	425.	700.
279	851	New York	White-Mellon				
		a	Upper case district letter in lower left.	50.00	100.	350.	700.
		b	Lower case district letter in lower left.	60.00	125.	350.	600.
		c	Blue seal to left of district letters.	275.	325.	500.	1250.
280	852	Philadelphia	Burke-McAdoo	110.	525.	750.	825.
281	853	Philadelphia	Burke-Glass	60.00	—	500.	1100.
282	854	Philadelphia	Burke-Houston	65.00	150.	425.	650.
283	855	Philadelphia	White-Mellon				
		a	Upper case district letter in lower left.	100.	150.	300.	575.
		b	Lower case district letter in lower left.	100.	150.	1000.	1500.
		c	Blue seal to left of district letters.	100.	150.	450.	600.
284	856	Cleveland	Burke-McAdoo	150.	300.	800.	1000.
285	857	Cleveland	Burke-Glass	320.	575.	1250.	4000.
286	858	Cleveland	Burke-Houston	100.	200.	450.	1600.
287	859	Cleveland	White-Mellon				
		a	Upper case district letter in lower left.	60.00	100.	375.	775.
		b	Lower case district letter in lower left.	75.00	100.	425.	875.
		c	Blue seal to left of district letters.	70.00	150.	400.	1050.
288	860	Richmond	Burke-McAdoo	75.00	200.	1100.	1500.
289	861	Richmond	Burke-Glass	90.00	400.	2100.	2750.
290	862	Richmond	Burke-Houston	85.00	175.	1000.	1400.
291	863	Richmond	White-Mellon				
		a	Upper Case District letter in lower left.	60.00	135.	450.	1300.
		b	Lower case district letter in lower left.	60.00	5200.	—	—
		c	Blue seal to left of district letter.	—	Rare	—	—
292	864	Atlanta	Burke-McAdoo	60.00	225.	1500.	2000.
293	865	Atlanta	Burke-Glass	100.	700.	1300.	1500.
294	866	Atlanta	Burke-Houston	60.00	225.	550.	1275.
295	867	Atlanta	White-Mellon				
		a	Upper case district letter in lower left.	60.00	200.	600.	800.
		b	Lower case district letter in lower left.	150.	1000.	5200.	6000.
		c	Blue seal to left of district letter.	—	Rare	—	—

KL#	Fr#	Bank	Signatures	Fine		XF CH CU (63)	Gem CU (65)
296	868	Chicago	Burke-McAdoo	100.	300.	400.	650.
297	869	Chicago	Burke-Glass	100.	175.	600.	2000.
298	870	Chicago	Burke-Houston	100.	200.	350.	875.
299	871	Chicago	White-Mellon				
		a Upper case district letter in lower left.		90.00	150.	650.	950.
		b Lower case district letter in lower left.		60.00	200.	600.	725.
		c Blue seal to left of district letter.		100.	275.	550.	1200.
300	872	St. Louis	Burke-McAdoo	75.00	750.	1250.	1450.
301	873	St. Louis	Burke-Glass	80.00	325.	900.	1000.
302	874	St. Louis	Burke-Houston	75.00	300.	575.	825.
303	875	St. Louis	White-Mellon				
		a Upper case district letter in lower left.		100.	200.	950.	1200.
		b Lower case district letter in lower left.		100.	200.	1300.	1500.
304	876	Minneapolis	Burke-McAdoo	240.	375.	875.	1300.
305	877	Minneapolis	Burke-Glass	80.00	300.	900.	5000.
306	878	Minneapolis	Burke-Houston	100.	325.	650.	—
307	879	Minneapolis	White-Mellon				
		a Upper case district letter at lower left.		75.00	195.	500.	1500.
		b Lower case district letter at lower left.		75.00	195.	350.	700.
308	880	Kansas City	Burke-McAdoo	100.	400.	675.	1500.
309	881	Kansas City	Burke-Glass	90.00	475.	1500.	2000.
310	882	Kansas City	Burke-Houston	100.	400.	600.	1250.
311	883	Kansas City	White-Mellon				
		a Upper case district letter at lower left.		100.	400.	600.	650.
		b Lower case district letter at lower left.		300.	700.	2000.	2500.
312	884	Dallas	Burke-McAdoo	250.	500.	1250.	2000.
313	885	Dallas	Burke-Glass	275.	1950.	—	—
314	886	Dallas	Burke-Houston	250.	500.	900.	2000.
315	887	Dallas	White-Mellon				
		a Upper case district letter at lower left.		70.00	175.	500.	1000.
		b Lower case district letter at lower left.		200.	400.	850.	1200.
		c Blue seal to left of district letter.		—	Rare	—	—
316	888	San Francisco	Burke-McAdoo	70.00	1100.	1500.	1750.
317	889	San Francisco	Burke-Glass	195.	1500.	—	—
318	890	San Francisco	Burke-Houston	100.	250.	550.	800.
319	891	San Francisco	White-Mellon				
		a Upper case district letter at lower left.		100.	400.	600.	800.
		b Lower case district letter at lower left.		150.	925.	1400.	1750.
		c Blue seal to left of district letter.		400.	800.	1900.	2250.

Federal Reserve Bank Notes
1915

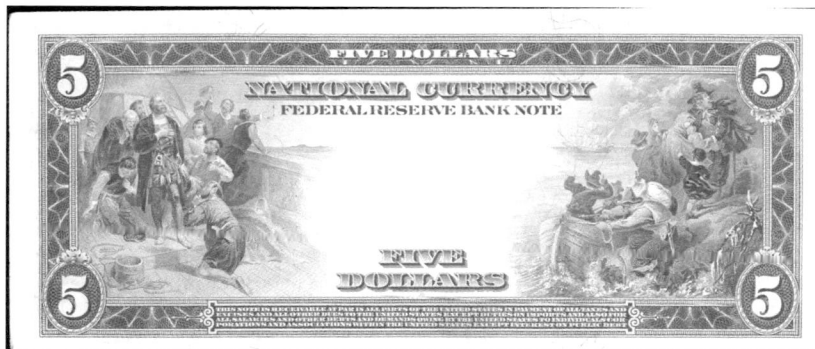

Abraham Lincoln at left.
Columbus discovery of land at left and Landing of the Pilgrims at right.

KL#	Fr#	Bank	Federal Sigs.	Bank Sigs.	Fine	XF	CH CU (63)	Gem CU (65)
320	788	Atlanta	Teehee-Burke	Bell-Wellborn	400.	2000.	4000.	5000.
321	789	Atlanta	Teehee-Burke	Pike-McCord	400.	750.	4000.	5000.
322	793	Chicago	Teehee-Burke	McLallen-McDougal	500.	1300.	2500.	3000.
323	800	Kansas City	Teehee-Burke	Anderson-Miller	450.	700.	2200.	2300
324	801	Kansas City	Teehee-Burke	Cross-Miller	2000.	9500.	—	25,000.
325	802	Kansas City	Teehee-Burke	Helm-Miller	500.	6000.	—	—
326	805	Dallas	Teehee-Burke	Hoopes-Van Zandt	550.	3500.	—	8000.
327	806	Dallas	Teehee-Burke	Talley-Van Zandt	550.	4000.	5000.	6000.
328	808	San Francisco	Teehee-Burke	Clerk-Lynch	500.	1750.	3000.	7000.

1918

KL#	Fr#	Bank	Federal Sigs.	Bank Sigs.	Fine	XF	CH CU (63)	Gem CU (65)
329	781	Boston	Teehee-Burke	Bullen-Morss	700.	7500.	—	—
330	782	New York	Teehee-Burke	Hendricks-Strong	225.	650.	2000.	2875.
331	783	Philadelphia	Teehee-Burke	Hardt-Passmore	375.	750.	4000.	5000.
332	784	Philadelphia	Teehee-Burke	Dyer-Passmore	375.	1500.	2500.	3000.
333	785	Cleveland	Teehee-Burke	Baxter-Fancher	375.	500.	1350.	1700.
334	786	Cleveland	Teehee-Burke	Davis-Fancher	550.	1750.	3000.	4250.
335	787	Cleveland	Elliott-Burke	Davis-Fancher	300.	750.	2500.	3000.
336	790	Atlanta	Teehee-Burke	Pike-McCord	375.	650.	1850.	2100.
337	791	Atlanta	Teehee-Burke	Bell-Wellborn	375.	650.	—	—
338	792	Atlanta	Elliott-Burke	Bell-Wellborn	500.	3000.	4000.	5000.
339	794	Chicago	Teehee-Burke	McCloud-McDougal	375.	600.	1100.	2525.
340	795	Chicago	Teehee-Burke	Cramer-McDougal	2525.	3500.	12,500.	—
341	796	St. Louis	Teehee-Burke	Attebery-Wells	375.	675.	2000.	3500.
342	797	St. Louis	Teehee-Burke	Attebery-Biggs	375.	1850.	—	—
343	798	St. Louis	Elliott-Burke	White-Biggs	375.	1700.	4000.	5000.
344	799	Minneapolis	Teehee-Burke	Cook-Wold	375.	1025.	3220.	4000.
345	803	Kansas City	Teehee-Burke	Anderson-Miller	375.	750.	2200.	2750.
346	804	Kansas City	Elliott-Burke	Helm-Miller	375.	1100.	2000.	2250.
347	807	Dallas	Teehee-Burke	Talley-Van Zandt	375.	4600.	—	—

Dated May 20, 1914.

348	809	San Francisco	Teehee-Burke	Clerk-Lynch	375.	2750.	3500.	4500.

Dated May 18, 1914.

348A	809a	San Francisco	Teehee-Burke	Clerk-Lynch	1750.	2700.	17,100.	—

Demand Notes
Ten Dollars

Abraham Lincoln at left, eagle at top center, Art at right.

KL#	Fr#	Payable at:	VG	Fine	VF
349	8-a	Boston, Type one: "For the" hand signed.	—	Very Rare.	—
350	8	Boston, Type two: "For the" engraved.	10,000.	18,000.	22,000.
351	6a	New York, Type one: "For the" hand signed.	10,000.	18,000.	55,000.
352	6	New York, Type two: "For the" engraved.	4000.	9000.	20,000.
353	7a	Philadelphia, Type one: "For the" hand signed.	12,000.	20,000.	100,000.
354	7	Philadelphia, Type two: "For the" engraved.	3750.	5000.	22,000.
356	10	St. Louis, Type two: "For the" engraved.	15,000.	12,000.	75,000.
357	9a	Cincinnati, Type one: "For the" hand signed.	9000.	17,500.	373,000.
358	9	Cincinnati, Type two: "For the" engraved.	—	16,000.	20,000.

United States Notes

Abraham Lincoln at left, eagle at top center, Art at right. One red serial number. First Obligation inscription (in octalobe) at center.

KL#	Fr#	Series	Signatures	Seal	Fine	XF	CH CU (63)	Gem CU (65)
359	93	1862	Chittenden-Spinner	Small red	6200.	7000.	13,800.	16,000.

Abraham Lincoln at left, eagle at top center, Art at right. One red serial number. Second Obligation inscription (in circle) at center.

American Bank Note Co. upper border.

KL#	Fr#	Series	Signatures	Seal	Fine	XF	CH CU (63)	Gem CU (65)
360	94	1862	Chittenden-Spinner	Small red	800.	3000.	8000.	—

Abraham Lincoln at left, eagle at top center, Art at right.
Second Obligation inscription (in circle) at center.

National Bank Note Co. lower border.

KL#	Fr#	Series	Signatures	Seal	Fine	XF	CH CU (63)	Gem CU (65)
360A	95	1863	Chittenden-Spinner	Small red	1500.	3400.	10,000.	12,500.

American Bank Note Co. lower border.

KL#	Fr#	Series	Signatures	Seal	Fine	XF	CH CU (63)	Gem CU (65)
360B	95a	1863	Chittenden-Spinner	Small red	2000.	7500.	15,750.	26,000.

Abraham Lincoln at left, eagle at top center, Art at right. Two red serial
numbers. Second Obligation inscription (in circle) at center.

American Bank Note Co. lower border.

KL#	Fr#	Series	Signatures	Seal	Fine	XF	CH CU (63)	Gem CU (65)
361	95b	1863	Chittenden-Spinner	Small red	1450.	3750.	10,000.	21,150.

Daniel Webster at lower left, Small eagle at lower center,
Pocahontas presented at Court at right.

American Bank Note Co. upper and lower borders. Red serial numbers.

KL#	Fr#	Series	Signatures	Seal	Fine	XF	CH CU (63)	Gem CU (65)
362	96	1869	Allison-Spinner	Large red	900.	3000.	6250.	9500.

Bureau of Engraving and Printing at upper face,
National Bank Note Co. on back.

KL#	Fr#	Series	Signatures	Seal	Fine	XF	CH CU (63)	Gem CU (65)
363	97	1875	Allison-New	Small red	4000.	14,000.	—	—

Series A in lower right face.

KL#	Fr#	Series	Signatures	Seal	Fine	XF	CH CU (63)	Gem CU (65)
364	98	1875	Allison-New		1000.	3000.	4500.	12,500.
365	99	1878	Allison-Gilfillan	Small red	700.	3200.	4750.	5500.

Daniel Webster at lower left, Small eagle at lower center,
Pocahontas presented at Court at right. Red serial numbers.

KL#	Fr#	Series	Signatures	Seal	Fine	XF	CH CU (63)	Gem CU (65)
366	100	1880	Scofield-Gilfillan	Large brown	600.	1200.	3000.	3750.
367	101	1880	Bruce-Gilfillan	Large brown	650.	1750.	2400.	3850.
368	102	1880	Bruce-Wyman	Large brown	500.	1350.	2500.	4750.

Daniel Webster at lower left, Small eagle at lower center,
Pocahontas presented at Court at right. Blue serial numbers.

KL#	Fr#	Series	Signatures	Seal	Fine	XF	CH CU (63)	Gem CU (65)
369	103	1880	Bruce-Wyman	Large red	500.	1250.	2500.	3900.
370	104	1880	Rosecrans-Jordan	Large red	400.	1650.	3500.	6250.
371	105	1880	Rosecrans-Hyatt	Large red	400.	1000.	2100.	3000.
372	106	1880	Rosecrans-Hyatt	Red spikes	400.	1400.	2400.	3750.
373	107	1880	Rosecrans-Huston	Red spikes	400.	1000.	2000.	3350.
374	108	1880	Rosecrans-Huston	Large brown	450.	1350.	2200.	3100.
375	109	1880	Rosecrans-Nebeker	Large brown	—	Rare	—	—

KL#	Fr#	Series	Signatures	Seal	Fine	XF	CH CU (63)	Gem CU (65)
376	110	1880	Rosecrans-Nebeker	Small red	375.	1400.	2000.	3250.
377	111	1880	Tillman-Morgan	Small red	500.	1400.	1750.	3000.
378	112	1880	Bruce-Roberts	Small red	825.	1500.	4250.	7750.
379	113	1880	Lyons-Roberts	Small red	500.	1400.	1800.	3000.

*American Bison Pablo at center, Meriweather Lewis at left and
William Clark at right. Red serial numbers. Large "X TEN" at left.
Progress standing at center.*

KL#	Fr#	Series	Signatures	Seal	Fine	XF	CH CU (63)	Gem CU (65)
380	114	1901	Lyons-Roberts	Small red	650.	2200.	5000.	9500.
381	115	1901	Lyons-Treat	Small red	800.	2400.	5500.	10,000.
382	116	1901	Vernon-Treat	Small red	650.	2250.	6250.	9500.
383	117	1901	Vernon-McClung	Small red	800.	2300.	15,000.	25,000.
384	118	1901	Napier-McClung	Small red	800.	2000.	7000.	8000.
385	119	1901	Parker-Burke	Small red	700.	2300.	4850.	7250.
386	120	1901	Teehee-Burke	Small red	900.	2500.	4600.	10,000.
387	121	1901	Elliott-White	Small red	500.	2250.	5000.	7000.
388	122	1901	Speelman-White	Small red	600.	2300.	4400.	8250.

Andrew Jackson at center. Red serial numbers.
Large "X DOLLARS" at right. 10 in ornate design at left and right ends.

KL#	Fr#	Series	Signatures	Seal	Fine	XF	CH CU (63)	Gem CU (65)
389	123	1923	Speelman-White	Small red	1000.	5750.	11,500.	18,500.

Compound Interest Treasury Notes

Salmon P. Chase at left, Eagle of the Capitol at center, Peace at right.
Redemption values at six month intervals at center.

KL#	FR#	Act	Overprint Date	Signatures	VG	Fine	XF
390	190	1863	June 10, 1864	Chittenden-Spinner	3000.	6000.	12,500.
391	190-A	1864	July 15, 1864	Chittenden-Spinner	4000.	6500.	17,500.
392	190b	1864	Aug. 15-Dec. 15,1864	Colby-Spinner	3000.	7000.	17,500.

Interest Bearing Notes

Salmon P. Chase at left, Eagle of the Capitol at center, Peace at right.

KL#	FR#	Act	Signatures	VG	Fine	XF
393	196	1863	Chittenden-Spinner	4000.	8000.	30,000.
393A	196a	1863	Chittenden-Spinner	4000.	8000.	19,000.

Refunding Certificates

Benjamin Franklin at upper left. Vertical format back, payable to order.

KL#	FR#	Signatures	Payable to...	VG	Fine	XF
394	213	Scofield-Gilfillan	To Order.	—	—	370,000.

Benjamin Franklin at upper left. Horizontal back, payable to Bearer.

KL#	FR#	Signatures	Payable to...	VG	Fine	XF
395	214	Scofield-Gilfillan	To Bearer.	1000.	2250.	6000.

National Gold Bank Notes

Franklin and Electricity, 1752 at left, America Seizing Lightning at right.
Various U.S. Gold Coins.

KL#	Fr#	Series	Issuing Bank	Location	Good	Fine	VF
396	1142	Orig.	First Nat'l Gold Bank	San Francisco	2400.	20,000.	45,000.
397	1143	Orig.	Nat'l Gold Bank & Trust Co.	San Francisco	4000.	10,000.	—
398	1144	Orig.	Nat'l Gold Bank of D.O. Mills	Sacramento	4000.	28,000.	69,000.
399	1146	Orig.	First Nat'l Gold Bank	Stockton	4000.	20,000.	—
400	1145	Orig.	First Nat'l Gold Bank	Santa Barbara	17,500.	54,000.	75,000.
401	1148	Orig.	Farmers' Nat'l Gold Bank	San Jose	4000.	33,000.	—
402	1149	Orig.	First Nat'l Gold Bank	Petaluma	4000.	18,000.	86,250.
403	1150	1875	First Nat'l Gold Bank	Petaluma	4000.	40,250.	—
404	1151	Orig.	First Nat'l Gold Bank	Oakland	4000.	15,000.	—
405	1151a	1875	Union Nat'l Gold Bank	Oakland	—	92,000.	—
406	1147	1875	First Nat'l Gold Bank	Stockton	4000.	12,000.	—

Silver Certificates

Robert Morris at upper left.

Place of Deposit: New York.

KL#	Fr#	Series	CounterSigned by:	Fine	XF	CH CU (63)
407	284	1878	J.C. Hopper, Asst. U.S. Treasurer	—	—	89,000.

Place of Deposit: New York.

408	283	1878	W.G. White, Asst. U.S. Treasurer	—	253,000.	—

Place of Deposit: Washington, D.C.

409	285a	1878	A.U. Wyman, Asst. U.S. Treasurer	—	30,000.	50,000.

Payable at: New York.

410	284a	1878	T. Hillhouse, Asst. U.S. Treasurer	—	Rare	—

Payable at: New York.

411	286	1880	T. Hillhouse, Asst. U.S. Treasurer	—	10,000.	30,000.

Robert Morris at upper left.
Blue serial numbers, with large "X" below center seal.

KL#	Fr#	Series	Signatures	Seal	Fine	XF	CH CU (63)	Gem CU (65)
412	287	1880	Scofield-Gilfillan	Large brown	2250.	8500.	32,000.	—
413	288	1880	Bruce-Gilfillan	Large brown	1700.	8500.	15,300.	33,000.
414	289	1880	Bruce-Wyman	Large brown	1750.	8500.	14,000.	19,000.

Robert Morris at upper left.
Blue serial numbers, without large "X" below center seal.

KL#	Fr#	Series	Signatures	Seal	Fine	XF	CH CU (63)	Gem CU (65)
415	290	1880	Bruce-Wyman	Large red	3500.	30,000.	40,000.	50,000.

Thomas A. Hendricks at center.

KL#	Fr#	Series	Signatures	Seal	Fine	XF	CH CU (63)	Gem CU (65)
416	291	1886	Rosecrans-Jordan	Small red	1250.	5000.	20,000.	25,000.
417	292	1886	Rosecrans-Hyatt	Small red	1250.	6000.	12,000.	25,000.
418	293	1886	Rosecrans-Hyatt	Large red	1250.	4000.	16,100.	25,000.
419	294	1886	Rosecrans-Huston	Large red	1000.	4000.	12,000.	25,000.
420	295	1886	Rosecrans-Huston	Large brown	1250.	7600.	22,000.	25,000.
421	296	1886	Rosecrans-Nebeker	Large brown	1000.	5750.	12,000.	35,000.
422	297	1886	Rosecrans-Nebeker	Small red	3500.	9000.	20,000.	42,500.
423	298	1891	Rosecrans-Nebeker	Small red	700.	1700.	8250.	10,000.
424	299	1891	Tillman-Morgan	Small red	550.	3000.	7500.	9000.
425	300	1891	Bruce-Roberts	Small red	650.	2000.	4250.	12,000.
426	301	1891	Lyons-Roberts	Small red	650.	2000.	5000.	12,500.

Thomas A. Hendricks at center. Large "X TEN" at left.

KL#	Fr#	Series	Signatures	Seal	Fine	XF	CH CU (63)	Gem CU (65)
427	302	1908	Vernon-Treat	Small blue	500.	1250.	6500.	7750.
428	303	1908	Vernon-McClung	Small blue	800.	2000.	5500.	7750.
429	304	1908	Parker-Burke	Small blue	600.	2750.	7000.	9000.

Treasury or Coin Notes

General Philip Sheridan at center.

KL#	Fr#	Series	Signatures	Seal	Fine	XF	CH CU (63)	Gem CU (65)
430	366	1890	Rosecrans-Huston	Large brown	1400.	6750.	9000.	25,500.
431	367	1890	Rosecrans-Nebeker	Large brown	1850.	4500.	20,700.	31,000.
432	368	1890	Rosecrans-Nebeker	Small red	1000.	5000.	7000.	17,000.

KL#	Fr#	Series	Signatures	Seal	Fine	XF	CH CU (63)	Gem CU (65)
433	369	1891	Rosecrans-Nebeker	Small red	1250.	1900.	4000.	6500.
434	370	1891	Tillman-Morgan	Small red	1000.	1800.	4300.	6000.
435	371	1891	Bruce-Roberts	Small red	1250.	2850.	5000.	6325.

Gold Certificates

Michael Hillegas at center. Large "X TEN" at left.

KL#	Fr#	Issue	Signatures	Fine	XF	CH CU (63)	Gem CU (65)
436	1167	1907	Vernon-Treat	175.	635.	3000.	3600.
437	1168	1907	Vernon-McClung	175.	675.	4500.	5000.
438	1169	1907	Napier-McClung	100.	500.	3450.	3600.
439	1170	1907	Napier-Thompson	450.	1250.	—	34,500.
440	1171	1907	Parker-Burke	225.	500.	1800.	4500.
441	1172	1907	Teehee-Burke	150.	650.	1500.	5000.

Michael Hillegas at center. Legal Tender clause and large "X TEN" at left.

KL#	Fr#	Issue	Signatures	Fine	XF	CH CU (63)	Gem CU (65)
442	1173	1922	Speelman-White	200.	450.	1350.	2250.

Michael Hillegas at center.
Legal Tender clause and large "X TEN" at left. Small serial number.

KL#	Fr#	Issue	Signatures	Fine	XF	CH CU (63)	Gem CU (65)
442A	1173a	1922	Speelman-White	200.	500.	1150.	2250.

Federal Reserve Notes
1914

Andrew Jackson at center. Red Seal. Farming at left and Industry at right.

KL#	Fr#	Bank	Signatures	Fine	XF	CH CU (63)	Gem CU (65)
443	892	Boston	Burke-McAdoo				
			a Plate Letter at upper left.	550.	1100.	3200.	7500.
			b District # and letter above plate letter at upper left.	800.	2750.	4000.	6000.
444	893	New York	Burke-McAdoo				
			a Plate letter at upper left.	500.	900.	2500.	5500.
			b District # and letter above plate letter at upper left.	400.	1100.	2000.	4250.
445	894	Philadelphia	Burke-McAdoo				
			a Plate letter at upper right.	800.	2000.	4000.	7000.
			b District # and letter above plate letter at upper left.	400.	1000.	3500.	5750.
446	895	Cleveland	Burke-McAdoo				
			a Plate letter at upper right.	850.	2500.	4000.	5750.
			b District # and letter above plate letter at upper left.	375.	1250.	2500.	5750.
447	896	Richmond	Burke-McAdoo				
			a Plate letter at upper left.	800.	2500.	6500.	7250.
			b District # and letter above plate letter at upper left.	800.	1750.	4000.	5750.
448	897	Atlanta	Burke-McAdoo				
			a Plate letter at upper left.	300.	2500.	4000.	5750.
			b District # and letter above plate letter at upper left.	1000.	2000.	8000.	9000.
449	898	Chicago	Burke-McAdoo				
			a Plate letter at upper left.	400.	1250.	4500.	6000.
			b District # and letter above plate letter at upper left.	300.	1250.	3250.	5000.

KL#	Fr#	Bank	Signatures	Fine	XF	CH CU (63)	Gem CU (65)
450	899	St. Louis	Burke-McAdoo				
		a Plate letter at upper left.		600.	1300.	2800.	5800.
		b District # and letter above plate letter at upper left.		850.	1500.	3700.	5750.
451	900	Minneapolis	Burke-McAdoo				
		a Plate letter at upper right.		700.	1250.	3500.	11,000.
		b District # and letter above plate letter at upper left.		400.	3000.	4000.	9000.
452	901	Kansas City	Burke-McAdoo				
		a Plate letter at upper left.		500.	3500.	3750.	—
		b District # and letter above plate letter at upper left.		700.	3500.	8000.	—
453	902	Dallas	Burke-McAdoo				
		a Plate letter at upper left.		600.	3500.	4750.	5750.
		b District # and letter above plate letter at upper left.		1000.	5500.	7500.	8000.
454	903	San Francisco	Burke-McAdoo				
		a Plate letter at upper left.		400.	3000.	5250.	6000.
		b District # and letter above plate letter at upper left.		600.	3500.	5000.	5750.

Andrew Jackson at center. Blue Seal. Farming at left and Industry at right.

KL#	Fr#	Bank	Signatures	Fine	XF	CH CU (63)	Gem CU (65)
455	904	Boston	Burke-McAdoo	110.	240.	900.	1100.
456	905	Boston	Burke-Glass	100.	750.	1150.	1300.
457	906	Boston	Burke-Houston	110.	750.	1150.	1300.
458	907	Boston	White-Mellon				
		a Upper case district letter at lower left.		70.00	175.	425.	775.
		b Lower case district letter at lower left.		300.	375.	500.	1200.
459	908	New York	Burke-McAdoo	80.00	240.	975.	1100.
460	909	New York	Burke-Glass	100.	300.	3000.	3350.
461	910	New York	Burke-Houston	70.00	175.	600.	900.
462	911	New York	White-Mellon				
		a Upper case district letter at lower left.		100.	225.	500.	800.
		b Lower case district letter at lower left.		90.00	150.	450.	650.
		c Blue seal to left of district letter.		110.	250.	700.	1000.
463	912	Philadelphia	Burke-McAdoo	125.	320.	1150.	1300.
464	913	Philadelphia	Burke-Glass	85.00	625.	2000.	3000.
465	914	Philadelphia	Burke-Houston	125.	325.	575.	1100.
466	915	Philadelphia	White-Mellon				
		a Upper case district letter at lower left.		75.00	230.	500.	825.
		c Blue seal to left of district letter.		105.	250.	800.	1100.
467	916	Cleveland	Burke-McAdoo	155.	240.	2800.	3250.
468	917	Cleveland	Burke-Glass	90.00	700.	2000.	2500.
469	918	Cleveland	Burke-Houston	85.00	240.	675.	1100.

KL#	Fr#	Bank	Signatures	Fine	XF	CH CU (63)	Gem CU (65)
470	919	Cleveland	White-Mellon				
		a	Upper case district letter at lower left.	85.00	225.	650.	1100.
		b	Lower case district letter at lower left.	150.	450.	1750.	2500.
		c	Blue seal to left of district letter.	125.	350.	2350.	2750.
471	920	Richmond	Burke-McAdoo	105.	225.	575.	1100.
472	921	Richmond	Burke-Glass	110.	1400.	2400.	2750.
473	922	Richmond	Burke-Houston	55.00	240.	825.	1100.
474	923	Richmond	White-Mellon	85.00	125.	575.	1250.
475	924	Atlanta	Burke-McAdoo	310.	1275.	2400.	2750.
476	925	Atlanta	Burke-Glass	200.	500.	700.	1100.
477	926	Atlanta	Burke-Houston	245.	400.	2100.	2600.
478	927	Atlanta	White-Mellon				
		a	Upper case district letter at lower left.	110.	240.	1500.	2000.
		b	Lower case district letter at lower left.	110.	750.	2000.	2300.
479	928	Chicago	Burke-McAdoo	75.00	200.	500.	1000.
480	929	Chicago	Burke-Glass	75.00	450.	1300.	2400.
481	930	Chicago	Burke-Houston	110.	240.	500.	825.
482	931	Chicago	White-Mellon				
		a	Upper case district letter at lower left.	95.00	200.	525.	2000.
		b	Lower case district letter at lower left.	105.	275.	800.	900.
		c	Blue seal to left of district letter.	115.	350.	2250.	3000.
483	932	St. Louis	Burke-McAdoo	110.	240.	1200.	1350.
484	933	St. Louis	Burke-Glass	110.	900.	1500.	1750.
485	934	St. Louis	Burke-Houston	75.00	250.	575.	1100.
486	935	St. Louis	White-Mellon	155.	420.	750.	1875.
487	936	Minneapolis	Burke-McAdoo	90.00	275.	1250.	1350.
488	937	Minneapolis	Burke-Glass	150.	525.	2850.	3000.
489	938	Minneapolis	Burke-Houston	125.	620.	1350.	1500.
490	939	Minneapolis	White-Mellon	80.00	200.	575.	1350.
491	940	Kansas City	Burke-McAdoo	105.	240.	450.	1000.
492	941	Kansas City	Burke-Glass	430.	925.	3750.	4500.
493	942	Kansas City	Burke-Houston	125.	275.	700.	2300.
494	943	Kansas City	White-Mellon				
		a	Upper case district letter at lower left.	110.	240.	1250.	1750.
		c	Blue seal to left of district letter.	—	Rare	—	—
495	944	Dallas	Burke-McAdoo	110.	230.	1000.	1300.
496	945	Dallas	Burke-Glass	1250.	2300.	7000.	9000.
497	946	Dallas	Burke-Houston	65.00	240.	1500.	2000.
498	947	Dallas	White-Mellon	110.	240.	1350.	1750.
499	948	San Francisco	Burke-McAdoo	320.	—	—	—
500	949	San Francisco	Burke-Glass	295.	2300.	—	—
501	950	San Francisco	Burke-Houston	295.	875.	2250.	4500.
502	951	San Francisco	White-Mellon				
		a	Upper case district letter at lower left.	110.	150.	675.	1200.
		b	Lower case district letter at lower left.	400.	600.	2000.	2500.
		c	Blue seal to left of district letter.	400.	600.	2000.	2300.

Federal Reserve Bank Notes
1915

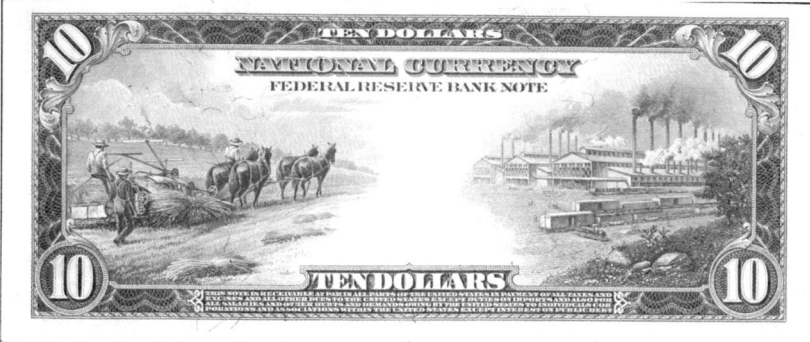

Andrew Jackson at center. Farming at left and Industry at right.

KL#	Fr#	Bank	Federal Sigs.	Bank Sigs.	Fine	XF	CH CU (63)	Gem CU (65)
503	811	Atlanta	Teehee-Burke	Bell-Wellborn	2500.	15,000.	—	—
504	813	Chicago	Teehee-Burke	McLallen-McDougal	1100.	4000.	7000.	11,500.
505	816	Kansas City	Teehee-Burke	Anderson-Miller	1500.	3500.	7000.	8500.
506	817	Kansas City	Teehee-Burke	Cross-Miller	1050.	3800.	5500.	6500.
507	818	Kansas City	Teehee-Burke	Helm-Miller	1750.	43,000.	—	—
508	819	Dallas	Teehee-Burke	Hoopes-Van Zandt	1800.	3800.	—	11,000.
509	820	Dallas	Teehee-Burke	Gilbert-Van Zandt	—	48,875.	—	—
510	821	Dallas	Teehee-Burke	Talley-Van Zandt	—	16,000.	—	—

1918

KL#	Fr#	Bank	Federal Sigs.	Bank Sigs.	Fine	XF	CH CU (63)	Gem CU (65)
511	810	New York	Teehee-Burke	Hendricks-Strong	1250.	4500.	—	14,250.
512	812	Atlanta	Elliott-Burke	Bell-Wellborn	1200.	3100.	—	—
513	814	Chicago	Teehee-Burke	McCloud-McDougal	900.	5500.	7500.	9000.
514	815	St. Louis	Teehee-Burke	Attebery-Wells	1380.	4500.	—	8000.

Demand Notes
Twenty Dollars

America at center, standing with sword and shield.

KL#	Fr#	Payable at:	VG	Fine	VF
515	13a	Boston - Type One	—	—	200,000.
516	13	Boston	36,000.	—	62,500.
517	11a	New York	41,400.	—	80,000.
518	11	New York	21,000.	80,000.	100,000.
520	12	Philadelphia	115,000.	—	100,000.
522	14	Cincinnati	—	2500.	—
522A	15	St. Louis	Unknown in private hands		

United States Notes

America at center, standing with sword and shield. One red serial number.
Second Obligation inscription (in octolobe) at center.

KL#	Fr#	Series	Signatures	Seal	Fine	XF	CH CU (63)	Gem CU (65)
523	124	1862	Chittenden-Spinner	Small red	2300.	16,100.	22,500.	—

Second Obligation inscription (in oval) at center.

American Bank Note Co. lower border.

524	125	1862	Chittenden-Spinner	Small red	2500.	6750.	17,500.	—

*America at center, standing with sword and shield. Two red serial
numbers. Second Obligation inscription (in oval) at center.*

National Bank Note Co. American Bank Note Co.

KL#	Fr#	Series	Signatures	Seal	Fine	XF	CH CU (63)	Gem CU (65)
525	126	1863	Chittenden-Spinner	Small red	3000.	6750.	17,825.	20,000.

America at center, standing with sword and shield.
Second Obligation inscription (in oval) at center.

KL#	Fr#	Series	Signatures	Seal	Fine	XF	CH CU (63)	Gem CU (65)
525A	126a	1863	Chittenden-Spinner	Small red	3700.	15,000.	—	—
525B	126b	1863	Chittenden-Spinner	Small red	2000.	4000.	17,500.	30,000.

Alexander Hamilton at left, Liberty at right. Blue serial numbers.
Central Legal Tender clause flanked by XX and 20

American Bank Note Co. in lower border.

KL#	Fr#	Series	Signatures	Seal	Fine	XF	CH CU (63)	Gem CU (65)
526	127	1869	Allison-Spinner	Large red	2900.	8000.	18,500.	46,000.

Alexander Hamilton at left, Liberty at right.
Blue serial numbers. "XX" twice in red.

KL#	Fr#	Series	Signatures	Seal	Fine	XF	CH CU (63)	Gem CU (65)
527	128	1875	Allison-New	Small red	1225.	2750.	5000.	8000.
528	129	1878	Allison-Gilfillan	Small red	900.	1100.	3000.	5750.

Alexander Hamilton at left, Liberty at right. Blue serial numbers.

KL#	Fr#	Series	Signatures	Seal	Fine	XF	CH CU (63)	Gem CU (65)
529	130	1880	Scofield-Gilfillan	Large brown	3000.	4250.	—	—
530	131	1880	Bruce-Gilfillan	Large brown	850.	2500.	—	—
531	132	1880	Bruce-Wyman	Large brown	750.	3250.	15,000.	—
532	133	1880	Bruce-Wyman	Large red	1000.	4000.	10,000.	17,000.
533	134	1880	Rosecrans-Jordan	Large red	500.	1600.	5500.	7500.
534	135	1880	Rosecrans-Hyatt	Large red	400.	1750.	3250.	5000.
535	136	1880	Rosecrans-Hyatt	Red spikes	800.	1500.	2000.	4250.
536	137	1880	Rosecrans-Huston	Red spikes	400.	1250.	2250.	5500.
537	138	1880	Rosecrans-Huston	Large brown	650.	2250.	4000.	7750.
538	139	1880	Rosecrans-Nebeker	Large brown	1250.	3000.	3500.	10,000.
539	140	1880	Rosecrans-Nebeker	Small red	600.	1000.	2000.	3750.
540	141	1880	Tillman-Morgan	Small red	300.	1250.	2250.	3800.
541	142	1880	Bruce-Roberts	Small red	300.	1250.	2800.	4000.
542	143	1880	Lyons-Roberts	Small red	400.	1250.	4500.	6000.
543	144	1880	Vernon-Treat	Small red	375.	1250.	4150.	4500.
544	145	1880	Vernon-McClung	Small red	485.	1650.	6000.	—

Alexander Hamilton at left, Liberty at right. Red serial numbers.

KL#	Fr#	Series	Signatures	Seal	Fine	XF	CH CU (63)	Gem CU (65)
545	146	1880	Teehee-Burke	Small red	485.	1000.	5250.	6000.
546	147	1880	Elliott-White	Small red	275.	1000.	2000.	4100.

Compound Interest Treasury Notes

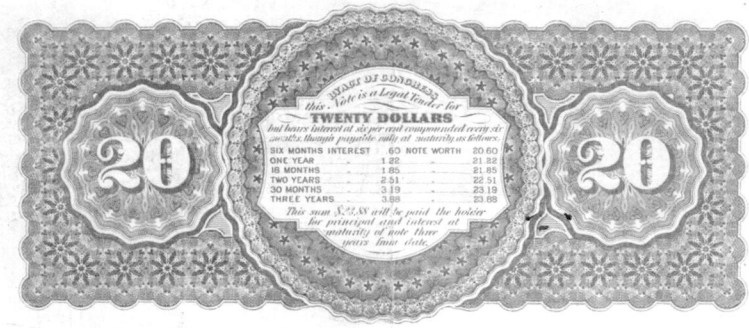

Victory at left, motor at lower center, Abraham Lincoln at right.
Interest table at six month intervals at center.

KL#	FR#	Act	Overprint Date	Signatures	VG	Fine	XF
547	191	1864	July 14, 1864	Chittenden-Spinner	—	—	92,000.
548	191a	1864	Aug. 15, 1864-Oct. 16, 1865	Colby-Spinner	5000.	7750.	32,500.

Interest Bearing Notes

Victory at left, motor at lower center, Abraham Lincoln at right.
Clause within central diamond frame.

KL#	FR#	Act	Signatures	VG	Fine	XF
549	197	1863	Chittenden-Spinner	6500.	74,750.	—
549a	197a		Chittenden-Spinner	5000.	20,000.	45,000.

Gold Certificates

Eagle on shield at left, large "20" in green underprint.

KL#	Fr#	Issue/Act/Series	Signatures	Fine	XF	CH CU (63)	Gem CU (65)
550	1166b	First/1863	Colby-Spinner	—	500,000.	—	—

James Garfield at right. Eagle on ocean telegraph.

KL#	Fr#	Series	Signatures	Seal	Fine	XF	CH CU (63)	Gem CU (65)
551	1175	1882	Thos. C. Acton, Asst. U.S. Treasurer	Brown	—	—	—	
552	1174	1882	Bruce-Gilfillan	Brown	2500.	—	—	—
553	1176	1882	Bruce-Wyman	Brown	4500.	20,000.	44,000.	138,000.
554	1177	1882	Rosecrans-Huston	Large brown	4100.	18,500.	—	—
555	1178	1882	Lyons-Roberts	Small red	750.	4000.	10,000.	15,000.

George Washington at center, "$20" at left. Great Seal.

KL#	Fr#	Series	Signatures	Seal	Fine	XF	CH CU (63)	Gem CU (65)
556	1179	1905	Lyons-Roberts	Small red	2500.	18,500.	30,000.	80,000.
557	1180	1905	Lyons-Treat	Small red	1750.	10,000.	25,000.	50,000.

George Washington at center, "XX" at left. Great Seal.

558	1181	1906	Vernon-Treat	Gold	260.	1000.	2500.	3000.
559	1182	1906	Vernon-McClung	Gold	225.	900.	4750.	1.00
560	1183	1906	Napier-McClung	Gold	200.	900.	3500.	4000.
561	1184	1906	Napier-Thompson	Gold	750.	1800.	9500.	12,500.

KL#	Fr#	Series	Signatures	Seal	Fine	XF	CH CU (63)	Gem CU (65)
562	1185	1906	Parker-Burke	Gold	200.	850.	2000.	6325.
563	1186	1906	Teehee-Burke	Gold	300.	725.	2250.	5500.

George Washington at center, Legal tender clause and "XX" at left.
Great Seal.

KL#	Fr#	Series	Signatures	Seal	Fine	XF	CH CU (63)	Gem CU (65)
564	1187	1922	Speelman-White	Gold	220.	700.	1750.	4000.

National Gold Bank Notes

Battle of Lexington, 1775 at left, Loyalty at right.
Various U.S. Gold Coins.

KL#	Fr#	Series	Issuing Bank	Location	Good	Fine	VF
566	1152	Orig.	First Nat'l Gold Bank	San Francisco	10,000.	40,000.	50,000.
567	1154	Orig.	Nat'l Gold Bank of D.O. Mills	Sacramento	8000.	30,000.	—
568	1155	Orig.	First Nat'l Gold Bank	Stockton	8000.	25,500.	—
569	1159a	Orig.	First Nat'l Gold Bank	Santa Barbara	10,000.	30,000.	—
570	1156	Orig.	Farmers' Nat'l Gold Bank	San Jose	12,000.	35,000.	—
571	1153	1875	First Nat'l Gold Bank	San Francisco	12,000.	25,000.	—
572	1157	1875	First Nat'l Gold Bank	Petaluma	—	15,000.	—
573	1158	Orig.	First Nat'l Gold Bank	Oakland	12,000.	30,000	—
574	1159	Orig.	Union Nat'l Gold Bank	Oakland	—	150,000.	—

Silver Certificates

Stephen Decatur at right.

Place of Deposit: New York.; Rare.

KL#	Fr#	Series	CounterSigned by:	Fine	XF	CH CU (63)
575	305	1878	J.C. Hopper, Asst. U.S. Treasurer	—	—	—

Place of Deposit: Washington, D.C.

KL#	Fr#	Series	CounterSigned by:	Fine	XF	CH CU (63)
576	306	1878	A.U. Wyman, Asst. U.S. Treasurer	7500.	15,000.	—

Place of Deposit: New York.

KL#	Fr#	Series	CounterSigned by:	Fine	XF	CH CU (63)
577	307	1878	T. Hillhouse, Asst. U.S. Treasurer	5000.	25,000.	75,000.

Place of Deposit: New York.

KL#	Fr#	Series	CounterSigned by:	Fine	XF	CH CU (63)
578	308	1880	T. Hillhouse, Asst. U.S. Treasurer	7500.	20,000.	47,500.

Stephen Decatur at right. Large brown "XX" under seal at center.

KL#	Fr#	Series	Signatures	Seal	Fine	XF	CH CU (63)	Gem CU (65)
579	309	1880	Scofield-Gilfillan	Large brown	4200.	12,500.	—	—
580	310	1880	Bruce-Gilfillan	Large brown	3000.	22,425.	—	—
581	311	1880	Bruce-Wyman	Large brown	4000.	15,000.	—	—

Stephen Decatur at right.

KL#	Fr#	Series	Signatures	Seal	Fine	XF	CH CU (63)	Gem CU (65)
582	312	1880	Bruce-Wyman	Small red	4250.	22,000.		—

Daniel Manning at center flanked by Agriculture and Industry.
Clause within central double diamond frame design.

KL#	Fr#	Series	Signatures	Seal	Fine	XF	CH CU (63)	Gem CU (65)
583	313	1886	Rosecrans-Hyatt	Large red	5000.	50,000.	60,000.	100,000.
584	314	1886	Rosecrans-Huston	Large brown	2750.	24,150.	30,000.	45,000.
585	315	1886	Rosecrans-Nebeker	Large brown	3750.	27,750.	—	—
586	316	1886	Rosecrans-Nebeker	Small red	4000.	35,000.	60,000.	200,000.

Daniel Manning at center flanked by Agriculture and Industry.
"Series 1891" upper right and lower left.

KL#	Fr#	Series	Signatures	Seal	Fine	XF	CH CU (63)	Gem CU (65)
587	317	1891	Rosecrans-Nebeker	Small red	1200.	4000.	12,000.	35,250.
588	318	1891	Tillman-Morgan	Small red	750.	3750.	12,000.	18,000.
589	319	1891	Bruce-Roberts	Small red	1250.	3750.	12,000.	18,000.
590	320	1891	Lyons-Roberts	Small red	1500.	3750.	16,000.	18,000.

Daniel Manning at center flanked by Agriculture and Industry.
Large blue "XX" at left.

KL#	Fr#	Series	Signatures	Seal	Fine	XF	CH CU (63)	Gem CU (65)
591	321	1891	Parker-Burke	Small blue	750.	3300.	6750.	10,600.

Large and small size signature varieties are known.

592	322	1891	Teehee-Burke	Small blue	900.	3500.	12,000.	18,000.

Treasury or Coin Notes

John Marshall at left.

KL#	Fr#	Series	Signatures	Seal	Fine	XF	CH CU (63)	Gem CU (65)
593	372	1890	Rosecrans-Huston	Large brown	4000.	21,000.	75,000.	161,000.
594	373	1890	Rosecrans-Nebeker	Large brown	7500.	16,000.	25,000.	40,000.
595	374	1890	Rosecrans-Nebeker	Small red	3500.	9000.	21,000.	40,259.

KL#	Fr#	Series	Signatures	Seal	Fine	XF	CH CU (63)	Gem CU (65)
596	375	1891	Tillman-Morgan	Small red	2850.	7000.	10,000.	15,500.
597	375a	1891	Bruce-Roberts	Small red	10,500.	—	—	—

Federal Reserve Notes

1914

Grover Cleveland at center. Red Seal.
Auto and steam train at left, tug and ocean liner at right.

KL#	Fr#	Bank	Signatures	Fine	XF	CH CU (63)	Gem CU (65)
598	952	Boston	Burke-McAdoo				
		a Plate letter at upper left.		550.	2250.	8000.	9000.
		b District # and letter above plate letter at upper left.		1500.	3750.	6800.	9000.
599	953	New York	Burke-McAdoo				
		a Plate letter at upper left.		450.	3000.	6400.	13,500.
		b District # and letter above plate letter at upper left.		450.	2000.	6800.	9500.
600	954	Philadelphia	Burke-McAdoo				
		a Plate letter at upper left.		575.	6450.	8000.	9000.
		b District # and letter above plate letter at upper left.		675.	2750.	6800.	9000.
601	955	Cleveland	Burke-McAdoo				
		a Plate letter at upper left.		875.	4400.	6800.	9000.
		b District # and letter above plate letter at upper left.		700.	2500.	6800.	9000.
602	956	Richmond	Burke-McAdoo				
		a Plate letter at upper left.		1000.	5000.	6800.	9000.
		b District # and letter above plate letter at upper left.		1000.	5000.	6800.	9000.
603	957	Atlanta	Burke-McAdoo				
		a Plate letter at upper left.		—	—	—	—
604	958	Chicago	Burke-McAdoo				
		a Plate letter at upper left.		525.	1500.	—	—
		b District # and letter above plate letter at upper left.		600.	2300.	10,000.	—

KL#	Fr#	Bank	Signatures	Fine	XF	CH CU (63)	Gem CU (65)
605	959	St. Louis	Burke-McAdoo				
		a Plate letter at upper left.		550.	3500.	6800.	9000.
		b District # and letter above plate letter at upper left.		725.	3500.	6800.	9000.
606	960	Minneapolis	Burke-McAdoo				
		a Plate letter at upper left.		725.	4500.	6800.	9000.
		b District # and letter above plate letter at upper left.		2250.	3750.	6800.	9000.
607	961	Kansas City	Burke-McAdoo				
		a Plate letter at upper left.		500.	4000.	6800.	9000.
		b District # and letter above plate letter at upper left.		1000.	—	—	—
608	962	Dallas	Burke-McAdoo				
		a Plate letter at upper left.		—	4600.	—	—
609	963	San Francisco	Burke-McAdoo				
		a Plate letter at upper left.		1000.	3750.	6800.	9000.
		b District # and letter above plate letter at upper left.		1000.	4500.	6800.	9000.

Grover Cleveland at center. Blue Seal.
Auto and steam train at left, tug and ocean liner at right.

KL#	Fr#	Bank	Signatures		Fine	XF	CH CU (63)	Gem CU (65)
610	964	Boston	Burke-McAdoo	145.	1200.	2000.	2250.	
611	965	Boston	Burke-Glass	—	750.	—	—	
612	966	Boston	Burke-Houston	115.	400.	1500.	2000.	
613	967	Boston	White-Mellon	145.	400	725.	2300.	
614	968	New York	Burke-McAdoo	175.	275.	1300.	1500.	
615	969	New York	Burke-Glass	200.	500.		2000.	
616	970	New York	Burke-Houston	175.	400.	725.	950.	
617	971	New York	White-Mellon					
		a Upper case district letter at lower left 75.00			150.	750.	2550.	
		b Lower case district eltter at lower left.	175.		350.	900.	1275.	
		c Blue seal to left of district letter.	—		—	—	—	
618	972	Philadelphia	Burke-McAdoo	80.00	400.	2750.	3000.	
619	973	Philadelphia	Burke-Glass	175.	300.	1750.	3000.	
620	974	Philadelphia	Burke-Houston	125.	400.	1200.	1400.	
621	975	Philadelphia	White-Mellon	185.	300.	750.	1750.	
622	976	Cleveland	Burke-McAdoo	215.	325.	1800.	2000.	
623	977	Cleveland	Burke-Glass	85.00	500.	2300.	2725.	
624	978	Cleveland	Burke-Houston	215.	400.	1500.	1850.	
625	979	Cleveland	White-Mellon					
		a Upper case district letter at lower left.	125.		300.	800.	1975.	
		b Lower case district letter at lower left.	200.		700.	1500.	2000.	
626	980	Richmond	Burke-McAdoo	400.	1300.	2350.	2800.	
627	981	Richmond	Burke-Glass	400.	1150.	2350.	2800.	

KL#	Fr#	Bank	Signatures	Fine	XF	CH CU (63)	Gem CU (65)
628	982	Richmond	Burke-Houston	100.	375.	725.	950.
629	983	Richmond	White-Mellon				
		a Upper case district letter at lower left.		215.	425.	1750.	2000.
		b Lower case district letter at lower left.		—	—	—	—
630	984	Atlanta	Burke-McAdoo	150.	350.	600.	2100.
632	986	Atlanta	Burke-Houston	215.	400.	1100.	1250.
633	987	Atlanta	White-Mellon				
		a Upper case district letter at lower left.		110.	145.	725.	1550.
		b Lower case district letter at lower left.		—	Rare	—	—
634	988	Chicago	Burke-McAdoo	215.	400.	1250.	1400.
635	989	Chicago	Burke-Glass	100.	350.	1250.	2500.
636	990	Chicago	Burke-Houston	215.	325.	1400.	1850.
637	991	Chicago	White-Mellon				
		c Blue seal to left of district letter.		450.	1000.	2500.	3000.
637	991	Chicago	White-Mellon				
		b Lower case district letter at lower left.		100.	400.	1200.	1650.
637	991	Chicago	White-Mellon				
		a Upper case district letter at lower left.		75.00	400.	1200.	1650.
638	992	St. Louis	Burke-McAdoo	75.00	400.	750.	950.
639	993	St. Louis	Burke-Glass	175.	2425.	—	—
640	994	St. Louis	Burke-Houston	150.	400.	725.	950.
641	995	St. Louis	White-Mellon	60.00	400.	725.	950.
642	996	Minneapolis	Burke-McAdoo	215.	300.	1750.	2000.
643	997	Minneapolis	Burke-Glass	215.	2575.	—	—
644	998	Minneapolis	Burke-Houston	215.	400.	800.	950.
645	999	Minneapolis	White-Mellon	250.	350.	575.	2500.
646	1000	Kansas City	Burke-McAdoo	150.	400.	600.	1500.
647	1001	Kansas City	Burke-Glass	—	—	—	—
648	1002	Kansas City	Burke-Houston	110.	250.	1275.	1500.
649	1003	Kansas City	White-Mellon	150.	400.	725.	1425.
650	1004	Dallas	Burke-McAdoo	100.	250.	725.	950.
651	1005	Dallas	Burke-Glass	500.	6000.	—	—
652	1006	Dallas	Burke-Houston	70.00	400.	3500.	3750.
653	1007	Dallas	White-Mellon	150.	325.	1300.	1500.
654	1008	San Francisco	Burke-McAdoo	215.	1000.	4300.	—
655	1009	San Francisco	Burke-Glass	140.	1750.	3900.	—
656	1010	San Francisco	Burke-Houston	140.	375.	725.	950.
657	1011	San Francisco	White-Mellon				
		a Upper case district letter at lower left.		150.	200.	400.	2300.
		b Lower case district letter at lower left.		175.	700.	1500.	2000.
		c Blue seal to left of district letter.		300.	700.	2300.	2650.

Federal Reserve Bank Notes

1915

Grover Cleveland at center.
Auto and steam train at left, tug and ocean liner at right.

KL#	Fr#	Bank	Federal Sigs.	Bank Sigs.	Fine	XF	CH CU (63)	Gem CU (65)
658	822	Atlanta	Teehee-Burke	Bell-Wellborn	Unique	—	—	—
659	822a	Atlanta	Teehee-Burke	Pike-McCord	—	22,500.	—	—
660	824	Chicago	Teehee-Burke	McLallen-McDougal	2250.	10,350.	16,000.	20,000.
661	826	Kansas City	Teehee-Burke	Anderson-Miller	1700.	6500.	—	—
662	827	Kansas City	Teehee-Burke	Cross-Miller	1500.	27,600.	—	—
663	828	Dallas	Teehee-Burke	Hoopes-Van Zandt	2100.	5225.	—	—
664	829	Dallas	Teehee-Burke	Gilbert-Van Zandt	5000.	20,000.	—	—
665	830	Dallas	Teehee-Burke	Talley-Van Zandt	15,000.	—	—	—

1918

KL#	Fr#	Bank	Federal Sigs.	Bank Sigs.	Fine	XF	CH CU (63)	Gem CU (65)
666	823	Atlanta	Elliott-Burke	Bell-Wellborn	2300.	6000.	12,000.	13,500.
667	825	St. Louis	Teehee-Burke	Attebery-Wells	2500.	18,800.	—	—

United States Notes

Fifty Dollars

Alexander Hamilton at left.
First Obligation inscription (in circle) at center.

KL#	Fr#	Series	Signatures	Seal	Fine	XF	CH CU (63)	Gem CU (65)
668	148	1862	Chittenden-Spinner	Small red	32,500.	43,125.	—	—

Alexander Hamilton at left.
National Bank Note Co. at top. Second Obligation inscription.

KL#	Fr#	Series	Signatures	Seal	Fine	XF	CH CU (63)	Gem CU (65)
670	150	1863	Chittenden-Spinner	Small red	12,500.	29,900.	—	—

Peace standing at left, Henry Clay at right. Blue serial numbers.

KL#	Fr#	Series	Signatures	Seal	Fine	XF	CH CU (63)	Gem CU (65)
671	151	1869	Allison-Spinner	Large red	21,500.	60,000.	200,000.	275,000.

Benjamin Franklin at left, America at right.
Ornate red "L" twice at center. Blue serial numbers.

KL#	Fr#	Series	Signatures	Seal	Fine	XF	CH CU (63)	Gem CU (65)
672	152	1874	Allison-Spinner	Small red	10,000.	18,500.	38,000.	87,500.
673	153	1875	Allison-Spinner	Small red	—	Rare	—	—
674	154	1878	Allison-Gilfillan	Small red	5000.	20,000.	800,000.	100,000.

Benjamin Franklin at left, America at right. Blue serial numbers.

KL#	Fr#	Series	Signatures	Seal	Fine	XF	CH CU (63)	Gem CU (65)
675	155	1880	Bruce-Gilfillan	Large brown	7000.	28,000.	32,500.	48,750.
676	156	1880	Bruce-Wyman	Large brown	5000.	10,000.	32,500.	48,750.
677	157	1880	Rosecrans-Jordan	Large red	6000.	14,000.	32,500.	48,750.
678	158	1880	Rosecrans-Hyatt	Large red	10,000.	20,000.	61,000.	67,500.
679	159	1880	Rosecrans-Hyatt	Red spikes	6750.	12,000.	40,000.	47,500.
680	160	1880	Rosecrans-Huston	Red spikes	4750.	46,000.	—	—
681	161	1880	Rosecrans-Huston	Large brown	4500.	10,000.	12,000.	25,000.

KL#	Fr#	Series	Signatures	Seal	Fine	XF	CH CU (63)	Gem CU (65)
682	162	1880	Tillman-Morgan	Small red	2250.	11,000.	22,500.	36,000.
683	163	1880	Bruce-Roberts	Small red	35,250.	—	—	—
684	164	1880	Lyons-Roberts	Small red	2250.	7500.	15,000.	32,000.

Compound Interest Treasury Notes

Liberty standing at left, Alexander Hamilton at right.

KL#	FR#	Act	Overprint Date	Signatures	VG	Fine	XF
685	192	1863	June 10, 1864	Chittenden-Spinner —	—	75,000.	
686	192-A	1864	July 15, 1864	Chittenden-Spinner Three known.——	—		
687	192-B	1864	Aug. 15, 1864-Sept. 1, 1865	Colby-Spinner Two known.16,000.30,000.60,000.			

Andrew Jackson at left, Justice seated at center, Salmon P. Chase at right.

687a	202a	1861	March 2, 1861	Chittenden-Spinner	—	—	368,000.

Interest Bearing Notes

Liberty standing at left, Alexander Hamilton at right.

KL#	FR#	Act	Term	Signatures	VG	Fine	XF
688	198	1863	One year	Chittenden-Spinner	10,000.	22,000.	92,000.

Female holding Caduceus at left, Justice seated with shield at center, Loyalty standing at right.

| 689 | 203 | 1863 | Two years | Chittenden-Spinner | 15,000. | 30,000. | 65,000. |

Eagle at center pearched on rock.

| 690 | 207 | 1861 | Three years | Chittenden-Spinner | — | — | 172,500. |

Eagle at center pearched on shield.

| 691 | 212 | 1864 | Three years | Colby-Spinner | — | 65,000. | — |
| 692 | 212d | 1865 | Three years | Colby-Spinner | — | 70,000. | 100,000. |

Gold Certificates

Silas Wright at left. Countersigned.

KL#	Fr#	Series	Signatures	Seal	Fine	XF	CH CU (63)	Gem CU (65)
693	1189	1882	Bruce-Gilfillan	Brown	—	39,000.	—	—
694	1188	1882	Bruce-Gilfillan	Brown	—	30,000.	—	—
695	1190	1882	Bruce-Wyman	Brown	20,000.	43,500.	—	—
696	1191	1882	Rosecrans-Hyatt	Large red	—	Rare	—	—
697	1192	1882	Rosecrans-Huston	Large brown	—	30,000.	—	—
697a	1192a	1882	Rosecrans-Huston	Small red	—	300,000.	—	—
698	1193	1882	Lyons-Roberts	Small red	1100.	6000.	17,000.	30,000.
699	1194	1882	Lyons-Treat	Small red	1100.	20,000.	—	—
700	1195	1882	Vernon-Treat	Small red	1500.	5000.	10,000.	16,500.
701	1196	1882	Vernon-McClung	Small red	2000.	5000.	30,000.	—

Silas Wright at left.

KL#	Fr#	Series	Signatures	Seal	Fine	XF	CH CU (63)	Gem CU (65)
702	1197	1882	Napier-McClung	Small red	1500.	5000.	18,500.	40,000.

Ulysses S. Grant at center.

KL#	Fr#	Series	Signatures	Seal	Fine	XF	CH CU (63)	Gem CU (65)
703	1198	1913	Parker-Burke	Gold	700.	4400.	7500.	20,000.
704	1199	1913	Teehee-Burke	Gold	450.	3750.	8000.	17,250.

Large and small serial number varieties exist.

KL#	Fr#	Series	Signatures	Seal	Fine	XF	CH CU (63)	Gem CU (65)
705	1200	1922	Speelman-White	Gold	500.	1950.	7250.	11,500.

National Gold Bank Notes

Washington Crossing the Delaware at left, Prayer for Victory at right.
Various U.S. Gold Coins.

KL#	Fr#	Series	Issuing Bank	Location	Good	Fine	VF
706	1160	Orig.	First Nat'l Gold Bank	San Francisco	—	Rare	373,750.
707	1161	Orig.	Farmers' Nat'l Gold Bank	San Jose	—	Rare	—

Silver Certificates

Edward Everett at right.

Payable at: Washington, D.C. Large "FIFTY" below center seal.

KL#	Fr#	Series	Signatures	Good	Fine	VF
708	324c	1878	A.U. Wyman, Asst. U.S. Treasurer	—	37,000.	—
			Payable at: New York.			
709	324	1878	T. Hillhouse, Asst. U.S. Treasurer	—	Rare	—
			Payable at: San Francisco.			
710	324a	1878	R.M. Anthony, Asst. U.S. Treasurer	—	Rare	—

Edward Everett at right. Large "FIFTY" in center, brown "L" below.

KL#	Fr#	Series	Signatures	Seal	Fine	XF	CH CU (63)	Gem CU (65)
711	325	1880	Scofield-Gilfillan	Large brown	Rare	—	—	—
712	326	1880	Bruce-Gilfillan	Large brown	20,000.	60,000.	—	—
713	327	1880	Bruce-Wyman	Large brown	30,000.	115,000.	—	—

Edward Everett at right. Large "FIFTY" in center.

KL#	Fr#	Series	Signatures	Seal	Fine	XF	CH CU (63)	Gem CU (65)
714	328	1880	Rosecrans-Huston	Large brown	10,000.	70,000.	75,000.	130,000.
715	329	1880	Rosecrans-Nebeker	Small red	27,500.	50,000.	—	—

Edward Everett at right.

KL#	Fr#	Series	Signatures	Seal	Fine	XF	CH CU (63)	Gem CU (65)
716	330	1891	Rosecrans-Nebeker	Small red	22,500.	37,500.	—	—
717	331	1891	Tillman-Morgan	Small red	4500.	11,250.	30,000.	40,000.
718	332	1891	Bruce-Roberts	Small red	22,000.	40,000.	—	—
719	333	1891	Lyons-Roberts	Small red	3000.	11,000.	—	—
720	334	1891	Vernon-Treat	Small red	2200.	8500.	16,000.	26,000.
721	335	1891	Parker-Burke	Blue	1750.	5200.	11,000.	17,000.

Treasury or Coin Notes

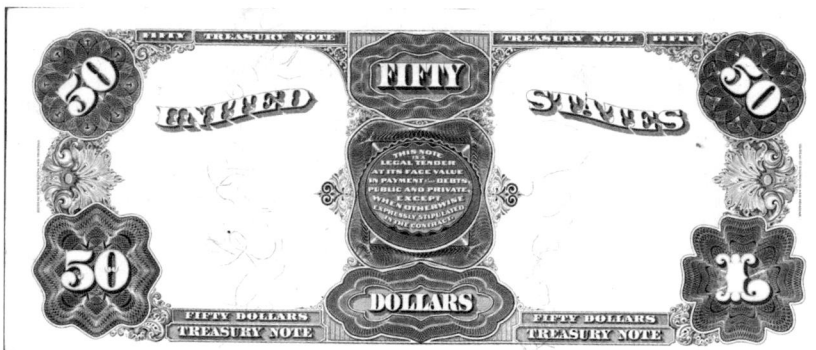

William H. Seward at center.

KL#	Fr#	Series	Signatures	Seal	Fine	XF	CH CU (63)	Gem CU (65)
722	376	1891	Rosecrans-Nebeker	Small red	—	138,000.	300,000.	—

Federal Reserve Notes
1914

Ulysses S. Grant at center. Red Seal.
Panama at center, ocean liner and battleship flanking.

KL#	Fr#	Bank	Signatures	Fine	XF	CH CU (63)	Gem CU (65)
723	1012	Boston	Burke-McAdoo				
		a	Plate letter at upper left.	2750.	10,000.	12,000.	15,000.
		b	District # and letter above plate letter at upper left.	2750.	14,500.	25,000.	40,000.
724	1013	New York	Burke-McAdoo				
		a	Plate letter at upper left	1265.	15,000.	—	—
		b	District # and letter above plate letter at upper left.	—	5500.	—	—
725	1014	Philadelphia	Burke-McAdoo				
		a	Plate letter at upper left.	—	15,000.	20,000.	—
		b	District # and letter above plate letter at upper left.	—	8000.	—	—
726	1015	Cleveland	Burke-McAdoo				
		a	Plate letter at upper left.	2750.	13,000.	20,000.	25,000.
		b	District # and letter above plate letter at upper left.	2750.	4500.	12,000.	15,000.
727	1016	Richmond	Burke-McAdoo				
		a	Plate letter at upper left.	2300.	5000.	12,000.	15,000.
		b	District # and letter above plate letter at upper left.	3250.	4500.	12,000.	15,000.
728	1017	Atlanta	Burke-McAdoo				
		a	Plate letter at upper left.	3500.	—	—	—
729	1018	Chicago	Burke-McAdoo				
		a	Plate letter at upper left.	—	69,000.	—	—
		b	District # and letter above plate letter at upper left.	1150.	—	—	—
730	1019	St. Louis	Burke-McAdoo				
		a	Plate letter at upper left.	3225.	6500.	12,000.	15,000.
		b	District # and letter above plate letter at upper left.	3000.	4500.	12,000.	15,000.

KL#	Fr#	Bank	Signatures	Fine	XF	CH CU (63)	Gem CU (65)
731	1020	Minneapolis	Burke-McAdoo				
		a Plate letter at upper left.		4000.	50,000.	—	—
		b District # and letter above plate letter at upper left.		3000.	10,500.	—	—
732	1021	Kansas City	Burke-McAdoo				
		a Plate letter at upper left.		4600.	—	—	—
		b District # and letter above plate letter at upper left.		22,500.	—	—	—
733	1022	Dallas	Burke-McAdoo				
		a Plate letter at upper left.		2250.	—	—	—
734	1023	San Francisco	Burke-McAdoo				
		a Plate letter at upper left.		2750.	4500.	12,000.	15,000.
		b District # and letter above plate letter at upper left.		2775.	4500.	12,000.	15,000.

Ulysses S. Grant at center. Blue Seal.
Panama at center, ocean liner and battleship flanking.

KL#	Fr#	Bank	Signatures	Fine	XF	CH CU (63)	Gem CU (65)
735	1024	Boston	Burke-McAdoo		300.	1500.	3500.	5000.
736	1025	Boston	Burke-Glass		250.	1600.	5750.	6000.
737	1026	Boston	Burke-Houston		580.	3000.	9000.	11,500.
739	1028	New York	Burke-McAdoo		350.	1100.	2900.	5000.
740	1029	New York	Burke-Glass		230.	1500.	2900.	5000.
741	1030	New York	Burke-Houston		400.	800.	4000.	5000.
742	1031	New York	White-Mellon					
		a Upper case district letter at lower left.		200.	700.	2500.	3000.
		b Lower case district letter at lower left.		400.	3000.	4000.	5000.
743	1032	Philadelphia	Burke-McAdoo		400.	700.	1750.	2750.
744	1033	Philadelphia	Burke-Glass		245.	6000.	9000.	11,500.
745	1034	Philadelphia	Burke-Houston		200.	800.	2750.	3500.
746	1035	Philadelphia	White-Mellon		175.	700.	2250.	5500.
747	1036	Cleveland	Burke-McAdoo		325.	1000.	3000.	3500.
748	1037	Cleveland	Burke-Glass		200.	2500.	4500.	5750.
749	1038	Cleveland	Burke-Houston		440.	1800.	2250.	3750.
750	1039	Cleveland	White-Mellon					
		a Upper case district letter at lower left.		400.	900.	—	—
		b Lower case district letter at lower left.		425.	1250.	4200.	—
751	1040	Richmond	Burke-McAdoo		200.	750.	3250.	5000.
752	1041	Richmond	Burke-Glass		500.	1500.	9000.	11,500.
753	1042	Richmond	Burke-Houston		175.	1000.	4000.	5000.
754	1043	Richmond	White-Mellon		225.	900.	4000.	6300.
755	1044	Atlanta	Burke-McAdoo		325.	1500.	3200.	4750.
756	1045	Atlanta	Burke-Glass		2000.	15,000.	—	—
757	1046	Atlanta	Burke-Houston		350.	800.	2550.	3750.
758	1047	Atlanta	White-Mellon		500.	925.	2950.	4850.
759	1048	Chicago	Burke-McAdoo		300.	1100.	2250.	9000.
760	1049	Chicago	Burke-Glass		250.	775.	2250.	3750.
761	1050	Chicago	Burke-Houston		475.	1350.	2250.	3750.
762	1051	Chicago	White-Mellon		400.	900.	2250.	3750.
763	1052	St. Louis	Burke-McAdoo		250.	1000.	2700.	4500.
764	1053	St. Louis	Burke-Glass		175.	900.	2750.	3750.
765	1054	St. Louis	Burke-Houston		375.	900.	3000.	6325.
767	1056	Minneapolis	Burke-McAdoo		250.	1000.	2750.	5750.
769	1058	Minneapolis	Burke-Houston		—	4250.	—	—
771	1060	Kansas City	Burke-McAdoo		475.	1500.	3000.	3750.
774	1063	Kansas City	White-Mellon		1725.	6000.	—	—
775	1064	Dallas	Burke-McAdoo		580.	2250.	2500.	—
777	1066	Dallas	Burke-Houston		—	30,000.	—	—
779	1068	San Francisco	Burke-McAdoo		150.	700.	3500.	4500.
781	1070	San Francisco	Burke-Houston		350.	1500.	2250.	3750.
782	1071	San Francisco	White-Mellon		230.	1100.	—	—

Federal Reserve Bank Notes
1918

Ulysses S. Grant at center.
Panama at center, ocean liner and battleship flanking.

KL#	Fr#	Bank	Federal Sigs.	Bank Sigs.	Fine	XF	CH CU (63)	Gem CU (65)
783	831	St. Louis	Teehee-Burke	Attebery-Wells	10,000.	20,000.	32,500	40,000.

United States Notes
One Hundred Dollars

Large Eagle at upper left. Red serial numbers.
First Obligation inscription (in circle) at center.

KL#	Fr#	Series	Signatures	Seal	Fine	XF	CH CU (63)	Gem CU (65)
784	165	1862	Chittenden-Spinner	Small red	30,000.	60,000.	75,000.	125,000.

Large Eagle at upper left. Red serial numbers.
Second Obligation inscription.

American Bank Note Co. or National Bank Note Co. imprint.

KL#	Fr#	Series	Signatures	Seal	Fine	XF	CH CU (63)	Gem CU (65)
785	166	1862	Chittenden-Spinner	Small red	—	—	Unique	—

Large Eagle at upper left. Second Obligation inscription.

KL#	Fr#	Series	Signatures	Seal	Fine	VF	CH CU (63)
786	167	1863	Chittenden-Spinner	Small red	—	—	—

Abraham Lincoln at left, Reconstruction vignette at right.
Red serial numbers.

KL#	Fr#	Series	Signatures	Seal	Fine	XF	CH CU (63)	Gem CU (65)
787	168	1869	Allison-Spinner	Large red	17,500.	105,000.	135,000.	185,000.

Abraham Lincoln at left, Reconstruction vignette at right. Series of 1875 at upper left and lower right face. Blue serial numbers.

KL#	Fr#	Series	Signatures	Seal	Fine	XF	CH CU (63)	Gem CU (65)
788	169	1875	Allison-New	Small red	19,500.	40,000.	65,000.	80,000.
789	170	1875	Allison-Wyman	Small red	15,000.	40,000.	65,000.	80,000.

Abraham Lincoln at left, Reconstruction vignette at right. Series 1878 at upper left face. Blue serial numbers.

KL#	Fr#	Series	Signatures	Seal	Fine	VF	XF
790	171	1878	Allison-Gilfillan	Small red	15,000.	30,000	—

Abraham Lincoln at left, Reconstruction vignette at right. Series 1880
at upper left face. Blue serial numbers.

KL#	Fr#	Series	Signatures	Seal	Fine	XF	CH CU (63)	Gem CU (65)
791	172	1880	Bruce-Gilfillan	Large brown	13,250.	30,000.	97,750.	110,000.
792	173	1880	Bruce-Wyman	Large brown	25,300.	30,000.	75,000.	91,000.
793	174	1880	Rosecrans-Jordan	Large red	14,000.	37,000.	75,000.	91,000.

Abraham Lincoln at left, Reconstruction vignette at right. Series 1880
at upper left. Blue serial numbers.

794	175	1880	Rosecrans-Hyatt	Large red	—	Rare	—	—
795	176	1880	Rosecrans-Hyatt	Red spikes	15,000.	37,500.	65,000.	91,000.
796	177	1880	Rosecrans-Huston	Red spikes	9200.	40,000.	65,000.	80,000.
797	178	1000	Rosecrans-Huston	Large brown	9000.	40,000.	65,000.	80,000.

Abraham Lincoln at left, Reconstruction vignette at right.
Series 1880 at upper left. Blue serial numbers.

KL#	Fr#	Series	Signatures	Seal	Fine	XF	CH CU (63)	Gem CU (65)
798	179	1880	Tillman-Morgan	Small red	10,000.	17,500.	85,000.	95,000.
799	180	1880	Bruce-Roberts	Small red	12,500.	30,000.	35,000.	45,000.
800	181	1880	Lyons-Roberts	Small red	6000.	25,000.	35,000.	45,000.
801	182	1880	Napier-McClung	Small red	Unknown	—	—	—

Compound Interest Treasury Notes

Guardian vignette at lower left, George Washington at center,
Justice and shield at lower right.

KL#	FR#	Act	Overprint Date	Signatures	VG	Fine	XF
802	193	1863	June 10, 1864	Chittenden-Spinner	—	41,400.	—
803	193a	1864	July 15, 1864	Chittenden-Spinner	—	—	—
804	193b	1864	Aug. 15, 1864-Sept. 1, 1865	Colby-Spinner	—	34,500.	—

Interest Bearing Notes

KL#	FR#	Act	Term	Signatures	VG	Fine	XF
805	199	1863	One year	Chittenden-Spinner	—	—	—

Farmer and Mechanics at lower left, Treasury Building at upper center,
In the Turret at lower right.

806	204	1863	Two years	Chittenden-Spinner	—	—	—

General Winfield Scott facing left at top center.

807	208	1861	Three years	Chittenden-Spinner	Unknown	—	—
808	212a	1864	Three years	Colby-Spinner	—	45,000.	86,250.

General Winfield Scott facing right at top center.

809	212e	1865	Three years	Colby-Spinner	—	—	2,100,000.

Gold Certificates

Eagle on shield at left.

KL#	Fr#	Issue/Act/Series	Signatures	Fine	XF	CH CU (63)	Gem CU (65)
810	1166c	First/1863	Colby-Spinner	—	—	Rare	—

Thomas H. Benton at left.

KL#	Fr#	Issue/Act/Series		Signatures	Fine	XF	CH CU (63)	Gem CU (65)
811	1166h	Second/1870		Allison-Spinner			Unkown in private hands.	
812	1166m	Third/1863/1875		Allison-New	—	—	Rare	—

KL#	Fr#	Series	Signatures	Seal	Fine	XF	CH CU (63)	Gem CU (65)
813	1202	1882	Thos. C. Acton, Asst. U.S. Treasurer	Brown	—	Rare	—	
814	1201	1882	Bruce-Gilfillan	Brown	—	Rare	—	—
815	1203	1882	Bruce-Wyman	Brown	285,000.	—	—	—
816	1204	1882	Rosecrans-Hyatt	Large red	Rare	—	—	—
817	1205	1882	Rosecrans-Huston	Large brown	90,000.	—	—	—
818	1206	1882	Lyons-Roberts	Small red	1150.	4000.	9000.	14,500.
819	1207	1882	Lyons-Treat	Small red	3750.	9000.	14,000.	40,500.
820	1208	1882	Vernon-Treat	Small red	3000.	9000.	16,500.	20,000.
821	1209	1882	Vernon-McClung	Small red	1100.	3000.	8750.	24,000.
822	1210	1882	Napier-McClung	Small red	1650.	4000.	10,000.	19,500.
823	1211	1882	Napier-Thompson	Small red	1150.	6300.	9500.	11,500.
824	1212	1882	Napier-Burke	Small red	1150.	3300.	9000.	14,500.
825	1213	1882	Parker-Burke	Small red	1150.	6300.	9000.	36,225.
826	1214	1882	Teehee-Burke	Small red	675.	4000.	12,000.	16,000.

KL#	Fr#	Series	Signatures	Seal	Fine	XF	CH CU (63)	Gem CU (65)
827	1215	1922	Speelman-White	Small red	675.	3000.	7000.	19,000.

National Gold Bank Notes

Battle of Lake Erie at left, Union at right. Various U.S. Gold Coins.

KL#	Fr#	Series	Issuing Bank	Location	Good	Fine	VF
828	1162	Orig.	First Nat'l Gold Bank	San Francisco	—	258,000.	—
829	1163	1875	First Nat'l Gold Bank	San Francisco	—	Rare	—
830	1164	Orig.	First Nat'l Gold Bank	Santa Barbara	—	Rare	—
831	1165	Orig.	First Nat'l Gold Bank	Petaluma	100,000.	—	—
832	1166	Orig.	Union Nat'l Gold Bank	Oakland	—	Rare	—

Silver Certificates

James Monroe at left.

Place of Deposit: Washington, D.C. Large "100" at bottom center.

KL#	Fr#	Series	CounterSigned by:	VG	Fine	XF
833	337b	1878	A.U. Wyman, Asst. U.S. Treasurer	—	Rare	—

Place of Deposit: San Francisco. Note: R.M. Anthony was really the bookkeeper for the Asst. Treasurer.

834	337	1878	R.M. Anthony, Asst. U.S. Treasurer	—	Rare	—

Place of Deposit: New York.

835	336	1878	W.G. White, Asst. U.S. Treasurer	—	Rare	—

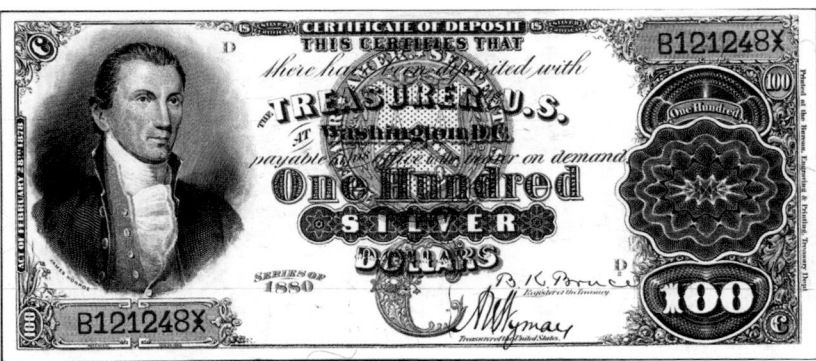

KL#	Fr#	Series	Signatures	Seal	Fine	XF	CH CU (63)	Gem CU (65)
836	338	1880	Scofield-Gilfillan	Large brown	—	Extremely Rare	—	—
837	339	1880	Bruce-Gilfillan	Large brown	—	Extremely Rare	—	—
838	340	1880	Bruce-Wyman	Large brown	20,000.	45,000.	—	—
839	341	1880	Rosecrans-Huston	Large brown	20,000.	145,000.	220,000.	—
840	342	1880	Rosecrans-Nebeker	Small red	28,000.	125,000.	180,000.	210,000.

KL#	Fr#	Series	Signatures	Seal	Fine	XF	CH CU (63)	Gem CU (65)
841	343	1891	Rosecrans-Nebeker	Small red	10,350.	50,000.	—	—
842	344	1891	Tillman-Morgan	Small red	9000.	43,125.	—	—

Treasury or Coin Notes

Admiral David G. Farragut at right. Large "100".

KL#	Fr#	Series	Signatures	Seal	Fine	XF	CH CU (63)	Gem CU (65)
843	377	1890	Rosecrans-Huston	Large brown	—	170,000.	356,500.	—

Admiral David G. Farragut at right.

KL#	Fr#	Series	Signatures	Seal	Fine	XF	CH CU (63)	Gem CU (65)
844	378	1891	Rosecrans-Nebeker	Small red	90,000.	150,000.	—	—

Federal Reserve Notes
1914

Benjamin Franklin at center. Red Seal.
Vignettes of Labor, Plenty, America, Peace and Commerce.

KL#	Fr#	Bank	Signatures	Fine	XF	CH CU (63)	Gem CU (65)
845	1072	Boston	Burke-McAdoo				
		a	Plate letter at upper right.	1750.	12,500.	29,000.	40,250.
		b	District # and letter above plate letter at upper left.	1725.	11,000.	29,000.	38,500.
846	1073	New York	Burke-McAdoo				
		a	Plate letter at upper left.	1750.	6000.	29,000.	40,000.
		b	District # and letter above plate letter at upper left.	1750.	7500.	29,000.	40,000.
847	1074	Philadelphia	Burke-McAdoo				
		a	Plate letter at upper left.	2100.	5000.	29,000.	40,000.
		b	District # and letter above plate letter at upper left.	2300.	5000.	29,000.	40,000.
848	1075	Cleveland	Burke-McAdoo				
		a	Plate letter at upper left.	5000.	7000.	29,000.	40,000.
		b	District # and letter above plate letter at upper left.	2750.	11,000.	29,000.	40,000.
849	1076	Richmond	Burke-McAdoo				
		a	Plate letter at upper left.	2185.	5000.	29,000.	40,000.
		b	District # and letter above plate letter at upper left.	—	—	29,000.	40,000.
850	1077	Atlanta	Burke-McAdoo				
		a	Plate letter at upper left.	2500.	30,000.	32,500.	40,000.
		b	District # and letter above plate letter at upper left.	1750.	30,000.	32,500.	40,000.
851	1078	Chicago	Burke-McAdoo				
		a	Plate letter at upper left.	3000.	3750.	29,000.	40,000.
		b	District # and letter above plate letter at upper left.	2000.	5000.	17,500.	40,000.
852	1079	St. Louis	Burke-McAdoo				
		a	Plate letter at upper left.	2500.	9500.	29,000.	40,000.
		b	District # and letter above plate letter at upper left.	2500.	12,500.	29,000.	40,000.

KL#	Fr#	Bank	Signatures	Fine	XF	CH CU (63)	Gem CU (65)
853	1080	Minneapolis	Burke-McAdoo				
		a Plate letter at upper left.		8625.	12,500.	29,000.	40,000.
		b District # and letter above plate letter at upper left.	5000.	12,500.	29,000.	40,000.
854	1081	Kansas City	Burke-McAdoo				
		a Plate letter at upper left.		2350.	—	—	—
		b District # and letter above plate letter at upper left.	—	—	—	—
855	1082	Dallas	Burke-McAdoo				
		a Plate letter at upper left.		5600.	13,000.	29,000.	40,000.
		b District # and letter above plate letter at upper left.	7500.	32,100.	35,000.	40,000.
856	1083	San Francisco	Burke-McAdoo				
		a Plate letter at upper left.		2550.	4500.	29,000.	40,000.
		b District # and letter above plate letter at upper left.	2450.	6000.	29,000.	40,000.

Benjamin Franklin at center. Blue Seal.
Vignettes of Labor, Plenty, America, Peace and Commerce.

KL#	Fr#	Bank	Signatures	Fine	XF	CH CU (63)	Gem CU (65)
857	1084	Boston	Burke-McAdoo	400.	2250.	8100.	12,500.
858	1085	Boston	Burke-Glass	500.	5000.	—	—
860	1087	Boston	White-Mellon	800.	1600.	8100.	11,500.
861	1088	New York	Burke-McAdoo	400.	1350.	3500.	7000.
862	1089	New York	Burke-Glass	700.	2100.	—	—
863	1090	New York	Burke-Houston	550.	1400.	3500.	4500.
864	1091	New York	White-Mellon	350.	—	—	7500.
865	1092	Philadelphia	Burke-McAdoo	400.	1500.	3500.	4500.
868	1095	Philadelphia	White-Mellon	400.	3500.	5000.	9000.
869	1096	Cleveland	Burke-McAdoo	1000.	—	—	—
870	1097	Cleveland	Burke-Glass	600.	1500.	2750.	3000.
871	1098	Cleveland	Burke-Houston	625.	1500.	4250.	5350.
872	1099	Cleveland	White-Mellon	750.	1200.	5000.	6000.
873	1100	Richmond	Burke-McAdoo	750.	1850.	—	—
874	1101	Richmond	Burke-Glass	400.	5750.	7500.	—
877	1104	Atlanta	Burke-McAdoo	550.	1200.	2400.	4500.
879	1106	Atlanta	Burke-Houston	400.	8500.	9000.	10,000.
880	1107	Atlanta	White-Mellon	400.	1500.	7500.	8000.
881	1108	Chicago	Burke-McAdoo	450.	1250.	5100.	6000.
883	1110	Chicago	Burke-Houston	375.	1025.	2800.	6600.
885	1112	St. Louis	Burke-McAdoo	500.	1500.	3500.	4500.
889	1116	Minneapolis	Burke-McAdoo	450.	1500.	5750.	7000.
892	1119	Minneapolis	White-Mellon	750.	1850.	3500.	6000.
893	1120	Kansas City	Burke-McAdoo	500.	1600.	4500.	6000.
896	1123	Kansas City	White-Mellon	750.	1000.	5500.	7500.
897	1124	Dallas	Burke-McAdoo	750.	1500.	5500.	7500.
900	1127	Dallas	White-Mellon	750.	9800.	—	—
901	1128	San Francisco	Burke-McAdoo	600.	1500.	2500.	4200.
903	1130	San Francisco	Burke-Houston	625.	2100.	5250.	6250.
904	1131	San Francisco	White-Mellon	450.	1750.	6500.	7250.

United States Notes
Five Hundred Dollars

Albert Gallatin at center.

First Obligation inscription on back. Red serial number.

KL#	Fr#	Series	Signatures	Seal	Fine	XF	CH CU (63)	Gem CU (65)
904a	183a	1862	Chittenden-Spinner	Small red	—	Extremely Rare		—

Second Obligation inscription on back. Red serial number.

905	183b	1862	Chittenden-Spinner	Small red	—	Extremely Rare		—
906	183c	1863	Chittenden-Spinner	Small red	—	—	540,000.	—

Justice seated at left, John Quincy Adams at right. Blue serial numbers.

907	184	1869	Allison-Spinner	Large red	—	Extremely Rare		—

Victory at left, Brigadier General Joseph K. Mansfield at right.

KL#	Fr#	Series	Signatures	Seal	Fine	XF	CH CU (63)
908	185a	1874	Allison-Spinner	Small red	—		Extremely Rare
909	185b	1875	Allison-New	Small red	—		Extremely Rare
910	185c	1875	Allison-Wyman	Small red	—		Extremely Rare
911	185d	1878	Allison-Gilfillan	Small red	—		27,600.—
912	185e	1880	Scofield-Gilfillan	Large brown	—		Extremely Rare
913	185f	1880	Bruce-Wyman	Large brown	—		Extremely Rare
914	185g	1880	Rosecrans-Jordan	Large red	—		Extremely Rare
915	185h	1880	Rosecrans-Hyatt	Large red	—		Extremely Rare
916	185-i	1880	Rosecrans-Huston	Large red	—	700,000.	—
917	185j	1880	Rosecrans-Nebeker	Small red	—		Extremely Rare
918	185k	1880	Tillman-Morgan	Small red	—		Extremely Rare
919	185l	1880	Bruce-Roberts	Small red	—	411,000.	—
920	185m	1880	Lyons-Roberts	Small red	—	—	150,000.
921	185n	1880	Napier-McClung	Small red Not issued	—	—	—

Compound Interest Treasury Notes

The Standard Bearer at left, New Ironsides at right.

KL#	FR#	Act	Overprint Date	Signatures	VG	Fine	XF
922	194	1863	June 10, 1864	Chittenden-Spinner	—	Extremely Rare	—
923	194a	1864	July 15, 1864	Chittenden-Spinner	—	Extremely Rare	—
924	194-B	1864	Aug. 15, 1864-Oct. 1, 1865	Colby-Spinner	—	Extremely Rare	—

Interest Bearing Notes

KL#	FR#	Act	Term	Signatures	VG	Fine	XF
925	200	1863	One year	Chittenden-Spinner	—	Extremely Rare	—
925A	-	1861	Two years	Chittenden-Spinner	—	Extremely Rare	—

Liberty and Union at left, Eagle on nest at top center.

926	205	1863	Two years	Chittenden-Spinner	—	Extremely Rare	

Justice at left, George Washington at top center, Transportation at right.

927	209	1861	Three years	Chittenden-Spinner	—	Extremely Rare	

Mortar at lower left, Alexander Hamilton at top center,
George Washington at right.

928	212b	1864	Three years	Colby-Spinner	—	Extremely Rare	—
929	212f	1865	Three years	Colby-Spinner	—	8000.	—

Gold Certificates

Abraham Lincoln at left.

KL#	Fr#	Issue/Act/Series	Signatures	VG	Fine	XF
930	1160d	First/1863	Colby-Spinner		Unknown in private hands	
931	1166l	Second/1870	Allison-Spinner		Extremely Rare	
932	1166n	Third/1875	Allison-New		Unknown in private hands	

Abraham Lincoln at left. Countersigned. Eagle on flag.

KL#	Fr#	Series	Signatures	Fine	XF	CH CU (63)	Gem CU (65)
933	1215b	1882	Bruce-Gilfillan			Unknown in private hands	
934	1215a	1882	Bruce-Gilfillan			Extremely Rare	
935	1215c	1882	Bruce-Wyman			Extremely Rare	
936	1215d	1882	Rosecrans-Hyatt			Extremely Rare	
937	1216	1882	Lyons-Roberts	10,500.	40,250.	—	—
938	1216a	1882	Parker-Burke	11,000.	40,250.	—	—
939	1216b	1882	Teehee-Burke	10,400.	25,000.	—	—

Abraham Lincoln at left. Eagle on flag.

KL#	Fr#	Issue/Act/Series	Signatures	Fine	XF	Gem CU (65)
940	1217	1922	Speelman-White	10,000.	50,000.	—

National Gold Bank Notes

Civilization at left, Arrival of the Sirius at right. Various U.S. Gold Coins.

KL#	Fr#	Series	Issuing Bank	Location	Good	Fine	VF
941	-	1875	First Nat'l Gold Bank	San Francisco		Unknown in private hands	
942	-	Orig.	Nat'l Gold Bank & Trust Co.	San Francisco		Unknown in private hands	
943	-	Orig.	Nat'l Gold Bank of				
			D.O. Mills and Company	Sacramento		Unknown in private hands	

Silver Certificates

Charles Sumner at right.

Place of Deposit: New York.

KL#	Fr#	Series	CounterSigned by:	Fine	XF	CH CU (63)	Gem CU (65)
944	345a	1878	W.G. White, Asst. U.S. Treasurer	—	—	Unique	—

Place of Deposit: New York.

| 945 | 345a | 1878 | J.C. Hopper, Asst. U.S. Treasurer | | | Unknown in private hands | |

Place of Deposit: New York.

| 946 | 345a | 1878 | T. Hillhouse, Asst. U.S. Treasurer | — | — | Not issued | — |

Place of Deposit: San Francisco.

| 947 | 345a | 1878 | R.M. Anthony, Asst. U.S. Treasurer | | | Unknown in private hands | |

Place of Deposit: Washington, D.C.

| 948 | 345a | 1878 | A.U. Wyman, Asst. U.S. Treasurer | — | — | Unique | — |

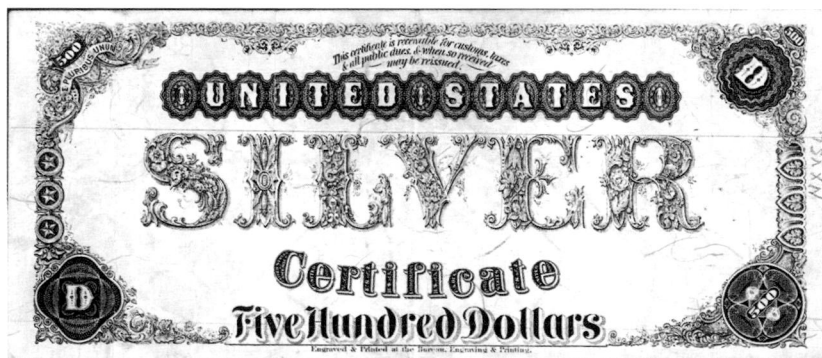

KL#	Fr#	Series	Signatures	Seal	Fine	XF	CH CU (63)	Gem CU (65)
949	345b	1880	Scofield-Gilfillan	Brown			Unknown in private hands	
950	345c	1880	Bruce-Gilfillan	Brown	—	420,000.	—	—
951	345d	1880	Bruce-Wyman	Brown			Extremely Rare	

Federal Reserve Notes
1918

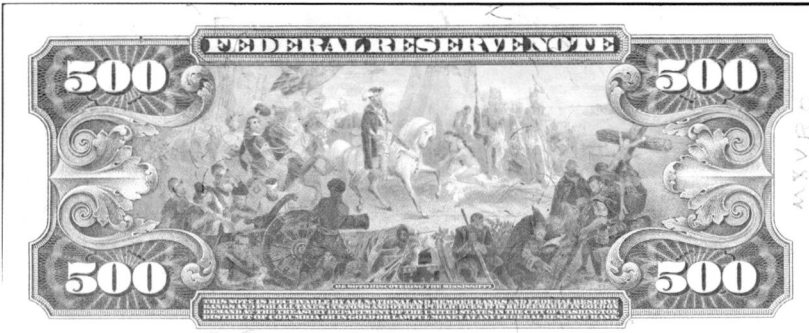

John Marshall at center. DeSoto Discovering the Mississippi.

KL#	Fr#	Bank	Signatures	Fine	XF	CH CU (63)	Gem CU (65)
952	1132	Boston	Burke-Glass	13,500.	40,000.	—	—
953	1132	New York	Burke-Glass	7750.	—	—	—
954	1132	New York	White-Mellon	7750.	40,000.	—	—
955	1132	Philadelphia	Burke-Glass	22,500.	60,000.	—	—
956	1132	Cleveland	Burke Glass	10,500.	30,000.	—	—
957	1132	Richmond	Burke-Glass	Unknown in private hands			
958	1132	Atlanta	Burke-Glass	—	—	75,000.	—
960	1132	Chicago	Burke-Glass	8500.	25,000.	—	—
961	1132	St. Louis	Burke-Glass	30,000.	34,500.	—	—
962	1132	Minneapolis	Burke-Glass	140,000.	126,500.	—	—
963	1132	Kansas City	Burke-Glass	12,000.	22,000.	—	—
964	1132	Dallas	Burke-Glass	6000.	40,250.	—	—
965	1132	San Francisco	Burke-Glass	10,750.	34,000.	95,000.	—
965A	1132	San Francisco	Burke-Houston	—	Extremely Rare		—
965B	1132	San Francisco	White-Mellon	—	Extremely Rare		—

United States Notes
One Thousand Dollars

Robert Morris at center.

First Obligation inscription on back. Red serial number.

KL#	Fr#	Series	Signatures	Seal	Fine	XF	CH CU (63)	Gem CU (65)
966	186a	1862	Chittenden-Spinner	Small red	Unknown in issued form			

Second Obligation inscription on back. Red serial number.

| 967 | 186b | 1862 | Chittenden-Spinner | Small red | Unknown in issued form | | | |

Red serial number.

| 968 | 186c | 1863 | Chittenden-Spinner | Small red | 650,000. | — | — | — |

Robert Morris at center. ABNCo imprint. Blue serial number.

KL#	Fr#	Series	Signatures	Seal	Fine	XF	CH CU (63)	Gem CU (65)
969	186d	1863	Chittenden-Spinner	Small red	—	1,200,000.	—	—

Robert Morris at center. ABNCo imprint.

969A	186e	1863	Chittenden-Spinner	Small red	—	—	Unique	—

Columbus in his study at left, DeWitt Clinton at center.

969B	186f	1869	Allison-Spinner	Large red	—	Extremely Rare	—	—

KL#	Fr#	Series	Signatures	Seal	Fine	XF	CH CU (63)	Gem CU (65)
970	187a	1878	Allison-Gilfillan	Small red	—	Extremely Rare		—
971	187b	1880	Bruce-Wyman	Large brown	—	750,000.	—	—

KL#	Fr#	Series	Signatures	Seal	Fine	XF	CH CU (63)	Gem CU (65)
972	187c	1880	Rosecrans-Jordan	Large red	—	—	Unique	—
973	187d	1880	Rosecrans-Hyatt	Large red	—	—	Unique	—
974	187e	1880	Rosecrans-Huston	Large red	—	—	Unique	—
975	187f	1880	Rosecrans-Nebeker	Large brown	—	—	Unique	—
976	187g	1880	Tillman-Morgan	Small red	—	—	Extremely Rare	—
978	187i	1880	Bruce-Roberts	Small red	—	—	Unique	—
979	187j	1880	Lyons-Roberts	Small red	—	283,000.	—	—
980	187k	1880	Vernon-Treat	Small red	—	—	Extremely Rare	—
981	187l	1880	Napier-McClung	Small red	—	—	Not issued	—

Compound Interest Treasury Notes

KL#	FR#	Act	Overprint Date	Signatures	VG	Fine	XF
982	195	1864	July 15, 1864	Chittenden-Spinner	—	Unknown	—
983	195a	1864	Aug. 15, 1864– Sept. 15, 1865	Colby-Spinner	—	Unknown	—

Interest Bearing Notes

Justice at left, eagle with shield at center, Liberty holding flag at right.

KL#	FR#	Act	Term	Signatures	VG	Fine	XF
984	201	1863	One year	Chittenden-Spinner	—	Unknown	—
984A	-	1861	Two years	Chittenden-Spinner	—	Unknown	—

Naval engagement between the Guerriere and the Constitution at left,
Discovery of the Mississippi by DeSoto at right.

985	206	1863	Two years	Chittenden-Spinner	—	Unknown	—

Salmon P. Chase at center.

986	210	1861	Three years	Chittenden-Spinner	—	Unknown	—

Justice with shield at lower center.

987	212c	1864	Three years	Colby-Spinner	—	Unknown	—
988	212g	1865	Three years	Colby-Spinner	—	Extremely Rare	—

Gold Certificates

Eagle on shield at left.

KL#	Fr#	Issue/Act/Series	Signatures	Seal	Fine	XF	CH CU (63)	Gem CU (65)
989	1166e	First/1863	Colby-Spinner	—	—	—	Unique	—

Alexander Hamilton at left.

KL#	Fr#	Issue/Act/Series	Signatures	Seal	Fine	XF	CH CU (63)	Gem CU (65)
990	1166j	Second/1870	Allison-Spinner	—	—	—	Unique	—
991	1166o	Third/1863/1875	Allison-New	—	—	—	Unknown	—

Alexander Hamilton at right. Countersigned.

KL#	Fr#	Issue/Act/Series	Signatures	Seal	Fine	XF	CH CU (63)	Gem CU (65)
992	1218a	1882	Bruce-Gilfillan	Large brown	—	—	Extremely Rare	—

Alexander Hamilton at right.

KL#	Fr#	Series	Signatures	Seal	Fine	XF	CH CU (63)	Gem CU (65)
993	1218	1882	Bruce-Gilfillan	Large brown	—	—	Unknown	—
994	1218b	1882	Bruce-Wyman	Large brown	—	—	Unique	—
995	1218c	1882	Rosecrans-Hyatt	Large red	—	—	Unique	—
996	1218d	1882	Rosecrans-Huston	Large brown	—	950,000.	—	—
997	1218e	1882	Rosecrans-Nebeker	Small red	—		Extremely Rare	—
998	1218f	1882	Lyons-Roberts	Small red	—	—	—	—
999	1218g	1882	Lyons-Treat	Small red	—	230,000.	—	—

Alexander Hamilton at center. Great Seal.

KL#	Fr#	Series	Signatures	Seal	Fine	XF	CH CU (63)	Gem CU (65)
1000	1219	1907	Vernon-Treat	Small red	—		Extremely Rare	—
1001	1219a	1907	Vernon-McClung	Small red	15,000.	—	Unknown	—
1002	1219b	1907	Napier-McClung	Small red	125,500.	287,000.	Unique	—
1003	1219c	1907	Napier-Burke	Small red	—	37,500.	—	—
1004	1219d	1907	Parker-Burke	Small red	—		Extremely Rare	—
1005	1219e	1907	Teehee-Burke	Small red	—	60,000.	180,000.	241,500.
1006	1220	1922	Speelman-White	Small red	—	75,000.	—	—

Silver Certificates

William Marcy at left.

Place of Deposit: Washington D.C.

KL#	Fr#	Series	Signatures	Seal	Fine	XF	CH CU (63)	Gem CU (65)
1007	346a	1878	A.U. Wyman, Asst. U.S. Treasurer		—	—	Unknown	—

Place of Deposit: San Francisco

1008	346a	1878	R.M. Anthony, Asst. U.S. Treasurer		—	—	Unknown	—

Place of Deposit: New York

1009	346a	1878	Unknown signers		—	—	Unknown	—
1010	346b	1880	Scofield-Gilfillan	Large brown	—	—	Unknown	—
1011	346c	1880	Bruce-Gilfillan	Large brown	—	—	Unknown	—
1012	346d	1880	Bruce-Wyman	Large brown	—	580,000.	—	—

Liberty holding shield at left, William Marcy at right.

1013	346e	1891	Tillman-Morgan	Small red	—	—	Extremely Rare	—

Treasury or Coin Notes

Major General George G. Meade at left. Large "1000".

KL#	Fr#	Series	Signatures	Seal	Fine	XF	CH CU (63)	Gem CU (65)
1014	379a	1890	Rosecrans-Huston	Large brown	—1,095,000.		—	—
1015	379b	1890	Rosecrans-Nebeker	Small red	—	Extremely Rare		—

Major General George G. Meade at left.

KL#	Fr#	Series	Signatures	Seal	Fine	XF	CH CU (63)	Gem CU (65)
1016	379d	1891	Rosecrans-Nebeker	Small red		Unknown in private hands		
1017	379c	1891	Tillman-Morgan	Small red	—2,100,000.		—	—

Federal Reserve Notes
1918

Alexander Hamilton at center. Eagle on flag.

KL#	Fr#	Bank	Signatures	Fine	XF	CH CU (63)	Gem CU (65)
1018	1133	Boston	Burke-Glass	35,000.	37,375.	—	—
1019	1133	New York	Burke-Glass	11,500.	27,600.	—	—
1020	1133	New York	Burke-Houston	17,000.	38,000.	—	—
1022	1133	Philadelphia	Burke-Glass	—	—	45,000.	95,000.
1023	1133	Cleveland	Burke-Glass	6000.	17,500.	85,000.	95,000.
1024	1133	Richmond	Burke-Glass	Unknown in private hands—	—	—	—
1025	1133	Atlanta	Burke-Glass	11,500.	20,000.	75,000.	—
1026	1133	Atlanta	White-Mellon	—	25,300.	—	—
1027	1133	Chicago	Burke-Glass	8500.	20,000.	—	—
1028	1133	St. Louis	Burke-Glass	17,000.	—	—	—
1029	1133	Minneapolis	Burke-Glass	—	80,000.	—	—
1030	1133	Kansas City	Burke-Glass	—	—	39,000.	45,000.
1031	1133	Dallas	Burke-Glass	—	50,000.	—	—
1032	1133	San Francisco	Burke-Glass	10,000.	35,000.	24,000.	32,500.
1033	1133	San Francisco	White-Mellon	—	30,000.	65,000.	—

Interest Bearing Notes
Five Thousand Dollars

Altar of Liberty vignette at center.

KL#	FR#	Act	Term	Signatures	VG	Fine	XF
1044	202	1863	One year	Chittenden-Spinner	—	Unknown	—

Justice at left and America at upper center.

| 1045 | 211 | 1861 | Three years | Chittenden-Spinner | — | Unknown | — |
| 1045A | 211 | 1865 | Three years | Colby-Spinner | — | Unknown | — |

James Madison at left. Large eagle on shield.

| 1045B | 188 | | | Scofield-Gilfillan | — | Unknown | — |

Gold Certificates

Eagle on shield at left, large 5000 as underprint.
Value within fancy border.

KL#	Fr#	Issue/Act/Series	Signatures	Seal	Fine	XF	CH CU (63)	Gem CU (65)
1046	1166f	First/1863	Colby-Spinner	—	—	Unique	—

James Madison at left.

| 1047 | 1166k | Second/1870 | Allison-New | — | — | Unknown | — |
| 1048 | - | Third/1863/1875 | Allison-New | — | — | Unknown | — |

Other signature varieties were issued in Series 1882 but none are known.

| 1059 | 1221j | 1882 | Teehee-Burke | Small red — | Extremely Rare | — |

Series 1888 were uniface transfer documents,
not intended for general circulation. None are known.

Federal Reserve Notes
1918

James Madison at center. Washington Resigning his Commission.

KL#	Fr#	Bank	Signatures	Fine	XF	CH CU (63)	Gem CU (65)
1060	1134	Boston	Burke-Glass	—	—	Unknown	—
1061	1134	New York	Burke-Glass	—	Extremely Rare	—
1062	1134	Cleveland	Burke-Glass	—	—	Unique	—
1063	1134	Richmond	Burke-Glass	—	—	Unknown	—
1065	1134	Chicago	Burke-Glass	—	—	Unique	—
1066	1134	St. Louis	Burke-Glass	—	—	Unknown	—
1067	1134	San Francisco	Burke-Glass	—	—	Unique	—

Gold Certificates
Ten Thousand Dollars

KL#	Fr#	Issue/Act/Series	Signatures	Seal	Fine	XF	CH CU (63)	Gem CU (65)
1068	1166g	First/1863	Colby-Spinner		—	—	Unknown	—

Andrew Jackson at left.

KL#	Fr#	Issue/Act/Series	Signatures	Seal	Fine	XF	CH CU (63)	Gem CU (65)
1069	1166l	Second/1870	Allison-New		—	—	Unknown	—
1070	1166q	Third/1875	Allison-New		—	—	Unique	—

Andrew Jackson at left. Eagle on flag at right.

KL#	Fr#	Issue/Act/Series	Signatures	Seal	Fine	XF	CH CU (63)	Gem CU (65)
1078	1223g	1882	Teehee-Burke	Small red	—		Extremely Rare	—

Other signature varieties were issued in Series 1882 but, none are known.
Series 1888 were uniface transfer documents, not intended for general circulation.

KL#	Fr#	Issue/Act/Series	Signatures	Seal	Fine	XF	CH CU (63)	Gem CU (65)
1078A	1224	1888	Rosecrans-Hyatt	Large red	—	—	Unknown	—
1078B	1224a	1888	Rosecrans-Nebeker	Small red	—	—	Unknown	—
1079	1225		Lyons-Roberts		1750.	2500.	3300.	7800.
1079A	1225		Lyons-Treat		1750.	2500.	4000.	8400.
1079B	1225		Vernon-Treat		1750.	2500.	4000.	7800.
1079C	1225		Vernon-McClung		1750.	2500.	4000.	7800.
1079D	1225		Napier-McClung		1750.	2500.	4000.	7800.
1079E	1225		Napier-Burke		1750.	2500.	4000.	7800.
1079F	1225		Parker-Burke		1750.	2500.	4000.	7800.
1079G	1225		Teehee-Burke		1750.	2500.	4000.	7800.

All outstanding 1900 $10,000 Gold Certificates are the result of a 1935 fire
in a Treasury storage area in Washington, D.C. While fighting the fire,
a quantity of these redeemed and cancelled notes were thrown out into the street,
where the scattered notes were picked up by passers-by.

Federal Reserve Notes
1918

Salmon P. Chase at center. Embarkation of the Pilgrims.

KL#	Fr#	Bank	Signatures	Fine	XF	CH CU (63)	Gem CU (65)
1080	1135	Boston	Burke-Glass	—	—	Unknown	—
1081	1135	New York	Burke-Glass	—		Extremely Rare	—
1082	1135	Cleveland	Burke-Glass	—	—	Unique	—
1083	1135	Richmond	Burke-Glass	—	—	Unknown	—
1084	1135	St. Louis	Burke-Glass	—	—	Unknown	—
1085	1135	San Francisco	Burke-Glass	—		Extremely Rare	—

Small Size Currency

United States Notes

When the switch to the smaller, current size U.S. currency was made in July, 1929, the United States Notes (Legal Tender Notes), bearing red Treasury, seals and serial numbers, were included, although denominations were pared back to only $1, $2, $5 and $100 notes.

The Red Seal $1 is especially popular with collectors in that it was issued only in one series (1928) and in fewer than two million notes. The 1928 $1 Legal Tenders were principally released in Puerto Rico more than 20 years after the notes had been printed. Star notes of the type are especially sought-after and command a strong premium, even in circulated grades.

The small size U.S. Note remained current in the $2 denomination until July, 1965, and in the $5 value until November, 1967. The last issue of Red Seal $100s was in 1968.

The obligation for small size U.S. Notes began in Series 1928 as: "This note is a legal tender at its face value for all debts public and private except duties on imports and interest on the public debt." Under terms of the Act of May 12, 1933, the clause was amended to read: "This note is a legal tender at its face value for all debts public and private." Beginning in Series 1963, it was changed to: "This note is legal tender for all debts, public and private."

Gold Certificates

With the rest of the U.S. currency, the change to smaller notes in 1929 affected the Gold Certificates. Most noticeably, the type lost its distinguishing gold-colored back design as the general configuration of the notes was standardized in all types. The seal and serial numbers continued in gold ink. Among the small size notes, Gold Certificate denominations continued from $10-$10,000, nominally intended for circulation, and even included the $100,000 Gold Certificate of Series 1934, for use in fiscal channels. Like the $100, $1,000 and $10,000 gold notes of Series 1934, the $100,000s were never released to general circulation and may not be legally held by collectors.

Likewise, Series 1928A Gold Certificates were printed in denominations of $10, 20 and $100, though never released.

The small size gold notes were a short series, cut off by the Gold Reserve Act of 1933, which required the surrender of all Gold Certificates (a restriction which was lifted in 1964). For practical purposes the collectibility of the type is thus limited to the Series 1928 notes in the $10, $20, $50 and $100 denominations, which are currently in strong demand in uncirculated condition. Star notes are especially in demand.

Silver Certificates

From the 1929 release date of the small size U.S. currency issues, until Silver Certificate legislation was abolished by a Congressional Act on June 4, 1963, small size Silver Certificates, distinguished by their blue Treasury seal and serial number, were issued in denominations of $1, $5, and $10.

The earliest small size silver notes were redeemable for "One Silver Dollar," (or the appropriate number) as had been the large size issues. A change in the redemption clause, however, was made with the Silver Purchase Act of 1934, which specified the certificates be redeemable for silver dollars or silver bullion. At that time the wording on the notes was changed to read: "One Dollar in Silver." In March, 1964, by order of the Secretary of the Treasury, redemption in silver dollars was halted, and on June 24, 1968, redemption in silver bullion was also discontinued. Like all U.S. currency issued since 1861, Silver Certificates retain their status as legal tender, though today they are convertible only into current U.S. Federal Reserve Notes.

Federal Reserve Notes

Virtually the only type of U.S. paper money encountered in circulation today is the Federal Reserve Note, in denominations of $1-$100. Beginning with the Series 1990 $100 and $50 notes new security features have been added, including a metallic strip and micro-printing. A second printing plant was opened at Fort Worth, Texas in 1990, with the notes identified by a "FW" prefix on the face plate check number. A full redesign of the $5, $10, $20, $50, and $100 notes occured starting in 1995 series with the introduction of the off-centered "big head" notes. With the 2004 series color began to be added to the $10, $20 and $50 notes.

Authorization continued in the small size period for FRNs to be issued in denominations from $5-$10,000. With the demise of the Silver Certificate $1 bill in 1963, that denomination was moved into the FRN realm. The Bicentennial in 1976 led to the re-introduction of the $2 note, which had last been issued as a United States Note in 1966, in the guise of a green-seal Federal Reserve Note.

No Federal Reserve Note of denomination higher than $100 has been printed since 1945, and since 1969 all notes of $500 and higher face value have been actively retired as they are turned into the Federal Reserve System.

Federal Reserve Bank Notes

The small size Federal Reserve Bank Notes were an emergency currency issue authorized March 9, 1933, to inject cash into the economy to combat heavy withdrawals from the Federal Reserve System in the first months of that year.

FRBNs in the small size were printed on currency stock prepared for the regular Series 1929 National Currency. Changes consisted of overprinting several elements. The President (and sometimes Cashier) title at the bottom of the notes was obliterated, and replaced with Governor, and the appropriate signatures of those Federal Reserve Bank officers engraved. There are, however, three exceptions to the Cashier-Governor combination on the small size FRBNs. On the notes of the Chicago bank, the signatures are those of the Assistant Deputy Governor and Governor; for New York, the signature of the Deputy Governor replaces that of the Cashier, and in the St. Louis district, the Controller signed instead of the Cashier.

In the places where the National Bank's charter number would have been imprinted, the proper district letter of the issuing bank appears in heavy black block type. At top of the note, near the obligation, a line was added to read: "or by like deposit of other securities."

Like the regular National Bank Notes of the small size era, the Treasury seal and serial number on the Federal Reserve Bank Notes are in brown ink.

Collector demand for this type has been almost non-existent until recent years. Now, however, the true rarity of some banks and denominations ($5-$100), especially in star notes, is being appreciated.

WWII Emergency Notes

Emergency conditions during World War II brought about several interesting and collectible varieties, of small size U.S. currency.

North African Invasion Notes

When U.S. armed forces hit the beaches of North Africa in 1942 to begin the advance into Axis-held Europe from the south, special currency was issued to the troops which could be easily identified and demonetized in the event of military reverse and the capture of large quantities of the cash.

The notes were normal Silver Certificates, with blue serial numbers, but with Treasury seals printed in yellow. All bearing the Julian-Morgenthau signature combination, the $1 denominations were issued in Series 1935A, the $5s in Series 1934A and $10s in Series 1934 and 1934A. The 1934 $10 notes are quite scarce, especially as star notes.

Hawaii Overprints

As an economic defense precaution against Japanese invasion and occupation of Hawaii, specially marked U.S. currency was issued there in July, 1942, to replace other types in circulation. Distinguished by brown seal and serial numbers, and by "HAWAII" overprints on face and back, such notes could have been declared worthless in the event large numbers of them were captured.

The $1 notes used as emergency currency were Silver Certificates of Series 1935A, while $5s, $10s, and $20s were overprinted examples of San Francisco-district Federal Reserve Notes; the $5s in Series 1934 and '34A, the $10s in Series 1934A only, and the $20s in Series 1934 and '34A. All notes bear the Julian-Morgenthau combination.

By late October, 1944, the emergency monetary conditions were declared ended, and normal currency returned to use in Hawaii, and the Hawaii-overprinted notes went on to do further duty during the occupation of formerly Japanese-held islands in the Pacific.

R & S Experimentals

To test different types of security paper during World War II, when it was not known whether supplies of normal U.S. bank note paper could be maintained, an experimental run of notes was produced using normal, and new special paper.

Notes on the special paper were overprinted with a large red S in the lower right corner, while a control group on regular paper was printed with a large red R in the same location. Exactly 1,184,000 of each type were released to circulation, all Silver Certificates bearing Series 1935A designation and the Julian Morgenthau signature combination. The tests proved to be inconclusive, so no change in bank note paper resulted, but collectors were left with an interesting variety that is especially challenging in uncirculated condition, and truly rare in star note form.

Because unscrupulous persons have applied phony R and S overprints to regular Series 1935A $1 Silver Certificates in an effort to pass them off as the higher-value experimental issue, collectors should be aware of the serial number ranges of the genuine issues. Serial numbers for the genuine R notes run from S70884001C through S72068000C; while those for the S notes are S73884001C through S75068000C.

United States Notes
One Dollar

KL#	Fr#	Series	Signatures	Fine	XF	CH CU (63)	Gem CU (65)
1444	1500	1928	Woods-Woodin	125.	225.	400.	600.
1444☆	1500	1928☆	Woods-Woodin	2000.	12,500.	18,000.	45,000.

Silver Certificates

KL#	Fr#	Series	Signatures	Fine	XF	CH CU (63)	Gem CU (65)
1445	1600	1928	Tate-Mellon	25.00	50.00	110.	125.

KL#	Fr#	Series	Signatures	Fine	XF	CH CU (63)	Gem CU (65)
1445☆	1600	1928☆	Tate-Mellon	85.00	175.	575.	1560.
1446	1601	1928A	Woods-Mellon	25.00	45.00	80.00	100.
1446☆	1601	1928A☆	Woods-Mellon	80.00	200.	450.	700.
1447	1602	1928B	Woods-Mills	25.00	45.00	100.	135.
1447☆	1602	1928B☆	Woods-Mills	125.	350.	1650.	2500.
1448	1603	1928C	Woods-Woodin	125.	425.	775.	900.
1448☆	1603	1928C☆	Woods-Woodin	5000.	8000.	25,000.	45,000.
1449	1604	1928D	Julian-Woodin	60.00	200.	500.	750.
1449☆	1604	1928D☆	Julian-Woodin	5000.	10,000.	23,000.	61,000.
1450	1605	1928E	Julian-Morgenthau	400.	800.	1500.	3200.
1450☆	1605	1928E☆	Julian-Morgenthau	10,000.	15,000.	75,000.	145,000.
1451	1606	1934	Julian-Morgenthau	25.00	40.00	100.	150.
1451☆	1606	1934☆	Julian-Morgenthau	75.00	300.	775.	2100.

KL#	Fr#	Series	Signatures	Fine	XF	CH CU (63)	Gem CU (65)
1452	1607	1935	Julian-Morgenthau	10.00	15.00	40.00	100.
1452☆	1607	1935☆	Julian-Morgenthau	50.00	150.	900.	1550.
1453	1608	1935A	Julian-Morgenthau	3.00	6.00	20.00	40.00
1453☆	1608	1935A☆	Julian-Morgenthau	25.00	75.00	175.	225.
1454	1611	1935B	Julian-Vinson	3.00	5.00	22.00	40.00
1454☆	1611	1935B☆	Julian-Vinson	10.00	80.00	250.	500.
1455	1612	1935C	Julian-Snyder	2.00	4.00	20.00	40.00
1455☆	1612	1935C☆	Julian-Snyder	15.00	35.00	125.	200.
1456	1613	1935D	Clark-Snyder	3.00	11.00	22.00	35.00
			Wide back, 4 digit plate #5015 or less				
1456☆	1613	1935D☆	Clark-Snyder	8.00	40.00	200.	250.
			Wide back, 4 digit plate #5015 or less				
1456A	1613	1935D	Clark-Snyder	3.00	6.00	20.00	35.00
			Narrow back, 4 digit plate #5017 or greater				
1456A☆	1613	1935D☆	Clark-Snyder	8.00	40.00	80.00	350.
			Narrow back, 4 digit plate #5017 or greater				
1457	1614	1935E	Priest-Humphrey	3.00	4.00	18.00	30.00
1457☆	1614	1935E☆	Priest-Humphrey	3.00	11.00	25.00	50.00
1458	1615	1935F	Priest-Anderson	3.00	4.00	18.00	23.00
1458☆	1615	1935F☆	Priest-Anderson	3.00	10.00	45.00	70.00
1459	1616	1935G	Smith-Dillon	3.00	5.00	18.00	23.00
1459☆	1616	1935G☆	Smith-Dillon	8.00	10.00	100.	200.
1460	1617	1935G	Smith-Dillon	3.00	10.00	85.00	100.
1460☆	1617	1935G☆	Smith-Dillon	35.00	65.00	150.	350.

KL#	Fr#	Series	Signatures	Fine	XF	CH CU (63)	Gem CU (65)
1461	1618	1935H	Granahan-Dillon	3.00	5.00	25.00	35.00
1461☆	1618	1935H☆	Granahan-Dillon	5.00	20.00	100.	150.
1462	1619	1957	Priest-Anderson	3.00	4.00	10.00	20.00
1462☆	1619	1957☆	Priest-Anderson	3.00	5.00	25.00	35.00
1463	1620	1957A	Smith-Dillon	3.00	4.00	17.00	20.00
1463☆	1620	1957A☆	Smith-Dillon	3.00	8.00	25.00	35.00
1464	1621	1957B	Granahan-Dillon	3.00	3.00	6.00	8.00
1464☆	1621	1957B☆	Granahan-Dillon	3.00	6.00	12.00	30.00

Federal Reserve Notes
Series 1963 Granahan-Dillon

KL#	Fr#	District	Fine	XF	CH CU (63)	Gem CU (65)
1465	1900A	Boston	FV	3.00	6.00	7.00
1465☆	1900A ☆	Boston	FV	4.00	8.00	10.00
1466	1900B	New York	FV	3.00	6.00	10.00

KL#	Fr#	District	Fine	XF	CH CU (63)	Gem CU (65)
1466☆	1900B ☆	New York	FV	4.00	7.00	8.00
1467	1900C	Philadelphia	FV	3.00	5.00	6.00
1467☆	1900C ☆	Philadelphia	FV	4.00	7.00	10.00
1468	1900D	Cleveland	FV	3.00	5.00	6.00
1468☆	1900D ☆	Cleveland	FV	4.00	8.00	10.00
1469	1900E	Richmond	FV	3.00	8.00	10.00
1469☆	1900E ☆	Richmond	FV	4.00	10.00	12.00
1470	1900F	Atlanta	FV	3.00	6.00	7.00
1470☆	1900F ☆	Atlanta	FV	4.00	9.00	10.00
1471	1900G	Chicago	FV	3.00	5.00	7.00
1471☆	1900G ☆	Chicago	FV	4.00	8.00	10.00
1472	1900H	St. Louis	FV	3.00	6.00	7.00
1472☆	1900H ☆	St. Louis	FV	4.00	12.00	15.00
1473	1900I	Minneapolis	FV	3.00	6.00	8.00
1473☆	1900I ☆	Minneapolis	FV	5.00	9.00	15.00
1474	1900J	Kansas City	FV	3.00	6.00	7.00
1474☆	1900J ☆	Kansas City	FV	4.00	9.00	10.00
1475	1900K	Dallas	FV	3.00	8.00	10.00
1475☆	1900K ☆	Dallas	FV	5.00	13.00	15.00
1476	1900L	San Francisco	FV	4.00	8.00	10.00
1476☆	1900L ☆	San Francisco	FV	5.00	30.00	35.00

A Word About Star Notes

In our listings there are often two entries for each catalog number.
For example:

KL#	Fr#	District	Fine	XF	CH CU (63)	Gem CU (65)
1501	1903A	Boston	FV	2.00	7.00	8.00
1501☆	1903A☆	Boston	FV	5.00	10.00	12.00

The first listing has a serial number format of
letter - eight digits - letter.

The second listing refers to a bank note with a serial number format of
letter - eight digits - star.

This star at the end of the serial number refers to a replacement note,
one which replaces a note damaged during the production process.
There are fewer of these printed and therefore they are more expensive.

Series 1963A Granahan-Fowler

KL#	Fr#	District	Fine	XF	CH CU (63)	Gem CU (65)
1477	1901A	Boston	FV	2.00	5.00	9.00
1477☆	1901A ☆	Boston	FV	3.00	10.00	12.00
1478	1901B	New York	FV	3.00	5.00	9.00
1478☆	1901B ☆	New York	FV	4.00	10.00	12.00
1479	1901C	Philadelphia	FV	3.00	5.00	9.00
1479☆	1901C ☆	Philadelphia	FV	4.00	10.00	12.00
1480	1901D	Cleveland	FV	3.00	5.00	8.00
1480☆	1901D ☆	Cleveland	FV	3.00	9.00	10.00
1481	1901E	Richmond	FV	2.00	5.00	9.00
1481☆	1901E ☆	Richmond	FV	4.00	9.00	10.00
1482	1901F	Atlanta	FV	3.00	5.00	9.00
1482☆	1901F ☆	Atlanta	FV	4.00	10.00	12.00
1483	1901G	Chicago	FV	3.00	5.00	9.00
1483☆	1901G ☆	Chicago	FV	4.00	10.00	11.00
1484	1901H	St. Louis	FV	3.00	5.00	9.00
1484☆	1901H ☆	St. Louis	FV	4.00	12.00	13.00
1485	1901I	Minneapolis	FV	3.00	7.00	9.00
1485☆	1901I ☆	Minneapolis	FV	4.00	12.00	15.00
1486	1901J	Kansas City	FV	3.00	5.00	10.00
1486☆	1901J ☆	Kansas City	FV	4.00	10.00	12.00
1487	1901K	Dallas	FV	3.00	5.00	10.00
1487☆	1901K ☆	Dallas	FV	4.00	10.00	12.00
1488	1901L	San Francisco	FV	3.00	5.00	10.00
1488☆	1901L ☆	San Francisco	FV	4.00	8.00	10.00

Series 1963B Granahan-Barr

KL#	Fr#	District	Fine	XF	CH CU (63)	Gem CU (65)
1490	1902B	New York	FV	3.00	8.00	10.00
1490☆	1902B ☆	New York	FV	6.00	20.00	25.00
1493	1902E	Richmond	FV	3.00	9.00	12.00
1493☆	1902E ☆	Richmond	FV	7.00	20.00	25.00

KL#	Fr#	District	Fine	XF	CH CU (63)	Gem CU (65)
1495	1902G	Chicago	FV	3.00	9.00	12.00
1495☆	1902G ☆	Chicago	FV	6.00	20.00	25.00
1498	1902J	Kansas City	FV	2.00	10.00	12.00
1500	1902L	San Francisco	FV	6.00	9.00	12.00
1500☆	1902L ☆	San Francisco	FV	13.00	25.00	30.00

Series 1969 Elston-Kennedy

KL#	Fr#	District	Fine	XF	CH CU (63)	Gem CU (65)
1501	1903A	Boston	FV	2.00	7.00	8.00
1501☆	1903A ☆	Boston	FV	5.00	10.00	12.00
1502	1903B	New York	FV	2.00	7.00	8.00
1502☆	1903B ☆	New York	FV	5.00	10.00	12.00
1503	1903C	Philadelphia	FV	2.00	7.00	8.00
1503☆	1903C ☆	Philadelphia	FV	5.00	10.00	12.00
1504	1903D	Cleveland	FV	2.00	7.00	8.00
1504☆	1903D ☆	Cleveland	FV	5.00	10.00	12.00
1505	1903E	Richmond	FV	2.00	7.00	8.00
1505☆	1903E ☆	Richmond	FV	5.00	10.00	12.00
1506	1903F	Atlanta	FV	2.00	7.00	8.00
1506☆	1903F ☆	Atlanta	FV	5.00	10.00	12.00
1507	1903G	Chicago	FV	2.00	7.00	8.00
1507☆	1903G ☆	Chicago	FV	5.00	10.00	12.00
1508	1903H	St. Louis	FV	2.00	7.00	8.00
1508☆	1903H ☆	St. Louis	FV	5.00	10.00	12.00
1509	1903I	Minneapolis	FV	3.00	7.00	8.00
1509☆	1903I ☆	Minneapolis	2.00	8.00	30.00	35.00
1510	1903J	Kansas City	FV	2.00	7.00	8.00
1510☆	1903J ☆	Kansas City	FV	5.00	10.00	15.00
1511	1903K	Dallas	FV	2.00	8.00	12.00
1511☆	1903K ☆	Dallas	FV	5.00	10.00	12.00
1512	1903L	San Francisco	FV	2.00	8.00	10.00
1512☆	1903L ☆	San Francisco	FV	5.00	12.00	15.00

Series 1969A Kabis-Kennedy

KL#	Fr#	District	Fine	XF	CH CU (63)	Gem CU (65)
1513	1904A	Boston	FV	2.00	8.00	10.00
1513☆	1904A ☆	Boston	FV	5.00	10.00	15.00
1514	1904B	New York	FV	2.00	5.00	8.00
1514☆	1904B ☆	New York	FV	5.00	10.00	12.00
1515	1904C	Philadelphia	FV	2.00	5.00	9.00
1515☆	1904C ☆	Philadelphia	FV	3.00	10.00	12.00
1516	1904D	Cleveland	FV	2.00	7.00	9.00
1516☆	1904D ☆	Cleveland	FV	5.00	10.00	15.00
1517	1904E	Richmond	FV	2.00	6.00	8.00
1517☆	1904E ☆	Richmond	FV	3.00	10.00	11.00
1518	1904F	Atlanta	FV	2.00	6.00	8.00
1518☆	1904F ☆	Atlanta	FV	5.00	10.00	11.00
1519	1904G	Chicago	FV	2.00	6.00	8.00
1519☆	1904G ☆	Chicago	FV	5.00	8.00	10.00
1520	1904H	St. Louis	FV	2.00	5.00	10.00
1520☆	1904H ☆	St. Louis	FV	5.00	8.00	15.00
1521	1904I	Minneapolis	FV	2.00	7.00	10.00
1521☆	1904I ☆	Minneapolis	FV	10.00	30.00	35.00
1522	1904J	Kansas City	FV	2.00	5.00	12.00
1522☆	1904J ☆	Kansas City	FV	3.00	25.00	30.00
1523	1904K	Dallas	FV	2.00	8.00	10.00
1524	1904L	San Francisco	FV	2.00	7.00	10.00
1524☆	1904L ☆	San Francisco	FV	5.00	8.00	10.00

Series 1969B Kabis-Connally

KL#	Fr#	District	Fine	XF	CH CU (63)	Gem CU (65)
1525	1905A	Boston	FV	2.00	5.00	9.00
1525☆	1905A ☆	Boston	FV	4.00	9.00	15.00
1526	1905B	New York	FV	2.00	5.00	8.00
1526☆	1905B ☆	New York	FV	3.00	9.00	12.00
1527	1905C	Philadelphia	FV	2.00	5.00	8.00

KL#	Fr#	District	Fine	XF	CH CU (63)	Gem CU (65)
1527☆	1905C ☆	Philadelphia	FV	3.00	10.00	11.00
1528	1905D	Cleveland	FV	2.00	5.00	9.00
1528☆	1905D ☆	Cleveland	FV	3.00	10.00	11.00
1529	1905E	Richmond	FV	2.00	5.00	8.00
1529☆	1905E ☆	Richmond	FV	3.00	10.00	11.00
1530	1905F	Atlanta	FV	2.00	5.00	8.00
1530☆	1905F ☆	Atlanta	FV	3.00	10.00	11.00
1531	1905G	Chicago	FV	2.00	5.00	8.00
1531☆	1905G ☆	Chicago	FV	3.00	7.00	8.00
1532	1905H	St. Louis	FV	2.00	5.00	8.00
1532☆	1905H ☆	St. Louis	FV	3.00	10.00	11.00
1533	1905I	Minneapolis	FV	2.00	7.00	10.00
1533☆	1905I ☆	Minneapolis	5.00	15.00	35.00	40.00
1534	1905J	Kansas City	FV	2.00	5.00	9.00
1534☆	1905J ☆	Kansas City	FV	3.00	10.00	12.00
1535	1905K	Dallas	FV	2.00	5.00	9.00
1535☆	1905K ☆	Dallas	FV	3.00	10.00	11.00
1536	1905L	San Francisco	FV	2.00	5.00	8.00
1536☆	1905L ☆	San Francisco	FV	3.00	9.00	10.00

Series 1969C Banuelos-Connally

KL#	Fr#	District	Fine	XF	CH CU (63)	Gem CU (65)
1538	1906B	New York	FV	3.00	7.00	9.00
1540	1906D	Cleveland	FV	4.00	9.00	11.00
1540☆	1906D ☆	Cleveland	5.00	15.00	50.00	60.00
1541	1906E	Richmond	FV	3.00	10.00	12.00
1541☆	1906E ☆	Richmond	3.00	13.00	50.00	75.00
1542	1906F	Atlanta	FV	3.00	7.00	9.00
1542☆	1906F ☆	Atlanta	2.00	10.00	35.00	60.00
1543	1906G	Chicago	FV	3.00	7.00	9.00
1543☆	1906G ☆	Chicago	2.00	10.00	25.00	30.00
1544	1906H	St. Louis	FV	3.00	6.00	9.00
1544☆	1906H ☆	St. Louis	3.00	10.00	30.00	45.00
1545	1906I	Minneapolis	FV	3.00	7.00	9.00
1545☆	1906I ☆	Minneapolis	10.00	15.00	35.00	45.00
1546	1906J	Kansas City	FV	3.00	6.00	9.00
1546☆	1906J ☆	Kansas City	2.00	10.00	25.00	30.00
1547	1906K	Dallas	FV	3.00	7.00	9.00
1547☆	1906K ☆	Dallas	5.00	15.00	35.00	45.00
1548	1906L	San Francisco	FV	2.00	7.00	9.00
1548☆	1906L ☆	San Francisco	50.00	100.	175.	200.

Series 1969D Banuelos-Shultz

KL#	Fr#	District	Fine	XF	CH CU (63)	Gem CU (65)
1561	1907A	Boston	FV	2.00	7.00	9.00
1561☆	1907A ☆	Boston	2.00	10.00	25.00	30.00
1562	1907B	New York	FV	2.00	7.00	9.00
1562☆	1907B ☆	New York	FV	5.00	9.00	15.00
1563	1907C	Philadelphia	FV	2.00	7.00	9.00
1563☆	1907C ☆	Philadelphia	FV	5.00	10.00	12.00
1564	1907D	Cleveland	FV	3.00	7.00	9.00
1564☆	1907D ☆	Cleveland	FV	4.00	10.00	12.00
1565	1907E	Richmond	FV	2.00	7.00	9.00
1565☆	1907E ☆	Richmond	FV	5.00	10.00	12.00
1566	1907F	Atlanta	FV	4.00	7.00	9.00
1566☆	1907F ☆	Atlanta	FV	5.00	10.00	12.00
1567	1907G	Chicago	FV	2.00	7.00	9.00
1567☆	1907G ☆	Chicago	FV	5.00	8.00	10.00
1568	1907H	St. Louis	FV	2.00	7.00	9.00
1568☆	1907H ☆	St. Louis	FV	5.00	10.00	12.00
1569	1907I	Minneapolis	FV	2.00	7.00	9.00
1570	1907J	Kansas City	FV	2.00	7.00	9.00
1570☆	1907J ☆	Kansas City	FV	5.00	9.00	10.00
1571	1907K	Dallas	FV	2.00	7.00	9.00
1571☆	1907K ☆	Dallas	FV	5.00	9.00	10.00
1572	1907L	San Francisco	FV	2.00	7.00	9.00
1572☆	1907L ☆	San Francisco	FV	5.00	9.00	10.00

Series 1974 Neff-Simon

KL#	Fr#	District	Fine	XF	CH CU (63)	Gem CU (65)
1573	1908A	Boston	FV	2.00	6.00	8.00
1573☆	1908A ☆	Boston	FV	4.00	9.00	10.00
1574	1908B	New York	FV	2.00	6.00	8.00
1574☆	1908B ☆	New York	FV	4.00	9.00	10.00
1575	1908C	Philadelphia	FV	2.00	5.00	8.00

KL#	Fr#	District	Fine	XF	CH CU (63)	Gem CU (65)
1575☆	1908C ☆	Philadelphia	FV	4.00	15.00	25.00
1576	1908D	Cleveland	FV	2.00	5.00	8.00
1576☆	1908D ☆	Cleveland	FV	10.00	30.00	35.00
1577	1908E	Richmond	FV	2.00	5.00	8.00
1577☆	1908E ☆	Richmond	FV	5.00	10.00	12.00
1578	1908F	Atlanta	FV	2.00	5.00	8.00
1578☆	1908F ☆	Atlanta	FV	4.00	13.00	15.00
1579	1908G	Chicago	FV	2.00	5.00	8.00
1579☆	1908G ☆	Chicago	FV	4.00	10.00	11.00
1580	1908H	St. Louis	FV	2.00	5.00	8.00
1580☆	1908H ☆	St. Louis	FV	4.00	9.00	12.00
1581	1908I	Minneapolis	FV	2.00	5.00	8.00
1581☆	1908I ☆	Minneapolis	FV	12.00	45.00	50.00
1582	1908J	Kansas City	FV	2.00	5.00	8.00
1582☆	1908J ☆	Kansas City	FV	4.00	9.00	10.00
1583	1908K	Dallas	FV	2.00	5.00	8.00
1583☆	1908K ☆	Dallas	FV	4.00	25.00	30.00
1584	1908L	San Francisco	FV	2.00	5.00	8.00
1584☆	1908L ☆	San Francisco	FV	4.00	9.00	12.00

Series 1977 Morton-Blumenthal

KL#	Fr#	District	Fine	XF	CH CU (63)	Gem CU (65)
1585	1909A	Boston	FV	2.00	6.00	8.00
1585☆	1909A ☆	Boston	FV	3.00	25.00	30.00
1586	1909B	New York	FV	2.00	6.00	8.00
1586☆	1909B ☆	New York	FV	4.00	10.00	12.00
1587	1909C	Philadelphia	FV	2.00	6.00	8.00
1587☆	1909C ☆	Philadelphia	FV	4.00	15.00	20.00
1588	1909D	Cleveland	FV	3.00	7.00	8.00
1588☆	1909D ☆	Cleveland	FV	10.00	15.00	20.00
1589	1909E	Richmond	FV	2.00	6.00	8.00
1589☆	1909E ☆	Richmond	FV	4.00	9.00	12.00
1590	1909F	Atlanta	FV	2.00	5.00	8.00
1590☆	1909F ☆	Atlanta	FV	4.00	9.00	15.00
1591	1909G	Chicago	FV	2.00	5.00	8.00
1591☆	1909G ☆	Chicago	FV	4.00	9.00	12.00
1592	1909H	St. Louis	FV	2.00	5.00	8.00
1592☆	1909H ☆	St. Louis	FV	4.00	12.00	15.00
1593	1909I	Minneapolis	FV	2.00	6.00	8.00
1593☆	1909I ☆	Minneapolis	FV	6.00	12.00	20.00
1594	1909J	Kansas City	FV	2.00	6.00	8.00
1594☆	1909J ☆	Kansas City	FV	4.00	10.00	12.00
1595	1909K	Dallas	FV	2.00	6.00	8.00
1595☆	1909K ☆	Dallas	FV	4.00	10.00	12.00
1596	1909L	San Francisco	FV	2.00	6.00	8.00
1596☆	1909L ☆	San Francisco	FV	4.00	9.00	12.00

Series 1977A Morton-Miller

KL#	Fr#	District	Fine	XF	CH CU (63)	Gem CU (65)
1597	1910A	Boston	FV	2.00	6.00	8.00
1597☆	1910A ☆	Boston	FV	7.00	25.00	30.00
1598	1910B	New York	FV	2.00	20.00	25.00
1598☆	1910B ☆	New York	FV	3.00	10.00	30.00
1599	1910C	Philadelphia	FV	2.00	6.00	8.00
1599☆	1910C ☆	Philadelphia	FV	4.00	9.00	15.00
1600	1910D	Cleveland	FV	2.00	6.00	8.00
1600☆	1910D ☆	Cleveland	FV	3.00	12.00	15.00
1601	1910E	Richmond	FV	2.00	6.00	8.00
1601☆	1910E ☆	Richmond	FV	3.00	9.00	12.00
1602	1910F	Atlanta	FV	2.00	6.00	8.00
1602☆	1910F ☆	Atlanta	FV	3.00	10.00	12.00
1603	1910G	Chicago	FV	2.00	6.00	8.00
1603☆	1910G ☆	Chicago	FV	3.00	15.00	20.00
1604	1910H	St. Louis	FV	2.00	6.00	8.00
1604☆	1910H☆	St. Louis	FV	4.00	10.00	12.00
1605	1910I	Minneapolis	FV	6.00	20.00	25.00
1605☆	1910I ☆	Minneapolis	FV	6.00	25.00	35.00
1606	1910J	Kansas City	FV	2.00	6.00	8.00
1606☆	1910J ☆	Kansas City	FV	4.00	10.00	12.00
1607	1910K	Dallas	FV	2.00	6.00	8.00
1607☆	1910K ☆	Dallas	FV	4.00	10.00	12.00
1608	1910L	San Francisco	FV	2.00	6.00	8.00
1608☆	1910L ☆	San Francisco	FV	4.00	10.00	12.00

Series 1981 Buchanan-Regan

KL#	Fr#	District	Fine	XF	CH CU (63)	Gem CU (65)
3500	1911A	Boston	FV	2.00	5.00	8.00
3500☆	1911A ☆	Boston	FV	7.00	40.00	50.00
3501	1911B	New York	FV	2.00	7.00	8.00
3501☆	1911B ☆	New York	FV	4.00	12.00	15.00
3502	1911C	Philadelphia	FV	2.00	7.00	8.00
3502☆	1911C ☆	Philadelphia	FV	35.00	125.	150.

KL#	Fr#	District	Fine	XF	CH CU (63)	Gem CU (65)
3503	1911D	Cleveland	FV	2.00	7.00	9.00
3503☆	1911D ☆	Cleveland	FV	8.00	13.00	15.00
3504	1911E	Richmond	FV	2.00	7.00	9.00
3504☆	1911E ☆	Richmond	FV	7.00	20.00	25.00
3505	1911F	Atlanta	FV	2.00	7.00	9.00
3505☆	1911F ☆	Atlanta	FV	7.00	15.00	20.00
3506	1911G	Chicago	FV	2.00	7.00	9.00
3506☆	1911G ☆	Chicago	FV	5.00	15.00	20.00
3507	1911H	St. Louis	FV	2.00	5.00	9.00
3507☆	1911H ☆	St. Louis	FV	4.00	12.00	20.00
3508	1911I	Minneapolis	FV	2.00	7.00	9.00
3508☆	1911I ☆	Minneapolis	FV	8.00	20.00	25.00
3509	1911J	Kansas City	FV	2.00	7.00	9.00
3509☆	1911J ☆	Kansas City	FV	5.00	15.00	20.00
3510	1911K	Dallas	FV	2.00	7.00	9.00
3510☆	1911K ☆	Dallas	FV	4.00	20.00	25.00
3511	1911L	San Francisco	FV	2.00	6.00	8.00
3511☆	1911L ☆	San Francisco	FV	5.00	12.00	15.00

Series 1981A Ortega-Regan

KL#	Fr#	District	Fine	XF	CH CU (63)	Gem CU (65)
3600	1912A	Boston	FV	2.00	6.00	8.00
3601	1912B	New York	FV	2.00	6.00	8.00
3601☆	1912B ☆	New York	FV	5.00	12.00	15.00
3602	1912C	Philadelphia	FV	2.00	6.00	8.00
3602A	-	Philadelphia - Back plate #129 at left	FV	2.00	8.00	12.00
3603	1912D	Cleveland	FV	2.00	6.00	8.00
3604	1912E	Richmond	FV	2.00	6.00	8.00
3604☆	1912E ☆	Richmond	FV	5.00	15.00	20.00
3605	1912F	Atlanta	FV	2.00	6.00	8.00
3605A	-	Atlanta - Back plate #129 at left	FV	2.00	6.00	0.00
3606	1912G	Chicago	FV	2.00	6.00	8.00
3606☆	1912G ☆	Chicago	FV	5.00	15.00	20.00
3607	1912H	St. Louis	FV	2.00	6.00	8.00
3607A	-	St. Louis - Back plate #129 at left	FV	2.00	6.00	8.00
3608	1912I	Minneapolis	FV	2.00	6.00	8.00
3608A	-	Minneapolis - Back plate #129 at left	FV	2.00	6.00	8.00
3609	1912J	Kansas City	FV	2.00	6.00	8.00
3610	1912K	Dallas	FV	2.00	6.00	8.00
3610☆	1912K ☆	Dallas	250.	550.	1300.	1850.
3611	1912L	San Francisco	FV	2.00	6.00	8.00
3611☆	1912L ☆	San Francisco	FV	5.00	20.00	25.00
3611A	-	San Francisco - Back plate #129 at left	FV	2.00	6.00	8.00

Series 1985 Ortega-Baker

KL#	Fr#	District	Fine	XF	CH CU (63)	Gem CU (65)
3700	1913A	Boston	FV	FV	6.00	9.00

KL#	Fr#	District	Fine	XF	CH CU (63)	Gem CU (65)
3700A	-	Boston - Back plate #129 at left	FV	FV	6.00	9.00
3701	1913B	New York	FV	FV	6.00	8.00
3701A	-	New York - Back plate #129 at left	FV	FV	6.00	8.00
3702	1913C	Philadelphia	FV	FV	6.00	8.00
3703	1913D	Cleveland	FV	FV	6.00	8.00
3703A	-	Cleveland - Back plate #129 at left	FV	FV	6.00	8.00
3704	1913E	Richmond	FV	FV	6.00	8.00
3704☆	1913E ☆	Richmond	FV	FV	15.00	20.00
3704A	-	Richmond - Back plate #129 at left	FV	FV	6.00	8.00
3705	1913F	Atlanta	FV	FV	5.00	8.00
3705A	-	Atlanta - Back plate #129 at left	FV	FV	5.00	8.00
3706	1913G	Chicago	FV	FV	6.00	8.00
3706☆	1913G ☆	Chicago	2.00	4.00	8.00	10.00
3706A	-	Chicago - Back plate #129 at left	FV	FV	6.00	8.00
3707	1913H	St. Louis	FV	FV	15.00	20.00
3707☆	1913H ☆	St. Louis	40.00	400.	1500.	1750.
3707A	-	St. Louis - Back plate #129 at left	FV	FV	6.00	8.00
3708	1913I	Minneapolis	FV	FV	6.00	8.00
3708☆	1913I ☆	Minneapolis	FV	2.00	15.00	20.00
3709	1913J	Kansas City	FV	FV	6.00	8.00
3710	1913K	Dallas	FV	FV	5.00	8.00
3710☆	1913K ☆	Dallas	FV	2.00	15.00	20.00
3711	1913L	San Francisco	FV	FV	6.00	8.00
3711☆	1913L ☆	San Francisco	FV	2.00	15.00	20.00
3711A	-	San Francisco - Back plate #129 at left	FV	FV	6.00	8.00

Series 1988 Ortega-Brady

KL#	Fr#	District	Fine	XF	CH CU (63)	Gem CU (65)
3772	1914A	Boston	FV	2.00	9.00	11.00
3772☆	1914A ☆	Boston	FV	5.00	15.00	20.00
3773	1914B	New York	FV	2.00	9.00	11.00
3773☆	1914B ☆	New York	FV	5.00	15.00	20.00
3774	1914C	Philadelphia	FV	2.00	9.00	11.00
3775	1914D	Cleveland	FV	2.00	9.00	11.00
3776	1914E	Richmond	FV	2.00	9.00	11.00
3776☆	1914E ☆	Richmond	FV	5.00	15.00	20.00
3777	1914F	Atlanta	FV	2.00	9.00	11.00
3777☆	1914F ☆	Atlanta	100.	250.	650.	1000.
3778	1914G	Chicago	FV	2.00	9.00	11.00
3779	1914H	St. Louis	FV	2.00	9.00	11.00
3780	1914I	Minneapolis	FV	2.00	9.00	11.00
3781	1914J	Kansas City	FV	2.00	9.00	11.00
3781☆	1914J ☆	Kansas City	FV	5.00	15.00	20.00
3782	1914K	Dallas	FV	2.00	9.00	11.00
3782☆	1914K ☆	Dallas	FV	5.00	30.00	35.00
3783	1914L	San Francisco	FV	2.00	9.00	11.00
3783☆	1914L ☆	San Francisco	FV	5.00	15.00	20.00

Series 1988A Villalpando-Brady - DC

KL#	Fr#	District	Fine	XF	CH CU (63)	Gem CU (65)
3844	1915A	Boston	FV	2.00	6.00	8.00
3845	1915B	New York	FV	2.00	6.00	8.00
3845☆	1915B ☆	New York	FV	3.00	10.00	12.00
3846	1915C	Philadelphia	FV	2.00	6.00	8.00
3847	1915D	Cleveland	FV	2.00	6.00	8.00
3847☆	1915D ☆	Cleveland	FV	4.00	10.00	12.00
3848	1915E	Richmond	FV	2.00	6.00	8.00
3848☆	1915E ☆	Richmond	FV	3.00	10.00	12.00
3849	1915F	Atlanta	FV	2.00	6.00	8.00
3849☆	1915F ☆	Atlanta	FV	3.00	10.00	12.00
3850	1915G	Chicago	FV	2.00	6.00	8.00
3850 ☆	1915G ☆	Chicago	FV	3.00	15.00	20.00
3851	1915H	St. Louis	FV	2.00	6.00	8.00
3851☆	1915H ☆	St. Louis	FV	2.00	15.00	17.00
3852	1915I	Minneapolis	FV	2.00	6.00	8.00
3852☆	1915I ☆	Minneapolis	FV	5.00	25.00	35.00
3853	1915J	Kansas City	FV	2.00	6.00	8.00
3854	1915K	Dallas	FV	2.00	6.00	8.00
3854☆	1915K ☆	Dallas	FV	4.00	20.00	25.00
3855	1915L	San Francisco	FV	2.00	6.00	8.00
3855☆	1915L ☆	San Francisco	FV	4.00	20.00	25.00

Series 1988A Villalpando-Brady - FW

KL#	Fr#	District	Fine	XF	CH CU (63)	Gem CU (65)
3861	1916F	Atlanta	FV	2.00	6.00	8.00
3862	1916G	Chicago	FV	2.00	6.00	8.00
3862☆	1916G ☆	Chicago	FV	4.00	20.00	25.00
3863	1916H	St. Louis	FV	2.00	6.00	8.00
3864	1916I	Minneapolis	13.00	65.00	350.	500.
3865	1916J	Kansas City	FV	2.00	6.00	8.00
3866	1916K	Dallas	FV	2.00	6.00	8.00
3867	1916L	San Francisco	FV	2.00	6.00	8.00
3867☆	1916L ☆	San Francisco	FV	4.00	10.00	12.00

Series 1993 Withrow-Bentsen - DC

KL#	Fr#	District	Fine	XF	CH CU (63)	Gem CU (65)
4012	1918A	Boston	FV	2.00	6.00	8.00
4013	1918B	New York	FV	2.00	6.00	8.00
4013☆	1918B ☆	New York	FV	2.00	10.00	12.00
4014	1918C	Philadelphia	FV	2.00	6.00	8.00
4014☆	1918C ☆	Philadelphia	25.00	75.00	200.	250.
4015	1918D	Cleveland	FV	2.00	6.00	8.00
4016	1918E	Richmond	FV	2.00	6.00	8.00
4017	1918F	Atlanta	FV	2.00	6.00	8.00
4017☆	1918F ☆	Atlanta	FV	2.00	12.00	15.00
4018	1918G	Chicago	FV	2.00	6.00	8.00
4023	1918L	San Francisco	FV	3.00	6.00	8.00

Series 1993 Withrow-Bentsen - FW

KL#	Fr#	District	Fine	XF	CH CU (63)	Gem CU (65)
4023A	1916G	Chicago	FV	2.00	6.00	8.00
4023A☆	1916G ☆	Chicago	FV	2.00	10.00	12.00
4023B	1919H	St. Louis	FV	2.00	6.00	8.00
4023C	1919I	Minneapolis	35.00	100.	175.	200.
4023D	1919K	Dallas	FV	2.00	6.00	8.00
4023D☆	1919K ☆	Dallas	FV	4.00	10.00	12.00
4023E	1919L	San Francisco	FV	2.00	6.00	8.00

Series 1995 Withrow-Rubin - DC

KL#	Fr#	District	Fine	XF	CH CU (63)	Gem CU (65)
4235	1921A	Boston	FV	FV	4.00	5.00
4235☆	1921A ☆	Boston	FV	2.00	7.00	10.00
4236	1921B	New York	FV	FV	4.00	5.00
4236☆	1921B ☆	New York	FV	2.00	12.00	15.00
4237	1921C	Philadelphia	FV	FV	4.00	5.00
4237☆	1921C ☆	Philadelphia	FV	2.00	6.00	7.00
4238	1921D	Cleveland	FV	FV	4.00	5.00
4238☆	1921D ☆	Cleveland	FV	2.00	6.00	7.00
4239	1921E	Richmond	FV	FV	4.00	5.00
4239☆	1921E ☆	Richmond	FV	2.00	6.00	7.00
4240	1921F	Atlanta	FV	FV	4.00	5.00
4240☆	1921F ☆	Atlanta	FV	2.00	6.00	7.00
4241	1921G	Chicago	FV	FV	4.00	5.00
4242	1921I	Minneapolis	FV	FV	4.00	5.00
4243	1921J	Kansas City	FV	FV	4.00	5.00
4244	1921L	San Francisco	FV	FV	4.00	5.00

Series 1995 Withrow-Rubin - FW

KL#	Fr#	District	Fine	XF	CH CU (63)	Gem CU (65)
4245	1922D	Cleveland	FV	FV	4.00	5.00
4246	1922F	Atlanta	FV	FV	4.00	5.00
4246☆	1922F ☆	Atlanta	FV	FV	7.00	9.00
4247	1922G	Chicago	FV	FV	4.00	5.00
4247☆	1922G ☆	Chicago	FV	2.00	6.00	7.00
4248	1922H	St. Louis	FV	FV	4.00	5.00
4249	1922I	Minneapolis	FV	FV	4.00	5.00
4249☆	1922I ☆	Minneapolis	FV	2.00	6.00	7.00
4250	1922J	Kansas City	FV	FV	4.00	5.00
4250☆	1922J ☆	Kansas City	FV	2.00	6.00	7.00
4251	1922K	Dallas	FV	FV	4.00	5.00
4251☆	1922K ☆	Dallas	FV	10.00	35.00	50.00
4252	1922L	San Francisco	FV	FV	4.00	5.00
4252☆	1922L ☆	San Francisco	FV	2.00	7.00	8.00

Series 1999 Withrow-Summers - DC

KL#	Fr#	District	Fine	XF	CH CU (63)	Gem CU (65)
4500	1924A	Boston	FV	FV	3.00	4.00
4500☆	1924A ☆	Boston	FV	2.00	6.00	7.00
4501	1924B	New York	FV	FV	5.00	4.00
4501☆	1924B ☆	New York	FV	2.00	6.00	7.00
4502	1924C	Philadelphia	FV	FV	3.00	4.00
4502☆	1924C ☆	Philadelphia	FV	FV	6.00	7.00
4503	1924D	Cleveland	FV	FV	3.00	4.00
4503☆	1924D ☆	Cleveland	FV	10.00	75.00	100.
4504	1924E	Richmond	FV	FV	3.00	4.00
4504☆	1924E ☆	Richmond	FV	2.00	6.00	7.00
4505	1924F	Atlanta	FV	FV	3.00	4.00

Series 1999 Withrow-Summers - FW

KL#	Fr#	District	Fine	XF	CH CU (63)	Gem CU (65)
4506	1925F	Atlanta	FV	FV	3.00	4.00
4506☆	1925F ☆	Atlanta	5.00	25.00	100.	140.
4507	1925G	Chicago	FV	FV	5.00	4.00
4508	1925H	St. Louis	FV	FV	10.00	6.00
4508☆	1925H ☆	St. Louis	FV	FV	8.00	10.00
4509	1925I	Minneapolis	FV	2.00	10.00	7.00
4510	1925J	Kansas City	FV	FV	5.00	4.00
4511	1925K	Dallas	FV	FV	3.00	4.00
4512	1925L	San Francisco	FV	FV	3.00	4.00
4512☆	1925L ☆	San Francisco	FV	2.00	6.00	7.00

Series 2001 Marin-O'Neill - DC

KL#	Fr#	District	Fine	XF	CH CU (63)	Gem CU (65)
4571	1926A	Boston	FV	FV	3.00	4.00
4571☆	1926A ☆	Boston	FV	2.00	6.00	7.00
4572	1926B	New York	FV	FV	3.00	4.00
4573	1926C	Philadelphia	FV	FV	3.00	4.00
4573☆	1926C ☆	Philadelphia	FV	2.00	6.00	8.00
4574	1926D	Cleveland	FV	FV	3.00	4.00
4575	1926E	Richmond	FV	FV	3.00	4.00
4576	1926F	Atlanta	FV	FV	3.00	4.00
4576☆	1926F ☆	Atlanta	FV	FV	6.00	7.00
4577	1926H	St. Louis	FV	50.00	85.00	100.
4577☆	1926H☆	St. Louis	5.00	25.00	60.00	70.00
4578	1926I	Minneapolis	FV	FV	3.00	4.00
4579	1926J	Kansas City	FV	FV	3.00	4.00

Series 2001 Marin-O'Neill - FW

KL#	Fr#	District	Fine	XF	CH CU (63)	Gem CU (65)
4580	1927F	Atlanta	FV	FV	3.00	4.00
4581	1927G	Chicago	FV	FV	3.00	4.00
4581☆	1927G ☆	Chicago	FV	2.00	6.00	7.00
4582	1927H	St. Louis	FV	FV	3.00	4.00
4583	1927I	Minneapolis	FV	FV	10.00	12.00
4584	1927J	Kansas City	FV	FV	10.00	12.00
4585	1927K	Dallas	FV	FV	3.00	4.00
4585☆	1927K ☆	Dallas	FV	2.00	12.00	15.00
4586	1927L	San Francisco	FV	FV	25.00	30.00
4586☆	1927L ☆	San Francisco	FV	2.00	6.00	7.00

Series 2003 Marin-Snow - DC

KL#	Fr#	District	Fine	XF	CH CU (63)	Gem CU (65)
4653	1928A	Boston	FV	FV	3.00	4.00
4653☆	1928A ☆	Boston	FV	FV	6.00	7.00
4654	1928B	New York	FV	FV	3.00	4.00
4654☆	1928B ☆	New York	FV	FV	6.00	7.00
4655	1928C	Philadelphia	FV	FV	3.00	4.00
4656	1928D	Cleveland	FV	FV	3.00	4.00
4656☆	1928D ☆	Cleveland	10.00	50.00	125.	150.
4657	1928E	Richmond	FV	FV	3.00	4.00
4657☆	1928E ☆	Richmond	FV	2.00	6.00	7.00
4658	1928F	Atlanta	FV	FV	3.00	4.00
4658☆	1928F ☆	Atlanta	FV	2.00	6.00	7.00

Series 2003 Marin-Snow - FW

KL#	Fr#	District	Fine	XF	CH CU (63)	Gem CU (65)
4658A	-	Philadelphia	FV	FV	8.00	15.00
4659	1929F	Atlanta	FV	FV	3.00	4.00
4659☆	1929F ☆	Atlanta	FV	FV	6.00	7.00
4660	1929G	Chicago	FV	FV	3.00	4.00
4660☆	1929G ☆	Chicago	FV	2.00	20.00	25.00
4661	1929H	St. Louis	FV	FV	3.00	4.00
4662	1929I	Minneapolis	FV	FV	3.00	4.00
4663	1929J	Kansas City	FV	FV	25.00	30.00
4664	1929K	Dallas	FV	FV	7.00	9.00
4664☆	1929K ☆	Dallas	FV	FV	6.00	7.00
4665	1929L	San Francisco	FV	FV	3.00	4.00
4665☆	1929L ☆	San Francisco	FV	FV	7.00	9.00

Series 2003A Cabral-Snow - DC

KL#	Fr#	District	Fine	XF	CH CU (63)	Gem CU (65)
4666	-	Boston	FV	FV	3.00	4.00
4667	-	New York	FV	FV	3.00	4.00
4667☆	-	New York	5.00	20.00	100.	125.
4668	-	Philadelphia	FV	FV	25.00	30.00
4668☆	-	Philadelphia	FV	2.00	6.00	7.00
4669	-	Cleveland	FV	FV	3.00	4.00
4670	-	Richmond	FV	FV	3.00	4.00
4670☆	-	Richmond	FV	2.00	6.00	7.00
4671	-	Atlanta	FV	FV	3.00	4.00
4671☆	-	Atlanta	FV	2.00	6.00	7.00

Series 2003A Cabral-Snow - FW

KL#	Fr#	District	Fine	XF	CH CU (63)	Gem CU (65)
4671A	-	Atlanta	FV	FV	2.00	3.00
4671A☆	-	Atlanta	FV	4.00	6.00	7.00
4671B	-	Chicago	FV	FV	3.00	4.00
4671B☆	-	Chicago	FV	3.00	6.00	7.00

KL#	Fr#	District	Fine	XF	CH CU (63)	Gem CU (65)
4671C	-	St. Louis	FV	FV	3.00	4.00
4671D	-	Minneapolis	FV	FV	3.00	4.00
4671E	-	Kansas City	FV	FV	3.00	4.00
4671E☆	-	Kansas City	FV	3.00	8.00	10.00
4671F	-	Dallas	FV	FV	3.00	4.00
4671F☆	-	Dallas	FV	3.00	25.00	30.00
4671G	-	San Francisco	FV	FV	3.00	4.00

Series 2006 Cabral-Paulson - DC

KL#	Fr#	District	Fine	XF	CH CU (63)	Gem CU (65)
4797	-	Boston	FV	FV	3.00	4.00
4798	-	New York	FV	FV	3.00	4.00
4798☆	-	New York	FV	FV	10.00	15.00
4799	-	Philadelphia	FV	FV	3.00	4.00
4800	-	Cleveland `	FV	FV	3.00	4.00
4801	-	Richmond	FV	FV	3.00	4.00
4801A	-	Atlanta	FV	FV	3.00	4.00
4801A☆	-	Atlanta	FV	2.00	6.00	7.00

Series 2006 Cabral-Paulson - FW

KL#	Fr#	District	Fine	XF	CH CU (63)	Gem CU (65)
4801B	-	Boston	FV	FV	3.00	4.00
4801C☆	-	New York	FV	FV	6.00	7.00
4801D	-	Philadelphia	FV	FV	3.00	4.00
4801D☆	-	Philadelphia	FV	FV	6.00	7.00
4801E	-	Richmond	FV	FV	3.00	4.00
4802	-	Atlanta	FV	FV	3.00	4.00
4802☆	-	Atlanta	FV	2.00	50.00	65.00
4803	-	Chicago	FV	FV	3.00	4.00
4803☆	-	Chicago	FV	2.00	10.00	15.00
4804	-	St. Louis	FV	FV	3.00	4.00
4805	-	Minneapolis	FV	FV	3.00	4.00
4806	-	Kansas City	FV	FV	3.00	4.00
4806☆	-	Kansas City	FV	2.00	6.00	7.00
4807	-	Dallas	FV	FV	3.00	4.00
4807☆	-	Dallas	FV	3.00	6.00	7.00
4808	-	San Francisco	FV	FV	3.00	4.00
4808☆	-	San Francisco	FV	3.00	50.00	55.00
4808E	-	Cleveland	FV	FV	3.00	4.00

Series 2009 Rios-Geithner - DC

KL#	Fr#	District	Fine	XF	CH CU (63)	Gem CU (65)
4911	-	Boston	FV	FV	3.00	4.00
4911☆	-	Boston	FV	FV	5.00	8.00
4912	-	New York	FV	FV	3.00	4.00

Series 2009 Rios-Geithner - FW

KL#	Fr#	District	Fine	XF	CH CU (63)	Gem CU (65)
4915A	-	New York	FV	FV	3.00	4.00
4916	-	Atlanta	FV	FV	3.00	4.00
4917	-	Chicago	FV	FV	3.00	4.00
4918	-	St. Louis	FV	FV	3.00	4.00
4921	-	Dallas	FV	FV	3.00	4.00
4922	-	San Francisco	FV	FV	3.00	4.00

Federal Reserve Notes - Web Press

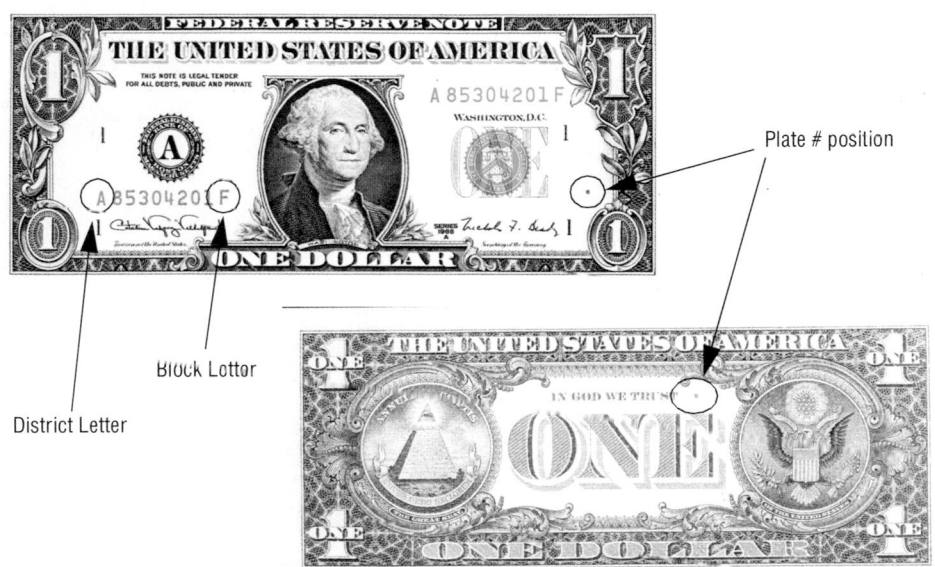

Plate # position

Block Letter

District Letter

KL#	Series	District - Block Letter	Fine	XF	CH CU (63)	Gem CU (65)
WP1	1988A	A - E		10.00	22.50	45.0065.00
WP2	1988A	A - F		4.00	7.75	40.0060.00
WP3	1988A	A - G		30.00	50.00	400.600.
WP4	1988A	B - L		100.	350.	1000.3000.
WP5	1988A	C - A		4.00	10.00	45.0065.00
WP6	1988A	E - I		4.00	10.00	40.0060.00
WP7	1988A	E - K		4.00	10.00	45 0065.00
WP8	1988A	F -		225.	600.	750.1000.
WP9	1988A	F - L		15.00	50.00	200.250.
WP10	1988A	F - M		10.00	40.00	125.150.
WP11	1988A	F - N		10.00	40.00	125.150.
WP12	1988A	F - U		4.00	7.75	40.0060.00
WP13	1988A	F - V		4.00	7.75	40.0060.00
WP14	1988A	G - P		6.00	25.00	90.00105.
WP15	1988A	G - Q		10.00	30.00	60.0070.00
WP16	1993	B - H		5.00	10.00	20.0030.00
WP17	1993	C - A		4.00	6.00	15.0025.00
WP18	1995	A - C		4.00	6.00	17.0027.50
WP19	1995	A - D		4.00	10.00	30.0040.00
WP20	1995	B - H		4.00	8.00	17.0027.50
WP21	1995	D - C		5.00	10.00	20.0030.00
WP22	1995	F - D		5.00	10.00	17.0027.50

Silver Certificates - Hawaii Emergency

Ovpt: HAWAII on face and back of 1935 A series.

KL#	Fr#	Series	Signatures	Fine	XF	CH CU (63)	Gem CU (65)
1609	2300	1935A	Julian-Morgenthau	45.00	70.00	200.	250.
1609☆	2300	1935A☆	Julian-Morgenthau	325.	700.	1750.	4500.

Silver Certificates - Experimental Issue

Red "R" at lower right.

KL#	Fr#	Series	Fine	XF	CH CU (63)	Gem CU (65)
1611	1609	1935A	75.00	150.	450.	625.
1611☆	1609	1935A☆	2000.	2700.	7000.	14,000.

Red "S" at lower right.

KL#	Fr#	Series	Fine	XF	CH CU (63)	Gem CU (65)
1612	1610	1935A	75.00	150.	500.	625.
1612☆	1610	1935A☆	2000.	3000.	7000.	10,000.

Silver Certificates - North Africa Emergency

Yellow seal on face.

KL#	Fr#	Series	Signatures	Fine	XF	CH CU (63)	Gem CU (65)
1610a	2306	1935Aa	Julian-Morgenthau	45.00	95.00	250.	325.
1610☆	2306	1935A☆	Julian-Morgenthau	225.	550.	3000.	5000.

United States Notes
Two Dollars

KL#	Fr#	Series	Signatures	Fine	XF	CH CU (63)	Gem CU (65)
1613	1501	1928	Tate-Mellon	20.00	75.00	250.	375.
1613☆	1501	1928☆	Tate-Mellon	300.	1000.	1500.	2800.
1614	1502	1928A	Woods-Mellon	50.00	90.00	475.	1000.
1614☆	1502	1928A☆	Woods-Mellon	700.	2500.	4000.	1.00
1615	1503	1928B	Woods-Mills	75.00	300.	800.	2000.
1615☆	1503	1928B☆	Woods-Mills	10,000.	50,000.	65,000.	100,000.
1616	1504	1928C	Julian-Morgenthau	25.00	65.00	225.	275.
1616☆	1504	1928C☆	Julian-Morgenthau	300.	900.	3000.	8050.
1617	1505	1928D	Julian-Morgenthau	20.00	45.00	125.	150.
1617☆	1505	1928D☆	Julian-Morgenthau	225.	275.	425.	1500.
1617A		1928D	Julian-Morgenthau	20.00	45.00	125.	200.
1617A☆		1928D☆	Julian-Morgenthau	75.00	275.	475.	2750.
1618	1506	1928E	Julian-Vinson	30.00	50.00	150.	300.
1618☆	1506	1928E☆	Julian-Vinson	2500.	5000.	14,375.	18,000.
1619	1507	1928F	Julian-Snyder	15.00	25.00	100.	100.
1619☆	1507	1928F☆	Julian-Snyder	75.00	125.	650.	1475.
1620	1508	1928G	Clark-Snyder	10.00	25.00	70.00	125.
1620☆	1508	1928G☆	Clark-Snyder	75.00	150.	350.	800.

KL#	Fr#	Series	Signatures	Fine	XF	CH CU (63)	Gem CU (65)
1621	1509	1953	Priest-Humphrey	10.00	15.00	35.00	70.00
1621☆	1509	1953☆	Priest-Humphrey	20.00	40.00	100.	230.
1622	1510	1953A	Priest-Anderson	8.00	12.00	25.00	45.00
1622☆	1510	1953A☆	Priest-Anderson	15.00	35.00	100.	200.
1623	1511	1953B	Smith-Dillon	7.00	10.00	25.00	40.00
1623☆	1511	1953B☆	Smith-Dillon	15.00	40.00	100.	150.
1624	1512	1953C	Granahan-Dillon	7.00	10.00	20.00	40.00
1624☆	1512	1953C☆	Granahan-Dillon	15.00	30.00	85.00	185.

KL#	Fr#	Series	Signatures	Fine	XF	CH CU (63)	Gem CU (65)
1625	1513	1963	Granahan-Dillon	7.00	15.00	22.00	35.00
1625☆	1513	1963☆	Granahan-Dillon	10.00	20.00	60.00	100.
1626	1514	1963A	Granahan-Fowler	7.00	9.00	20.00	30.00
1626☆	1514	1963A☆	Granahan-Fowler	10.00	35.00	100.	125.

Federal Reserve Notes
Series 1976 Neff-Simon

KL#	Fr#	District	Fine	XF	CH CU (63)	Gem CU (65)
1627	1935A	Boston	FV	3.00	10.00	12.00
1627☆	1935A ☆	Boston	FV	5.00	20.00	30.00
1628	1935B	New York	FV	3.00	9.00	12.00
1628☆	1935B ☆	New York	FV	5.00	20.00	30.00
1629	1935C	Philadelphia	FV	3.00	9.00	12.00
1629☆	1935C ☆	Philadelphia	FV	5.00	25.00	30.00
1630	1935D	Cleveland	FV	3.00	9.00	12.00
1630☆	1935D ☆	Cleveland	FV	6.00	25.00	35.00
1631	1935E	Richmond	FV	3.00	9.00	12.00
1631☆	1935E ☆	Richmond	FV	15.00	75.00	100.
1632	1935F	Atlanta	FV	3.00	10.00	12.00
1632☆	1935F ☆	Atlanta	FV	6.00	25.00	35.00
1633	1935G	Chicago	FV	3.00	12.00	15.00
1633☆	1935G ☆	Chicago	FV	15.00	60.00	70.00
1634	1935H	St. Louis	FV	3.00	25.00	30.00
1634☆	1935H ☆	St. Louis	FV	6.00	25.00	35.00
1635	1935I	Minneapolis	FV	3.00	20.00	25.00
1635☆	1935I ☆	Minneapolis	25.00	75.00	175.	250.
1636	1935J	Kansas City	FV	3.00	20.00	25.00
1636☆	1935J ☆	Kansas City	10.00	65.00	175.	200.
1637	1935K	Dallas	FV	3.00	9.00	12.00
1637☆	1935K ☆	Dallas	FV	6.00	30.00	40.00
1638	1935L	San Francisco	FV	3.00	10.00	15.00
1638☆	1935L ☆	San Francisco	FV	7.00	55.00	75.00

Series 1995 Withrow-Rubin

KL#	Fr#	District	Fine	XF	CH CU (63)	Gem CU (65)
4222☆	1936A ☆	Boston	2.00	10.00	50.00	75.00
4223☆	1936B ☆	New York	2.00	10.00	40.00	50.00
4224☆	1936C ☆	Philadelphia	2.00	10.00	40.00	50.00
4225☆	1936D ☆	Cleveland	2.00	10.00	40.00	50.00
4226☆	1936E ☆	Richmond	2.00	10.00	40.00	50.00

KL#	Fr#	District	Fine	XF	CH CU (63)	Gem CU (65)
4227	1936F	Atlanta	2.00	4.00	9.00	10.00
4227☆	1936F ☆	Atlanta	2.00	10.00	50.00	75.00
4228☆	1936G ☆	Chicago	2.00	8.00	50.00	75.00
4229☆	1936H ☆	St. Louis	2.00	10.00	50.00	75.00
4230☆	1936I ☆	Minneapolis	2.00	10.00	50.00	75.00
4231☆	1936J ☆	Kansas City	2.00	10.00	50.00	75.00
4232☆	1936K ☆	Dallas	2.00	10.00	50.00	75.00
4233☆	1936L ☆	San Francisco	2.00	10.00	50.00	75.00

Premium Millennium Federal Reserve Set (12 notes).
In original packaging. Total production 9,999 sets.

KL#	Fr#	District	Fine	XF	CH CU (63)	Gem CU (65)
4234☆	- ☆			—	40.00	50.00

Series 2003 Marin-Snow - FW

KL#	Fr#	District	Fine	XF	CH CU (63)	Gem CU (65)
4672☆	1937A@☆	Boston	—	—	40.00	50.00
4673☆	1937B@☆	New York	—	—	40.00	50.00

KL#	Fr#	District	Fine	XF	CH CU (63)	Gem CU (65)
4674☆	1937C ☆	Philadelphia	—	—	40.00	50.00
4675☆	1937D ☆	Cleveland	—	—	40.00	50.00
4676☆	1937E ☆	Richmond	—	—	40.00	50.00
4677☆	1937F ☆	Atlanta	—	—	40.00	50.00
4678☆	1937G ☆	Chicago	—	—	40.00	50.00
4679☆	1937H ☆	St. Louis	—	—	40.00	50.00
4680	1937I	Minneapolis	FV	6.00	9.00	50.00
4680☆	1937I ☆	Minneapolis	FV	8.00	40.00	50.00
4681☆	1937J ☆	Kansas City	—	—	40.00	50.00
4682☆	1937K ☆	Dallas	—	—	40.00	50.00
4683☆	1937L ☆	San Francisco	—	—	40.00	50.00

Series 2003A Cabral-Snow - FW

KL#	Fr#	District	Fine	XF	CH CU (63)	Gem CU (65)
4684A	-	Boston	—	—	8.00	10.00
4684B	-	New York	—	—	8.00	10.00
4684C	-	Philadelphia	—	—	8.00	10.00
4684D	-	Cleveland	—	—	8.00	10.00
4684E	-	Richmond	—	—	8.00	10.00
4684F	-	Atlanta	3.00	5.00	8.00	10.00
4684F☆	-	Atlanta	9.00	25.00	100.	150.
4684G	-	Chicago	—	—	8.00	10.00
4684H	-	St. Louis	—	—	8.00	10.00
4684I	-	Minneapolis	—	—	8.00	10.00
4684J	-	Kansas City	—	—	8.00	10.00
4684K	-	Dallas	—	—	8.00	10.00
4684L	-	San Francisco	—	—	8.00	10.00

United States Notes

Five Dollars

KL#	Fr#	Series	Signatures	Fine	XF	CH CU (63)	Gem CU (65)
1639	1525	1928	Woods-Mellon	15.00	35.00	125.	250.
1639☆	1525	1928☆	Woods-Mellon	175.	450.	1500.	4000.
1640	1526	1928A	Woods-Mills	20.00	50.00	150.	400.
1640☆	1526	1928A☆	Woods-Mills	475.	2500.	12,500.	13,000.
1641	1527	1928B	Julian-Morgenthau	15.00	30.00	85.00	140.
1641☆	1527	1928B☆	Julian-Morgenthau	90.00	350.	875.	2000.
1642	1528	1928C	Julian-Morgenthau	13.00	30.00	100.	125.
1642☆	1528	1928C☆	Julian-Morgenthau	90.00	300.	575.	1500.
1643	1529	1928D	Julian-Vinson	30.00	75.00	225.	325.
1643☆	1529	1928D☆	Julian-Vinson	500.	2000.	6500.	7000.
1644	1530	1928E	Julian-Snyder	15.00	25.00	90.00	175.
1644☆	1530	1928E☆	Julian-Snyder	90.00	275.	700.	1500.
1645	1531	1928F	Clark-Snyder	10.00	50.00	90.00	100.
1645☆	1531	1928F☆	Clark-Snyder	140.	250.	650.	900.
1646	1532	1953	Priest-Humphrey	10.00	15.00	35.00	60.00
1646☆	1532	1953☆	Priest-Humphrey	30.00	80.00	375.	425.

KL#	Fr#	Series	Signatures	Fine	XF	CH CU (63)	Gem CU (65)
1647	1533	1953A	Priest-Anderson	10.00	18.00	40.00	50.00
1647☆	1533	1953A☆	Priest-Anderson	25.00	75.00	200.	325.
1648	1534	1953B	Smith-Dillon	10.00	15.00	35.00	60.00
1648☆	1534	1953B☆	Smith-Dillon	40.00	75.00	225.	450.
1649	1535	1953C	Granahan-Dillon	10.00	25.00	60.00	70.00
1649☆	1535	1953C☆	Granahan-Dillon	55.00	95.00	250.	325.

KL#	Fr#	Series	Signatures	Fine	XF	CH CU (63)	Gem CU (65)
1650	1536	1963	Granahan-Dillon	8.00	15.00	35.00	75.00
1650☆	1536	1963☆	Granahan-Dillon	10.00	35.00	110.	150.

Silver Certificates

KL#	Fr#	Series	Signatures	Fine	XF	CH CU (63)	Gem CU (65)
1651	1650	1934	Julian-Morgenthau	15.00	40.00	80.00	165.
1651☆	1650	1934☆	Julian-Morgenthau	35.00	175.	400.	950.
1652	1651	1934A	Julian-Morgenthau	15.00	30.00	45.00	75.00
1652☆	1651	1934A☆	Julian-Morgenthau	40.00	60.00	250.	500.
1653	1652	1934B	Julian-Vinson	10.00	25.00	110.	125.
1653☆	1652	1934B☆	Julian-Vinson	65.00	550.	1250.	2000.
1654	1653	1934C	Julian-Snyder	10.00	30.00	50.00	160.
1654☆	1653	1934C☆	Julian-Snyder	40.00	85.00	350.	500.
1655	1654	1934D	Clark-Snyder	10.00	20.00	55.00	100.
1655☆	1654	1934D☆	Clark-Snyder	50.00	100.	275.	475.
1656	1655	1953	Priest-Humphrey	10.00	25.00	45.00	75.00
1656☆	1655	1953☆	Priest-Humphrey	20.00	45.00	120.	225.
1657	1656	1953A	Priest-Anderson	8.00	15.00	40.00	
1657☆	1656	1953A☆	Priest-Anderson	15.00	35.00	95.00	125.
1658	1657	1953B	Smith-Dillon	8.00	15.00	30.00	65.00
1658☆	1657	1953B☆	Smith-Dillon	1500.	8000.	14,500.	16,000.

Federal Reserve Bank Notes

KL#	Fr#	Series	District	Fine	XF	CH CU (63)	Gem CU (65)
1659	1850A	1929	Boston	25.00	60.00	200.	300.
1659☆	1850A	1929☆	Boston	1000.	4000.	10,500.	12,500.
1660	1850B	1929	New York	20.00	50.00	200.	400.
1660☆	1850B	1929☆	New York	1250.	1850.	3500.	4500.
1661	1850C	1929	Philadelphia	20.00	75.00	250.	600.
1661☆	1850C	1929☆	Philadelphia	300.	1000.	3000.	4000.
1662	1850D	1929	Cleveland	20.00	75.00	375.	400.
1662☆	1850D	1929☆	Cleveland	400.	650.	4000.	5000.
1664	1850F	1929	Atlanta	35.00	50.00	700.	900.
1664☆	1850F	1929☆	Atlanta	400.	650.	2700.	3750.
1665	1850G	1929	Chicago	20.00	55.00	150.	575.
1665☆	1850G	1929☆	Chicago	300.	500.	2000.	3500.
1666	1850H	1929	St. Louis	625.	2000.	5500.	7000.
1666☆	1850H	1929☆	St. Louis	3000.	8000.	15,000.	20,000.
1667	1850I	1929	Minneapolis	40.00	300.	900.	5500.
1667☆	1850I	1929☆	Minneapolis	3000.	4000.	8000.	10,000.
1668	1850J	1929	Kansas City	75.00	150.	315.	325.
1668☆	1850J	1929☆	Kansas City	260.	550.	3500.	5000.
1669	1850K	1929	Dallas	55.00	75.00	325.	525.
1669☆	1850K	1929☆	Dallas	1000.	30,000.	—	—
1670	1850L	1929	San Francisco	450.	2500.	10,000.	12,000.
1670☆	1850L	1929☆	San Francisco	1.00	—	—	—

Federal Reserve Notes
Series 1928 Tate-Mellon

KL#	Fr#	District	Fine	XF	Ofl CU (63)	Gem CU (65)
1671	1950A	Boston	500.	1500.	5000.	7500.
1671☆	1950A ☆	Boston	55.00	100.	750.	1200.
1672	1950B	New York	20.00	100.	750.	1000.
1672☆	1950B ☆	New York	100.	750.	1500.	2500.
1673	1950C	Philadelphia	20.00	100.	550.	750.
1673☆	1950C ☆	Philadelphia	350.	1000.	2500.	4000.
1674	1950D	Cleveland	20.00	75.00	300.	500.
1674☆	1950D ☆	Cleveland	200.	800.	2500.	3500.
1675	1950E	Richmond	20.00	150.	1250.	3000.
1675☆	1950E ☆	Richmond	75.00	1500.	5000.	8000.
1676	1950F	Atlanta	20.00	100.	400.	1000.
1676☆	1950F ☆	Atlanta	300	1400.	4000.	6000.
1677	1950G	Chicago	15.00	55.00	250.	475.
1677☆	1950G ☆	Chicago	150.	450.	1250.	2300.
1678	1950H	St. Louis	75.00	400.	1500.	2000.
1678☆	1950H ☆	St. Louis	40.00	2000.	6000.	7500.
1679	1950I	Minneapolis	125.	350.	2000.	3500.
1679☆	1950I ☆	Minneapolis	1500.	3000.	8000.	10,000.
1680	1950J	Kansas City	25.00	125.	500.	750.
1680☆	1950J ☆	Kansas City	350.	1500.	3000.	5000.
1681	1950K	Dallas	20.00	100.	400.	500.
1681☆	1950K ☆	Dallas	300.	1250.	4000.	6000.
1682	1950L	San Francisco	20.00	200.	500.	550.
1682☆	1950L ☆	San Francisco	500.	2750.	7000.	8500.

Series 1928A Woods-Mellon

KL#	Fr#	District	Fine	XF	CH CU (63)	Gem CU (65)
1683	1951A	Boston	75.00	275.	800.	1500.
1683☆	1951A ☆	Boston	500.	1750.	5000.	10,000.
1684	1951B	New York	12.00	75.00	250.	300.
1684☆	1951B ☆	New York	250.	2500.	7000.	10,000.
1685	1951C	Philadelphia	12.00	75.00	250.	400.
1685☆	1951C ☆	Philadelphia	350.	1500.	3500.	4500.
1686	1951D	Cleveland	12.00	50.00	250.	375.
1686☆	1951D ☆	Cleveland	100.	700.	2500.	3500.
1687	1951E	Richmond	15.00	100.	450.	700.
1687☆	1951E ☆	Richmond	100.	2750.	6000.	7500.
1688	1951F	Atlanta	25.00	250.	1000.	2500.
1688☆	1951F ☆	Atlanta	500.	3250.	7500.	9000.
1689	1951G	Chicago	15.00	75.00	200.	400.
1689☆	1951G ☆	Chicago	125.	350.	1250.	4000.
1690	1951H	St. Louis	17.00	100.	250.	275.
1690☆	1951H ☆	St. Louis	200.	3500.	8250.	10,000.
1691	1951I	Minneapolis	90.00	750.	4750.	7000.
1691☆	1951I ☆	Minneapolis	—	—	—	—
1692	1951J	Kansas City	25.00	300.	550.	1150.
1692☆	1951J ☆	Kansas City	—	—	—	—
1693	1951K	Dallas	—	—	—	—
1693☆	1951K ☆	Dallas	200.	1000.	4000.	6000.
1694	1951L	San Francisco	50.00	200.	500.	800.
1694☆	1951L ☆	San Francisco	—	—	—	—

Series 1928B Woods-Mellon

KL#	Fr#	District	Fine	XF	CH CU (63)	Gem CU (65)
1695	1952A	Boston	12.00	25.00	100.	150.
1695☆	1952A ☆	Boston	100.	800.	2000.	3000.
1696	1952B	New York	12.00	25.00	75.00	150.
1696☆	1952B ☆	New York	75.00	700.	1500.	2000.
1697	1952C	Philadelphia	15.00	30.00	100.	225.
1697☆	1952C ☆	Philadelphia	100.	450.	1000.	1500.
1698	1952D	Cleveland	12.00	25.00	100.	150.
1698☆	1952D ☆	Cleveland	100.	625.	2000.	3000.
1699	1952E	Richmond	12.00	25.00	90.00	125.
1699☆	1952E ☆	Richmond	100.	650.	2000.	2750.
1700	1952F	Atlanta	12.00	25.00	100.	150.
1700☆	1952F ☆	Atlanta	100.	500.	2000.	2600.
1701	1952G	Chicago	12.00	25.00	200.	300.
1701☆	1952G ☆	Chicago	—	—	—	—
1702	1952H	St. Louis	12.00	25.00	75.00	150.
1702☆	1952H ☆	St. Louis	200.	400.	800.	1600.
1703	1952I	Minneapolis	25.00	75.00	200.	400.
1703☆	1952I ☆	Minneapolis	100.	1750.	5000.	7000.

KL#	Fr#	District	Fine	XF	CH CU (63)	Gem CU (65)
1704	1952J	Kansas City	12.00	100.	400.	600.
1704☆	1952J ☆	Kansas City	—	—	—	—
1705	1952K	Dallas	14.00	40.00	300.	400.
1705☆	1952K ☆	Dallas	100.	500.	1000.	2000.
1706	1952L	San Francisco	12.00	25.00	175.	350.
1706☆	1952L ☆	San Francisco	100.	800.	2000.	2500.

Series 1928C Woods-Mills

KL#	Fr#	District	Fine	XF	CH CU (63)	Gem CU (65)
1710	1953D	Cleveland	—	—	Unknown	—
1712	1953F	Atlanta	300.	600.	10,000.	25,000.
1718	1953L	San Francisco	—	—	Unknown	—

Series 1928D Woods-Woodin

KL#	Fr#	District	Fine	XF	CH CU (63)	Gem CU (65)
1724	1954F	Atlanta	750.	2500.	9000.	10,000.

Series 1934 Julian-Morgenthau

KL#	Fr#	District	Fine	XF	CH CU (63)	Gem CU (65)
1731	1955A	Boston	10.00	20.00	90.00	125.
1731☆	1955A ☆	Boston	150.	750.	1400.	2000.

KL#	Fr#	District	Fine	XF	CH CU (63)	Gem CU (65)
1732	1955B	New York	10.00	20.00	80.00	100.
1732☆	1955B ☆	New York	100.	400.	850.	1500.
1733	1955C	Philadelphia	10.00	20.00	80.00	100.
1733☆	1955C ☆	Philadelphia	125.	550.	900.	1500.
1734	1955D	Cleveland	10.00	20.00	80.00	100.
1734☆	1955D ☆	Cleveland	125.	550.	900.	1250.
1735	1955E	Richmond	10.00	20.00	90.00	125.
1735☆	1955E ☆	Richmond	125.	550.	900.	1250.
1736	1955F	Atlanta	10.00	20.00	100.	125.
1736☆	1955F ☆	Atlanta	125.	550.	900.	1250.
1737	1955G	Chicago	10.00	25.00	90.00	140.
1737☆	1955G ☆	Chicago	130.	275.	700.	1125.
1738	1955H	St. Louis	10.00	20.00	80.00	120.
1738☆	1955H ☆	St. Louis	125.	375.	500.	1250.
1739	1955I	Minneapolis	12.00	35.00	250.	300.
1739☆	1955I ☆	Minneapolis	125.	525.	1000.	1750.
1740	1955J	Kansas City	10.00	20.00	70.00	100.
1740☆	1955J ☆	Kansas City	125.	550.	900.	1250.
1741	1955K	Dallas	10.00	20.00	100.	125.
1741☆	1955K ☆	Dallas	125.	750.	1500.	2000.
1742	1955L	San Francisco	10.00	20.00	80.00	120.
1742☆	1955L ☆	San Francisco	125.	550.	1250.	1750.

Series 1934A Julian-Morgenthau

KL#	Fr#	District	Fine	XF	CH CU (63)	Gem CU (65)
1743	1957A	Boston	10.00	20.00	70.00	75.00
1743☆	1957A ☆	Boston	30.00	80.00	350.	600.
1744	1957B	New York	10.00	20.00	65.00	70.00
1744☆	1957B ☆	New York	25.00	75.00	350.	500.
1745	1957C	Philadelphia	10.00	15.00	60.00	80.00
1745☆	1957C ☆	Philadelphia	30.00	80.00	350.	650.
1746	1957D	Cleveland	12.00	50.00	300.	350.
1746☆	1957D ☆	Cleveland	30.00	80.00	350.	600.
1747	1957E	Richmond	10.00	20.00	40.00	125.
1747☆	1957E ☆	Richmond	30.00	100.	500.	600.
1748	1957F	Atlanta	15.00	40.00	75.00	100.
1748☆	1957F ☆	Atlanta	40.00	150.	500.	600.
1749	1957G	Chicago	10.00	20.00	60.00	65.00
1749☆	1957G ☆	Chicago	20.00	75.00	350.	400.
1750	1957H	St. Louis	10.00	20.00	60.00	75.00
1750☆	1957H ☆	St. Louis	20.00	75.00	350.	400.
1754	1957L	San Francisco	10.00	20.00	65.00	70.00
1754☆	1957L ☆	San Francisco	20.00	75.00	350.	400.

A Word About Star Notes

In our listings there are often two entries for each catalog number.
For example:

KL#	Fr#	District	Fine	XF	CH CU (63)	Gem CU (65)
1686	1951D	Cleveland	12.00	50.00	175.	200.
1686☆	1951D☆	Cleveland	100.	250.	800.	2000.

The first listing has a serial number format of
letter - eight digits - letter.

The second listing refers to a bank note with a serial number format of
letter - eight digits - star.

This star at the end of the serial number refers to a replacement note,
one which replaces a note damaged during the production process.
There are fewer of these printed and therefore they are more expensive.

Series 1934B Julian-Vinson

KL#	Fr#	District	Fine	XF	CH CU (63)	Gem CU (65)
1755	1958A	Boston	10.00	20.00	60.00	125.
1755☆	1958A ☆	Boston	75.00	200.	1500.	1750.
1756	1958B	New York	10.00	20.00	50.00	80.00
1756☆	1958B ☆	New York	60.00	150.	1000.	1250.
1757	1958C	Philadelphia	10.00	20.00	50.00	80.00
1757☆	1958C ☆	Philadelphia	75.00	200.	1000.	1250.
1758	1958D	Cleveland	10.00	25.00	75.00	125.
1758☆	1958D ☆	Cleveland	75.00	225.	650.	1000.
1759	1958E	Richmond	10.00	20.00	70.00	85.00
1759☆	1958E ☆	Richmond	75.00	200.	1500.	1750.
1760	1958F	Atlanta	10.00	20.00	70.00	100.
1760☆	1958F ☆	Atlanta	100.	250.	1600.	1800.
1761	1958G	Chicago	10.00	20.00	70.00	125.
1761☆	1958G ☆	Chicago	75.00	200.	1500.	1800.
1762	1958H	St. Louis	12.00	25.00	80.00	110.
1762☆	1958H ☆	St. Louis	75.00	200.	1000.	1250.
1763	1958I	Minneapolis	15.00	30.00	100.	200.
1763☆	1958I ☆	Minneapolis	75.00	200.	800.	1000.
1764	1958J	Kansas City	200.	1500.	5000.	—
1766	1958L	San Francisco	10.00	20.00	70.00	95.00
1766☆	1958L ☆	San Francisco	75.00	300.	8500.	10,000.

Series 1934C Julian-Snyder

KL#	Fr#	District	Fine	XF	CH CU (63)	Gem CU (65)
1767	1959A	Boston	10.00	20.00	75.00	85.00
1767☆	1959A ☆	Boston	50.00	250.	800.	1000.
1768	1959B	New York	20.00	50.00	90.00	125.
1768☆	1959B ☆	New York	50.00	250.	625.	800.
1769	1959C	Philadelphia	10.00	20.00	60.00	75.00
1769☆	1959C ☆	Philadelphia	50.00	250.	800.	1000.
1770	1959D	Cleveland	10.00	20.00	80.00	140.
1770☆	1959D ☆	Cleveland	50.00	250.	800.	1250.

KL#	Fr#	District	Fine	XF	CH CU (63)	Gem CU (65)
1771	1959E	Richmond	10.00	20.00	60.00	75.00
1771☆	1959E ☆	Richmond	50.00	250.	800.	2100.
1772	1959F	Atlanta	10.00	20.00	75.00	85.00
1772☆	1959F ☆	Atlanta	50.00	250.	1000.	1250.
1773	1959G	Chicago	10.00	20.00	60.00	640.
1773☆	1959G ☆	Chicago	50.00	250.	600.	800.
1774	1959H	St. Louis	10.00	20.00	75.00	90.00
1774☆	1959H☆	St. Louis	50.00	250.	800.	1000.
1775	1959I	Minneapolis	15.00	40.00	125.	150.
1775☆	1959I ☆	Minneapolis	100.	350.	1200.	2000.
1776	1959J	Kansas City	20.00	20.00	100.	90.00
1776☆	1959J ☆	Kansas City	50.00	250.	750.	1000.
1777	1959K	Dallas	14.00	35.00	75.00	100.
1777☆	1959K ☆	Dallas	100.	250.	1000.	1500.
1778	1959L	San Francisco	10.00	20.00	60.00	85.00
1778☆	1959L ☆	San Francisco	50.00	150.	750.	1000.

Series 1934D Clark-Snyder

KL#	Fr#	District	Fine	XF	CH CU (63)	Gem CU (65)
1779	1960A	Boston	10.00	20.00	60.00	75.00
1779☆	1960A ☆	Boston	40.00	250.	650.	900.
1780	1960B	New York	10.00	25.00	90.00	140.
1780☆	1960B ☆	New York	75.00	300.	700.	4600.
1781	1960C	Philadelphia	10.00	20.00	100.	110.
1781☆	1960C ☆	Philadelphia	50.00	250.	550.	2300.
1782	1960D	Cleveland	10.00	20.00	60.00	75.00
1782☆	1960D ☆	Cleveland	50.00	300.	900.	2550.
1783	1960E	Richmond	10.00	20.00	60.00	1100.
1783☆	1960E ☆	Richmond	50.00	500.	1500.	2150.
1784	1960F	Atlanta	150.	250.	500.	800.
1784☆	1960F ☆	Atlanta	50.00	800.	3000.	4000.
1785	1960G	Chicago	10.00	20.00	90.00	100.
1785☆	1960G ☆	Chicago	50.00	200.	500.	700.
1786	1960H	St. Louis	10.00	20.00	60.00	75.00
1786☆	1960H☆	St. Louis	50.00	250.	600.	1000.
1787	1960I	Minneapolis	15.00	40.00	400.	550.
1787☆	1960I ☆	Minneapolis	100.	600.	1400.	1900.
1788	1960J	Kansas City	10.00	20.00	100.	125.
1788☆	1960J ☆	Kansas City	50.00	350.	3000.	4000.
1789	1960K	Dallas	15.00	35.00	75.00	400.
1789☆	1960K ☆	Dallas	50.00	250.	3500.	4000.
1790	1960L	San Francisco	10.00	20.00	65.00	100.
1790☆	1960L ☆	San Francisco	50.00	250.	650.	900.

Series 1950 Clark-Snyder

KL#	Fr#	District	Fine	XF	CH CU (63)	Gem CU (65)
1791	1961A	Boston	8.00	12.00	50.00	60.00
1791☆	1961A ☆	Boston	35.00	75.00	300.	500.
1792	1961B	New York	8.00	12.00	40.00	50.00
1792☆	1961B ☆	New York	30.00	60.00	400.	600.
1793	1961C	Philadelphia	10.00	12.00	40.00	50.00
1793☆	1961C ☆	Philadelphia	25.00	75.00	350.	400.
1794	1961D	Cleveland	8.00	12.00	55.00	70.00
1794☆	1961D ☆	Cleveland	25.00	75.00	400.	750.
1795	1961E	Richmond	8.00	12.00	40.00	50.00
1795☆	1961E ☆	Richmond	30.00	100.	300.	475.
1796	1961F	Atlanta	8.00	12.00	50.00	60.00
1796☆	1961F ☆	Atlanta	30.00	75.00	300.	400.
1797	1961G	Chicago	8.00	12.00	45.00	60.00
1797☆	1961G ☆	Chicago	30.00	110.	350.	475.
1798	1961H	St. Louis	8.00	12.00	40.00	60.00
1798☆	1961H ☆	St. Louis	300.	—	—	—
1799	1961I	Minneapolis	9.00	20.00	60.00	85.00
1799☆	1961I ☆	Minneapolis	500.	450.	1250.	1500.
1800	1961J	Kansas City	8.00	15.00	40.00	60.00
1800☆	1961J ☆	Kansas City	30.00	75.00	200.	300.
1801	1961K	Dallas	8.00	12.00	40.00	80.00
1801☆	1961K ☆	Dallas	40.00	100.	300.	500.
1802	1961L	San Francisco	8.00	12.00	40.00	70.00
1802☆	1961L ☆	San Francisco	40.00	100.	300.	600.

Series 1950A Priest-Humphrey

KL#	Fr#	District	Fine	XF	CH CU (63)	Gem CU (65)
1803	1962A	Boston	10.00	18.00	25.00	35.00
1803☆	1962A ☆	Boston	10.00	20.00	60.00	75.00
1804	1962B	New York	10.00	18.00	25.00	35.00
1804☆	1962B ☆	New York	10.00	20.00	60.00	80.00
1805	1962C	Philadelphia	10.00	18.00	25.00	35.00

KL#	Fr#	District	Fine	XF	CH CU (63)	Gem CU (65)
1805☆	1962C ☆	Philadelphia	10.00	20.00	60.00	75.00
1806	1962D	Cleveland	10.00	18.00	25.00	35.00
1806☆	1962D ☆	Cleveland	10.00	20.00	60.00	75.00
1807	1962E	Richmond	10.00	18.00	25.00	35.00
1807☆	1962E ☆	Richmond	10.00	20.00	60.00	75.00
1808	1962F	Atlanta	10.00	18.00	25.00	35.00
1808☆	1962F ☆	Atlanta	10.00	20.00	60.00	75.00
1809	1962G	Chicago	9.00	15.00	20.00	30.00
1809☆	1962G ☆	Chicago	10.00	20.00	60.00	75.00
1810	1962H	St. Louis	10.00	18.00	25.00	35.00
1810☆	1962H ☆	St. Louis	25.00	50.00	150.	200.
1811	1962I	Minneapolis	15.00	20.00	40.00	50.00
1811☆	1962I ☆	Minneapolis	25.00	100.	300.	400.
1812	1962J	Kansas City	10.00	18.00	25.00	35.00
1812☆	1962J ☆	Kansas City	15.00	30.00	100.	125.
1813	1962K	Dallas	15.00	20.00	40.00	60.00
1813☆	1962K ☆	Dallas	25.00	50.00	165.	200.
1814	1962L	San Francisco	10.00	18.00	25.00	35.00
1814☆	1962L ☆	San Francisco	15.00	25.00	200.	300.

Series 1950B Priest-Anderson

KL#	Fr#	District	Fine	XF	CH CU (63)	Gem CU (65)
1815	1963A	Boston	12.00	20.00	30.00	40.00
1815☆	1963A ☆	Boston	10.00	20.00	60.00	75.00
1816	1963B	New York	10.00	15.00	20.00	30.00
1816☆	1963B ☆	New York	15.00	22.00	65.00	85.00
1817	1963C	Philadelphia	12.00	20.00	30.00	40.00
1817☆	1963C ☆	Philadelphia	10.00	20.00	60.00	75.00
1818	1963D	Cleveland	15.00	30.00	100.	125.
1818☆	1963D ☆	Cleveland	15.00	22.00	50.00	65.00
1820	1963F	Atlanta	12.00	20.00	30.00	40.00
1820☆	1963F ☆	Atlanta	10.00	20.00	60.00	75.00
1821	1963G	Chicago	12.00	20.00	30.00	40.00
1821☆	1963G ☆	Chicago	10.00	20.00	60.00	80.00
1822	1963H	St. Louis	12.00	20.00	30.00	40.00
1822☆	1963H ☆	St. Louis	10.00	20.00	60.00	75.00
1823	1963I	Minneapolis	12.00	20.00	35.00	50.00
1823☆	1963I ☆	Minneapolis	20.00	50.00	250.	350.
1824	1963J	Kansas City	12.00	20.00	30.00	40.00
1824☆	1963J ☆	Kansas City	15.00	22.00	50.00	85.00
1825	1963K	Dallas	12.00	20.00	30.00	45.00
1825☆	1963K ☆	Dallas	18.00	30.00	80.00	100.
1826	1963L	San Francisco	12.00	20.00	50.00	65.00
1826☆	1963L ☆	San Francisco	18.00	30.00	80.00	100.

Series 1950C Smith-Dillon

KL#	Fr#	District	Fine	XF	CH CU (63)	Gem CU (65)
1827	1964A	Boston	8.00	10.00	15.00	20.00
1827☆	1964A ☆	Boston	15.00	30.00	75.00	125.
1828	1964B	New York	8.00	10.00	15.00	20.00
1828☆	1964B ☆	New York	10.00	18.00	40.00	60.00
1829	1964C	Philadelphia	8.00	10.00	15.00	20.00
1829☆	1964C ☆	Philadelphia	10.00	18.00	40.00	125.
1830	1964D	Cleveland	8.00	10.00	15.00	20.00
1830☆	1964D ☆	Cleveland	10.00	18.00	40.00	50.00
1831	1964E	Richmond	8.00	10.00	15.00	20.00
1831☆	1964E ☆	Richmond	18.00	30.00	75.00	125.
1832	1964F	Atlanta	8.00	10.00	15.00	20.00
1832☆	1964F ☆	Atlanta	15.00	25.00	60.00	75.00
1833	1964G	Chicago	10.00	12.00	25.00	35.00
1833☆	1964G ☆	Chicago	25.00	35.00	100.	135.
1834	1964H	St. Louis	8.00	10.00	15.00	25.00
1834☆	1964H ☆	St. Louis	25.00	50.00	225.	400.
1835	1964I	Minneapolis	10.00	12.00	25.00	40.00
1835☆	1964I ☆	Minneapolis	30.00	50.00	150.	300.
1836	1964J	Kansas City	8.00	10.00	15.00	20.00
1836☆	1964J ☆	Kansas City	20.00	30.00	75.00	100.
1837	1964K	Dallas	15.00	25.00	50.00	75.00
1837☆	1964K ☆	Dallas	25.00	50.00	150.	400.
1838	1964L	San Francisco	8.00	10.00	15.00	20.00
1838☆	1964L ☆	San Francisco	20.00	40.00	120.	150.

Series 1950D Granahan-Dillon

KL#	Fr#	District	Fine	XF	CH CU (63)	Gem CU (65)
1839	1965A	Boston	8.00	10.00	15.00	25.00
1839☆	1965A ☆	Boston	15.00	30.00	75.00	100.
1840	1965B	New York	8.00	10.00	15.00	20.00
1840☆	1965B ☆	New York	15.00	20.00	40.00	60.00
1841	1965C	Philadelphia	8.00	10.00	15.00	20.00

KL#	Fr#	District	Fine	XF	CH CU (63)	Gem CU (65)
1841☆	1965C ☆	Philadelphia	15.00	25.00	50.00	70.00
1842	1965D	Cleveland	8.00	10.00	15.00	20.00
1842☆	1965D ☆	Cleveland	15.00	25.00	50.00	70.00
1843	1965E	Richmond	8.00	10.00	15.00	20.00
1843☆	1965E ☆	Richmond	15.00	30.00	175.	250.
1844	1965F	Atlanta	8.00	10.00	15.00	25.00
1844☆	1965F ☆	Atlanta	15.00	30.00	70.00	90.00
1845	1965G	Chicago	8.00	10.00	15.00	20.00
1845☆	1965G ☆	Chicago	10.00	20.00	45.00	60.00
1846	1965H	St. Louis	8.00	10.00	15.00	20.00
1846☆	1965H ☆	St. Louis	15.00	30.00	70.00	160.
1847	1965I	Minneapolis	10.00	12.00	25.00	35.00
1847☆	1965I ☆	Minneapolis	30.00	70.00	250.	450.
1848	1965J	Kansas City	8.00	10.00	15.00	20.00
1848☆	1965J ☆	Kansas City	15.00	30.00	60.00	75.00
1849	1965K	Dallas	8.00	10.00	50.00	100.
1849☆	1965K ☆	Dallas	25.00	50.00	100.	210.
1850	1965L	San Francisco	15.00	25.00	50.00	70.00
1850☆	1965L ☆	San Francisco	30.00	70.00	150.	200.

Series 1950E Granahan-Fowler

KL#	Fr#	District	Fine	XF	CH CU (63)	Gem CU (65)
1852	1966B	New York	9.00	12.00	25.00	35.00
1852☆	1966B ☆	New York	15.00	30.00	70.00	150.
1853	1966G	Chicago	20.00	40.00	160.	200.
1853☆	1966G ☆	Chicago	75.00	150.	325.	550.
1854	1966L	San Francisco	15.00	25.00	40.00	50.00
1854☆	1966L ☆	San Francisco	20.00	45.00	200.	525.

Series 1963 Granahan-Dillon

KL#	Fr#	District	Fine	XF	CH CU (63)	Gem CU (65)
1855	1967A	Boston	8.00	10.00	28.00	30.00
1855☆	1967A ☆	Boston	20.00	45.00	70.00	125.
1856	1967B	New York	8.00	10.00	28.00	30.00
1856☆	1967B ☆	New York	20.00	45.00	60.00	100.
1857	1967C	Philadelphia	8.00	10.00	28.00	30.00
1857☆	1967C ☆	Philadelphia	20.00	45.00	60.00	100.
1858	1967D	Cleveland	8.00	10.00	28.00	30.00
1858☆	1967D ☆	Cleveland	20.00	45.00	60.00	100.
1859	1967F	Atlanta	8.00	10.00	28.00	30.00
1859☆	1967F ☆	Atlanta	20.00	45.00	70.00	100.
1860	1967G	Chicago	8.00	10.00	28.00	30.00
1860☆	1967G ☆	Chicago	15.00	35.00	60.00	75.00
1861	1967H	St. Louis	8.00	10.00	28.00	30.00
1861☆	1967H ☆	St. Louis	15.00	45.00	70.00	125.
1861A	1967J	Kansas City	8.00	10.00	28.00	30.00
1861A☆	1967J ☆	Kansas City	15.00	45.00	70.00	100.
1862	1967K	Dallas	8.00	10.00	28.00	150.
1862☆	1967K ☆	Dallas	15.00	45.00	70.00	100.
1863	1967L	San Francisco	8.00	10.00	28.00	30.00
1863☆	1967L ☆	San Francisco	15.00	45.00	60.00	65.00

Series 1963A Granahan-Fowler

KL#	Fr#	District	Fine	XF	CH CU (63)	Gem CU (65)
1864	1968A	Boston	8.00	10.00	23.00	25.00
1864☆	1968A ☆	Boston	10.00	25.00	40.00	43.00
1865	1968B	New York	8.00	10.00	23.00	25.00
1865☆	1968B ☆	New York	15.00	30.00	40.00	43.00
1866	1968C	Philadelphia	8.00	10.00	23.00	25.00
1866☆	1968C ☆	Philadelphia	15.00	30.00	40.00	43.00
1867	1968D	Cleveland	8.00	10.00	23.00	25.00
1867☆	1968D ☆	Cleveland	15.00	30.00	40.00	43.00
1868	1968E	Richmond	8.00	10.00	23.00	25.00
1868☆	1968E ☆	Richmond	15.00	30.00	40.00	43.00

KL#	Fr#	District	Fine	XF	CH CU (63)	Gem CU (65)
1869	1968F	Atlanta	8.00	10.00	23.00	25.00
1869☆	1968F ☆	Atlanta	15.00	40.00	60.00	65.00
1870	1968G	Chicago	8.00	10.00	23.00	25.00
1870☆	1968G ☆	Chicago	15.00	40.00	60.00	65.00
1871	1968H	St. Louis	7.00	10.00	23.00	25.00
1871☆	1968H ☆	St. Louis	15.00	25.00	35.00	45.00
1872	1968I	Minneapolis	8.00	15.00	30.00	35.00
1872☆	1968I ☆	Minneapolis	15.00	40.00	80.00	100.
1873	1968J	Kansas City	8.00	10.00	23.00	25.00
1873☆	1968J ☆	Kansas City	15.00	30.00	60.00	65.00
1874	1968K	Dallas	8.00	10.00	23.00	25.00
1874☆	1968K ☆	Dallas	15.00	22.00	35.00	150.
1875	1968L	San Francisco	8.00	10.00	23.00	25.00
1875☆	1968L ☆	San Francisco	15.00	22.00	35.00	40.00

Series 1969 Elston-Kennedy

KL#	Fr#	District	Fine	XF	CH CU (63)	Gem CU (65)
1876	1969A	Boston	6.00	7.00	20.00	23.00
1876☆	1969A ☆	Boston	10.00	30.00	50.00	53.00
1877	1969B	New York	6.00	7.00	20.00	23.00
1877☆	1969B ☆	New York	10.00	20.00	40.00	45.00
1878	1969C	Philadelphia	6.00	7.00	20.00	23.00
1878☆	1969C ☆	Philadelphia	10.00	30.00	50.00	140.
1879	1969D	Cleveland	6.00	7.00	20.00	23.00
1879☆	1969D ☆	Cleveland	10.00	20.00	40.00	45.00
1880	1969E	Richmond	6.00	7.00	20.00	23.00
1880☆	1969E ☆	Richmond	10.00	30.00	50.00	55.00
1881	1969F	Atlanta	6.00	7.00	20.00	23.00
1881☆	1969F ☆	Atlanta	10.00	25.00	40.00	45.00
1882	1969G	Chicago	6.00	7.00	20.00	23.00
1882☆	1969G ☆	Chicago	10.00	25.00	40.00	45.00
1883	1969H	St. Louis	6.00	7.00	20.00	23.00
1883☆	1969H ☆	St. Louis	15.00	35.00	60.00	65.00
1884	1969I	Minneapolis	10.00	25.00	40.00	45.00
1884☆	1969I ☆	Minneapolis	15.00	45.00	145.	185.
1885	1969J	Kansas City	6.00	7.00	20.00	23.00
1885☆	1969J ☆	Kansas City	15.00	30.00	50.00	55.00
1886	1969K	Dallas	6.00	7.00	20.00	23.00
1886☆	1969K ☆	Dallas	15.00	30.00	50.00	55.00
1887	1969L	San Francisco	6.00	7.00	20.00	23.00
1887☆	1969L ☆	San Francisco	15.00	30.00	50.00	55.00

Series 1969A Kabis-Connally

KL#	Fr#	District	Fine	XF	CH CU (63)	Gem CU (65)
1888	1970A	Boston	6.00	8.00	22.00	25.00
1888☆	1970A ☆	Boston	10.00	30.00	65.00	70.00
1889	1970B	New York	6.00	8.00	22.00	25.00
1889☆	1970B ☆	New York	15.00	32.00	65.00	70.00
1890	1970C	Philadelphia	6.00	8.00	22.00	25.00
1890☆	1970C ☆	Philadelphia	15.00	32.00	70.00	75.00
1891	1970D	Cleveland	6.00	8.00	22.00	25.00
1891☆	1970D ☆	Cleveland	15.00	32.00	75.00	80.00
1892	1970E	Richmond	6.00	8.00	22.00	25.00
1892☆	1970E ☆	Richmond	15.00	32.00	75.00	80.00
1893	1970F	Atlanta	6.00	8.00	22.00	25.00
1893☆	1970F ☆	Atlanta	15.00	32.00	75.00	80.00
1894	1970G	Chicago	6.00	8.00	22.00	25.00
1894☆	1970G ☆	Chicago	15.00	32.00	65.00	70.00
1895	1970H	St. Louis	6.00	8.00	22.00	25.00
1895☆	1970H ☆	St. Louis	15.00	30.00	70.00	75.00
1896	1970I	Minneapolis	6.00	10.00	28.00	30.00
1896☆	1970I ☆	Minneapolis	20.00	40.00	85.00	90.00
1897	1970J	Kansas City	6.00	8.00	23.00	25.00
1897☆	1970J ☆	Kansas City	15.00	35.00	75.00	80.00
1898	1970K	Dallas	6.00	8.00	28.00	30.00
1898☆	1970K ☆	Dallas	20.00	40.00	80.00	85.00
1899	1970L	San Francisco	6.00	8.00	23.00	25.00
1899☆	1970L ☆	San Francisco	15.00	35.00	75.00	80.00

Series 1969B Banuelos-Connally

KL#	Fr#	District	Fine	XF	CH CU (63)	Gem CU (65)
1900	1971A	Boston	15.00	30.00	75.00	80.00
1901	1971B	New York	10.00	30.00	75.00	100.
1901☆	1971B ☆	New York	50.00	100.	225.	275.
1902	1971C	Philadelphia	10.00	30.00	75.00	80.00
1903	1971D	Cleveland	10.00	30.00	75.00	80.00
1904	1971E	Richmond	10.00	30.00	75.00	80.00
1904☆	1971E ☆	Richmond	50.00	100.	225.	235.
1905	1971F	Atlanta	10.00	30.00	75.00	80.00
1905☆	1971F ☆	Atlanta	50.00	125.	175.	200.
1906	1971G	Chicago	10.00	30.00	75.00	125.
1906☆	1971G ☆	Chicago	50.00	125.	200.	250.
1907	1971H	St. Louis	10.00	30.00	75.00	80.00
1908	1971I	Minneapolis	20.00	100.	175.	200.
1909	1971J	Kansas City	10.00	30.00	75.00	80.00
1909☆	1971J ☆	Kansas City	30.00	100.	225.	230.
1910	1971K	Dallas	10.00	30.00	75.00	80.00
1911	1971L	San Francisco	10.00	30.00	75.00	80.00
1911☆	1971L ☆	San Francisco	30.00	100.	225.	230.

Series 1969C Banuelos-Shultz

KL#	Fr#	District	Fine	XF	CH CU (63)	Gem CU (65)
1912	1972A	Boston	FV	7.00	20.00	23.00
1912☆	1972A ☆	Boston	15.00	30.00	60.00	65.00
1913	1972B	New York	FV	7.00	20.00	23.00
1913☆	1972B ☆	New York	15.00	30.00	60.00	65.00
1914	1972C	Philadelphia	FV	7.00	20.00	23.00
1914☆	1972C ☆	Philadelphia	15.00	30.00	60.00	65.00
1915	1972D	Cleveland	FV	7.00	20.00	23.00
1915☆	1972D ☆	Cleveland	15.00	35.00	65.00	70.00
1916	1972E	Richmond	FV	7.00	20.00	23.00
1916☆	1972E ☆	Richmond	15.00	35.00	70.00	75.00
1917	1972F	Atlanta	FV	7.00	20.00	23.00
1917☆	1972F ☆	Atlanta	15.00	35.00	65.00	70.00
1918	1972G	Chicago	FV	7.00	20.00	23.00
1919	1972H	St. Louis	FV	7.00	20.00	23.00
1919☆	1972H ☆	St. Louis	10.00	35.00	65.00	70.00
1920	1972I	Minneapolis	FV	7.00	25.00	30.00
1921	1972J	Kansas City	FV	7.00	20.00	23.00
1921☆	1972J ☆	Kansas City	15.00	35.00	65.00	70.00
1922	1972K	Dallas	FV	7.00	20.00	23.00
1922☆	1972K ☆	Dallas	15.00	35.00	65.00	70.00
1923	1972L	San Francisco	FV	7.00	20.00	23.00
1923☆	1972L ☆	San Francisco	15.00	35.00	65.00	70.00

Series 1974 Neff-Simon

KL#	Fr#	District	Fine	XF	CH CU (63)	Gem CU (65)
1924	1973A	Boston	FV	7.00	15.00	18.00
1924☆	1973A ☆	Boston	6.00	25.00	40.00	43.00
1925	1973B	New York	FV	7.00	15.00	18.00
1925☆	1973B ☆	New York	6.00	25.00	40.00	43.00
1926	1973C	Philadelphia	5.00	7.00	15.00	18.00
1926☆	1973C ☆	Philadelphia	6.00	20.00	35.00	38.00
1927	1973D	Cleveland	FV	7.00	15.00	18.00

KL#	Fr#	District	Fine	XF	CH CU (63)	Gem CU (65)
1927☆	1973D ☆	Cleveland	6.00	25.00	40.00	43.00
1928	1973E	Richmond	FV	7.00	15.00	18.00
1928☆	1973E ☆	Richmond	6.00	25.00	40.00	43.00
1929	1973F	Atlanta	FV	7.00	350.	400.
1929☆	1973F ☆	Atlanta	6.00	20.00	35.00	38.00
1930	1973G	Chicago	FV	7.00	15.00	18.00
1930☆	1973G ☆	Chicago	6.00	20.00	35.00	38.00
1931	1973H	St. Louis	FV	7.00	15.00	18.00
1931☆	1973H ☆	St. Louis	8.00	40.00	75.00	80.00
1932	1973I	Minneapolis	FV	7.00	15.00	18.00
1932☆	1973I ☆	Minneapolis	6.00	20.00	35.00	38.00
1933	1973J	Kansas City	FV	7.00	15.00	18.00
1933☆	1973J ☆	Kansas City	6.00	20.00	35.00	38.00
1934	1973K	Dallas	FV	7.00	15.00	18.00
1934☆	1973K ☆	Dallas	6.00	25.00	40.00	45.00
1935	1973L	San Francisco	FV	7.00	15.00	18.00
1935☆	1973L ☆	San Francisco	6.00	20.00	35.00	38.00

Series 1977 Morton-Blumenthal

KL#	Fr#	District	Fine	XF	CH CU (63)	Gem CU (65)
1936	1974A	Boston	FV	7.00	15.00	18.00
1936☆	1974A ☆	Boston	6.00	20.00	40.00	43.00
1937	1974B	New York	FV	7.00	15.00	18.00
1937☆	1974B ☆	New York	6.00	20.00	40.00	43.00
1938	1974C	Philadelphia	FV	7.00	15.00	18.00
1938☆	1974C ☆	Philadelphia	6.00	20.00	40.00	75.00
1939	1974D	Cleveland	FV	7.00	15.00	50.00
1939☆	1974D ☆	Cleveland	6.00	20.00	40.00	43.00
1940	1974E	Richmond	FV	7.00	15.00	18.00
1940☆	1974E ☆	Richmond	6.00	20.00	40.00	43.00
1941	1974F	Atlanta	FV	7.00	15.00	18.00
1941☆	1974F ☆	Atlanta	6.00	20.00	40.00	43.00
1942	1974G	Chicago	FV	7.00	15.00	18.00
1942☆	1974G ☆	Chicago	6.00	20.00	40.00	43.00
1943	1974H	St. Louis	FV	7.00	15.00	18.00
1943☆	1974H ☆	St. Louis	7.00	35.00	70.00	75.00
1944	1974I	Minneapolis	FV	7.00	15.00	18.00
1945	1974J	Kansas City	FV	7.00	15.00	18.00
1945☆	1974J ☆	Kansas City	6.00	23.00	45.00	48.00
1946	1974K	Dallas	FV	7.00	15.00	18.00
1946☆	1974K ☆	Dallas	6.00	20.00	40.00	43.00
1947	1974L	San Francisco	FV	7.00	15.00	18.00
1947☆	1974L ☆	San Francisco	6.00	20.00	40.00	43.00

Series 1977A Morton-Miller

KL#	Fr#	District	Fine	XF	CH CU (63)	Gem CU (65)
1948	1975A	Boston	7.00	10.00	35.00	38.00
1948☆	1975A ☆	Boston	20.00	60.00	135.	140.
1949	1975B	New York	7.00	10.00	35.00	38.00
1949☆	1975B ☆	New York	10.00	30.00	60.00	65.00
1950	1975C	Philadelphia	7.00	10.00	35.00	38.00
1950☆	1975C ☆	Philadelphia	10.00	30.00	60.00	65.00
1951	1975D	Cleveland	7.00	10.00	35.00	38.00
1951☆	1975D ☆	Cleveland	18.00	50.00	125.	130.
1952	1975E	Richmond	7.00	10.00	35.00	38.00
1952☆	1975E ☆	Richmond	18.00	50.00	125.	130.
1953	1975F	Atlanta	7.00	10.00	35.00	38.00
1953☆	1975F ☆	Atlanta	10.00	30.00	60.00	65.00
1954	1975G	Chicago	7.00	10.00	35.00	38.00
1954☆	1975G☆	Chicago	20.00	30.00	60.00	65.00
1955	1975H	St. Louis	7.00	10.00	35.00	38.00
1955☆	1975H ☆	St. Louis	20.00	60.00	160.	155
1956	1975I	Minneapolis	7.00	10.00	35.00	38.00
1956☆	1975I ☆	Minneapolis	18.00	100.	225.	300.
1957	1975J	Kansas City	7.00	10.00	35.00	38.00
1957☆	1975J ☆	Kansas City	18.00	50.00	125.	130.
1958	1975K	Dallas	7.00	10.00	35.00	38.00
1958☆	1975K ☆	Dallas	15.00	40.00	80.00	85.00
1959	1975L	San Francisco	7.00	10.00	35.00	38.00
1959☆	1975L ☆	San Francisco	10.00	30.00	60.00	65.00

Series 1981 Buchanan-Regan

KL#	Fr#	District	Fine	XF	CH CU (63)	Gem CU (65)
3512	1976A	Boston	FV	8.00	25.00	28.00
3513	1976B	New York	FV	8.00	25.00	28.00
3513☆	1976B ☆	New York	7.00	20.00	225.	500.
3514	1976C	Philadelphia	FV	8.00	25.00	28.00
3514☆	1976C ☆	Philadelphia	7.00	100.	130.	150.

KL#	Fr#	District	Fine	XF	CH CU (63)	Gem CU (65)
3515	1976D	Cleveland	FV	8.00	25.00	28.00
3515☆	1976D ☆	Cleveland	7.00	20.00	50.00	53.00
3516	1976E	Richmond	FV	8.00	25.00	28.00
3516☆	1976E ☆	Richmond	7.00	20.00	50.00	53.00
3517	1976F	Atlanta	FV	8.00	25.00	28.00
3517☆	1976F ☆	Atlanta	20.00	55.00	90.00	100.
3518	1976G	Chicago	FV	8.00	25.00	28.00
3518☆	1976G ☆	Chicago	7.00	20.00	60.00	75.00
3519	1976H	St. Louis	FV	8.00	25.00	28.00
3519☆	1976H ☆	St. Louis	10.00	35.00	150.	260.
3520	1976I	Minneapolis	FV	15.00	45.00	60.00
3520☆	1976I ☆	Minneapolis	10.00	450.	1000.	2000.
3521	1976J	Kansas City	FV	8.00	25.00	28.00
3521☆	1976J ☆	Kansas City	10.00	35.00	70.00	75.00
3522	1976K	Dallas	FV	8.00	25.00	28.00
3522☆	1976K ☆	Dallas	7.00	20.00	50.00	53.00
3523	1976L	San Francisco	FV	8.00	25.00	28.00
3523☆	1976L ☆	San Francisco	7.00	20.00	50.00	53.00

Series 1981A Ortega-Regan

KL#	Fr#	District	Fine	XF	CH CU (63)	Gem CU (65)
3612	1977A	Boston	7.00	15.00	30.00	33.00
3613	1977B	New York	7.00	15.00	30.00	33.00
3613☆	1977B ☆	New York	65.00	165.	200.	225.
3614	1977C	Philadelphia	7.00	15.00	30.00	33.00
3615	1977D	Cleveland	7.00	15.00	30.00	33.00
3616	1977E	Richmond	7.00	15.00	30.00	33.00
3617	1977F	Atlanta	7.00	15.00	30.00	33.00
3618	1977G	Chicago	7.00	15.00	30.00	33.00
3619	1977H	St. Louis	7.00	15.00	30.00	33.00
3620	1977I	Minneapolis	7.00	15.00	30.00	33.00
3621	1977J	Kansas City	7.00	15.00	30.00	33.00
3622	1977K	Dallas	7.00	15.00	30.00	33.00
3623	1977L	San Francisco	7.00	15.00	30.00	33.00
3623☆	1977L ☆	San Francisco	7.00	25.00	75.00	78.00

Series 1985 Ortega-Baker

KL#	Fr#	District	Fine	XF	CH CU (63)	Gem CU (65)
3712	1978A	Boston	FV	7.00	15.00	18.00
3713	1978B	New York	FV	7.00	15.00	18.00
3713☆	1978B ☆	New York	6.00	30.00	60.00	63.00
3714	1978C	Philadelphia	FV	7.00	15.00	18.00
3714☆	1978C ☆	Philadelphia	6.00	25.00	75.00	80.00
3715	1978D	Cleveland	FV	7.00	15.00	18.00
3716	1978E	Richmond	FV	7.00	15.00	18.00
3716☆	1978E ☆	Richmond	6.00	30.00	60.00	63.00
3717	1978F	Atlanta	FV	7.00	15.00	18.00
3717☆	1978F ☆	Atlanta	6.00	30.00	60.00	63.00
3718	1978G	Chicago	FV	7.00	15.00	18.00
3718☆	1978G ☆	Chicago	6.00	30.00	60.00	63.00
3719	1978H	St. Louis	FV	7.00	15.00	18.00
3720	1978I	Minneapolis	FV	7.00	15.00	18.00
3721	1978J	Kansas City	FV	7.00	15.00	18.00
3722	1978K	Dallas	FV	7.00	15.00	18.00
3722☆	1978K ☆	Dallas	6.00	30.00	60.00	80.00
3723	1978L	San Francisco	FV	7.00	15.00	18.00
3723☆	1978L ☆	San Francisco	6.00	30.00	60.00	63.00

Series 1988 Ortega-Brady

KL#	Fr#	District	Fine	XF	CH CU (63)	Gem CU (65)
3784	1979A	Boston	FV	7.00	15.00	18.00
3784☆	1979A ☆	Boston	6.00	30.00	70.00	75.00
3785	1979B	New York	FV	7.00	15.00	18.00
3785☆	1979B ☆	New York	6.00	25.00	50.00	53.00
3786	1979C	Philadelphia	FV	7.00	15.00	18.00
3787	1979D	Cleveland	FV	7.00	15.00	18.00
3788	1979E	Richmond	FV	7.00	15.00	18.00
3789	1979F	Atlanta	FV	7.00	15.00	18.00
3789☆	1979F ☆	Atlanta	6.00	25.00	50.00	53.00
3790	1979G	Chicago	FV	7.00	15.00	18.00

KL#	Fr#	District	Fine	XF	CH CU (63)	Gem CU (65)
3791	1979H	St. Louis	FV	7.00	15.00	18.00
3792	1979I	Minneapolis	FV	15.00	40.00	43.00
3793	1979J	Kansas City	FV	7.00	15.00	18.00
3794	1979K	Dallas	FV	7.00	15.00	18.00
3795	1979L	San Francisco	FV	7.00	15.00	18.00

Series 1988A Villalpando-Brady

KL#	Fr#	District	Fine	XF	CH CU (63)	Gem CU (65)
3856	1980A	Boston	FV	7.00	15.00	18.00
3856☆	1980A ☆	Boston	6.00	15.00	40.00	43.00
3857	1980B	New York	FV	7.00	15.00	18.00
3857☆	1980B ☆	New York	6.00	15.00	40.00	43.00
3858	1980C	Philadelphia	FV	7.00	15.00	18.00
3859	1980D	Cleveland	FV	7.00	15.00	18.00
3859☆	1980D ☆	Cleveland	6.00	15.00	40.00	43.00
3860	1980E	Richmond	FV	7.00	15.00	18.00
3860☆	1980E ☆	Richmond	6.00	15.00	40.00	250.

Series 1988A Villalpando-Brady - FW

KL#	Fr#	District	Fine	XF	CH CU (63)	Gem CU (65)
3860A	1980F	Atlanta	FV	7.00	15.00	18.00
3860A☆	1980F ☆	Atlanta	6.00	15.00	40.00	43.00
3860B	1980G	Chicago	FV	7.00	15.00	18.00
3860B☆	1980G ☆	Chicago	6.00	15.00	40.00	43.00
3860C	1980H	St. Louis	FV	7.00	15.00	18.00
3860C☆	1980H ☆	St. Louis	250.	1250.	2000.	2250.
3860D	1980I	Minneapolis	FV	7.00	15.00	18.00
3860D☆	1980I ☆	Minneapolis	6.00	15.00	40.00	43.00
3860E	1980J	Kansas City	FV	7.00	15.00	18.00
3860F	1980K	Dallas	FV	7.00	15.00	18.00
3860F☆	1980K ☆	Dallas	6.00	15.00	40.00	43.00
3860G	1980L	San Francisco	FV	7.00	15.00	18.00

Series 1993 Withrow-Bentsen - DC

KL#	Fr#	District	Fine	XF	CH CU (63)	Gem CU (65)
4024	1982A	Boston	FV	7.00	15.00	18.00
4025	1982B	New York	FV	7.00	15.00	18.00
4025☆	1982B ☆	New York	6.00	10.00	40.00	50.00
4026	1982C	Philadelphia	FV	7.00	15.00	18.00
4026☆	1982C ☆	Philadelphia	6.00	7.00	15.00	18.00
4029	1982F	Atlanta	FV	7.00	15.00	18.00

Series 1993 Withrow-Bentsen - FW

KL#	Fr#	District	Fine	XF	CH CU (63)	Gem CU (65)
4030	1982G	Chicago	FV	7.00	15.00	18.00
4030☆	1982G ☆	Chicago	6.00	10.00	40.00	50.00
4031	1982H	St. Louis	FV	7.00	15.00	18.00
4031☆	1982H ☆	St. Louis	6.00	10.00	40.00	50.00
4032	1982I	Minneapolis	50.00	150.	600.	1000.
4033	1982J	Kansas City	FV	7.00	15.00	18.00
4034	1982K	Dallas	FV	7.00	15.00	18.00
4035	-	San Francisco	FV	7.00	15.00	18.00
4035☆	- ☆	San Francisco	6.00	10.00	40.00	50.00

Series 1995 Withrow-Rubin - DC

KL#	Fr#	District	Fine	XF	CH CU (63)	Gem CU (65)
4096	1984A	Boston	FV	6.00	10.00	13.00
4096☆	1984A ☆	Boston	6.00	10.00	35.00	40.00
4097	1984B	New York	FV	6.00	10.00	13.00
4097☆	1984B ☆	New York	6.00	10.00	30.00	35.00
4098	1984C	Philadelphia	FV	6.00	10.00	13.00
4099	1984D	Cleveland	FV	6.00	10.00	13.00
4100	1984E	Richmond	FV	6.00	10.00	13.00
4101	1984F	Atlanta	FV	6.00	10.00	13.00

Series 1995 Withrow-Rubin - FW

KL#	Fr#	District	Fine	XF	CH CU (63)	Gem CU (65)
4101A	1981A	Boston	FV	FV	10.00	13.00
4101B	1984B	New York	FV	FV	10.00	13.00
4101C	1984C	Philadelphia	FV	FV	10.00	13.00
4101D	1984D	Cleveland	FV	FV	10.00	13.00
4101D☆	1984D ☆	Cleveland	FV	10.00	30.00	35.00
4101E	1984E	Richmond	FV	FV	10.00	13.00
4101F	1984F	Atlanta	FV	FV	10.00	13.00
4101F☆	1984F ☆	Atlanta	FV	10.00	50.00	60.00
4102	1984G	Chicago	FV	6.00	10.00	13.00
4102☆	1984G ☆	Chicago	6.00	10.00	25.00	28.00
4103	1984H	St. Louis	FV	6.00	10.00	13.00

KL#	Fr#	District	Fine	XF	CH CU (63)	Gem CU (65)
4104	1984I	Minneapolis	FV	6.00	30.00	40.00
4105	1984J	Kansas City	FV	6.00	10.00	13.00
4106	1984K	Dallas	FV	6.00	10.00	13.00
4107	1984L	San Francisco	FV	6.00	10.00	13.00

Series 1999 Withrow-Summers - DC

KL#	Fr#	District	Fine	XF	CH CU (63)	Gem CU (65)
4513	1986A	Boston	FV	6.00	10.00	13.00
4514	1986B	New York	FV	6.00	10.00	13.00
4515	1986C	Philadelphia	FV	6.00	10.00	13.00
4516	1986D	Cleveland	FV	6.00	10.00	13.00
4517	1986E	Richmond	FV	6.00	10.00	13.00
4517☆	1986E ☆	Richmond	6.00	10.00	20.00	23.00

Series 1999 Withrow-Summers - FW

KL#	Fr#	District	Fine	XF	CH CU (63)	Gem CU (65)
4518	1987A	Boston	FV	6.00	10.00	13.00
4518☆	1987A ☆	Boston	6.00	10.00	20.00	23.00
4519	1987B	New York	FV	6.00	10.00	13.00
4519☆	1987B ☆	New York	6.00	10.00	20.00	23.00
4520	1987C	Philadelphia	FV	6.00	10.00	13.00
4521	1987D	Cleveland	FV	6.00	10.00	13.00
4522	1987E	Richmond	FV	6.00	10.00	13.00
4522☆	1987E ☆	Richmond	6.00	10.00	20.00	23.00
4523	1987F	Atlanta	FV	6.00	10.00	13.00
4523☆	1987F ☆	Atlanta	6.00	8.00	20.00	23.00
4524	1987G	Chicago	FV	6.00	10.00	13.00
4524☆	1987G ☆	Chicago	6.00	8.00	20.00	23.00
4525	1987H	St. Louis	FV	6.00	10.00	13.00
4526	1987I	Minneapolis	FV	6.00	10.00	13.00
4527	1987J	Kansas City	FV	6.00	10.00	13.00
4527☆	1987J ☆	Kansas City	6.00	8.00	20.00	23.00
4528	1987K	Dallas	FV	6.00	10.00	13.00
4528☆	1987K ☆	Dallas	6.00	6.00	10.00	13.00
4529	1987L	San Francisco	FV	6.00	10.00	13.00

Series 2001 Marin-O'Neill - FW

KL#	Fr#	District	Fine	XF	CH CU (63)	Gem CU (65)
4587	1989A	Boston	FV	7.00	15.00	18.00
4588	1989B	New York	FV	7.00	15.00	18.00
4589	1989C	Philadelphia	FV	7.00	15.00	18.00
4590	1989D	Cleveland	FV	7.00	15.00	18.00
4591	1989E	Richmond	FV	7.00	15.00	18.00
4592	1989F	Atlanta	FV	7.00	15.00	18.00
4593	1989G	Chicago	FV	7.00	15.00	18.00
4594	1989H	St. Louis	FV	7.00	15.00	18.00
4595	1989I	Minneapolis	FV	10.00	35.00	45.00
4596	1989J	Kansas City	FV	10.00	40.00	18.00
4597	1989K	Dallas	FV	7.00	15.00	18.00
4597☆	1989K ☆	Dallas	6.00	10.00	35.00	38.00
4598	1989L	San Francisco	FV	7.00	15.00	18.00
4598☆	1989I ☆	San Francisco	6.00	10.00	35.00	38.00

Series 2003 Marin-Snow - DC

KL#	Fr#	District	Fine	XF	CH CU (63)	Gem CU (65)
4685A	-	Boston	FV	7.00	15.00	18.00
4685C	-	Philadelphia	FV	7.00	15.00	18.00
4685D	-	Cleveland	FV	7.00	15.00	18.00
4685F	-	Atlanta	FV	7.00	15.00	18.00
4685G	-	Chicago	FV	7.00	15.00	18.00
4685G☆	-	Chicago	6.00	10.00	35.00	38.00

Series 2003 Marin-Snow - FW

KL#	Fr#	District	Fine	XF	CH CU (63)	Gem CU (65)
4688	1990A	Boston	FV	7.00	15.00	18.00
4689	1990B	New York	FV	7.00	15.00	18.00
4690	1990C	Philadelphia	FV	7.00	15.00	18.00

KL#	Fr#	District	Fine	XF	CH CU (63)	Gem CU (65)
4690☆	1990C ☆	Philadelphia	FV	7.00	35.00	38.00
4691	1990D	Cleveland	FV	7.00	15.00	18.00
4692	1990E	Richmond	FV	7.00	15.00	18.00
4693	1990F	Atlanta	FV	7.00	15.00	18.00
4694	1990G	Chicago	FV	7.00	15.00	18.00
4695	1990H	St. Louis	FV	7.00	15.00	18.00
4696	1990I	Minneapolis	FV	7.00	40.00	55.00
4697	1990J	Kansas City	FV	7.00	15.00	18.00
4698	1990K	Dallas	FV	7.00	15.00	18.00
4699	1990L	San Francisco	FV	7.00	15.00	18.00
4699☆	1990L ☆	San Francisco	6.00	10.00	35.00	38.00

Series 2003A Cabral-Snow - FW

KL#	Fr#	District	Fine	XF	CH CU (63)	Gem CU (65)
4850	-	Boston	FV	7.00	15.00	18.00
4851	-	New York	FV	7.00	15.00	18.00
4851☆	-	New York	FV	10.00	35.00	38.00
4852	-	Philadelphia	FV	7.00	15.00	18.00
4853	-	Richmond	FV	7.00	15.00	18.00
4854	-	Cleveland	FV	7.00	15.00	18.00
4855	-	Atlanta	FV	7.00	15.00	18.00
4855☆	-	Atlanta	6.00	10.00	35.00	38.00
4856	-	Chicago	FV	7.00	15.00	18.00
4856☆	-	Chicago	6.00	10.00	35.00	38.00
4857	-	St. Louis	FV	7.00	15.00	18.00
4858	-	Minneapolis	FV	7.00	15.00	18.00
4859	-	Kansas City	FV	7.00	15.00	18.00
4860	-	Dallas	FV	7.00	15.00	18.00
4861	-	San Francisco	FV	7.00	15.00	18.00

Series 2006 Cabral-Paulson - FW

KL#	Fr#	District	Fine	XF	CH CU (63)	Gem CU (65)
4862	-	Atlanta	FV	7.00	15.00	18.00
4863	-	Chicago	FV	7.00	15.00	18.00
4864	-	Minneapolis	FV	19.00	35.00	45.00

Colorized.

KL#	Fr#	District	Fine	XF	CH CU (63)	Gem CU (65)
4870	-	Boston	FV	7.00	15.00	18.00
4870☆	-	Boston	6.00	10.00	35.00	38.00
4871	-	New York	FV	7.00	15.00	18.00
4872	-	Philadelphia	FV	7.00	15.00	18.00
4873	-	Richmond	FV	7.00	15.00	18.00
4874	-	Atlanta	FV	7.00	15.00	18.00
4874☆	-	Atlanta	6.00	10.00	30.00	35.00
4875	-	Chicago	FV	7.00	15.00	17.00
4875☆	-	Chicago	6.00	10.00	30.00	35.00
4876	-	St. Louis	FV	7.00	15.00	18.00
4877	-	Minneapolis	FV	7.00	15.00	18.00
4878	-	Kansas City	FV	7.00	15.00	17.00
4879	-	Dallas	FV	7.00	15.00	17.00
4880	-	San Francisco	FV	7.00	15.00	17.00
4880☆	-	San Francisco	6.00	10.00	30.00	35.00

Federal Reserve Notes - Hawaii Emergency

KL#	Fr#	Series	Signatures	Fine	XF	CH CU (63)	Gem CU (65)
1960	2301	1934	Julian-Morgenthau	75.00	200.	500.	1000.

Silver Certificates - North Africa Emergency

KL#	Fr#	Series	Signatures	Fine	XF	CH CU (63)	Gem CU (65)
1962	2307	1934A	Julian-Morgenthau	70.00	100.	375.	500.
1962☆	2307	1934A☆	Julian-Morgenthau	325.	600.	3000.	5250.

Gold Certificates
Ten Dollars

KL#	Fr#	Series	Signatures	VF	XF	CH CU (63)	Gem CU (65)
1963	2400	1928	Woods-Mellon	150.	275.	500.	1350.
1963☆	2400	1928☆	Woods-Mellon	450.	1000.	3500.	7000.

Silver Certificates

KL#	Fr#	Series	Signatures	VF	XF	CH CU (63)	Gem CU (65)
1964	1700	1933	Julian-Woodin	3500.	12,000.	20,000.	28,250.
1964☆	1700	1933☆	Julian-Woodin	—	—	Rare	—
1966	1701	1934	Julian-Morgenthau	30.00	60.00	200.	275.
1966☆	1701	1934☆	Julian-Morgenthau	50.00	500.	850.	1500.
1967	1702	1934A	Julian-Morgenthau	35.00	125.	550.	850.
1967☆	1702	1934A☆	Julian-Morgenthau	140.	400.	1500.	4000.
1968	1703	1934B	Julian-Vinson	125.	325.	2000.	4700.
1968☆	1703	1934B☆	Julian-Vinson	1150.	5200.	18,000.	20,000.

KL#	Fr#	Series	Signatures	VF	XF	CH CU (63)	Gem CU (65)
1969	1704	1934C	Julian-Snyder	20.00	50.00	175.	350.
1969☆	1704	1934C☆	Julian-Snyder	80.00	150.	475.	600.
1970	1705	1934D	Clark-Snyder	30.00	40.00	200.	275.
1970☆	1705	1934D☆	Clark-Snyder	100.	450.	4500.	6000.
1971	1706	1953	Priest-Humphrey	30.00	75.00	150.	225.
1971☆	1706	1953☆	Priest-Humphrey	60.00	150.	500.	700.
1972	1707	1953A	Priest-Anderson	40.00	125.	200.	450.
1972☆	1707	1953A☆	Priest-Anderson	60.00	200.	625.	1100.
1973	1708	1953B	Smith-Dillon	25.00	75.00	175.	250.

Federal Reserve Bank Notes

KL#	Fr#	Series	District	Fine	XF	CH CU (63)	Gem CU (65)
1974	1860A	1929	Boston	30.00	75.00	235.	375.
1974☆	1860A	1929☆	Boston	2500.	5000.	10,000.	13,400.
1975	1860B	1929	New York	100.	140.	300.	400.
1975☆	1860B	1929☆	New York	165.	450.	2400.	3250.
1976	1860C	1929	Philadelphia	20.00	65.00	225.	1250.
1976☆	1860C	1929☆	Philadelphia	350.	1250.	3300.	3750.
1977	1860D	1929	Cleveland	20.00	70.00	175.	300.
1977☆	1860D	1929☆	Cleveland	150.	900.	2500.	3500.
1978	1860E	1929	Richmond	25.00	100.	350.	750.
1978☆	1860E	1929☆	Richmond	500.	1500.	9000.	11,400.
1979	1860F	1929	Atlanta	20.00	75.00	700.	750.
1979☆	1860F	1929☆	Atlanta	1500.	3000.	6000.	7000.
1980	1860G	1929	Chicago	30.00	70.00	125.	250.
1980☆	1860G	1929☆	Chicago	585.	2500.	—	—
1981	1860H	1929	St. Louis	20.00	60.00	200.	325.
1981☆	1860H	1929☆	St. Louis	250.	900.	3500.	3350.
1982	1860I	1929	Minneapolis	25.00	75.00	300.	675.
1982☆	1860I	1929☆	Minneapolis	400.	1200.	3500.	4700.
1983	1860J	1929	Kansas City	25.00	50.00	275.	500.
1983☆	1860J	1929☆	Kansas City	250.	700.	2600.	3700.
1984	1860K	1929	Dallas	300.	750.	2500.	3500.
1984☆	1860K	1929☆	Dallas	5000.	30,000.	—	—
1985	1860L	1929	San Francisco	75.00	150.	6900.	—
1985☆	1860L	1929☆	San Francisco	650.	2000.	5000.	7500.

Federal Reserve Notes
Series 1928 Tate-Mellon

KL#	Fr#	District	Fine	XF	CH CU (63)	Gem CU (65)
1986	2000A	Boston	35.00	150.	500.	1500.
1986☆	2000A ☆	Boston	500.	1000.	3000.	4000.
1987	2000B	New York	35.00	75.00	300.	460.
1987☆	2000B ☆	New York	150.	450.	1125.	1250.
1988	2000C	Philadelphia	40.00	75.00	400.	700.
1988☆	2000C ☆	Philadelphia	150.	600.	1500.	4750.
1989	2000D	Cleveland	35.00	50.00	250.	325.
1989☆	2000D ☆	Cleveland	150.	350.	950.	1500.
1990	2000E	Richmond	40.00	225.	1000.	1250.
1990☆	2000E ☆	Richmond	250.	1500.	5000.	—
1991	2000F	Atlanta	40.00	60.00	400.	500.
1991☆	2000F ☆	Atlanta	300.	950.	9750.	11,000.
1992	2000G	Chicago	35.00	60.00	300.	400.
1992☆	2000G ☆	Chicago	150.	475.	1500.	2000.
1993	2000H	St. Louis	60.00	125.	300.	425.
1993☆	2000H ☆	St. Louis	200.	500.	—	—
1994	2000I	Minneapolis	30.00	100.	500.	600.
1994☆	2000I ☆	Minneapolis	500.	800.	2000.	3000.
1995	2000J	Kansas City	50.00	125.	300.	450.
1995☆	2000J ☆	Kansas City	225.	450.	1750.	4000.
1996	2000K	Dallas	35.00	100.	250.	500.
1996☆	2000K ☆	Dallas	1000.	2500.	5000.	—
1997	2000L	San Francisco	35.00	75.00	500.	750.
1997☆	2000L ☆	San Francisco	325.	1500.	4000.	5000.

Series 1928A Woods-Mellon

KL#	Fr#	District	Fine	XF	CH CU (63)	Gem CU (65)
1998	2001A	Boston	45.00	275.	1500.	—
1998☆	2001A ☆	Boston	1500.	—	—	—
1999	2001B	New York	25.00	100.	400.	900.
1999☆	2001B ☆	New York	400.	900.	2000.	—
2000	2001C	Philadelphia	60.00	125.	900.	1750.
2000☆	2001C ☆	Philadelphia	300.	—	—	—
2001	2001D	Cleveland	35.00	60.00	250.	750.
2001☆	2001D ☆	Cleveland	175.	750.	1250.	1500.
2002	2001E	Richmond	50.00	200.	1500.	2500.
2002☆	2001E ☆	Richmond	300.	—	—	—
2003	2001F	Atlanta	35.00	60.00	450.	750.
2003☆	2001F ☆	Atlanta	—	—	—	—
2004	2001G	Chicago	65.00	125.	500.	1500.
2004☆	2001G ☆	Chicago	—	—	—	600.
2005	2001H	St. Louis	—	150.	500.	600.
2005☆	2001H ☆	St. Louis	250.	550.	1500.	—
2006	2001I	Minneapolis	450.	1200.	6000.	—
2007	2001J	Kansas City	350.	1500.	3250.	3500.
2008	2001K	Dallas	400.	1200.	2500.	3000.
2009	2001L	San Francisco	65.00	300.	1000.	2250.
2009☆	2001L ☆	San Francisco	250.	450.	2500.	—

Series 1928B Woods-Mellon

KL#	Fr#	District	Fine	XF	CH CU (63)	Gem CU (65)
2010	2002A	Boston	18.00	30.00	80.00	100.
2010☆	2002A ☆	Boston	60.00	300.	975.	1250.
2011	2002B	New York	18.00	30.00	100.	175.
2011☆	2002B ☆	New York	75.00	250.	900.	1000.
2012	2002C	Philadelphia	18.00	35.00	90.00	225.
2012☆	2002C ☆	Philadelphia	75.00	200.	1100.	1150.
2013	2002D	Cleveland	18.00	50.00	120.	140.
2013☆	2002D ☆	Cleveland	75.00	175.	1000.	1300.
2014	2002E	Richmond	18.00	30.00	100.	120.
2014☆	2002E ☆	Richmond	65.00	150.	900.	1000.
2015	2002F	Atlanta	18.00	30.00	120.	140.
2015☆	2002F ☆	Atlanta	65.00	200.	1750.	2250.
2016	2002G	Chicago	18.00	60.00	400.	900.
2016☆	2002G ☆	Chicago	50.00	75.00	300.	650.
2017	2002H	St. Louis	18.00	30.00	85.00	100.
2017☆	2002H ☆	St. Louis	375.	600.	1750.	2250.
2018	2002I	Minneapolis	18.00	30.00	140.	325.
2018☆	2002I ☆	Minneapolis	140.	350.	1000.	1100.
2019	2002J	Kansas City	18.00	30.00	90.00	125.
2019☆	2002J ☆	Kansas City	125.	450.	2400.	2500.

KL#	Fr#	District	Fine	XF	CH CU (63)	Gem CU (65)
2020	2002K	Dallas	35.00	125.	250.	300.
2021	2002L	San Francisco	18.00	25.00	90.00	150.
2021☆	2002L ☆	San Francisco	60.00	400.	1100.	1200.

Series 1928C Woods-Mills

KL#	Fr#	District	Fine	XF	CH CU (63)	Gem CU (65)
2022	2003B	New York	75.00	400.	600.	1000.
2023	2003D	Cleveland	200.	700.	2500.	4500.
2023☆	2003D ☆	Cleveland	10,000.	20,000.	50,000.	55,000.
2024	2003E	Richmond	575.	5000.	12,500.	15,000.
2026	2003G	Chicago	65.00	225.	300.	550.

Series 1934 Julian-Morgenthau

KL#	Fr#	District	Fine	XF	CH CU (63)	Gem CU (65)
2027	2004A	Boston	15.00	25.00	100.	150.
2027☆	2004A ☆	Boston	35.00	75.00	800.	2000.
2028	2004B	New York	15.00	30.00	75.00	100.
2028☆	2004B ☆	New York	45.00	175.	1275.	1500.
2029	2004C	Philadelphia	15.00	30.00	100.	125.
2029☆	2004C ☆	Philadelphia	45.00	70.00	800.	1000.
2030	2004D	Cleveland	15.00	30.00	100.	150.
2030☆	2004D ☆	Cleveland	45.00	150.	900.	1100.
2031	2004E	Richmond	15.00	35.00	120.	150.
2031☆	2004E ☆	Richmond	150.	400.	1500.	1750.
2032	2004F	Atlanta	25.00	40.00	150.	200.
2032☆	2004F ☆	Atlanta	100.	350.	1100.	1400.
2033	2004G	Chicago	15.00	40.00	90.00	135.
2033☆	2004G ☆	Chicago	50.00	175.	800.	1000.
2034	2004H	St. Louis	15.00	50.00	150.	200.
2034☆	2004H ☆	St. Louis	175.	400.	1200.	1500.
2035	2004I	Minneapolis	15.00	40.00	100.	150.

KL#	Fr#	District	Fine	XF	CH CU (63)	Gem CU (65)
2035☆	2004I ☆	Minneapolis	45.00	325.	525.	1500.
2036	2004J	Kansas City	15.00	40.00	100.	150.
2036☆	2004J ☆	Kansas City	45.00	350.	900.	1100.
2037	2004K	Dallas	15.00	75.00	225.	550.
2037☆	2004K ☆	Dallas	170.	450.	1800.	2250.
2038	2004L	San Francisco	15.00	40.00	100.	150.
2038☆	2004L ☆	San Francisco	95.00	450.	1500.	1800.

Series 1934A Julian-Morgenthau

KL#	Fr#	District	Fine	XF	CH CU (63)	Gem CU (65)
2039	2006A	Boston	11.00	12.00	40.00	50.00
2039☆	2006A ☆	Boston	20.00	40.00	225.	300.
2040	2006B	New York	11.00	12.00	40.00	50.00
2040☆	2006B ☆	New York	20.00	40.00	200.	400.
2041	2006C	Philadelphia	11.00	12.00	40.00	50.00
2041☆	2006C ☆	Philadelphia	20.00	35.00	150.	250.
2042	2006D	Cleveland	11.00	12.00	40.00	50.00
2042☆	2006D ☆	Cleveland	20.00	40.00	250.	575.
2043	2006E	Richmond	11.00	12.00	40.00	50.00
2043☆	2006E ☆	Richmond	25.00	50.00	250.	300.
2044	2006F	Atlanta	11.00	12.00	40.00	50.00
2044☆	2006F ☆	Atlanta	20.00	75.00	400.	500.
2045	2006G	Chicago	11.00	12.00	25.00	40.00
2045☆	2006G ☆	Chicago	25.00	45.00	275.	525.
2046	2006H	St. Louis	11.00	12.00	40.00	50.00
2046☆	2006H ☆	St. Louis	25.00	60.00	200.	250.
2047	2006I	Minneapolis	11.00	15.00	50.00	60.00
2047☆	2006I ☆	Minneapolis	30.00	75.00	400.	500.
2048	2006J	Kansas City	11.00	12.00	45.00	60.00
2048☆	2006J ☆	Kansas City	25.00	50.00	250.	300.
2049	2006K	Dallas	11.00	12.00	45.00	60.00
2049☆	2006K ☆	Dallas	40.00	100.	400.	500.
2050	2006L	San Francisco	11.00	15.00	45.00	60.00
2050☆	2006L ☆	San Francisco	35.00	80.00	350.	400.

Series 1934B Julian-Vinson

KL#	Fr#	District	Fine	XF	CH CU (63)	Gem CU (65)
2051	2007A	Boston	15.00	25.00	100.	150.
2051☆	2007A ☆	Boston	30.00	150.	700.	700.
2052	2007B	New York	15.00	25.00	75.00	85.00
2052☆	2007B ☆	New York	20.00	85.00	450.	500.
2053	2007C	Philadelphia	15.00	25.00	100.	100.
2053☆	2007C ☆	Philadelphia	25.00	150.	500.	725.
2054	2007D	Cleveland	17.00	40.00	150.	200.
2054☆	2007D ☆	Cleveland	50.00	250.	375.	425.
2055	2007E	Richmond	13.00	25.00	50.00	175.
2055☆	2007E ☆	Richmond	30.00	150.	700.	900.
2056	2007F	Atlanta	13.00	25.00	575.	1000.
2056☆	2007F ☆	Atlanta	30.00	150.	700.	1000.
2057	2007G	Chicago	13.00	35.00	75.00	125.
2057☆	2007G ☆	Chicago	90.00	225.	450.	650.
2058	2007H	St. Louis	13.00	25.00	50.00	100.
2058☆	2007H ☆	St. Louis	25.00	150.	500.	700.
2059	2007I	Minneapolis	20.00	45.00	100.	150.
2059☆	2007I ☆	Minneapolis	35.00	300.	1200.	1500.
2060	2007J	Kansas City	13.00	25.00	50.00	125.
2060☆	2007J ☆	Kansas City	25.00	250.	500.	2200.
2061	2007K	Dallas	20.00	25.00	150.	150.
2061☆	2007K ☆	Dallas	35.00	300.	1250.	1500.
2062	2007L	San Francisco	13.00	25.00	50.00	100.
2062☆	2007L ☆	San Francisco	160.	360.	900.	1000.

Series 1934C Julian-Snyder

KL#	Fr#	District	Fine	XF	CH CU (63)	Gem CU (65)
2063	2008A	Boston	11.00	15.00	50.00	50.00
2063☆	2008A ☆	Boston	35.00	75.00	400.	400.
2064	2008B	New York	11.00	15.00	40.00	40.00
2064☆	2008B ☆	New York	25.00	50.00	250.	525.
2065	2008C	Philadelphia	11.00	15.00	40.00	40.00

KL#	Fr#	District	Fine	XF	CH CU (63)	Gem CU (65)
2065☆	2008C ☆	Philadelphia	30.00	60.00	275.	400.
2066	2008D	Cleveland	11.00	15.00	45.00	45.00
2066☆	2008D ☆	Cleveland	35.00	75.00	275.	400.
2067	2008E	Richmond	11.00	15.00	50.00	50.00
2067☆	2008E ☆	Richmond	35.00	80.00	500.	400.
2068	2008F	Atlanta	11.00	15.00	50.00	50.00
2068☆	2008F ☆	Atlanta	35.00	80.00	500.	400.
2069	2008G	Chicago	11.00	30.00	50.00	75.00
2069☆	2008G ☆	Chicago	25.00	160.	300.	975.
2070	2008H	St. Louis	11.00	15.00	50.00	50.00
2070☆	2008H ☆	St. Louis	35.00	75.00	300.	325.
2071	2008I	Minneapolis	11.00	15.00	75.00	75.00
2071☆	2008I ☆	Minneapolis	50.00	300.	1000.	900.
2072	2008J	Kansas City	11.00	15.00	50.00	85.00
2072☆	2008J ☆	Kansas City	20.00	45.00	400.	400.
2073	2008K	Dallas	11.00	15.00	50.00	50.00
2073☆	2008K ☆	Dallas	40.00	85.00	450.	450.
2074	2008L	San Francisco	11.00	15.00	40.00	40.00
2074☆	2008L ☆	San Francisco	35.00	75.00	500.	400.

Series 1934D Clark-Snyder

KL#	Fr#	District	Fine	XF	CH CU (63)	Gem CU (65)
2075	2009A	Boston	12.00	20.00	60.00	60.00
2075☆	2009A ☆	Boston	65.00	125.	700.	700.
2076	2009B	New York	11.00	15.00	60.00	50.00
2076☆	2009B ☆	New York	25.00	70.00	450.	450.
2077	2009C	Philadelphia	11.00	20.00	60.00	75.00
2077☆	2009C ☆	Philadelphia	30.00	90.00	500.	650.
2078	2009D	Cleveland	11.00	17.00	50.00	75.00
2078☆	2009D ☆	Cleveland	30.00	125.	550.	650.
2079	2009E	Richmond	11.00	15.00	60.00	75.00
2079☆	2009E ☆	Richmond	65.00	250.	1000.	1650.
2080	2009F	Atlanta	12.00	15.00	60.00	75.00
2080☆	2009F ☆	Atlanta	65.00	90.00	900.	1000.
2081	2009G	Chicago	11.00	30.00	90.00	100.
2081☆	2009G ☆	Chicago	90.00	225.	475.	700.
2082	2009H	St. Louis	12.00	15.00	75.00	100.
2082☆	2009H ☆	St. Louis	150.	200.	800.	900.
2083	2009I	Minneapolis	20.00	45.00	125.	150.
2083☆	2009I ☆	Minneapolis	100.	300.	1400.	1500.
2084	2009J	Kansas City	15.00	15.00	100.	125.
2084☆	2009J ☆	Kansas City	65.00	125.	800.	900.
2085	2009K	Dallas	12.00	20.00	100.	150.
2085☆	2009K ☆	Dallas	125.	200.	1400.	1500.
2086	2009L	San Francisco	11.00	20.00	115.	125.
2086☆	2009L ☆	San Francisco	200.	475.	1350.	1500.

Series 1950 Clark-Snyder

KL#	Fr#	District	Fine	XF	CH CU (63)	Gem CU (65)
2087	2010A	Boston	FV	20.00	80.00	125.
2087☆	2010A ☆	Boston	25.00	110.	500.	800.
2088	2010B	New York	FV	20.00	75.00	100.
2088☆	2010B ☆	New York	20.00	100.	425.	750.
2089	2010C	Philadelphia	FV	25.00	75.00	100.
2089☆	2010C ☆	Philadelphia	25.00	100.	600.	750.
2090	2010D	Cleveland	FV	20.00	75.00	100.
2090☆	2010D ☆	Cleveland	25.00	125.	500.	750.
2091	2010E	Richmond	FV	20.00	75.00	100.
2091☆	2010E ☆	Richmond	35.00	125.	450.	750.
2092	2010F	Atlanta	FV	25.00	75.00	100.
2092☆	2010F ☆	Atlanta	35.00	125.	500.	750.
2093	2010G	Chicago	FV	20.00	70.00	100.
2093☆	2010G ☆	Chicago	20.00	125.	500.	600.
2094	2010H	St. Louis	FV	20.00	75.00	100.
2094☆	2010H ☆	St. Louis	25.00	150.	600.	750.
2095	2010I	Minneapolis	FV	20.00	90.00	100.
2095☆	2010I ☆	Minneapolis	50.00	250.	900.	1000.
2096	2010J	Kansas City	20.00	75.00	320.	450.
2096☆	2010J ☆	Kansas City	35.00	125.	600.	750.
2097	2010K	Dallas	FV	20.00	75.00	100.
2097☆	2010K ☆	Dallas	35.00	125.	400.	750.
2098	2010L	San Francisco	FV	15.00	75.00	100.
2098☆	2010L ☆	San Francisco	25.00	125.	600.	750.

Series 1950A Priest-Humphrey

KL#	Fr#	District	Fine	XF	CH CU (63)	Gem CU (65)
2099	2011A	Boston	FV	30.00	70.00	90.00
2099☆	2011A ☆	Boston	25.00	115.	200.	275.
2100	2011B	New York	FV	30.00	70.00	90.00
2100☆	2011B ☆	New York	25.00	90.00	150.	200.
2101	2011C	Philadelphia	FV	30.00	70.00	90.00

KL#	Fr#	District	Fine	XF	CH CU (63)	Gem CU (65)
2101☆	2011C ☆	Philadelphia	25.00	30.00	300.	325.
2102	2011D	Cleveland	FV	30.00	70.00	90.00
2102☆	2011D ☆	Cleveland	25.00	125.	225.	375.
2103	2011E	Richmond	FV	30.00	70.00	90.00
2103☆	2011E ☆	Richmond	25.00	125.	300.	375.
2104	2011F	Atlanta	FV	30.00	70.00	90.00
2104☆	2011F ☆	Atlanta	25.00	125.	450.	600.
2105	2011G	Chicago	FV	30.00	70.00	90.00
2105☆	2011G ☆	Chicago	25.00	150.	250.	375.
2106	2011H	St. Louis	FV	30.00	100.	125.
2106☆	2011H ☆	St. Louis	25.00	150.	250.	375.
2107	2011I	Minneapolis	FV	30.00	100.	110.
2107☆	2011I ☆	Minneapolis	25.00	150.	300.	475.
2108	2011J	Kansas City	FV	30.00	70.00	90.00
2108☆	2011J ☆	Kansas City	25.00	150.	300.	325.
2109	2011K	Dallas	FV	30.00	70.00	90.00
2109☆	2011K ☆	Dallas	25.00	150.	300.	325.
2110	2011L	San Francisco	FV	30.00	60.00	90.00
2110☆	2011L ☆	San Francisco	25.00	100.	200.	275.

Series 1950B Priest-Anderson

KL#	Fr#	District	Fine	XF	CH CU (63)	Gem CU (65)
2111	2012A	Boston	FV	20.00	40.00	45.00
2111☆	2012A ☆	Boston	15.00	75.00	150.	160.
2112	2012B	New York	FV	20.00	35.00	45.00
2112☆	2012B ☆	New York	15.00	75.00	125.	160.
2113	2012C	Philadelphia	FV	20.00	35.00	45.00
2113☆	2012C ☆	Philadelphia	15.00	75.00	150.	160.
2114	2012D	Cleveland	FV	20.00	40.00	45.00
2114☆	2012D ☆	Cleveland	15.00	75.00	150.	160.
2115	2012E	Richmond	FV	20.00	35.00	45.00
2115☆	2012E ☆	Richmond	15.00	75.00	150.	160.
2116	2012F	Atlanta	FV	15.00	35.00	40.00
2116☆	2012F ☆	Atlanta	15.00	75.00	150.	160.
2117	2012G	Chicago	FV	15.00	35.00	40.00
2117☆	2012G ☆	Chicago	15.00	65.00	125.	150.
2118	2012H	St. Louis	FV	12.00	35.00	40.00
2118☆	2012H ☆	St. Louis	15.00	75.00	170.	180.
2119	2012I	Minneapolis	FV	20.00	40.00	45.00
2120	2012J	Kansas City	FV	20.00	40.00	45.00
2120☆	2012J ☆	Kansas City	15.00	70.00	175.	200.
2121	2012K	Dallas	FV	20.00	40.00	45.00
2121☆	2012K ☆	Dallas	15.00	60.00	150.	325.
2122	2012L	San Francisco	FV	20.00	40.00	45.00
2122☆	2012L ☆	San Francisco	15.00	75.00	150.	160.

Series 1950C Smith-Dillon

KL#	Fr#	District	Fine	XF	CH CU (63)	Gem CU (65)
2123	2013A	Boston	FV	25.00	50.00	65.00
2123☆	2013A ☆	Boston	70.00	150.	300.	375.
2124	2013B	New York	FV	25.00	50.00	65.00
2124☆	2013B ☆	New York	60.00	120.	275.	300.
2125	2013C	Philadelphia	FV	25.00	50.00	65.00
2125☆	2013C ☆	Philadelphia	90.00	125.	300.	475.
2126	2013D	Cleveland	FV	30.00	75.00	75.00
2126☆	2013D ☆	Cleveland	85.00	175.	300.	1000.
2127	2013E	Richmond	FV	30.00	55.00	85.00
2127☆	2013E ☆	Richmond	85.00	125.	300.	425.
2128	2013F	Atlanta	FV	30.00	50.00	150.
2128☆	2013F ☆	Atlanta	85.00	125.	350.	425.
2129	2013G	Chicago	FV	30.00	50.00	70.00
2129☆	2013G ☆	Chicago	55.00	125.	350.	375.
2130	2013H	St. Louis	FV	40.00	75.00	90.00
2130☆	2013H ☆	St. Louis	60.00	75.00	150.	325.
2131	2013I	Minneapolis	FV	45.00	85.00	100.
2131☆	2013I ☆	Minneapolis	75.00	90.00	250.	375.
2132	2013J	Kansas City	FV	45.00	75.00	110.
2132☆	2013J ☆	Kansas City	60.00	100.	300.	325.
2133	2013K	Dallas	FV	40.00	75.00	90.00
2133☆	2013K ☆	Dallas	60.00	85.00	250.	325.
2134	2013L	San Francisco	FV	45.00	85.00	100.
2134☆	2013L ☆	San Francisco	60.00	85.00	250.	325.

Series 1950D Granahan-Dillon

KL#	Fr#	District	Fine	XF	CH CU (63)	Gem CU (65)
2135	2014A	Boston	FV	20.00	50.00	70.00
2135☆	2014A ☆	Boston	FV	45.00	200.	225.
2136	2014B	New York	FV	20.00	45.00	65.00
2136☆	2014B ☆	New York	20.00	50.00	150.	275.
2137	2014C	Philadelphia	FV	20.00	55.00	75.00

KL#	Fr#	District	Fine	XF	CH CU (63)	Gem CU (65)
2137☆	2014C ☆	Philadelphia	FV	45.00	200.	275.
2138	2014D	Cleveland	FV	20.00	55.00	75.00
2138☆	2014D ☆	Cleveland	FV	45.00	200.	275.
2139	2014E	Richmond	FV	20.00	50.00	75.00
2139☆	2014E ☆	Richmond	15.00	60.00	200.	325.
2140	2014F	Atlanta	FV	20.00	50.00	70.00
2140☆	2014F ☆	Atlanta	15.00	60.00	250.	325.
2141	2014G	Chicago	FV	20.00	55.00	70.00
2141☆	2014G ☆	Chicago	15.00	65.00	250.	325.
2142	2014H	St. Louis	FV	20.00	55.00	70.00
2142☆	2014H ☆	St. Louis	15.00	65.00	250.	325.
2144	2014J	Kansas City	FV	20.00	50.00	175.
2144☆	2014J ☆	Kansas City	15.00	30.00	150.	325.
2145	2014K	Dallas	FV	20.00	50.00	80.00
2145☆	2014K ☆	Dallas	15.00	50.00	275.	325.
2146	2014L	San Francisco	FV	20.00	100.	125.
2146☆	2014L ☆	San Francisco	FV	30.00	225.	250.

Series 1950E Granahan-Fowler

KL#	Fr#	District	Fine	XF	CH CU (63)	Gem CU (65)
2147	2015B	New York	15.00	55.00	100.	135.
2147☆	2015B ☆	New York	35.00	160.	500.	700.
2148	2015G	Chicago	15.00	55.00	125.	175.
2148☆	2015G ☆	Chicago	35.00	160.	250.	475.
2149	2015L	San Francisco	20.00	65.00	125.	150.
2149☆	2015L ☆	San Francisco	90.00	200.	400.	650.

Series 1963 Granahan-Dillon

KL#	Fr#	District	Fine	XF	CH CU (63)	Gem CU (65)
2150	2010A	Boston	FV	15.00	50.00	55.00
2150☆	2016A ☆	Boston	25.00	75.00	120.	150.
2151	2016B	New York	FV	15.00	50.00	55.00
2151☆	2016B ☆	New York	25.00	35.00	60.00	80.00
2152	2016C	Philadelphia	FV	15.00	50.00	55.00
2152☆	2016C ☆	Philadelphia	15.00	40.00	125.	175.
2153	2016D	Cleveland	FV	15.00	50.00	55.00
2153☆	2016D ☆	Cleveland	15.00	50.00	100.	135.
2154	2016E	Richmond	FV	15.00	50.00	55.00
2154☆	2016E ☆	Richmond	15.00	50.00	120.	150.
2155	2016F	Atlanta	FV	15.00	50.00	55.00
2155☆	2016F ☆	Atlanta	15.00	40.00	80.00	110.
2156	2016G	Chicago	FV	15.00	50.00	55.00
2156☆	2016G ☆	Chicago	15.00	40.00	80.00	150.
2157	2016H	St. Louis	FV	15.00	50.00	55.00
2157☆	2016H ☆	St. Louis	15.00	40.00	80.00	110.
2159	2016J	Kansas City	FV	25.00	70.00	75.00
2159☆	2016J ☆	Kansas City	15.00	50.00	120.	150.
2160	2016K	Dallas	FV	25.00	60.00	75.00
2160☆	2016K ☆	Dallas	15.00	50.00	375.	450.
2161	2016L	San Francisco	FV	15.00	50.00	53.00
2161☆	2016L ☆	San Francisco	15.00	50.00	100.	150.

Series 1963A Granahan-Fowler

KL#	Fr#	District	Fine	XF	CH CU (63)	Gem CU (65)
2162	2017A	Boston	FV	20.00	50.00	55.00
2162☆	2017A ☆	Boston	FV	40.00	90.00	150.
2163	2017B	New York	FV	20.00	50.00	55.00
2163☆	2017B ☆	New York	FV	40.00	80.00	85.00
2164	2017C	Philadelphia	FV	20.00	50.00	55.00
2164☆	2017C ☆	Philadelphia	FV	40.00	80.00	85.00
2165	2017D	Cleveland	FV	20.00	50.00	55.00
2165☆	2017D ☆	Cleveland	FV	40.00	90.00	120.
2166	2017E	Richmond	FV	20.00	50.00	55.00
2166☆	2017E ☆	Richmond	FV	40.00	85.00	120.
2167	2017F	Atlanta	FV	20.00	50.00	55.00
2167☆	2017F ☆	Atlanta	FV	40.00	80.00	85.00
2168	2017G	Chicago	FV	20.00	50.00	55.00
2168☆	2017G ☆	Chicago	FV	40.00	80.00	85.00
2169	2017H	St. Louis	FV	20.00	50.00	55.00
2169☆	2017H ☆	St. Louis	FV	40.00	80.00	85.00
2170	2017I	Minneapolis	FV	20.00	47.00	50.00
2170☆	2017I ☆	Minneapolis	FV	40.00	80.00	85.00
2171	2017J	Kansas City	FV	20.00	60.00	70.00
2171☆	2017J ☆	Kansas City	FV	40.00	90.00	120.
2172	2017K	Dallas	FV	20.00	60.00	70.00
2172☆	2017K ☆	Dallas	FV	40.00	90.00	120.
2173	2017L	San Francisco	FV	20.00	55.00	50.00
2173☆	2017L ☆	San Francisco	FV	40.00	85.00	100.

Series 1969 Elston-Kennedy

KL#	Fr#	District	Fine	XF	CH CU (63)	Gem CU (65)
2174	2018A	Boston	FV	15.00	38.00	42.00
2174☆	2018A ☆	Boston	FV	40.00	70.00	77.00
2175	2018B	New York	FV	15.00	38.00	42.00
2175☆	2018B ☆	New York	FV	40.00	70.00	77.00

KL#	Fr#	District	Fine	XF	CH CU (63)	Gem CU (65)
2176	2018C	Philadelphia	FV	15.00	38.00	42.00
2176☆	2018C ☆	Philadelphia	FV	40.00	70.00	77.00
2177	2018D	Cleveland	FV	15.00	38.00	42.00
2177☆	2018D ☆	Cleveland	FV	40.00	100.	125.
2178	2018E	Richmond	FV	15.00	38.00	42.00
2178☆	2018E ☆	Richmond	FV	40.00	100.	125.
2179	2018F	Atlanta	FV	15.00	38.00	42.00
2179☆	2018F ☆	Atlanta	FV	40.00	70.00	77.00
2180	2018G	Chicago	FV	15.00	38.00	42.00
2180☆	2018G ☆	Chicago	FV	40.00	70.00	77.00
2181	2018H	St. Louis	FV	15.00	38.00	42.00
2181☆	2018H ☆	St. Louis	50.00	100.	200.	225.
2182	2018I	Minneapolis	FV	15.00	38.00	42.00
2182☆	2018I ☆	Minneapolis	FV	40.00	70.00	77.00
2183	2018J	Kansas City	FV	15.00	38.00	42.00
2183☆	2018J ☆	Kansas City	FV	40.00	70.00	225.
2184	2018K	Dallas	FV	15.00	38.00	42.00
2184☆	2018K ☆	Dallas	FV	40.00	70.00	77.00
2185	2018L	San Francisco	FV	15.00	38.00	42.00
2185☆	2018L ☆	San Francisco	FV	40.00	70.00	77.00

Series 1969A Kabis-Connally

KL#	Fr#	District	Fine	XF	CH CU (63)	Gem CU (65)
2186	2019A	Boston	FV	15.00	35.00	37.00
2186☆	2019A ☆	Boston	FV	20.00	60.00	62.00
2187	2019B	New York	FV	15.00	35.00	37.00
2187☆	2019B ☆	New York	FV	20.00	60.00	62.00
2188	2019C	Philadelphia	FV	15.00	35.00	37.00
2188☆	2019C ☆	Philadelphia	FV	20.00	60.00	62.00
2189	2019D	Cleveland	FV	15.00	45.00	47.00
2189☆	2019D ☆	Cleveland	FV	20.00	60.00	62.00
2190	2019E	Richmond	FV	15.00	40.00	42.00
2190☆	2019E ☆	Richmond	FV	20.00	150.	225.
2191	2019F	Atlanta	FV	15.00	45.00	47.00
2191☆	2019F ☆	Atlanta	FV	20.00	75.00	95.00
2192	2019G	Chicago	FV	15.00	35.00	37.00
2192☆	2019G ☆	Chicago	FV	20.00	75.00	85.00
2193	2019H	St. Louis	FV	15.00	35.00	37.00
2193☆	2019H ☆	St. Louis	FV	20.00	60.00	95.00
2194	2019I	Minneapolis	FV	15.00	45.00	47.00
2195	2019J	Kansas City	FV	15.00	40.00	42.00
2196	2019K	Dallas	FV	15.00	45.00	47.00
2196☆	2019K ☆	Dallas	FV	20.00	60.00	95.00
2197	2019L	San Francisco	FV	15.00	40.00	37.00
2197☆	2019L ☆	San Francisco	FV	20.00	75.00	95.00

Series 1969B Banuelos-Connally

KL#	Fr#	District	Fine	XF	CH CU (63)	Gem CU (65)
2198	2020A	Boston	25.00	75.00	175.	200.
2199	2020B	New York	FV	50.00	150.	165.
2199☆	2020B ☆	New York	25.00	100.	200.	220.
2200	2020C	Philadelphia	FV	50.00	150.	165.
2201	2020D	Cleveland	FV	50.00	150.	165.
2202	2020E	Richmond	FV	50.00	150.	165.
2202☆	2020E ☆	Richmond	25.00	75.00	600.	750.
2203	2020F	Atlanta	FV	50.00	150.	165.
2203☆	2020F ☆	Atlanta	25.00	75.00	300.	325.
2204	2020G	Chicago	FV	50.00	150.	165.
2204☆	2020G ☆	Chicago	FV	50.00	250.	275.
2205	2020H	St. Louis	FV	75.00	175.	200.
2205☆	2020H ☆	St. Louis	25.00	75.00	250.	275.
2206	2020I	Minneapolis	25.00	75.00	350.	375.
2207	2020J	Kansas City	25.00	75.00	175.	200.
2207☆	2020J ☆	Kansas City	25.00	75.00	600.	750.
2208	2020K	Dallas	FV	50.00	150.	165.
2209	2020L	San Francisco	25.00	75.00	350.	375.
2209☆	2020L ☆	San Francisco	FV	50.00	150.	200.

Series 1969C Banuelos-Shultz

KL#	Fr#	District	Fine	XF	CH CU (63)	Gem CU (65)
2210	2021A	Boston	FV	20.00	40.00	42.00
2210☆	2021A ☆	Boston	12.00	50.00	125.	135.
2211	2021B	New York	FV	20.00	40.00	42.00
2211☆	2021B ☆	New York	FV	25.00	75.00	90.00
2212	2021C	Philadelphia	FV	25.00	50.00	60.00
2212☆	2021C ☆	Philadelphia	12.00	35.00	80.00	90.00
2213	2021D	Cleveland	FV	20.00	40.00	42.00
2213☆	2021D ☆	Cleveland	12.00	30.00	80.00	90.00
2214	2021E	Richmond	FV	20.00	40.00	42.00

KL#	Fr#	District	Fine	XF	CH CU (63)	Gem CU (65)
2214☆	2021E ☆	Richmond	15.00	35.00	75.00	80.00
2215	2021F	Atlanta	FV	20.00	40.00	42.00
2215☆	2021F ☆	Atlanta	12.00	35.00	80.00	90.00
2216	2021G	Chicago	FV	20.00	40.00	42.00
2216☆	2021G ☆	Chicago	12.00	35.00	100.	120.
2217	2021H	St. Louis	FV	20.00	40.00	42.00
2217☆	2021H ☆	St. Louis	12.00	35.00	100.	120.
2218	2021I	Minneapolis	FV	20.00	40.00	42.00
2218☆	2021I ☆	Minneapolis	15.00	60.00	140.	160.
2219	2021J	Kansas City	FV	20.00	40.00	42.00
2219☆	2021J ☆	Kansas City	15.00	60.00	120.	150.
2220	2021K	Dallas	FV	20.00	40.00	42.00
2220☆	2021K ☆	Dallas	15.00	50.00	120.	150.
2221	2021L	San Francisco	FV	20.00	40.00	45.00
2221☆	2021L ☆	San Francisco	15.00	50.00	120.	150.

Series 1974 Neff-Simon

KL#	Fr#	District	Fine	XF	CH CU (63)	Gem CU (65)
2222	2022A	Boston	FV	15.00	35.00	42.00
2222☆	2022A ☆	Boston	FV	25.00	70.00	75.00
2223	2022B	New York	FV	15.00	35.00	40.00
2223☆	2022B ☆	New York	FV	25.00	70.00	62.00
2224	2022C	Philadelphia	FV	15.00	40.00	42.00
2224☆	2022C ☆	Philadelphia	FV	25.00	70.00	75.00
2225	2022D	Cleveland	FV	15.00	35.00	42.00
2225☆	2022D ☆	Cleveland	FV	30.00	70.00	75.00
2226	2022E	Richmond	FV	15.00	40.00	42.00
2226☆	2022E ☆	Richmond	FV	25.00	60.00	65.00
2227	2022F	Atlanta	FV	15.00	35.00	42.00
2227☆	2022F ☆	Atlanta	FV	25.00	65.00	55.00
2228	2022G	Chicago	FV	15.00	35.00	42.00
2228☆	2022G ☆	Chicago	FV	25.00	55.00	60.00
2229	2022H	St. Louis	FV	15.00	35.00	42.00
2229☆	2022H ☆	St. Louis	FV	25.00	85.00	95.00
2230	2022I	Minneapolis	FV	15.00	35.00	42.00
2230☆	2022I ☆	Minneapolis	FV	25.00	120.	140.
2231	2022J	Kansas City	FV	15.00	35.00	42.00
2231☆	2022J ☆	Kansas City	FV	25.00	60.00	65.00
2232	2022K	Dallas	FV	15.00	35.00	42.00
2232☆	2022K ☆	Dallas	FV	25.00	60.00	65.00
2233	2022L	San Francisco	FV	15.00	35.00	42.00
2233☆	2022L ☆	San Francisco	FV	25.00	60.00	65.00

Series 1977 Morton-Blumenthal

KL#	Fr#	District	Fine	XF	CH CU (63)	Gem CU (65)
2234	2023A	Boston	FV	15.00	35.00	42.00
2234☆	2023A ☆	Boston	FV	25.00	100.	150.
2235	2023B	New York	FV	15.00	35.00	42.00
2235☆	2023B ☆	New York	FV	25.00	70.00	75.00
2236	2023C	Philadelphia	FV	15.00	35.00	42.00
2236☆	2023C ☆	Philadelphia	FV	25.00	125.	165.
2237	2023D	Cleveland	FV	15.00	35.00	42.00
2237☆	2023D ☆	Cleveland	FV	25.00	200.	300.
2238	2023E	Richmond	FV	15.00	40.00	42.00
2238☆	2023E ☆	Richmond	FV	25.00	60.00	65.00
2239	2023F	Atlanta	FV	15.00	35.00	42.00
2239☆	2023F ☆	Atlanta	FV	25.00	100.	125.
2240	2023G	Chicago	FV	15.00	35.00	42.00
2240☆	2023G ☆	Chicago	FV	20.00	55.00	65.00
2241	2023H	St. Louis	FV	15.00	35.00	42.00
2241☆	2023H ☆	St. Louis	FV	25.00	100.	125.
2242	2023I	Minneapolis	FV	15.00	35.00	45.00
2242☆	2023I ☆	Minneapolis	15.00	50.00	150.	200.
2243	2023J	Kansas City	FV	15.00	35.00	42.00
2243☆	2023J ☆	Kansas City	FV	25.00	60.00	65.00
2244	2023K	Dallas	FV	15.00	35.00	42.00
2244☆	2023K ☆	Dallas	FV	25.00	60.00	65.00
2245	2023L	San Francisco	FV	15.00	35.00	42.00
2245☆	2023L ☆	San Francisco	FV	25.00	120.	145.

Series 1977A Morton-Miller

KL#	Fr#	District	Fine	XF	CH CU (63)	Gem CU (65)
2246	2024A	Boston	FV	15.00	35.00	37.00
2246☆	2024A ☆	Boston	FV	20.00	100.	125.
2247	2024B	New York	FV	15.00	35.00	40.00
2247☆	2024B ☆	New York	FV	20.00	60.00	70.00
2248	2024C	Philadelphia	FV	15.00	35.00	40.00

KL#	Fr#	District	Fine	XF	CH CU (63)	Gem CU (65)
2249	2024D	Cleveland	FV	15.00	35.00	40.00
2249☆	2024D ☆	Cleveland	FV	20.00	70.00	85.00
2250	2024E	Richmond	FV	15.00	35.00	40.00
2250☆	2024E ☆	Richmond	FV	20.00	80.00	90.00
2251	2024F	Atlanta	FV	15.00	35.00	35.00
2251☆	2024F ☆	Atlanta	FV	20.00	150.	175.
2252	2024G	Chicago	FV	15.00	35.00	40.00
2252☆	2024G ☆	Chicago	FV	20.00	65.00	75.00
2253	2024H	St. Louis	FV	15.00	35.00	40.00
2253☆	2024H ☆	St. Louis	FV	20.00	125.	145.
2254	2024I	Minneapolis	FV	15.00	50.00	60.00
2254☆	2024I ☆	Minneapolis	FV	20.00	200.	240.
2255	2024J	Kansas City	FV	15.00	35.00	40.00
2255☆	2024J ☆	Kansas City	FV	20.00	90.00	115.
2256	2024K	Dallas	FV	15.00	35.00	40.00
2256☆	2024K ☆	Dallas	FV	20.00	60.00	80.00
2257	2024L	San Francisco	FV	15.00	35.00	40.00
2257☆	2024L ☆	San Francisco	FV	20.00	70.00	80.00

Series 1981 Buchanan-Regan

KL#	Fr#	District	Fine	XF	CH CU (63)	Gem CU (65)
3524	2025A	Boston	FV	20.00	40.00	42.00
3524☆	2025A ☆	Boston	15.00	30.00	100.	105.
3525	2025B	New York	FV	20.00	40.00	42.00
3525☆	2025B ☆	New York	15.00	50.00	125.	135.
3526	2025C	Philadelphia	FV	20.00	40.00	42.00
3526☆	2025C ☆	Philadelphia	15.00	50.00	125.	135.
3527	2025D	Cleveland	FV	20.00	40.00	42.00
3527☆	2025D ☆	Cleveland	15.00	50.00	120.	125.
3528	2025E	Richmond	FV	20.00	40.00	42.00
3528☆	2025E ☆	Richmond	15.00	50.00	100.	110.
3529	2025F	Atlanta	FV	20.00	40.00	42.00
3529☆	2025F ☆	Atlanta	15.00	50.00	225.	275.
3530	2025G	Chicago	FV	20.00	50.00	55.00
3530☆	2025G ☆	Chicago	15.00	50.00	100.	105.
3531	2025H	St. Louis	FV	20.00	50.00	55.00
3532	2025I	Minneapolis	FV	20.00	50.00	55.00
3532☆	2025I ☆	Minneapolis	15.00	50.00	150.	160.
3533	2025J	Kansas City	FV	20.00	50.00	55.00
3534	2025K	Dallas	FV	20.00	40.00	42.00
3535	2025L	San Francisco	FV	20.00	40.00	42.00
3535☆	2025L ☆	San Francisco	15.00	50.00	100.	105.

Series 1981A Ortega-Regan

KL#	Fr#	District	Fine	XF	CH CU (63)	Gem CU (65)
3624	2026A	Boston	FV	20.00	45.00	47.00
3625	2026B	New York	FV	20.00	45.00	47.00
3625☆	2026B ☆	New York	15.00	45.00	400.	500.
3626	2026C	Philadelphia	FV	20.00	45.00	47.00
3627	2026D	Cleveland	FV	20.00	45.00	47.00
3628	2026E	Richmond	FV	20.00	40.00	47.00
3628☆	2026E ☆	Richmond	15.00	45.00	100.	120.
3629	2026F	Atlanta	FV	20.00	40.00	47.00
3629☆	2026F ☆	Atlanta	15.00	45.00	100.	125.
3630	2026G	Chicago	FV	20.00	40.00	47.00
3631	2026H	St. Louis	FV	20.00	65.00	67.00
3632	2026I	Minneapolis	FV	20.00	40.00	47.00
3633	2026J	Kansas City	FV	20.00	40.00	47.00
3634	2026K	Dallas	FV	20.00	40.00	47.00
3635	2026L	San Francisco	FV	20.00	45.00	47.00

Series 1985 Ortega-Baker

KL#	Fr#	District	Fine	XF	CH CU (63)	Gem CU (65)
3724	2027A	Boston	FV	20.00	35.00	42.00
3724☆	2027A ☆	Boston	FV	35.00	60.00	75.00
3725	2027B	New York	FV	20.00	35.00	72.00
3725☆	2027B ☆	New York	FV	35.00	60.00	75.00
3726	2027C	Philadelphia	FV	20.00	35.00	42.00
3727	2027D	Cleveland	FV	20.00	35.00	42.00
3727☆	2027D ☆	Cleveland	FV	40.00	95.00	105.
3728	2027E	Richmond	FV	20.00	35.00	42.00
3729	2027F	Atlanta	FV	20.00	35.00	42.00
3729☆	2027F ☆	Atlanta	FV	45.00	150.	200.
3730	2027G	Chicago	FV	20.00	35.00	42.00
3731	2027H	St. Louis	FV	20.00	35.00	42.00
3731☆	2027H ☆	St. Louis	FV	30.00	70.00	75.00
3732	2027I	Minneapolis	FV	20.00	40.00	42.00
3733	2027J	Kansas City	FV	20.00	35.00	42.00

KL#	Fr#	District	Fine	XF	CH CU (63)	Gem CU (65)
3734	2027K	Dallas	FV	20.00	35.00	42.00
3734☆	2027K ☆	Dallas	FV	30.00	60.00	70.00
3735	2027L	San Francisco	FV	20.00	35.00	42.00
3735☆	2027L ☆	San Francisco	FV	30.00	80.00	85.00

Series 1988A Villalpando-Brady

KL#	Fr#	District	Fine	XF	CH CU (63)	Gem CU (65)
3868	2029A	Boston	FV	20.00	35.00	42.00
3868☆	2029A ☆	Boston	15.00	50.00	100.	105.
3869	2029B	New York	FV	20.00	35.00	42.00
3869☆	2029B ☆	New York	15.00	50.00	100.	105.
3870	2029C	Philadelphia	FV	20.00	35.00	42.00
3871	2029D	Cleveland	FV	20.00	35.00	42.00
3871☆	2029D ☆	Cleveland	15.00	50.00	100.	105.
3872	2029E	Richmond	FV	20.00	35.00	42.00
3873	2029F	Atlanta	FV	20.00	35.00	42.00
3874	2029G	Chicago	FV	20.00	35.00	42.00
3875	2029H	St. Louis	FV	20.00	35.00	42.00
3876	2029I	Minneapolis	FV	20.00	35.00	42.00
3877	2029J	Kansas City	FV	20.00	35.00	42.00
3878	2029K	Dallas	FV	20.00	35.00	42.00
3879	2029L	San Francisco	FV	20.00	35.00	42.00
3879☆	2029L ☆	San Francisco	15.00	50.00	100.	105.

Series 1990 Villalpando-Brady

KL#	Fr#	District	Fine	XF	CH CU (63)	Gem CU (65)
4000	2030A	Boston	FV	FV	20.00	27.00
4001	2030B	New York	FV	FV	20.00	27.00
4001☆	2030B ☆	New York	FV	15.00	60.00	67.00
4002	2030C	Philadelphia	FV	FV	20.00	27.00
4002☆	2030C ☆	Philadelphia	FV	15.00	50.00	55.00
4003	2030D	Cleveland	FV	FV	20.00	27.00
4004	2030E	Richmond	FV	FV	20.00	27.00
4005	2030F	Atlanta	FV	FV	20.00	27.00

KL#	Fr#	District	Fine	XF	CH CU (63)	Gem CU (65)
4006	2030G	Chicago	FV	FV	20.00	27.00
4006☆	2030G ☆	Chicago	FV	15.00	55.00	60.00
4007	2030H	St. Louis	FV	FV	20.00	27.00
4007☆	2030H ☆	St. Louis	FV	15.00	75.00	42.00
4008	2030I	Minneapolis	FV	FV	20.00	27.00
4009	2030J	Kansas City	FV	FV	20.00	27.00
4010	2030K	Dallas	FV	FV	20.00	27.00
4011	2030L	San Francisco	FV	FV	20.00	27.00

Series 1993 Withrow-Bentsen

KL#	Fr#	District	Fine	XF	CH CU (63)	Gem CU (65)
4036	2031A	Boston	FV	FV	20.00	22.00
4037	2031B	New York	FV	FV	20.00	22.00
4037☆	2031B ☆	New York	FV	25.00	55.00	52.00
4038	2031C	Philadelphia	FV	FV	20.00	22.00
4038☆	2031C ☆	Philadelphia	FV	25.00	60.00	52.00
4039	2031D	Cleveland	FV	FV	20.00	22.00
4041	2031F	Atlanta	FV	FV	20.00	22.00
4042	2031G	Chicago	FV	FV	20.00	260.
4042☆	2031G ☆	Chicago	FV	25.00	65.00	52.00
4043	2031H	St. Louis	FV	FV	20.00	22.00
4045	2031J	Kansas City	FV	FV	20.00	22.00
4047	2031L	San Francisco	FV	FV	20.00	22.00

Series 1995 Withrow-Rubin

KL#	Fr#	District	Fine	XF	CH CU (63)	Gem CU (65)
4108	2032A	Boston	FV	FV	25.00	27.00
4109	2032B	New York	FV	FV	25.00	27.00
4109☆	2032B ☆	New York	FV	25.00	50.00	52.00
4110	2032C	Philadelphia	FV	FV	25.00	27.00
4111	2032D	Cleveland	FV	FV	25.00	27.00
4111☆	2032D ☆	Cleveland	FV	25.00	50.00	52.00
4112	2032E	Richmond	FV	FV	20.00	22.00

KL#	Fr#	District	Fine	XF	CH CU (63)	Gem CU (65)
4112☆	2032E ☆	Richmond	FV	25.00	60.00	65.00
4113	2032F	Atlanta	FV	FV	20.00	22.00
4113☆	2032F ☆	Atlanta	FV	25.00	75.00	65.00
4114	2032G	Chicago	FV	FV	20.00	22.00
4114☆	2032G ☆	Chicago	FV	25.00	40.00	52.00
4115	2032H	St. Louis	FV	FV	35.00	22.00
4115☆	2032H ☆	St. Louis	FV	25.00	45.00	42.00
4116	2032I	Minneapolis	FV	FV	20.00	22.00
4117	2032J	Kansas City	FV	FV	20.00	22.00
4118	2032K	Dallas	FV	FV	20.00	22.00
4119	2032L	San Francisco	FV	FV	20.00	22.00
4119☆	2032L ☆	San Francisco	FV	20.00	50.00	42.00

Series 1999 Withrow-Summers - DC

KL#	Fr#	District	Fine	XF	CH CU (63)	Gem CU (65)
4530	2033A	Boston	FV	FV	20.00	22.00
4531	2033B	New York	FV	FV	20.00	22.00
4532	2033C	Philadelphia	FV	FV	20.00	22.00
4532☆	2033C ☆	Philadelphia	FV	FV	45.00	47.00
4533	2033D	Cleveland	FV	FV	25.00	27.00
4533☆	2033D ☆	Cleveland	FV	FV	45.00	47.00
4534	2033E	Richmond	FV	FV	25.00	27.00
4534☆	2033E ☆	Richmond	FV	FV	45.00	47.00
4535	2033F	Atlanta	FV	FV	25.00	27.00
4536	2033G	Chicago	FV	FV	25.00	27.00
4537	2033H	St. Louis	FV	FV	25.00	27.00
4538	2033I	Minneapolis	FV	FV	100.	125.
4539	2033J	Kansas City	FV	FV	25.00	27.00
4540	2033K	Dallas	FV	FV	25.00	27.00
4541	2033L	San Francisco	FV	FV	25.00	27.00

Series 1999 Withrow-Summers - FW

KL#	Fr#	District	Fine	XF	CH CU (63)	Gem CU (65)
4542☆	2034A ☆	Boston	FV	FV	45.00	47.00
4543☆	2034B ☆	New York	FV	FV	100.	125.
4544	2034F	Atlanta	FV	FV	20.00	22.00
4544☆	2034F ☆	Atlanta	FV	FV	30.00	32.00
4545	2034G	Chicago	FV	FV	20.00	22.00
4546	2034J	Kansas City	FV	FV	20.00	22.00
4547	2034K	Dallas	FV	FV	20.00	22.00
4547☆	2034K ☆	Dallas	FV	FV	30.00	32.00
4548	2034L	San Francisco	FV	FV	20.00	22.00

Series 2001 Marin-O'Neill - DC

KL#	Fr#	District	Fine	XF	CH CU (63)	Gem CU (65)
4599	2035A	Boston	FV	FV	20.00	22.00
4600	2035B	New York	FV	FV	20.00	22.00
4600☆	2035B ☆	New York	FV	40.00	110.	115.
4601	2035C	Philadelphia	FV	FV	20.00	22.00
4602	2035D	Cleveland	FV	FV	20.00	22.00
4602☆	2035D ☆	Cleveland	FV	FV	35.00	37.00
4603	2035E	Richmond	FV	FV	20.00	22.00
4604	2035F	Atlanta	FV	FV	20.00	22.00
4605☆	2035G ☆	Chicago	FV	FV	35.00	37.00
4606	2035H	St. Louis	FV	FV	20.00	22.00
4607	2035I	Minneapolis	FV	FV	20.00	22.00

A Word About Star Notes

In our listings there are often two entries for each catalog number.
For example:

KL#	Fr#	District	Fine	XF	CH CU (63)	Gem CU (65)
1501	1903A	Boston	FV	2.00	7.00	8.00
1501☆	1903A☆	Boston	FV	5.00	10.00	12.00

The first listing has a serial number format of letter - eight digits - letter.

The second listing refers to a bank note with a serial number format of
letter - eight digits - star.

This star at the end of the serial number refers to a replacement note,
one which replaces a note damaged during the production process.
There are fewer of these printed and therefore they are more expensive.

Series 2001 Marin-O'Neill - FW

KL#	Fr#	District	Fine	XF	CH CU (63)	Gem CU (65)
4608	2036A	Boston	FV	FV	20.00	22.00
4609	2036B	New York	FV	FV	20.00	22.00
4610	2036E	Richmond	FV	FV	20.00	22.00
4611	2036F	Atlanta	FV	FV	20.00	22.00
4612	2036G	Chicago	FV	FV	20.00	22.00
4613	2036H	St. Louis	FV	FV	20.00	22.00
4614	2036I	Minneapolis	FV	FV	20.00	22.00
4615	2036K	Dallas	FV	FV	25.00	27.00
4615☆	2036K ☆	Dallas	FV	FV	35.00	37.00
4616	2036L	San Francisco	FV	FV	20.00	22.00

Series 2003 Marin-Snow - DC

KL#	Fr#	District	Fine	XF	CH CU (63)	Gem CU (65)
4700	2037A	Boston	FV	FV	15.00	17.00
4701	2037B	New York	FV	FV	15.00	17.00
4702	2037C	Philadelphia	FV	FV	15.00	17.00
4703	2037D	Cleveland	FV	FV	15.00	17.00
4703☆	2037D ☆	Cleveland	FV	FV	35.00	37.00
4704	2037E	Richmond	FV	FV	15.00	17.00
4705	2037F	Atlanta	FV	FV	15.00	17.00
4706	2037G	Chicago	FV	FV	15.00	17.00
4707	2037H	St. Louis	FV	FV	15.00	17.00
4707☆	2037H ☆	St. Louis	FV	FV	100.	125.
4708	2037I	Minneapolis	FV	FV	15.00	17.00
4709	2037J	Kansas City	FV	FV	15.00	17.00
4710	2037K	Dallas	FV	FV	15.00	17.00
4711	2037L	San Francisco	FV	FV	15.00	17.00

Series 2003 Marin-Snow - FW

KL#	Fr#	District	Fine	XF	CH CU (63)	Gem CU (65)
4712	-	Boston	FV	FV	15.00	17.00
4713	-	New York	FV	FV	15.00	17.00
4714	-	Philadelphia	FV	FV	15.00	17.00
4715	-	Cleveland	FV	FV	15.00	17.00
4716	-	Richmond	FV	FV	15.00	17.00
4717	-	Atlanta	FV	FV	15.00	17.00
4718	-	Chicago	FV	FV	15.00	17.00
4719	-	Minneapolis	FV	FV	15.00	17.00

Series 2004A Cabral-Snow - FW

KL#	Fr#	District	Fine	XF	CH CU (63)	Gem CU (65)
4770	-	Boston	FV	FV	13.00	15.00
4770☆	-	Boston	FV	FV	35.00	45.00
4771	-	New York	FV	FV	15.00	17.00
4771☆	-	New York	FV	FV	35.00	75.00
4772	-	Philadelphia	FV	FV	15.00	17.00
4773	-	Cleveland	FV	FV	15.00	17.00
4774	-	Richmond	FV	FV	15.00	17.00
4775	-	Atlanta	FV	FV	15.00	17.00
4775☆	-	Atlanta	FV	FV	30.00	45.00
4776	-	Chicago	FV	FV	15.00	75.00
4776☆	-	Chicago	FV	FV	100.	175.
4777	-	St. Louis	FV	FV	15.00	17.00
4778	-	Minneapolis	FV	FV	15.00	17.00
4779	-	Kansas City	FV	FV	15.00	17.00
4780	-	Dallas	FV	FV	15.00	17.00
4781	-	San Francisco	FV	FV	15.00	20.00
4781☆	-	San Francisco	FV	FV	35.00	55.00

Series 2006 Cabral-Paulson - FW

KL#	Fr#	District	Fine	XF	CH CU (63)	Gem CU (65)
4885	-	Boston	FV	FV	15.00	20.00
4886	-	New York	FV	FV	15.00	20.00
4886☆	-	New York	FV	FV	30.00	35.00
4887	-	Philadelphia	FV	FV	15.00	20.00
4887☆	-	Philadelphia	FV	FV	35.00	37.00
4888	-	Cleveland	FV	FV	15.00	20.00
4890	-	Atlanta	FV	FV	15.00	20.00
4891	-	Chicago	FV	FV	15.00	20.00
4891☆	-	Chicago	FV	FV	30.00	35.00
4892	-	St. Louis	FV	FV	15.00	20.00
4893	-	Minneapolis	FV	FV	15.00	20.00
4894	-	Kansas City	FV	FV	15.00	20.00
4895	-	Dallas	FV	FV	15.00	20.00
4896	-	San Francisco	FV	FV	15.00	20.00

Series 2009 Rios-Geithner - FW

KL#	Fr#	District	Fine	XF	CH CU (63)	Gem CU (65)
4935	-	Boston	FV	FV	15.00	20.00
4936	-	New York	FV	FV	15.00	20.00
4936☆	-	New York	FV	FV	35.00	37.00
4937	-	Philadelphia	FV	FV	15.00	20.00
4938	-	Cleveland	FV	FV	15.00	20.00
4938☆	-	Cleveland	FV	FV	35.00	37.00
4939	-	Richmond	FV	FV	15.00	20.00
4940	-	Atlanta	FV	FV	15.00	20.00
4941	-	Chicago	FV	FV	15.00	20.00
4942	-	St. Louis	FV	FV	15.00	20.00
4943	-	Minneapolis	FV	FV	15.00	20.00
4944	-	Kansas City	FV	FV	15.00	20.00
4945	-	Dallas	FV	FV	15.00	20.00
4946	-	San Francisco	FV	FV	15.00	20.00

Federal Reserve Notes - Hawaii Emergency

KL#	Fr#	Series	Signatures	Fine	XF	CH CU (63)	Gem CU (65)
2258	2303	1934A	Julian-Morgenthau	100.	250.	600.	1400.

Silver Certificates - North Africa Emergency

KL#	Fr#	Series	Signatures	Fine	XF	CH CU (63)	Gem CU (65)
2259	2308	1934	Julian-Morgenthau	3200.	9000.	17,500.	27,500.
2259☆	2308	1934☆	Julian-Morgenthau	—	—	—	—
2260	2309	1934A	Julian-Morgenthau	60.00	150.	325.	500.
2260☆	2309	1934A☆	Julian-Morgenthau	275.	475.	1200.	4600.

Gold Certificates
Twenty Dollars

KL#	Fr#	Series	Signatures	VF	XF	CH CU (63)	Gem CU (65)
2261	2402	1928	Woods-Mellon	155.	250.	800.	1600.
2261☆	2402	1928☆	Woods-Mellon	500.	1250.	9000.	14,000.

Federal Reserve Bank Notes

KL#	Fr#	Series	District	Fine	XF	CH CU (63)	Gem CU (65)
2262	1870A	1929	Boston	30.00	75.00	300.	525.
2262☆	1870A	1929☆	Boston	1250.	2500.	—	—
2263	1870B	1929	New York	35.00	50.00	165.	325.
2263☆	1870B	1929☆	New York	250.	600.	—	—
2264	1870C	1929	Philadelphia	35.00	110.	275.	375.

KL#	Fr#	Series	District	Fine	XF	CH CU (63)	Gem CU (65)
2264☆	1870C	1929☆	Philadelphia	125.	650.	—	—
2265	1870D	1929	Cleveland	30.00	70.00	350.	690.
2265☆	1870D	1929☆	Cleveland	3700.	4500.	—	—
2266	1870E	1929	Richmond	30.00	175.	500.	800.
2266☆	1870E	1929☆	Richmond	300.	900.	3500.	6000.
2267	1870F	1929	Atlanta	35.00	150.	375.	800.
2267☆	1870F	1929☆	Atlanta	1250.	3500.	—	—
2268	1870G	1929	Chicago	30.00	60.00	170.	225.
2268☆	1870G	1929☆	Chicago	775.	2500.	—	—
2269	1870H	1929	St. Louis	30.00	100.	150.	275.
2269☆	1870H	1929☆	St. Louis	270.	800.	3000.	5000.
2270	1870I	1929	Minneapolis	30.00	100.	275.	400.
2270☆	1870I	1929☆	Minneapolis	475.	1500.	5000.	8200.
2271	1870J	1929	Kansas City	35.00	50.00	450.	800.
2271☆	1870J	1929☆	Kansas City	750.	900.	1750.	2900.
2272	1870K	1929	Dallas	175.	650.	3500.	10,000.
2272☆	1870K	1929☆	Dallas	5000.	10,000.	—	—
2273	1870L	1929	San Francisco	100.	135.	425.	4500.
2273☆	1870L	1929☆	San Francisco	1850.	3000.	—	—

Federal Reserve Notes

Series 1928 Tate-Mellon

KL#	Fr#	District	Fine	XF	CH CU (63)	Gem CU (65)
2274	2050A	Boston	175.	500.	2500.	4000.
2274☆	2050A ☆	Boston	100.	1000.	5000.	—
2275	2050B	New York	50.00	100.	300.	400.
2275☆	2050B ☆	New York	75.00	400.	2000.	—
2276	2050C	Philadelphia	70.00	150.	500.	1000.
2276☆	2050C ☆	Philadelphia	150.	400.	2000.	—
2277	2050D	Cleveland	50.00	125.	200.	300.
2277☆	2050D ☆	Cleveland	150.	275.	1000.	3200.
2278	2050E	Richmond	50.00	85.00	250.	500.

KL#	Fr#	District	Fine	XF	CH CU (63)	Gem CU (65)
2278☆	2050E ☆	Richmond	175.	800.	3000.	—
2279	2050F	Atlanta	55.00	100.	275.	425.
2279☆	2050F ☆	Atlanta	175.	900.	3000.	4500.
2280	2050G	Chicago	35.00	95.00	225.	300.
2280☆	2050G ☆	Chicago	100.	500.	2000.	2500.
2281	2050H	St. Louis	40.00	75.00	250.	400.
2281☆	2050H ☆	St. Louis	100.	720.	2500.	2950.
2282	2050I	Minneapolis	40.00	125.	250.	525.
2282☆	2050I ☆	Minneapolis	200.	600.	2750.	5300.
2283	2050J	Kansas City	40.00	75.00	225.	300.
2283☆	2050J ☆	Kansas City	100.	600.	2000.	8050.
2284	2050K	Dallas	55.00	150.	1500.	2500.
2284☆	2050K ☆	Dallas	1000.	3000.	6500.	—
2285	2050L	San Francisco	40.00	75.00	350.	400.
2285☆	2050L ☆	San Francisco	100.	600.	4400.	—

Series 1928A Woods-Mellon

KL#	Fr#	District	Fine	XF	CH CU (63)	Gem CU (65)
2286	2051A	Boston	60.00	250.	500.	1500.
2286☆	2051A ☆	Boston	600.	1200.	4000.	7000.
2287	2051B	New York	60.00	200.	600.	2300.
2287☆	2051B ☆	New York	600.	3000.	5000.	7000.
2288	2051C	Philadelphia	60.00	150.	400.	500.
2288☆	2051C ☆	Philadelphia	1750.	3000.	5000.	8000.
2289	2051D	Cleveland	60.00	150.	450.	800.
2289☆	2051D ☆	Cleveland	600.	3000.	5000.	7000.
2290	2051E	Richmond	60.00	150.	500.	700.
2290☆	2051E ☆	Richmond	600.	2750.	5250.	—
2291	2051F	Atlanta	75.00	150.	400.	650.
2291☆	2051F ☆	Atlanta	—	—	—	—
2292	2051G	Chicago	60.00	100.	400.	1500.
2292☆	2051G ☆	Chicago	—	—	—	—
2293	2051H	St. Louis	75.00	175.	350.	800.
2293☆	2051H ☆	St. Louis	600.	1200.	4000.	7000.
2294	2051J	Kansas City	75.00	200.	325.	700.
2294☆	2051J ☆	Kansas City	600.	1200.	4000.	9000.
2295	2051K	Dallas	60.00	200.	450.	500.
2295☆	2051K ☆	Dallas	600.	1200.	4000.	8000.

Series 1928B Woods-Mellon

KL#	Fr#	District	Fine	XF	CH CU (63)	Gem CU (65)
2296	2052A	Boston	30.00	50.00	150.	250.
2296☆	2052A ☆	Boston	140.	600.	1200.	2250.
2297	2052B	New York	30.00	50.00	175.	250.
2297☆	2052B ☆	New York	140.	300.	1000.	1600.
2298	2052C	Philadelphia	30.00	50.00	125.	350.
2298☆	2052C ☆	Philadelphia	140.	300.	1500.	3000.
2299	2052D	Cleveland	30.00	50.00	150.	300.
2299☆	2052D ☆	Cleveland	140.	300.	1500.	3000.
2300	2052E	Richmond	30.00	50.00	240.	500.
2300☆	2052E ☆	Richmond	140.	350.	1500.	3500.
2301	2052F	Atlanta	60.00	750.	1500.	2000.
2301☆	2052F ☆	Atlanta	140.	350.	1500.	3500.
2302	2052G	Chicago	30.00	60.00	100.	125.
2302☆	2052G ☆	Chicago	140.	350.	1000.	2100.
2303	2052H	St. Louis	30.00	50.00	75.00	200.
2303☆	2052H ☆	St. Louis	140.	350.	1500.	3000.
2304	2052I	Minneapolis	30.00	60.00	375.	500.
2304☆	2052I ☆	Minneapolis	140.	750.	2000.	4500.
2305	2052J	Kansas City	30.00	50.00	125.	250.
2305☆	2052J ☆	Kansas City	140.	750.	1500.	3000.
2306	2052K	Dallas	30.00	60.00	200.	400.
2306☆	2052K ☆	Dallas	140.	750.	1500.	3500.
2307	2052L	San Francisco	30.00	50.00	170.	350.
2307☆	2052L ☆	San Francisco	140.	600.	1500.	3500.

Series 1928C Woods-Mills

KL#	Fr#	District	Fine	XF	CH CU (63)	Gem CU (65)
2308	2053G	Chicago	225.	600.	2250.	4100.
2309	2053L	San Francisco	200.	900.	5000.	6000.

Series 1934 Julian-Morgenthau

KL#	Fr#	District	Fine	XF	CH CU (63)	Gem CU (65)
2310	2054A	Boston	25.00	40.00	100.	125.
2310☆	2054A ☆	Boston	50.00	100.	500.	750.
2311	2054B	New York	25.00	40.00	75.00	105.
2311☆	2054B ☆	New York	50.00	100.	500.	1000.
2312	2054C	Philadelphia	25.00	40.00	85.00	100.
2312☆	2054C ☆	Philadelphia	50.00	100.	500.	1000.
2313	2054D	Cleveland	25.00	40.00	85.00	100.
2313☆	2054D ☆	Cleveland	50.00	125.	500.	1000.
2314	2054E	Richmond	25.00	40.00	85.00	185.
2314☆	2054E ☆	Richmond	70.00	150.	500.	1000.
2315	2054F	Atlanta	25.00	40.00	70.00	100.
2315☆	2054F ☆	Atlanta	70.00	150.	500.	1000.
2316	2054G	Chicago	25.00	40.00	85.00	100.
2316☆	2054G ☆	Chicago	50.00	100.	500.	1000.
2317	2054H	St. Louis	25.00	40.00	85.00	100.
2317☆	2054H ☆	St. Louis	50.00	100.	500.	1000.
2318	2054I	Minneapolis	25.00	40.00	85.00	100.
2318☆	2054I ☆	Minneapolis	100.	275.	1250.	2000.
2319	2054J	Kansas City	25.00	40.00	85.00	100.
2319☆	2054J ☆	Kansas City	50.00	100.	500.	1000.
2320	2054K	Dallas	25.00	40.00	85.00	200.
2320☆	2054K ☆	Dallas	70.00	180.	650.	1000.
2321	2054L	San Francisco	25.00	40.00	85.00	100.
2321☆	2054L ☆	San Francisco	70.00	150.	500.	1000.

Series 1934A Julian-Morgenthau

KL#	Fr#	District	Fine	XF	CH CU (63)	Gem CU (65)
2322	2055A	Boston	25.00	40.00	75.00	135.
2322☆	2055A ☆	Boston	70.00	125.	500.	875.
2323	2055B	New York	20.00	30.00	60.00	300.
2323☆	2055B ☆	New York	40.00	75.00	250.	875.

KL#	Fr#	District	Fine	XF	CH CU (63)	Gem CU (65)
2324	2055C	Philadelphia	22.00	30.00	75.00	135.
2324☆	2055C ☆	Philadelphia	55.00	90.00	500.	875.
2325	2055D	Cleveland	22.00	30.00	75.00	135.
2325☆	2055D ☆	Cleveland	55.00	90.00	500.	750.
2326	2055E	Richmond	22.00	30.00	75.00	160.
2326☆	2055E ☆	Richmond	50.00	90.00	500.	875.
2327	2055F	Atlanta	25.00	35.00	75.00	135.
2327☆	2055F ☆	Atlanta	50.00	85.00	500.	875.
2328	2055G	Chicago	22.00	30.00	70.00	135.
2328☆	2055G ☆	Chicago	55.00	300.	500.	875.
2329	2055H	St. Louis	25.00	35.00	75.00	135.
2329☆	2055H ☆	St. Louis	55.00	90.00	500.	875.
2330	2055I	Minneapolis	25.00	45.00	100.	200.
2330☆	2055I ☆	Minneapolis	70.00	125.	550.	1000.
2331	2055J	Kansas City	25.00	35.00	75.00	135.
2331☆	2055J ☆	Kansas City	55.00	90.00	500.	875.
2332	2055K	Dallas	25.00	35.00	75.00	135.
2332☆	2055K ☆	Dallas	70.00	125.	500.	1000.
2333	2055L	San Francisco	22.00	50.00	300.	600.
2333☆	2055L ☆	San Francisco	40.00	80.00	500.	900.

Series 1934B Julian-Vinson

KL#	Fr#	District	Fine	XF	CH CU (63)	Gem CU (65)
2334	2056A	Boston	25.00	35.00	100.	185.
2334☆	2056A ☆	Boston	75.00	200.	900.	1550.
2335	2056B	New York	22.00	32.00	100.	185.
2335☆	2056B ☆	New York	65.00	135.	750.	1250.
2336	2056C	Philadelphia	25.00	35.00	125.	185.
2336☆	2056C ☆	Philadelphia	80.00	150.	750.	1400.
2337	2056D	Cleveland	25.00	50.00	100.	185.
2337☆	2056D ☆	Cleveland	75.00	200.	500.	1000.
2338	2056E	Richmond	25.00	32.00	100.	185.
2338☆	2056E ☆	Richmond	80.00	150.	750.	1400.
2339	2056F	Atlanta	25.00	35.00	85.00	185.
2339☆	2056F ☆	Atlanta	80.00	150.	700.	1550.
2340	2056G	Chicago	25.00	32.00	100.	150.
2340☆	2056G ☆	Chicago	65.00	175.	750.	1250.
2341	2056H	St. Louis	25.00	35.00	100.	185.
2341☆	2056H ☆	St. Louis	80.00	150.	750.	1400.
2342	2056I	Minneapolis	25.00	40.00	100.	185.
2342☆	2056I ☆	Minneapolis	75.00	200.	750.	1550.
2343	2056J	Kansas City	25.00	35.00	100.	185.
2343☆	2056J ☆	Kansas City	75.00	200.	700.	1550.
2344	2056K	Dallas	25.00	40.00	100.	185.
2344☆	2056K ☆	Dallas	75.00	200.	900.	2000.
2345	2056L	San Francisco	25.00	40.00	100.	185.
2345☆	2056L ☆	San Francisco	75.00	200.	900.	1550.

Series 1934C Julian-Snyder

KL#	Fr#	District	Fine	XF	CH CU (63)	Gem CU (65)
2346	2057A	Boston	25.00	40.00	100.	135.
2346☆	2057A ☆	Boston	65.00	150.	375.	400.
2347	2057B	New York	25.00	35.00	70.00	135.
2347☆	2057B ☆	New York	85.00	150.	800.	1000.
2348	2057C	Philadelphia	25.00	40.00	90.00	100.
2348☆	2057C ☆	Philadelphia	55.00	150.	600.	1000.
2349	2057D	Cleveland	25.00	40.00	100.	150.
2349☆	2057D ☆	Cleveland	85.00	125.	475.	850.
2350	2057E	Richmond	30.00	40.00	100.	125.
2350☆	2057E ☆	Richmond	85.00	125.	650.	1000.
2351	2057F	Atlanta	25.00	40.00	100.	135.
2351☆	2057F ☆	Atlanta	55.00	150.	800.	1250.
2352	2057G	Chicago	25.00	40.00	100.	135.
2352☆	2057G ☆	Chicago	55.00	120.	400.	1000.
2353	2057II	St. Louis	25.00	40.00	100.	135.
2353☆	2057H ☆	St. Louis	80.00	150.	650.	1000.
2354	2057I	Minneapolis	25.00	45.00	100.	135.
2354☆	2057I ☆	Minneapolis	100.	250.	600.	1250.
2355	2057J	Kansas City	25.00	40.00	100.	135.
2355☆	2057J ☆	Kansas City	100.	200.	600.	1000.
2356	2057K	Dallas	25.00	40.00	100.	135.
2356☆	2057K ☆	Dallas	100.	275.	600.	1000.
2357	2057L	San Francisco	25.00	40.00	100.	135.
2357☆	2057L ☆	San Francisco	100.	125.	525.	1000.

Series 1934D Clark-Snyder

KL#	Fr#	District	Fine	XF	CH CU (63)	Gem CU (65)
2358	2058A	Boston	FV	30.00	75.00	150.
2358☆	2058A ☆	Boston	125.	400.	1350.	1375.
2359	2058B	New York	FV	30.00	75.00	150.
2359☆	2058B ☆	New York	80.00	150.	650.	1000.

KL#	Fr#	District	Fine	XF	CH CU (63)	Gem CU (65)
2360	2058C	Philadelphia	FV	30.00	95.00	125.
2360☆	2058C ☆	Philadelphia	80.00	100.	800.	1000.
2361	2058D	Cleveland	FV	30.00	95.00	175.
2361☆	2058D ☆	Cleveland	100.	450.	1100.	2200.
2362	2058E	Richmond	FV	30.00	95.00	150.
2362☆	2058E ☆	Richmond	75.00	200.	1000.	1375.
2363	2058F	Atlanta	FV	30.00	95.00	150.
2363☆	2058F ☆	Atlanta	75.00	200.	1100.	1500.
2364	2058G	Chicago	FV	25.00	75.00	150.
2364☆	2058G ☆	Chicago	75.00	200.	750.	1000.
2365	2058H	St. Louis	FV	25.00	95.00	150.
2365☆	2058H ☆	St. Louis	75.00	200.	1000.	1350.
2366	2058I	Minneapolis	FV	40.00	120.	150.
2366☆	2058I ☆	Minneapolis	75.00	200.	750.	1250.
2367	2058J	Kansas City	FV	30.00	95.00	150.
2367☆	2058J ☆	Kansas City	75.00	200.	750.	1000.
2368	2058K	Dallas	FV	35.00	95.00	150.
2368☆	2058K ☆	Dallas	75.00	200.	750.	1250.
2369	2058L	San Francisco	FV	35.00	95.00	150.
2369☆	2058L ☆	San Francisco	75.00	200.	1300.	1550.

Series 1950 Clark-Snyder

KL#	Fr#	District	Fine	XF	CH CU (63)	Gem CU (65)
2370	2059A	Boston	FV	35.00	70.00	90.00
2370☆	2059A ☆	Boston	40.00	250.	450.	625.
2371	2059B	New York	FV	35.00	70.00	90.00
2371☆	2059B ☆	New York	40.00	250.	400.	625.
2372	2059C	Philadelphia	FV	35.00	70.00	90.00
2372☆	2059C ☆	Philadelphia	40.00	250.	400.	625.
2373	2059D	Cleveland	FV	35.00	50.00	90.00
2373☆	2059D ☆	Cleveland	40.00	250.	450.	625.
2374	2059E	Richmond	FV	35.00	70.00	90.00
2374☆	2059E ☆	Richmond	40.00	250.	450.	625.
2375	2059F	Atlanta	FV	35.00	70.00	90.00
2375☆	2059F ☆	Atlanta	45.00	250.	700.	625.
2376	2059G	Chicago	FV	35.00	50.00	90.00
2376☆	2059G ☆	Chicago	40.00	200.	275.	300.
2377	2059H	St. Louis	FV	35.00	70.00	90.00
2377☆	2059H ☆	St. Louis	40.00	250.	550.	625.
2378	2059I	Minneapolis	FV	35.00	70.00	90.00
2378☆	2059I ☆	Minneapolis	40.00	300.	600.	650.
2379	2059J	Kansas City	FV	35.00	70.00	90.00
2379☆	2059J ☆	Kansas City	40.00	250.	550.	625.
2380	2059K	Dallas	FV	35.00	90.00	110.
2380☆	2059K ☆	Dallas	40.00	300.	700.	750.
2381	2059L	San Francisco	FV	35.00	65.00	90.00
2381☆	2059L ☆	San Francisco	40.00	250.	450.	625.

Series 1950A Priest-Humphrey

KL#	Fr#	District	Fine	XF	CH CU (63)	Gem CU (65)
2382	2060A	Boston	FV	30.00	75.00	85.00
2382☆	2060A ☆	Boston	75.00	150.	250.	375.
2383	2060B	New York	FV	30.00	50.00	75.00
2383☆	2060B ☆	New York	75.00	150.	200.	375.
2384	2060C	Philadelphia	FV	30.00	70.00	85.00
2384☆	2060C ☆	Philadelphia	75.00	150.	250.	375.
2385	2060D	Cleveland	FV	30.00	70.00	75.00
2385☆	2060D ☆	Cleveland	75.00	150.	150.	375.
2386	2060E	Richmond	FV	30.00	70.00	85.00
2386☆	2060E ☆	Richmond	75.00	150.	250.	375.
2387	2060F	Atlanta	FV	30.00	70.00	85.00
2387☆	2060F ☆	Atlanta	70.00	100.	250.	375.
2388	2060G	Chicago	FV	30.00	80.00	90.00
2388☆	2060G ☆	Chicago	75.00	150.	250.	375.
2389	2060H	St. Louis	FV	30.00	70.00	75.00
2389☆	2060H ☆	St. Louis	75.00	150.	250.	375.
2390	2060I	Minneapolis	FV	30.00	70.00	85.00
2390☆	2060I ☆	Minneapolis	75.00	175.	300.	425.
2391	2060J	Kansas City	FV	30.00	70.00	75.00
2391☆	2060J ☆	Kansas City	75.00	160.	275.	400.
2392	2060K	Dallas	FV	30.00	70.00	85.00
2392☆	2060K ☆	Dallas	75.00	160.	275.	400.
2393	2060L	San Francisco	FV	30.00	70.00	75.00
2393☆	2060L ☆	San Francisco	75.00	160.	275.	400.

Series 1950B Priest-Anderson

KL#	Fr#	District	Fine	XF	CH CU (63)	Gem CU (65)
2394	2061A	Boston	FV	30.00	60.00	75.00
2394☆	2061A ☆	Boston	50.00	175.	500.	550.
2395	2061B	New York	FV	30.00	50.00	75.00
2395☆	2061B ☆	New York	35.00	125.	250.	476.
2396	2061C	Philadelphia	FV	30.00	60.00	75.00

KL#	Fr#	District	Fine	XF	CH CU (63)	Gem CU (65)
2396☆	2061C ☆	Philadelphia	35.00	175.	375.	425.
2397	2061D	Cleveland	FV	30.00	60.00	75.00
2397☆	2061D ☆	Cleveland	35.00	150.	225.	375.
2398	2061E	Richmond	FV	30.00	60.00	75.00
2398☆	2061E ☆	Richmond	35.00	175.	350.	425.
2399	2061F	Atlanta	FV	30.00	60.00	75.00
2399☆	2061F ☆	Atlanta	35.00	175.	350.	425.
2400	2061G	Chicago	FV	30.00	50.00	75.00
2400☆	2061G ☆	Chicago	35.00	150.	225.	250.
2401	2061H	St. Louis	FV	30.00	60.00	75.00
2401☆	2061H ☆	St. Louis	35.00	150.	300.	375.
2402	2061I	Minneapolis	FV	30.00	60.00	75.00
2402☆	2061I ☆	Minneapolis	35.00	150.	200.	375.
2403	2061J	Kansas City	FV	30.00	60.00	75.00
2403☆	2061J ☆	Kansas City	35.00	175.	225.	250.
2404	2061K	Dallas	FV	30.00	60.00	75.00
2404☆	2061K ☆	Dallas	35.00	175.	350.	425.
2405	2061L	San Francisco	FV	30.00	60.00	75.00
2405☆	2061L ☆	San Francisco	35.00	175.	350.	435.

Series 1950C Smith-Dillon

KL#	Fr#	District	Fine	XF	CH CU (63)	Gem CU (65)
2406	2062A	Boston	FV	35.00	50.00	90.00
2406☆	2062A ☆	Boston	30.00	125.	350.	500.
2407	2062B	New York	FV	35.00	50.00	80.00
2407☆	2062B ☆	New York	30.00	125.	300.	650.
2408	2062C	Philadelphia	FV	35.00	50.00	90.00
2408☆	2062C ☆	Philadelphia	30.00	125.	350.	500.
2409	2062D	Cleveland	FV	35.00	70.00	80.00
2409☆	2062D ☆	Cleveland	30.00	125.	300.	500.
2410	2062E	Richmond	FV	35.00	70.00	80.00
2410☆	2062E ☆	Richmond	30.00	125.	350.	500.
2411	2062F	Atlanta	FV	35.00	70.00	80.00
2411☆	2062F ☆	Atlanta	30.00	125.	350.	500.
2412	2062G	Chicago	FV	35.00	70.00	80.00
2412☆	2062G ☆	Chicago	30.00	125.	250.	450.
2413	2062H	St. Louis	FV	35.00	60.00	80.00
2413☆	2062H ☆	St. Louis	30.00	125.	300.	500.
2414	2062I	Minneapolis	FV	35.00	60.00	80.00
2414☆	2062I ☆	Minneapolis	30.00	125.	300.	450.
2415	2062J	Kansas City	FV	35.00	50.00	80.00
2415☆	2062J ☆	Kansas City	30.00	125.	350.	450.
2416	2062K	Dallas	FV	40.00	60.00	90.00
2416☆	2062K ☆	Dallas	75.00	125.	425.	750.
2417	2062L	San Francisco	FV	35.00	60.00	80.00
2417☆	2062L ☆	San Francisco	30.00	125.	400.	500.

Series 1950D Granahan-Dillon

KL#	Fr#	District	Fine	XF	CH CU (63)	Gem CU (65)
2418	2063A	Boston	FV	35.00	425.	500.
2418☆	2063A ☆	Boston	35.00	140.	225.	325.
2419	2063B	New York	FV	35.00	75.00	90.00
2419☆	2063B ☆	New York	45.00	140.	175.	400.
2419A	2063C	Philadelphia	FV	35.00	75.00	90.00
2419A☆	2063C ☆	Philadelphia	65.00	125.	200.	300.
2420	2063D	Cleveland	FV	35.00	75.00	90.00
2420☆	2063D ☆	Cleveland	65.00	125.	200.	300.
2421	2063E	Richmond	FV	35.00	75.00	90.00
2421☆	2063E ☆	Richmond	45.00	140.	225.	325.
2422	2063F	Atlanta	FV	35.00	75.00	90.00
2422☆	2063F ☆	Atlanta	40.00	125.	200.	525.
2423	2063G	Chicago	FV	35.00	65.00	90.00
2423☆	2063G ☆	Chicago	40.00	125.	150.	300.
2424	2063H	St. Louis	FV	35.00	75.00	90.00
2424☆	2063H ☆	St. Louis	45.00	150.	250.	350.
2424A	2063I	Minneapolis	22.00	35.00	125.	140.
2424A☆	2063I ☆	Minneapolis	55.00	175.	750.	900.
2425	2063J	Kansas City	FV	35.00	125.	140.
2425☆	2063J ☆	Kansas City	40.00	125.	250.	300.
2426	2063K	Dallas	FV	35.00	75.00	90.00
2426☆	2063K ☆	Dallas	40.00	125.	200.	300.
2427	2063L	San Francisco	FV	35.00	75.00	90.00
2427☆	2063L ☆	San Francisco	40.00	125.	200.	300.

Series 1950E Granahan-Fowler

KL#	Fr#	District	Fine	XF	CH CU (63)	Gem CU (65)
2428	2064B	New York	25.00	55.00	100.	125.
2428☆	2064B ☆	New York	200.	300.	750.	1500.
2429	2064G	Chicago	25.00	70.00	175.	225.
2429☆	2064G ☆	Chicago	200.	400.	1000.	1500.
2430	2064L	San Francisco	25.00	70.00	175.	200.
2430☆	2064L ☆	San Francisco	200.	400.	800.	1000.

Series 1963 Granahan-Dillon

KL#	Fr#	District	Fine	XF	CH CU (63)	Gem CU (65)
2431	2065A	Boston	FV	35.00	75.00	100.
2431☆	2065A ☆	Boston	40.00	100.	220.	250.
2432	2065B	New York	FV	35.00	60.00	77.00
2432☆	2065B ☆	New York	40.00	75.00	150.	175.
2433	2065D	Cleveland	FV	35.00	75.00	100.
2433☆	2065D ☆	Cleveland	40.00	100.	175.	225.
2434	2065E	Richmond	FV	35.00	75.00	77.00
2434☆	2065E ☆	Richmond	40.00	100.	200.	225.
2435	2065F	Atlanta	FV	35.00	75.00	100.
2435☆	2065F ☆	Atlanta	70.00	100.	200.	225.
2436	2065G	Chicago	FV	35.00	95.00	125.
2436☆	2065G ☆	Chicago	40.00	75.00	175.	200.
2437	2065H	St. Louis	FV	35.00	75.00	100.
2437☆	2065H ☆	St. Louis	40.00	100.	170.	225.
2438	2065J	Kansas City	FV	35.00	125.	375.
2438☆	2065J ☆	Kansas City	40.00	100.	225.	800.
2439	2065K	Dallas	FV	35.00	75.00	100.
2439☆	2065K ☆	Dallas	40.00	100.	200.	225.
2440	2065L	San Francisco	FV	35.00	75.00	100.
2440☆	2065L ☆	San Francisco	40.00	100.	175.	225.

Series 1963A Granahan-Fowler

KL#	Fr#	District	Fine	XF	CH CU (63)	Gem CU (65)
2441	2066A	Boston	FV	30.00	60.00	62.00
2441☆	2066A ☆	Boston	35.00	75.00	150.	160.
2442	2066B	New York	FV	30.00	60.00	62.00
2442☆	2066B ☆	New York	35.00	75.00	150.	160.
2443	2066C	Philadelphia	FV	30.00	60.00	62.00
2443☆	2066C ☆	Philadelphia	35.00	75.00	150.	160.
2444	2066D	Cleveland	FV	30.00	60.00	62.00
2444☆	2066D ☆	Cleveland	35.00	75.00	150.	160.
2445	2066E	Richmond	FV	30.00	60.00	62.00
2445☆	2066E ☆	Richmond	35.00	75.00	150.	160.
2446	2066F	Atlanta	FV	30.00	60.00	62.00
2446☆	2066F ☆	Atlanta	35.00	75.00	150.	175.
2447	2066G	Chicago	FV	30.00	60.00	62.00
2447☆	2066G ☆	Chicago	35.00	75.00	150.	160.
2448	2066H	St. Louis	FV	30.00	60.00	62.00
2448☆	2066H ☆	St. Louis	35.00	75.00	150.	160.
2449	2066I	Minneapolis	FV	30.00	60.00	62.00
2449☆	2066I ☆	Minneapolis	35.00	75.00	250.	300.
2450	2066J	Kansas City	FV	30.00	60.00	62.00
2450☆	2066J ☆	Kansas City	35.00	75.00	150.	160.
2451	2066K	Dallas	FV	30.00	60.00	62.00
2451☆	2066K ☆	Dallas	35.00	75.00	150.	160.
2452	2066L	San Francisco	FV	30.00	60.00	62.00
2452☆	2066L ☆	San Francisco	35.00	75.00	150.	160.

Series 1969 Elston-Kennedy

KL#	Fr#	District	Fine	XF	CH CU (63)	Gem CU (65)
2453	2067A	Boston	FV	30.00	60.00	62.00
2453☆	2067A ☆	Boston	35.00	70.00	140.	150.
2454	2067B	New York	FV	30.00	60.00	62.00
2454☆	2067B ☆	New York	30.00	65.00	120.	135.
2455	2067C	Philadelphia	FV	30.00	60.00	62.00

KL#	Fr#	District	Fine	XF	CH CU (63)	Gem CU (65)
2455	2067C	Philadelphia	FV	30.00	60.00	62.00
2455☆	2067C ☆	Philadelphia	35.00	70.00	140.	150.
2456	2067D	Cleveland	FV	30.00	60.00	62.00
2456☆	2067D ☆	Cleveland	30.00	65.00	140.	155.
2457	2067E	Richmond	FV	30.00	60.00	62.00
2457☆	2067E ☆	Richmond	30.00	65.00	140.	155.
2458	2067F	Atlanta	FV	30.00	60.00	62.00
2458☆	2067F ☆	Atlanta	35.00	70.00	140.	150.
2459	2067G	Chicago	FV	30.00	60.00	62.00
2459☆	2067G ☆	Chicago	35.00	65.00	200.	225.
2460	2067H	St. Louis	FV	30.00	60.00	62.00
2461	2067I	Minneapolis	FV	30.00	60.00	62.00
2461☆	2067I ☆	Minneapolis	35.00	70.00	150.	165.
2462	2067J	Kansas City	FV	30.00	60.00	62.00
2462☆	2067J ☆	Kansas City	35.00	70.00	140.	150.
2463	2067K	Dallas	FV	30.00	60.00	62.00
2463☆	2067K ☆	Dallas	35.00	70.00	140.	150.
2464	2067L	San Francisco	FV	30.00	60.00	62.00
2464☆	2067L ☆	San Francisco	35.00	65.00	125.	135.

Series 1969A Kabis-Connally

KL#	Fr#	District	Fine	XF	CH CU (63)	Gem CU (65)
2465	2068A	Boston	FV	40.00	80.00	90.00
2466	2068B	New York	FV	40.00	70.00	85.00
2466☆	2068B ☆	New York	35.00	70.00	125.	150.
2467	2068C	Philadelphia	FV	40.00	80.00	90.00
2468	2068D	Cleveland	FV	40.00	75.00	85.00
2468☆	2068D ☆	Cleveland	35.00	75.00	150.	160.
2469	2068E	Richmond	FV	40.00	80.00	85.00
2469☆	2068E ☆	Richmond	35.00	70.00	140.	150.
2470	2068F	Atlanta	FV	40.00	80.00	90.00
2471	2068G	Chicago	FV	40.00	80.00	85.00
2471☆	2068G ☆	Chicago	35.00	70.00	140.	150.
2472	2068H	St. Louis	FV	40.00	70.00	90.00
2472☆	2068H ☆	St. Louis	35.00	70.00	140.	150.
2473	2068I	Minneapolis	FV	40.00	70.00	90.00
2473☆	2068I ☆	Minneapolis	45.00	90.00	160.	190.
2474	2068J	Kansas City	FV	40.00	90.00	100.
2475	2068K	Dallas	FV	40.00	80.00	95.00
2475☆	2068K ☆	Dallas	35.00	70.00	140.	150.
2476	2068L	San Francisco	FV	40.00	75.00	85.00
2476☆	2068L ☆	San Francisco	35.00	70.00	160.	175.

Series 1969B Banuelos-Connally

KL#	Fr#	District	Fine	XF	CH CU (63)	Gem CU (65)
2477	2069B	New York	35.00	45.00	200.	220.
2477☆	2069B ☆	New York	125.	250.	450.	550.
2478	2069D	Cleveland	50.00	105.	250.	275.
2479	2069E	Richmond	50.00	100.	225.	240.
2480	2069F	Atlanta	50.00	100.	200.	220.
2480☆	2069F ☆	Atlanta	175.	350.	425.	500.
2481	2069G	Chicago	50.00	100.	150.	200.
2481☆	2069G ☆	Chicago	125.	175.	600.	750.
2482	2069H	St. Louis	50.00	105.	250.	275.
2483	2069I	Minneapolis	60.00	125.	400.	450.
2484	2069J	Kansas City	60.00	125.	250.	325.
2484☆	2069J ☆	Kansas City	140.	275.	800.	900.
2485	2069K	Dallas	45.00	105.	200.	230.
2486	2069L	San Francisco	45.00	100.	175.	220.
2486☆	2069L ☆	San Francisco	140.	275.	800.	900.

Series 1969C Banuelos-Shultz

KL#	Fr#	District	Fine	XF	CH CU (63)	Gem CU (65)
2487	2070A	Boston	FV	30.00	60.00	62.00
2487☆	2070A ☆	Boston	30.00	60.00	135.	145.
2488	2070B	New York	FV	30.00	60.00	62.00
2488☆	2070B ☆	New York	30.00	60.00	120.	130.
2489	2070C	Philadelphia	FV	30.00	60.00	62.00
2489☆	2070C ☆	Philadelphia	30.00	60.00	135.	140.
2490	2070D	Cleveland	FV	30.00	60.00	70.00
2490☆	2070D ☆	Cleveland	30.00	60.00	140.	145.
2491	2070E	Richmond	FV	30.00	60.00	62.00
2491☆	2070E ☆	Richmond	30.00	60.00	120.	130.
2492	2070F	Atlanta	FV	30.00	60.00	62.00
2492☆	2070F ☆	Atlanta	30.00	60.00	175.	200.
2493	2070G	Chicago	FV	30.00	60.00	62.00
2493☆	2070G ☆	Chicago	30.00	60.00	150.	175.

KL#	Fr#	District	Fine	XF	CH CU (63)	Gem CU (65)
2494	2070H	St. Louis	FV	30.00	60.00	62.00
2494☆	2070H☆	St. Louis	40.00	80.00	170.	185.
2495	2070I	Minneapolis	FV	30.00	60.00	62.00
2495☆	2070I ☆	Minneapolis	30.00	60.00	175.	200.
2496	2070J	Kansas City	FV	30.00	60.00	62.00
2496☆	2070J ☆	Kansas City	40.00	80.00	180.	185.
2497	2070K	Dallas	FV	30.00	60.00	62.00
2497☆	2070K ☆	Dallas	35.00	70.00	150.	175.
2498	2070L	San Francisco	FV	30.00	60.00	62.00
2498☆	2070L ☆	San Francisco	35.00	70.00	175.	200.

A Word About Star Notes

In our listings there are often two entries for each catalog number.
For example:

KL#	Fr#	District	Fine	XF	CH CU (63)	Gem CU (65)
2302	2052G	Chicago	30.00	60.00	100.	125.
2302☆	2052G☆	Chicago	140.	350.	1000.	2100.

The first listing has a serial number format of letter - eight digits - letter.

The second listing refers to a bank note with a serial number format of
letter - eight digits - star.

This star at the end of the serial number
refers to a replacement note, one which replaces a note
damaged during the production process. There are fewer of
these printed and therefore they are more expensive.

Series 1974 Neff-Simon

KL#	Fr#	District	Fine	XF	CH CU (63)	Gem CU (65)
2499	2071A	Boston	FV	30.00	60.00	62.00
2499☆	2071A ☆	Boston	25.00	40.00	115.	135.
2500	2071B	New York	FV	30.00	60.00	562.
2500☆	2071B ☆	New York	25.00	40.00	125.	135.
2501	2071C	Philadelphia	FV	30.00	60.00	62.00
2501☆	2071C ☆	Philadelphia	25.00	40.00	125.	135.
2502	2071D	Cleveland	FV	30.00	60.00	62.00
2502☆	2071D ☆	Cleveland	25.00	40.00	125.	135.
2503	2071E	Richmond	FV	30.00	55.00	62.00
2503☆	2071E ☆	Richmond	25.00	40.00	125.	135.
2504	2071F	Atlanta	FV	30.00	55.00	60.00
2504☆	2071F ☆	Atlanta	25.00	40.00	80.00	90.00
2505	2071G	Chicago	FV	30.00	55.00	62.00
2505☆	2071G ☆	Chicago	25.00	40.00	115.	125.
2506	2071H	St. Louis	FV	30.00	55.00	62.00
2506☆	2071H ☆	St. Louis	25.00	40.00	110.	125.
2507	2071I	Minneapolis	FV	30.00	55.00	62.00
2507☆	2071I ☆	Minneapolis	25.00	40.00	110.	125.
2508	2071J	Kansas City	FV	30.00	55.00	62.00
2508☆	2071J ☆	Kansas City	25.00	40.00	110.	125.
2509	2071K	Dallas	FV	30.00	55.00	62.00
2509☆	2071K ☆	Dallas	25.00	40.00	110.	125.
2510	2071L	San Francisco	FV	30.00	55.00	62.00
2510☆	2071L ☆	San Francisco	25.00	40.00	105.	120.

Series 1977 Morton-Blumenthal

KL#	Fr#	District	Fine	XF	CH CU (63)	Gem CU (65)
2511	2072A	Boston	22.00	30.00	60.00	62.00
2511☆	2072A ☆	Boston	25.00	50.00	100.	110.
2512	2072B	New York	FV	30.00	60.00	62.00
2512☆	2072B ☆	New York	25.00	50.00	100.	110.

KL#	Fr#	District	Fine	XF	CH CU (63)	Gem CU (65)
2513	2072C	Philadelphia	FV	30.00	60.00	62.00
2513☆	2072C ☆	Philadelphia	25.00	50.00	100.	110.
2514	2072D	Cleveland	FV	30.00	60.00	62.00
2514☆	2072D ☆	Cleveland	25.00	50.00	100.	110.
2515	2072E	Richmond	FV	30.00	60.00	62.00
2515☆	2072E ☆	Richmond	25.00	50.00	100.	110.
2516	2072F	Atlanta	FV	30.00	60.00	62.00
2516☆	2072F ☆	Atlanta	25.00	50.00	100.	110.
2517	2072G	Chicago	FV	30.00	60.00	62.00
2517☆	2072G ☆	Chicago	25.00	50.00	100.	110.
2518	2072H	St. Louis	FV	30.00	60.00	62.00
2518☆	2072H ☆	St. Louis	25.00	50.00	100.	110.
2519	2072I	Minneapolis	FV	30.00	65.00	67.00
2519☆	2072I ☆	Minneapolis	25.00	50.00	110.	130.
2520	2072J	Kansas City	FV	30.00	60.00	62.00
2520☆	2072J ☆	Kansas City	25.00	50.00	100.	110.
2521	2072K	Dallas	FV	30.00	60.00	62.00
2521☆	2072K ☆	Dallas	25.00	50.00	100.	110.
2522	2072L	San Francisco	FV	30.00	60.00	62.00
2522☆	2072L ☆	San Francisco	25.00	50.00	100.	110.

Series 1981 Buchanan-Regan

KL#	Fr#	District	Fine	XF	CH CU (63)	Gem CU (65)
3536	2073A	Boston	FV	35.00	75.00	80.00
3536☆	2073A ☆	Boston	35.00	90.00	125.	130.
3537	2073B	New York	FV	35.00	60.00	77.00
3537☆	2073B ☆	New York	35.00	90.00	125.	185.
3538	2073C	Philadelphia	FV	35.00	75.00	77.00
3538☆	2073C ☆	Philadelphia	45.00	90.00	150.	185.
3539	2073D	Cleveland	FV	35.00	75.00	77.00
3539☆	2073D ☆	Cleveland	45.00	90.00	150.	185.
3540	2073E	Richmond	FV	35.00	75.00	77.00
3540☆	2073E ☆	Richmond	45.00	90.00	165.	185.
3541	2073F	Atlanta	FV	35.00	75.00	77.00
3541☆	2073F ☆	Atlanta	45.00	90.00	165.	185.
3542	2073G	Chicago	FV	35.00	75.00	77.00
3542☆	2073G ☆	Chicago	45.00	90.00	140.	185.
3543	2073H	St. Louis	FV	35.00	75.00	77.00
3543☆	2073H ☆	St. Louis	45.00	90.00	140.	185.
3544	2073I	Minneapolis	FV	35.00	95.00	115.
3544☆	2073I ☆	Minneapolis	45.00	90.00	250.	275.
3545	2073J	Kansas City	FV	35.00	75.00	77.00
3545☆	2073J ☆	Kansas City	45.00	90.00	150.	185.
3546	2073K	Dallas	FV	35.00	75.00	77.00
3546☆	2073K ☆	Dallas	45.00	90.00	175.	185.
3547	2073L	San Francisco	FV	35.00	75.00	77.00
3547☆	2073L ☆	San Francisco	45.00	90.00	150.	200.

Series 1981A Ortega-Regan

KL#	Fr#	District	Fine	XF	CH CU (63)	Gem CU (65)
3636	2074A	Boston	FV	30.00	60.00	62.00
3637	2074B	New York	FV	30.00	50.00	62.00
3638	2074C	Philadelphia	FV	30.00	60.00	62.00
3638☆	2074C ☆	Philadelphia	35.00	70.00	100.	105.
3639	2074D	Cleveland	FV	30.00	60.00	62.00
3639☆	2074D ☆	Cleveland	35.00	70.00	100.	105.
3640	2074E	Richmond	FV	30.00	60.00	62.00
3641	2074F	Atlanta	FV	30.00	60.00	62.00
3641☆	2074F ☆	Atlanta	35.00	70.00	100.	105.
3642	2074G	Chicago	FV	30.00	50.00	62.00
3643	2074H	St. Louis	FV	30.00	50.00	62.00
3644	2074I	Minneapolis	FV	30.00	60.00	62.00
3645	2074J	Kansas City	FV	30.00	60.00	62.00
3646	2074K	Dallas	FV	30.00	60.00	62.00
3647	2074L	San Francisco	FV	30.00	60.00	62.00
3647☆	2074L ☆	San Francisco	35.00	70.00	100.	105.

Series 1985 Ortega-Baker

KL#	Fr#	District	Fine	XF	CH CU (63)	Gem CU (65)
3736	2075A	Boston	FV	25.00	50.00	52.00
3736☆	2075A ☆	Boston	FV	35.00	75.00	77.00
3737	2075B	New York	FV	25.00	40.00	52.00
3737☆	2075B ☆	New York	FV	35.00	75.00	77.00
3738	2075C	Philadelphia	FV	25.00	50.00	52.00
3738☆	2075C ☆	Philadelphia	FV	35.00	75.00	77.00
3739	2075D	Cleveland	FV	25.00	50.00	52.00
3739☆	2075D ☆	Cleveland	FV	35.00	75.00	77.00
3740	2075E	Richmond	FV	25.00	50.00	52.00
3740☆	2075E ☆	Richmond	FV	35.00	75.00	77.00
3741	2075F	Atlanta	FV	25.00	50.00	52.00
3742	2075G	Chicago	FV	25.00	50.00	52.00
3742☆	2075G ☆	Chicago	FV	35.00	70.00	77.00
3743	2075H	St. Louis	FV	25.00	50.00	52.00
3744	2075I	Minneapolis	FV	25.00	50.00	52.00
3745	2075J	Kansas City	FV	25.00	50.00	52.00
3745☆	2075J ☆	Kansas City	FV	35.00	75.00	77.00
3746	2075K	Dallas	FV	25.00	50.00	52.00
3746☆	2075K ☆	Dallas	FV	35.00	75.00	77.00
3747	2075L	San Francisco	FV	25.00	50.00	52.00
3747☆	2075L ☆	San Francisco	FV	35.00	75.00	77.00

Series 1988A Villalpando-Brady

KL#	Fr#	District	Fine	XF	CH CU (63)	Gem CU (65)
3880	2076A	Boston	FV	30.00	60.00	62.00
3881	2076B	New York	FV	30.00	60.00	62.00
3881☆	2076B ☆	New York	25.00	50.00	100.	105.
3882	2076C	Philadelphia	FV	30.00	60.00	62.00
3882☆	2076C ☆	Philadelphia	FV	30.00	100.	105.
3883	2076D	Cleveland	FV	30.00	60.00	62.00
3884	2076E	Richmond	FV	30.00	60.00	65.00
3885	2076F	Atlanta	FV	30.00	60.00	62.00
3885☆	2076F ☆	Atlanta	25.00	50.00	100.	105.
3886	2076G	Chicago	FV	30.00	60.00	62.00
3886☆	2076G ☆	Chicago	25.00	50.00	100.	105.
3887	2076H	St. Louis	FV	30.00	60.00	62.00
3888	2076I	Minneapolis	FV	30.00	60.00	62.00
3889	2076J	Kansas City	FV	30.00	60.00	62.00
3890	2076K	Dallas	FV	30.00	60.00	62.00
3890☆	2076K ☆	Dallas	25.00	50.00	100.	105.
3891	2076L	San Francisco	FV	30.00	60.00	62.00

Series 1990 Villalpando-Brady

KL#	Fr#	District	Fine	XF	CH CU (63)	Gem CU (65)
3952	2077A	Boston	FV	25.00	40.00	47.00
3952☆	2077A ☆	Boston	FV	35.00	70.00	72.00
3953	2077B	New York	FV	25.00	45.00	47.00
3953☆	2077B ☆	New York	FV	35.00	70.00	72.00
3954	2077C	Philadelphia	FV	25.00	45.00	47.00
3955	2077D	Cleveland	FV	25.00	45.00	47.00
3955☆	2077D ☆	Cleveland	FV	35.00	70.00	72.00
3956	2077E	Richmond	FV	25.00	40.00	47.00
3956☆	2077E ☆	Richmond	FV	35.00	70.00	72.00
3957	2077F	Atlanta	FV	25.00	40.00	47.00

KL#	Fr#	District	Fine	XF	CH CU (63)	Gem CU (65)
3957☆	2077F ☆	Atlanta	FV	35.00	100.	110.
3958	2077G	Chicago	FV	25.00	40.00	47.00
3958☆	2077G ☆	Chicago	FV	35.00	70.00	72.00
3959	2077H	St. Louis	FV	25.00	45.00	47.00
3959☆	2077H ☆	St. Louis	FV	40.00	70.00	85.00
3960	2077I	Minneapolis	FV	25.00	45.00	47.00
3960☆	2077I ☆	Minneapolis	FV	40.00	80.00	85.00
3961	2077J	Kansas City	FV	25.00	45.00	47.00
3962	2077K	Dallas	FV	25.00	45.00	47.00
3963	2077L	San Francisco	FV	25.00	45.00	47.00

Series 1993 Withrow-Bentsen - DC

KL#	Fr#	District	Fine	XF	CH CU (63)	Gem CU (65)
4048	2079A	Boston	FV	FV	40.00	42.00
4048☆	2079A ☆	Boston	FV	25.00	60.00	62.00
4049	2079B	New York	FV	FV	45.00	47.00
4049☆	2079B ☆	New York	FV	25.00	50.00	52.00
4050	2079C	Philadelphia	FV	FV	40.00	42.00
4051	2079D	Cleveland	FV	FV	40.00	42.00
4051☆	2079D ☆	Cleveland	FV	25.00	60.00	62.00
4052	2079E	Richmond	FV	FV	40.00	42.00
4052☆	2079E ☆	Richmond	FV	30.00	70.00	75.00
4053	2079F	Atlanta	FV	FV	45.00	47.00
4053A	2079H	St. Louis	FV	FV	45.00	47.00
4053B☆	2079L ☆	San Francisco	FV	25.00	60.00	62.00

Series 1993 Withrow-Bentsen - FW

KL#	Fr#	District	Fine	XF	CH CU (63)	Gem CU (65)
4054	2079G	Chicago	FV	FV	40.00	42.00
4055	2079H	St. Louis	FV	FV	45.00	47.00
4057	2079J	Kansas City	FV	FV	40.00	42.00
4058	2079K	Dallas	FV	FV	45.00	47.00
4059	2079L	San Francisco	FV	FV	40.00	42.00

Series 1995 Withrow-Rubin - DC

KL#	Fr#	District	Fine	XF	CH CU (63)	Gem CU (65)
4121	2081B	New York	FV	FV	40.00	42.00
4121☆	2081B ☆	New York	FV	FV	50.00	52.00
4122	2081C	Philadelphia	FV	FV	45.00	47.00
4123	2081D	Cleveland	FV	FV	45.00	47.00
4123☆	2081D ☆	Cleveland	FV	25.00	70.00	75.00
4124	2081E	Richmond	FV	FV	45.00	47.00

Series 1995 Withrow-Rubin - FW

KL#	Fr#	District	Fine	XF	CH CU (63)	Gem CU (65)
4125	2081F	Atlanta	FV	FV	45.00	47.00
4125☆	2081F ☆	Atlanta	FV	25.00	60.00	62.00
4126	2081G	Chicago	FV	FV	40.00	42.00
4127	2081H	St. Louis	FV	FV	45.00	47.00
4128	2081I	Minneapolis	FV	FV	45.00	47.00
4129	2081J	Kansas City	FV	FV	45.00	47.00
4130	2081K	Dallas	FV	FV	45.00	47.00
4131	2081L	San Francisco	FV	FV	40.00	42.00

Series 1996 Withrow-Rubin - DC

KL#	Fr#	District	Fine	XF	CH CU (63)	Gem CU (65)
4162	2083A	Boston	FV	FV	30.00	37.00
4162☆	2083A ☆	Boston	FV	FV	35.00	52.00

KL#	Fr#	District	Fine	XF	CH CU (63)	Gem CU (65)
4163	2083B	New York	FV	FV	30.00	37.00
4163☆	2083B ☆	New York	FV	FV	35.00	52.00
4164	2083C	Philadelphia	FV	FV	30.00	37.00
4164☆	2083C ☆	Philadelphia	FV	FV	40.00	47.00
4165	2083D	Cleveland	FV	FV	30.00	37.00
4165☆	2083D ☆	Cleveland	FV	FV	40.00	52.00
4166	2083E	Richmond	FV	FV	30.00	37.00
4166☆	2083E ☆	Richmond	FV	FV	40.00	52.00
4167	2083F	Atlanta	FV	FV	40.00	47.00
4167☆	2083F ☆	Atlanta	FV	FV	40.00	52.00

Series 1996 Withrow-Rubin - FW

KL#	Fr#	District	Fine	XF	CH CU (63)	Gem CU (65)
4168	2083G	Chicago	FV	FV	30.00	37.00
4168☆	2083G ☆	Chicago	FV	FV	30.00	52.00
4169	2083H	St. Louis	FV	FV	30.00	37.00
4169☆	2083H ☆	St. Louis	FV	45.00	150.	165.
4170	2083I	Minneapolis	FV	FV	35.00	37.00
4171	2083J	Kansas City	FV	FV	35.00	37.00
4172	2083K	Dallas	FV	FV	35.00	37.00
4173	2083L	San Francisco	FV	FV	35.00	37.00
4173☆	2083L ☆	San Francisco	FV	25.00	50.00	175.

Series 1999 Withrow-Summers - DC

KL#	Fr#	District	Fine	XF	CH CU (63)	Gem CU (65)
4549	2085A	Boston	FV	FV	30.00	32.00
4549☆	2085A ☆	Boston	FV	FV	60.00	62.00
4550	2085B	New York	FV	FV	30.00	32.00
4550☆	2085B ☆	New York	FV	FV	45.00	62.00
4551	2085C	Philadelphia	FV	FV	30.00	32.00
4552	2085D	Cleveland	FV	FV	30.00	32.00
4552☆	2085D ☆	Cleveland	FV	FV	60.00	62.00
4553	2085E	Richmond	FV	FV	30.00	32.00

Series 1999 Withrow-Summers - FW

KL#	Fr#	District	Fine	XF	CH CU (63)	Gem CU (65)
4553A☆	- ☆	New York	FV	FV	60.00	62.00
4553B	-	Cleveland	FV	FV	30.00	32.00
4554	2085F	Atlanta	FV	FV	30.00	32.00
4555	2085G	Chicago	FV	FV	30.00	32.00
4555☆	2085G ☆	Chicago	FV	FV	60.00	62.00
4556	2085H	St. Louis	FV	FV	30.00	32.00
4557	2085I	Minneapolis	FV	FV	30.00	32.00
4558	2085J	Kansas City	FV	FV	30.00	32.00
4559	2085L	San Francisco	FV	FV	30.00	32.00
4559☆	2085L ☆	San Francisco	FV	FV	60.00	62.00

Series 2001 Marin-O'Neill - DC

KL#	Fr#	District	Fine	XF	CH CU (63)	Gem CU (65)
4617	2087B	New York	FV	FV	30.00	32.00
4617☆	2087B ☆	New York	25.00	65.00	125.	130.
4618	2087D	Cleveland	FV	FV	30.00	32.00
4619	2087E	Richmond	FV	FV	30.00	32.00

Series 2001 Marin-O'Neill - FW

KL#	Fr#	District	Fine	XF	CH CU (63)	Gem CU (65)
4620	2088B	New York	FV	FV	30.00	32.00
4621	2088E	Richmond	FV	FV	30.00	32.00
4622	2088F	Atlanta	FV	FV	30.00	32.00
4623	2088G	Chicago	FV	FV	30.00	32.00
4623☆	2088G ☆	Chicago	FV	25.00	50.00	52.00
4624	2088H	St. Louis	FV	FV	30.00	32.00
4625	2088I	Minneapolis	FV	FV	30.00	32.00
4626	2088J	Kansas City	FV	FV	30.00	32.00
4626☆	2088J ☆	Kansas City	FV	25.00	50.00	52.00
4627	2088K	Dallas	FV	FV	30.00	32.00
4628	2088L	San Francisco	FV	FV	30.00	32.00
4628☆	2088L ☆	San Francisco	FV	25.00	50.00	42.00

Series 2004 Marin-Snow - DC

KL#	Fr#	District	Fine	XF	CH CU (63)	Gem CU (65)
4733	2089A	Boston	FV	FV	30.00	32.00
4733☆	2089A ☆	Boston	FV	FV	50.00	52.00
4734	2089B	New York	FV	FV	30.00	32.00
4734☆	2089B ☆	New York	FV	40.00	150.	165.
4735	2089C	Philadelphia	FV	FV	30.00	32.00
4735☆	2089C ☆	Philadelphia	FV	FV	50.00	52.00
4736	2089D	Cleveland	FV	FV	30.00	32.00
4737	2089E	Richmond	FV	FV	30.00	32.00
4737☆	2089E ☆	Richmond	FV	25.00	100.	125.
4738	2089F	Atlanta	FV	FV	30.00	32.00

Series 2004 Marin-Snow - FW

KL#	Fr#	District	Fine	XF	CH CU (63)	Gem CU (65)
4739	2090D	Cleveland	FV	FV	30.00	32.00
4740	2090E	Richmond	FV	FV	30.00	32.00
4741	2090F	Atlanta	FV	FV	30.00	32.00
4741☆	2090F ☆	Atlanta	FV	FV	50.00	52.00
4742	2090G	Chicago	FV	FV	30.00	32.00
4742☆	2090G ☆	Chicago	FV	FV	50.00	52.00
4743	2090H	St. Louis	FV	FV	30.00	32.00
4744	2090I	Minneapolis	FV	FV	30.00	32.00
4745	2090J	Kansas City	FV	FV	30.00	32.00
4745☆	2090J ☆	Kansas City	FV	FV	50.00	52.00
4746	2090K	Dallas	FV	FV	30.00	32.00
4746☆	2090K ☆	Dallas	FV	FV	50.00	52.00
4747	2090L	San Francisco	FV	FV	30.00	32.00
4747☆	2090L ☆	San Francisco	FV	FV	50.00	52.00

Series 2004A Cabral-Snow - DC

KL#	Fr#	District	Fine	XF	CH CU (63)	Gem CU (65)
4782	-	Boston	FV	FV	30.00	32.00
4782☆	-	Boston	FV	FV	50.00	52.00
4783	-	New York	FV	FV	30.00	32.00
4783☆	-	New York	FV	FV	125.	225.
4784	-	Philadelphia	FV	FV	30.00	32.00
4785	-	Cleveland	FV	FV	30.00	32.00
4786	-	Richmond	FV	FV	30.00	32.00
4786☆	-	Richmond	FV	FV	50.00	52.00
4787	-	Atlanta	FV	FV	30.00	32.00
4787☆	-	Atlanta	FV	FV	50.00	52.00
4788	-	Chicago	FV	FV	30.00	32.00
4788A	-	St. Louis	FV	FV	30.00	32.00
4789	-	Minneapolis	FV	FV	30.00	32.00
4790	-	Kansas City	FV	FV	30.00	32.00

Series 2004A Cabral-Snow - FW

KL#	Fr#	District	Fine	XF	CH CU (63)	Gem CU (65)
4791	-	Atlanta	FV	FV	30.00	32.00
4792	-	St. Louis	FV	FV	30.00	32.00
4793	-	Minneapolis	FV	FV	30.00	32.00
4794	-	Kansas City	FV	FV	30.00	32.00
4795	-	Dallas	FV	FV	30.00	32.00
4795☆	-	Dallas	FV	FV	50.00	52.00
4796	-	San Francisco	FV	FV	30.00	32.00
4796☆	-	San Francisco	FV	FV	50.00	52.00

Series 2006 Cabral-Paulson - DC

KL#	Fr#	District	Fine	XF	CH CU (63)	Gem CU (65)
4810	-	Boston	FV	FV	30.00	32.00
4811	-	New York	FV	FV	30.00	32.00
4812	-	Philadelphia	FV	FV	30.00	32.00
4813	-	Cleveland	FV	FV	30.00	32.00
4814	-	Richmond	FV	FV	30.00	32.00
4814☆	-	Richmond	FV	FV	50.00	52.00
4815	-	Atlanta	FV	FV	30.00	32.00
4815☆	-	Atlanta	FV	FV	50.00	52.00
4816	-	Chicago	FV	FV	30.00	32.00
4816☆	-	Chicago	FV	FV	50.00	52.00
4817	-	St. Louis	FV	FV	30.00	32.00
4818	-	Minneapolis	FV	FV	30.00	32.00
4819	-	Kansas City	FV	FV	30.00	32.00
4820	-	Dallas	FV	FV	30.00	32.00
4820☆	-	Dallas	FV	FV	50.00	52.00
4821	-	San Francisco	FV	FV	30.00	32.00
4821☆	-	San Francisco	FV	FV	50.00	52.00

Series 2006 Cabral-Paulson - FW

KL#	Fr#	District	Fine	XF	CH CU (63)	Gem CU (65)
4821A☆	-	Boston	FV	FV	50.00	52.00
4821D	-	Cleveland	FV	FV	30.00	32.00
4821F	-	Atlanta	FV	FV	30.00	32.00
4821G	-	Chicago	FV	FV	30.00	32.00
4821H	-	St. Louis	FV	FV	30.00	32.00
4821I	-	Minneapolis	FV	FV	30.00	32.00
4821J	-	Kansas City	FV	FV	30.00	32.00
4821K	-	Dallas	FV	FV	30.00	32.00
4821L	-	San Francisco	FV	FV	30.00	32.00

Series 2009 Rios-Geithner - DC

KL#	Fr#	District	Fine	XF	CH CU (63)	Gem CU (65)
4947	-	Boston	FV	FV	30.00	32.00
4948	-	New York	FV	FV	30.00	32.00
4948☆	-	New York	FV	FV	50.00	55.00
4949	-	Philadelphia	FV	FV	30.00	32.00
4950	-	Cleveland	FV	FV	30.00	32.00
4950☆	-	Cleveland	FV	FV	50.00	55.00
4951	-	Richmond	FV	FV	30.00	32.00
4951☆	-	Richmond	FV	FV	50.00	55.00
4952	-	Atlanta	FV	FV	30.00	32.00
4952☆	-	Atlanta	FV	FV	50.00	55.00
4953	-	St. Louis	FV	FV	30.00	32.00

Series 2009 Rios-Geithner - FW

KL#	Fr#	District	Fine	XF	CH CU (63)	Gem CU (65)
4954	-	Cleveland	FV	FV	30.00	32.00
4956	-	Chicago	FV	FV	30.00	32.00
4956☆	-	Chicago	FV	FV	50.00	55.00
4959	-	Kansas City	FV	FV	30.00	32.00
4959☆	-	Kansas City	FV	FV	50.00	55.00
4961	-	San Francisco	FV	FV	30.00	32.00

Federal Reserve Notes - Hawaii Emergency

KL#	Fr#	Series	Signatures	Fine	XF	CH CU (63)	Gem CU (65)
2523	2304	1934	Julian-Morgenthau	700.	900.	1750.	—

Gold Certificates
Fifty Dollars

KL#	Fr#	Series	Signatures	VF	XF	CH CU (63)	Gem CU (65)
2525	2404	1928	Woods-Mellon	400.	1000.	2750.	5050.
2525☆	2404	1928☆	Woods-Mellon	3825.	9000.	20,000.	24,750.

Federal Reserve Bank Notes

KL#	Fr#	Series	District	Fine	XF	CH CU (63)	Gem CU (65)
2526	1880B	1929	New York	75.00	150.	400.	725.
2526☆	1880B	1929☆	New York	400.	920.	3000.	5700.
2527	1880D	1929	Cleveland	475.	115.	700.	800.
2527☆	1880D	1929☆	Cleveland	350.	800.	7000.	5000.

KL#	Fr#	Series	District	Fine	XF	CH CU (63)	Gem CU (65)
2528	1880G	1929	Chicago	85.00	150.	250.	1625.
2528☆	1880G	1929☆	Chicago	3000.	7500.	—	—
2529	1880I	1929	Minneapolis	65.00	185.	375.	950.
2529☆	1880I	1929☆	Minneapolis	—	—	—	—
2530	1880J	1929	Kansas City	75.00	—	325.	520.
2530☆	1880J	1929☆	Kansas City	550.	1000.	1500.	4750.
2531	1880K	1929	Dallas	200.	1000.	4000.	—
2531☆	1880K	1929☆	Dallas	375.	1725.	7000.	9800.
2532	1880L	1929	San Francisco	75.00	150.	375.	725.
2532☆	1880L	1929☆	San Francisco	3000.	5250.	—	—

Federal Reserve Notes

Series 1928 Woods-Mellon

KL#	Fr#	District	Fine	XF	CH CU (63)	Gem CU (65)
2533	2100A	Boston	150.	500.	2000.	2500.
2533☆	2100A ☆	Boston	3000.	7500.	13,000.	—
2534	2100B	New York	110.	200.	660.	900.
2534☆	2100B ☆	New York	250.	700.	2000.	2500.
2535	2100C	Philadelphia	100.	300.	400.	1400.
2535☆	2100C ☆	Philadelphia	550.	1000.	3000.	1.00
2536	2100D	Cleveland	100.	225.	750.	1150.
2536☆	2100D ☆	Cleveland	300.	750.	3000.	5200.
2537	2100E	Richmond	100.	250.	4500.	6000.
2537☆	2100E ☆	Richmond	250.	700.	3500.	11,500.
2538	2100F	Atlanta	100.	375.	550.	1250.
2538☆	2100F ☆	Atlanta	250.	700.	3000.	4000.
2539	2100G	Chicago	85.00	225.	500.	1025.
2539☆	2100G ☆	Chicago	250.	600.	1600.	2750.
2540	2100H	St. Louis	110.	400.	800.	1100.
2540☆	2100H ☆	St. Louis	325.	375.	3000.	3750.
2541	2100I	Minneapolis	85.00	750.	2500.	4000.
2541☆	2100I ☆	Minneapolis	200.	600.	2500.	—
2542	2100J	Kansas City	85.00	150.	3000.	5500.
2542☆	2100J ☆	Kansas City	300.	3000.	7000.	—
2543	2100K	Dallas	100.	350.	2000.	3000.
2543☆	2100K ☆	Dallas	750.	4500.	—	—
2544	2100L	San Francisco	100.	225.	775.	1750.
2544☆	2100L ☆	San Francisco	200.	1200.	3000.	4000.

Series 1928A Woods-Mellon

KL#	Fr#	District	Fine	XF	CH CU (63)	Gem CU (65)
2545	2101A	Boston	70.00	125.	525.	650.
2546	2101B	New York	70.00	115.	250.	400.
2547	2101C	Philadelphia	70.00	90.00	350.	400.
2548	2101D	Cleveland	70.00	90.00	275.	425.
2549	2101E	Richmond	70.00	90.00	525.	575.
2550	2101F	Atlanta	80.00	120.	525.	800.
2551	2101G	Chicago	70.00	110.	400.	525.
2551☆	2101G ☆	Chicago	1000.	3500.	12,500.	13,500.
2552	2101H	St. Louis	75.00	110.	350.	450.
2553	2101I	Minneapolis	75.00	200.	1100.	1275.
2554	2101J	Kansas City	75.00	110.	800.	1100.
2555	2101K	Dallas	60.00	85.00	2000.	2100.
2556	2101L	San Francisco	65.00	95.00	1000.	1300.

Series 1934 Julian-Morgenthau

KL#	Fr#	District	Fine	XF	CH CU (63)	Gem CU (65)
2557	2102A	Boston	FV	60.00	200.	400.
2557☆	2102A ☆	Boston	100.	175.	750.	900.
2558	2102B	New York	FV	60.00	200.	220.
2558☆	2102B ☆	New York	100.	175.	575.	625.
2559	2102C	Philadelphia	FV	60.00	200.	250.
2559☆	2102C ☆	Philadelphia	100.	175.	800.	850.
2560	2102D	Cleveland	FV	60.00	200.	225.
2560☆	2102D ☆	Cleveland	100.	600.	1000.	1100.
2561	2102E	Richmond	FV	60.00	225.	275.
2561☆	2102E ☆	Richmond	100.	175.	8.00	1150.
2562	2102F	Atlanta	FV	60.00	225.	475.
2562☆	2102F ☆	Atlanta	100.	425.	925.	1200.
2563	2102G	Chicago	FV	75.00	225.	300.
2563☆	2102G ☆	Chicago	100.	200.	575.	1300.
2564	2102H	St. Louis	55.00	65.00	250.	360.
2564☆	2102H ☆	St. Louis	100.	375.	500.	1300.

KL#	Fr#	District	Fine	XF	CH CU (63)	Gem CU (65)
2565	2102I	Minneapolis	300.	1000.	2200.	2500.
2565☆	2102I ☆	Minneapolis	100.	200.	900.	1200.
2566	2102J	Kansas City	55.00	65.00	200.	250.
2566☆	2102J ☆	Kansas City	100.	200.	750.	1000.
2567	2102K	Dallas	55.00	65.00	250.	275.
2567☆	2102K ☆	Dallas	100.	200.	1125.	1500.
2568	2102L	San Francisco	FV	60.00	225.	400.
2568☆	2102L ☆	San Francisco	100.	200.	750.	1150.

Series 1934A Julian-Morgenthau

KL#	Fr#	District	Fine	XF	CH CU (63)	Gem CU (65)
2569	2103A	Boston	70.00	125.	350.	450.
2569☆	2103A ☆	Boston	125.	500.	1125.	1500.
2570	2103B	New York	65.00	125.	275.	350.
2570☆	2103B ☆	New York	80.00	500.	825.	1200.
2571	2103D	Cleveland	75.00	100.	250.	325.
2571☆	2103D ☆	Cleveland	125.	500.	1125.	1500.
2572	2103E	Richmond	75.00	100.	250.	325.
2572☆	2103F ☆	Richmond	250.	500.	975.	1500.
2573	2103F	Atlanta	75.00	100.	300.	400.
2573☆	2103F ☆	Atlanta	125.	500.	1125.	1500.
2574	2103G	Chicago	70.00	95.00	225.	325.
2574☆	2103G ☆	Chicago	100.	400.	975.	1500.
2575	2103H	St. Louis	75.00	125.	225.	500.
2575☆	2103H ☆	St. Louis	125.	500.	1125.	1500.
2576	2103I	Minneapolis	80.00	200.	375.	500.
2577	2103J	Kansas City	75.00	125.	375.	500.
2578	2103K	Dallas	75.00	125.	300.	1500.
2579	2103L	San Francisco	75.00	125.	375.	1500.

Series 1934B Julian-Vinson

KL#	Fr#	District	Fine	XF	CH CU (63)	Gem CU (65)
2580	2104C	Philadelphia	65.00	125.	400.	500.
2580☆	2104C ☆	Philadelphia	300.	1250.	3500.	4650.
2581	2104D	Cleveland	70.00	200.	400.	500.
2581☆	2104D ☆	Cleveland	300.	1000.	3500.	4650.
2582	2104E	Richmond	70.00	125.	400.	600.
2582☆	2104E ☆	Richmond	300.	1050.	3500.	4650.
2583	2104F	Atlanta	70.00	125.	400.	600.
2584	2104G	Chicago	70.00	125.	400.	600.
2585	2104H	St. Louis	70.00	125.	400.	600.
2586	2104I	Minneapolis	100.	250.	550.	925.
2587	2104J	Kansas City	70.00	125.	500.	600.
2587☆	2104J ☆	Kansas City	300.	1250.	3500.	4650.
2588	2104K	Dallas	100.	135.	550.	750.
2589	2104L	San Francisco	70.00	175.	450.	600.

Series 1934C Julian-Snyder

KL#	Fr#	District	Fine	XF	CH CU (63)	Gem CU (65)
2590	2105A	Boston	75.00	125.	300.	500.
2591	2105B	New York	75.00	110.	220.	350.
2591☆	2105B ☆	New York	250.	600.	1500.	2350.
2592	2105C	Philadelphia	80.00	125.	300.	515.
2592☆	2105C ☆	Philadelphia	250.	650.	1500.	2350.
2593	2105D	Cleveland	75.00	100.	250.	425.
2593☆	2105D ☆	Cleveland	250.	750.	1500.	3750.
2594	2105E	Richmond	75.00	110.	225.	450.
2594☆	2105E ☆	Richmond	250.	600.	1500.	2350.
2595	2105F	Atlanta	125.	125.	1000.	1250.
2596	2105G	Chicago	75.00	110.	250.	425.
2597	2105H	St. Louis	75.00	110.	250.	425.
2598	2105I	Minneapolis	80.00	125.	300.	475.
2598☆	2105I ☆	Minneapolis	250.	600.	1500.	2350.
2599	2105J	Kansas City	75.00	110.	175.	200.
2600	2105K	Dallas	75.00	110.	250.	300.
2600☆	2105K ☆	Dallas	250.	600.	1500.	2000.

Series 1934D Clark-Snyder

KL#	Fr#	District	Fine	XF	CH CU (63)	Gem CU (65)
2601	2106A	Boston	100.	150.	300.	500.
2601☆	2106A ☆	Boston	1200.	1750.	4000.	5500.
2602	2106B	New York	100.	150.	250.	550.
2602☆	2106B ☆	New York	800.	1500.	3000.	5500.
2603	2106C	Philadelphia	75.00	110.	400.	550.
2603☆	2106C ☆	Philadelphia	800.	1500.	3000.	4500.
2604	2106E	Richmond	85.00	175.	500.	750.
2605	2106F	Atlanta	75.00	200.	400.	650.
2605☆	2106F ☆	Atlanta	875.	2100.	4000.	6250.
2606	2106G	Chicago	80.00	125.	250.	450.
2606☆	2106G ☆	Chicago	500.	1500.	3000.	4000.
2607	2106K	Dallas	75.00	125.	400.	1100.

Series 1950 Clark-Snyder

KL#	Fr#	District	Fine	XF	CH CU (63)	Gem CU (65)
2608	2107A	Boston	80.00	125.	175.	300.
2608☆	2107A ☆	Boston	175.	375.	575.	900.
2609	2107B	New York	80.00	110.	135.	200.
2609☆	2107B ☆	New York	175.	375.	450.	700.
2610	2107C	Philadelphia	80.00	125.	150.	225.
2610☆	2107C ☆	Philadelphia	175.	400.	600.	900.
2611	2107D	Cleveland	80.00	125.	170.	350
2611☆	2107D ☆	Cleveland	175.	400.	490.	800.
2612	2107E	Richmond	80.00	125.	150.	300.
2612☆	2107E ☆	Richmond	175.	350.	490.	700.
2613	2107F	Atlanta	80.00	125.	190.	350.
2613☆	2107F ☆	Atlanta	175.	400.	600.	900.
2614	2107G	Chicago	70.00	100.	200.	350.
2614☆	2107G ☆	Chicago	200.	275.	375.	800.
2615	2107H	St. Louis	70.00	100.	135.	325.
2615☆	2107H ☆	St. Louis	225.	450.	650.	1000.
2616	2107I	Minneapolis	85.00	250.	320.	575.
2616☆	2107I ☆	Minneapolis	375.	750.	1125.	1600.
2617	2107J	Kansas City	70.00	100.	150.	300.
2617☆	2107J ☆	Kansas City	300.	500.	675.	1000.
2618	2107K	Dallas	80.00	110.	150.	1250.
2618☆	2107K ☆	Dallas	225.	350.	450.	800.
2619	2107L	San Francisco	70.00	100.	150.	300.
2619☆	2107L ☆	San Francisco	225.	325.	500.	900.

Series 1950A Priest-Humphrey

KL#	Fr#	District	Fine	XF	CH CU (63)	Gem CU (65)
2620	2108A	Boston	75.00	100.	190.	375.
2620☆	2108A ☆	Boston	125.	350.	450.	850.
2621	2108B	New York	75.00	100.	135.	250.
2621☆	2108B ☆	New York	125.	250.	300.	600.
2622	2108C	Philadelphia	75.00	100.	135.	275.

KL#	Fr#	District	Fine	XF	CH CU (63)	Gem CU (65)
2622☆	2108C ☆	Philadelphia	125.	250.	300.	600.
2623	2108D	Cleveland	75.00	100.	135.	275.
2623☆	2108D ☆	Cleveland	125.	250.	300.	600.
2624	2108E	Richmond	75.00	100.	135.	300.
2624☆	2108E ☆	Richmond	125.	300.	375.	650.
2625	2108F	Atlanta	75.00	125.	150.	350.
2625☆	2108F ☆	Atlanta	125.	300.	525.	900.
2626	2108G	Chicago	75.00	100.	170.	300.
2626☆	2108G ☆	Chicago	125.	250.	340.	635.
2627	2108H	St. Louis	75.00	100.	150.	375.
2627☆	2108H ☆	St. Louis	125.	250.	300.	625.
2628	2108J	Kansas City	75.00	125.	150.	325.
2628☆	2108J ☆	Kansas City	150.	300.	300.	625.
2629	2108K	Dallas	75.00	100.	150.	325.
2629☆	2108K ☆	Dallas	175.	350.	375.	700.
2630	2108L	San Francisco	75.00	100.	150.	375.
2630☆	2108L ☆	San Francisco	175.	350.	375.	700.

Series 1950B Priest-Anderson

KL#	Fr#	District	Fine	XF	CH CU (63)	Gem CU (65)
2631	2109A	Boston	60.00	80.00	115.	300.
2631☆	2109A ☆	Boston	70.00	200.	265.	500.
2632	2109B	New York	60.00	80.00	75.00	200.
2632☆	2109B ☆	New York	70.00	200.	190.	375.
2633	2109C	Philadelphia	60.00	80.00	115.	225.
2633☆	2109C ☆	Philadelphia	70.00	200.	265.	450.
2634	2109D	Cleveland	60.00	80.00	115.	225.
2634☆	2109D ☆	Cleveland	70.00	200.	265.	450.
2635	2109E	Richmond	60.00	80.00	115.	250.
2635☆	2109E ☆	Richmond	70.00	200.	340.	500.
2636	2109G	Chicago	60.00	80.00	115.	225.
2636☆	2109G ☆	Chicago	70.00	200.	240.	450.
2637	2109H	St. Louis	60.00	80.00	115.	300.
2637☆	2109H ☆	St. Louis	70.00	200.	340.	525.
2638	2109J	Kansas City	60.00	80.00	115.	250.
2638☆	2109J ☆	Kansas City	70.00	200.	340.	500.
2639	2109K	Dallas	60.00	80.00	190.	300.
2639☆	2109K ☆	Dallas	70.00	200.	340.	500.
2640	2109L	San Francisco	55.00	80.00	115.	250.
2640☆	2109L ☆	San Francisco	70.00	200.	340.	500.

Series 1950C Smith-Dillon

KL#	Fr#	District	Fine	XF	CH CU (63)	Gem CU (65)
2641	2110A	Boston	52.00	70.00	95.00	300.
2641☆	2110A ☆	Boston	125.	300.	420.	800.
2642	2110B	New York	52.00	70.00	75.00	300.
2642☆	2110B ☆	New York	125.	300.	375.	700.
2643	2110C	Philadelphia	52.00	70.00	175.	300.
2643☆	2110C ☆	Philadelphia	125.	300.	375.	700.
2644	2110D	Cleveland	52.00	70.00	95.00	300.
2644☆	2110D ☆	Cleveland	125.	300.	375.	700.
2645	2110E	Richmond	52.00	70.00	95.00	300.
2645☆	2110E ☆	Richmond	125.	300.	525.	900.
2646	2110G	Chicago	52.00	70.00	95.00	300.
2646☆	2110G ☆	Chicago	125.	300.	300.	675.
2047	2110II	St. Louis	52.00	70.00	225.	300.
2647☆	2110H ☆	St. Louis	125.	350.	375.	700.
2648	2110I	Minneapolis	52.00	70.00	210.	225.
2648☆	2110I ☆	Minneapolis	250.	500.	900.	2000.
2649	2110J	Kansas City	52.00	70.00	115.	300.
2649☆	2110J ☆	Kansas City	125.	350.	450.	1100.
2650	2110K	Dallas	52.00	70.00	95.00	300.
2650☆	2110K ☆	Dallas	125.	350.	525.	800.
2651	2110L	San Francisco	52.00	70.00	95.00	300.
2651☆	2110L ☆	San Francisco	125.	350.	450.	1100.

Series 1950D Granahan-Dillon

KL#	Fr#	District	Fine	XF	CH CU (63)	Gem CU (65)
2652	2111A	Boston	55.00	100.	150.	200.
2652☆	2111A ☆	Boston	125.	300.	450.	950.
2653	2111B	New York	55.00	100.	165.	375.
2653☆	2111B ☆	New York	110.	250.	450.	850.
2654	2111C	Philadelphia	55.00	75.00	95.00	225.
2654☆	2111C ☆	Philadelphia	110.	250.	400.	850.
2655	2111D	Cleveland	55.00	75.00	90.00	95.00

KL#	Fr#	District	Fine	XF	CH CU (63)	Gem CU (65)
2655☆	2111D ☆	Cleveland	110.	250.	375.	850.
2656	2111E	Richmond	55.00	75.00	95.00	350.
2656☆	2111E ☆	Richmond	110.	250.	425.	850.
2657	2111F	Atlanta	55.00	65.00	80.00	350.
2657☆	2111F ☆	Atlanta	125.	300.	375.	750.
2658	2111G	Chicago	55.00	75.00	95.00	350.
2658☆	2111G ☆	Chicago	110.	200.	375.	600.
2659	2111H	St. Louis	55.00	100.	125.	200.
2659☆	2111H ☆	St. Louis	110.	250.	400.	700.
2660	2111I	Minneapolis	55.00	100.	165.	225.
2660☆	2111I ☆	Minneapolis	150.	350.	650.	800.
2661	2111J	Kansas City	55.00	100.	150.	225.
2661☆	2111J ☆	Kansas City	150.	250.	400.	650.
2662	2111K	Dallas	55.00	100.	225.	350.
2662☆	2111K ☆	Dallas	150.	350.	650.	800.
2663	2111L	San Francisco	55.00	100.	200.	275.
2663☆	2111L ☆	San Francisco	125.	250.	400.	450.
2663☆	2111L ☆	San Francisco	125.	250.	400.	450.

Series 1950E Granahan-Fowler

KL#	Fr#	District	Fine	XF	CH CU (63)	Gem CU (65)
2664	2112B	New York	60.00	150.	275.	400.
2664☆	2112B ☆	New York	250.	450.	1000.	2150.
2665	2112G	Chicago	100.	150.	500.	600.
2665☆	2112G ☆	Chicago	300.	500.	2200.	3000.
2666	2112L	San Francisco	160.	200.	325.	600.
2666☆	2112L ☆	San Francisco	350.	550.	1500.	2100.

Series 1963A Granahan-Fowler

KL#	Fr#	District	Fine	XF	CH CU (63)	Gem CU (65)
2667	2113A	Boston	FV	75.00	80.00	150.
2667☆	2113A ☆	Boston	70.00	150.	300.	550.
2668	2113B	New York	FV	75.00	80.00	150.
2668☆	2113B ☆	New York	70.00	150.	200.	450.
2669	2113C	Philadelphia	FV	75.00	180.	250.
2669☆	2113C ☆	Philadelphia	70.00	150.	200.	450.
2670	2113D	Cleveland	FV	75.00	80.00	150.
2670☆	2113D ☆	Cleveland	70.00	150.	250.	450.
2671	2113E	Richmond	FV	75.00	80.00	150.
2671☆	2113E ☆	Richmond	70.00	150.	240.	550.
2672	2113F	Atlanta	FV	75.00	80.00	150.
2672☆	2113F ☆	Atlanta	100.	150.	200.	475.
2673	2113G	Chicago	FV	75.00	80.00	150.
2673☆	2113G ☆	Chicago	100.	150.	200.	520.
2674	2113H	St. Louis	FV	75.00	80.00	150.
2674☆	2113H ☆	St. Louis	70.00	150.	350.	450.
2675	2113I	Minneapolis	FV	75.00	150.	250.
2675☆	2113I ☆	Minneapolis	70.00	150.	400.	650.
2676	2113J	Kansas City	FV	75.00	80.00	150.
2676☆	2113J ☆	Kansas City	100.	200.	450.	475.
2677	2113K	Dallas	FV	75.00	80.00	150.
2677☆	2113K ☆	Dallas	100.	200.	500.	600.
2678	2113L	San Francisco	FV	75.00	80.00	150.
2678☆	2113L ☆	San Francisco	100.	200.	250.	600.

Series 1969 Elston-Kennedy

KL#	Fr#	District	Fine	XF	CH CU (63)	Gem CU (65)
2679	2114A	Boston	FV	60.00	150.	175.
2680	2114B	New York	FV	60.00	100.	170.
2680☆	2114B ☆	New York	70.00	125.	175.	275.
2681	2114C	Philadelphia	FV	60.00	100.	170.
2681☆	2114C ☆	Philadelphia	125.	225.	275.	375.
2682	2114D	Cleveland	FV	60.00	100.	150.
2682☆	2114D ☆	Cleveland	FV	60.00	300.	400.
2683	2114E	Richmond	FV	60.00	100.	210.
2683☆	2114E ☆	Richmond	125.	275.	250.	300.
2684	2114F	Atlanta	70.00	100.	150.	250.
2685	2114G	Chicago	FV	60.00	75.00	150.
2685☆	2114G ☆	Chicago	75.00	125.	200.	275.
2686	2114H	St. Louis	70.00	100.	200.	250.
2687	2114I	Minneapolis	70.00	100.	150.	225.
2688	2114J	Kansas City	FV	75.00	100.	220.
2688☆	2114J ☆	Kansas City	150.	275.	450.	600.
2689	2114K	Dallas	FV	75.00	200.	250.
2689☆	2114K ☆	Dallas	150.	200.	220.	245.
2690	2114L	San Francisco	FV	75.00	150.	400.
2690☆	2114L ☆	San Francisco	90.00	150.	400.	475.

Series 1969A Kabis-Connally

KL#	Fr#	District	Fine	XF	CH CU (63)	Gem CU (65)
2691	2115A	Boston	FV	75.00	120.	150.
2691☆	2115A ☆	Boston	60.00	100.	300.	400.
2692	2115B	New York	FV	75.00	125.	175.
2692☆	2115B ☆	New York	60.00	90.00	200.	275.
2693	2115C	Philadelphia	FV	75.00	125.	150.
2694	2115D	Cleveland	FV	75.00	100.	150.
2695	2115E	Richmond	FV	75.00	100.	2000.
2695☆	2115E ☆	Richmond	125.	250.	350.	525.

KL#	Fr#	District	Fine	XF	CH CU (63)	Gem CU (65)
2696	2115F	Atlanta	FV	75.00	150.	2000.
2696☆	2115F ☆	Atlanta	125.	250.	675.	875.
2697	2115G	Chicago	FV	60.00	100.	150.
2697☆	2115G ☆	Chicago	70.00	125.	150.	275.
2698	2115H	St. Louis	FV	75.00	150.	200.
2699	2115I	Minneapolis	FV	75.00	150.	175.
2700	2115J	Kansas City	FV	75.00	150.	175.
2701	2115K	Dallas	FV	75.00	100.	175.
2701☆	2115K ☆	Dallas	125.	250.	400.	575.
2702	2115L	San Francisco	FV	75.00	100.	175.
2702☆	2115L ☆	San Francisco	85.00	175.	250.	450.

A Word About Star Notes

In our listings there are often two entries for each catalog number.
For example:

KL#	Fr#	District	Fine	XF	CH CU (63)	Gem CU (65)
2641	2110A	Boston	52.00	70.00	95.00	300.
2641☆	2110A ☆	Boston	125.	300.	420.	800.

The first listing has a serial number format of letter - eight digits - letter.

The second listing refers to a bank note with a serial number format of
letter - eight digits - star.

This star at the end of the serial number refers to a replacement note,
one which replaces a note damaged during the production process.
There are fewer of these printed and therefore they are more expensive.

Series 1969B Banuelos-Connally

KL#	Fr#	District	Fine	XF	CH CU (63)	Gem CU (65)
2703	2116A	Boston	150.	700.	1250.	—
2704	2116B	New York	125.	600.	1000.	—
2705	2116E	Richmond	300.	700.	1000.	—
2706	2116F	Atlanta	135.	700.	1000.	—
2707	2116G	Chicago	275.	325.	400.	—
2708	2116K	Dallas	125.	700.	2500.	2750.
2708☆	2116K ☆	Dallas	300.	1300.	2100.	—

Series 1969C Banuelos-Shultz

KL#	Fr#	District	Fine	XF	CH CU (63)	Gem CU (65)
2709	2117A	Boston	FV	65.00	95.00	130.
2709☆	2117A ☆	Boston	75.00	200.	340.	425.
2710	2117B	New York	FV	65.00	75.00	110.
2710☆	2117B ☆	New York	75.00	150.	265.	325.
2711	2117C	Philadelphia	FV	65.00	75.00	120.
2711☆	2117C ☆	Philadelphia	75.00	150.	225.	350.
2712	2117D	Cleveland	FV	65.00	75.00	125.
2712☆	2117D ☆	Cleveland	70.00	125.	185.	350.
2713	2117E	Richmond	FV	65.00	75.00	125.
2713☆	2117E ☆	Richmond	100.	200.	300.	375.
2714	2117F	Atlanta	FV	75.00	135.	175.
2714☆	2117F ☆	Atlanta	125.	250.	265.	425.
2715	2117G	Chicago	FV	55.00	75.00	125.
2715☆	2117G ☆	Chicago	75.00	90.00	100.	125.
2716	2117H	St. Louis	FV	65.00	75.00	125.
2716☆	2117H ☆	St. Louis	100.	200.	300.	425.
2717	2117I	Minneapolis	FV	75.00	115.	140.
2717☆	2117I ☆	Minneapolis	100.	200.	325.	425.
2718	2117J	Kansas City	FV	75.00	95.00	130.
2718☆	2117J ☆	Kansas City	75.00	150.	210.	325.

KL#	Fr#	District	Fine	XF	CH CU (63)	Gem CU (65)
2719	2117K	Dallas	FV	75.00	95.00	110.
2719☆	2117K ☆	Dallas	100.	200.	300.	425.
2720	2117L	San Francisco	FV	75.00	115.	140.
2720☆	2117L ☆	San Francisco	75.00	150.	190.	325.

Series 1974 Neff-Simon

KL#	Fr#	District	Fine	XF	CH CU (63)	Gem CU (65)
2721	2118A	Boston	FV	70.00	115.	140.
2721☆	2118A☆	Boston	70.00	125.	150.	225.
2722	2118B	New York	FV	65.00	75.00	125.
2722☆	2118B☆	New York	70.00	125.	135.	220.
2723	2118C	Philadelphia	FV	70.00	115.	140.
2723☆	2118C☆	Philadelphia	70.00	125.	225.	300.
2724	2118D	Cleveland	FV	70.00	75.00	140.
2724☆	2118D☆	Cleveland	70.00	125.	150.	240.
2725	2118E	Richmond	FV	70.00	75.00	140.
2725☆	2118E☆	Richmond	70.00	125.	150.	240.
2726	2118F	Atlanta	FV	70.00	75.00	140.
2726☆	2118F☆	Atlanta	70.00	125.	150.	275.
2727	2118G	Chicago	FV	50.00	55.00	125.
2727☆	2118G☆	Chicago	70.00	75.00	100.	225.
2728	2118H	St. Louis	FV	75.00	170.	225.
2728☆	2118H☆	St. Louis	70.00	125.	265.	310.
2729	2118I	Minneapolis	FV	75.00	115.	175.
2729☆	2118I☆	Minneapolis	70.00	125.	265.	300.
2730	2118J	Kansas City	FV	75.00	115.	175.
2730☆	2118J☆	Kansas City	70.00	125.	265.	300.
2731	2118K	Dallas	FV	75.00	115.	175.
2731☆	2118K☆	Dallas	70.00	125.	265.	300.
2732	2118L	San Francisco	FV	75.00	115.	175.
2732☆	2118L☆	San Francisco	70.00	125.	300.	400.

Series 1977 Morton-Blumenthal

KL#	Fr#	District	Fine	XF	CH CU (63)	Gem CU (65)
2733	2119A	Boston	FV	50.00	75.00	100.
2733☆	2119A☆	Boston	75.00	125.	135.	225.
2734	2119B	New York	FV	55.00	75.00	100.
2734☆	2119B☆	New York	75.00	100.	115.	400.
2735	2119C	Philadelphia	FV	55.00	75.00	100.
2735☆	2119C☆	Philadelphia	75.00	125.	225.	275.
2736	2119D	Cleveland	FV	55.00	75.00	100.
2736☆	2119D☆	Cleveland	75.00	125.	150.	225.
2737	2119E	Richmond	FV	55.00	75.00	100.
2737☆	2119E☆	Richmond	75.00	125.	150.	200.
2738	2119F	Atlanta	FV	55.00	75.00	110.
2738☆	2119F☆	Atlanta	75.00	125.	150.	250.
2739	2119G	Chicago	FV	75.00	100.	125.
2739☆	2119G☆	Chicago	75.00	125.	150.	250.
2740	2119H	St. Louis	FV	75.00	90.00	150.
2740☆	2119H☆	St. Louis	75.00	125.	150.	250.
2741	2119I	Minneapolis	FV	100.	225.	300.
2742	2119J	Kansas City	FV	80.00	90.00	300.
2742☆	2119J☆	Kansas City	60.00	70.00	225.	250.
2743	2119K	Dallas	FV	80.00	90.00	140.
2743☆	2119K☆	Dallas	75.00	125.	190.	275.
2744	2119L	San Francisco	FV	50.00	55.00	125.
2744☆	2119L☆	San Francisco	75.00	125.	150.	275.

Series 1981 Buchanan-Regan

KL#	Fr#	District	Fine	XF	CH CU (63)	Gem CU (65)
3548	2120A	Boston	FV	70.00	115.	165.
3549	2120B	New York	FV	70.00	95.00	165.
3549☆	2120B☆	New York	75.00	150.	190.	375.
3550	2120C	Philadelphia	FV	70.00	115.	165.
3551	2120D	Cleveland	FV	70.00	115.	165.
3551☆	2120D☆	Cleveland	75.00	150.	225.	325.

KL#	Fr#	District	Fine	XF	CH CU (63)	Gem CU (65)
3552	2120E	Richmond	FV	70.00	115.	150.
3553	2120F	Atlanta	FV	70.00	115.	165.
3553☆	2120F☆	Atlanta	75.00	150.	225.	325.
3554	2120G	Chicago	FV	70.00	115.	165.
3554☆	2120G☆	Chicago	75.00	150.	225.	325.
3555	2120H	St. Louis	FV	70.00	115.	165.
3556	2120I	Minneapolis	FV	70.00	115.	165.
3556☆	2120I☆	Minneapolis	75.00	150.	275.	325.
3557	2120J	Kansas City	FV	70.00	115.	165.
3557☆	2120J☆	Kansas City	75.00	150.	225.	325.
3558	2120K	Dallas	FV	70.00	115.	165.
3559	2120L	San Francisco	FV	70.00	115.	165.
3559☆	2120L☆	San Francisco	75.00	150.	210.	325.

Series 1981A Ortega-Regan

KL#	Fr#	District	Fine	XF	CH CU (63)	Gem CU (65)
3648	2121A	Boston	FV	75.00	100.	165.
3649	2121B	New York	FV	75.00	100.	125.
3649☆	2121B☆	New York	100.	175.	275.	350.
3651	2121D	Cleveland	FV	75.00	100.	165.
3652	2121E	Richmond	FV	75.00	100.	165.
3652☆	2121E☆	Richmond	75.00	175.	250.	300.
3653	2121F	Atlanta	FV	75.00	100.	165
3654	2121G	Chicago	FV	75.00	100.	165.
3655	2121H	St. Louis	FV	75.00	100.	165.
3656	2121I	Minneapolis	FV	75.00	100.	165.
3657	2121J	Kansas City	FV	75.00	100.	165.
3658	2121K	Dallas	FV	75.00	100.	165.
3659	2121L	San Francisco	FV	75.00	100.	165.
3659☆	2121L☆	San Francisco	75.00	150.	300.	375.

Series 1985 Ortega-Baker

KL#	Fr#	District	Fine	XF	CH CU (63)	Gem CU (65)
3748	2122A	Boston	FV	60.00	75.00	100.
3748☆	2122A☆	Boston	75.00	100.	350.	400.
3749	2122B	New York	FV	60.00	75.00	100.
3749☆	2122B☆	New York	75.00	100.	250.	325.
3750	2122C	Philadelphia	FV	60.00	90.00	100.
3751	2122D	Cleveland	FV	60.00	75.00	100.
3751☆	2122D☆	Cleveland	75.00	100.	350.	375.
3752	2122E	Richmond	FV	60.00	75.00	100.
3753	2122F	Atlanta	FV	60.00	75.00	100.
3754	2122G	Chicago	FV	60.00	75.00	100.
3754☆	2122G☆	Chicago	75.00	100.	250.	300.
3755	2122H	St. Louis	FV	60.00	75.00	100.
3756	2122I	Minneapolis	FV	60.00	75.00	100.
3757	2122J	Kansas City	FV	60.00	75.00	100.
3758	2122K	Dallas	FV	60.00	75.00	100.
3759	2122L	San Francisco	FV	60.00	75.00	100.

Series 1988 Ortega-Brady

KL#	Fr#	District	Fine	XF	CH CU (63)	Gem CU (65)
3820	2123A	Boston	FV	60.00	150.	175.
3821	2123B	New York	FV	60.00	100.	125.
3821☆	2123B☆	New York	75.00	150.	300.	325.
3823	2123D	Cleveland	FV	60.00	150.	175.
3824	2123E	Richmond	FV	60.00	150.	175.
3826	2123G	Chicago	FV	60.00	100.	200.
3829	2123J	Kansas City	FV	60.00	150.	175.
3831	2123L	San Francisco	FV	60.00	150.	175.

Series 1990 Villalpando-Brady

KL#	Fr#	District	Fine	XF	CH CU (63)	Gem CU (65)
3964	2124A	Boston	FV	FV	75.00	80.00
3965	2124B	New York	FV	FV	75.00	80.00
3965☆	2124B☆	New York	FV	60.00	100.	110.
3966	2124C	Philadelphia	FV	FV	75.00	80.00
3966☆	2124C☆	Philadelphia	FV	60.00	125.	140.
3967	2124D	Cleveland	FV	FV	75.00	80.00
3968	2124E	Richmond	FV	FV	75.00	80.00
3970	2124G	Chicago	FV	300.	425.	475.
3970☆	2124G☆	Chicago	FV	60.00	100.	110.
3971	2124H	St. Louis	FV	FV	75.00	80.00
3972	2124I	Minneapolis	FV	FV	75.00	80.00
3973	2124J	Kansas City	FV	FV	75.00	80.00
3973☆	2124J☆	Kansas City	FV	60.00	125.	150.
3974	2124K	Dallas	FV	FV	75.00	80.00
3975	2124L	San Francisco	FV	FV	75.00	80.00

Series 1993 Withrow-Bentsen

KL#	Fr#	District	Fine	XF	CH CU (63)	Gem CU (65)
4060	2125A	Boston	FV	FV	70.00	80.00
4061	2125B	New York	FV	FV	70.00	80.00
4061☆	2125B☆	New York	FV	75.00	100.	140.
4063	2125D	Cleveland	FV	FV	70.00	80.00
4063☆	2125D☆	Cleveland	FV	75.00	135.	150.
4064	2125E	Richmond	FV	FV	70.00	80.00
4066	2125G	Chicago	FV	FV	90.00	110.
4066☆	2125G☆	Chicago	FV	75.00	100.	135.
4067	2125H	St. Louis	FV	FV	70.00	80.00
4069	2125J	Kansas City	FV	FV	70.00	80.00
4070	2125K	Dallas	FV	FV	70.00	80.00

Series 1996 Withrow-Rubin

KL#	Fr#	District	Fine	XF	CH CU (63)	Gem CU (65)
4150	2126A	Boston	FV	FV	70.00	75.00
4151	2126B	New York	FV	FV	70.00	75.00
4151☆	2126B☆	New York	FV	70.00	90.00	100.
4152	2126C	Philadelphia	FV	FV	70.00	75.00
4153	2126D	Cleveland	FV	FV	70.00	75.00
4154	2126E	Richmond	FV	FV	70.00	75.00
4155	2126F	Atlanta	FV	FV	70.00	75.00
4156	2126G	Chicago	FV	FV	60.00	65.00
4156☆	2126G☆	Chicago	FV	70.00	90.00	110.
4157	2126H	St. Louis	FV	FV	60.00	65.00
4158	2126I	Minneapolis	FV	FV	60.00	65.00
4159	2126J	Kansas City	FV	FV	60.00	65.00
4159☆	2126J☆	Kansas City	FV	70.00	95.00	110.
4160	2126K	Dallas	FV	FV	60.00	65.00
4161	2126L	San Francisco	FV	FV	60.00	65.00
4161☆	2126L☆	San Francisco	FV	70.00	90.00	110.

Series 2001 Marin-O'Neill - DC

KL#	Fr#	District	Fine	XF	CH CU (63)	Gem CU (65)
4629	2127A	Boston	FV	FV	75.00	85.00
4630	2127B	New York	FV	FV	70.00	80.00
4630☆	2127B☆	New York	100.	125.	250.	300.
4631	2127C	Philadelphia	FV	FV	70.00	80.00
4632	2127D	Cleveland	FV	FV	70.00	80.00
4633	2127E	Richmond	FV	FV	70.00	80.00
4633☆	2127E☆	Richmond	75.00	100.	125.	175.
4634	2127F	Atlanta	FV	FV	70.00	80.00
4635	2127G	Chicago	FV	FV	80.00	90.00
4636	2127H	St. Louis	FV	FV	80.00	90.00
4637	2127I	Minneapolis	FV	FV	80.00	90.00
4638	2127J	Kansas City	FV	FV	75.00	85.00
4639	2127K	Dallas	FV	FV	70.00	80.00
4640	2127L	San Francisco	FV	FV	70.00	80.00

Series 2004 Marin-Snow - FW

KL#	Fr#	District	Fine	XF	CH CU (63)	Gem CU (65)
4752	2128A	Boston	FV	FV	75.00	80.00
4753	2128B	New York	FV	FV	70.00	80.00
4754	2128C	Philadelphia	FV	FV	70.00	80.00
4755	2128D	Cleveland	FV	FV	70.00	80.00
4756	2128E	Richmond	FV	FV	85.00	95.00
4756☆	2128E☆	Richmond	FV	125.	150.	225.
4757	2128F	Atlanta	FV	FV	70.00	80.00
4758	2128G	Chicago	FV	FV	70.00	80.00
4758☆	2128G☆	Chicago	FV	FV	85.00	95.00
4759	2128H	St. Louis	FV	FV	70.00	80.00
4760	2128I	Minneapolis	FV	FV	70.00	80.00
4761	2128J	Kansas City	FV	FV	70.00	80.00
4762	2128K	Dallas	FV	FV	70.00	80.00
4762☆	2128K☆	Dallas	FV	75.00	150.	175.
4763	2128L	San Francisco	FV	FV	70.00	80.00
4763☆	2128I☆	San Francisco	FV	FV	85.00	110.

Series 2004A Cabral-Snow - FW

KL#	Fr#	District	Fine	XF	CH CU (63)	Gem CU (65)
4763A	-	Boston	FV	FV	95.00	100.
4763B	-	New York	FV	FV	70.00	73.00
4763C	-	Richmond	FV	FV	70.00	73.00
4763C☆	-	Richmond	FV	FV	90.00	95.00
4763D	-	Atlanta	FV	FV	70.00	73.00
4763E	-	Chicago	FV	FV	70.00	73.00
4763F	-	Kansas City	FV	FV	70.00	73.00

Series 2006 Cabral-Paulson - FW

KL#	Fr#	District	Fine	XF	CH CU (63)	Gem CU (65)
4825	-	Boston	FV	FV	75.00	80.00
4825☆	-	Boston	FV	FV	90.00	95.00
4826	-	New York	FV	FV	75.00	325.
4827	-	Philadelphia	FV	FV	70.00	73.00
4828	-	Cleveland	FV	FV	75.00	80.00
4829	-	Richmond	FV	FV	75.00	80.00
4830	-	Atlanta	FV	FV	70.00	80.00
4831	-	Chicago	FV	FV	70.00	80.00
4831☆	-	Chicago	FV	FV	90.00	95.00
4832	-	St. Louis	FV	FV	75.00	80.00
4833	-	Minneapolis	FV	FV	75.00	80.00
4834	-	Kansas City	FV	FV	70.00	80.00
4835	-	Dallas	FV	FV	75.00	80.00
4836	-	San Francisco	FV	FV	75.00	80.00

Series 2009 Rios-Geithner - FW

KL#	Fr#	District	Fine	XF	CH CU (63)	Gem CU (65)
4964	-	Philadelphia	FV	FV	75.00	80.00
4967	-	Atlanta	FV	FV	75.00	80.00
4968	-	Chicago	FV	FV	75.00	80.00
4968☆	-	Chicago	FV	FV	90.00	95.00

United States Notes
One Hundred Dollars

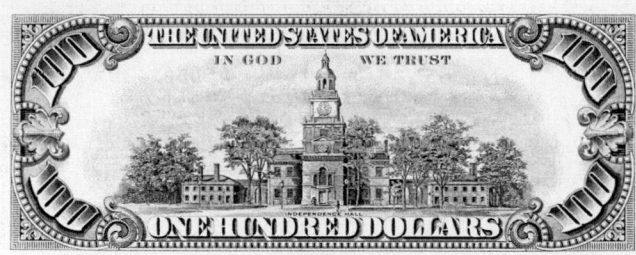

KL#	Fr#	Series	Signatures	Fine	XF	CH CU (63)	Gem CU (65)
2745	1550	1966	Granahan-Fowler	125.	300.	375.	1100.
2745☆	1550	1966☆	Granahan-Fowler	225.	525.	1400.	2550.

KL#	Fr#	Series	Signatures	Fine	XF	CH CU (63)	Gem CU (65)
2746	1551	1966A	Elston-Kennedy	150.	225.	600.	1550.

Gold Certificates

KL#	Fr#	Series	Signatures	VF	XF	CH CU (63)	Gem CU (65)
2747	2405	1928	Woods-Mellon	550.	1250.	4025.	25,000.
2747☆	2405	1928☆	Woods-Mellon	9000.	15,000.	30,000.	50,000.
2748	-	1934	Julian-Morgenthau	—	—	—	—

Federal Reserve Bank Notes

KL#	Fr#	Series	District	Fine	XF	CH CU (63)	Gem CU (65)
2749	1890B	1929	New York	130.	165.	300.	2000.
2749☆	1890B	1929☆	New York	1100.	3500.	—	—
2751	1890D	1929	Cleveland	125.	175.	275.	600.
2751☆	1890D	1929☆	Cleveland	1500.	4000.	8000.	—
2752	1890E	1929	Richmond	150.	275.	650.	2500.
2752☆	1890E	1929☆	Richmond	2500.	7500.	10,500.	15,000.
2754	1890G	1929	Chicago	125.	150.	325.	900.
2754☆	1890G	1929☆	Chicago	1000.	4000.	5350.	5750.

KL#	Fr#	Series	District	Fine	XF	CH CU (63)	Gem CU (65)
2756	1890I	1929	Minneapolis	150.	175.	850.	1625.
2756☆	1890I	1929☆	Minneapolis	6000.	13,000.	—	—
2757	1890J	1929	Kansas City	125.	190.	500.	1175.
2757☆	1890J	1929☆	Kansas City	425.	600.	1150.	2000.
2758	1890K	1929	Dallas	300.	500.	725.	3300.
2758☆	1890K	1929☆	Dallas	23,000.	25,000.	30,000.	—

Federal Reserve Notes

Series 1928 Woods-Mellon

KL#	Fr#	District	Fine	XF	CH CU (63)	Gem CU (65)
2760	2150A	Boston	150.	300.	900.	1500.
2760☆	2150A☆	Boston	—	—	4000.	6500.
2761	2150B	New York	150.	350.	750.	4000.
2761☆	2150B☆	New York	300.	1500.	2500.	5000.
2762	2150C	Philadelphia	115.	225.	750.	2000.
2762☆	2150C☆	Philadelphia	350.	675.	2500.	4500.
2763	2150D	Cleveland	115.	225.	900.	1500.
2763☆	2150D☆	Cleveland	200.	750.	2500.	3750.
2764	2150E	Richmond	115.	300.	800.	1200.
2764☆	2150E☆	Richmond	1000.	3000.	7000.	8500.
2765	2150F	Atlanta	115.	275.	900.	1500.
2765☆	2150F☆	Atlanta	150.	7000.	10,000.	12,500.
2766	2150G	Chicago	115.	225.	600.	1450.
2766☆	2150G☆	Chicago	150.	850.	2500.	6500.
2767	2150H	St. Louis	115.	250.	1000.	4000.
2767☆	2150H☆	St. Louis	200.	1200.	4000.	4500.
2768	2150I	Minneapolis	115.	450.	2500.	7500.
2768☆	2150I☆	Minneapolis	200.	2500.	6000.	7500.
2769	2150J	Kansas City	115.	225.	825.	3000.
2769☆	2150J☆	Kansas City	1500.	2500.	6000.	6500.
2770	2150K	Dallas	115.	600.	600.	3500.
2770☆	2150K☆	Dallas	—	—	—	—
2771	2150L	San Francisco	115.	225.	1500.	2000.
2771☆	2150L☆	San Francisco	3225.	4500.	6000.	7500.

Series 1928A Woods-Mellon

KL#	Fr#	District	Fine	XF	CH CU (63)	Gem CU (65)
2772	2151A	Boston	FV	200.	350.	450.
2773	2151B	New York	FV	175.	250.	350.
2773☆	2151B☆	New York	1000.	—	—	—
2774	2151C	Philadelphia	FV	200.	300.	800.
2775	2151D	Cleveland	FV	185.	325.	450.
2776	2151D	Richmond	FV	210.	325.	500.
2777	2151E	Atlanta	FV	195.	600.	1500.
2778	2151G	Chicago	FV	165.	275.	400.
2779	2151H	St. Louis	200.	275.	325.	750.
2779☆	2151H☆	St. Louis	2500.	8000.	15,000.	18,000.
2780	2151I	Minneapolis	FV	195.	400.	1500.
2781	2151J	Kansas City	FV	210.	450.	600.
2782	2151K	Dallas	FV	225.	400.	700.
2783	2151L	San Francisco	FV	185.	400.	600.

Series 1934 Julian-Morganthau

KL#	Fr#	District	Fine	XF	CH CU (63)	Gem CU (65)
2784	2152A	Boston	FV	130.	150.	350.
2784☆	2152A☆	Boston	FV	900.	1500.	1750.
2785	2152B	New York	FV	130.	145.	350.
2785☆	2152B☆	New York	FV	500.	700.	1500.
2786	2152C	Philadelphia	125.	180.	175.	350.
2786☆	2152C☆	Philadelphia	575.	1275.	1500.	1700.
2787	2152D	Cleveland	FV	175.	225.	350.
2787☆	2152D☆	Cleveland	125.	400.	1500.	2300.
2788	2152E	Richmond	FV	175.	200.	350.
2788☆	2152E☆	Richmond	150.	300.	1500.	2250.
2789	2152F	Atlanta	FV	210.	200.	350.
2789☆	2152F☆	Atlanta	FV	1650.	1750.	2000.
2790	2152G	Chicago	FV	110.	275.	300.

KL#	Fr#	District	Fine	XF	CH CU (63)	Gem CU (65)
2790☆	2152G☆	Chicago	150.	200.	320.	—
2791	2152H	St. Louis	FV	135.	175.	350.
2791☆	2152H☆	St. Louis	150.	300.	1500.	1800.
2792	2152I	Minneapolis	FV	175.	225.	575.
2792☆	2152I☆	Minneapolis	150.	400.	1500.	2000.
2793	2152J	Kansas City	FV	175.	375.	425.
2793☆	2152J☆	Kansas City	FV	300.	1500.	2000.
2794	2152K	Dallas	FV	175.	200.	375.
2794☆	2152K☆	Dallas	FV	300.	2000.	2500.
2795	2152L	San Francisco	FV	175.	225.	400.
2795☆	2152L☆	San Francisco	FV	300.	1200.	1700.

Series 1934A Julian-Morgenthau

KL#	Fr#	District	Fine	XF	CH CU (63)	Gem CU (65)
2784A	2153A	Boston	FV	225.	500.	600.
2784A☆	2153A☆	Boston	FV	400.	1500.	—
2785A	2153B	New York	FV	135.	225.	250.
2785A☆	2153B☆	New York	175.	350.	700.	1500.
2786A	2153C	Philadelphia	FV	180.	400.	475.
2786A☆	2153C☆	Philadelphia	FV	400.	1500.	—
2787A	2153D	Cleveland	FV	180.	400.	475.
2787A☆	2153D☆	Cleveland	150.	300.	1500.	—
2788A	2153E	Richmond	FV	180.	400.	475.
2788A☆	2153E☆	Richmond	200.	425.	1500.	2000.
2789A	2153F	Atlanta	FV	180.	400.	500.
2789A☆	2153F☆	Atlanta	200.	425.	1500.	2000.
2790A	2153G	Chicago	FV	180.	225.	275.
2790A☆	2153G☆	Chicago	200.	500.	2100.	1300.
2791A	2153H	St. Louis	FV	180.	400.	500.
2791A☆	2153H☆	St. Louis	—	—	—	—
2792A	2153I	Minneapolis	FV	180.	225.	400.
2792A☆	2153I☆	Minneapolis	—	—	—	—
2793A	2153J	Kansas City	FV	180.	400.	550.
2793A☆	2153J☆	Kansas City	—	—	—	—
2794A	2153K	Dallas	FV	180.	400.	500.
2794A☆	2153K☆	Dallas	—	—	—	—
2795A	2153L	San Francisco	FV	180.	400.	600.
2795A☆	2153L☆	San Francisco	750.	1000.	2000.	—

Series 1934B Julian-Vinson

KL#	Fr#	District	Fine	XF	CH CU (63)	Gem CU (65)
2796	2154A	Boston	FV	350.	425.	600.
2797	2154C	Philadelphia	—	—	—	—
2798	2154D	Cleveland	FV	350.	450.	1100.
2799	2154E	Richmond	100.	225.	450.	800.
2799☆	2154E☆	Richmond	800.	2200.	4500.	6500.
2800	2154F	Atlanta	FV	300.	450.	650.
2800☆	2154F☆	Atlanta	—	—	—	—
2801	2154G	Chicago	FV	300.	450.	650.
2801☆	2154G☆	Chicago	—	—	—	—
2802	2154H	St. Louis	FV	300.	450.	750.
2802☆	2154H☆	St. Louis	650.	2200.	4000.	6500.
2803	2154I	Minneapolis	FV	300.	450.	650.
2803☆	2154I☆	Minneapolis	800.	2200.	4500.	6500.
2804	2154J	Kansas City	FV	300.	450.	650.
2804☆	2154J☆	Kansas City	—	—	—	—
2805	2154K	Dallas	FV	300.	500.	2530.
2805☆	2154K☆	Dallas	800.	2200.	4000.	6500.

Series 1934C Julian-Snyder

KL#	Fr#	District	Fine	XF	CH CU (63)	Gem CU (65)
2806	2155A	Boston	FV	175.	500.	1600.
2807	2155B	New York	—	—	—	—
2808	2155C	Philadelphia	FV	200.	500.	750.
2809	2155D	Cleveland	FV	200.	500.	700.
2809☆	2155D☆	Cleveland	400.	2250.	4500.	6500.
2809A	2155E	Richmond	100.	250.	300.	400.
2809A☆	2155E☆	Richmond	300.	2000.	3000.	6000.
2810	2155F	Atlanta	FV	200.	400.	1300.
2810☆	2155F☆	Atlanta	500.	1200.	3750.	4500.
2811	2155G	Chicago	FV	200.	300.	400.
2811☆	2155G☆	Chicago	425.	1200.	3000.	4250.

KL#	Fr#	District	Fine	XF	CH CU (63)	Gem CU (65)
2812	2155H	St. Louis	FV	165.	175.	299.
2812☆	2155H☆	St. Louis	500.	1200.	3750.	5000.
2813	2155I	Minneapolis	FV	200.	350.	400.
2814	2155J	Kansas City	FV	200.	450.	600.
2815	2155K	Dallas	FV	200.	575.	600.
2815☆	2155K☆	Dallas	—	—	—	—
2816	2155L	San Francisco	FV	200.	450.	1150.
2816☆	2155L☆	San Francisco	750.	2000.	4500.	7500.

Series 1934D Clark-Snyder

KL#	Fr#	District	Fine	XF	CH CU (63)	Gem CU (65)
2817	2156B	New York	750.	2500.	5000.	—
2818	2156C	Philadelphia	FV	350.	600.	750.
2818☆	2156C☆	Philadelphia	750.	3000.	6000.	—
2819	2156F	Atlanta	FV	350.	750.	1000.
2819☆	2156F☆	Atlanta	750.	3000.	6000.	—
2820	2156G	Chicago	175.	400.	500.	1000.
2820☆	2156G☆	Chicago	1000.	2750.	6000.	8000.
2821	2156H	St. Louis	FV	350.	500.	2300.
2822	2156K	Dallas	FV	350.	750.	—

Series 1950 Clark-Snyder

KL#	Fr#	District	Fine	XF	CH CU (63)	Gem CU (65)
2823	2157A	Boston	FV	300.	450.	700.
2823☆	2157A☆	Boston	250.	700.	1300.	1900.
2824	2157B	New York	FV	275.	350.	600.
2824☆	2157B☆	New York	FV	700.	1300.	1900.
2825	2157C	Philadelphia	FV	200.	400.	600.
2825☆	2157C☆	Philadelphia	FV	275.	1500.	1900.
2826	2157D	Cleveland	FV	200.	400.	600.
2826☆	2157D☆	Cleveland	1.00	275.	1500.	2000.
2827	2157E	Richmond	FV	200.	400.	700.

KL#	Fr#	District	Fine	XF	CH CU (63)	Gem CU (65)
2827☆	2157E☆	Richmond	FV	275.	1500.	2000.
2828	2157F	Atlanta	FV	200.	400.	700.
2829	2157G	Chicago	FV	200.	400.	700.
2830	2157H	St. Louis	FV	200.	400.	700.
2831	2157I	Minneapolis	FV	200.	450.	700.
2831☆	2157I☆	Minneapolis	FV	200.	400.	700.
2832	2157J	Kansas City	FV	200.	450.	700.
2832☆	2157J☆	Kansas City	250.	750.	1500.	2000.
2833	2157K	Dallas	FV	200.	450.	700.
2834	2157L	San Francisco	FV	200.	450.	700.

Series 1950A Priest-Humphrey

KL#	Fr#	District	Fine	XF	CH CU (63)	Gem CU (65)
2835	2158A	Boston	FV	FV	200.	400.
2835☆	2158A☆	Boston	150.	250.	400.	850.
2836	2158B	New York	FV	FV	200.	375.
2836☆	2158B☆	New York	150.	250.	350.	700.
2837	2158C	Philadelphia	FV	FV	200.	400.
2837☆	2158C☆	Philadelphia	150.	250.	400.	700.
2838	2158D	Cleveland	FV	FV	225.	350.
2838☆	2158D☆	Cleveland	150.	250.	700.	900.
2839	2158E	Richmond	FV	FV	240.	350.
2839☆	2158E☆	Richmond	125.	250.	400.	900.
2840	2158F	Atlanta	FV	FV	240.	400.
2840☆	2158F☆	Atlanta	125.	250.	400.	800.
2841	2158G	Chicago	FV	FV	240.	400.
2841☆	2158G☆	Chicago	125.	250.	400.	700.
2842	2158H	St. Louis	FV	FV	240.	350.
2842☆	2158H☆	St. Louis	125.	250.	400.	700.
2843	2158I	Minneapolis	FV	FV	240.	400.
2843☆	2158I☆	Minneapolis	125.	250.	520.	800.
2844	2158J	Kansas City	FV	FV	240.	400.
2844☆	2158J☆	Kansas City	125.	250.	560.	800.
2845	2158K	Dallas	FV	FV	240.	400.
2846	2158L	San Francisco	FV	125.	240.	400.
2846☆	2158L☆	San Francisco	125.	250.	400.	800.

Series 1950B Priest-Anderson

KL#	Fr#	District	Fine	XF	CH CU (63)	Gem CU (65)
2847	2159A	Boston	FV	185.	190.	205.
2847☆	2159A☆	Boston	—	—	—	—
2848	2159B	New York	FV	110.	160.	350.
2848☆	2159B☆	New York	150.	275.	280.	550.
2849	2159C	Philadelphia	FV	125.	275.	350.
2849☆	2159C☆	Philadelphia	150.	300.	320.	600.
2850	2159D	Cleveland	FV	185.	1.00	350.
2850☆	2159D☆	Cleveland	200.	300.	400.	500.
2851	2159E	Richmond	FV	140.	180.	325.
2851☆	2159E☆	Richmond	—	—	—	—
2852	2159F	Atlanta	FV	185.	240.	450.
2852☆	2159F☆	Atlanta	175.	275.	400.	700.
2853	2159G	Chicago	FV	150.	160.	450.
2853☆	2159G☆	Chicago	175.	215.	240.	725.
2854	2159H	St. Louis	FV	150.	180.	400.
2854☆	2159H☆	St. Louis	175.	275.	320.	400.
2855	2159I	Minneapolis	FV	185.	240.	325.
2855☆	2159I☆	Minneapolis	175.	275.	560.	925.
2856	2159J	Kansas City	FV	185.	200.	325.
2856☆	2159J☆	Kansas City	175.	200.	225.	245.
2857	2159K	Dallas	FV	185.	200.	450.
2857☆	2159K☆	Dallas	175.	275.	440.	800.
2858	2159L	San Francisco	FV	185.	225.	350.
2858☆	2159L☆	San Francisco	175.	275.	320.	800.

Series 1950C Smith-Dillon

KL#	Fr#	District	Fine	XF	CH CU (63)	Gem CU (65)
2859	2160A	Boston	FV	FV	225.	275.
2859☆	2160A☆	Boston	150.	300.	400.	700.
2860	2160B	New York	FV	FV	180.	275.
2860☆	2160B☆	New York	150.	300.	440.	750.

KL#	Fr#	District	Fine	XF	CH CU (63)	Gem CU (65)
2861☆	2160C☆	Philadelphia	150.	300.	440.	750.
2862	2160D	Cleveland	FV	FV	200.	275.
2862☆	2160D☆	Cleveland	150.	300.	440.	750.
2863	2160E	Richmond	FV	FV	200.	275.
2863☆	2160E☆	Richmond	150.	300.	440.	750.
2864	2160F	Atlanta	FV	FV	200.	275.
2864☆	2160F☆	Atlanta	150.	300.	440.	700.
2865	2160G	Chicago	FV	FV	220.	275.
2865☆	2160G☆	Chicago	150.	300.	440.	750.
2866	2160H	St. Louis	FV	FV	175.	275.
2866☆	2160H☆	St. Louis	150.	260.	300.	750.
2867	2160I	Minneapolis	FV	FV	200.	275.
2867☆	2160I☆	Minneapolis	—	—	—	—
2868	2160J	Kansas City	FV	FV	200.	275.
2868☆	2160J☆	Kansas City	—	—	—	—
2869	2160K	Dallas	FV	FV	200.	275.
2869☆	2160K☆	Dallas	150.	300.	440.	750.
2870	2160L	San Francisco	FV	FV	180.	275.
2870☆	2160L☆	San Francisco	150.	300.	440.	700.

Series 1950D Granahan-Dillon

KL#	Fr#	District	Fine	XF	CH CU (63)	Gem CU (65)
2871	2161A	Boston	FV	FV	180.	300.
2871☆	2161A☆	Boston	175.	275.	560.	750.
2872	2161B	New York	FV	FV	160.	300.
2872☆	2161B☆	New York	175.	275.	400.	650.
2873	2161C	Philadelphia	FV	FV	180.	300.
2873☆	2161C☆	Philadelphia	FV	225.	560.	800.
2874	2161D	Cleveland	FV	FV	180.	300.
2874☆	2161D☆	Cleveland	175.	275.	400.	475.
2875	2161E	Richmond	FV	FV	225.	325.
2875☆	2161E☆	Richmond	175.	275.	400.	1600.
2876	2161F	Atlanta	FV	FV	225.	300.
2876☆	2161F☆	Atlanta	175.	275.	600.	900.
2877	2161G	Chicago	FV	FV	200.	300.
2877☆	2161G☆	Chicago	175.	275.	400.	450.
2878	2161H	St. Louis	FV	FV	200.	300.
2878☆	2161H☆	St. Louis	175.	275.	700.	900.
2879	2161I	Minneapolis	FV	FV	225.	275.
2879☆	2161I☆	Minneapolis	175.	275.	700.	900.
2880	2161J	Kansas City	FV	FV	225.	300.
2880☆	2161J☆	Kansas City	175.	275.	700.	900.
2881	2161K	Dallas	FV	175.	200.	300.
2881☆	2161K☆	Dallas	FV	225.	400.	900.
2882	2161L	San Francisco	FV	175.	180.	325.
2882☆	2161L☆	San Francisco	FV	225.	440.	750.

Series 1950E Granahan-Fowler

KL#	Fr#	District	Fine	XF	CH CU (63)	Gem CU (65)
2883	2162B	New York	FV	200.	250.	275.
2883☆	2162B ☆	New York	250.	400.	2500.	3000.
2884	2162G	Chicago	150.	300.	550.	900.
2884☆	2162G ☆	Chicago	—	—	—	—
2885	2162L	San Francisco	110.	140.	300.	375.
2885☆	2162L ☆	San Francisco	600.	800.	3500.	3750.

Series 1963A Granahan-Fowler

KL#	Fr#	District	Fine	XF	CH CU (63)	Gem CU (65)
2886	2163A	Boston	FV	120.	150.	200.
2886☆	2163A☆	Boston	125.	225.	300.	750.
2887	2163B	New York	FV	FV	135.	200.
2887☆	2163B☆	New York	125.	175.	225.	300.
2888	2163C	Philadelphia	FV	FV	150.	200.
2888☆	2163C☆	Philadelphia	125.	175.	375.	450.
2889	2163D	Cleveland	FV	FV	125.	140.
2889☆	2163D☆	Cleveland	125.	175.	220.	300.
2890	2163E	Richmond	FV	FV	150.	200.
2890☆	2163E☆	Richmond	125.	175.	375.	450.
2891	2163F	Atlanta	FV	FV	150.	200.
2891☆	2163F☆	Atlanta	125.	175.	450.	750.

KL#	Fr#	District	Fine	XF	CH CU (63)	Gem CU (65)
2892	2163G	Chicago	FV	FV	135.	200.
2892☆	2163G ☆	Chicago	125.	175.	225.	325.
2893	2163H	St. Louis	FV	FV	150.	200.
2893☆	2163H ☆	St. Louis	FV	125.	300.	375.
2894	2163I	Minneapolis	FV	FV	150.	425.
2894☆	2163I ☆	Minneapolis	125.	175.	450.	550.
2895	2163J	Kansas City	FV	FV	150.	200.
2895☆	2163J ☆	Kansas City	125.	175.	450.	525.
2896	2163K	Dallas	FV	FV	150.	200.
2896☆	2163K ☆	Dallas	125.	175.	450.	700.
2897	2163L	San Francisco	FV	FV	150.	200.
2897☆	2163L ☆	San Francisco	125.	175.	215.	400.

Series 1969 Elston-Kennedy

KL#	Fr#	District	Fine	XF	CH CU (63)	Gem CU (65)
2898	2164A	Boston	FV	FV	140.	225.
2898☆	2164A☆	Boston	125.	200.	280.	400.
2899	2164B	New York	FV	FV	140.	225.
2899☆	2164B☆	New York	125.	200.	240.	400.
2900	2164C	Philadelphia	FV	FV	140.	225.
2900☆	2164C☆	Philadelphia	125.	200.	280.	400.
2901	2164D	Cleveland	FV	FV	150.	225.
2901☆	2164D☆	Cleveland	125.	200.	420.	475.
2902	2164E	Richmond	FV	FV	140.	225.
2902☆	2164E ☆	Richmond	110.	120.	125.	150.
2903	2164F	Atlanta	FV	FV	140.	225.
2903☆	2164F ☆	Atlanta	125.	200.	280.	400.
2904	2164G	Chicago	FV	FV	120.	225.
2904☆	2164G☆	Chicago	125.	200.	280.	400.
2905	2164H	St. Louis	FV	FV	140.	225.
2905☆	2164H☆	St. Louis	125.	200.	320.	575.
2906	2164I	Minneapolis	FV	FV	140.	225.
2906☆	2164I ☆	Minneapolis	125.	200.	300.	575.
2907	2164J	Kansas City	FV	FV	140.	225.
2907☆	2164J ☆	Kansas City	125.	200.	280.	450.
2908	2164K	Dallas	FV	FV	140.	225.
2908☆	2164K☆	Dallas	125.	200.	280.	400.
2909	2164L	San Francisco	FV	FV	140.	225.
2909☆	2164L☆	San Francisco	125.	200.	280.	300.

Series 1969A Kabis-Connally

KL#	Fr#	District	Fine	XF	CH CU (63)	Gem CU (65)
2909A	2165A	Boston	FV	FV	180.	235.
2909A☆	2165A☆	Boston	125.	150.	260.	500.
2909B	2165B	New York	FV	FV	140.	200.
2909B☆	2165B☆	New York	125.	150.	220.	300.
2909C	2165C	Philadelphia	FV	FV	180.	235.
2909C☆	2165C☆	Philadelphia	125.	150.	260.	325.
2909D	2165D	Cleveland	FV	FV	180.	225.
2909D☆	2165D☆	Cleveland	125.	150.	260.	325.
2909E	2165E	Richmond	FV	FV	200.	250.
2909E☆	2165E☆	Richmond	125.	150.	275.	325.
2909F	2165F	Atlanta	FV	FV	180.	235.
2909F☆	2165F☆	Atlanta	125.	150.	480.	600.
2909G	2165G	Chicago	FV	FV	140.	200.
2909G☆	2165G☆	Chicago	125.	150.	245.	300.
2909H	2165H	St. Louis	FV	FV	180.	225.
2909H☆	2165H☆	St. Louis	125.	150.	320.	400.
2909I	2165I	Minneapolis	FV	FV	180.	225.
2909J	2165J	Kansas City	FV	FV	180.	225.
2909K	2165K	Dallas	FV	FV	180.	250.
2909K☆	2165K☆	Dallas	125.	150.	300.	435.
2909L	2165L	San Francisco	FV	FV	180.	250.
2909L☆	2165L☆	San Francisco	125.	150.	260.	325.

Series 1969C Banuelos-Shultz

KL#	Fr#	District	Fine	XF	CH CU (63)	Gem CU (65)
2910	2166A	Boston	FV	FV	150.	225.
2910☆	2166A☆	Boston	150.	225.	375.	475.
2911	2166B	New York	FV	FV	135.	225.
2911☆	2166B☆	New York	150.	225.	225.	375.
2912	2166C	Philadelphia	FV	FV	150.	225.
2912☆	2166C☆	Philadelphia	150.	225.	450.	500.

KL#	Fr#	District	Fine	XF	CH CU (63)	Gem CU (65)
2913	2166D	Cleveland	FV	FV	150.	225.
2913☆	2166D☆	Cleveland	150.	225.	450.	500.
2914	2166E	Richmond	FV	FV	150.	225.
2914☆	2166E ☆	Richmond	150.	225.	300.	375.
2915	2166F	Atlanta	FV	FV	150.	225.
2915☆	2166F ☆	Atlanta	150.	225.	450.	500.
2916	2166G	Chicago	FV	FV	150.	225.
2916☆	2166G☆	Chicago	150.	225.	200.	250.
2917	2166H	St. Louis	FV	FV	140.	165.
2917☆	2166H☆	St. Louis	150.	225.	450.	500.
2918	2166I	Minneapolis	FV	FV	170.	225.
2918☆	2166I ☆	Minneapolis	150.	225.	375.	425.
2919	2166J	Kansas City	FV	FV	150.	225.
2919☆	2166J ☆	Kansas City	150.	225.	375.	450.
2920	2166K	Dallas	FV	FV	150.	225.
2920☆	2166K☆	Dallas	150.	225.	375.	475.
2921	2166L	San Francisco	FV	FV	150.	225.
2921☆	2166L ☆	San Francisco	150.	225.	300.	375.

A Word About Star Notes

In our listings there are often two entries for each catalog number.
For example:

KL#	Fr#	District	Fine	XF	CH CU (63)	Gem CU (65)
2901	2164D	Cleveland	FV	FV	150.	225.
2901☆	2164D ☆	Cleveland	125.	200.	420.	475.

The first listing has a serial number format of letter - eight digits - letter.

The second listing refers to a bank note with a serial number format of
letter - eight digits - star.

This star at the end of the serial number refers to a replacement note,
one which replaces a note damaged during the production process.
There are fewer of these printed and therefore they are more expensive.

Series 1974 Neff-Simon

KL#	Fr#	District	Fine	XF	CH CU (63)	Gem CU (65)
2922	2167A	Boston	FV	FV	135.	200.
2922☆	2167A ☆	Boston	125.	200.	285.	350.
2923	2167B	New York	FV	FV	115.	200.
2923☆	2167B ☆	New York	125.	200.	150.	350.
2924	2167C	Philadelphia	FV	FV	135.	200.
2924☆	2167C ☆	Philadelphia	125.	200.	225.	625.
2925	2167D	Cleveland	FV	FV	135.	200.
2925☆	2167D ☆	Cleveland	125.	200.	375.	450.
2926	2167E	Richmond	FV	FV	135.	200.
2926☆	2167E ☆	Richmond	125.	200.	285.	350.
2927	2167F	Atlanta	FV	FV	135.	200.
2927☆	2167F ☆	Atlanta	125.	200.	285.	350.
2928	2167G	Chicago	FV	FV	115.	200.
2928☆	2167G ☆	Chicago	125.	200.	245.	350.
2929	2167H	St. Louis	FV	FV	135.	200.
2929☆	2167H ☆	St. Louis	125.	200.	286.	350.
2930	2167I	Minneapolis	FV	FV	135.	200.
2930☆	2167I ☆	Minneapolis	125.	130.	135.	140.
2931	2167J	Kansas City	FV	FV	135.	200.
2931☆	2167J ☆	Kansas City	125.	200.	285.	350.
2932	2167K	Dallas	FV	FV	265.	300.
2932☆	2167K ☆	Dallas	125.	200.	285.	350.
2933	2167L	San Francisco	FV	FV	135.	200.
2933☆	2167L ☆	San Francisco	125.	200.	210.	220.

Series 1977 Morton-Blumenthal

KL#	Fr#	District	Fine	XF	CH CU (63)	Gem CU (65)
2934	2168A	Boston	FV	FV	130.	175.
2934☆	2168A ☆	Boston	FV	175.	300.	340.
2935	2168B	New York	FV	FV	130.	175.
2935☆	2168B ☆	New York	FV	200.	300.	340.

KL#	Fr#	District	Fine	XF	CH CU (63)	Gem CU (65)
2936	2168C	Philadelphia	FV	FV	130.	175.
2936☆	2168C☆	Philadelphia	FV	125.	175.	200.
2937	2168D	Cleveland	FV	FV	130.	175.
2937☆	2168D☆	Cleveland	FV	175.	225.	340.
2938	2168E	Richmond	FV	FV	130.	175.
2938☆	2168E☆	Richmond	FV	175.	300.	340.
2939	2168F	Atlanta	FV	FV	200.	225.
2939☆	2168F☆	Atlanta	FV	175.	450.	500.
2940	2168G	Chicago	FV	FV	115.	175.
2940☆	2168G☆	Chicago	FV	175.	225.	340.
2941	2168H	St. Louis	FV	FV	130.	175.
2941☆	2168H☆	St. Louis	FV	175.	225.	375.
2942	2168I	Minneapolis	FV	FV	300.	350.
2942☆	2168I ☆	Minneapolis	FV	175.	300.	340.
2943	2168J	Kansas City	FV	FV	130.	175.
2943☆	2168J☆	Kansas City	FV	175.	225.	500.
2944	2168K	Dallas	FV	FV	130.	175.
2944☆	2168K☆	Dallas	FV	175.	300.	340.
2944A	2168L	San Francisco	FV	FV	130.	175.
2944A☆	2168L☆	San Francisco	FV	175.	225.	340.

Series 1981 Buchanan-Regan

KL#	Fr#	District	Fine	XF	CH CU (63)	Gem CU (65)
3560	2169A	Boston	FV	FV	140.	225.
3561	2169B	New York	FV	FV	140.	225.
3562	2169C	Philadelphia	FV	FV	160.	225.
3563	2169D	Cleveland	FV	FV	160.	225.
3564	2169E	Richmond	FV	FV	140.	225.
3564☆	2169E ☆	Richmond	225.	600.	3000.	3300.
3565	2169F	Atlanta	FV	FV	220.	225.
3566	2169G	Chicago	FV	FV	140.	225.
3567	2169H	St. Louis	FV	FV	140.	225.
3568	2169I	Minneapolis	FV	FV	140.	200.
3569	2169J	Kansas City	FV	FV	140.	225.
3570	2169K	Dallas	FV	FV	140.	225.
3571	2169L	San Francisco	FV	FV	140.	225.

Series 1981A Ortega-Regan

KL#	Fr#	District	Fine	XF	CH CU (63)	Gem CU (65)
3660	2170A	Boston	FV	125.	160.	225.
3661	2170B	New York	FV	125.	140.	225.
3662	2170C	Philadelphia	FV	125.	200.	225.
3663	2170D	Cleveland	FV	125.	160.	225.
3664	2170E	Richmond	FV	125.	160.	225.
3665	2170F	Atlanta	FV	125.	160.	225.
3666	2170G	Chicago	FV	125.	140.	225.
3667	2170H	St. Louis	FV	125.	160.	225.
3668	2170I	Minneapolis	FV	125.	160.	225.
3670	2170K	Dallas	FV	125.	160.	225.
3671	2170L	San Francisco	FV	125.	175.	225.
3671☆	2170L ☆	San Francisco	375.	750.	550.	600.

Series 1985 Ortega-Baker

KL#	Fr#	District	Fine	XF	CH CU (63)	Gem CU (65)
3760	2171A	Boston	FV	FV	150.	175.
3761	2171B	New York	FV	FV	150.	175.
3762	2171C	Philadelphia	FV	FV	150.	175.
3763	2171D	Cleveland	FV	FV	150.	175.
3763☆	2171D☆	Cleveland	125.	225.	400.	450.
3764	2171E	Richmond	FV	FV	150.	175.
3765	2171F	Atlanta	FV	FV	150.	175.
3766	2171G	Chicago	FV	FV	150.	175.
3767	2171H	St. Louis	FV	FV	150.	175.
3768	2171I	Minneapolis	FV	FV	150.	175.
3769	2171J	Kansas City	FV	FV	200.	225.
3769☆	2171J ☆	Kansas City	125.	225.	400.	450.
3770	2171K	Dallas	FV	FV	150.	175.
3770☆	2171K☆	Dallas	125.	225.	500.	550.
3771	2171L	San Francisco	FV	FV	150.	175.

Series 1988 Ortega-Brady

KL#	Fr#	District	Fine	XF	CH CU (63)	Gem CU (65)
3832	2172A	Boston	FV	FV	175.	200.
3833	2172B	New York	FV	FV	160.	200.
3833☆	2172B ☆	New York	150.	250.	450.	500.
3834	2172C	Philadelphia	FV	FV	175.	200.
3835	2172D	Cleveland	FV	FV	175.	200.
3836	2172E	Richmond	FV	FV	175.	200.
3838	2172G	Chicago	FV	FV	175.	200.
3839	2172H	St. Louis	FV	FV	175.	200.
3841	2172J	Kansas City	FV	FV	175.	200.
3843	2172L	San Francisco	FV	FV	175.	200.

Series 1990 Villalpando-Brady

KL#	Fr#	District	Fine	XF	CH CU (63)	Gem CU (65)
3976	2173A	Boston	FV	FV	150.	150.
3977	2173B	New York	FV	FV	140.	150.
3977☆	2173B☆	New York	FV	175.	175.	225.
3978	2173C	Philadelphia	FV	FV	150.	170.
3978☆	2173C☆	Philadelphia	FV	175.	225.	225.
3979	2173D	Cleveland	FV	FV	150.	150.
3980	2173E	Richmond	FV	FV	150.	150.
3981	2173F	Atlanta	FV	FV	150.	225.
3982	2173G	Chicago	FV	FV	125.	150.
3982☆	2173G☆	Chicago	FV	150.	175.	225.
3983	2173H	St. Louis	FV	FV	150.	150.
3984	2173I	Minneapolis	FV	FV	150.	150.
3985	2173J	Kansas City	FV	FV	150.	160.
3985☆	2173J☆	Kansas City	FV	175.	225.	225.
3986	2173K	Dallas	FV	FV	150.	200.
3986☆	2173K☆	Dallas	FV	175.	225.	475.
3987	2173L	San Francisco	FV	FV	150.	175.
3987☆	2173L☆	San Francisco	FV	175.	225.	250.

Series 1993 Withrow-Bentsen

KL#	Fr#	District	Fine	XF	CH CU (63)	Gem CU (65)
4072	2174A	Boston	FV	FV	160.	175.
4073	2174B	New York	FV	FV	160.	175.
4073☆	2174B☆	New York	FV	150.	200.	225.
4074	2174C	Philadelphia	FV	FV	160.	175.
4074☆	2174C☆	Philadelphia	FV	150.	160.	165.
4075	2174D	Cleveland	FV	FV	160.	175.
4075☆	2174D☆	Cleveland	FV	150.	200.	225.
4076	2174E	Richmond	FV	FV	160.	175.
4077	2174F	Atlanta	FV	FV	160.	175.
4078	2174G	Chicago	FV	FV	200.	225.
4079	2174H	St. Louis	FV	FV	160.	175.
4079☆	2174H☆	St. Louis	FV	250.	400.	1000.
4080	2174I	Minneapolis	FV	175.	250.	275.
4081	2174J	Kansas City	FV	FV	160.	225.
4082	2174K	Dallas	FV	FV	160.	175.
4083	2174L	San Francisco	FV	FV	160.	175.
4083☆	2174L☆	San Francisco	FV	150.	200.	225.

Series 1996 Withrow-Rubin

KL#	Fr#	District	Fine	XF	CH CU (63)	Gem CU (65)
4132	2175A	Boston	FV	FV	125.	135.
4132☆	2175A☆	Boston	FV	FV	150.	175.

KL#	Fr#	District	Fine	XF	CH CU (63)	Gem CU (65)
4133	2175B	New York	FV	FV	120.	135.
4133☆	2175B ☆	New York	FV	FV	135.	165.
4134	2175C	Philadelphia	FV	FV	120.	135.
4135	2175D	Cleveland	FV	FV	120.	135.
4135☆	2175D ☆	Cleveland	FV	300.	900.	1600.
4136	2175E	Richmond	FV	FV	120.	135.
4136☆	2175E ☆	Richmond	FV	FV	145.	175.
4137	2175F	Atlanta	FV	FV	120.	135.
4137☆	2175F ☆	Atlanta	FV	FV	160.	225.
4138	2175G	Chicago	FV	FV	120.	135.
4138☆	2175G ☆	Chicago	FV	FV	160.	185.
4139	2175H	St. Louis	FV	FV	120.	135.
4140	2175I	Minneapolis	FV	FV	120.	135.
4141	2175J	Kansas City	FV	FV	120.	135.
4142	2175K	Dallas	FV	FV	125.	135.
4142☆	2175K ☆	Dallas	FV	FV	160.	185.
4143	2175L	San Francisco	FV	FV	120.	135.

Series 1999 Withrow-Summers - DC

KL#	Fr#	District	Fine	XF	CH CU (63)	Gem CU (65)
4560	2176A	Boston	FV	FV	125.	150.
4560☆	2176A ☆	Boston	FV	FV	150.	175.
4561	2176B	New York	FV	FV	125.	150.
4561☆	2176B ☆	New York	FV	FV	200.	225.
4562	2176C	Philadelphia	FV	FV	260.	150.
4563	2176D	Cleveland	FV	FV	135.	150.
4564	2176E	Richmond	FV	FV	125.	150.
4565	2176F	Atlanta	FV	FV	135.	150.
4566	2176G	Chicago	FV	FV	125.	150.
4567	2176H	St. Louis	FV	FV	125.	150.
4568	2176I	Minneapolis	FV	FV	125.	150.
4569	2176J	Kansas City	FV	FV	125.	150.
4570	2176K	Dallas	FV	FV	125.	150.

Series 2001 Marin-O'Neill - DC

KL#	Fr#	District	Fine	XF	CH CU (63)	Gem CU (65)
4641	2177A	Boston	FV	FV	125.	150.
4642	2177B	New York	FV	FV	135.	150.
4642☆	2177B ☆	New York	FV	125.	300.	200.
4643	2177C	Philadelphia	FV	ΓV	135.	150.
4644	2177D	Cleveland	FV	FV	125.	150.
4644☆	2177D ☆	Cleveland	FV	125.	150.	200.
4645	2177E	Richmond	FV	FV	125.	150.
4645☆	2177E ☆	Richmond	FV	125.	150.	200.
4646	2177F	Atlanta	FV	FV	125.	150.
4646☆	2177F ☆	Atlanta	FV	125.	175.	250.
4647	2177G	Chicago	FV	FV	125.	150.
4648	2177H	St. Louis	FV	FV	125.	150.
4649	2177I	Minneapolis	FV	FV	140.	150.
4650	2177J	Kansas City	FV	FV	135.	150.
4651	2177K	Dallas	FV	FV	125.	150.
4652	2177L	San Francisco	FV	FV	125.	150.

Series 2003 Marin-Snow - DC

KL#	Fr#	District	Fine	XF	CH CU (63)	Gem CU (65)
4720	2178A	Boston	FV	FV	135.	150.
4721	2178B	New York	FV	FV	125.	150.
4721☆	2178B ☆	New York	FV	125.	200.	225.
4722	2178C	Philadelphia	FV	FV	135.	150.
4723	2178D	Cleveland	FV	FV	135.	150.
4724	2178E	Richmond	FV	FV	125.	150.
4725	2178F	Atlanta	FV	FV	125.	150.
4725☆	2178F ☆	Atlanta	FV	125.	175.	200.
4726	2178G	Chicago	FV	FV	140.	150.
4727	2178H	St. Louis	FV	FV	135.	150.
4728	2178I	Minneapolis	FV	FV	135.	150.
4729	2179J	Kansas City	FV	FV	135.	150.
4730	2178K	Dallas	FV	FV	125.	150.
4730☆	2178K ☆	Dallas	FV	125.	175.	200.
4731	2178L	San Francisco	FV	FV	125.	150.
4731☆	2178L ☆	San Francisco	FV	FV	200.	225.

Series 2003A Cabral-Snow - DC

KL#	Fr#	District	Fine	XF	CH CU (63)	Gem CU (65)
4732A	-	Boston	FV	FV	135.	150.
4732B	-	New York	FV	FV	135.	150.
4732B☆	-	New York	FV	125.	250.	300.
4732C	-	Philadelphia	FV	FV	125.	150.
4732D	-	Cleveland	FV	FV	135.	150.
4732E	-	Richmond	FV	FV	125.	150.
4732F	-	Atlanta	FV	FV	125.	150.
4732G	-	Chicago	FV	FV	125.	150.
4732G☆	-	Chicago	FV	125.	175.	200.
4732H	-	St. Louis	FV	FV	135.	150.
4732H☆	-	St. Louis	FV	125.	175.	200.
4732I	-	Minneapolis	FV	FV	130.	150.
4732J	-	Kansas City	FV	FV	125.	150.
4732K	-	Dallas	FV	FV	125.	150.
4732L	-	San Francisco	FV	FV	135.	150.
4732L☆	-	San Francisco	FV	125.	200.	225.

Series 2006 Cabral-Paulson - DC

KL#	Fr#	District	Fine	XF	CH CU (63)	Gem CU (65)
4837	-	Boston	FV	FV	125.	150.
4837☆	-	Boston	FV	125.	175.	200.
4838	-	New York	FV	FV	120.	150.
4838☆	-	New York	FV	125.	175.	200.
4839	-	Philadelphia	FV	FV	125.	150.

KL#	Fr#	District	Fine	XF	CH CU (63)	Gem CU (65)
4840	-	Cleveland	FV	FV	125.	150.
4841	-	Richmond	FV	FV	125.	150.
4841☆	-	Richmond	FV	125.	175.	200.
4842	-	Atlanta	FV	FV	125.	150.
4843	-	Chicago	FV	FV	125.	150.
4844	-	St. Louis	FV	FV	125.	150.
4845	-	Minneapolis	FV	FV	135.	150.
4846	-	Kansas City	FV	FV	125.	150.
4847	-	Dallas	FV	FV	125.	150.
4847☆	-	Dallas	FV	125.	175.	200.
4848	-	San Francisco	FV	FV	125.	150.
4848☆	-	San Francisco	FV	125.	175.	200.

Series 2006 Cabral-Paulson - FW

KL#	Fr#	District	Fine	XF	CH CU (63)	Gem CU (65)
4849B	-	New York	FV	FV	125.	150.
4849B☆	-	New York	FV	125.	175.	200.
4849J	-	Kansas City	FV	FV	125.	150.
4849L	-	San Francisco	FV	FV	125.	150.
4849L☆	-	San Francisco	FV	125.	175.	200.

Series 2006A Rios-Geithner - DC

KL#	Fr#	District	Fine	XF	CH CU (63)	Gem CU (65)
4898	-	Boston	FV	FV	125.	150.
4899	-	New York	FV	FV	125.	150.

Series 2009 Rios-Geithner - DC

KL#	Fr#	District	Fine	XF	CH CU (63)	Gem CU (65)
4974	-	Boston	—	—	—	—
4974☆	-	Boston	—	—	—	—
4975	-	New York	—	—	—	—
4975☆	-	New York	—	—	—	—
4976	-	Philadelphia	—	—	—	—
4977	-	Cleveland	—	—	—	—
4978	-	Richmond	—	—	—	—

Series 2009 Rios-Geithner - FW

KL#	Fr#	District	Fine	XF	CH CU (63)	Gem CU (65)
4979	-	Atlanta	—	—	—	—
4979☆	-	Atlanta	—	—	—	—
4980	-	Chicago	—	—	—	—
4981	-	St. Louis	—	—	—	—
4981☆	-	St. Louis	—	—	—	—
4982	-	Minneapolis	—	—	—	—
4983	-	Kansas City	—	—	—	—
4983☆	-	Kansas City	—	—	—	—
4984	-	Dallas	—	—	—	—
4984☆	-	Dallas	—	—	—	—
4985	-	San Francisco	—	—	—	—
4985☆	-	San Francisco	—	—	—	—

Gold Certificates
Five Hundred Dollars

KI #	Fr#	Series	Signatures	VF	XF	CH CU (63)	Gem CU (65)
2945	2407	1928	Woods-Mellon	8500.	13,000.	50,000	75,000.

Federal Reserve Notes
Series 1928 Woods-Mellon

KL#	Fr#	District	Fine	XF	CH CU (63)	Gem CU (65)
2946	2000A	Boston	2200.	12,000.	17,500.	20,000.
2946☆	2000A ☆	Boston	30,000.	100,000.	—	—
2947	2200B	New York	650.	1350.	4000.	5500.
2947☆	2200B ☆	New York	25,000.	100,000.	—	—
2948	2200C	Philadelphia	800.	1350.	4000.	8225.
2948☆	2200C ☆	Philadelphia	30,000.	50,000.	—	—
2949	2200D	Cleveland	850.	1500.	4000.	9400.
2949☆	2200D ☆	Cleveland	25,000.	97,750.	—	—
2950	2200E	Richmond	700.	1650.	4250.	6500.
2950☆	2200E ☆	Richmond	25,000.	100,000.	—	—
2951	2200F	Atlanta	850.	1500.	3000.	7500.
2951☆	2200F ☆	Atlanta	20,000.	40,000.	—	—
2952	2200G	Chicago	750.	1150.	4000.	5000.
2952☆	2200G ☆	Chicago	5000.	20,000.	—	—
2953	2200H	St. Louis	850.	1350.	3250.	4000.
2953☆	2200H ☆	St. Louis	—	—	—	—
2954	2200I	Minneapolis	850.	1300.	7500.	8500.
2954☆	2200I ☆	Minneapolis	—	—	—	—
2955	2200J	Kansas City	750.	1300.	5500.	6500.
2955☆	2200J ☆	Kansas City	—	—	—	—
2956	2200K	Dallas	850.	1300.	8500.	9500.
2956☆	2200K ☆	Dallas	—	—	—	—
2957	2200L	San Francisco	675.	1300.	6500.	9500.
2957☆	2200L ☆	San Francisco	—	—	—	—

Series 1934 Julian-Morgenthau

KL#	Fr#	District	Fine	XF	CH CU (63)	Gem CU (65)
2958	2201A	Boston	700.	1000.	1750.	2550.
2958☆	2201A ☆	Boston	1500.	4500.	—	—
2959	2201B	New York	700.	1075.	1850.	2750.
2959☆	2201B ☆	New York	1750.	—	6000.	—
2960	2201C	Philadelphia	750.	1000.	1950.	2750.
2960☆	2201C ☆	Philadelphia	1500.	4000.	6000.	—
2961	2201D	Cleveland	750.	900.	3500.	4500.
2961☆	2201D ☆	Cleveland	1500.	3000.	6000.	—
2962	2201E	Richmond	750.	1000.	2100.	4500.
2962☆	2201E ☆	Richmond	1500.	3000.	6000.	—
2963	2201F	Atlanta	750.	950.	1950.	3250.
2963☆	2201F ☆	Atlanta	2100.	3000.	20,000.	—
2964	2201G	Chicago	600.	950.	1750.	2600.
2964☆	2201G ☆	Chicago	1500.	4500.	9000.	10,800.
2965	2201H	St. Louis	650.	925.	2100.	2600.
2965☆	2201H ☆	St. Louis	2500.	5500.	10,000.	—
2966	2201I	Minneapolis	750.	1000.	3750.	5000.
2966☆	2201I ☆	Minneapolis	3000.	7500.	9000.	—
2967	2201J	Kansas City	750.	975.	2100.	2900.

KL#	Fr#	District	Fine	XF	CH CU (63)	Gem CU (65)
2967☆	2201J ☆	Kansas City	3000.	7500.	10,000.	—
2968	2201K	Dallas	750.	1025.	4000.	—
2968☆	2201K ☆	Dallas	2250.	—	9000.	—
2969	2201L	San Francisco	659.	900.	2000.	6000.
2969☆	2201L ☆	San Francisco	1700.	6000.	7000.	—

Series 1934A Julian-Morgenthau

KL#	Fr#	District	Fine	XF	CH CU (63)	Gem CU (65)
2971	2202B	New York	750.	850.	1400.	3250.
2971☆	2202B ☆	New York	2000.	4000.	—	—
2972	2202C	Philadelphia	650.	825.	1750.	3750.
2973	2202D	Cleveland	750.	1150.	2750.	5000.
2974	2202E	Richmond	600.	800.	2500.	4000.
2974☆	2202E ☆	Richmond	2000.	4000.	10,000.	—
2974A	-	Atlanta	675.	900.	1750.	2000.
2975	2202G	Chicago	700.	850.	2000.	3500.
2975☆	2202G ☆	Chicago	2000.	4000.	—	—
2976	2202H	St. Louis	750.	925.	1700.	2600.
2977	2202I	Minneapolis	750.	1000.	2750.	9000.
2978	2202J	Kansas City	700.	950.	2000.	—
2978☆	2202J ☆	Kansas City	—	—	—	—
2979	2202K	Dallas	750.	1150.	5500.	6500.
2980	2202L	San Francisco	750.	1000.	2250.	5500.
2980☆	2202L ☆	San Francisco	3000.	3750.	8000.	—

Series 1934B Julian-Vinson

KL#	Fr#	District	Fine	XF	CH CU (63)	Gem CU (65)
2981	2203F	Atlanta	—	Specimens Only		—

Series 1934C Julian-Snyder

KL#	Fr#	District	Fine	XF	CH CU (63)	Gem CU (65)
2982	2204A	Boston	—	—	—	—
2983	2204B	New York	—	Specimens Only		—

Gold Certificates
One Thousand Dollars

KL#	Fr#	Series	Signatures	VF	XF	CH CU (63)	Gem CU (65)
2984	2408	1928	Woods-Mellon	8000.	15,000.	35,000.	40,000.
2984A	2408A	1934	Julian-Morgenthau	17,500.	22,500.	—	—

Federal Reserve Notes
Series 1928 Woods-Mellon

KL#	Fr#	District	Fine	XF	CH CU (63)	Gem CU (65)
2985	2210A	Boston	4000.	6000.	—	—
2985☆	2210A ☆	Boston	2500.	6000.	—	—

KL#	Fr#	District	Fine	XF	CH CU (63)	Gem CU (65)
2986	2210B	New York	1500.	2750.	5300.	7000.
2986☆	2210B ☆	New York	20,000.	45,000.	76,500.	—
2987	2210C	Philadelphia	3200.	3500.	6000.	8000.
2987☆	2210C ☆	Philadelphia	15,000.	45,000.	—	—
2988	2210D	Cleveland	1600.	2100.	9000.	13,750.
2988☆	2210D ☆	Cleveland	30,000.	65,000.	—	—
2989	2210E	Richmond	1675.	3000.	6000.	12,000.
2989☆	2210E ☆	Richmond	25,000.	60,000.	—	—
2990	2210F	Atlanta	1600.	2550.	4500.	5025.
2990☆	2210F ☆	Atlanta	25,000.	60,000.	—	—
2991	2210G	Chicago	1350.	2250.	4500.	9000.
2991☆	2210G ☆	Chicago	20,000.	65,000.	—	—
2902	2210H	St. Louis	1400.	2100.	3200.	—
2992☆	2210H ☆	St. Louis	20,000.	65,000.	39,000.	47,500.
2993	2210I	Minneapolis	1600.	2000.	15,000.	—
2993☆	2210I ☆	Minneapolis	20,000.	65,000.	—	—
2994	2210J	Kansas City	1350.	2250.	6000.	9000.
2994☆	2210J ☆	Kansas City	10,000.	20,000.	—	—
2995	2210K	Dallas	1800.	3200.	8500.	17,750.
2995☆	2210K ☆	Dallas	2000.	6500.	—	17,500.
2996	2210L	San Francisco	1450.	2750.	6000.	—
2996☆	2210L ☆	San Francisco	—	—	—	—

Series 1934 Julian-Morgenthau

KL#	Fr#	District	Fine	XF	CH CU (63)	Gem CU (65)
2997	2211A	Boston	1250.	2000.	5000.	6325.
2997☆	2211A ☆	Boston	3000.	7500.	15,000.	—
2998	2211B	New York	1450.	2300.	5000.	3800.
2998☆	2211B ☆	New York	3000.	8000.	12,000.	13,200.
2999	2211C	Philadelphia	1350.	1800.	6500.	—
2999☆	2211C ☆	Philadelphia	2500.	8000.	15,000.	—
3000	2211D	Cleveland	1300.	2200.	6000.	—
3000☆	2211D ☆	Cleveland	2500.	8000.	15,000.	—
3001	2211E	Richmond	1500.	3750.	13,000.	—
3001☆	2211E ☆	Richmond	—	—	—	—
3002	2211F	Atlanta	1500.	2250.	5250.	—
3002☆	2211F ☆	Atlanta	3500.	8000.	15,000.	—
3003	2211G	Chicago	1375.	2000.	5000.	7000.
3003☆	2211G ☆	Chicago	3500.	8000.	15,000.	—
3004	2211H	St. Louis	1350.	1800.	4200.	—
3004☆	2211H ☆	St. Louis	3500.	7500.	15,000.	—
3005	2211I	Minneapolis	1500.	1900.	4500.	6000.
3005☆	2211I ☆	Minneapolis	3500.	8000.	10,000.	—
3006	2211J	Kansas City	1600.	1850.	3500.	—
3006☆	2211J ☆	Kansas City	2750.	5000.	15,000.	—

KL#	Fr#	District	Fine	XF	CH CU (63)	Gem CU (65)
3007	2211K	Dallas	1350.	1900.	3000.	7000.
3007☆	2211K ☆	Dallas	2500.	3500.	4500.	6000.
3008	2211L	San Francisco	1500.	1900.	6000.	6650.
3008☆	2211L ☆	San Francisco	3500.	5000.	15,000.	—

Series 1934A Julian-Morgenthau

KL#	Fr#	District	Fine	XF	CH CU (63)	Gem CU (65)
3009	2212A	Boston	1375.	1800.	2600.	5000.
3009☆	2212A ☆	Boston	—	—	—	—
3010	2212B	New York	1500.	1610.	3700.	4700.
3010☆	2212B ☆	New York	15,000.	30,000.	—	—
3011	2212C	Philadelphia	1500.	1900.	4500.	6000.
3011☆	2212C ☆	Philadelphia	—	—	—	—
3012	2212D	Cleveland	1500.	2500.	3900.	5000.
3012☆	2212D ☆	Cleveland	—	—	—	—
3013	2212E	Richmond	1500.	3100.	12,000.	—
3013☆	2212E ☆	Richmond	—	—	—	—
3014	2212F	Atlanta	1500.	1900.	3450.	5200.
3014☆	2212F ☆	Atlanta	—	—	—	—
3015	2212G	Chicago	1300.	2150.	3500.	6000.
3015☆	2212G ☆	Chicago	2000.	15,000.	23,000.	25,000.
3016	2212H	St. Louis	1350.	1800.	2900.	5000.
3016☆	2212H ☆	St. Louis	—	—	—	—
3017	2212I	Minneapolis	1500.	3500.	12,500.	15,000.
3017☆	2212I ☆	Minneapolis	—	—	—	—
3018	2212J	Kansas City	1300.	1850.	3800.	—
3018☆	2212J ☆	Kansas City	—	—	—	—
3019	2212L	San Francisco	1500.	1950.	3500.	—
3019☆	2212L ☆	San Francisco	—	—	—	—

Series 1934C Julian-Snyder

KL#	Fr#	District	Fine	XF	CH CU (63)	Gem CU (65)
3020	2213A	Boston	—	—	—	—
3021	2213B	New York	—	2100.	Specimens Only	—

Gold Certificates

Five Thousand Dollars

KL#	Fr#	Series	Signatures	VF	XF	CH CU (63)	Gem CU (65)
3022	2410	1928	Woods-Mellon	—	—	Unique	—

Federal Reserve Notes

Series 1928 Woods-Mellon

KL #	Fr#	District	Fine	XF	CH CU (63)	Gem CU (65)
3023	2220A	Boston	20,000.	105,000.	125,000.	—
3024	2220B	New York	20,000.	105,000.	125,000.	—
3025	2220D	Cleveland	20,000.	105,000.	125,000.	—
3026	2220E	Richmond	20,000.	105,000.	125,000.	—
3027	2220F	Atlanta	20,000.	105,000.	125,000.	—
3028	2220G	Chicago	20,000.	105,000.	150,000.	—
3029	2220J	Kansas City	20,000.	130,000.	150,000.	—
3030	2220K	Dallas	20,000.	135,000.	150,000.	—
3031	2220L	San Francisco	20,000.	105,000.	125,000.	—

Series 1934 Julian-Morgenthau

KL#	Fr#	District	Fine	XF	CH CU (63)	Gem CU (65)
3032	2221A	Boston	20,000.	70,000.	125,000.	—
3033	2221B	New York	20,000.	70,000.	125,000.	—
3034	2221C	Philadelphia	20,000.	70,000.	125,000.	—
3035	2221D	Cleveland	20,000.	70,000.	125,000.	—
3036	2221E	Richmond	20,000.	70,000.	125,000.	—
3037	2221F	Atlanta	20,000.	70,000.	125,000.	—
3038	2221G	Chicago	20,000.	68,000.	125,000.	195,500.
3039	2221H	St. Louis	20,000.	69,000.	130,000.	—
3040	2221J	Kansas City	20,000.	80,000.	125,000.	—
3041	2221K	Dallas	20,000.	65,000.	100,000.	—
3042	2221L	San Francisco	20,000.	70,000.	125,000.	—

Series 1934A Julian-Morgenthau

KL#	Fr#	District	Fine	XF	CH CU (63)	Gem CU (65)
3043	2222H	St. Louis	—	—	—	—

Series 1934B Julian-Vinson

KL#	Fr#	District	Fine	XF	CH CU (63)	Gem CU (65)
3044	2223A	Boston	—	—	—	—
3045	2223B	New York	—	—	—	—

Gold Certificates

Ten Thousand Dollars

KL#	Fr#	Series	Signatures	VF	XF	CH CU (63)	Gem CU (65)
3046	2411	1928	Woods-Mellon	—	—	Unique	—
3046A	2411A	1934	Julian-Morgenthau	—		Extremely Rare	—

Federal Reserve Notes

Series 1928 Woods-Mellon

KL#	Fr#	District	Fine	XF	CH CU (63)	Gem CU (65)
3047	2230A	Boston	—	—	—	—
3048	2230B	New York	—	—	—	—
3049	2230D	Cleveland	—	175,000.	—	—
3050	2230E	Richmond	—	195,500.	—	—
3051	2230F	Atlanta	—	170,000.	—	—
3052	2230G	Chicago	—	—	—	—
3053	2230H	St. Louis	—	—	—	—
3054	2230I	Minneapolis	—	—	—	—
3055	2230J	Kansas City	—	—	—	—
3056	2230K	Dallas	—	—	—	—
3057	2230L	San Francisco	—	—	—	—

Series 1934 Julian-Morgenthau

KL#	Fr#	District	Fine	XF	CH CU (63)	Gem CU (65)
3058	2231A	Boston	46,000.	70,000.	90,000.	105,000.
3059	2231B	New York	46,000.	70,000.	90,000.	105,000.
3060	2231C	Philadelphia	46,000.	85,000.	95,000.	115,000.
3061	2231D	Cleveland	46,000.	70,000.	85,000.	105,000.
3062	2231E	Richmond	46,000.	85,000.	95,000.	105,000.
3063	2231F	Atlanta	46,000.	80,000.	85,000.	105,000.
3064	2231G	Chicago	46,000.	80,000.	85,000.	105,000.
3065	2231H	St. Louis	46,000.	80,000.	90,000.	110,000.
3066	2231J	Kansas City	46,000.	69,000.	85,000.	105,000.
3067	2231K	Dallas	46,000.	67,250.	85,000.	105,000.
3068	2231L	San Francisco	75,000.	103,000.	150,000.	175,000.

Series 1934A Julian-Morgenthau

KL#	Fr#	District	Fine	XF	CH CU (63)	Gem CU (65)
3069	2232G	Chicago	Specimens Only	—	161,000.	—

Series 1934B Julian-Vinson

KL#	Fr#	District	Fine	XF	CH CU (63)	Gem CU (65)
3070	2233B	New York	—	Unknown in Private Hands		—

National Bank Notes

In the 72 years of their issue more than 14,000 "home town" banks across the United States, the $17,000,000,000 ($17 billion) worth of National Bank Notes issued between December, 1863, and May, 1935, represent a widely collected series of United States paper money.

Their long and historically, as well as financially, interesting life began with the National Currency Act being signed into law by President Abraham Lincoln on Feb. 25, 1863. The dual aim of the legislation was to provide a ready and steady market for the sale of United States bonds issued to finance Federal involvement in the Civil War, and to create a sound bank currency to replace the generally insecure issues of the state banks then in circulation.

While National Bank Notes were only one of seven different types of U.S. paper money in circulation virtually simultaneously during and after the Civil War, they represent more interesting variations and types than any other. For more than half a century, from the implementation of the National Currency Act in 1863 until the creation of the Federal Reserve System in 1914, the National Bank Notes were an important part of the paper money in circulation.

The composition of these notes and the individual histories behind each of the issuing banks and its officers present unlimited fascination for the modern hobbyist.

The National Currency era came to an end in May, 1935, when the Comptroller of the Currency shipped the last National Bank Notes to the issuing bank. The United States bonds which the banks had purchased to secure the value of their Nationals in circulation were called in for payment, ending nearly three-quarters of a century of an important era of "Main Street Banking."

Six distinct series make up the National Bank Note issue; four in large size, two in small size. Large size Nationals are comprised of 1) The Original Series, 2) Series of 1875, 3) Series of 1882 and 4) Series of 1902. In small size, there are the Series of 1929, Type 1 and Type 2. Within each of the large size series, there are several varieties and subtypes.

Alternatively, the Nationals are sometimes grouped according to Charter Period, thus: First Charter, Original Series and Series of 1875; Second Charter, Series of 1882; Third Charter, Series of 1902, and Small Size.

The terms Charter Period and Charter Number are particularly important to National Bank Notes and refer to the issuing authority of each particular bank.

The original National Currency Act of 1863 provided that banks organized under its provisions be chartered as National Banks for a period of 20 years.

In anticipation of the expiration of those first charters in February, 1883, an act was passed on July 12, 1882, extending the banks' existence for another 20 years. A similar extension was granted with an Act of Congress on April 12, 1902, and just before the 1922 expiration date, the National Currency Act was amended to provide 99-year lives for all National banks. This, in turn, was amended five years later, on Feb. 25, 1927, with the endowment of perpetual succession of their corporate identity on National banks.

A better understanding of National Bank Notes as a whole can be gained by a study of the several unique component parts of the National Currency issues.

Charter Number. Upon the approval of its organization as a National Bank, the Comptroller would issue each bank a unique charter number, designating its place on the roster of all such banks. Charter No. 1 was issued to The First National Bank of Philadelphia in June, 1863. Charter No. 14320, the highest to appear on a National Bank Note, was issued in early 1935 to The Liberty National Bank & Trust Company, Louisville, Ky.

The very earliest Original Series National Bank Notes were not required to have their charter number imprinted. However, when it was discovered that notes being presented at the Treasury for redemption could not be quickly sorted, an Act of June 20, 1874, was passed, requiring the charter number be overprinted twice on the face of each note. In the 1882 revision of the National Currency Act, the printing of the charter number as part of the engraved border design in six different places on the face of the note was required; this to facilitate the redemption of partial notes. The 1882 act also required the surcharge of the number on the face, and its printing in the center of the back, giving rise to the popular Series 1882 Brown Back type notes. The Aldrich-Vreeland Act of May 30, 1908, provided for dropping the charter number from the back of the note, thus creating the 1882 Date Back and Value Back series.

The Series of 1902 notes, authorized by the Act of April 12, 1902, again provided for the engraving of the charter number six times on the face border, and overprinting of the number twice on the face.

The small size National Bank Notes which debuted in 1929 were no longer printed from plates specially engraved for each bank. Rather, for the Type 1 notes, the charter number was overprinted twice in black on the face, along with the bank, city and state names, and the officers' signatures. On the Type 2 small size Nationals, the charter number was printed an extra two times on the face, in brown ink, matching the Treasury seal and serial numbers.

Bank Title. Each National bank's title, once approved by the Comptroller of the Currency, was engraved on the face of all currency printing plates for that bank. On large size Nationals, the title, along with city and state of the bank's location, is printed in a variety of bold and interesting type faces in the center of the note. On small size Nationals, the title is printed to the left of the portrait. Prior to May 1, 1886, it took an act of Congress to change the title of a National Bank. Legislation on that date, though, gave the banks authority to change their name upon a vote of the stockholders, and with the approval of the Comptroller of the Currency.

Date. While the engraved date near the title on the face of all large size National Bank Notes remains something of an enigma, it is generally believed to have been chosen by the Comptroller of the Currency to represent the approximate date of issue for the note. This is not an absolute indicator of issue, though, and thus has little significance to the collector.

Treasury Serial Number. From the first issues of National Bank Notes of Dec. 21, 1863, to Aug. 22, 1925, all National Bank Notes carried a U.S. Treasury serial number on the face of the note. On all notes except the $1 and $2, the Treasury serial number appears somewhere in the upper right of the note. On the First Charter $1 and $2 notes, the Treasury number runs vertically at the left end of the note. After Aug. 22, 1925, the Treasury number was replaced by a second impression of the issuing bank's serial number.

Bank Serial Number. Found on all National Bank Notes, except for the small size Type 2 notes, it indicates how many impressions of a particular plate configuration had been printed for a bank. For the Type 2 small size notes, the bank serial number is an indicator of how many notes of a particular denomination had been issued by a bank.

Treasury Signatures. On all National Bank Notes, the engraved signatures of the Register of the Treasury and the Treasurer of the U.S. appear on the face, usually just above center, the Register's to the left of the bank title, and the Treasurer's to the right; though there are exceptions to this placement. The particular combination of these signatures can pinpoint the period in which a plate was engraved for a given bank.

Bank Officers' Signatures. The original National Currency Act of 1863 required that each National Bank Note be signed by the Cashier and the bank's President or Vice President. These signatures, whether pen autographed, rubber stamped, or engraved, always appear at the bottom of the face of the note, the Cashier to the left, the President (or VP) to the right. The signatures gave a local stamp of approval to this type of currency, probably an important consideration when it was first issued and at a time when paper money was often distrusted. The thousands of persons whose signatures appear on National Bank Notes help give each individual note a unique history not found in other forms of U.S. currency.

Treasury Seal. Found on the face of all National Bank Notes, the overprinted Treasury seal was the final Federal authentication of the note, giving each note its validity as circulating currency. Generally found on the right side of the note's face, it varies in color (red, brown, blue), size and embellishment (8 or 12 scallops, 34 or 40 rays).

Geographic Letters. From 1902-1924, large block letters were overprinted with and near the bank's charter number on each National Bank Note to facilitate sorting at central redemption points. Each letter stood for a particular geographic area of the country where the issuing bank was located: N for New England, E for Eastern, S for Southern, M for Midwest, W for Western and P for Pacific.

Plate Position Letters. On all large size National Bank Notes, a letter from A through D appears twice on the face of the note to indicate from which position (top, 2nd, 3rd or bottom) on a printing plate the note had been produced. Because of the great variety of plate configurations used, there is little significance attached by collectors to plate letters, except perhaps in the case of bank serial number 1 notes, in which case the A-position notes might be of greater value.

Among small size Nationals, the plate position letter is part of the serial number. On Series 1929 Nationals, the prefix letter of the serial number is the plate position. Since 1929s were printed six-up in a sheet, the plate positions letters (prefix) run from A through F.

Denominations. National Bank Notes were authorized, over the course of their history, in denominations of $1, $2, $3, $5, $10, $20, $50, $100, $500, $1,000, and $10,000. No notes of the $3 or $10,000 denomination were printed. No surviving $1,000 Nationals are known, although the Treasury still reports 21 outstanding. Only three, of a reported-outstanding 173, $500 Nationals are known in collections. It should also be noted that not all banks issued all denominations in all series.

Circulation. While the original National Banking Act of Feb. 25, 1863, authorized state, as well as National, banks to issue circulating currency upon deposit of U.S. bonds with the Treasury as security, no state banks took advantage of this privilege before it was withdrawn from them by the Act of June 3, 1864, leaving the National banks in a monopoly position as far as bank-issued currency.

The 1863 legislation allowed National banks to issue notes to the total of 90% of the market value of specified series of United States bonds which they had deposited with the Treasurer of the United States. The revision of June 3, 1864, limited the total amount of National Bank Notes in circulation to $300 million; while a provision to apportion that total was added in March 3, 1865, legislation. That act - which also imposed a 10% tax on state bank notes in circulation, effectively killing them off-specified that half of the circulation be apportioned on the basis of population, and half on the basis of banking capital.

In 1870, additional circulation of $54 million was added to the total, and measures taken to more equitably distribute it, while a $500,000 circulation per bank limit was imposed. In 1875, the restrictions on a per bank basis, as well as total circulation, were taken off. In 1900, banks were allowed to issue notes to the full 100% market value of their bond deposits, instead of the 90%.

The circulation privilege was effectively withdrawn in favor of the Federal Reserve Bank System in July, 1935, when the last of the U.S. bonds carrying that privilege were called in. No new bonds of the type have been issued since.

Closing. A National bank could wind up its affairs in one of three manners, as specified by law.

A bank which violated provisions of the current legislation or charter, or which refused to redeem its notes, could be placed in charge of a receiver by order of the Comptroller of the Currency. It may have been allowed to reopen if it could be proved to be sound. If not, the receiver liquidated the bank's assets so as to provide for meeting the greatest amount of the bank's liabilities.

A bank could also go into voluntary liquidation on a two-thirds vote of the stockholders. Such might be done to allow the bank to be absorbed by or to absorb and consolidate with another bank, either National or state.

After Nov. 18, 1918, a National Bank could also close its corporate doors by consolidating with another bank, but not liquidating its assets.

National Bank Note Chronology

Act of Feb. 25, 1863. The original National Currency Act allowed banks with more than $50,000 capital to organize as National banks. Before starting business as such, the bank was required to deposit with the Treasurer of the United States, specified U.S. bonds to the amount of not less than one-third of its capital stock. With that deposit, the Comptroller of the Currency would issue the bank its "Certificate of Authority to Commence Business," its charter. Banks organized under this act were given a corporate life of 20 years from the date of the act.

Act of June 3, 1864. This act provided that any National bank now organized would have a 20-year charter from the date of organization. It also required that bonds deposited against note-issue be registered, interest bearing U.S. bonds.

Act of March 3, 1865. Besides provision mentioned in the earlier text, this allowed state banks with branches to convert to National status. At that time, National banks were not allowed to establish branch banks.

Act of July 12, 1870. This act provided for the organization of National Gold Banks. Subject to greater restrictions than other National Banks, the National Gold Banks could issue currency only to the total of 80% of their deposited bonds, and had to maintain in their vaults gold and silver equal to 25 % of their circulation.

Act of Feb. 14, 1880. The act permitted the conversion of National Gold Banks to regular National banks, and allowed them to keep their original date of organization.

Act of July 12, 1882. This act created the Second Charter Period, allowing National banks to extend their charters for another 20 years.

Act of March 14, 1900. This act greatly increased the number of National banks by allowing the organization of banks with a minimum of $25,000 capital in localities of fewer than 3,000 population.

Act of April 12, 1902. This act created the Third Charter Period by extending the charters of banks chartered or re-chartered under the 1882 act for another 20 years.

Act of May 30, 1908. A response to the financial panic of 1907, this act, known as the Aldrich-Vreeland Act, allowed the formation of voluntary National Currency Associations. To form such an association required at least 10 National banks with a total of at least $50 million in capital and a surplus of at least 2. After formation, such associations could deposit "other securities" against which they could circulate notes to the extent of 75% of their value. These other securities were usually short-term notes, payable within six months. Due to expire on June 30, 1914, the act was extended by the Federal Reserve Act of Dec. 23, 1913, to June 30, 1915, when it did expire.

Act of July 1, 1922. The act provided that all National banks then in existence would have a corporate life of 99 years from the date of the legislation. All National banks organized after this date would have a corporate existence of 99 years from the date of organization.

Act of Feb. 25, 1927. This act provided perpetual corporate life for all National banks then in existence or to be organized in the future. It also allowed National banks to establish branch banks and for the assumption of state banks by National banks.

First Charter Notes

Although the First Charter Period ran from Feb. 25, 1863, through July 11, 1882, notes of the First Charter type were issued until 1902, a 40-year period. This was due to the authorizing legislation which granted a National bank a charter good for 20 years from the date of reorganization, not the date of the National Bank Act (Feb. 25, 1863). Once a bank was chartered in this period, it issued the same type of notes for 20 years, despite the fact that the Second Charter Period may have come into effect (July 12, 1902) during the course of that time. When the bank's original 20-year charter expired, and it was re-chartered under the Second (or even Third) Period, it would begin issue of Second (or Third) Period notes, as appropriate to the date of its charter extension.

During the First Charter period, two different series of notes were issued, Original Series and Series of 1875.

Notes of the Original Series appeared in denominations from $1 through $1,000, and are distinguishable principally by their lack of overprinted charter numbers, although some banks did issue Original Series notes with charter numbers surcharged. The nearly identical Series 1875 notes all have red (or in rare cases, black) charter numbers imprinted, along with the notation at the left of the bank title "Series 1875."

Serial numbers of First Charter notes appear in either red or blue, with the blue variety being the scarcer.

Obligation of the face of the note reads: "This note is secured by bonds of the United States deposited with the U.S. Treasurer in Washington ... The (name and location of bank) will pay the bearer on demand – dollars." On back, there is the inscription: "This note is receivable at par in all parts of the United States, in payment of all taxes and excises and other dues to the United States, except duties on imports, and also for all salaries and other debts and demands owing by the United States to individuals, corporations and associations within the United States except interest on the public debt."

Second Charter Notes

Three distinct note issues make up the National Currency of the Second Charter Period, July 12, 1882, through April 11, 1902. These types differ principally in their back designs for which collectors have evolved the nicknames Brown Back, Date Back and Value Back.

Like the notes of the First Charter Period, the Second Charter Period currency was issued for a span of 40 years, until 1922, when all charters had to be renewed.

The Brown Backs of Series 1882 were placed in circulation that year, and were issued until 1908. The Brown Backs take their name from the large charter number printed on the back in the center of two cartouches of geometric design in brown ink. All other printing on back was also in the brown shades which matched the predominant color of the note's face.

Called Date Backs because of the large 1882-1908 dates on their green-printed backs, the second issue of Series 1882 Nationals was a result of the previously described Aldrich-Vreeland Act. Denominations from $5-$100 were in circulation from June, 1908, to July, 1916, and the $50s and $100s continued current in this type until 1922. Date Back 1882 Nationals were issued only by banks which had issued Brown Backs, and the charter of which were still in force. Those banks whose charter expired in the 1908-1916 period were re-chartered and issued notes of the Third Charter Period.

The expiration of the Aldrich-Vreeland Act in 1915 gave rise to the third type of Series 1882 Nationals, the rare Value Backs (sometimes called Denomination Backs). As implied, the name comes from the large spelled-out indication of value in the center of the back design. As a type, they are the rarest of National Bank Notes, having been issued in the period 1916-1922 by banks which had issued the Date Back type and for which the charter was still in effect. Naturally, this number dwindled each successive year as banks were re-chartered and their note issues switched to the Third Period types.

The Date Back and Value Back notes of Series 1882 were something of emergency issues, produced at a time when it was felt an increase in the supply of currency in circulation was needed to combat hard times. Accordingly, for their issue, the Treasury accepted certain securities other than U.S. bonds on deposit against circulation. This addition is stated on the obligations of these notes.

Third Charter Notes

Passed to extend the life of those National banks whose charters were coming to expiration beginning in 1902, the Currency Act of April 12, 1902, created the Third Charter Period and the three distinct types of National Currency issued thereunder.

In 1922, Congress did away with the need for continual renewing of charters every 20 years by granting National banks perpetual charters to operate.

Issued from 1902 until they were replaced by the small size National Currency in 1929, the Third Charter Nationals represented a change in design to distinguish them from the notes of the Second Charter Period.

The first issue of the Third Charter Period was the popular and often-rare Red Seals. Issued only from 1902-1908, due to the intervention of the Aldrich-Vreeland Emergency Money Act, the Red Seals were issued for a shorter period and by fewer banks than the other two Third Charter types. Their rarity, and the fact that they were issued by every U.S. state and Territory except Hawaii, make them a challenge among collectors who seek to build a state set of this type.

The latter two issues of the Third Charter Period both feature blue Treasury seals, and are principally distinguished by their backs.

The Series 1902 Date Back carries the dates 1902 and 1908 in the white space on the upper back. Like the Second Charter Date Backs, they are something of an emergency issue, having been released during the term of the Aldrich-Vreeland Act, 1908-1915, with the $50s and $100, as in Series 1882, being issued later, until 1926.

Upon expiration of that emergency currency measure, the issues of the Third Charter Period continued with the 1902 Plain Backs, named thus for their lack of the 1902-1908 dates on back. The most plentiful of all National Bank Notes, they were issued from 1915 to 1929, when they were superceded by the small size issue.

Small Size Nationals

When the rest of the currency classes were "down-sized" in July, 1929, the National Bank Notes were included. At the same time, their designs were standardized to fit in with the other types of notes in the same denominations.

Two separate types of small size Nationals were issued. Type 1, current from July, 1929-May, 1933, is distinguished chiefly by the appearance of the bank charter number only twice on the face of the note, in heavy black numerals. Serial numbers of the Type 1 notes consisted of a prefix letter A through F (corresponding to the note's position on the printing plate), six digits and the suffix A (or B, in the case of Ch. No. 2379, The Chase N.B., New York City, the only bank to issue more than six million small size notes in any denomination). The Type 2 Series 1929 Nationals had the same two charter imprints as Type 1, but had an extra pair in brown ink alongside the serial numbers. Serial numbering of the Type 2 notes was also different, being made up of prefix letter A (B only in the case of The Bank of America National Trust and Savings Association of San Francisco) along with six digits.

The obligation was changed on the Series 1929 Nationals, to read "follows: "National Currency secured by United States bonds deposited with the Treasurer of the United States of America ... The (bank name and city/state) will pay to the bearer on demand – dollars." At right, across the brown Treasury seal, was the obligation: "Redeemable in lawful money of the United States at United States Treasury or at the bank of issue."

The calling in of the bonds which secured the National Currency issue ended this Golden Era for U.S. paper money in May, 1935.

Surviving National Bank Notes

Of the approximately $17 billion worth of National Currency issued between 1863-1935, it is estimated that some $50 million worth remain outstanding today, with most knowledgeable observers in agreement that the surviving amount is about equally divided between large and small size issues, representing about 3/10 of 1% of the total issue.

Valuations By Type

Concordia clasping hands before altar. Spiked red seal.
Landing of the Pilgrims at center, state seal at left.

KL#	FR#	Type	Denom.	Signatures	VG	VF	CH CU (63)	Gem CU (65)
1086	380	Orig	$1	Colby-Spinner	600.	950.	3100.	4000.
1087	381	Orig	$1	Jeffries-Spinner	1900.	4650.	14,000.	15,000.
1088	382	Orig	$1	Allison-Spinner	600.	950.	3100.	4000.

Concordia clasping hands before altar. Scalloped red seal.

KL#	FR#	Type	Denom.	Signatures	VG	VF	CH CU (63)	Gem CU (65)
1089	383	1875	$1	Allison-New	600.	950.	3100.	4000.
1090	384	1875	$1	Allison-Wyman	600.	950.	3100.	4000.
1091	385	1875	$1	Allison-Gilfillan	600.	950.	3100.	4000.
1092	386	1875	$1	Scofield-Gilfillan	600.	950.	3100.	4000.

Female seated holding flag at left, large "2" on its side at top right.
Spiked red seal. Sir Walter Raleigh presenting corn and tobacco at center.

KL#	FR#	Type	Denom.	Signatures	VG	VF	CH CU (63)	Gem CU (65)
1093	387	Orig	$2	Colby-Spinner	1750.	4000.	10,500.	24,000.
1094	388	Orig	$2	Jeffries-Spinner	4750.	8000.	15,000.	26,000.
1095	389	Orig	$2	Allison-Spinner	1750.	4000.	10,500.	24,000.

Female seated holding flag at left, large "2" on its side at top right.
Scalloped red seal.

KL#	FR#	Type	Denom.	Signatures	VG	VF	CH CU (63)	Gem CU (65)
1096	390	1875	$2	Allison-New	1750.	4000.	10,500.	24,000.
1097	391	1875	$2	Allison-Wyman	1750.	4000.	12,750.	24,000.
1098	392	1875	$2	Allison-Gilfillan	1750.	4000.	12,750.	24,000.
1099	393	1875	$2	Scofield-Gilfillan	1750.	4000.	12,750.	24,000.

Columbus in sight of land at left,
America presented to the Old World at right. Spiked red seal.
Landing of Columbus at center.

KL#	FR#	Type	Denom.	Signatures	VG	VF	CH CU (63)	Gem CU (65)
1100	394	Orig	$5	Chittenden-Spinner	750.	1650.	5000.	6750.
1101	397	Orig	$5	Colby-Spinner	750.	1650.	5000.	6750.
1102	398	Orig	$5	Jeffries-Spinner	5750.	9850.	20,000.	22,750.
1103	399	Orig	$5	Allison-Spinner	750.	1650.	5000.	6750.

Columbus in sight of land at left,
America presented to the Old World at right. Scalloped red seal.
Bank charter number in black.

KL#	FR#	Type	Denom.	Signatures	VG	VF	CH CU (63)	Gem CU (65)
1104	401	1875	$5	Allison-New	-	Rare	-	-

Columbus in sight of land at left,
America presented to the Old World at right. Scalloped red seal.
Bank charter number in red.

KL#	FR#	Type	Denom.	Signatures	VG	VF	CH CU (63)	Gem CU (65)
1105	401	1875	$5	Allison-New	750.	1650.	5000.	6750.

Columbus in sight of land at left,
America presented to the Old World at right. Scalloped red seal.

KL#	FR#	Type	Denom.	Signatures	VG	VF	CH CU (63)	Gem CU (65)
1106	402	1875	$5	Allison-Wyman	750.	1650.	5000.	6750.
1107	403	1875	$5	Allison-Gilfillan	750.	1650.	5000.	6750.
1108	404	1875	$5	Scofield-Gilfillan	750.	1650.	5000.	6750.
1109	405	1875	$5	Bruce-Gilfillan	750.	1650.	5000.	6750.
1110	406	1875	$5	Bruce-Wyman	750.	1650.	5000.	6750.
1111	406A	1875	$5	Bruce-Jordan	-	Rare	-	-
1112	407	1875	$5	Rosecrans-Huston	750.	1650.	5000.	6750.
1113	408	1875	$5	Rosecrans-Jordan	750.	1650.	5000.	6750.

James A. Garfield at left. Charter number in brown field.

KL#	FR#	Type	Denom.	Signatures	VG	VF	CH CU (63)	Gem CU (65)
1114	466	'82BB	$5	Bruce-Gilfillan	375.	725.	2000.	5250.
1115	467	'82BB	$5	Bruce-Wyman	375.	725.	2000.	2750.
1116	468	'82BB	$5	Bruce-Jordan	375.	725.	2000.	2750.
1117	469	'82BB	$5	Rosecrans-Jordan	375.	725.	2000.	2750.
1118	470	'82BB	$5	Rosecrans-Hyatt	375.	725.	2000.	2750.
1119	471	'82BB	$5	Rosecrans-Huston	375.	725.	2000.	2750.
1120	472	'82BB	$5	Rosecrans-Nebeker	375.	725.	2000.	2750.
1121	473	'82BB	$5	Rosecrans-Morgan	375.	725.	2000.	2750.
1122	474	'82BB	$5	Tillman-Morgan	375.	725.	2000.	2750.
1123	475	'82BB	$5	Tillman-Roberts	375.	725.	2000.	2750.
1124	476	'82BB	$5	Bruce-Roberts	375.	725.	2000.	2750.
1125	477	'82BB	$5	Lyons-Roberts	375.	725.	2000.	2750.
1126	478	'82BB	$5	Vernon-Treat	375.	725.	2000.	2750.

George Washington at left, date in center, Capital Building at right.

KL#	FR#	Type	Denom.	Signatures	VG	VF	CH CU (63)	Gem CU (65)
1127	532	'82DB	$5	Rosecrans-Huston	350.	1100.	3500.	5250.
1128	533	'82DB	$5	Rosecrans-Nebeker	350.	625.	2000.	3500.
1129	533-A	'82DB	$5	Rosecrans-Morgan	825.	1500.	2500.	4250.
1130	534	'82DB	$5	Tillman-Morgan	350.	625.	2000.	3500.
1131	535	'82DB	$5	Tillman-Roberts	350.	625.	2000.	3500.
1132	536	'82DB	$5	Bruce-Roberts	350.	625.	2000.	3500.
1133	537	'82DB	$5	Lyons-Roberts	350.	625.	2000.	3500.
1134	538	'82DB	$5	Vernon-Treat	350.	625.	2000.	3500.
1135	538b	'82DB	$5	Napier-McClung	2150.	3300.	4000.	6500.

George Washington at left, value in center, Capital Building at right.

KL#	FR#	Type	Denom.	Signatures	VG	VF	CH CU (63)	Gem CU (65)
1136	573	'82VB	$5	Tillman-Morgan	500.	1050.	2650.	3500.
1137	573a	'82VB	$5	Tillman-Roberts	500.	1025.	2650.	3500.
1138	574	'82VB	$5	Lyons-Roberts	500.	1025.	2650.	3500.
1139	574a	'82VB	$5	Bruce-Roberts	500.	1025.	2650.	3500.
1140	575	'82VB	$5	Vernon-Treat	500.	1025.	2650.	3500.
1141	575a	'82VB	$5	Napier-McClung	500.	1025.	2650.	3500.
1142	575b	'82VB	$5	Teehee-Burke	-	Rare	-	-

Benjamin Harrison at left. Red seal. Landing of the Pilgrims at center.

KL#	FR#	Type	Denom.	Signatures	VG	VF	CH CU (63)	Gem CU (65)
1143	587	'02RS	$5	Lyons-Roberts	450.	750.	2000.	3000.
1144	588	'02RS	$5	Lyons-Treat	450.	750.	2000.	3000.
1145	589	'02RS	$5	Vernon-Treat	450.	750.	2000.	3000.

Benjamin Harrison at left. Dates flanking Landing of the Pilgrims at center.

KL#	FR#	Type	Denom.	Signatures	VG	VF	CH CU (63)	Gem CU (65)
1140	590	'02DB	$5	Lyons-Roberts	135.	350.	600.	800.
1147	591	'02DB	$5	Lyons-Treat	135.	350.	600.	900.
1148	592	'02DB	$5	Vernon-Treat	135.	350.	600.	900.
1149	593	'02DB	$5	Vernon-McClung	135.	350.	600.	900.
1150	594	'02DB	$5	Napier-McClung	250.	400.	700.	1050.
1151	595	'02DB	$5	Napier-Thompson	150.	550.	1700.	2000.
1152	596	'02DB	$5	Napier-Burke	135.	375.	700.	900.
1153	597	'02DB	$5	Parker-Burke	135.	400.	700.	900.
1154	597a	'02DB	$5	Teehee-Burke	250.	525.	1700.	1850.

Landing of the Pilgrims at center.

KL#	FR#	Type	Denom.	Signatures	VG	VF	CH CU (63)	Gem CU (65)
1155	598	'02PB	$5	Lyons-Roberts	100.	225.	600.	800.
1156	599	'02PB	$5	Lyons-Treat	100.	225.	600.	800.

KL#	FR#	Type	Denom.	Signatures	VG	VF	CH CU (63)	Gem CU (65)
1157	600	'02PB	$5	Vernon-McClung	100.	225.	600.	800.
1158	601	'02PB	$5	Vernon-Treat	100.	225.	600.	800.
1159	602	'02PB	$5	Napier-McClung	100.	225.	600.	750.
1160	603	'02PB	$5	Napier-Thompson	100.	225.	800.	1000.
1161	604	'02PB	$5	Napier-Burke	100.	225.	600.	800.
1162	605	'02PB	$5	Parker-Burke	100.	225.	600.	800.
1163	606	'02PB	$5	Teehee-Burke	100.	225.	600.	800.
1164	607	'02PB	$5	Elliott-Burke	100.	225.	600.	800.
1165	608	'02PB	$5	Elliott-White	100.	225.	600.	800.
1166	609	'02PB	$5	Speelman-White	100.	225.	600.	800.
1167	610	'02PB	$5	Woods-White	100.	225.	600.	800.
1168	611	'02PB	$5	Woods-Tate	100.	225.	600.	800.

Benjamin Harrison at left. Red seal.

KL#	FR#	Type	Denom.	Signatures	VG	VF	CH CU (63)	Gem CU (65)
1169	612	'02PB	$5	Jones-Woods	875.	1300.	2500.	3400.

Abraham Lincoln at center. Lincoln Memorial.

KI #	FR#	Type	Denom	Signatures	VG	VF	CH CU (63)	Com CU (66)
1170	1800-1	'29T1	$5	Jones-Woods	60.00	100.	275.	340.

KL#	FR#	Type	Denom.	Signatures	VG	VF	CH CU (63)	Gem CU (65)
1171	1800-2	'29T2	$5	Jones-Woods	75.00	125.	325.	450.

Franklin and Electricity at left, America Seizing Lightning at left. Spiked
red seal. DeSoto Discovering the Mississippi at center, state seal at left.

KL#	FR#	Type	Denom.	Signatures	VG	VF	CH CU (63)	Gem CU (65)
1172	409	Orig	$10	Chittenden-Spinner	1100.	2250.	10,000.	12,000.
1173	412	Orig	$10	Colby-Spinner	1100.	2250.	10,000.	12,000.
1174	413	Orig	$10	Jeffries-Spinner	-	Rare	-	-
1175	414	Orig	$10	Allison-Spinner	1100.	2250.	10,000.	12,000.

Franklin and Electricity at left,
America Seizing Lightning at left. Scalloped red seal.

KL#	FR#	Type	Denom.	Signatures	VG	VF	CH CU (63)	Gem CU (65)
1176	416	1875	$10	Allison-New	1000.	2000.	8000.	10,000.
1177	417	1875	$10	Allison-Wyman	1000.	2000.	8000.	10,000.
1178	418	1875	$10	Allison-Gilfillan	1000.	2000.	8000.	10,000.
1179	419	1875	$10	Scofield-Gilfillan	1000.	2000.	8000.	10,000.
1180	420	1875	$10	Bruce-Gilfillan	1000.	2000.	8000.	10,000.

KL#	FR#	Type	Denom.	Signatures	VG	VF	CH CU (63)	Gem CU (65)
1181	421	1875	$10	Bruce-Wyman	1000.	2000.	8000.	10,000.
1182	422	1875	$10	Rosecrans-Huston	1000.	2000.	8000.	10,000.
1183	423	1875	$10	Rosecrans-Nebeker	1000.	2000.	8000.	10,000.
1184	423a	1875	$10	Tillman-Morgan	-	Rare	-	-

Charter number on brown center, state seal at left.

KL#	FR#	Type	Denom.	Signatures	VG	VF	CH CU (63)	Gem CU (65)
1185	479	'82BB	$10	Bruce-Gilfillan	500.	775.	2000.	3000.
1186	480	'82BB	$10	Bruce-Wyman	500.	775.	2000.	3000.
1187	481	'82BB	$10	Bruce-Jordan	500.	775.	2000.	3000.

KL#	FR#	Type	Denom.	Signatures	VG	VF	CH CU (63)	Gem CU (65)
1188	482	'82BB	$10	Rosecrans-Jordan	500.	775.	2000.	3000.
1189	483	'82BB	$10	Rosecrans-Hyatt	500.	775.	2000.	3000.
1190	484	'82BB	$10	Rosecrans-Huston	500.	775.	2000.	3000.
1191	485	'82BB	$10	Rosecrans-Nebeker	500.	775.	2000.	3000.
1192	486	'82BB	$10	Rosecrans-Morgan	2000.	3850.	8000.	-
1193	487	'82BB	$10	Tillman-Morgan	500.	775.	2000.	3000.
1194	488	'82BB	$10	Tillman-Roberts	500.	775.	2000.	3000.
1195	489	'82BB	$10	Bruce-Roberts	500.	775.	2000.	3000.
1196	490	'82BB	$10	Lyons-Roberts	500.	775.	2000.	3000.
1197	491	'82BB	$10	Lyons-Treat	500.	775.	2000.	3000.
1198	492	'82BB	$10	Vernon-Treat	500.	775.	2000.	3000.

Franklin and Electricity at left, America Seizing Lightning at left. Scalloped blue seal. William P. Fessenden at left, dates at center, Mechanics at right.

KL#	FR#	Type	Denom.	Signatures	VG	VF	CH CU (63)	Gem CU (65)
1199	539	'82DB	$10	Rosecrans-Huston	400.	1200.	2500.	2800.
1200	540	'82DB	$10	Rosecrans-Nebeker	400.	1200.	2500.	2800.
1201	541	'82DB	$10	Rosecrans-Morgan	1700.	3250.	7000.	8000.
1202	542	'82DB	$10	Tillman-Morgan	400.	800.	2500.	2800.
1203	543	'82DB	$10	Tillman-Roberts	400.	800.	2500.	2800.
1204	544	'82DB	$10	Bruce-Roberts	400.	800.	2500.	2800.
1205	545	'82DB	$10	Lyons-Roberts	400.	800.	2500.	2800.
1206	546	'82DB	$10	Vernon-Treat	400.	800.	2500.	2800.
1207	547	'82DB	$10	Vernon-McClung	400.	800.	2500.	2800.
1208	548	'82DB	$10	Napier-McClung	400.	825.	2500.	2800.

William P. Fessenden at left, value at center, Mechanics at right.

KL#	FR#	Type	Denom.	Signatures	VG	VF	CH CU (63)	Gem CU (65)
1209	576	'82VB	$10	Tillman-Morgan	450.	825.	3000.	3500.
1210	576a	'82VB	$10	Tillman-Roberts	450.	825.	3000.	3500.
1211	576b	'82VB	$10	Bruce-Roberts	475.	1500.	5000.	6300.
1212	577	'82VB	$10	Lyons-Roberts	450.	825.	3000.	3500.
1213	578	'82VB	$10	Vernon-Treat	450.	825.	3000.	3500.
1214	579	'82VB	$10	Napier-McClung	450.	825.	3000.	3500.
1215	579b	'82VB	$10	Teehee-Burke	-	Rare	-	-

William McKinley at left. Red scalloped seal.
Liberty and Progress standing at center.

KL#	FR#	Type	Denom.	Signatures	VG	VF	CH CU (63)	Gem CU (65)
1216	613	'02RS	$10	Lyons-Roberts	400.	850.	2300.	2800.
1217	614	'02RS	$10	Lyons-Treat	400.	900.	2300.	2800.
1218	615	'02RS	$10	Vernon-Treat	400.	850.	2300.	2800.

William McKinley at left.
Date flanking top of Liberty and Progress standing at center.

KL#	FR#	Type	Denom.	Signatures	VG	VF	CH CU (63)	Gem CU (65)
1219	616	'02DB	$10	Lyons-Roberts	150.	350.	850.	1200.
1220	617	'02DB	$10	Lyons-Treat	150.	350.	850.	1200.
1221	618	'02DB	$10	Vernon-Treat	150.	350.	850.	1200.
1222	619	'02DB	$10	Vernon-McClung	150.	350.	850.	1200.
1223	620	'02DB	$10	Napier-McClung	150.	350.	850.	1200.
1224	621	'02DB	$10	Napier-Thompson	150.	350.	850.	1200.
1225	622	'02DB	$10	Napier-Burke	250.	350.	850.	1200.
1226	623	'02DB	$10	Parker-Burke	150.	350.	850.	1200.
1227	623a	'02DB	$10	Teehee-Burke	150.	350.	850.	1200.

Liberty and Progress standing at center.

KL#	FR#	Type	Denom.	Signatures	VG	VF	CH CU (63)	Gem CU (65)
1228	624	'02PB	$10	Lyons-Roberts	125.	250.	550.	625.
1229	625	'02PB	$10	Lyons-Treat	125.	250.	550.	625.
1230	626	'02PB	$10	Vernon-Treat	125.	250.	550.	625.
1231	627	'02PB	$10	Vernon-McClung	125.	250.	550.	625.
1232	628	'02PB	$10	Napier-McClung	125.	250.	550.	625.
1233	629	'02PB	$10	Napier-Thompson	125.	250.	1500.	1750.
1234	630	'02PB	$10	Napier-Burke	125.	250.	550.	625.
1235	631	'02PB	$10	Parker-Burke	125.	250.	550.	625.
1236	632	'02PB	$10	Teehee-Burke	125.	250.	550.	625.
1237	633	'02PB	$10	Elliott-Burke	125.	250.	550.	625.
1238	634	'02PB	$10	Elliott-White	125.	250.	550.	625.
1239	635	'02PB	$10	Speelman-White	125.	250.	550.	625.
1240	636	'02PB	$10	Woods-White	125.	500.	1700.	1850.
1241	637	'02PB	$10	Woods-Tate	125.	500.	1700.	1850.
1242	638	'02PB	$10	Jones-Woods	525.	1260.	2250.	2500.

Alexander Hamilton at center. Treasury Building.

KL#	FR#	Type	Denom.	Signatures	VG	VF	CH CU (63)	Gem CU (65)
1243	1801-1	'29T1	$10	Jones-Woods	70.00	100.	250.	275.

KL#	FR#	Type	Denom.	Signatures	VG	VF	CH CU (63)	Gem CU (65)
1244	1801-2	'29T2	$10	Jones-Woods	86.00	200.	400.	450.

Twenty Dollars

Battle of Lexington at left, Loyalty, female holding flag at right.
Spiked red seal. Baptism of Pocahontas

KL#	FR#	Type	Denom.	Signatures	VG	VF	CH CU (63)	Gem CU (65)
1245	424	Orig	$20	Chittenden-Spinner	2500.	4250.	10,500.	15,000.
1246	427	Orig	$20	Colby-Spinner	2500.	4250.	10,500.	15,000.
1247	428	Orig	$20	Jeffries-Spinner	-	Rare	-	-
1248	429	Orig	$20	Allison-Spinner	2500.	4250.	10,500.	15,000.

Battle of Lexington at left, Loyalty, female holding flag at right.
Scalloped red seal.

KL#	FR#	Type	Denom.	Signatures	VG	VF	CH CU (63)	Gem CU (65)
1249	431	1875	$20	Allison-New	1600.	3000.	10,500.	15,000.
1250	432	1875	$20	Allison-Wyman	1600.	3000.	10,500.	15,000.
1251	433	1875	$20	Allison-Gilfillan	1600.	3000.	10,500.	15,000.
1252	434	1875	$20	Scofield-Gilfillan	1600.	3000.	10,500.	15,000.

KL#	FR#	Type	Denom.	Signatures	VG	VF	CH CU (63)	Gem CU (65)
1253	435	1875	$20	Bruce-Gilfillan	1600.	3000.	10,500.	15,000.
1254	436	1875	$20	Bruce-Wyman	-	Rare	-	-
1255	437	1875	$20	Rosecrans-Huston	1600.	3000.	10,500.	15,000.
1256	438	1875	$20	Rosecrans-Nebeker	1600.	3000.	10,500.	15,000.
1257	439	1875	$20	Tillman-Morgan	-	Rare	-	-

Battle of Lexington at left, Loyalty, female holding flag at right. Scalloped blue seal. Charter number at center, state seal at left.

KL#	FR#	Type	Denom.	Signatures	VG	VF	CH CU (63)	Gem CU (65)
1258	493	'82BB	$20	Bruce-Gilfillan	575.	925.	2200.	4000.
1259	494	'82BB	$20	Bruce-Wyman	575.	925.	2200.	4000.
1260	495	'82BB	$20	Bruce-Jordan	575.	925.	2200.	4000.
1261	496	'82BB	$20	Rosecrans-Jordan	575.	925.	2200.	4000.
1262	497	'82BB	$20	Rosecrans-Hyatt	575.	925.	2200.	4000.
1263	498	'82BB	$20	Rosecrans-Huston	575.	925.	2200.	4000.

KL#	FR#	Type	Denom.	Signatures	VG	VF	CH CU (63)	Gem CU (65)
1264	499	'82BB	$20	Rosecrans-Nebeker	575.	925.	2200.	4000.
1265	500	'82BB	$20	Rosecrans-Morgan	-	Rare	-	-
1266	501	'82BB	$20	Tillman-Morgan	575.	925.	2200.	4000.
1267	502	'82BB	$20	Tillman-Roberts	575.	925.	2200.	4000.
1268	503	'82BB	$20	Bruce-Roberts	575.	925.	2200.	4000.
1269	504	'82BB	$20	Lyons-Roberts	575.	925.	2200.	4000.
1270	505	'82BB	$20	Lyons-Treat	575.	925.	2200.	4000.
1271	506	'82BB	$20	Vernon-Treat	575.	925.	2200.	4000.

Dates at center, state seal at left.

KI #	FR#	Type	Denom.	Signatures	VG	VF	CH CU (63)	Gem CU (65)
1272	549	'82DB	$20	Rosecrans-Huston	550.	800.	2000.	3500.
1273	550	'82DB	$20	Rosecrans-Nebeker	550.	800.	2000.	3500.
1274	551	'82DB	$20	Rosecrans-Morgan	-	Rare	-	-
1275	552	'82DB	$20	Tillman-Morgan	550.	800.	2000.	3500.
1276	553	'82DB	$20	Tillman-Roberts	550.	800.	2000.	3500.
1277	554	'82DB	$20	Bruce-Roberts	550.	800.	2000.	3500.
1278	555	'82DB	$20	Lyons-Roberts	550.	800.	2000.	3500.
1279	556	'82DB	$20	Vernon-Treat	550.	800.	2000.	3500.
1280	557	'82DB	$20	Napier-McClung	600.	1000.	2500.	4000.

Value at center, state seal at left.

KL#	FR#	Type	Denom.	Signatures	VG	VF	CH CU (63)	Gem CU (65)
1281	580	'82VB	$20	Tillman-Morgan	750.	1750.	4000.	5000.
1282	580a	'82VB	$20	Tillman-Roberts	-	5750.	-	-
1283	580b	'82VB	$20	Bruce-Roberts	-	Rare	-	-
1284	581	'82VB	$20	Lyons-Roberts	750.	1300.	4000.	5000.
1285	582	'82VB	$20	Lyons-Treat	750.	1300.	4000.	5000.
1286	583	'82VB	$20	Vernon-Treat	750.	1300.	4000.	5000.
1287	584	'82VB	$20	Napier-McClung	750.	1850.	4000.	5000.
1288	584a	'82VB	$20	Parker-Burke	-	Rare	-	-
1289	585	'82VB	$20	Teehee-Burke	750.	2100.	4000.	5000.

Hugh McCulloch at left. Red scalloped seal. Union and Civilization at left.

KL#	FR#	Type	Denom.	Signatures	VG	VF	CH CU (63)	Gem CU (65)
1290	639	'02RS	$20	Lyons-Roberts	500.	925.	2700.	4000.
1291	640	'02RS	$20	Lyons-Treat	500.	925.	2700.	4000.
1292	641	'02RS	$20	Vernon-Treat	500.	925.	2700.	4000.

Hugh McCulloch at left. Union and Civilization at left, dates at top center.

KL#	FR#	Type	Denom.	Signatures	VG	VF	CH CU (63)	Gem CU (65)
1293	642	'02DB	$20	Lyons-Roberts	175.	350.	800.	900.
1294	643	'02DB	$20	Lyons-Treat	175.	350.	800.	900.
1295	644	'02DB	$20	Vernon-Treat	175.	350.	800.	900.
1296	645	'02DB	$20	Vernon-McClung	175.	350.	800.	900.
1297	646	'02DB	$20	Napier McClung	175.	350.	800.	900.
1298	647	'02DB	$20	Napier-Thompson	175.	350.	800.	900.
1299	648	'02DB	$20	Napier-Burke	175.	350.	800.	900.
1300	649	'02DB	$20	Parker-Burke	175.	350.	800.	900.
1301	649a	'02DB	$20	Teehee-Burke	175.	350.	800.	900.

Union and Civilization at left.

KL#	FR#	Type	Denom.	Signatures	VG	VF	CH CU (63)	Gem CU (65)
1302	650	'02PB	$20	Lyons-Roberts	150.	300.	700.	825.
1303	651	'02PB	$20	Lyons-Treat	150.	300.	700.	825.
1304	652	'02PB	$20	Vernon-Treat	150.	300.	700.	825.

KL#	FR#	Type	Denom.	Signatures	VG	VF	CH CU (63)	Gem CU (65)
1305	653	'02PB	$20	Vernon-McClung	150.	300.	700.	825.
1306	654	'02PB	$20	Napier-McClung	150.	300.	700.	825.
1307	655	'02PB	$20	Napier-Thompson	150.	300.	700.	1700.
1308	656	'02PB	$20	Napier-Burke	150.	300.	700.	825.
1309	657	'02PB	$20	Parker-Burke	150.	300.	700.	825.
1310	658	'02PB	$20	Teehee-Burke	150.	300.	700.	825.
1311	659	'02PB	$20	Elliott-Burke	150.	300.	700.	825.
1312	660	'02PB	$20	Elliott-White	150.	300.	700.	825.
1313	661	'02PB	$20	Speelman-White	150.	300.	700.	825.
1314	662	'02PB	$20	Woods-White	400.	700.	2350.	2650.
1315	663	'02PB	$20	Woods-Tate	400.	700.	2350.	2650.
1316	663a	'02PB	$20	Jones-Woods	-	Rare	-	-

Andrew Jackson at center. White House.

KL#	FR#	Type	Denom.	Signatures	VG	VF	CH CU (63)	Gem CU (65)
1317	1802-1	'29T1	$20	Jones-Woods	75.00	125.	300.	350.

KL#	FR#	Type	Denom.	Signatures	VG	VF	CH CU (63)	Gem CU (65)
1318	1802-2	'29T2	$20	Jones-Woods	85.00	150.	450.	700.

Fifty Dollars

Washington Crossing the Delaware at left, Prayer for Victory at right.
Spiked red seal. Embarkation of the Pilgrims.

KL#	FR#	Type	Denom.	Signatures	VG	VF	CH CU (63)	Gem CU (65)
1319	440	Orig	$50	Chittenden-Spinner	15,000.	25,000.	30,000.	35,000.
1320	442	Orig	$50	Colby-Spinner	15,000.	25,000.	30,000.	35,000.
1321	443	Orig	$50	Allison-Spinner	15,000.	25,000.	30,000.	35,000.

Washington Crossing the Delaware at left, Prayer for Victory at right.
Scalloped red seal.

KL#	FR#	Type	Denom.	Signatures	VG	VF	CH CU (63)	Gem CU (65)
1322	444	1875	$50	Allison-New	15,000.	25,000.	30,000.	35,000.
1323	444a	1875	$50	Allison-Wyman	-	Rare	-	-
1324	445	1875	$50	Allison-Gilfillan	15,000.	22,500.	30,000.	35,000.
1325	446	1875	$50	Scofield-Gilfillan	15,000.	22,500.	30,000.	35,000.

KL#	FR#	Type	Denom.	Signatures	VG	VF	CH CU (63)	Gem CU (65)
1326	447	1875	$50	Bruce-Gilfillan	15,000.	22,500.	30,000.	35,000.
1327	448	1875	$50	Bruce-Wyman	15,000.	22,500.	30,000.	35,000.
1328	449	1875	$50	Rosecrans-Huston	15,000.	22,500.	30,000.	35,000.
1329	450	1875	$50	Rosecrans-Nebeker	15,000.	22,500.	30,000.	35,000.
1330	451	1875	$50	Tillman-Morgan	15,000.	22,500.	30,000.	35,000.

*Washington Crossing the Delaware at left, Prayer for Victory at right.
Scalloped brown seal. Large Charter number in center, state seal at left.*

KL#	FR#	Type	Denom.	Signatures	VG	VF	CH CU (63)	Gem CU (65)
1331	507	'82BB	$50	Bruce-Gilfillan	4500.	6000.	15,000.	20,000.
1332	508	'82BB	$50	Bruce-Wyman	4500.	6000.	15,000.	20,000.
1333	509	'82BB	$50	Bruce-Jordan	4500.	6000.	15,000.	20,000.

KL#	FR#	Type	Denom.	Signatures	VG	VF	CH CU (63)	Gem CU (65)
1334	510	'82BB	$50	Rosecrans-Jordan	4500.	6000.	15,000.	20,000.
1335	511	'82BB	$50	Rosecrans-Hyatt	4500.	6000.	15,000.	20,000.
1336	512	'82BB	$50	Rosecrans-Huston	3750.	6000.	15,000.	20,000.
1337	513	'82BB	$50	Rosecrans-Nebeker	4500.	6000.	15,000.	20,000.
1338	514	'82BB	$50	Rosecrans-Morgan	4500.	6000.	15,000.	20,000.

KL#	FR#	Type	Denom.	Signatures	VG	VF	CH CU (63)	Gem CU (65)
1339	515	'82BB	$50	Tillman-Morgan	4500.	6000.	15,000.	20,000.
1340	516	'82BB	$50	Tillman-Roberts	4500.	6000.	15,000.	20,000.
1341	517	'82BB	$50	Bruce-Roberts	4500.	6000.	15,000.	20,000.
1342	518	'82BB	$50	Lyons-Roberts	4500.	6000.	15,000.	20,000.
1343	518a	'82BB	$50	Vernon-Treat	6000.	8500.	17,500.	23,000.

Washington Crossing the Delaware at left, Prayer for Victory at right. Dates at center, heraldic eagle at each side.

KL#	FR#	Type	Denom.	Signatures	VG	VF	CH CU (63)	Gem CU (65)
1344	558	'82DB	$50	Rosecrans-Huston	4000.	6500.	16,000.	21,000.
1345	559	'82DB	$50	Rosecrans-Nebeker	4000.	6500.	16,000.	21,000.
1346	560	'82DB	$50	Tillman-Morgan	4000.	5500.	16,000.	21,000.
1347	561	'82DB	$50	Tillman-Roberts	4000.	6500.	16,000.	21,000.
1348	562	'82DB	$50	Bruce-Roberts	4000.	6500.	16,000.	21,000.
1349	563	'82DB	$50	Lyons-Roberts	4000.	6500.	16,000.	21,000.
1350	564	'82DB	$50	Vernon-Treat	4000.	6500.	16,000.	21,000.
1351	565	'82DB	$50	Napier-McClung	4000.	6500.	16,000.	21,000.

Value at center, heraldic eagle at each side.

KL#	FR#	Type	Denom.	Signatures	VG	VF	CH CU (63)	Gem CU (65)
1352	586	'82VB	$50	Lyons-Roberts 7 known	-	Rare	-	-

John Sherman at left. Red seal.
Mechanics and Navigation (Steam locomotive at right).

KL#	FR#	Type	Denom.	Signatures	VG	VF	CH CU (63)	Gem CU (65)
1353	664	'02RS	$50	Lyons-Roberts	5750.	6000.	16,000.	22,000.
1354	665	'02RS	$50	Lyons-Treat	5750.	6500.	16,000.	22,000.
1355	666	'02RS	$50	Vernon-Treat	5750.	6500.	16,000.	22,000.

John Sherman at left.
Date at center, Mechanics and Navigation (Steam locomotive at right).

KL#	FR#	Type	Denom.	Signatures	VG	VF	CH CU (63)	Gem CU (65)
1356	667	'02DB	$50	Lyons-Roberts	700.	825.	5500.	6800.
1357	668	'02DB	$50	Lyons-Roberts	750.	1300.	5500.	6800.
1358	669	'02DB	$50	Vernon-Treat	700.	825.	5500.	6800.
1359	670	'02DB	$50	Vernon-McClung	700.	825.	5500.	6800.
1360	671	'02DB	$50	Napier-McClung	700.	825.	5500.	6800.
1361	672	'02DB	$50	Napier-Thompson	700.	825.	5500.	6800.
1362	673	'02DB	$50	Napier-Burke	700.	825.	5500.	6800.
1363	674	'02DB	$50	Parker-Burke	700.	825.	5500.	6800.
1364	674a	'02DB	$50	Teehee-Burke	700.	825.	5500.	6800.

Mechanics and Navigation (Steam locomotive at right).

KL#	FR#	Type	Denom.	Signatures	VG	VF	CH CU (63)	Gem CU (65)
1365	675	'02PB	$50	Lyons-Roberts	700.	825.	5000.	7500.
1366	676	'02PB	$50	Lyons-Treat	700.	825.	5000.	7500.
1367	677	'02PB	$50	Vernon-Treat	700.	825.	5000.	7500.
1368	678	'02PB	$50	Vernon-McClung	700.	825.	5000.	7500.
1369	679	'02PB	$50	Napier-McClung	700.	825.	5000.	7500.
1370	679a	'02PB	$50	Napier-Thompson	700.	825.	5000.	7500.
1371	680	'02PB	$50	Napier-Burke	700.	825.	5000.	7500.
1372	681	'02PB	$50	Parker-Burke	700.	825.	5000.	7500.
1373	682	'02PB	$50	Teehee-Burke	700.	825.	5000.	7500.
1374	683	'02PB	$50	Elliott-Burke	700.	825.	5000.	7500.
1375	684	'02PB	$50	Elliott-White	700.	825.	5000.	7500.
1376	685	'02PB	$50	Speelman-White	700.	825.	5000.	7500.
1377	685a	'02PB	$50	Woods-White	700.	825.	5000.	7500.

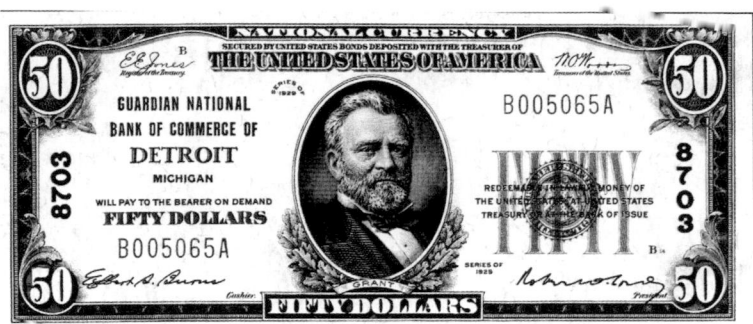

Ulysses S. Grant at center. Capitol Building.

KL#	FR#	Type	Denom.	Signatures	VG	VF	CH CU (63)	Gem CU (65)
1378	1803-1	'29T1	$50	Jones-Woods	90.00	145.	650.	800.
1379	1803-2	'29T2	$50	Jones-Woods	175.	450.	1000.	1200

One Hundred Dollars

Battle of Lake Erie at left, Union at right. Spiked red seal.
Trumbull's Declaration of Independence.

KL#	FR#	Type	Denom.	Signatures	VG	VF	CH CU (63)	Gem CU (65)
1380	452	Orig	$100	Chittenden-Spinner	17,000.	35,000.	47,500.	63,000.
1381	454	Orig	$100	Colby-Spinner	17,000.	35,000.	47,500.	63,000.
1382	455	Orig	$100	Allison-Spinner	17,000.	35,000.	47,500.	63,000.

Battle of Lake Erie at left, Union at right. Scalloped red seal.

KL#	FR#	Type	Denom.	Signatures	VG	VF	CH CU (63)	Gem CU (65)
1383	456	1875	$100	Allison-New	17,000.	35,000.	47,500.	63,000.
1384	457	1875	$100	Allison-Wyman	-	Rare	-	-
1385	458	1875	$100	Allison-Gilfillan	17,000.	35,000.	47,500.	63,000.
1386	459	1875	$100	Scofield-Gilfillan	17,000.	35,000.	47,500.	63,000.
1387	460	1875	$100	Bruce-Gilfillan	17,000.	35,000.	47,500.	63,000.
1388	461	1875	$100	Bruce-Wyman	17,000.	35,000.	47,500.	63,000.
1389	462	1875	$100	Rosecrans-Huston	-	Rare	-	-
1390	462a	1875	$100	Rosecrans-Nebeker	-	Rare	-	-
1391	463	1875	$100	Tillman-Morgan	-	Rare	-	-

Large Charter number at center.

KL#	FR#	Type	Denom.	Signatures	VG	VF	CH CU (63)	Gem CU (65)
1392	519	'82BB	$100	Bruce-Gilfillan	2250.	5500.	18,000.	22,000.
1393	520	'82BB	$100	Bruce-Wyman	2500.	5500.	18,000.	22,000.
1394	521	'82BB	$100	Bruce-Jordan	2500.	5500.	18,000.	22,000.
1395	522	'82BB	$100	Rosecrans-Jordan	2500.	5500.	18,000.	22,000.
1396	523	'82BB	$100	Rosecrans-Hyatt	2500.	5500.	18,000.	22,000.
1397	524	'82BB	$100	Rosecrans-Huston	2500.	5500.	18,000.	22,000.
1398	525	'82BB	$100	Rosecrans-Nebeker	2500.	5500.	18,000.	22,000.
1399	526	'82BB	$100	Rosecrans-Morgan	2500.	5500.	18,000.	22,000.
1400	527	'82BB	$100	Tillman-Morgan	2500.	5500.	18,000.	22,000.
1401	529	'82BB	$100	Bruce-Roberts	2500.	5500.	18,000.	22,000.

Battle of Lake Erie at left, Union at right. Scalloped red seal.
Large Charter number at center.

KL#	FR#	Type	Denom.	Signatures	VG	VF	CH CU (63)	Gem CU (65)
1401	528	'82BB	$100	Tillman-Roberts	2500.	5500.	18,000.	22,000.
1402	530	'82BB	$100	Lyons-Roberts	2500.	5500.	18,000.	22,000.
1403	531	'82BB	$100	Vernon-Treat	-	Rare	-	-

Date at center, eagles at sides.

KL#	FR#	Type	Denom.	Signatures	VG	VF	CH CU (63)	Gem CU (65)
1404	566	'82DB	$100	Rosecrans-Huston	7500.	8250.	19,250.	23,000.
1405	567	'82DB	$100	Rosecrans-Nebeker	7500.	8250.	19,250.	23,000.
1406	568	'82DB	$100	Tillman-Morgan	7500.	8250.	19,250.	23,000.
1407	569	'82DB	$100	Tillman-Roberts	7500.	8250.	19,250.	23,000.
1408	570	'82DB	$100	Bruce-Roberts	7500.	8250.	19,250.	23,000.
1409	571	'82DB	$100	Lyons-Roberts	7500.	8250.	19,250.	23,000.
1410	572	'82DB	$100	Vernon-Treat	7500.	8250.	19,250.	23,000.
1411	572a	'82DB	$100	Napier-McClung	-	Rare	-	-

Value at center, eagles at sides.

KL#	FR#	Type	Denom.	Signatures	VG	VF	CH CU (63)	Gem CU (65)
1412	586-A	'82VB	$100	Lyons-Roberts 5 known	-	Rare	-	-

John Knox at left. Red seal. Eagle on shield flanked by male figures and flags.

KL#	FR#	Type	Denom.	Signatures	VG	VF	CH CU (63)	Gem CU (65)
1413	686	'02RS	$100	Lyons-Roberts	6500.	8500.	18,500.	25,000.
1414	687	'02RS	$100	Lyons-Roberts	6500.	8500.	18,500.	25,000.
1415	688	'02RS	$100	Vernon-Treat	6500.	8500.	18,500.	25,000.

John Knox at left.
Dates above Eagle on shield flanked by male figures and flags.

KL#	FR#	Type	Denom.	Signatures	VG	VF	CH CU (63)	Gem CU (65)
1416	689	'02DB	$100	Lyons-Roberts	850.	1250.	7750.	8500.
1417	690	'02DB	$100	Lyons-Treat	850.	1250.	7750.	8500.
1418	691	'02DB	$100	Vernon-Treat	850.	1250.	7750.	8500.
1419	692	'02DB	$100	Vernon-McClung	850.	1250.	7750.	8500.
1420	693	'02DB	$100	Napier-McClung	850.	1250.	7750.	8500.
1421	694	'02DB	$100	Napier-Thompson	850.	1250.	7750.	8500.
1422	695	'02DB	$100	Napier-Burke	850.	1250.	7750.	8500.
1423	696	'02DB	$100	Parker-Burke	850.	1250.	7750.	8500.
1424	697	'02DB	$100	Teehee-Burke	850.	1250.	7750.	8500.

Eagle on shield flanked by male figures and flags.

KL#	FR#	Type	Denom.	Signatures	VG	VF	CH CU (63)	Gem CU (65)
1425	698	'02PB	$100	Lyons-Roberts	1100.	1750.	8000.	9000.
1426	699	'02PB	$100	Lyons-Treat	800.	1250.	8000.	9000.
1427	700	'02PB	$100	Vernon-Treat	800.	1250.	8000.	9000.
1428	701	'02PB	$100	Vernon-McClung	800.	1250.	8000.	9000.
1429	702	'02PB	$100	Napier-McClung	800.	1250.	8000.	9000.
1430	702a	'02PB	$100	Napier-Thompson	800.	1250.	8000.	9000.
1431	703	'02PB	$100	Parker-Burke	800.	1250.	8000.	9000.
1432	704	'02PB	$100	Teehee-Burke	800.	1250.	8000.	9000.
1433	705	'02PB	$100	Elliott-Burke	800.	1250.	8000.	9000.
1434	706	'02PB	$100	Elliott-White	800.	1250.	8000.	9000.
1435	707	'02PB	$100	Speelman-White	800.	1250.	8000.	9000.
1436	707a	'02PB	$100	Woods-White 2 known	-	Rare	-	-

Benjamin Franklin at center. Independence Hall.

KL#	FR#	Type	Denom.	Signatures	VG	VF	CH CU (63)	Gem CU (65)
1437	1804-1	'29T1	$100	Jones-Woods	175.	225.	425.	500.

KL#	FR#	Type	Denom.	Signatures	VG	VF	CH CU (63)	Gem CU (65)
1438	1804-2	'29T2	$100	Jones-Woods	225.	350.	1000.	1200.

Civilization vignette at left, The Arrival of the Sirius at right.
Spiked red seal. Trumbull's painting:
Surrender of General Burgoyne to General Gates at Saratoga.

KL#	FR#	Type	Denom.	Signatures	VG	VF	CH CU (63)	Gem CU (65)
1439	464	Orig	$500	Colby-Spinner	-	Rare	-	-

Civilization vignette at left, The Arrival of the Sirius at right.
Scalloped red seal.

KL#	FR#	Type	Denom.	Signatures	VG	VF	CH CU (63)	Gem CU (65)
1440	464	1875	$500	Colby-Spinner	-	-	Unique	-
1441	464	1875	$500	Allison-New	-	-	Unique	-

General Scott's entrance into Mexico City at left.
U.S. Capitol at right. Spiked red seal.
Trumbull's painting: Washington resigning his Commission.

KL#	FR#	Type	Denom.	Signatures	VG	VF	CH CU (63)	Gem CU (65)
1442	465	Orig	$1,000	Chittenden-Spinner s	-	Unknown in Private hand		-

General Scott's entrance into Mexico City at left.
U.S. Capitol at right. Scalloped red seal.

KL#	FR#	Type	Denom.	Signatures	VG	VF	CH CU (63)	Gem CU (65)
1443	465	1875	$1,000	Allison-Wyman	-	-	-	-

Original Series $1

(KL #1086-1088) (Fr #380-382)

	VG	VF	AU
Alabama	—	Rare	—
Colorado Territory	—	Rare	—
Connecticut	650.	1400.	2100.
Dakota Territory	4000.	7000.	9000.
Delaware	—	Rare	—
District of Columbia	—	Rare	—
Georgia	—	Rare	—
Illinois	600.	1350.	2000.
Indiana	600.	1350.	2000.
Iowa	600.	1350.	2000.
Kansas	600.	1350.	2000.
Kentucky	1100.	1900.	2500.
Louisiana	—	Rare	—
Maine	750.	1600.	2300.
Maryland	650.	1400.	2100.
Massachusetts	600.	1350.	2000.
Michigan	600.	1350.	2000.
Minnesota	600.	1350.	2000.
Missouri	600.	1350.	2000.
Montana Territory	—	Rare	—
Nebraska	600.	1350.	2000.
Nebraska Territory	—	Rare	—
New Hampshire	750.	1600.	2300.
New Jersey	600.	1350.	2000.
New Mexico Territory	—	Rare	—
New York	600.	1350.	2000.
North Carolina	650.	1400.	2100.
Ohio	600.	1350.	2000.
Pennsylvania	600.	1350.	2000.
Rhode Island	650.	1900.	2100.
South Carolina	—	Rare	—
Tennessee	650.	1400.	2100.
Texas	600.	1350.	2000.
Utah Territory	2500.	5000.	9000.
Vermont	750.	1600.	2300.
West Virginia	—	—	—
Wisconsin	600.	1350.	2000.
Wyoming Territory	—	Rare	—

Series 1875 $1

(KL #1089-1092) (Fr #383-386)

	VG	VF	AU
Connecticut	650.	1400.	2100.
Delaware	—	Rare	—
Georgia	—	Rare	—
Idaho Territory	—	—	—
Illinois	600.	1350.	2100.
Indiana	600.	1350.	2100.
Iowa	600.	1350.	2100.
Kansas	600.	1350.	2100.
Kentucky	1100.	1900.	2500.
Maine	400.	1100.	2200.
Massachusetts	600.	1350.	2000.
Michigan	600.	1350.	2000.
Minnesota	600.	1350.	2000.
Missouri	1500.	2350.	4000.

	VG	VF	AU
Nebraska	2000.	3000.	6000.
New Hampshire	850.	1200.	2500.
New Jersey	650.	1350.	2000.
New Mexico Territory	—	Rare	—
New York	600.	1200.	2000.
North Carolina	2000.	3000.	6000.
Ohio	600.	1300.	2000.
Pennsylvania	600.	1350.	2000.
Rhode Island	700.	1400.	2200.
Tennessee	2500.	4000.	6000.
Texas	4000.	6000.	10,000.
Vermont	650.	1300.	2750.
Wisconsin	650.	1350.	2100.

Original Series $2

(KL# 1093-1095) (Fr #387-389)

	VG	VF	AU
Connecticut	15,000.	3000.	6750.
Dakota Territory		Two known	
Delaware		Five known	
District of Columbia		Two known	
Idaho Territory		VF:Unique	
Illinois	2000.	5000.	8000.
Indiana	2000.	5000.	8500.
Iowa	2000.	5000.	8000.
Kansas	2000.	5000.	11,000.
Kentucky	2500.	5500.	11,000.
Louisiana	—	Rare	—
Maine	2500.	5500.	10,000.
Maryland	3000.	5000.	11,000.
Massachusetts	2000.	5000.	8500.
Michigan	2000.	5000.	9000.
Minnesota	2000.	5000.	9000.
Missouri	2000.	5000.	9000.
Montana Territory		Two known	
Nebraska		Three known	
Nebraska Territory		Three known	
New Hampshire	3000.	6000.	12,500.
New Jersey	2000.	5000.	8000.
New Mexico Territory		Four known	
New York	2000.	4500.	7500.
North Carolina	4000.	8000.	13,000.
Ohio	2000.	4500.	10,200.
Pennsylvania	2000.	5000.	11,000.
Rhode Island	2000.	5000.	7500.
Tennessee	4000.	6500.	14,000.
Utah Territory		Four known	
Vermont	2200.	5000.	10,000.
Wisconsin	222.	5000.	8.00
Wyoming Territory		VF:Unique	

Series 1875 $2

(KL #1096-1099) (Fr #390-393)

	VG	VF	AU
Colorado Territory	6000.	10,000.	18,000.
Connecticut	2000.	5000.	8000.
Delaware	—	Rare	—
Georgia	—	Rare	—
Illinois	1125.	5000.	8000.
Indiana	2000.	5000.	8000.
Iowa	2000.	5000.	8000.
Kansas	2200.	5500.	9000.
Kentucky	2500.	6000.	10,000.
Maine	2700.	6000.	10,000.
Massachusetts	2000.	5000.	8000.
Michigan	2000.	5000.	8000.
Minnesota	2000.	5000.	8000.
Missouri	—	Rare	—
Montana Territory	—	Rare	—
New Hampshire	3000.	6000.	13,000.
New Jersey	2000.	5000.	8000.
New York	2000.	4500.	6000.
North Carolina	4000.	8000.	13,000.
Ohio	2000.	4500.	7000.
Pennsylvania	2000.	4500.	7000.
Rhode Island	2000.	4500.	6000.
Texas		Unique	
Vermont	2500.	5500.	9000.
Wisconsin	2000.	5000.	8000.

Original Series $5

(KL #1100-1103) (Fr #394-399)

	VG	VF	AU
Alabama	1000.	1500.	2000.
Arkansas	—	Rare	—
Colorado Territory	7000.	10,000.	13,500.
Connecticut	750.	1600.	2100.
Dakota Territory	—	Rare	—
District of Columbia	700.	2000.	3000.
Florida	—	Rare	—
Georgia	5000.	8000.	13,000.
Illinois	700.	1600.	2500.
Indiana	700.	1600.	2500.
Iowa	700.	1600.	2500.
Kansas	750.	1700.	3500.
Kentucky	750.	1750.	3500.
Louisiana	1500.	2500.	5200.
Maine	1000.	1700.	3500.
Maryland	700.	1700.	250.
Massachusetts	700.	1700.	2500.
Michigan	700.	1700.	2500.
Minnesota	750.	1750.	2500.
Missouri	700.	1700.	2500.
Montana Territory	—	Rare	—
Nebraska	2200.	3300.	7000.
New Hampshire	750.	1600.	5000.
New Jersey	750.	1600.	2500.
New Mexico Territory	—	Rare	—
New York	650.	1550.	2400.
North Carolina	2200.	3400.	7000.

	VG	VF	AU
Ohio	600.	1550.	2400.
Pennsylvania	650.	1700.	2500.
Rhode Island	650.	1700.	2500.
South Carolina	2300.	4000.	8000.
Tennessee	1750.	3500.	7000.
Vermont	750.	1800.	3500.
Virginia	1400.	2300.	5000.
West Virginia	1400.	1700.	6000.
Wisconsin	700.	1700.	2500.

Series 1875 $5

(KL #1104-1113) (Fr #401-408)

	VG	VF	AU
Alabama	750.	1125.	2500.
Arizona Territory	—	Rare	—
Arkansas	—	Rare	—
California		VF:Unique	
Colorado	2250.	4000.	8000.
Colorado Territory	7000.	10,000.	14,000.
Connecticut	700.	1600.	2200.
Dakota Territory	—	Rare	—
Delaware	—	Rare	—
District of Columbia	1500.	2250.	3450.
Florida	—	Rare	—
Georgia	5000.	8000.	13,000.
Idaho Territory	—	Rare	—
Illinois	700.	1600.	2000.
Indiana	700.	1600.	2200.
Iowa	700.	1600.	2800.
Kansas	700.	1800.	3400.
Kentucky	700.	1800.	3300.
Louisiana	1700.	2800.	5300.
Maine	1200.	1900.	3500.
Maryland	1200.	1900.	3000.
Massachusetts	700.	1500.	2300.
Michigan	700.	1600.	2800.
Minnesota	800.	1600.	3200.
Missouri	700.	1500.	2000.
Montana	—	Rare	—
Montana Territory	—	Rare	—
Nebraska	2100.	3300.	6500.
New Hampshire	750.	1750.	4750.
New Jersey	700.	1600.	2750.
New Mexico Territory	—	Rare	—
New York	600.	900.	1900.
North Carolina	2200.	3400.	7000.
North Dakota	—	Rare	—
Ohio	600.	1500.	2500.
Pennsylvania	600.	1500.	2200.
Rhode Island	600.	1500.	3200.
South Carolina	700.	1500.	3200.
South Dakota	—	Rare	—
Tennessee	1850.	3500.	7000.
Texas	5000.	8000.	13,000.
Utah Territory	—	Rare	—
Vermont	700.	1800.	3400.
Virginia	1500.	2400.	5000.
Washington	—	Rare	—
West Virginia	2000.	3000.	5500.

	VG	VF	AU
Wisconsin	700.	1500.	2300.
Wyoming	4000.	7000.	12,000.
Wyoming Territory	—	Rare	—

	VG	VF	AU
Washington Territory	—	Rare	—
West Virginia	650.	750.	1400.
Wisconsin	400.	650.	1200.
Wyoming	—	Rare	—

1882 Brown Back $5
(KL #1114-1126) (Fr #466-478)

	VG	VF	AU
Alabama	750.	1750.	2750.
Arizona Territory	—	Rare	—
Arkansas	2000.	3000.	9000.
California	400.	600.	2000.
Colorado	600.	1200.	3750.
Connecticut	750.	1100.	2000.
Dakota Territory	—	8000.	—
Delaware	2500.	5000.	12,000.
District of Columbia	400.	600.	1200.
Florida	2500.	3500.	6000.
Georgia	750.	1750.	2750.
Hawaii	2500.	5000.	8000.
Idaho	—	Rare	—
Idaho Territory	—	Rare	—
Illinois	400.	600.	1200.
Indian Territory	3400.	6000.	10,000.
Indiana	400.	600.	1200.
Iowa	400.	600.	1200.
Kansas	450.	650.	1250.
Kentucky	700.	1000.	1500.
Louisiana	800.	1400.	2000.
Maine	700.	1000.	1700.
Maryland	750.	1100.	2000.
Massachusetts	400.	600.	1200.
Michigan	400.	600.	1200.
Minnesota	450.	650.	1250.
Mississippi	2000.	4000.	6000.
Missouri	400.	600.	1200.
Montana	1500.	2500.	7000.
Montana Territory	—	Rare	—
Nebraska	500.	750.	13,060.
New Hampshire	550.	800.	1400.
New Jersey	400.	600.	1200.
New Mexico Territory	3000.	6500.	10,000.
New York	400.	5500.	1100.
North Carolina	900.	1500.	2000.
North Dakota	—	Rare	—
Ohio	400.	600.	1200.
Oklahoma	2000.	5000.	7500.
Oklahoma Territory	3500.	5500.	9500.
Oregon	2000.	4000.	7000.
Pennsylvania	400.	600.	1200.
Rhode Island	450.	550.	1300.
South Carolina	1500.	3000.	5000.
South Dakota	2000.	3400.	7000.
Tennessee	500.	700.	2000.
Texas	500.	700.	1800.
Utah	2200.	4000.	9600.
Utah Territory		Unique	
Vermont	700.	900.	1750.
Virginia	700.	900.	1750.
Washington	1100.	2500.	5000.

1882 Date Back $5
(KL #1127-1135) (Fr #532-538-B)

	VG	VF	AU
Alabama	700.	1200.	1700.
Arizona Territory	—	Rare	—
California	400.	700.	1200.
Colorado	700.	1200.	2700.
Connecticut	900.	1100.	2000.
Delaware	—	Rare	—
District of Columbia	700.	950.	2000.
Florida	650.	2000.	3200.
Georgia	650.	1000.	2000.
Hawaii	2250.	4500.	6750.
Idaho	—	Rare	—
Illinois	400.	700.	1200.
Indiana	400.	700.	1200.
Iowa	400.	700.	1200.
Kansas	550.	850.	1350.
Kentucky	450.	750.	1100.
Louisiana	500.	850.	2250.
Maine	—	Rare	—
Maryland	400.	700.	1200.
Massachusetts	400.	700.	1200.
Michigan	400.	700.	1200.
Minnesota	400.	700.	1200.
Mississippi	—	Rare	—
Missouri	400.	700.	1200.
Montana	—	Rare	—
Nebraska	450.	800.	1300.
New Hampshire	800.	1250.	2000.
New Jersey	400.	700.	1200.
New Mexico	2000.	3250.	5500.
New Mexico Territory	3000.	5000.	12,000.
New York	400.	700.	1100.
North Carolina	500.	900.	1300.
North Dakota	1200.	2750.	4500.
Ohio	400.	700.	1200.
Oklahoma	400.	700.	1200.
Oregon		Unique	
Pennsylvania	400.	700.	1200.
Rhode Island	800.	1100.	2000.
South Carolina	800.	1300.	3000.
South Dakota		Unique	
Tennessee	400.	700.	1200.
Texas	400.	700.	1200.
Utah	850.	1100.	2150.
Vermont	850.	1100.	2150.
Virginia	650.	800.	1300.
Washington	1700.	2750.	4500.
West Virginia	800.	950.	1500.
Wisconsin	400.	800.	1100.
Wyoming		Unique	

1882 Value Back $5

(KL #1136-1142) (Fr #573-575-B)

	VG	VF	AU
Alabama	600.	1300.	3400.
California	550.	1000.	1900.
Colorado	—	Rare	—
Connecticut	550.	1100.	3800.
District of Columbia	700.	2000.	4350.
Florida	900.	3000.	4800.
Georgia	650.	2000.	3400.
Hawaii		Unique	
Idaho		Unique	
Illinois	550.	800.	1700.
Indiana	550.	800.	1750.
Iowa	550.	800.	1750.
Kansas	600.	850.	2000.
Kentucky	550.	800.	1700.
Maine		Rare	—
Maryland	550.	825.	2000.
Massachusetts	550.	825.	2250.
Michigan	550.	825.	2250.
Minnesota	550.	825.	1950.
Missouri		Rare	—
Nebraska	600.	900.	2000.
New Hampshire	—	Rare	—
New Jersey	550.	850.	2000.
New Mexico	1250.	3000.	6000.
New York	550.	800.	2000.
North Carolina	750.	1500.	2750.
North Dakota		Rare	—
Ohio	550.	800.	1600.
Oklahoma	600.	900.	2000.
Pennsylvania	600.	800.	1750.
South Dakota		Unique	
Texas	600.	850.	1600.
Utah		Unique	
Virginia	600.	850.	1600.
Washington		Unique	
West Virginia	625.	850.	2500.
Wisconsin	550.	850.	1300.

1902 Red Seal $5

(KL #1143-1145) (Fr #587-589)

	VG	VF	AU
Alabama	500.	1200.	2100.
Alaska	10,000.	25,000.	30,000.
Arkansas	700.	1400.	3150.
California	400.	800.	1700.
Colorado	900.	1500.	3750.
Connecticut	400.	700.	1350.
Delaware	3000.	7500.	13,500.
District of Columbia	400.	1000.	2000.
Florida	1800.	3000.	5500.
Georgia	1000.	1750.	4500.
Idaho	1500.	2500.	5000.
Illinois	400.	700.	900.
Indian Territory	1500.	2500.	4500.
Indiana	400.	700.	1000.
Iowa	400.	700.	1000.

	VG	VF	AU
Kansas	400.	700.	1000.
Kentucky	450.	1000.	2500.
Louisiana	500.	900.	2000.
Maine	400.	700.	1200.
Maryland	400.	700.	1000.
Massachusetts	400.	700.	1000.
Michigan	400.	700.	1000.
Minnesota	400.	700.	1000.
Mississippi	1350.	2400.	4125.
Missouri	400.	700.	1000.
Montana	2250.	5500.	11,250.
Nebraska	450.	700.	1500.
Nevada	4500.	8000.	13,500.
New Hampshire	400.	700.	1200.
New Jersey	400.	700.	1000.
New York	400.	700.	1000.
North Carolina	2250.	4200.	6600.
North Dakota	1950.	3000.	6000.
Ohio	400.	700.	1000.
Oklahoma Territory	1500.	2800.	6000.
Oregon	1500.	3000.	6000.
Pennsylvania	400.	700.	1000.
Rhode Island	400.	700.	1000.
South Carolina	3000.	4800.	7500.
Tennessee	400.	900.	2000.
Texas	400.	700.	1200.
Vermont	400.	800.	2000.
Virginia	400.	800.	1500.
Washington	1350.	2600.	4500.
West Virginia	400.	800.	2000.
Wisconsin	400.	700.	1100.

1902 Date Back $5

(KL #1146-1154) (Fr #590-597-A)

	VG	VF	AU
Alabama	125.	350.	600.
Alaska	—	Rare	—
Arizona	1350.	3000.	4250.
Arkansas	135.	325.	600.
California	125.	325.	600.
Colorado	150.	325.	625.
Connecticut	135.	250.	600.
Delaware	275.	550.	1200.
District of Columbia	160.	250.	600.
Florida	175.	300.	600.
Georgia	150.	375.	600.
Hawaii	—	Rare	—
Idaho	250.	375.	800.
Illinois	135.	325.	600.
Indiana	135.	250.	600.
Iowa	135.	360.	600.
Kansas	135.	260.	600.
Kentucky	165.	325.	650.
Louisiana	165.	325.	625.
Maine	165.	325.	625.
Maryland	135.	325.	600.
Massachusetts	135.	325.	600.
Michigan	135.	325.	600.
Minnesota	135.	325.	600.

	VG	VF	AU		VG	VF	AU
Mississippi	225.	350.	825.	Nebraska	100.	150.	250.
Missouri	150.	300.	600.	Nevada	600.	1200.	2000.
Montana	200.	450.	700.	New Hampshire	140.	235.	300.
Nebraska	125.	300.	600.	New Jersey	100.	150.	250.
Nevada	800.	1850.	3000.	New Mexico	200.	300.	750.
New Hampshire	160.	300.	600.	New York	100.	150.	250.
New Jersey	135.	275.	600.	North Carolina	110.	165.	250.
New Mexico	350.	825.	1200.	North Dakota	125.	200.	325.
New Mexico Territory	3000.	5000.	7000.	Ohio	100.	150.	250.
New York	125.	350.	600.	Oklahoma	110.	165.	250.
North Carolina	150.	325.	600.	Oregon	110.	165.	250.
North Dakota	150.	350.	625.	Pennsylvania	100.	150.	250.
Ohio	125.	325.	600.	Rhode Island	125.	200.	325.
Oklahoma	125.	325.	600.	South Carolina	125.	200.	325.
Oregon	140.	325.	650.	South Dakota	125.	200.	325.
Pennsylvania	125.	325.	600.	Tennessee	110.	165.	275.
Rhode Island	125.	325.	600.	Texas	100.	150.	250.
South Carolina	125.	325.	600.	Utah	140.	190.	325.
South Dakota	175.	375.	625.	Vermont	140.	235.	400.
Tennessee	135.	325.	600.	Virginia	110.	165.	275.
Texas	135.	325.	600.	Washington	125.	225.	450.
Utah	135.	350.	650.	West Virginia	125.	225.	450.
Vermont	200.	375.	650.	Wisconsin	100.	150.	250.
Virginia	135.	375.	600.	Wyoming	350.	500.	1000.
Washington	150.	375.	600.				
West Virginia	150.	350.	600.				
Wisconsin	125.	325.	600.				
Wyoming	450.	875.	1450.				

1929 Type 1 $5

(KL #1170) (Fr #1800-1)

	VG	VF	AU
Alabama	—	110	185.
Alaska	—	9000.	15,000.
Arizona	—	360.	750.
Arkansas	—	150.	275.
California	—	100.	175.
Colorado	—	100.	185.
Connecticut	—	135.	250
Delaware	—	350.	700.
District of Columbia	—	150.	275.
Florida	—	115.	185.
Georgia	—	105.	180.
Hawaii	—	350.	700.
Idaho	—	350.	700.
Illinois	—	100.	165.
Indiana	—	110.	185.
Iowa	—	100.	165.
Kansas	—	100.	165.
Kentucky	—	110.	175.
Louisiana	—	150.	275.
Maine	—	150.	275.
Maryland	—	110.	165.
Massachusetts	—	100.	150.
Michigan	—	105.	155.
Minnesota	—	105.	155.
Mississippi	—	105.	285.
Missouri	—	105.	155.
Montana	—	150.	275.
Nebraska	—	105.	155.
Nevada	—	150.	275.
New Hampshire	—	110.	160.
New Jersey	—	105.	155.

1902 Plain Back $5

(KL #1155-1169) (Fr #598-612)

	VG	VF	AU
Alabama	110.	225.	250.
Alaska	—	Rare	—
Arizona	1200.	2200.	4000.
Arkansas	110.	160.	250.
California	100.	150.	250.
Colorado	125.	200.	325.
Connecticut	110.	165.	250.
Delaware	225.	450.	1000
District of Columbia	140.	150.	250.
Florida	125.	200.	325.
Georgia	110.	165.	275.
Hawaii	700.	1500.	3000.
Idaho	200.	300.	950.
Illinois	100.	150.	250.
Indiana	100.	150.	250.
Iowa	100.	150.	250.
Kansas	100.	150.	250.
Kentucky	110.	165.	275.
Louisiana	150.	250.	275.
Maine	140.	235.	400.
Maryland	110.	165.	275.
Massachusetts	100.	150.	250.
Michigan	100.	150.	250.
Minnesota	100.	150.	250.
Mississippi	200.	300.	400.
Missouri	100.	150.	250.
Montana	165.	275.	350.

	VG	VF	AU		VG	VF	AU
New Mexico	—	200.	350.	Ohio	—	120.	180.
New York	—	100.	150.	Oklahoma	—	120.	180.
North Carolina	—	115.	165.	Oregon	—	180.	310.
North Dakota	—	165.	250.	Pennsylvania	—	115.	175.
Ohio	—	105.	155.	Rhode Island	—	100.	175.
Oklahoma	—	100.	155.	South Carolina	—	175.	300.
Oregon	—	165.	285.	South Dakota	—	185.	300.
Pennsylvania	—	100.	150.	Tennessee	—	165.	185.
Rhode Island	—	100.	150.	Texas	—	165.	275.
South Carolina	—	150.	275.	Utah	—	165.	275.
South Dakota	—	150.	275.	Vermont	—	165.	275.
Tennessee	—	55.00	155.	Virginia	—	160.	300.
Texas	—	150.	295.	Washington	—	180.	275.
Utah	—	165.	265.	West Virginia	—	180.	300.
Vermont	—	160.	260.	Wisconsin	—	165.	275.
Virginia	—	50.00	150.	Wyoming	—	390.	775.
Washington	—	50.00	150.				
West Virginia	—	150.	250.				
Wisconsin	—	150.	250.				
Wyoming	—	375.	750.				

1929 Type 2 $5

(KL #1171) (Fr #1800-2)

	VG	VF	AU
Alabama	—	125.	200.
Alaska	—	10,500.	18,000.
Arizona	—	375.	775.
Arkansas	—	165.	290.
California	—	105.	190.
Colorado	—	115.	200.
Connecticut	—	150.	265.
Delaware	—	265.	725.
District of Columbia	—	165.	290.
Florida	—	130.	200.
Georgia	—	120.	200.
Hawaii	—	365.	725.
Idaho	—	365.	725.
Illinois	—	115.	165.
Indiana	—	125.	200.
Iowa	—	110.	190.
Kansas	—	115.	190.
Kentucky	—	125.	200.
Louisiana	—	165.	300.
Maine	—	165.	300.
Maryland	—	125.	190.
Massachusetts	—	115.	175.
Michigan	—	120.	180.
Minnesota	—	120.	180.
Mississippi	—	180.	310.
Missouri	—	120.	180.
Montana	—	165.	300.
Nebraska	—	120.	180.
Nevada	—	165.	300.
New Hampshire	—	125.	185.
New Jersey	—	120.	185.
New Mexico	—	220.	375.
New York	—	115.	175.
North Carolina	—	130.	190.
North Dakota	—	180.	275.

Original Series $10

(KL #1172-1175) (Fr #409-414)

	VG	VF	AU
Alabama		Unique	
Colorado Territory	6750.	10,500.	21,000.
Connecticut	1700.	3000.	5000.
Delaware	2450.	6000.	7500.
District of Columbia	2000.	4500.	6500.
Florida	—	Rare	—
Georgia	2800.	5600.	7500.
Idaho Territory	—	Rare	—
Illinois	1700.	3000.	4000.
Indiana	1700.	3000.	4000.
Iowa	1700.	3000.	4000.
Kansas	2000.	4000.	6500.
Kentucky	1800.	3200.	4200.
Louisiana	3500.	7000.	9000.
Maine	1800.	3000.	4500.
Maryland	1700.	3000.	4000.
Massachusetts	1700.	3000.	4000.
Michigan	1700.	3000.	4000.
Minnesota	1700.	3000.	4000.
Missouri	1700.	3000.	4000.
Montana	—	Rare	—
Nebraska	2500.	4000.	5000.
New Hampshire	1700.	2500.	4000.
New Jersey	1700.	3000.	4000.
New York	1700.	3000.	4000.
North Carolina	2500.	6000.	7000.
Ohio	1700.	3000.	4000.
Pennsylvania	1700.	3000.	4000.
Rhode Island	1700.	3000.	4000.
South Carolina	2500.	5000.	6000.
Tennessee	2200.	4800.	5500.
Texas	8000.	16,000.	16,000.
Vermont	1700.	3000.	4000.
Virginia	1900.	3300.	5000.
West Virginia	1800.	3200.	4300.
Wisconsin	1700.	3000.	4000.

Series 1875 $10

(KL #1176-1184) (Fr #416-423-A)

	VG	VF	AU
Alabama		VF:Unique	
Arkansas	—	Rare	—
California	3750.	7500.	12,000.
Colorado	3750.	6000.	10,500.
Colorado Territory	6750.	10,500.	19,500.
Connecticut	1500.	3000.	4000.
Dakota Territory	—	Rare	—
Delaware	2500.	4000.	7500.
District of Columbia	1500.	3000.	5650.
Florida	—	Rare	—
Georgia	2500.	4000.	5650.
Idaho Territory	—	Rare	—
Illinois	1500.	3000.	4000.
Indiana	1500.	3000.	4000.
Iowa	1500.	3000.	4000.
Kansas	1800.	3000.	5400.
Kentucky	1500.	3000.	4000.
Louisiana	3000.	4000.	9000.
Maine	1500.	3000.	4000.
Maryland	1500.	3000.	4000.
Massachusetts	1500.	3000.	4000.
Michigan	1500.	3000.	4000.
Minnesota	1500.	3000.	4000.
Missouri	1500.	3000.	4000.
Montana	—	Rare	—
Nebraska	2000.	3200.	4500.
Nebraska Territory	—	Rare	—
New Hampshire	1500.	3000.	4000.
New Jersey	1500.	3000.	4000.
New Mexico Territory	—	Rare	—
New York	1500.	3000.	4000.
North Carolina	2000.	4000.	6000.
North Dakota	—	Rare	—
Ohio	1500.	3000.	4000
Oregon	3500.	5500.	11,000.
Pennsylvania	1500.	3000.	4000.
Rhode Island	1500.	3000.	4000.
South Carolina	2000.	4000.	6000.
South Dakota		VF:Unique	
Tennessee	1500.	3000.	4500.
Texas	6000.	10,000.	16,000.
Vermont	1500.	3000.	4000.
Virginia	1500.	3000.	4000.
West Virginia	1500.	3000.	4000.
Wisconsin	1500.	3000.	4000.
Wyoming	3000.	4900.	6000.
Wyoming Territory	—	Rare	—

1882 Brown Back $10

(KL #1185-1198) (Fr #479-492)

	VG	VF	AU
Alabama	700.	1100.	2500.
Arizona Territory	—	Rare	—
Arkansas	—	Rare	—
California	600.	900.	1750.
Colorado	725.	1300.	3000.

	VG	VF	AU
Connecticut	600.	900.	1800.
Dakota Territory		VF:Unique	
Delaware	1000.	3000.	6000.
District of Columbia	600.	900.	1750.
Florida	1400.	5000.	7500.
Georgia	725.	1050.	2500.
Hawaii	2000.	3500.	7500.
Idaho	—	Rare	—
Idaho Territory		VF:Unique	
Illinois	600.	900.	1600.
Indian Territory	2500.	4500.	7000.
Indiana	600.	900.	1600.
Iowa	600.	900.	1600.
Kansas	600.	950.	1700.
Kentucky	725.	1100.	1700.
Louisiana	1000.	1600.	2000.
Maine	725.	1100.	1900.
Maryland	600.	900.	1700.
Massachusetts	600.	1100.	1700.
Michigan	600.	1100.	1700.
Minnesota	625.	1150.	1700.
Mississippi	2000.	4000.	6000.
Missouri	600.	1100.	1700.
Montana	2000.	4000.	6000.
Montana Territory	—	Rare	—
Nebraska	725.	1150.	1800.
Nevada		VF: Unique	
New Hampshire	800.	1200.	2000.
New Jersey	600.	1100.	1650.
New Mexico Territory	2400.	5000.	8000.
New York	600.	1100.	1600.
North Carolina	900.	1600.	2200.
North Dakota	1300.	3200.	4750.
Ohio	600.	1100.	1600.
Oklahoma	2500.	4000.	6000.
Oklahoma Territory	2500.	4000.	6000.
Oregon	1400.	2500.	3750.
Pennsylvania	600.	1100.	1600.
Rhode Island	600.	1150.	1750.
South Carolina	1500.	2750.	4000
South Dakota	1500.	2750.	4000.
Tennessee	850.	1200.	2000.
Texas	900.	1500.	2000.
Utah	1400.	2750.	4000.
Utah Territory	3500.	6500.	10,000.
Vermont	800.	1250.	2000.
Virginia	600.	1300.	2000.
Washington	1500.	2750.	4000.
Washington Territory		VF:Unique	
West Virginia	800.	1200.	2000.
Wisconsin	600.	1100.	1500.
Wyoming	2500.	5000.	7000.
Wyoming Territory		VF:Unique	

1882 Date Back $10

(KL #1199-1208) (Fr #539-548)

	VG	VF	AU
Alabama	650.	1200.	1700.
Arizona		Unique	

	VG	VF	AU		VG	VF	AU
Arkansas		Unique		Hawaii	1500.	5500.	10,000.
California	550.	800.	1500.	Idaho	1400.	4000.	7800.
Colorado	600.	1400.	2100.	Illinois	450.	800.	1600.
Connecticut	650.	1250.	1700.	Indiana	450.	800.	170.
Delaware	1200.	4000.	6000.	Iowa	450.	800.	1700.
District of Columbia	650.	1200.	1600.	Kansas	475.	825.	1700.
Florida	1250.	3000.	5000.	Kentucky	475.	850.	1700.
Georgia	600.	1200.	1700.	Louisiana	—	Rare	—
Hawaii	3000.	6250.	8000.	Maine	—	Rare	—
Idaho		Unique		Maryland	500.	900.	1600.
Illinois	550.	800.	1600.	Massachusetts	525.	925.	1900.
Indiana	550.	800.	1600.	Michigan	450.	900.	1700.
Iowa	550.	800.	1600.	Minnesota	450.	900.	1700.
Kansas	550.	800.	1500.	Mississippi		Unique	
Kentucky	550.	800.	1500.	Missouri	475.	950.	2000.
Louisiana	650.	900.	2000.	Montana	2350.	4300.	8500.
Maine	—	Rare	—	Nebraska	450.	900.	1700.
Maryland	600.	1000.	1700.	New Hampshire	850.	2000.	4000.
Massachusetts	550.	800.	1500.	New Jersey	500.	1000.	2600.
Michigan	550.	800.	1500.	New Mexico	1750.	3250.	5850.
Minnesota	550.	850.	1500.	New York	450.	900.	1700.
Mississippi	1625.	3250.	5850.	North Carolina	900.	1700.	2500.
Missouri	550.	800.	1500.	North Dakota	1200.	2250.	3000.
Montana	1150.	2500.	4500.	Ohio	450.	900.	2000.
Nebraska	550.	850.	1500.	Oklahoma	1000.	1600.	3100.
New Hampshire	775.	925.	2500.	Oregon	1750.	3750.	5000.
New Jersey	500.	800.	1500.	Pennsylvania	450.	900.	1700.
New Mexico	—	Rare	—	South Carolina	1400.	3000.	4000.
New Mexico Territory	2500.	5500.	7000.	South Dakota	800.	2000.	3000.
New York	550.	800.	1500.	Tennessee	500.	1500.	3000.
North Carolina	600.	1200.	2080.	Texas	550.	900.	1700.
North Dakota	800.	1400.	2750.	Utah	1400.	3750.	6250.
Ohio	550.	800.	1500.	Vermont	—	Rare	—
Oklahoma	550.	850.	1500.	Virginia	500.	950.	1700.
Oregon	1500.	2750.	3500.	Washington	1400.	3000.	5000.
Pennsylvania	550.	800.	1500.	West Virginia	500.	925.	1600.
Rhode Island	700.	1000.	2500.	Wisconsin	550.	900.	1700.
South Carolina	1000.	1500.	3500.	Wyoming	2150.	3750.	6250.
South Dakota	1000.	1500.	3500.				
Tennessee	600.	850.	1800.				
Texas	600.	825.	1600.				
Utah	—	Rare	—				
Vermont	—	Rare	—				
Virginia	550.	800.	1600.				
Washington	800.	1600.	2500.				
West Virginia	550.	900.	1600.				
Wisconsin	550.	900.	1500.				
Wyoming	2340.	4250.	7800.				

1902 Red Seal $10

(KL #1216-1218) (Fr #613-615)

	VG	VF	AU
Alabama	675.	1275.	2250.
Alaska		VF:Unique	
Arizona Territory	—	Rare	—
Arkansas	700.	1250.	2000.
California	650.	1100.	150.
Colorado	950.	1800.	3500.
Connecticut	650.	1100.	1500.
Delaware	3375.	7500.	13,500.
District of Columbia	650.	1100.	2000.
Florida	2500.	4800.	9000.
Georgia	1700.	3600.	7200.
Idaho	3000.	5250.	7500.
Illinois	650.	1100.	1500.
Indian Territory	1950.	3300.	6700.
Indiana	650.	1100.	1500.
Iowa	650.	1100.	1500.
Kansas	650.	1100.	1500.

1882 Value Back $10

(KL #1209-1215) (Fr #576-579-B)

	VG	VF	AU
Alabama	550.	1500.	3100.
Arizona	—	Rare	—
Arkansas		Unique	
California	450.	850.	1600.
Colorado	850.	2200.	4000.
Connecticut	550.	2200.	3000.
Georgia	600.	2000.	3000.

	VG	VF	AU		VG	VF	AU
Kentucky	750.	1400.	2500.	Louisiana	175.	350.	500.
Louisiana	1200.	2250.	4500.	Maine	200.	400.	750.
Maine	650.	1100.	2000.	Maryland	175.	350.	400.
Maryland	650.	1100.	1500.	Massachusetts	175.	350.	400.
Massachusetts	650.	1100.	1500.	Michigan	175.	350.	400.
Michigan	650.	1100.	1500.	Minnesota	175.	350.	400.
Minnesota	650.	1100.	1500.	Mississippi	200.	400.	600.
Mississippi	1500.	2500.	4500.	Missouri	175.	350.	400.
Missouri	650.	1100.	1500.	Montana	350.	700.	1000.
Montana	2500.	5850.	11,250.	Nebraska	200.	400.	600.
Nebraska	650.	1100.	1500.	Nevada	1500.	2750.	4000.
Nevada	3000.	5250.	9000.	New Hampshire	175.	350.	450.
New Hampshire	650.	1100.	2000.	New Jersey	175.	350.	400.
New Jersey	650.	1100.	1500.	New Mexico	450.	900.	1350.
New Mexico Territory	2400.	4800.	7500.	New Mexico Territory	3250.	5000.	8500.
New York	650.	1100.	1500.	New York	175.	350.	400.
North Carolina	1800.	3375.	5400.	North Carolina	175.	350.	400.
North Dakota	800.	1750.	3200.	North Dakota	250.	400.	800.
Ohio	650.	1100.	1500.	Ohio	175.	350.	400.
Oklahoma	—	Rare	—	Oklahoma	200.	4000.	800.
Oklahoma Territory	1800.	3600.	6750.	Oregon	200.	400.	800.
Oregon	1650.	3300.	6300.	Pennsylvania	175.	350.	400.
Pennsylvania	650.	1100.	1500.	Puerto Rico		Unique	
Puerto Rico	—	Rare	—	Rhode Island	200.	375.	425.
Rhode Island	650.	1100.	1500.	South Carolina	200.	375.	475.
South Carolina	1650.	2550.	3900.	South Dakota	250.	450.	800.
South Dakota	1200.	2400.	3750.	Tennessee	175.	350.	400.
Tennessee	650.	1100.	2000.	Texas	175.	350.	400.
Texas	650.	1100.	1500.	Utah	200.	475.	700.
Utah	3375.	6750.	12,750.	Vermont	200.	475.	650.
Vermont	650.	1100.	1500.	Virginia	175.	350.	400.
Virginia	650.	1100.	1500.	Washington	175.	350.	400.
Washington	1500.	2700.	4800.	West Virginia	175.	350.	400.
West Virginia	650.	1100.	2000.	Wisconsin	175.	350.	400.
Wisconsin	650.	1100.	1500.	Wyoming	750	1300.	2400.
Wyoming	—	Rare	—				

1902 Date Back $10

(KL #1219-1227) (Fr #616-623-A)

	VG	VF	AU
Alabama	175.	350.	700.
Alaska		Unique	
Arizona	1750.	3500.	5650.
Arizona Territory	—	Rare	—
Arkansas	175.	350.	500.
California	175.	350.	400.
Colorado	200.	400.	500.
Connecticut	175.	350.	500.
Delaware	400.	650.	1000.
District of Columbia	175.	350.	450.
Florida	300.	600.	1000.
Georgia	175.	350.	500.
Hawaii	—	Rare	—
Idaho	375.	700.	1000.
Illinois	175.	350.	400.
Indiana	175.	350.	400.
Iowa	175.	350.	400.
Kansas	175.	350.	500.
Kentucky	175.	350.	450.

1902 Plain Back $10

(KL #1228-1242) (Fr #624-638)

	VG	VF	AU
Alabama	125.	150.	300.
Alaska	—	Rare	—
Arizona	—	Rare	—
Arkansas	135.	225.	400.
California	125.	200.	300.
Colorado	125.	200.	350.
Connecticut	125.	200.	350.
Delaware	275.	375.	700.
District of Columbia	125.	200.	300.
Florida	220.	275.	500.
Georgia	125.	200.	300.
Hawaii	1500.	3000.	4500.
Idaho	275.	600.	800.
Illinois	125.	200.	300.
Indiana	125.	200.	300.
Iowa	125.	200.	300.
Kansas	125.	200.	300.
Kentucky	125.	200.	300.
Louisiana	125.	200.	300.
Maine	125.	200.	310.

	VG	VF	AU		VG	VF	AU
Maryland	125.	200.	300.	Mississippi	—	200.	400.
Massachusetts	125.	200.	300.	Missouri	—	90.00	150.
Michigan	125.	200.	300.	Montana	—	200.	450.
Minnesota	125.	200.	300.	Nebraska	—	90.00	150.
Mississippi	125.	200.	350.	Nevada	—	450.	700.
Missouri	125.	200.	300.	New Hampshire	—	90.00	15.00
Montana	250.	400.	650.	New Jersey	—	90.00	150.
Nebraska	125.	200.	300.	New Mexico	—	200.	400.
Nevada	1100.	1750.	3000.	New York	—	90.00	150.
New Hampshire	150.	225.	500.	North Carolina	—	90.00	100.
New Jersey	125.	200.	300.	North Dakota	—	200.	400.
New Mexico	450.	700.	1250.	Ohio	—	90.00	150.
New York	125.	200.	300.	Oklahoma	—	90.00	150.
North Carolina	125.	200.	300.	Oregon	—	90.00	150.
North Dakota	175.	300.	600.	Pennsylvania	—	90.00	150.
Ohio	125.	200.	300.	Rhode Island	—	90.00	150.
Oklahoma	135.	210.	325.	South Carolina	—	150.	250.
Oregon	135.	210.	325.	South Dakota	—	225.	450.
Pennsylvania	125.	200.	300.	Tennessee	—	90.00	150.
Rhode Island	125.	200.	300.	Texas	—	90.00	150.
South Carolina	135.	210.	350.	Utah	—	90.00	150.
South Dakota	150.	250.	500.	Vermont	—	90.00	150.
Tennessee	125.	200.	300.	Virginia	—	90.00	150.
Texas	125.	200.	300.	Washington	—	90.00	150.
Utah	135.	225.	300.	West Virginia	—	90.00	150.
Vermont	135.	250.	450.	Wisconsin	—	90.00	150.
Virginia	125.	200.	300.	Wyoming	—	350.	500.
Washington	125.	200.	300.				
West Virginia	125.	200.	300.				
Wisconsin	125.	200.	300.				
Wyoming	450.	800.	1400.				

1929 Type 2 $10

(KL #1244) (Fr #1801-2)

	VG	VF	AU
Alabama	—	175.	250.
Alaska	—	12,000.	24,000.
Arizona	—	400.	800.
Arkansas	—	175.	250.
California	—	175.	250.
Colorado	—	175.	250.
Connecticut	—	175.	250.
Delaware	—	300.	650.
District of Columbia	—	175.	250.
Florida	—	175.	250.
Georgia	—	150.	250.
Hawaii	—	375.	800.
Idaho	—	300.	600.
Illinois	—	175.	250.
Indiana	—	175.	250.
Iowa	—	175.	250.
Kansas	—	175.	250.
Kentucky	—	175.	250.
Louisiana	—	175.	250.
Maine	—	175.	250.
Maryland	—	175.	250.
Massachusetts	—	175.	250.
Michigan	—	175.	250.
Minnesota	—	175.	250.
Mississippi	—	225.	375.
Missouri	—	175.	250.
Montana	—	300.	500.
Nebraska	—	175.	250.

1929 Type 1 $10

(KL #1243) (Fr #1801-1)

	VG	VF	AU
Alabama	—	60.00	90.00
Alaska	—	11,250.	18,750.
Arizona	—	375.	650.
Arkansas	—	90.00	150.
California	—	90.00	150.
Colorado	—	90.00	150.
Connecticut	—	90.00	150.
Delaware	—	375.	700.
District of Columbia	—	90.00	150.
Florida	—	90.00	150.
Georgia	—	90.00	150.
Hawaii	—	300.	500.
Idaho	—	250.	500.
Illinois	—	90.00	150.
Indiana	—	90.00	150.
Iowa	—	90.00	150.
Kansas	—	90.00	150.
Kentucky	—	90.00	150.
Louisiana	—	90.00	150.
Maine	—	90.00	150.
Maryland	—	90.00	150.
Massachusetts	—	90.00	150.
Michigan	—	90.00	150.
Minnesota	—	90.00	150.

	VG	VF	AU
Nevada	—	450.	750.
New Hampshire	—	175.	250.
New Jersey	—	175.	250.
New Mexico	—	175.	250.
New York	—	175.	250.
North Carolina	—	175.	250.
North Dakota	—	175.	250.
Ohio	—	175.	250.
Oklahoma	—	175.	250.
Oregon	—	175.	250.
Pennsylvania	—	175.	250.
Rhode Island	—	175.	250.
South Carolina	—	225.	300.
South Dakota	—	275.	350.
Tennessee	—	175.	250.
Texas	—	175.	250.
Utah	—	175.	250.
Vermont	—	200.	250.
Virginia	—	175.	250.
Washington	—	175.	250.
West Virginia	—	175.	250.
Wisconsin	—	175.	250.
Wyoming	—	400.	700.

Original Series $20

(KL #1245-1248) (Fr #424-429)

	VG	VF	AU
Arkansas	—	Rare	—
Connecticut	2500.	3500.	10,500.
Delaware	—	Rare	—
Georgia	—	Rare	—
Illinois	2500.	3500.	6900.
Indiana	2500.	3500.	7200.
Iowa	—	Rare	—
Kentucky	2500.	3500.	7800.
Maine	2500.	4000.	8600.
Maryland	2500.	4000.	9500
Massachusetts	2500.	4500.	5275.
Michigan	2500.	4500.	6000.
Missouri	2500.	4500.	6000.
Nebraska Territory		VF:Unique	
New Hampshire		VF:Unique	
New Jersey	2500.	4500.	7000.
New York	2500.	4500.	4700.
North Carolina	—	Rare	—
Ohio	2500.	4500.	4050.
Pennsylvania	2500.	4500.	4700.
Rhode Island	2500.	4500.	8200.
Tennessee	3000.	5000.	8400.
Texas	10,000.	15,000.	25,000.
Vermont	2500.	4500.	8800.
Virginia	2500.	4500.	9750.
West Virginia	3000.	4000.	9750.
Wisconsin	2500.	4500.	6800.

Series 1875 $20

(KL #1249-1257) (Fr #431-439)

	VG	VF	AU
Alabama	—	Rare	—
California	—	Rare	—
Colorado	—	Rare	—
Colorado Territory	—	Rare	—
Connecticut	3000.	4000.	7000.
Dakota Territory	—	Rare	—
Delaware	—	Rare	—
District of Columbia	—	Rare	—
Georgia	—	Rare	—
Illinois	2500.	3500.	4800.
Indiana	3000.	4000.	6800.
Iowa	3000.	4000.	6600.
Kansas	—	Rare	—
Kentucky	2500.	3500.	5400
Louisiana	—	Rare	—
Maine	3000.	4000.	6000.
Maryland	3000.	4000.	7200.
Massachusetts	2500.	3500.	3750.
Michigan	3000.	4000.	4200.
Minnesota		VF:Unique	
Missouri	2500.	3500.	4050.
Montana	—	Rare	—
Montana Territory		VF:Unique	
Nebraska	—	Rare	—
Nevada	—	Rare	—
New Hampshire	3000.	2700.	4000.
New Jersey	2500.	3500.	5100.
New Mexico Territory	—	Rare	—
New York	2500.	3500.	3300.
North Carolina	—	Rare	—
North Dakota	—	Rare	—
Ohio	2500.	3500.	3750.
Oregon		Two known	
Pennsylvania	2500.	3500.	3300.
Rhode Island	2500.	3500.	5700.
South Carolina	—	Rare	—
South Dakota	—	Rare	—
Tennessee	3000.	4000.	6000.
Texas	9000.	13,500.	22,500.
Utah		VF:Unique	
Vermont	2500.	3500.	6000.
Virginia	3000.	4000.	6750.
West Virginia	3000.	4000.	6900.
Wisconsin	2500.	3500.	4750.
Wyoming Territory	—	Rare	—

1882 Brown Back $20

(KL #1258-1271) (Fr #493-506)

	VG	VF	AU
Alabama	600.	950.	2000.
Arizona Territory	—	Rare	—
Arkansas	—	Rare	—
California	550.	850.	2000.
Colorado	650.	1000.	2200.
Connecticut	550.	850.	2000.
Delaware	1250.	3000.	7000.

	VG	VF	AU
District of Columbia	550.	850.	2000.
Florida	1000.	3000.	7000.
Georgia	600.	900.	2600.
Hawaii	4000.	8000.	11,000.
Idaho	—	Rare	—
Illinois	550.	850.	2000.
Indian Territory	3000.	5250.	8000.
Indiana	550.	850.	2000.
Iowa	550.	850.	2000.
Kansas	550.	850.	2100.
Kentucky	550.	850.	2000.
Louisiana	600.	1000.	2250.
Maine	550.	900.	2000.
Maryland	550.	850.	2000.
Massachusetts	550.	850.	2000.
Michigan	550.	850.	2000.
Minnesota	550.	850.	2000.
Mississippi	—	Rare	—
Missouri	550.	850.	2000.
Montana	3000.	4800.	8000.
Nebraska	550.	850.	2100.
New Hampshire	550.	850.	2200.
New Jersey	550.	850.	2000.
New Mexico Territory	—	Rare	—
New York	550.	850.	2000.
North Carolina	1000.	1750.	3500.
North Dakota	1500.	4000.	7000.
Ohio	550.	850.	2000.
Oklahoma	1600.	4200.	7500.
Oklahoma Territory	1550.	4300.	7000.
Oregon	1550.	4300.	5000.
Pennsylvania	550.	850.	2000.
Rhode Island	600.	900.	2300.
South Carolina	1000.	2000.	5000.
South Dakota	1550.	3000.	6000.
Tennessee	650.	950.	2700.
Texas	650.	950.	2700.
Utah	1550.	4300.	7000.
Vermont	550.	850.	2750.
Virginia	600.	900.	2200.
Washington	1400.	3400.	5000.
Washington Territory		Unique	
West Virginia	600.	900.	2250.
Wisconsin	550.	850.	2000.
Wyoming	3000.	6500.	8000.

	VG	VF	AU
Florida	1750.	4000.	5500.
Georgia	650.	1000.	2700.
Hawaii	—	Rare	—
Idaho	—	Rare	—
Illinois	650.	1000.	2000.
Indiana	650.	1000.	2000.
Iowa	650.	1000.	2100.
Kansas	700.	1100.	1500.
Kentucky	700.	1100.	2100.
Louisiana	700.	1100.	2400.
Maine	900.	1500.	3200.
Maryland	650.	1000.	2100.
Massachusetts	650.	1000.	2100.
Michigan	650.	1000.	2100.
Minnesota	650.	1000.	2150.
Mississippi	1200.	3000.	6000.
Missouri	650.	1000.	2000.
Montana	1200.	2700.	4500.
Nebraska	650.	1000.	2100.
New Hampshire	900.	1750.	3000.
New Jersey	650.	1000.	2000.
New Mexico	2450.	3600.	5800.
New Mexico Territory		Unique	
New York	650.	1000.	2000.
North Carolina	700.	1200.	2800.
North Dakota	750.	1200.	3300.
Ohio	650.	1000.	2000.
Oklahoma	650.	1000.	2000.
Oregon	750.	1400.	3600.
Pennsylvania	650.	1000.	2000.
Rhode Island	—	Rare	—
South Carolina	700.	1400.	3000.
South Dakota	700.	1400.	3300.
Tennessee	650.	1200.	2800.
Texas	650.	1000.	2000.
Utah	—	Rare	—
Vermont		Unique	
Virginia	750.	1100.	2300.
Washington	1250.	2500.	3250.
West Virginia	650.	1000.	2000.
Wisconsin	650.	1000.	2100.
Wyoming	3600.	4800.	7200.

1882 Date Back $20

(KL #1272-1280) (Fr #549-557)

	VG	VF	AU
Alabama	700.	1100.	2400.
Alaska		Unique	
Arizona	—	Rare	—
Arizona Territory		Unique	
Arkansas	—	Rare	—
California	650.	1000.	2000.
Colorado	700.	1100.	3000.
Connecticut	650.	1000.	2000.
Delaware	2450.	5000.	7500.
District of Columbia	650.	1000.	2600.

1882 Value Back $20

(KL #1281-1289) (Fr #580-585)

	VG	VF	AU
Alabama	700.	1200.	3400.
Arizona	—	Rare	—
California	700.	1200.	2000.
Colorado	1200.	2500.	4500.
Connecticut	700.	1700.	3500.
Georgia	750.	1500.	3900.
Hawaii	—	Rare	—
Idaho		Unique	
Illinois	700.	1200.	2400.
Indiana	700.	1400.	2500.
Iowa	700.	1400.	2400.
Kansas	700.	1350.	2350.
Kentucky	750.	1200.	2000.

	VG	VF	AU		VG	VF	AU
Maine	—	Rare	—	New Hampshire	850.	1850.	2000.
Maryland	750.	1300.	2600.	New Jersey	600.	1850.	2000.
Massachusetts	800.	1650.	3100.	New Mexico Territory	2700.	5500.	7750.
Michigan	700.	1200.	2000.	New York	600.	1850.	2000.
Minnesota	700.	1200.	1950.	North Carolina	2000.	3650.	5000.
Missouri	700.	1200.	1950.	North Dakota	1800.	2850.	5350.
Montana	—	Rare	—	Ohio	600.	1850.	1750.
Nebraska	700.	1200.	2000.	Oklahoma	—	Rare	—
New Hampshire	1000.	2200.	3900.	Oklahoma Territory	2000.	3850.	5800.
New Jersey	750.	1300.	2850.	Oregon	—	Rare	—
New Mexico	—	Rare	—	Pennsylvania	600.	1500.	1100.
New York	700.	1200.	2200.	Puerto Rico	—	Rare	—
North Carolina	850.	1800.	4400.	Rhode Island	750.	1850.	2250.
North Dakota	—	Rare	—	South Carolina	—	Rare	—
Ohio	700.	1200.	2500.	South Dakota	1600.	2200.	4500.
Oklahoma	750.	2000.	4150.	Tennessee	700.	1900.	2700.
Oregon	—	Rare	—	Texas	600.	1850.	2000.
Pennsylvania	700.	1200.	2200.	Utah		Unique	
South Carolina	100.	2400.	4400.	Virginia	600.	1850.	2350.
South Dakota	900.	2100.	3450.	Washington	1550.	2850.	4350.
Tennessee	—	Rare	—	West Virginia	850.	2000.	3000.
Texas	700.	1200.	2150.	Wisconsin	600.	1850.	2000.
Virginia	700.	1350.	2700.	Wyoming	4000.	6000.	9500.
Washington	—	Rare	—				
West Virginia	850.	1750.	2900.				
Wisconsin	700.	1200.	1950.				
Wyoming	—	Rare	—				

1902 Date Back $20

(KL #1293-1301) (Fr #642-649-A)

1902 Red Seal $20

(KL #1290-1292) (Fr #639-641)

	VG	VF	AU
Alabama	650.	1850.	2200.
Alaska		Unique	
Arizona Territory		Unique	
Arkansas	—	Rare	—
California	600.	1850.	2200.
Colorado	1050.	2500.	5300.
Connecticut	600.	1850.	2000.
District of Columbia	600.	1850.	2200.
Florida	1000.	2200.	5000.
Georgia	650.	2500.	5000.
Idaho		Unique	
Illinois	600.	1850.	2000.
Indian Territory	2150.	3800.	5250.
Indiana	600.	1850.	2000.
Iowa	600.	1850.	2000.
Kansas	600.	1850.	2000.
Kentucky	600.	1850.	2000.
Louisiana	600.	1850.	2000.
Maine	650.	1850.	2000.
Maryland	650.	1850.	2000.
Massachusetts	650.	1000.	1850.
Michigan	600.	1850.	2000.
Minnesota	600.	1850.	2000.
Mississippi	2000.	3400.	4700.
Missouri	600.	1850.	2000.
Montana	3000.	6000.	11,000.
Nebraska	600.	1850.	2000.
Nevada	—	Rare	—

	VG	VF	AU
Alabama	200.	350.	500.
Arizona	2750.	4000.	6750.
Arizona Territory	—	Rare	—
Arkansas	200.	350.	650.
California	200.	350.	600.
Colorado	200.	350.	600.
Connecticut	200.	350.	500.
Delaware	400.	600.	1000.
District of Columbia	200.	350.	500.
Florida	200.	350.	500.
Georgia	200.	350.	500.
Hawaii		Unique	
Idaho	400.	650.	1350.
Illinois		350.	500.
Indiana	200.	350.	500.
Iowa	200.	350.	500.
Kansas	200.	350.	500.
Kentucky	200.	350.	500.
Louisiana	250.	425.	650.
Maine	225.	400.	650.
Maryland	200.	350.	500.
Massachusetts	200.	350.	500.
Michigan	200.	350.	500.
Minnesota	200.	350.	500.
Mississippi	250.	400.	550.
Missouri	200.	350.	500.
Montana	550.	900.	1550.
Nebraska	200.	350.	500.
Nevada	1750.	2500.	4500.
New Hampshire	200.	350.	500.
New Jersey	200.	350.	500.
New Mexico	750.	1100.	1750.

	VG	VF	AU		VG	VF	AU
New Mexico Territory	4500.	5500.	9250.	Oklahoma	175.	300.	450.
New York	200.	350.	500.	Oregon	175.	300.	450.
North Carolina	225.	375.	525.	Pennsylvania	175.	300.	450.
North Dakota	300.	350.	500.	Rhode Island	180.	300.	450.
Ohio	200.	350.	500.	South Carolina	175.	300.	450.
Oklahoma	225.	375.	600.	South Dakota	200.	325.	500.
Oregon	235.	400.	600.	Tennessee	175.	300.	450.
Pennsylvania	200.	350.	500.	Texas	175.	300.	450.
Rhode Island	200.	350.	500.	Utah	200.	300.	450.
South Carolina	225.	375.	550.	Vermont	200.	300.	450.
South Dakota	300.	500.	10,005.	Virginia	175.	300.	450.
Tennessee	200.	350.	500.	Washington	185.	300.	450.
Texas	200.	350.	500.	West Virginia	180.	300.	450.
Utah	225.	375.	550.	Wisconsin	175.	300.	450.
Vermont	200.	350.	500.	Wyoming	600.	925.	1450.
Virginia	200.	350.	500.				
Washington	200.	350.	500.				
West Virginia	200.	350.	500.				
Wisconsin	200.	350.	500.				
Wyoming	675.	950.	1750.				

1902 Plain Back $20

(KL #1302-1316) (Fr #650-663-A)

	VG	VF	AU
Alabama	200.	300.	600.
Alaska	—	Rare	—
Arizona	1800.	3500.	5750.
Arkansas	200.	300.	450.
California	175.	300.	450.
Colorado	200.	300.	450.
Connecticut	175.	300.	450.
Delaware	750.	1100.	1400.
District of Columbia	200.	350.	450.
Florida	200.	300.	450.
Georgia	200.	300.	450.
Idaho	300.	550.	1000.
Illinois	175.	300.	450.
Indiana	175.	300.	450.
Iowa	175.	300.	450.
Kansas	175.	300.	450.
Kentucky	175.	300.	450.
Louisiana	200.	350.	450.
Maine	175.	325.	450.
Maryland	185.	300.	450.
Massachusetts	175.	300.	450.
Michigan	175.	270.	450.
Minnesota	175.	270.	450.
Mississippi	275.	425.	700.
Missouri	200.	300.	450.
Montana	450.	800.	1250.
Nebraska	200.	300.	450.
Nevada	1400.	3000.	4250.
New Hampshire	200.	300.	450.
New Jersey	175.	300.	400.
New Mexico	650.	950.	1500.
New York	175.	300.	450.
North Carolina	175.	300.	450.
North Dakota	300.	550.	700.
Ohio	175.	300.	450.

1929 Type 1 $20

(KL #1317) (Fr #1802-1)

	VG	VF	AU
Alabama	—	85.00	200.
Alaska	—	11,250.	22,500.
Arizona	—	400.	800.
Arkansas	—	85.00	200.
California	—	85.00	200.
Colorado	—	85.00	200.
Connecticut	—	85.00	200.
Delaware	—	300.	600.
District of Columbia	—	85.00	200.
Florida	—	85.00	200.
Georgia	—	85.00	200.
Idaho	—	200.	350.
Illinois	—	85.00	200.
Indiana	—	85.00	200.
Iowa	—	85.00	200.
Kansas	—	85.00	200.
Kentucky	—	85.00	200.
Louisiana	—	85.00	200.
Maine	—	90.00	210.
Maryland	—	85.00	200.
Massachusetts	—	85.00	200.
Michigan	—	85.00	200.
Minnesota	—	85.00	200.
Mississippi	—	125.	250.
Missouri	—	85.00	200.
Montana	—	150.	300.
Nebraska	—	85.00	200.
Nevada	—	350.	700.
New Hampshire	—	85.00	230.
New Jersey	—	85.00	200.
New Mexico	—	150.	300.
New York	—	85.00	200.
North Carolina	—	85.00	200.
North Dakota	—	120.	240.
Ohio	—	85.00	200.
Oklahoma	—	85.00	200.
Oregon	—	85.00	200.
Pennsylvania	—	85.00	200.
Rhode Island	—	100.	240.
South Carolina	—	200.	300.

	VG	VF	AU
South Dakota	—	215.	330.
Tennessee	—	85.00	200.
Texas	—	85.00	200.
Utah	—	85.00	200.
Vermont	—	85.00	200.
Virginia	—	85.00	200.
Washington	—	85.00	200.
West Virginia	—	85.00	200.
Wisconsin	—	85.00	200.
Wyoming	—	350.	700.

1929 Type 2 $20

(KL #1318) (Fr #1802-2)

	VG	VF	AU
Alabama	—	150.	300.
Alaska	—	12,000.	24,000.
Arizona	—	450.	900.
Arkansas	—	175.	400.
California	—	150.	300.
Colorado	—	150.	300.
Connecticut	—	150.	300.
Delaware	—	450.	700.
District of Columbia	—	150.	300.
Florida	—	150.	300.
Georgia	—	150.	300.
Idaho	—	250.	500.
Illinois	—	150.	300.
Indiana	—	150.	300.
Iowa	—	150.	300.
Kansas	—	150.	300.
Kentucky	—	150.	300.
Louisiana	—	150.	300.
Maine	—	160.	310.
Maryland	—	160.	310.
Massachusetts	—	150.	300.
Michigan	—	150.	300.
Minnesota	—	150.	300.
Mississippi	—	160.	310.
Missouri	—	150.	300.
Montana	—	250.	450.
Nebraska	—	150.	300.
Nevada	—	375.	750.
New Hampshire	—	160.	320.
New Jersey	—	150.	300.
New Mexico	—	160.	320.
New York	—	150.	300.
North Carolina	—	160.	310.
North Dakota	—	225.	400.
Ohio	—	150.	300.
Oklahoma	—	150.	300.
Oregon	—	160.	320.
Pennsylvania	—	150.	300.
Rhode Island	—	200.	350.
South Carolina	—	160.	310.
South Dakota	—	250.	350.
Tennessee	—	150.	300.
Texas	—	150.	300.
Utah	—	160.	310.
Vermont	—	220.	350.

	VG	VF	AU
Virginia	—	160.	310.
Washington	—	160.	310.
West Virginia	—	150.	300.
Wisconsin	—	150.	300.
Wyoming	—	400.	800.

Original Series $50

(KL #1319-1321) (Fr #440-443)

	VG	VF	AU
Georgia		One known	
Illinois		15,000.	—
Indiana		One known	
Iowa		VF:Unique	
Kentucky		One known	
Louisiana	—	Rare	—
Maine		One known	
Maryland		One known	
Massachusetts		Nine known	
Missouri		One known	
New York		Two known	
Ohio		Four known	
Pennsylvania		Two known	
Tennessee		One known	

Series 1875 $50

(KL #1322-1330) (Fr #444-451)

	VG	VF	AU
Alabama		One known	
California		Two known	
Colorado Territory		One known	
Georgia		VF:Unique	
Illinois		Six known	
Indiana		Two known	
Iowa		Five known	
Kansas		One known	
Kentucky		Five known	
Louisiana		One known	
Maine		One known	
Maryland		Three known	
Massachusetts		Three known	
Michigan		Two known	
New Hampshire		Two known	
New Jersey		Two known	
New York		Seven known	
Ohio		Three known	
Pennsylvania		Nine known	
Tennessee		Five known	
Utah Territory		One known	
Wisconsin		One known	

1882 Brown Back $50

(KL #1331-1343) (Fr #507-518-A)

	VG	VF	AU
Alabama	Two known		
Arkansas	Three known		
California	5500.	11,500.	16,000.
Colorado	Six known		

	VG	VF	AU
Connecticut		Unique	
Delaware	Two known		
Georgia	Two known		
Illinois	5500.	6500.	10,000.
Indiana	5500.	7000.	10,500.
Iowa	5500.	6500.	9000.
Kansas	5500.	6500.	10,500.
Kentucky	5500.	6500.	10,000.
Louisiana	5500.	8000.	13,800.
Maryland	5500.	8500.	10,000.
Massachusetts	5500.	7000.	9000.
Michigan	Three known		
Minnesota	5500.	8000.	12,000.
Missouri	5500.	6700.	11,300.
Montana	Four known		
Nebraska	5500.	9700.	16,200.
New Jersey	Three known		
New Mexico Territory	Two known		
New York	5500.	6500.	8000.
North Carolina	Three known		
North Dakota		Unique	
Ohio	5500.	6500.	8000.
Oregon		Unique	
Pennsylvania	5500.	6500.	8000.
Rhode Island		Unique	
Tennessee	Three known		
Texas	5500.	8000.	9700.
Vermont	Four known		
Washington	Six known		
Wisconsin	Three known		

1882 Date Back $50
(KL #1344-1351) (Fr #558-565)

	VG	VF	AU
Arizona Territory		Unique	
California	5500.	6500.	9000.
Colorado	Two known		
Connecticut		Unique	
Delaware		Unique	
Illinois	5500.	6500.	7800.
Indiana	5500.	6500.	8800.
Iowa	5500.	6500.	8800.
Kansas	Two known		
Kentucky	5500.	6500.	8800.
Maryland	Two known		
Michigan	5500.	7600.	11,000.
Minnesota	Two known		
Missouri	Three known		
Montana	Three known		
Nebraska	Three known		
New Mexico	5000.	9750.	14,500.
New Mexico Territory	Two known		
New York	5500.	6500.	6500.
Ohio	5500.	6500.	6000.
Oklahoma	5500.	7500.	8000.
Pennsylvania	5500.	6500.	5000.
South Carolina		Unique	
Tennessee		Unique	
Texas	5500.	7500.	6750.
Washington		Unique	

1882 Value Back $50
(KL #1352) (Fr #586)

	VG	VF	AU
Louisiana		Four known	
Ohio		Three known	

1902 Red Seal $50
(KL #1353-1355) (Fr #664-666)

	VG	VF	AU
California	Two known		
Colorado		Unique	
Delaware		Unique	
Idaho		Unique	
Illinois	1900.	5500.	11,800.
Indiana		Two known	
Iowa		Two known	
Kansas	2500.	7600.	12,500.
Louisiana	Three known		
Maryland	Four known		
Massachusetts		Unique	
Missouri	1900.	5500.	11,800.
New Jersey	Three known		
New York	1900.	5500.	11,800.
Ohio	2000.	5600.	12,000.
Oregon	Two known		
Pennsylvania	1900.	5500.	11,800.
Puerto Rico	Two known		
Rhode Island	2500.	6250.	12,500.
South Dakota		Unique	
Tennessee	Two known		
Texas	Three known		
Virginia	Two known		
Washington	3000.	6500.	12,500.
Wisconsin	Two known		

1902 Date Back $50
(KL #1356-1364) (Fr #667-674-A)

	VG	VF	AU
Alabama	—	Rare	—
Arizona Territory	—	Rare	—
California	700.	2000.	3000.
Colorado	700.	2500.	3500.
Connecticut	700.	2000.	3000.
Delaware	2000.	4000.	6000.
Florida	—	Rare	—
Idaho	700.	2000.	3000.
Illinois	700.	2000.	3000.
Indiana	700.	2000.	3000.
Iowa	700.	2000.	3000.
Kansas	700.	2000.	3000.
Kentucky	700.	2000.	3000.
Louisiana	725.	2000.	3000.
Maine	—	Rare	—
Maryland	700.	2000.	3000.
Massachusetts	700.	2000.	3000.
Michigan	700.	2000.	3000.
Minnesota	700.	2000.	3000.
Mississippi	—	Rare	—

	VG	VF	AU
Missouri	700.	2000.	3000.
Montana	5000.	5000.	10,000.
Nebraska	700.	2000.	3000.
Nevada	4000.	5000.	10,000.
New Hampshire	2000.	5000.	8000.
New Jersey	700.	2000.	3000.
New York	700.	2000.	3000.
North Carolina	—	Rare	—
Ohio	750.	2500.	3000.
Oklahoma	700.	2500.	3000.
Oregon	725.	2500.	3000.
Pennsylvania	700.	2500.	3000.
Rhode Island	700.	2000.	3000.
South Dakota	850.	1500.	3000.
Tennessee	850.	2500.	3500.
Texas	700.	2000.	3000.
Utah	—	Rare	—
Vermont	1000.	2500.	4000.
Virginia	—	Rare	—
Washington	700.	2000.	3000.
Wisconsin	700.	2000.	3000.

1902 Plain Back $50

(KL #1365-1377) (Fr #675-685-A)

	VG	VF	AU
California	700.	1500.	2000.
Colorado	700.	1600.	3000.
Connecticut	700.	1500.	3000.
Delaware	2000.	4000.	7000.
District of Columbia	700.	2000.	3000.
Florida	2000.	4000.	8000.
Idaho	700.	1500.	3000.
Illinois	700.	1500.	2000.
Indiana	700.	1500.	3000.
Iowa	700.	1500.	3000.
Kansas	700.	1500.	3000.
Kentucky	700.	1500.	3000.
Louisiana	700.	1500.	3000.
Maryland	700.	1500.	3000.
Massachusetts	700.	1500.	3000
Michigan	700.	1500.	3000.
Minnesota	700.	1500.	3000.
Missouri	700.	1500.	3000.
Montana	3000.	5000.	10,000.
Nebraska	700.	1500.	2500.
Nevada	3000.	5000.	10,000.
New Hampshire	3000.	4500.	8000.
New Jersey	700.	1550.	3000.
New York	700.	1500.	2500.
North Carolina	—	Rare	—
North Dakota	—	Rare	—
Ohio	700.	1500.	2500.
Oklahoma	700.	1500.	2500.
Oregon	750.	2000.	3000.
Pennsylvania	700.	1500.	2500.
Rhode Island	700.	1600.	3000.
South Dakota	750.	2000.	3500.
Tennessee	750.	2000.	3500.
Texas	700.	1500.	3000.

	VG	VF	AU
Vermont	1000.	2000.	4000.
Washington	700.	1500.	3000.
West Virginia	2000.	3500.	5000.
Wisconsin	700.	1500.	3000.

1929 Type 1 $50

(KL #1378) (Fr #1803-1)

	VG	VF	AU
California	—	200.	400.
Colorado	—	210.	400.
Connecticut	—	320.	700.
Delaware	—	2000.	4000.
Florida	—	500.	800.
Hawaii	—	800.	2000.
Idaho	—	500.	1000.
Illinois	—	200.	500.
Indiana	—	200.	500.
Iowa	—	200.	500.
Kansas	—	200.	500.
Kentucky	—	200.	500.
Louisiana	—	200.	500.
Maryland	—	200.	500.
Massachusetts	—	200.	500.
Michigan	—	200.	500.
Minnesota	—	200.	500.
Mississippi	—	Rare	—
Missouri	—	200.	500.
Montana	—	650.	1250.
Nebraska	—	200.	500.
Nevada	—	1000.	2500.
New Hampshire	—	600.	1000.
New Jersey	—	200.	500.
New York	—	200.	500.
North Carolina	—	Rare	—
North Dakota	—	500.	1000.
Ohio	—	200.	500.
Oklahoma	—	200.	500.
Oregon	—	650.	1250.
Pennsylvania	—	200.	500.
Rhode Island	—	500.	1000.
South Dakota	—	650.	1400
Tennessee	—	400.	750.
Texas	—	200.	525.
Utah	—	500.	1000.
Vermont	—	750.	1250.
Washington	—	350.	750.
West Virginia	—	Rare	—
Wisconsin	—	200.	550.
Wyoming	—	Rare	—

1929 Type 2 $50

(KL #1379) (Fr #1803-2)

	VG	VF	AU
Arkansas	—	Rare	—
California	—	600.	1200.
Colorado	—	750.	1500.
Hawaii	—	1750.	3000.
Illinois	—	400.	1500.

	VG	VF	AU
Indiana	—	400.	1200.
Kansas	—	Rare	—
Kentucky	—	Rare	—
Louisiana	—	600.	1200.
Maryland	—	Rare	—
Michigan	—	750.	1500.
Minnesota	—	900.	2000.
Missouri	—	Rare	—
Nebraska	—	750.	1500.
New Jersey	—	Rare	—
New York	—	750.	1500.
Ohio	—	Rare	—
Oklahoma	—	600.	1000.
Pennsylvania	—	600.	1000.
Rhode Island	—	850.	1500.
Tennessee	—	800.	1500.
Texas	—	600.	1000.
Virginia	—	Rare	—
Wisconsin	—	Rare	—

Original Series $100

(KL #1380-1382) (Fr #452-455)

	VG	VF	AU
Connecticut		One known	
Illinois	—	—	—
Indiana	—	—	—
Iowa	—	—	—
Louisiana	—	—	—
Maine	—	—	—
Maryland	—	—	—
Massachusetts		Seven known	
New York	Seven known		
North Carolina	One known		
Ohio	Five known		
Pennsylvania	Four known		
Rhode Island			Unique
South Carolina			Unique
Texas	One known		
Utah Territory			Unique

Series 1875 $100

(KL #1383-1391) (Fr #456-463)

	VG	VF	AU
Alabama		Two known	
Connecticut		Two known	
Illinois		Two known	
Indiana		One known	
Iowa		One known	
Louisiana		One known	
Maine		One known	
Maryland		Two known	
Massachusetts		Four known	
New York		Eleven known	
Ohio		Eleven known	
Pennsylvania		Rare (Ten known	
Rhode Island		One known	
South Carolina		One known	
Utah Territory		One known	
Wisconsin		VF:Unique	

1882 Brown Back $100

(KL #1392-1403) (Fr #519-531)

	VG	VF	AU
Alabama	Five known		
California	6000.	7500.	23,000.
Colorado	Three known		
Delaware	Two known		
Florida	Three known		
Georgia	Four known		
Illinois	5500.	9000.	11,000.
Indian Territory		Unique	
Indiana	5500.	9000.	10,000.
Iowa	5500.	7500.	12,500.
Kansas	5500.	7500.	12,500.
Kentucky	5500.	7500.	12,500.
Louisiana	5500.	7500.	12,500.
Maryland	5500.	7500.	12,500.
Massachusetts	5500.	7500.	12,500.
Michigan		Unique	
Minnesota	Four known		
Missouri	5500.	8000.	13,500.
Montana	6000.	13,500.	20,000.
Nebraska	5500.	11,000.	—
New Hampshire	5500.	11,000.	—
New Jersey	5500.	11,000.	—
New Mexico Territory	Three known		
New York	5500.	8500.	12,500.
North Carolina	Two known		
North Dakota	Two known		
Ohio	5500.	7500.	12,500.
Oklahoma Territory	Three known		
Oregon		Unique	
Pennsylvania	5500.	8000.	12,500.
Rhode Island		Unique	
South Carolina		Unique	
Tennessee	Three known		
Texas	5500.	10,500.	20,000.
Utah Territory		Unique	
Vermont		Unique	
Virginia	—	—	Rare
Washington	5500.	11,200.	20,000.
West Virginia		Unique	

1882 Date Back $100

(KL #1404-1411) (Fr #566-572-A)

	VG	VF	AU
Alabama		Unique	
California	4500.	10,000.	17,000.
Colorado		Unique	
Delaware		Unique	
Georgia		Unique	
Hawaii		Unique	
Illinois	7500.	8250.	13,000.
Indiana	Two known		
Iowa	7500.	8250.	12,000.
Kansas		Unique	
Kentucky	7500.	8250.	11,000.
Maryland		Unique	
Massachusetts	7500.	8250.	10,000.

	VG	VF	AU
Minnesota		Unique	
Montana		Unique	
New Jersey		Unique	
New Mexico	4800.	9000.	15,000.
New York	8000.	8250.	13,000.
North Carolina	8000.	9000.	15,000.
North Dakota	—	Rare	—
Ohio	Three known		
Oklahoma	8000.	8500.	12,000.
Pennsylvania	8000.	8250.	10,000.
Texas	8000.	8500.	11,000.
Vermont		Unique	
Washington	Three known		

1882 Value Back $100

(KL #1412) (Fr #586-A)

	VG	VF	AU
Louisiana		Two known	
Ohio		Three known	

1902 Date Back $100

(KL #1416-1424) (Fr #689-697)

	VG	VF	AU
Alabama		Unique	
California	—	—	—
Colorado	2000.	4000.	8000.
Connecticut	2500.	5000.	10,000.
Delaware		Unique	
Florida		Unique	
Georgia		Unique	
Idaho	1000.	2000.	4000.
Illinois	1000.	1500.	3000.
Indiana	1000.	1500.	3000.
Iowa	1000.	1500.	3000.
Kansas	1000.	1500.	3000.
Kentucky	1000.	2000.	3000.
Louisiana	1000.	2000.	3000.
Maine		Unique	
Maryland	1000.	2000.	3000.
Massachusetts	1000.	2000.	3000.
Michigan	1000.	2000.	3000.
Minnesota		Unique	
Mississippi	4000.	8000.	15,000.
Missouri	1000.	1750.	4000.
Montana		Unique	
Nebraska	1000.	1750.	4000.
Nevada	5000.	10,000.	20,000.
New Hampshire	4000.	7000.	14,000.
New Jersey	3000.	5000.	10,000.
New York	1000.	1500.	3000.
North Carolina	—	Rare	—
North Dakota	—	Rare	—
Ohio	1000.	1500.	3000.
Oklahoma	1000.	1500.	3500.
Oregon	1500.	3000.	5000.
Pennsylvania	1000.	1500.	3000.
Puerto Rico	—	Rare	—
Rhode Island	1500.	3000.	6000.

	VG	VF	AU
South Dakota	1500.	3000.	7000.
Tennessee	1500.	4500.	9000.
Texas	1000.	1500.	4000.
Utah		Unique	
Vermont	3000.	6000.	10,000.
Virginia	—	Rare	—
Washington	1000.	2000.	3500.
Wisconsin	1000.	2000.	3500.

1902 Plain Back $100

(KL #1425-1436) (Fr #698-707-A)

	VG	VF	AU
California	1000.	1600.	2000.
Colorado	2000.	3000.	6000.
Connecticut	2000.	3100.	6000.
Delaware	3000.	5000.	10,000.
Idaho	1000.	1600.	2000.
Illinois	1000.	1600.	2000.
Indiana	1000.	1600.	2000.
Iowa	1000.	1600.	2000.
Kansas	1000.	1600.	2000.
Kentucky	1000.	1600.	2000.
Louisiana	1000.	1600.	2000.
Maryland	1000.	1600.	2000.
Massachusetts	1000.	1600.	2000.
Michigan	1000.	1600.	2000.
Mississippi	2200.	4000.	8000.
Missouri	1000.	1600.	2000.
Montana		Rare	—
Nebraska	1000.	1600.	2000.
Nevada	3500.	4000.	10,000.
New Hampshire	2000.	4000.	8000.
New Jersey	3500.	5000.	10,000.
New York	1000.	1600.	2000.
North Dakota	—	Rare	
Ohio	1000.	1600.	2000.
Oklahoma	1000.	1600.	2000.
Oregon	1000.	1600.	2500.
Pennsylvania	1000.	1600.	2000.
Rhode Island	1000.	1600.	2500.
South Dakota	1000.	2000.	3500.
Tennessee	1000.	2000.	3000.
Texas	1000.	1600.	2000.
Vermont	1000.	2000.	5000.
Washington	375.	750.	2000.
West Virginia		Unique	
Wisconsin	350.	700.	2000.

1929 Type 1 $100

(KL #1437) (Fr #1804-1)

	VG	VF	AU
California	—	225.	450.
Colorado	—	250.	500.
Connecticut	—	600.	1200.
Delaware	—	Rare	—
Florida	—	500.	1000.
Hawaii	—	600.	1250.
Idaho	—	500.	1000.

	VG	VF	AU
Illinois	—	225.	450.
Indiana	—	225.	450.
Iowa	—	225.	450.
Kansas	—	300.	600.
Kentucky	—	400.	800.
Louisiana	—	300.	600.
Maryland	—	250.	500.
Massachusetts	—	250.	500.
Michigan	—	225.	450.
Minnesota	—	250.	500.
Mississippi	—	Rare	—
Missouri	—	250.	500.
Montana	—	600.	1200.
Nebraska	—	250.	500.
Nevada	—	1500.	3000.
New Hampshire	—	450.	900.
New Jersey	—	250.	700.
New York	—	250.	700.
North Carolina	—	Rare	—
North Dakota	—	550.	1300.
Ohio	—	225.	600.
Oklahoma	—	225.	600.
Oregon	—	900.	2000.
Pennsylvania	—	225.	500.
Rhode Island	—	400.	1000.
South Dakota	—	750.	2000.
Tennessee	—	250.	800.
Texas	—	250.	800.
Vermont	—	475.	1200.
Washington	—	300.	850.
West Virginia	—	Rare	—
Wisconsin	—	300.	850.
Wyoming	—	Rare	—

1929 Type 2 $100
(KL #1438) (Fr #1804-2)

	VG	VF	AU
Arkansas	—	Rare	—
California	—	700.	1000.
Colorado	—	900.	1500.
Hawaii	—	Rare	—
Illinois	—	700.	1300.
Indiana	—	Rare	—
Kentucky	—	Rare	—
Louisiana	—	900.	1500.
Maryland	—	Rare	—
Michigan	—	Rare	—
Minnesota	—	900.	1500.
New Jersey	—	Rare	—
New York	—	Rare	—
Pennsylvania	—	900.	1500.
Rhode Island	—	1200.	2200.
Tennessee	—	Rare	—
Texas	—	1200.	1500.
Virginia	—	Rare	—

Pre-Civil War (1812-1861) United States Treasury Notes

Compiled by Russell Rulau

The first paper money issued by the United States government was not, as is often thought, the Interest Bearing Treasury Notes of 1861, these notes were actually the last in the long series of Treasury notes that commenced in 1812 as a consequence of the financial condition of the nation in the War of 1812.

The U.S. Treasury issued five separate series of notes between 1812 and 1815 with denominations ranging from $3 to $1,000. Though originally intended as loans to the government, they soon began to circulate since they were receivable for debts, taxes and duties due the federal government.

Neither the 1812-1815 notes nor later issues until 1861 were ever actually legal tender for all debts, public or private. This is an important distinction between them and the legal tender notes introduced in the Civil War. Compared to private bank notes of the period, however, they were "good as gold".

To provide bridge financing and spot cash, Congress authorized a whole series of interest-bearing Treasury notes – at 5.4% or 1.44 cents per day per $100 by acts of June 30, 1812; Feb. 25, 1813; March 4, 1814, and Feb. 24, 1815. By the 1815 act, Congress for the first time created a true currency with notes of $3 through $50 bearing no interest, but with those of $100 bearing the usual 5.4% annual interest

Specimen copies of all these notes, punch-canceled but bearing two of the three required signatures, were supplied to the chief customs houses at Baltimore, Boston, Charleston, New York and Philadelphia. Actual issued notes, whether unredeemed or canceled, bring the highest prices, unissued remainder notes sell well. Specimen notes, and printer's proofs, usually in excellent condition, bring slightly lower prices but are often the only notes available.

Of the 1814 issue, only about $40,000 remained outstanding in 1896 out of a total of $8.3 million. Of the 1815 $100 notes, note of the $1.5 million issued was unredeemed in 1896.

The 1815 "small bills" of $3 to $50 were issued to a total of $9,070,386. Some $5.6 million of these were funded into bonds, and in 1896 just $2,061 remained unredeemed.

The panic of 1837-1843 brought out eight more series of Treasury notes. These notes differed from the War of 1812 notes in that they were signed by the Treasurer of the United States and were engraved by Rawdon, Wright & Hatch (RWH) whereas the 1812-1815 notes had been signed by commissioners.

The Mexican War was responsible for the next two series of Treasury notes in 1846 and 1847, also signed by the U.S. Treasurer.

The severe financial conditions of the panic of 1857 resulted in the next three series of Treasury notes, issued form Dec. 1857 through March 1861. These notes were issued at competitive interest rates rather than predetermined rates. Confidence in the federal government was lacking and of the $10 million of 6% notes offered in Dec. 1860 only $70,000 was taken up! The remainder of these notes has to be offered at rates above 6%, with 10, 10.75, 11 and 12% being the largest. (Bids were received as high as 36%, but the Treasury rejected all bids above 12%.) The Acts of July 17 and Aug. 5, 1861 authorized the final issues of Treasury notes.

Most pre-Civil War Treasury notes bear the date of the act that authorized them, and an issue-date (in ink) as well. The catalog section is arranged by authorization (not issue) dates. All pre-Civil War Treasury notes are rare and seldom met with, many are unique.

A famed French politician and numismatist, Alexandre Vattemare, formed one of the largest private collections of the 1812-1815 notes. This collection sold in 1982 by Christie Manson & Woods International, mostly to one person, then re-auctioned in 2000 by R. M. Smtthe & Co.

The largest private collection ever assembled was by John J. Ford, Jr., buyer of much of the Vattemare 2000 offerings to add to his 40-year holds, and Stack's Rare Coins sold this group in late 2004. Heritage Currency Auctions offered another large group, the Taylor family holdings, in early 2005.

This section has been renumbered from previous editions, based on new information that has come to light from these recent offerings.

Bibliography:

Alexandre Vattemare Collection Sale, Christie Manson & Woods International, Sale of Sept., 17, 1982

J. W. Middendorf, II, Sale, Christies, March 22, 1994

John J. Ford, Jr. Sale, Stack's Rare Coins, Oct., 12, 2004

R.M. Smythe Sale. Memphis International Paper Money Show Auction, June 16, 2000.

Taylow Family Holdings Sale. Heritage Currency Auctions, Feb., 18-19, 2005.

Hessler, Gene. "An Illustrated History of U.S. Loans, 1775-1898" BNR Press, 1985 and 1988.

Knox, John Jay. "United States Notes: A history of the Various Issues of Paper Money", NY editions of 1884, 1885 and 1894.

Photos and note data courtesy of Larry Stevens, Eric P. Newman, Christie's, R. M. Smythe & Co., Stack's Rare Coins, and Heritage Currency Auctions.

PRINTER ABBREVIATIONS

ABNC	*American Bank Note Company*
NBNC	*National Bank Note Company*
MDF	*Murray, Draper, Fairman & Company*
RW&H	*Rawdon, Wright & Hatch*
RWH&E	*Rawdon, Wright, Hatch & Edson*
TC	*Toppan, Carpenter & Company*

WAR OF 1812

ACT OF JUNE 30, 1812

1 year notes at 5 2/5% interest. $5,000,000 authorized and issued.
No Issued notes are known to exist.

Murray, Draper, Fairman & Company

KL#		Denom.	Description	XF	AU
P1	a	$100	Single remainder.	8050.	17,250.
	b	$100	Remainder, sheet of two.	-	25,300.
P2		$1,000	Single remainder. (3 known).	21,850.	-

ACT OF FEBRUARY 25, 1813

1 year notes at 5 2/5% interest. $5,000,000 authorized and issued. No issued notes are known.

KL#	Denom.	Description	XF	AU
P3	$100	No description available.	-	-

ACT OF MARCH 4, 1814

1 Year notes at 5 2/5% interest. $10,000,000 authorized and issued. No issued ntoes are known.

KL#	Denom.	Description	XF	AU
P4	$20	No description available.	-	-
P5	$50	No description available.	-	-

Murray, Draper, Fairman & Company

KL#		Denom.	Description	XF	AU
P6		$100	Remainder with 2 signatures. (2 known).	29,900.	-

ACT OF DECEMBER 26, 1814

1 Year notes at 5 2/5% interest. $8,318,400 issued. No issued notes are known.

KL#		Denom.	Description	XF	AU
P7	a	$20	Remainder with 2 signatures. (About 15 known.)	12,650.	-
	b	$20	Remainder sheet of two.	-	12,650.
	c	$20	Proof on cardstock. (3 known)	-	5000.
P8		$50	No description available.	-	-

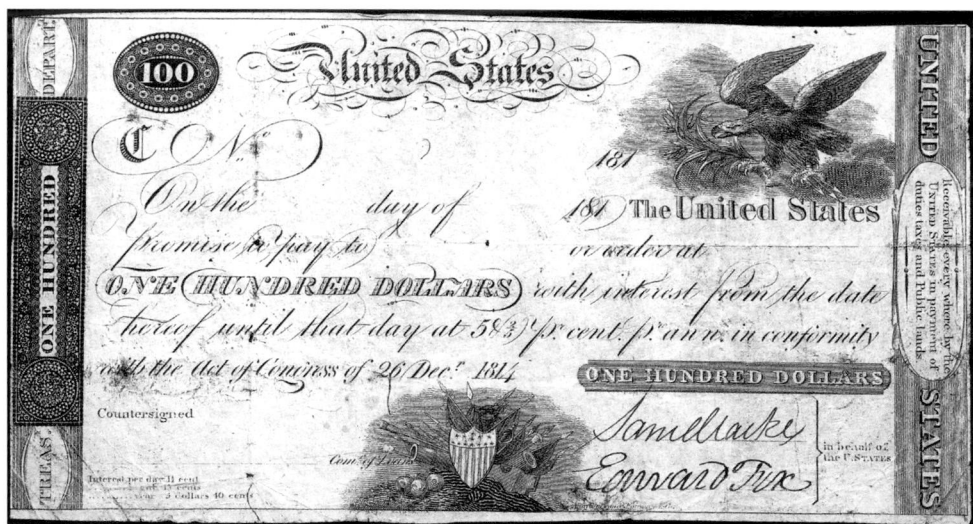

Imprint: Murray, Draper, Fairman & Company

KL#		Denom.	Description	XF	AU
P9	a	$100	Remainder with 2 signatures. (4 known).	22,425.	-
	b	$100	Proof on card. (2 known).	-	14,950.

ACT OF FEBRUARY 24, 1815

$3 to $50 notes without interest; $100 notes, indefinite interest at 5 2/5%
$3,392 issued in $3-50 notes; $4,969,400 issued in $100 notes.

KL#		Denom.	Description	XF	AU
P10	a	$3	Issued note. Signed by Joseph Nourse, F. W. McGeary and C. C. Biddle.	62,500.	-
	b	$3	Single remainder, unsigned. (5 known)	-	8250.
	c	$3	Remainder in sheet of four.	30,000.	-
	d	$3	Proof on cardstock.	-	5750.

KL#		Denom.	Description	XF	AU
P11	a	$5	Unsigned remainder. (About 13 known)	-	3750.

KL#		Denom.	Description	XF	AU
	b	$5	Two signature remainder sheet of 3.	-	12,750.
	c	$5	Proof on cardstock.	-	5000.

Murray, Draper, Fairman & Company

KL#	Denom.	Description	XF	AU
P12	$10	Remainder with two signatures. (3 known)	5000.	-

KL#	Denom.	Description	XF	AU
P13 a	$10	Remainder with 2 signatures. (17 known)	5250.	7000.
b	$10	Remainder sheet of three.	-	10,350.
c	$10	Single proof on India paper.	-	4000.
d	$10	Sheet of three proof on India paper.	-	19,000.

KL#	Denom.	Description	XF	AU
P14 a	$20	Unsigned remainder.	-	-
b	$20	Sheet of four unsigned remainders.	-	17,250.

KL#	Denom.	Description	XF	AU
c	$20	Proof on India paper. (3 known)	-	3750.

KI #	Denom.	Description	XF	AU
P15 a	$50	Issued, canceled note. Nourse, McGeary, Biddle signatures.	-	3750.

KL#	Denom.	Description	XF	AU
b	$50	Remainder, sheet of four (one signature).	19,750.	-
c	$50	Remainder, sheet of three.	-	23,250.
P16 a	$100	Unsigned remainder. (6 known)	8250.	-
b	$100	Unsigned remainder, sheet of three.	-	17,250.

KL#	Denom.	Description	XF	AU
c	$100	Proof on card.	8250.	-
d	$100	Proof, sheet of three.	-	21,000.

PANIC OF 1837

ACT OF OCTOBER 12, 1837

1 year notes issued at four different rates of interest 1 mill, 2%, 5% or 6%,
the rate written in by ink at time of issue. The 1-mil rate, which was nominal,
was used on notes intended to circulate as currency. $10,000,000 authorize

Face black, back orange. Rawdon, Wright & Hatch. 183 printed.

KL#	Denom.	Description	XF	AU
P17	$50	Unsigned remainder.	8000.	-

Rawdon, Wright & Hatch. Face black, back light orange.

KL#	Denom.	Description	XF	AU
P18	$100	Issued note, canceled.	6100.	-
P19	$500	No description availablc.	-	-
P20	$1,000	No description available.	-	-

Denomination, date, interest rate to be written in. Back orange. Rawdon, Wright & Hatch.

KL#	Denom.	Description	XF	AU
P20A	-	Unsigned remainder	1950.	-

ACT OF MAY 21, 1838

1 year ntoes at 6% interest. $6,888,809 issued.

KL#	Denom.	Description	XF	AU
P21	$50	No description available.	-	-

No description available.

KL#	Denom.	Description	XF	AU
P22	$100	No description available.	-	-
P23	$500	No description available.	-	-
P24	$1,000	No description available.	-	-

ACT OF MARCH 2, 1839

1 year notes at 2%, 5%, 5 2/5% or 6% interest, $3,857,276 issued

KL#	Denom.	Description	XF	AU
P25	$50	No description available.	-	-
P26	$100	No description available.	-	-
P27	$500	No description available.	-	-
P28	$1,000	No description available.	-	-

ACT OF MARCH 31, 1840

1 year notes at 2%, 5%, 5 2/5% or 6% interest, the rate written in by ink at time of issuance.

KL#	Denom.	Description	XF	AU
P29	$50	No description available.	-	-
		Knox drawing only available.		
P30	$100	Specimen.	-	-
P31	$500	No description available.	-	-
P32	$1,000	No description available.	-	-
P33	$10,000	No description available.	-	-

ACT OF JANUARY 31, 1842

1 year notes at 2% or 6% interest, $7,959,994 issued (including reissues).

KL#	Denom.	Description	XF	AU
P34	$50	No description available.	-	-
P35	$100	No description available.	-	-
P36	$500	No description available.	-	-
P37	$1,000	No description available.	-	-

PANIC OF 1837

ACT OF AUGUST 31, 1842

1 year notes at 2% or 6% interest. $3,025,554 issued.

Rawdon, Wright & Hatch.

KL#	Denom.	Description	XF	AU
P38	$50	Unissued remainder.	-	-

KL#	Denom.	Description	XF	AU
P39	$100	Unissued remainder.	-	-
P40	$500	No description available.	-	-

Rawdon, Wright & Hatch.

KL#	Denom.	Description	XF	AU
P41	$1,000	Unissued remainder.	-	-

ACT OF MARCH 3, 1843

1 year notes at 1 mill or 4% interest. $1,806,950 issued.

*Special Note: In 1887 there were only $83,425 outstanding
in all Treasury notes issued under acts prior to 1846!*

Rawdon, Wright & Hatch.

KL#	Denom.	Description	XF	AU
P42	$50	Issued note, cancelled. Very Rare.	-	-

MEXICAN WAR NOTES

ACT OF JULY 22, 1846

1 year notes at 1 mill or 5 2/5% interest. $7,687,800 issued.
Note: In 1887, only $5,900 was outstanding!

*Black print, red FIFTY protector near bottom center, blue serial #.
One mill. Rawdon, Wright & Hatch.*

KL#	Denom.	Description	XF	AU
P43 a	$50	Specimen.	-	5500.

KL#	Denom.	Description	XF	AU
b	$50	Face proof on India paper.	2500.	-
c	$50	Face proof on India paper, without red FIFTY protector.	2500.	-
P44	$100		-	-
P45	$500	No description available.	-	-
P46	$1,000	No description available.	-	-

MEXICAN WAR WARRANTS

ACT OF AUGUST 10, 1846

5 year warrants, interest not stated.

Black with red overprint. Rawdon, Wright, Hatch & Edson.

KL#	Denom.	Description	XF	AU
P46B	$1,000	Specimen.	-	-
		Blue with red overprint. Rawdon, Wright & Hatch.		
P46A	$500	Specimen.	-	-

MEXICAN WAR NOTES

ACT OF JANUARY 28, 1847

60 day or 1 or 2 year notes at 5 2/5% or 6% interest. $26,122,100 issued (including reissues).
Note: In 1887, only $950 or 6% notes were still outstanding!

Black face, orange back. One year note. Rawdon, Wright & Hatch.

KL#	Denom.	Description	XF	AU
P46C	$50	Specimen. Unique.		4250.

Black face, red back. Toppan, Carpenter & Company. Two year note.

KL#	Denom.	Description	XF	AU
P47 a	$50	Specimen.	-	4750.

KL#	Denom.	Description	XF	AU
b	$50	Proof on card.	4500.	8000.

Two year note. 184 printed. Rawdon, Wright, Hatch & Edson.

KL#	Denom.	Description	XF	AU
P48Ba	$100	Face and back proof on card.	-	4500.

KL#	Denom.	Description	XF	AU
b	$100	Face proof on India paper.	-	5000.

One year note. Black face, back orange. Rawdon, Wright & Hatch.

KL#	Denom.	Description	XF	AU
P48A	$100	Face and back proof. Unique.	-	5500.

184 printed. Rawdon, Wright, Hatch & Edson.

KL#	Denom.	Description	XF	AU
P48	$100	Face proof on card.	-	6000.

Two year note. Face black with red 500 protector. back brown. Rawdon, Wright, Hatch & Edson.

KL#	Denom.	Description	XF	AU
P49	$500	Specimen.	-	8500

Two year note. Toppan, Carpenter & Company.

KL#	Denom.	Description	XF	AU
P50Aa	$1,000	Face proof on India paper.	-	18,500.

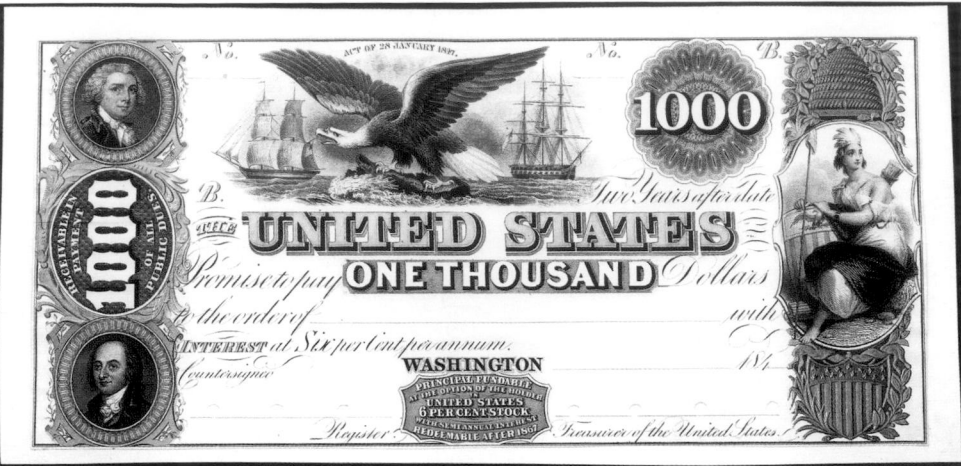

KL#	Denom.	Description	XF	AU
b	$1,000	Face and back proof.	-	18,500.
		One year note. Black face, orange back. Rawdon, Wright & Hatch.		
P50	$1,000	Specimen.	-	8500.
		Two year note. Rawdon, Wright, Hatch & Edson.		
P51	$5,000	Specimen, two sided.	-	-

Face black, back orange. Toppan, Carpenter & Company.

KL#	Denom.	Description	XF	AU
P52	$5,000	Proof on India paper on card.	-	22,000.

PANIC OF 1857

ACT OF DECEMBER 23, 1857
1 year notes at 3% to 6% interest. $20,000,000 authorized.
Note: In 1887, only $700 of all these notes were outstanding!

Black print, bronze-gold Treasury building underprint at right.

KL#	Denom.	Description	XF	AU
P53	$100	Face proof with counterfoil at left.	-	5500.
P54	$500	No description available.	-	-

Full green frame and green underprint protectors, black print.
Rawdon, Wright, Hatch & Edson.

KL#	Denom.	Description	XF	AU
P55	$1,000	Face proof on India paper. (3 known)	-	12,750.

ACT OF DECEMBER 17, 1860

1 year notes at 6% to 12% interest. $15,000,000 issued (most at rates of 10 3/4%, 11% or 12%).

KL#	Denom.	Description	XF	AU
P56	$50	No description available.	-	-
P57	$100	No description available.	-	-
P58	$500	No description available.	-	-

Black on green frame and underprint.
Rawdon, Wright, Hatch & Edson and American Bank Note Company.

KL#	Denom.	Description	XF	AU
P59 a	$1,000	Proof. Unique.	-	10,000.

KL#	Denom.	Description	XF	AU
b	$1,000	Two-sided specimen. Back green.	21,000.	-

ACT OF MARCH 2, 1861

1 or 2 year notes at 6% interest. $35,364,450 issued ($22.4 million in 2-year notes).
Two year, 6%. Black and orange face, blue back. National Bank Note Company.

KL#	Denom.	Description	XF	AU
P60Aa	$50	Face proof on India paper card.	-	16,250.

Black and orange; blue back. National Bank Note Company.

KL#	Denom.	Description	XF	AU
P60 a	$50	Issued note.	375,000.	-

KL#	Denom.	Description	XF	AU
b	$50	Proof.	-	-

Two year, 6%. Black and orange face, blue back. National Bank Note Company.

P60Ab	$50	Two sided proof.	-	-

Black and orange; green back.

KL#	Denom.	Description	XF	AU
P61	$100	Specimen.	-	30,000.

Black print, red 100 protector near bottom center. 60-day note.
Rawdon, Wright, Hatch & Edson.

KL#	Denom.	Description	XF	AU
P62	$100	Face specimen. Unique.	-	16,250.

60-day note, 6% interest. Black, green frame and underprint.
Rawdon, Wright, Hatch & Edson and American Bank Note Company.

KL#	Denom.	Description	XF	AU
P63	$500	Specimen.	-	21,000.

Black & green; brown back. 60-day note.
Imprint: American Bank Note Company and Rawdon, Wright, Hatch & Edson.

P64	$500	Specimen.	-	-

Two-year note, 6% interest. Black on green border and protectors.
National Bank Note Company.

KL#		Denom.	Description	XF	AU
P65	a	$500	Face proof.	-	25,000.
	b	$500	Face and back proof.	-	-

Two-year note, 6% interest. Black and green, orange back. National Bank Note Company.

KL#		Denom.	Description	XF	AU
P66	a	$1,000	Specimen.	-	-
	b	$1,000	Face proof on India paper on card.	-	30,000.
P67		$5,000	No description available.	-	-
P68		$5,000	No description available.	-	-

CIVIL WAR NOTES

ACT OF JULY 17 AND AUGUST 5, 1861

3 year notes at 7 3/10%. So-called "7-30s".
These are the first Treasury notes widely issued for circulation. $800,000,000-plus issued.
Black and green. American Bank Note Company.

KL#	Denom.	Description	XF	AU
P74	$20	Essay on card.	18,000.	-
		Black and green face, back green. American Bank Note Company.		
P75	$50	Issued note, uncancelled.	172,500.	-
P76	$100	Fragment of issued note.	-	-
		Green and black, back green. American Bank Note Company.		
P77 a	$500	Issued note, uncancelled.	300,000.	-
b	$500	Issued note, damaged and cancelled.	-	-
		No additional description available.		
P78	$1,000	Note fragment.	-	-
P79	$5,000	No description available.	-	-

ACTS NOT APPROVED

LOAN OF 1848

Black and red face, red back. Toppan, Carpenter & Company.

KL#	Denom.	Description	XF	AU
P80	$200	Essay.	-	-
		Rust color. Toppan, Carpenter& company.		
P81	$10,000	Essay.	-	-

ACT OF JUNE 14, 1858

Rust color.

KL#	Denom.	Description	XF	AU
P82	$5,000	Essay.	-	-

ACT OF JUNE 22, 1860

American Bank Note Company.

KL#	Denom.	Description	XF	AU
P83	$1,000	Essay.	-	-

KL#	Denom.	Description	XF	AU
P84	$5,000	Essay.	-	-

Encased Postage Stamps
&
Postage Stamp Envelopes

Encased Postage Stamps
By Len Glazer

Encased postage has always been among the most elusive of American numismatic items to collect, and consequently, among the most rewarding. With their natural appeal to numismatists, philatelists, and collectors of antique advertising media, demand has also been strong. This competition for scarce items, especially so in high grades of preservation, has meant a steady upward price progression that also makes Encased Postage Stamps desirable from an investment viewpoint.

While a complete set – by denomination, merchant and major variety – of Encased Postage has never been formed and likely never will be, it is entirely within the grasp of the determined numismatist to assemble a collection that is "complete" within self-set boundaries; that is, 6 denomination, by merchant, by type of merchant (medicinal, dry goods, etc.), by locality of issue, or by any other criteria.

While not generally collected along with the Gault encased postage stamps, the so-called Feuchtwanger rectangular encasement is a contemporary, though unsuccessful, competitor.

Approximately 31x61 mm, with a brass frame and no mica cover for the stamps, this item is generally found with a trio of 3-cent postage stamps; a face value of nine cents. The item is also found with other quantities of 3-cent stamps, though the originality of these other denominations is questionable.

Naturally, since the stamps are easily replaced, their condition has little bearing on the value.

Grading

Three factors must be considered in the grading of Encased Postage Stamps: the case itself, the enclosed stamp and the protective mica.

For the listings which follow, generally accepted standards for coin grading have been used to grade the cases. The accepted standards for grading unused U.S. postage stamps have been considered for that element. For the mica, terminology is that which has been in use since the collecting of Encased Postage Stamps began.

In referring to the price listing that follows, it should be made clear that unlike coins or stamps, which are bought and sold on the basis of generally accepted grading standards, Encased Postage Stamps are sold on the individual merits of the piece involved. This is the result of the many and varied states of preservation of each of the three main elements - case, stamp and mica - of these items.

The valuations quoted refer basically to the condition of the case. If the condition of the stamp and mica are consistent in their own way with that of the case, the valuations can be considered accurate at the time of this catalog's issue. If, however, either the stamp or the mica is significantly better or worse than the case, the value of the item as a whole may be more or less than the figure quoted.

Assume, for example, that a piece with a VF case holds a stamp that is Extremely Fine, protected by a piece of mica which is crazed (see mica grading). The stamp is obviously better than the case, and the crazed mica is also quite nice, though not perfect. The value of such a piece is definitely higher than the quoted VF price, and may be closer to the XF valuation.

Grading of Case

NEW - A condition unknown among Encased Postage Stamps. While there do, indeed, exist specimens which show no wear traces of circulation on the case, the condition of the stamp and/or mica will always contain some imperfection which prevents the accurate description of any Encased Postage Stamp as "New."

ABOUT NEW - The highest grade in which Encased Postage can practically be collected. Just a touch of rubbing on the case, which may or may not still retain some original silvering, if so issued.

EXTREMELY FINE - Higher than average grade, with a bit of noticeable wear on the case; still a very nice piece.

VERY FINE- The average grade for collectible Encased Postage Stamps. The case shows definite wear, but little or no flatness of the embossed lettering. Most catalog values are based on this grade.

FINE - A worn, but acceptable, piece. Generally the lowest undamaged or collectible grade of untampered Encased Postage, since the items did not circulate long enough to attain any greater degree of wear.

Grading of Stamp

In their usage with Encased Postage, stamps are generally described in one of the following degrees of brightness. Since the paper was protected by the mica, the only measurement of the state of preservation of the stamp can be the degree to which it was subjected to the fading effects of sunlight or other causes.

FULLY BRIGHT - A stamp that is 100% as vivid as the day it was issued.

NEAR FULL BRIGHT - Perhaps a spot or two of less than perfect brightness.

BRIGHT - A stamp which has lost some of its original color, but is still sharp and always acceptable.

TONED - A stamp which has darkened with age or exposure to light and other elements.

DULL or FADED - A stamp which has lost much of its color; the lowest generally collectable condition for an undamaged item.

Grading of Mica

Because it is a natural silicate mineral, mica of flawless, perfect quality probably does not exist in connection with its use in Encased Postage Stamps. Collectors are warned that only "perfect" mica generally encountered is acetate which has been used to repair a damaged Encased Postage Stamp. Upon close examination, some flaw can be found on virtually every mica piece used in this manner.

NEARLY PERFECT - The highest degree of preservation for a mica encasement.

CRAZED - Fine cracks in the surface, on the surface, or between the thin natural layers of mica. Separation beginning in its early stages. None of the crazing fully breaks the mica, exposing the stamp.

CRACKED -A break in the mica through to the stamp, but with no piece of the mica missing.

CHIPPED - A breaking of only the upper layer or layers of mica, with the chip or chips missing, though the mica beneath remains intact and the stamp protected.

BROKEN - A break in all layers of the mica, with some missing and the stamp exposed. The degree of broken or missing mica should be described.

Other Terms

Two other terms which the collector of Encased Postage will encounter also bear definition.

RIBBED FRAME - Some varieties of Encased Postage are known with cases which have fine parallel lines on the face (stamp side) of the metal case.

SILVERING - Many Encased Postage Stamps were issued with a thin silver wash on the case, to enhance their resemblance to the disappearing silver coinage of the day. More research is needed to determine which issues came with silvering, which came without and which, if any, were issued both ways. Since the silver wore off very quickly, even many high grade pieces have no traces of the original finish. A piece with a high percentage of silvering remaining is worth a premium, but those with just a trace of silver are not; though it is generally mentioned when describing an item for sale.

Rarity Ratings

When dealing with the relative rarity of Encased Postage Stamps, the collector must realize that all are scarce in terms of numismatic collectibles. Even the most common variety "Take Ayer's Pills" may not be easy to locate on the market at any given time.

Following years of study of major collections and auction offerings, and conversations with other specialists, the following table of rarity lists each piece in what we believe to be its correct order, and broken into six categories of rarity. While there may be some disagreement as to order within category, we believe most knowledgeable specialists will agree with the listing.

VERY RARE
1. Arthur M. Claflin
2. B. F. Miles
3. John W. Norris
4. Pearce, Tolle & Holton

RARE
5. White the Hatter
6. Sands' Ale
7. S. Steinfeld
8. Dougan
9. N.G. Taylor & Co.
10. Ellis McAlpin & Co.
11. L.C. Hopkins & Co.
12. Aerated Bread

VERY SCARCE
13. F. Buhl & Co.
14. Weir & Larminie
15. Lord & Taylor
16. H.A. Cook
17. Bailey & Co.

SCARCE
18. Schapker & Bussing
19. G.G. Evans
20. John Shillito & Co.
21. Mendum's Wine Emporium
22. North America Life Insurance Co.

COMMON
23. Tremont House
24. Joseph L. Bates
25. Kirkpatrick & Gault
26. Irving House
27. Brown's Bronchial Troches
28. Burnett's Cocoaine
29. J. Gault
30. Burnett's Cooking Extracts
31. Drake's Plantation Bitters

MOST COMMON
32. Take Ayer's Pills
33. Ayer's Cathartic Pills
34. Ayer's Sarsaparilla

Aerated Bread Co., New York

KL#	Denom.	Fine	VF	XF	AU
EPS1	1¢	800.	1250.	1500.	2500.

Ayer's Cathartic Pills

(Long Arrows variety)

KL#	Denom.	Fine	VF	XF	AU
EPS2	3¢	100.	175.	250.	800.
EPS3	5¢	125.	425.	500.	600.
EPS4	10¢	250.	500.	650.	1000.

(Short arrows variety)

KL#	Denom.	Fine	VF	XF	AU
EPS5	1¢	150.	225.	300.	975.
EPS6	3¢	100.	175.	250.	500.
EPS7	5¢	125.	275.	350.	600.
EPS8	10¢	200.	350.	500.	1000.
EPS9	12¢	300.	550.	1000.	1500.
EPS10	24¢	1200.	2000.	3000.	4500.
EPS11	30¢	1500.	3000.	4000.	5500.

Take Ayer's Pills

KL#	Denom.	Fine	VF	XF	AU
EPS12	1¢	150.	250.	325.	600.
EPS13	3¢	100.	150.	750.	875.
EPS14	5¢	100.	200.	300.	400.
EPS15	10¢	175.	375.	500.	850.

KL#	Denom.	Fine	VF	XF	AU
EPS16	12¢	300.	550.	1000.	1500.
EPS17	90¢		XF:Two known are both		

suspect as being counterfeit or altered.

Ayer's Sarsaparilla

(Small Ayer's)

KL#	Denom.	Fine	VF	XF	AU
EPS18	1¢	300.	625.	925.	1000.
EPS19	3¢	350.	550.	750.	1150.
EPS20	10¢	300.	625.	925.	1000.
EPS21	12¢	700.	1400.	2000.	3500.

(Medium Ayer's)

KL#	Denom.	Fine	VF	XF	AU
EPS22	1¢	150.	225.	300.	650.
EPS23	3¢	100.	175.	225.	750.
EPS24	5¢	150.	225.	300.	600.
EPS25	10¢	175.	300.	450.	850.
EPS26	12¢	300.	550.	1000.	5200.
EPS27	24¢	1200.	2000.	3000.	4500.
EPS28	30¢	1500.	3000.	4000.	5500.
EPS29	90¢	2500.	5000.	9000.	12,500.

(Large Ayer's)

KL#	Denom.	Fine	VF	XF	AU
EPS30	3¢	275.	400.	750.	1000.
EPS31	10¢	450.	700.	1000.	1500.

Bailey & Co., Philadelphia

KL#	Denom.	Fine	VF	XF	AU
EPS32	1¢	375.	550.	1265.	1500.
EPS33	3¢	375.	550.	1000.	1450.
EPS34	5¢	400.	650.	1300.	1800.
EPS35	10¢	400.	600.	1250.	1750.
EPS36	12¢	1000.	1500.	2500.	4000.

Joseph L. Bates
"Fancy Goods" as two words

KL#	Denom.	Fine	VF	XF	AU
EPS37	1¢	150.	225.	300.	925.
EPS38	3¢	350.	675.	850.	1100.
EPS39	10¢	200.	375.	600.	900.
EPS40	12¢	300.	550.	1000.	1500.

F. Buhl & Co., Detroit

KL#	Denom.	Fine	VF	XF	AU
EPS49	1¢	400.	650.	1400.	1750.
EPS50	3¢	400.	700.	1250.	1750.
EPS51	5¢	400.	650.	1100.	1500.
EPS52	10¢	750.	1000.	2000.	2500.
EPS53	12¢	750.	1500.	2000.	3000.

Joseph L. Bates
"Fancy Goods" as one word

KL#	Denom.	Fine	VF	XF	AU
EPS41	1¢	150.	225.	750.	850.
EPS42	3¢	300.	450.	650.	900.
EPS43	10¢	200.	375.	600.	900.

Burnett's Cocoaine Kalliston

KL#	Denom.	Fine	VF	XF	AU
EPS54	1¢	150.	250.	375.	650.
EPS55	3¢	125.	175.	275.	1050.
EPS56	5¢	150.	300.	425.	650.
FPS57	10¢	200.	550.	875.	1250.
EPS58	12¢	300.	550.	1000.	1500.
EPS59	24¢	1500.	2000.	3000.	4500.
EPS60	30¢	1750.	3000.	4000.	5500.
EPS61	90¢	2500.	5000.	9000.	12,500.

Brown's Bronchial Troches

KL#	Denom.	Fine	VF	XF	AU
EPS44	1¢	225.	375.	550.	700.
EPS45	3¢	175.	300.	400.	500.
EPS46	5¢	175.	575.	650.	725.
EPS47	10¢	250.	375.	500.	850.
EPS48	12¢	600.	1000.	1400.	2000.

Burnett's Cooking Extracts
(Plain frame)

KL#	Denom.	Fine	VF	XF	AU
EPS62	1¢	150.	250.	375.	825.
EPS63	3¢	150.	275.	425.	700.
EPS64	5¢	150.	250.	375.	600.
EPS65	10¢	200.	375.	550.	1000.

KL#	Denom.	Fine	VF	XF	AU
EPS66	12¢	300.	550.	1000.	1500.
EPS67	24¢	1500.	2000.	3000.	4500.
EPS68	30¢	1750.	3000.	4000.	5500.
EPS69	90¢	2500.	5000.	9000.	10,500.

(Ribbed frame)

KL#	Denom.	Fine	VF	XF	AU
EPS70	10¢	350.	650.	800.	1250.

A.M. Claflin, Hopkinton, R.I.

KL#	Denom.	Fine	VF	XF	AU
EPS71	1¢	3000.	6250.	12,750.	18,000.
EPS72	3¢	3000.	4000.	6000.	10,000.
EPS73	5¢	3000.	4000.	15,000.	18,000.
EPS74	12¢	3000.	5000.	7500.	12,500.

H.A. Cook, Evansville, Ind.

KL#	Denom.	Fine	VF	XF	AU
EPS75	5¢	350.	650.	1300.	1500.
EPS76	10¢	600.	1200.	2300.	3500.

Dougan, New York

KL#	Denom.	Fine	VF	XF	AU
EPS77	1¢	800.	1500.	2500.	3500.
EPS78	3¢	800.	1500.	2500.	3500.
EPS79	5¢	600.	1000.	2000.	3000.
EPS80	10¢	1000.	2000.	3000.	4000.

Drake's Plantation Bitters, New York

KL#	Denom.	Fine	VF	XF	AU
EPS81	1¢	175.	225.	650.	750.
EPS82	3¢	125.	275.	575.	650.
EPS83	5¢	200.	300.	400.	650.
EPS84	10¢	225.	375.	550.	850.
EPS85	12¢	300.	550.	1000.	1500.
EPS86	24¢	1500.	2500.	3000.	4500.
EPS87	30¢	2000.	3000.	4000.	5500.
EPS88	90¢	2750.	5500.	9000.	12,500.

Ellis, McAlpin & Co., Cincinnati

KL#	Denom.	Fine	VF	XF	AU
EPS89	1¢	600.	1250.	1850.	3000.
EPS90	3¢	600.	1250.	1750.	2500.
EPS91	5¢	800.	1650.	2300.	3200.
EPS92	10¢	600.	1250.	1750.	2500.
EPS93	12¢	800.	1500.	2250.	3500.
EPS94	24¢	1200.	2000.	3000.	4500.

G.G. Evans, Philadelphia

KL#	Denom.	Fine	VF	XF	AU
EPS95	1¢	300.	600.	900.	2125.
EPS96	3¢	400.	700.	1000.	2125.
EPS97	5¢	450.	750.	1250.	2000.
EPS98	10¢	450.	750.	1250.	2000.

J. Gault
(Plain frame)

KL#	Denom.	Fine	VF	XF	AU
EPS99	1¢	150.	225.	300.	600.
EPS100	2¢	-	12,000.	-	-
EPS101	3¢	150.	400.	2200.	2500.
EPS102	5¢	150.	250.	375.	700.
EPS103	10¢	200.	300.	500.	850.
EPS104	12¢	300.	550.	1000.	1500.
EPS105	24¢	1250.	2000.	3000.	4500.
EPS106	30¢	1500.	3000.	4000.	5500.
EPS107	90¢	2500.	5000.	9000.	12,500.

Irving House, N.Y.
(Hunt & Nash)
(Plain frame)

KL#	Denom.	Fine	VF	XF	AU
EPS119	1¢	150.	250.	350.	650.
EPS120	3¢	150.	250.	350.	550.
EPS121	5¢	400.	700.	1000.	2275.
EPS122	10¢	200.	300.	450.	850.
EPS123	12¢	300.	550.	1000.	1500.
EPS124	24¢	1250.	2000.	3000.	4500.
EPS125	30¢	1500.	3000.	4000.	5500.
EPS126	1¢	900.	1250.	2300.	3000.

(Ribbed frame)

KL#	Denom.	Fine	VF	XF	AU
EPS108	1¢	400.	700.	1000.	1250.
EPS109	3¢	400.	700.	1000.	1250.
EPS110	5¢	275.	450.	600.	800.
EPS111	10¢	300.	550.	700.	900.
EPS112	12¢	500.	800.	1500.	2000.
EPS113	24¢	1500.	2750.	3500.	5000.
EPS114	30¢	1750.	3000.	4000.	5500.

(Ribbed frame)

KL#	Denom.	Fine	VF	XF	AU
EPS127	3¢	400.	700.	1000.	1250.
EPS128	5¢	450.	750.	1500.	2100.
EPS129	10¢	350.	550.	750.	900.
EPS130	12¢	500.	800.	1500.	2000.
EPS131	24¢	1500.	2750.	3500.	5000.

L. C. Hopkins & Co., Cincinnati

KL#	Denom.	Fine	VF	XF	AU
EPS115	1¢	700.	1250.	1750.	2500.
EPS116	3¢	600.	1150.	1500.	2250.
EPS117	5¢	800.	1500.	2250.	3250.
EPS118	10¢	700.	1250.	1750.	4025.

Kirkpatrick & Gault, New York

KL#	Denom.	Fine	VF	XF	AU
EPS132	1¢	150.	225.	300.	600.
EPS133	3¢	125.	200.	275.	550.
EPS134	5¢	175.	350.	1380.	1500.
EPS135	10¢	200.	300.	500.	1100.
EPS136	12¢	300.	550.	1000.	1500.

KL#	Denom.	Fine	VF	XF	AU
EPS137	24¢	1250.	2000.	3000.	4500.
EPS138	30¢	1500.	3000.	4000.	5500.
EPS139	90¢	2500.	5000.	9000.	12,500.

Lord & Taylor, New York

KL#	Denom.	Fine	VF	XF	AU
EPS140	1¢	400.	650.	2100.	1750.
EPS141	3¢	400.	650.	1250.	1750.
EPS142	5¢	400.	650.	1250.	1750.
EPS143	10¢	400.	700.	1500.	2250.
EPS144	12¢	800.	1500.	2000.	3500.
EPS145	24¢	1500.	2500.	3500.	5000.
EPS146	30¢	2000.	4000.	5000.	7000.
EPS147	90¢	4000.	7500.	9000.	13,500.

B. F. Miles, Peoria

KL#	Denom.	Fine	VF	XF	AU
EPS154	5¢	3500.	7000.	9500.	12,000.

John W. Norris, Chicago

KL#	Denom.	Fine	VF	XF	AU
EPS155	1¢	750.	1000.	1700.	2750.
EPS156	3¢	1000.	1750.	3000.	4000.
EPS157	5¢	1000.	1750.	3000.	4000.
EPS158	10¢	1000.	1750.	3220.	4000.

Mendum's Family Wine Emporium, New York
(Plain frame)

KL#	Denom.	Fine	VF	XF	AU
EPS148	1¢	250.	350.	500.	1725.
EPS149	3¢	350.	500.	800.	1250.
EPS150	5¢	300.	450.	600.	1200.
EPS151	10¢	300.	450.	700.	1250.
EPS152	12¢	650.	1250.	1750.	2500.

(Ribbed frame)

KL#	Denom.	Fine	VF	XF	AU
EPS153	10¢	400.	700.	1000.	1750.

North America Life Insurance Co.,
(Straight "Insurance")

KL#	Denom.	Fine	VF	XF	AU
EPS159	1¢	175.	250.	350.	1625.
EPS160	3¢	175.	250.	350.	700.
EPS161	10¢	200.	375.	600.	1000.
EPS162	12¢	450.	1000.	1500.	2250.

(Curved "Insurance", trial piece)

KL#	Denom.	Fine	VF	XF	AU
EPS163	1¢	225.	500.	1000.	1500.
EPS164	10¢	300.	500.	750.	1250.

Pearce, Tolle & Holton, Cincinnati

KL#	Denom.	Fine	VF	XF	AU
EPS165	1¢	1000.	1750.	3000.	4000.
EPS166	3¢	800.	2175.	2500.	3500.
EPS167	5¢	1000.	1750.	3000.	4000.
EPS168	10¢	1100.	2000.	3500.	4750.

Sands' Ale

KL#	Denom.	Fine	VF	XF	AU
EPS169	5¢	800.	1500.	2500.	12,650.
EPS170	10¢	1000.	1750.	2750.	4000.
EPS171	30¢	2000.	3500.	5000.	7500.

Schapker & Bussing, Evansville, Ind.

KL#	Denom.	Fine	VF	XF	AU
EPS172	1¢	400.	700.	1000.	1750.
EPS173	3¢	225.	350.	600.	1625.
EPS174	5¢	450.	750.	1250.	2000.
EPS175	10¢	450.	800.	1250.	2000.
EPS176	12¢	500.	1250.	1750.	2750.

John Shillito & Co., Cincinnati

KL#	Denom.	Fine	VF	XF	AU
EPS177	1¢	400.	700.	1000.	1750.
EPS178	3¢	250.	350.	600.	1150.
EPS179	5¢	250.	450.	825.	1250.
EPS180	10¢	275.	425.	750.	1250.
EPS181	12¢	500.	1250.	1750.	2750.

S. Steinfeld, New York

KL#	Denom.	Fine	VF	XF	AU
EPS182	1¢	1000.	1700.	2500.	3500.
EPS183	10¢	1000.	1600.	2500.	3500.
EPS184	12¢	1000.	1750.	2750.	4500.

N. G. Taylor & Co., Philadelphia

KL#	Denom.	Fine	VF	XF	AU
EPS185	1¢	800.	1250.	1300.	2500.
EPS186	3¢	800.	1250.	1750.	2500.
EPS187	5¢	800.	1500.	2000.	2750.
EPS188	10¢	800.	1250.	1750.	2500.

Weir & Larminie, Montreal

KL#	Denom.	Fine	VF	XF	AU
EPS193	1¢	450.	750.	1250.	3300.
EPS194	3¢	400.	700.	1000.	1750.
EPS195	5¢	500.	800.	1500.	2250.
EPS196	10¢	600.	900.	1700.	2500.

Tremont House
(Gage Brothers & Drake),
Chicago

KL#	Denom.	Fine	VF	XF	AU
EPS189	1¢	150.	225.	300.	600.
EPS190	5¢	150.	300.	375.	650.
EPS191	10¢	200.	325.	450.	850.
EPS192	12¢	350.	600.	1250.	2000.

White the Hatter, New York

KL#	Denom.	Fine	VF	XF	AU
EPS197	1¢	750.	1000.	1650.	3000.
EPS198	3¢	800.	1500.	2000.	3500.
EPS199	5¢	900.	1750.	3000.	4000.
EPS200	10¢	800.	1500.	2500.	3500.

Postage Stamp Envelopes
By R.B. White

The introduction to these pages gives the background of the financial times preceding the introduction of Fractional Currency. In mid-1862, hard money was fast disappearing from circulation and postage stamps were pressed into service as a means of making small change.

The Postmaster General in hi s December report of 1862 said: "In the first quarter of the current year, ending September 20th, the number of stamps issued to postmasters was one hundred and four million dollars; there were calls for about two hundred millions, which would have been nearly sufficient to meet usual demands for the year. This extraordinary demand arose from the temporary use of these stamps as a currency for the public in lieu of the smaller denominations of specie, and ceased with the introduction of the so-called 'postal currency'."

But stamps were ill-suited for the wear and tear of commerce and at least in the early part of this period, the post office refused to exchange them for new issues. Before Gault produced his encased postage or the die-sinkers had produced their "copperheads" (more commonly now known as Civil War Tokens), a few enterprising printers produced small envelopes, approximately 70 x 35 mm in size, labeled with the value of the stamps contained and usually with an advertising message either for themselves or for some local merchant. This was mainly confined to the larger cities of the east. New York City had by far the most pieces, but Brooklyn, Boston, Albany, Cincinnati, Jersey City and Philadelphia are also represented.

The New York Central Railroad, in addition to envelopes, issued a stiff card with two slots by which the stamp or stamps are captured.

Some of these envelopes have the value of the stamps printed on them, others have blank spaces for hand written values. Occasionally the printed values are changed by hand.

The issues of J. Leach, stationer and printer in New York City, are by far the most common. They have been seen in five distinct types with multiple denominations within the types.

The first listing of Civil War postage stamp envelopes was published by Henry Russell Drowne in the *American Journal of Numismatics* in 1918. That article, primarily based on the Moreau hoard of 77 envelopes, reported that these pieces "were variously printed with black, blue, red and green ink on white, amber, lemon, pink, orange, violet, blue pale green, buff, manilla and brown paper." Red and blue ink on white paper was the most popular combination. Wood cuts and electrotypes were employed in the manufacture. One single piece bears a picture of Washington. All of the envelopes show evidence of having been hastily made and printed.

In the listings which follow, spaces have been left in the numbering system to accommodate future finds. No claim is made that the list is complete.

These pieces are all extremely rare. The most common probably having no more than half a dozen extant pieces. The pricing thus reflects the rarity of the firm name and the desirability of the design, legend and value. Drowne reported that the 25cts denomination is "by far the most common, about half as many are for 50cts, and a quarter for 10cts and 75 cts." All prices are for the envelope only; stamps may be included but there is really no way of knowing that they are original with the envelopes. Any stamps will increase the total value by their own philatelic value. Prices are for intact envelopes in very fine condition with no problems. Front-only specimens appear frequently and bring only 15% to 30% of the prices shown. A total of 110 different numbers are listed here; it is doubtful that 500 pieces total of all types still exist.

In the numbering system, a first number is assigned for each firm name or known major design type within that firm. The second number of the system is the stated value of the envelope in cents (blank value shown by 0); "hw" following the second number means the value was hand written. A question mark means that the value of the piece has not been reported. "Vars" means that minor varieties exist.

KL#	Name, address and notations	Value
5-10	American Express Co.	3750.

KL#	Name, address and notations	Value
10-50	American Music Hall	5500.
15-10	D. Appleton & Co. Booksellers & Stationer, NYC	1000.
15-15	D. Appleton & Co. Booksellers & Stationer, NYC	3250.
20-?	H. Armstrong, Hosiery, Laces, etc., 140 6th Ave. (NYC)	700.
25-?	Arthur, Gregory & Co., Stationer, 39 Nassau St., NYC	650.
25-50	Arthur, Gregory & Co., Stationer, 39 Nassau St., NYC	650.
27-25	C. van Benthuysen's Printing, Binding and Paper House., Albany, NY	1000.
30-25	Bennett & Reay, in linear border.	1100.
30-50	Bennett & Reay Envelopes, 5 & 7 Spruce St., NYC	1200.
32-25	Bennett & Reay, no border.	1000.
33-25	Bennett & Reay, 5 & 7 Spruce St., NYC	1000.

KL#	Name, address and notations	Value
35-25	Bergen & Tripp, Stationer, 114 Nassau St., (NYC)	775.
40-25	Berlin & Jones, Stationer, 134 William St., NYC	1000.
42-50	Berrian House Furnishing Establishment, 601 Broadway; Embree Stationer, 130 Grand St.	1000.

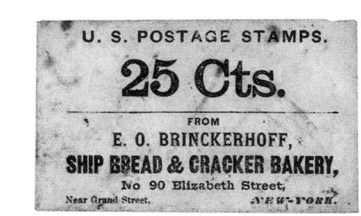

KL#	Name, address and notations	Value
45-25	E. O. Brinckerhoff, Ship Bread & Cracker Backery. NYC	6000.
55-15	Joseph Bryan, Clothing, 214 Fulton St., Brooklyn	4150.

KL#	Name, address and notations	Value
55-50	Joseph Bryan, Clothing, 214 Fulton St., Brooklyn	1200.
60-25	P.D. Braisted, Jr. Billiards, 14-16 4th Ave., NYC	650.

KL#	Name, address and notations	Value
65-25	August Brentano's Book Store, 639 Broadway, NYC	1625.
70-50	G.C. Brown, Tobacco, 669 Broadway, NYC	650.

KL#	Name, address and notations	Value

KL#	Name, address and notations	Value
75-25	Brown & Russell, Pewter Mug. Vertical format.	2000.

KL#	Name, address and notations	Value
80-25	Browning & Long, Salem, Mass.	3225.
85-25	John M. Burnett, Stationer, 51 William St., NYC	650.
85-25hw50	John M. Burnett, Stationer, 51 William St., NYC	650.

KL#	Name, address and notations	Value
90-10	Case's Market, Corner 3rd & 18th., NYC	2300.
95-50	John M. Burnett, Stationer, 51 William St., NYC	650.
95-25	Chas. T. Chickhaus, Tobacco, 176 Broadway, NYC	725.
100-?	Clarry & Reilley, Stationer, 12-14 Spruce St., NYC	725.

KL#	Name, address and notations	Value
105-50hw25	B.F. Corlies & Macy, Stationer, 33 Nassau St., NYC	1500.

KL#	Name, address and notations	Value
105 25	B.F. Corlies & Macy, Stationer, 33 Nassau St., NYC	1500.
105-50	B.F. Corlies & Macy, Stationer, 33 Nassau St., NYC. Red.	2200.
110-30	Crook & Duff, Bar-Lunch-Dining, 39-40 Park Row, (NYC)	800.
115-?	Cutter Tower & Co, Stationer, 128 Nassau St., NYC	650.

KL#	Name, address and notations	Value
120-25	Dawley, Stationer & Printer, 28, 30 & 32 Center St., NYC. Green.	1900.
125-15	T.Π. Dawley, for sale by:	1150.
125-25	T.R. Dawley, for sale by:	1000.
127-10	T.R. Dawley, Manufact'd by:	1100.
130-30	T.R. Dawley, Manufacturer.	1200.
130-25	T.R. Dawley, Manufacturer, Reade & Centre St., NYC.	1000.
130-10	T.R. Dawley, Manufacturer.	1000.
130-20	T.R. Dawley, Manufacturer.	1000.
130-50	T.R. Dawley, Manufacturer.	1725.
130-20hw50	T.R. Dawley, Manufacturer.	1850.
132-50	T.R. Dawley, Printer. Cor. Reade & Center Sts., NYC	1400.
135-25	T.R. Dawley, Steam Job Printer, Cor. Reade & Center Sts., NYC	800.

KL#	Name, address and notations	Value

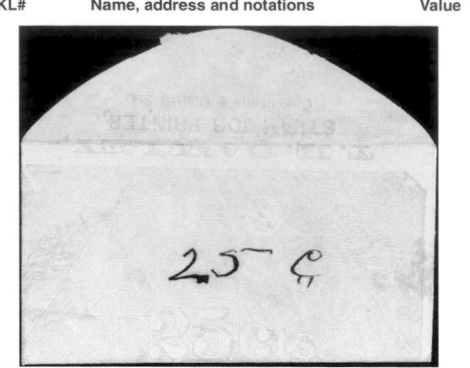

KL#	Name, address and notations	Value
135-25hw25	T.R. Dawley, Steam Job Printer, Cor. Reade & Center Sts., NYC	1000.
135-50	T.R. Dawley, Steam Job Printer, Cor. Reade & Center Sts., NYC	1000.
140-50	E.S. Dawson & Co., Saddlery, Coach & Trunk Hardware, Syracuse, NY	1625.
145-?hw25	Mad[ame] A. Doubet, Importer, 697 & 951 Broadway, (NYC)	725.

KL#	Name, address and notations	Value
150-25	John A. Dougan, Hatter.	6400.
155-25	Francis Duffy, Oysters & Dining, 239-241 8th Ave., NYC	1000.
160-?	Dunton & Ninesteel, Philadelphia, Penn.	2775.
165-50	Embree, Stationer, 130 Grand St., (NYC)	1000.
165-25	Embree, Stationer, 130 Grand St., (NYC)	1275.
170-25	Excelsior Envelope Manufactory	825.
172-50	Jno. C. Force, Brooklyn, NY	800.
175-25	Fox's Old Bowery Theatre (NYC)	2250.
180-?	German Opera, 485 Broadway, NYC	800.
180-25	German Opera, 485 Broadway, NYC	1500.

KL#	Name, address and notations	Value
185-75	Gould's Dining Rooms, 35 Nassau St., NYC	2300.
190-50	Arthur Gregory, NYC	1300.
195-25	Harlem & NY Navigation Co., Sylvan Shore & Sylvan Grove, (NYC) "LEGAL CURRENCY"	1500.
200-05	Harpel, Printers. Cincinnati. Ohio	2750.
200-20	Harpel, Printers. Cincinnati. Ohio	1900.

KL#	Name, address and notations	Value
205-25	Havana Agency	2300.
210-10	Irving House, Hotel, Broadway & 12th St., NYC	4900.
215-25	James, Hatter, 525 Broadway, (NYC)	650.
220-?	Hamilton Johnston, Stationer, 545 Broadway, (NYC) Washington portrait.	825.
222-25hw25	C.F. Hovey & Co. Boston. Blind embossed.	1000.
222-25hw37	Kinsley & Co. Express Forwarders, 72 Broadway & 13 New St., NYC	1000.
222-25	C.F. Hovey & Co., Boston. Blind embossed.	1600.
225-25	C.O. Jones, Stationer, 76 Cedar St., NYC	1500.
230-25	Kaiser & Waters, Stationer, 104 Fulton St., NYC	650.
230-50	Kaiser & Waters, Stationer, 104 Fulton St., NYC	650.
235-60	Kavanagh & Freeman, Billard & Saloon, 10th & Broadway, NYC	3700.
237-10	C. Knickerbocker, Stamp Currency.	1000.
240-20	Lansingh's Gent's Furnishings, Albany, NY	1500.
240-25	Lansingh's Gent's Furnishings, Albany, NY	650.
240-50	Lansingh's Gent's Furnishings, Albany, NY	2300.
250-10	J. Leach, Stationer, 86 Nassau St., NYC. Value in central diamond (vars.)	675.
250-15	J. Leach, Stationer, 86 Nassau St., NYC, Value in central diamond (vars.)	650.

KL#	Name, address and notations	Value
250-20	J. Leach, Stationer, 86 Nassau St., NYC. Value in central diamond (vars.)	575.

KL#	Name, address and notations	Value
250-25	J. Leach, Stationer, 86 Nassau St., NYC. Value in central diamond (vars.)	900.
250-30	J. Leach, Stationer, 86 Nassau St., NYC Value in central diamond (vars.)	650.

KL#	Name, address and notations	Value	KL#	Name, address and notations	Value

KL#	Name, address and notations	Value	KL#	Name, address and notations	Value
250-50	J. Leach, Stationer, 86 Nassau St., NYC. Value in central diamond (vars.)	575	255-50	J. Leach, Writing Paper, 86 Nassau St., NY, Eagle between "U" and "S" (vars.)	725.

KL#	Name, address and notations	Value	KL#	Name, address and notations	Value
250-75	J. Leach, Stationer, 86 Nassau St., NYC. Value in central diamond (vars.)	1000.	255-15	J. Leach, Writing Paper, 86 Nassau St., NY. Eagle between "U" and "S" (vars.)	575
			260-50	J. Leach, 86 Nassau St., NY. Large central oval with value (vars.)	575.
			260-25	J. Leach, 86 Nassau St., NY. Large central oval with value (vars.)	575.

KL#	Name, address and notations	Value
255-25	J. Leach, Writing Paper, 86 Nassau St., NY, Eagle between "U" and "S" (vars.)	575.

KL#	Name, address and notations	Value
265-25	J. Leach, Writing Paper, Envelopes; 86 Nassau St., NY. Flags at top corners	2775.
270-50	J. Leach, Stationer; 86 Nassau St., NY. Denomination in oval, flag left, shield right.	1000.
270-25	J. Leach, Stationer; 86 Nassau St., NY. Denomination in oval, flag left, shield right.	1000.
275-75	D.W. Lee, Stationer, 82 Nassau St., NYC	575.
280-?	R. Letson, Mercantile Dining Room, 256 Broadway, NYC	1000.

KL#	Name, address and notations	Value
282-30hw30	Henry W. Lincoln, Apothecary, Chestnut & Charles St., Boston.	1000.
282-30	Henry W. Lincoln, Apothecary, Chestnut & Charles Sts., Boston.	1000.

KL#	Name, address and notations	Value
285-25	J.W. Lingard, New Bowery Theatre, (NYC)	1000.
290-25	Macoy & Herwig, Stationer, 112-114 Broadway, (NYC)	650.
295-20	Hy Maillards, Confectionery, 621 Broadway, (NYC)	650.
295-25	Hy Maillards, Confectionery, 621 Broadway, (NYC)	650.
300-25hw	M. Markowitz	
300-100hw	M. Markowitz	3000.
305-50	Massasoit House, Springfield, Mass.	2550.

KL#	Name, address and notations	Value
305-25	Massasoit House, Springfield, Mass.	2775.

KL#	Name, address and notations	Value
305-10	Massasoit House, Springfield, Mass.	1725.
310-50	Frank McElroy, Stationers, 113 Nassau St. (NYC)	1000.
310-25	Frank McElroy, Stationers, 113 Nassau St. (NYC)	650.

KL#	Name, address and notations	Value
315-10	Metropolitan Hotel, NYC	1900.
320-25	Miller & Grant, Importers, Laces, 703 Broadway, NYC	725.

KL#	Name, address and notations	Value
325-25	Montezuma Dining Hall, 83 Nassau St., NYC	2550.
326-?	Morris Brothers, Minstrels, Boston. Blind embossed.	1000.

KL#	Name, address and notations	Value
327-25	Wm. Murphy, Stationer, 438 Canal St., NYC	1000.
328-25	Wm. Murphy, 438 Canal St., NYC.	4150.
330-25	W.H. Murphy (By D. Murphy's Sons). Stationers, 372 Pearl St., NYC	1000.
330-50	W.H. Murphy (by D. Murphy's Sons), Stationers, 372 Pearl St., NYC	650.
335-25	National Express Co., 74 Broadway, NYC	2550.
340-20	N.Y. Central R.R. Co., NYC.	725.
340-25	N.Y. Central R.R. Co., NYC.	2300.
340-10	N.Y. Central R.R. Co., NYC.	2300.

KL#	Name, address and notations	Value

U. S. POSTAGE STAMPS.

5 Cts.

N. Y. CENTRAL R. R. CO.

KL#	Name, address and notations	Value
340-05	N.Y. Central R.R. Co., NYC.	1000.

U. S. POSTAGE STAMPS.

50 Cts.

N. Y. CENTRAL R. R. CO.

KL#	Name, address and notations	Value
340-50	N.Y. Central R.R. Co., NYC.	1725.
345-50	N.Y. Consolidated Stage Co. (NYC)	1600.
350-50	N.Y. Consolidated Stage Co. (NYC)	1600.

25c. UNCLE SAM'S 25c.

CHRIS. O'NEILL'S

Wholesale & Retail Liquor Store,

Corner Hudson Av. & Prospect St.,

BROOKLYN.

25c. CHANGE. 25c.

KL#	Name, address and notations	Value
350-25	Chris O'Neills, Liquors, Hudson Ave., Brooklyn, NY "UNCLE SAM'S CHANGE"	800.
355-25	Niblos Garden - Wm Wheatley (Edwin Forrest) (NYC)	725.
355-50	Niblos Garden - Wm Wheatley (Edwin Forrest) (NYC)	3000.
360-25hw10	Nixon's Cremorne Garden, Palace of Music, 14th and 6th Ave. (NYC)	1000.
360-10	Nixon's Cremorne Garden, Palace of Music, 14th and 6th Ave., (NYC)	2700.

NIXON'S CREMORNE GARDEN.

PALACE OF MUSIC. } 14th STREET AND 6th AVENUE. { EQUESTRIAN SCHOOL.

Postage **25** Stamps.
CTS.

OPERA, PROMENADE,
BALLET, EQUESTRIANISM.

ADMISSION TWENTY-FIVE CENTS.

KL#	Name, address and notations	Value
360-25	Nixon's Cremorne Garden, Palace of Music, 14th and 6th Ave., (NYC), Hand stamp appears to read: "CREMORNE (GARD)EN"	725.

OYSTER BAY HOUSE,

553 Broadway.

25 cents.

UNITED STATES STAMPS.

KL#	Name, address and notations	Value
370-25	Oyster Bay House, 553 Broadway, NYC. Thick or thin rule line.	2500.
375-25	The Oyster House, 604 Broadway, NYC	650.

U. S.
POSTAGE STAMPS.

Paulding's Express.

25 Cts.

KL#	Name, address and notations	Value
380-?hw25	Paulding's Express	1000.
382-50	Pekin Tea House, 416 Broome St., Cor. Elm; Davis, Printer, 425 Broome St., NYC	2750.
385-?	Pettit & Crook's Dining Rooms, 100 Water St., NYC. "UNCLE SAM'S CHANGE"	000.

POMROY'S

699 Broadway, New York.

U. S. **POSTAGE STAMPS.**

50

KL#	Name, address and notations	Value
390-50	Pomroy's, 699 Broadway, NYC	2530.
395-50	Power, Bogarduc & Co., Steamship Line Pier 34, No. River, NYC	700.
400-50	S. Raynor, Envelope Manuf'r. 118 William St., NYC. Value in oval with eagle. Black or blue vars.	650.

U. S. POSTAGE STAMPS.

25 Cts.

S. Raynor, Envelope Manuf'r. 118 William St., N.Y.

KL#	Name, address and notations	Value
400-25	S. Raynor, Envelope Manuf'r. 118 William St., NYC. Value in rectangle within oval.	1125.
405-10	Capt. Tom Reeves' Billard Saloon, 214 Broadway, NYC	1500.

KL#	Name, address and notations	Value

(Capt. Tom Reeves' Billiard Saloon envelope image)

KL#	Name, address and notations	Value
405-25	Capt. Tom Reeves' Billard Saloon, 214 Broadway, NYC	800.

(Revere House envelope image)

KL#	Name, address and notations	Value
410-25	Revere House, 604, 606 & 608 Broadway, NYC	650.
415-25	W.B. Rice & Co., Boston, Mass.	2200.
420-25	Thomas Richardson, Chop Steak & Oyster House, 66 Maiden Lane, NYC	1725.
425-50	E.M. Riggin, Sanford House 336 Delaware Ave., Pine St. Wharf, Philadelphia	650.

(Wm. Robins Excelsior Envelopes image)

KL#	Name, address and notations	Value
430-25	Wm. Robins, Excelsior Envelopes, 49 & 51 Ann St., NYC. Value within rectangle. Black.	950.
430-50	Wm. Robins, Excelsior Envelopes, 49 & 51 Ann St., NYC. Value within rectangle, red.	950.
433-25	Wm. Robbins, value in oval.	950.

(R. Scovel, Stationer envelope image)

KL#	Name, address and notations	Value
435-25	R. Scovel, Stationer, 26 Nassau St., (NYC). Postage Stamps / 25 cts.	1250.

KL#	Name, address and notations	Value
437-25	R. Scovel, Stationer, 26 Nassau St., (NYC). Postage Stamps / 25 Cents.	1000.
440-25	Reuben Scovel, 26 Nassau St., (NYC). "GOVERNMENT CURRENCY"	650.
440-50	Reuben Scovel, 26 Nassau St., (NYC). "GOVERNMENT CURRENCY"	650.
445-25	Reuben Scovel, Stationer, 26 Nassau St., NYC	4850.
450-25	R. Scovel, Stationer, 26 Nassau St., NYC	2000.
455-50	C.C. Shelley, Stationer, 68 Barclay St., NYC	650.

(C.C. Shelley, Stationer envelope image)

KL#	Name, address and notations	Value
455-25	C.C. Shelley, Stationer, 68 Barclay St., NYC	650.

(H. Smith, Stationer envelope image — denomination 10)

KL#	Name, address and notations	Value
465-10	H. Smith, Stationer, 137 Williams St., NYC. Denomination in oval, flag left, shield right (vars.)	1150.

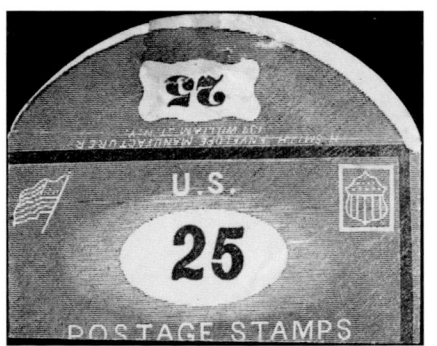

(H. Smith, Stationer envelope image — denomination 25)

KL#	Name, address and notations	Value
465-25	H. Smith, Stationer, 137 Williams St., NYC. Denomination in oval, flag left, shield right (vars.)	1750.

KL#	Name, address and notations	Value

KL#	Name, address and notations	Value
465-20	H. Smith, Stationer, 137 Williams St., NYC. Denomination in oval, flag left, shield right (vars.)	1150.

KL#	Name, address and notations	Value
465-50	H. Smith, Stationer, 137 Williams St., NYC. Denomination in oval, flag left, shield right (vars.)	1400.
465-13	H. Smith, Stationer, 137 Williams St., NYC. Denomination in oval, flag left, shield right (vars.)	575.
470-10hw10	H. Smith, Stationer, 137 Williams St., NYC. Fancy border, no flag, denomination below Postage Stamps. Red or blue vars.	1000.
470-15hw50	H. Smith, Stationer, 137 Williams St., NYC. Fancy border, no flag, denomination below Postage Stamps.	575.
470-50	H. Smith, Stationer, 137 Williams St., NYC. Fancy border, no flag, denomination below Postage Stamps	575.
470-25	H. Smith, Stationer, 137 Williams St., NYC. Fancy border, no flag, denomination below Postage Stamps.	1000.
475-?	Snow & Hapgood, 22 Court St., Boston (vars.)	2550.
475-15	Snow & Hapgood, 22 Court St., Boston (vars.)	1850.

KL#	Name, address and notations	Value
475-25	Snow & Hapgood, 22 Court St., Boston (vars.)	1000.
475-50	Snow & Hapgood, 22 Court St., Boston (vars.)	2300.
475-75	Snow & Hapgood, 22 Court St., Boston (vars.)	2250.
475-10	Snow & Hapgood, 22 Court St., Boston (vars.)	1400.

KL#	Name, address and notations	Value
480-25	Sonneborn, Stationer & Printer, 130 Nassau St., NYC (vars.)	2500.
485-25	Wm. Taylor, 555 Broadway, NYC	1400.
490-50	Taylor's Hotel, Exchange Place, Jersey City (vars.)	725.

KL#	Name, address and notations	Value
490-25	Taylor's Hotel, Exchange Place, Jersey City (vars.)	1400.
495-10	Dion Thomas, Stationer, 142 Nassau St., NYC	725.

KL#	Name, address and notations	Value
495-30	Dion Thomas, Stationer 142 Nassau St., NYC	2300.

KL#	Name, address and notations	Value

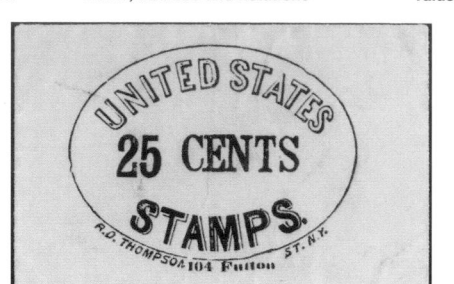

KL#	Name, address and notations	Value
505-25	R.D. Thompson, Stationer, 104 Fulton St., NYC (vars.)	950.
510-?	R.D. Thompson, Stationer, 162 William St., NYC	1000.

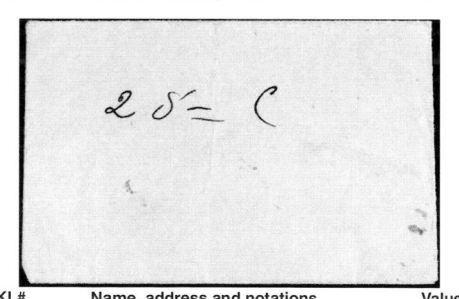

KL#	Name, address and notations	Value
512-50	Ticknor & Fields, Publishers, 135 Washington St., Boston.	1500.
515-25	G.W. & S. Turney, 77 Chatham St., NYC	650.
520-?	S.C. Upham, 403 Chestnut St., Philadelphia, Penn.	650.
525-25	Ward's Perfect Fitting Shirts.	3700.
530-25	David Walker, Stationer & Printer, 4 Park Place, NYC	1100.
530-50	David Walker, Stationer & Printer, 4 Park Place, NYC	1300.
535-25	Willard Looking Glasses, 269 Canal St. NYC	5500.
540-50	James Wiley, Wines & Liquors, 307 Broadway, NYC	650.
540-25	James Wiley, Wines & Liquors, 307 Broadway, NYC	650.
542-?	A. Williams & Co., Boston	1000.

KL#	Name, address and notations	Value
545-25	Blank - marked by hand. Envelope was perhaps hand made.	500.
550-hw25	Fare in the Box (handwritten)	2775.
555-10	U.S. / POSTAGE STAMPS / 10 CTS.	1800.
560-20	U.S. POSTAGE STAMPS 20 CENTS	1700.

KL#	Name, address and notations	Value

KL#	Name, address and notations	Value
565-25	U.S. POSTAGE STAMPS 25 CENTS (vars.)	500.
570-25	POSTAGE STAMPS 25 CENTS	500.
575-25	"UNITED STATES POSTAGE STAMPS" in oval	500.
580-30	U.S ./ POSTAGE STAMPS / 30 CTS.	1275.

KL#	Name, address and notations	Value
610-50	U.S. / POSTAGE STAMPS / 50 CTS.	500.

KL#	Name, address and notations	Value
620-75	U.S. / POSTAGE STAMPS / 75 / CENTS.	500.
625-75hw90	U.S. POSTAGE STAMPS 90 CENTS Hand changed from 75 cents.	650.

Fractional Currency Valuations

Paper Money Substitutes of the Civil War

The collector's first encounter with U.S. Postage and Fractional Currency invariably provokes two questions: What is it? Why was it issued? How was it used?

The first question is easily answered. Postage and Fractional Currency is genuine paper money of the United States issued during the 1862-1875 period in denominations of 3, 5, 10, 15, 25 and 50 cents.

Why paper money in denominations of less than the familiar dollar unit was required in commerce is less easily answered. The causes of this unusual issue of official "paper coins" at a time when people still demanded coins of high intrinsic value can only be found in the jumble of cause and effect that has been the catalyst of numismatic history from time immemorial.

It would be convenient to state, as has frequently been done, that within a few days of the outbreak of the Civil War all of the gold, silver and copper coins in circulation disappeared due to the desire of the timid to save something of universal value from the threatened wreck of the Union, and of the avaricious to hoard something which would possibly increase in value. Undoubtedly, fear and greed acted at once to trigger the hoarding instinct in some individuals, but on the whole, such an observation seems to be overdrawn. Contemporary newspaper accounts make little mention of a serious coin shortage until early in 1862.

It would appear that the initial hoarding of hard money was caused by little more than an ingrained distrust of paper money, an attitude more than justified by the nation's experience with non-metallic currency up to that time. The Yankee worker, whose livelihood was completely bound to the money earned tending the lathes and forges of the industrialized North, simply felt more secure when his paper wages had been converted to gold and silver. Consequently, he gave a cool reception to "Greenbacks," which could not be redeemed for either gold or silver and were suspiciously regarded as "faith paper." The reception grew progressively colder as the flood of paper dollars increased.

This expressed preference for coins inevitably depreciated Greenbacks in terms of the gold standard. Gold coins commanded a premium of three percent over U.S. and state paper money in January, 1862, the month following the general suspension of specie payment by banks and the Federal Treasury; six percent in June, 1862; 15 percent in July, and 32 percent by the end of 1862. Thereafter the depreciation of Greenbacks accelerated, until at one point in 1864 it required $285 in paper to purchase $100 in gold. The distrust of the Government's fiat paper was also maintained by the snowballing national debt, which reached its high-point of the war - $ 2.8 billion - in 1865.

A monetary situation whereby gold commanded a substantial premium over a like face value of paper dollars swiftly drove gold coins from commercial channels, effectively removing the United States from a gold standard. It also created a favorable condition for the exporting of silver coins, which disappeared from the marketplace, but at a less precipitous pace than gold.

In 1858 Canada had adopted a decimal system of coinage with a dollar unit similar to that of the United States. In lieu of a sufficient quantity of decimal coinage of British origin, Canada unofficially adopted the coinage of the United States and used it widely in domestic trade. The West Indies and many Latin American countries also imported large quantities of U.S. silver coinage for domestic use. Disappearance of gold from American trade channels and the willingness of foreign users of U.S. silver coins to pay for them with gold combined to produce a legal and highly profitable bullion trade which speculators and bankers found irresistible.

The discounting of Greenbacks in terms of gold enabled the exchange of paper money for silver coins, which were then exchanged for gold in Canada, the West Indies or Latin America. The gold was then returned to the United States, where it was used to purchase more Greenbacks at the metal's high premium rate. A safer round-robin to riches can hardly be imagined. Even in times of national crisis, pragmatic profit taking will attract more adherents than an idealistic consideration for the national good. During the last week of June and the first week of July, 1862, more than $25 million in subsidiary coins vanished from circulation in the North. The shortage of silver coins, particularly in the eastern United States, would not be relieved until the summer of 1876.

Illogically, the Philadelphia Mint continued a small but steady production of silver coins during the 1861 Although they were of no use to the nation's economy. Bullion dealers obtained them directly from the Mint and . sped them abroad. In 1863, nearly the entire production of silver coins was exported.

The withdrawal of subsidiary silver coins in the summer of 1862 all but paralyzed the institutions and practice of everyday commerce. The smallest denominations of official money available were discounted $5 Legal Tender Notes and the copper-nickel cents which had been fed into circulation in great quantities to retire demonetized Spanish silver coins and the large copper cents.

When first forced upon the public in 1857, the copper-nickel cent, which was intrinsically worth about 60 percent of face value, had been considered a nuisance; it was regularly discounted three percent and more in large transactions. But with the disappearance of silver coins, the ugly duckling became the belle of the ball. The erstwhile nuisance became the only alternative to walking, or going without a newspaper, or buying a pound of pomegranates and receiving change in kumquats and quince. Cents were bundled in bags of 25, 50 and 100 in a hopeless attempt to bridge the gap between the 1-cent piece and the $5 bill. By March 1863, the lowly cent commanded a premium of 20 percent, but few could be found.

The disappearance of nearly all official coinage from trade channels resulted in an outpouring of private emergency monies, some hoary with tradition, others as new and untried as the inspiration which gave them form. State bank notes of $1 and $2 denominations were cut into fractional parts. Other banks issued notes in denominations of $1.25, $1.50 and $1.75. Eastern cities issued their own fractional notes. Merchants, reviving a practice prevalent during the coin shortages of 1837 and 1857, made change in their own promissory notes or "shinplasters," which were notes of small value, redeemable in merchandise at the issuer's place of business. Unscrupulous merchants made change with their own notes even when they had sufficient specie on hand, knowing that the notes were not likely to be presented for redemption by other than their regular neighborhood customers. In like manner, private issues of the eminently collectible Civil War tokens began.

Most novel of the emergency monies called into use was the common postage stamp. The use of postage stamps as a low denomination medium of exchange was not a success, but it led directly to the issuing of the highly successful Postage and Fractional Currency series.

First issued by the Federal Government in 1847, by the time the Civil War began, the adhesive postage stamp had become a well-established part of the public routine. Inasmuch as they were of official origin, had a constant value throughout the country and were easily obtained, consideration of postage stamps as a medium of exchange for coin-deprived people was inevitable. In early July, 1862, Horace Greeley, publisher of the politically influential *New York Tribune,* suggested that stamps pasted on a half sheet of paper, with the other half folded over the stamps to afford them protection from wear, would make an excellent coin substitute. Other newspapers quickly endorsed the proposal, as did the coin-starved public.

Although there were surely those who attempted to do so, fragile, gummed stamps could not be carried loose in pocket or purse without soon becoming a crumpled, stuck-together, totally useless blob of colored paper.

Methods of affording the stamps a degree of protection were quickly devised. They were pasted on sheets of light vellum paper – with or without a protective flap – which also bore an advertising message and a large numeral indicating the total face value of the stamps. Stamps were also encased in small envelopes, on the outside of which was printed the value of the contents and an advertising message.

It soon became apparent that both methods of preparing stamps for the role of emergency money had as many drawbacks as advantages. Pasting the stamps on sheets of paper did not provide them sufficient protection from wear. Those enclosed in envelopes were better protected, but the method of protection provided an opportunity for petty larceny which wasn't neglected. Few recipients had the time to check the contents of each envelope to determine if it contained the proper denominational total of stamps, or if the stamps were unused, or if rectangles of colored paper had been substituted for the stamps.

The method of stamp packaging which best satisfied the dual requirements of visibility and protection was patented on Aug. 12, 1862, by a New England inventor named John Gault, who encased a single postage stamp in a round brass frame (25 mm in diameter) with a clear mica front piece through which the stamp could be viewed. The reverse of this case bore the advertising message of the participating merchant who purchased a quantity of Gault's "encased postage stamps" as a means of giving his customers the precise change required by their purchases.

Stamps encased by Gault were the 1-, 3-, 5-, 10-, 12-, 24-, 30-, and 90-cent denominations of the Series of 1861-1869. That series also contains a 2-cent and a 15-cent stamp, but the 2-cent stamp wasn't issued until July 6, 1863, and the 15-cent value came along on June 17, 1866. But for the eventual authorization of Postage and Fractional Currency, Gault's encased postage stamps would probably have become the chief means of "spending" postage stamps, although they, too, had their disadvantages. The protective mica shield was easily cracked, and the encased stamps cost the distributing merchant the face value of the stamps, plus about two cents per holder. In view of the 20 percent premium existing on official coins, the additional two cents was of little consequence in the instance of the higher denomination stamps, but in the case of the popular one-cent stamp, it meant an expenditure of three cents for every one-cent encased postage stamp obtained from Gault for monetary use.

The timing of the initiation of Gault's encased stamps also worked against their quantity distribution. At the time of their appearance in midsummer of 1862, the Postmaster General, Montgomery Blair, was still not reconciled to the idea of using postage stamps for money, and was doing his utmost to prevent quantity sales of stamps to anyone desiring them for coinage purposes.

All methods of using stamps for money that had been employed prior to July 17, 1862, suffered the ultimate disadvantage of being illegal, with the consequence that the holder of the stamps could neither redeem them at the post office nor exchange them for Treasury notes.

On that date, however, President Lincoln signed into law a measure proposed in self-defense by Treasury Secretary Salmon P. Chase, providing that "postage and other stamps of the United States" were to be received for all dues to the U.S. and were to be redeemable at any "designated depository" in sums less than $5. The law also prohibited the issue by "any private corporation, banking association, firm, or individual" of any note or token for a sum less than $5 – a provision that was widely ignored as the private sector continued its efforts to overcome a coin shortage in the face of which the Government seemed helpless.

The new law was not without its problems of practicality, either. The post office, already facing a stamp shortage before the gummed bits of paper had been declared legal tender, now had the almost impossible task of providing sufficient stamps for postal use as well as "coinage" use.

In addition, there was the problem of who would redeem nearly exhausted specimens of stamps which had been circulating for some time. Blair refused to take them in trade for new stamps and the Treasury would not exchange them for paper money because they hadn't issued them in the first place.

Blair's obstinacy ultimately melted before the heat of public pressure, and he agreed to redeem the masses of soiled and stuck-together stamps, but he continued to insist that the actual intent of the poorly-written law had been for the Treasury Department to print and distribute special stamps that would bear a general resemblance to postage stamps, but would be of a different design. A compromise was finally worked out whereby the Treasury Department would sell and redeem specially marked stamps which the post office would also accept for postage. Blair agreed to print the special stamps for the Treasury.

Before the stamps could be printed, a further decision was made to issue them in a larger, more convenient size, and to print them on a heavier, ungummed paper. Credit for the final form in which Postage Currency appeared is given to Gen. Francis Spinner, Treasurer of the United States. Spinner pasted unused postage stamps on small sheets of Treasury security paper of uniform size, signed his name to some of them and passed them out to his friends as samples of currency. Congress responded to Spinner's suggestion by authorizing the printing of reproductions of postage stamps on Treasury paper in arrangements patterned after Spinner's models. In this form, the "stamps" ceased to be stamps; they became, in effect, fractional Government promissory notes, a development not authorized by the initial enabling legislation of July 17, 1862. Nonetheless, the notes would be issued without legal authorization until passage of the Act of March 3, 1863, which provided for the issuing of fractional notes by the Federal Government.

Five issues of Postage and Fractional Currency in the total amount of $369 million were printed and released to circulation between Aug. 21, 1862, and Feb. 15, 1876, when a flood of silver from the Comstock Lode drove down silver bullion prices, reducing the intrinsic value of silver coins to a point below face, value, thereby insuring that they would remain in circulation. The silver price drop further augmented the supply of circulating silver by triggering a flow back to the United States – where they could be exchanged for their greater face value - of the hundreds of millions of silver coins which had been exported to Canada, the West Indies and Latin America since 1862.

Congressional Acts of Jan. 14, 1875, and April 17, 1876, provided for the redemption of Postage and Fractional Currency in silver coins, and all but about $1.8 million worth was returned to the Treasury for redemption. The outstanding notes remain legal tender and can purchase their face value equivalent in goods and services today.

FIRST ISSUE
August 2, 1862 - May 27,063
Denominations: 5¢, 10¢, 25¢, 50¢

The First Issue of U.S. Government stamp money is the only one of the five issues to be identified by name as Postage Currency. The initial printing of the First Issue was released through Army paymasters on Aug. 1, 1862, and was provided for general circulation a few weeks later.

Although it is a moot point, Postage Currency probably constitutes an illegal issue of fractional notes. Rather than being strictly "postage and other stamps of the United States," and despite being "receivable for postage stamps at any U.S. post office," Postage Currency took the form of reproductions of postage stamps printed on paper which carried the promise of the United States to exchange the currency for United States Notes, which gave Postage Currency the attributes of a promissory note, a development beyond the intent of the enabling Act of July 17, 1862.

The stamps reproduce on Postage Currency are the brown (sometimes buff) five-cent stamp of the Series of 1861, bearing the portrait of Thomas Jefferson, and the green ten-cent stamp of the same series, with George Washington's portrait. The 25- and 50-cent denominations bear multiple reproductions of the appropriate stamp. Various colors of paper were used in printing the four notes of the First Issue, but the color does not influence the collector value of the individual note. Faces of the notes are printed in a color approximating the color of the genuine postage stamp, backs are all printed in black.

An interesting feature of the First Issue is the existence of notes with both perforated and straight edges. Apparently, the idea of perforated Postage Currency was a carry-over from the postage stamp printing process and was discarded when the demand for Postage Currency exceeded the capacity of the perforating machines.

Inasmuch as the Bureau of Engraving and Printing had not yet been established, contracts for printing of the First Issue were awarded to private bank note printing companies. The National Bank Note Company printed the face, the American Bank Note Company, the back. The ABNC monogram appears on the backs of some notes.

Total value of Postage Currency issued was more than $20 million.

SECOND ISSUE
October 10, 1863 - February 23, 1867
Denominations: 5¢, 10¢, 25¢, 50¢

The Second Issue of a fractional currency, authorized by Congress on March 3, 1863, all but discarded the concept of postage stamp money. Notes continued to be "receivable for all United States postage stamps," but the identity of the notes was changed from Postage Currency to Fractional Currency, and the notes of the Second Issue did not bear a reproduction of a postage stamp, although the portrait of George Washington on all notes of this issue is the same as that appearing on the 24-cent stamp of the Series of 1861. The Second Issue was made necessary by the ease with which notes of the First Issue had been counterfeited.

All Second Issue notes have a slate-colored face with bronze oval surcharge centered on the portrait of Washington. Back of the 5-cent note is brown; the 10-cent, green; the 25-cent, violet, and the 50-cent note, red or reddish-orange. All backs have a large, bronze numerical outline overprinted.

Some specimen notes of this issue (and of the Third Issue) were printed on paper watermarked "C.S.A." in block letters, for Confederate States of America. The paper, made in England for the printing of Confederate States paper money, was contraband seized from a captured blockade runner.

First Issue notes had been printed by the National Bank Note Company and the American Bank Note Company both of New York - which were one concern in all respects but name - at a cost which the Treasury Department thought excessive. The Act of July 11, 1863, instructed the Treasury Department to undertake the printing of its own currency.

Although the primary purpose of Second Issue notes was to retire and replace First Issue notes, they were issued in excess of the requirement, to a total value of $23 million.

THIRD ISSUE
December 5, 1864 - August 16, 1869
Denominations: 3¢, 5¢, 10¢, (15¢ essay), 25¢, 50¢

Authorized by the Act of June 30, 1864, the Third Issue of Fractional Currency was necessitated by an increased demand for the low denomination notes and by the continuing counterfeiting of earlier issues. Counterfeits of the Second Issue were of better quality and even more numerous than those of the First Issue had been.

Third Issue notes provide the greatest number of varieties of any issue of Postage or Fractional Currency. Among these are varieties of paper, different colors of backs, ornamental and numerical value surcharges (or none at all), autographed or printed signatures, no signatures, and multiple designs for a single denomination.

In regard to varieties, the 10-cent note is particularly interesting. Through an oversight, the word CENTS does not appear anywhere on the note. The Third Issue varieties are too extensive to be within the scope of these remarks, but they are indicated and priced in the listing which follows.

The Act of June 30, 1864, contained a provision which, by amending the Act of March 3, 1863, authorized the Secretary of the Treasury to determine the form and denominations of Fractional Currency, the means by which it would be made, and the terms of note redemption. This authority permitted Secretary Chase to issue a 3-cent note to facilitate purchase of the new 3-cent first-class postage stamp. Need for the small note was eventually eliminated by the issue of nickel three-cent coins under the Act of March 3, 1865.

Little events can have lasting repercussions, as exemplified by the story of the 5-cent note of the Third Issue. Without the knowledge or authority of his superiors, Spencer M. Clark, then superintendent of the National Currency Bureau, had his likeness put on the 5-cent note of the Third Issue. Clark's presumptive act so angered Congress that a law was enacted April 7, 1866, prohibiting the placing of the likeness of a living person upon any "bonds, securities, notes, Fractional or Postal Currency of the United States." However, the wording of the law did not prohibit the likeness of a living person if the plate for the intended item had already been prepared.

Consequently, Clark's portrait didn't disappear from the nation's currency until the passage of May 17, 1866, legislation which authorized the issue of a nickel 5-cent piece and prohibited the issue of any note with a denomination of less than 10 cents.

Likewise unaffected were the Third Issue 25-cent note bearing the portrait of William Fessenden, and the 50-cent note portraying Francis E. Spinner, "The Father of Fractional Currency." The only note affected by the legislation was a proposed 15-cent denomination bearing the portraits of Generals Grant and Sherman, for which the plate had not yet been completed. This note was printed only as an essay, and in uniface form, with face and back being printed on separate pieces of paper.

All of the Third Issue notes were produced by the Treasury Department. Total face value was in excess of $86 million.

POSTAGE AND FRACTIONAL CURRENCY SHIELD

The Postage and Fractional Currency Shield was one of the measures by which the Treasury Department sought to overcome and prevent the wide-spread counterfeiting of Fractional Currency notes.

The shields consisted of a type set of the first three issues of Postage and Fractional Currency mounted on a heavy cardboard shield surmounted by an eagle and 13 stars. Size of the framed unit was 24 by 28 inches. The shields were made available to banks and other commercial institutions in 1866-67 to provide them with a file of genuine notes to use as a reference when checking suspect notes. Those qualified to receive the shield paid face value for the notes ($4.66), plus a presumed transportation charge, for a total cost believed to be $7.50.

The 39 closely-trimmed notes (20 faces and 19 backs) mounted on the shield are specimen notes printed on one side only. They include the scarce 15-cent Sherman/Grant essays and the two faces of the 3-cent note, which are distinguished by dark and light backgrounds to Washington's portrait. The shields upon which the notes were pasted are known in gray, pink and green, with gray being the most common.

Although the shields were produced in a quantity believed to be in excess of 4,500, it is presumed that fewer than 200 remain intact, with many of those folded, faded or water-stained. Apparently demand for the shields was less than the Treasury Department had anticipated and the surplus shields were carelessly stored - by common account in an old shed behind the Treasury Building. The number of intact shields was further reduced by early collectors who obtained them solely to secure the scarcer notes, which they removed from the shield.

FOURTH ISSUE
July 14, 1869 - February 16, 1875
Denominations: 10¢, 15¢, 25¢, 50¢

The Fourth Issue of Fractional Currency continued the refinements evident in the Second and Third Issues, and further diminished the pretense of stamp money with which the five issues of fractional notes were launched. The unaesthetic bronze overprintings were eliminated, and an improved type of paper - containing silk fibers – was used.

Three of the six designs (there are three different 50-cent notes) comprising the Fourth Issue make no mention of "stamps." Allegorical art claimed a greater role in note design than before; the 10-cent note bearing a representation of Liberty, and the 15-cent note, a representation of Columbia. The 25-cent and the trio of 50-cent notes bear definitive male portraits.

The Fourth Issue was produced outside the Treasury Department while the Bureau of Engraving and Printing experimented with new dry-printing operations that only succeeded in destroying nearly every hydraulic press the Government owned. Combined with increased demand for Legal Tender notes, the Treasury was forced to job out the production of the Fourth Issue Fractionals to the National and American Bank Note Companies

The total value of the Fourth Issue was more than $166 million.

FIFTH ISSUE
February 26, 1874 - February 15, 1876
Denominations: 10¢, 25¢, 50¢

The Fifth Issue of Fractional Currency was short and simple, consisting of but three notes, each of a different design. Why a change of design was thought necessary at that time is unclear, but the decision may reflect the Treasury Department's continuing disenchantment with the cost of notes produced by the two New York bank note firms.

Faces of the Fifth Issue were printed by the Bureau of Engraving and Printing, the backs by the Columbian Bank Note Company of Washington, D.C., and Joseph R. Carpenter of Philadelphia. Printing of this issue was terminated when the appropriations for the printing of Fractional Currency were exhausted.

Noteworthy varieties of the Fifth Issue include the green seal 10-cent note and the "long key" and "short key" 10- and 25-cent notes. All notes have faces printed in black, with green backs. All carry printed signatures.

Fifth Issue notes were printed to the total value of nearly $63 million, bringing the total value of all Postage and Fractional Currency issued to about $369 million, of which an estimated $1.8 million remains outstanding.

FIRST ISSUE "POSTAGE CURRENCY"

5 Cents

All notes have oval bronze ovpt. on face around head of Washington at center and large bronze outlined denomination numeral(s) on back.

KL#	Fr#	Date Description	Fine	XF	CU
3209	1228	17.7.1862. Brown. Perforated edges. Face, One 5 cent Jefferson stamp at center flanked by 5's. Back, Large 5 at center with ABNC's monogram.	45.00	125.	300.
3210	1229	Perforated edges. Face, One 5 cent Jefferson stamp at center flanked by 5's. Back, Large 5 at center without ABNC's monogram.	50.00	150.	325.
3211	1230	Straight edges. Face, One 5 cent Jefferson stamp at center flanked by 5's. Back, Large 5 at center with ABNC's monogram.	30.00	45.00	110.
3212	1231	Straight edges. Face, One 5 cent Jefferson stamp at center flanked by 5's. Back, Large 5 at center without ABNC's monogram.	50.00	150.	450.

10 Cents

KL#	Fr#	Date Description	Fine	XF	CU
3213	1240	17.7.1862. Green. Perforated edges. Face, One 10 cent Washington stamp at center flanked by 10's. Back, Large 10 at center with ABNC's monogram.	70.00	150.	375.
3214	1241	Perforated edges. Face, One 10 cent Washington stamp at center flanked by 10's. Back, Large 10 at center without ABNC's monogram.	75.00	200.	450.
3215	1242	Straight edges. Face, One 10 cent Washington stamp at center flanked by 10's. Back, Large 10 at center with ABNC's monogram.	30.00	70.00	115.
3216	1243	Straight edges. Face, One 10 cent Washington stamp at center flanked by 10's. Back, Large 10 at center without ABNC's monogram.	100.00	250.	400.

25 Cents

KL#	Fr#	Date	Description	Fine	XF	CU
3217	1279	17.7.1862. Brown. Perforated edges. Face, Horizontal row of five 5 cent Jefferson stamps. Back, Large 25 at center with ABNC's monogram.	60.00	125.	325.
3218	1280	Perforated edges. Face, Horizontal row of five 5 cent Jefferson stamps. Back, Large 25 at center without ABNC's monogram.	90.00	200.	425.
3219	1281	Straight edges. Face, Horizontal row of five 5 cent Jefferson stamps. Back, Large 25 at center with ABNC's monogram.	35.00	70.00	200.
3220	1282	Straight edges. Face, Horizontal row of five 5 cent Jefferson stamps. Back, Large 25 at center without ABNC's monogram.	100.	200.	600.

50 Cents

The brown seal was believed to have been caused by the sizing chemicals in the early stages of printing and must be between a rich chocolate brown to a rich purple brown.

KL#	Fr#	Date	Description	Fine	XF	CU
3221	1310	17.7.1862. Green. #12 perforated edges. Face, Horizontal row of five 10 cent Washington stamps. Back, Large 50 at center with ABNC's monogram.	70.00	200.	400.
3222	1310A	#14 perforated edges. Face, Horizontal row of five 10 cent Washington stamps. Back, Large 50 at center with ABNC's monogram.	—	—	—
3223	1311	Perforated edges. Face, Horizontal row of five 10 cent Washington stamps. Back, Large 50 at center without ABNC's monogram.	100.	300.	550.
3224	1312	Straight edges. Face, Horizontal row of five 10 cent Washington stamps. Back, Large 50 at center with ABNC's monogram.	45.00	80.00	200.
3225	1313	Straight edges. Face, Horizontal row of five 10 cent Washington stamps. Back, Large 50 at center without ABNC's monogram.	150.	400.	700.

SECOND ISSUE

5 Cents

*All notes have oval bronze ovpt. on face around head of Washington
at center and large bronze outlined denomination numeral(s) on back.*

KL#	Fr#	Date	Description	Fine	XF	CU
3226	1232	3.3.1863.	Face, George Washington at center flanked by 5's. Back, Large outlined 5 over smaller 5 on shield without overprint.	20.00	45.00	100.
3227	1233		Face, George Washington at center flanked by 5's. Back, Large outlined 5 over smaller 5 on shield with overprint: "18—63".	35.00	75.00	150.
3228	1234		Face, George Washington at center flanked by 5's. Back, Large outlined 5 over smaller 5 on shield with overprint: "18—63" and "S".	45.00	100.	200.
3229	1235		Fiber paper. Face, George Washington at center flanked by 5's. Back, Large outlined 5 over smaller 5 on shield with overprint: "18—63" and "R—1".	125.	275.	650.

10 Cents

KL#	Fr#	Date	Description	Fine	XF	CU
3230	1244		Face, George Washington at center flanked by 10's. Back, Large outlined 10 over smaller 10 on shield without overprint.	25.00	45.00	110.
3231	1245		Face, George Washington at center flanked by 10's. Back, Large outlined 10 over smaller 10 on shield with overprint: "18—63".	35.00	75.00	150.
3232	1246		Face, George Washington at center flanked by 10's. Back, Large outlined 10 over smaller 10 on shield with overprint: "18—63" and "S".	40.00	100.	225.
3233	1247		Face, George Washington at center flanked by 10's. Back, Large outlined 10 over smaller 10 on shield with overprint: "18—63" and "1".	60.00	175.	275.

KL#	Fr#	Date	Description	Fine	XF	CU
3234	1248		Face, George Washington at center flanked by 10's. Back, Large outlined 10 over smaller 10 on shield with overprint: "0—63".	700.	1350.	2500.
3235	1249		Fiber paper. Face, George Washington at center flanked by 10's. Back, Large outlined 10 over smaller 10 on shield with overprint: "18—63" and "T—1".	100.	220.	550.

25 Cents

KL#	Fr#	Date	Description	Fine	XF	CU
3236	1283	3.3.1863.	Face, George Washington at center flanked by 25's. Back, Large outlined 25 over smaller 25 on shield without overprint.	35.00	70.00	225.
3237	1284		Face, George Washington at center flanked by 25's. Back, Large outlined 25 over smaller 25 on shield with overprint: "18—63".	40.00	100.	275.
3238	1285		Face, George Washington at center flanked by 25's. Back, Large outlined 25 over smaller 25 on shield with overprint: "18—63"and "A".	35.00	90.00	200.
3239	1286		Face, George Washington at center flanked by 25's. Back, Large outlined 25 over smaller 25 on shield with overprint: "18—63" and "S".	35.00	90.00	250.
3240	—		Face, George Washington at center flanked by 25's. Back, Large outlined 25 over smaller 25 on shield with overprint: "18—63" and "1". Reported, not confirmed	—	—	—
3241	1288		Face, George Washington at center flanked by 25's. Back, Large outlined 25 over smaller 25 on shield with overprint: "18—63" and "2".	65.00	125.	300.
3242	1289		Fiber paper. Face, George Washington at center flanked by 25's. Back, Large outlined 25 over smaller 25 on shield with overprint: "18—63" and "T—1".	100.	200.	525.
3243	1290		Fiber paper. Face, George Washington at center flanked by 25's. Back, Large outlined 25 over smaller 25 on shield with overprint: "18—63" and "T—2".	80.00	175.	475.
3244	—		Face, George Washington at center flanked by 25's. Back, Large outlined 25 over smaller 25 on shield with overprint: "18—63" and "S—2". Reported, not confirmed	—	—	—

50 Cents

The brown seal was believed to have been caused by the sizing chemicals in the
early stages of printing and must be between a rich chocolate brown to a rich purple brown.

KL#	Fr#	Date	Description	Fine	XF	CU
3245	1316	3.3.1863. Face, George Washington at center flanked by 50's. Back, Large outlined 50 over smaller 50 on shield with overprint: "18—63".	50.00	100.	275.
3246	1317	Face, George Washington at center flanked by 50's. Back, Large outlined 50 over smaller 50 on shield with overprint: "18—63" and "A".	50.00	100.	300.
3247	1318	Face, George Washington at center flanked by 50's. Back, Large outlined 50 over smaller 50 on shield with overprint: "18—63" and "I".	45.00	100.	275.
3248	1320	Fiber paper. Face, George Washington at center flanked by 50's. Back, Large outlined 50 over smaller 50 on shield with overprint: "18—63" and "0—1".	90.00	225.	400.
3249	1321	Fiber paper. Face, George Washington at center flanked by 50's. Back, Large outlined 50 over smaller 50 on shield with overprint: "18—63" and "R—2".	100.	225.	375.
3250	1322	Fiber paper. Face, George Washington at center flanked by 50's. Back, Large outlined 50 over smaller 50 on shield with overprint: "18—63" and "T—1".	100.	200.	400.

THIRD ISSUE

3 Cents

KL#	Fr#	Date	Description	Fine	XF	CU
3252	1226	3.3.1863. Face, Portrait of Washington at center with light background. Back, Large 3 at center.	50.00	100.	150.
3253	1227	Face, Portrait of Washington at center with dark background. Back, Large 3 at center.	80.00	150.	275.

5 Cents

KL#	Fr#	Date	Description	Fine	XF	CU
3254	1236	3.3.1863. Red back. Face, Portrait of Clark at center. Back, 5 in each corner.	45.00	100.	250.
3255	1237		Red back. Face, Portrait of Clark at center with "a". Back, 5 in each corner.	50.00	125.	400.
3256	1238		Green back. Face, Portrait of Clark at center. Back, 5 in each corner.	35.00	80.00	150.
3257	1239		Green back. Face, Portrait of Clark at center with "a". Back, 5 in each corner.	40.00	90.00	175.

10 Cents

KL#	Fr#	Date	Description	Fine	XF	CU
3258	1251	3.3.1863. Small signature. Red back. Face, Portrait of Washington at center; bronze 10's in each corner. Back, Large outlined 10 at center.		45.00	100.	225.
3259	1252		Red back. Face, Portrait of Washington at center with one "1"; bronze 10's in each corner. Back, Large outlined 10 at center.	50.00	125.	375.
3260	1253		Large autographed signature. Face, Portrait of Washington at center; bronze 10's in each corner. Back, Large outlined 10 at center.	85.00	175.	275.
3261	1254		Large autographed signature. Face, Portrait of Washington at center; bronze 10's in each corner. Back, Large outlined 10 at center.	100.	200.	425.
3262	1255		Green back. Printed signature. Face, Portrait of Washington at center; bronze 10's in each corner. Back, Large outlined 10 at center.	25.00	50.00	100.
3263	1255A		Green back. Large autographed signature. Face, Portrait of Washington at center; bronze 10's in each corner. Back, Large outlined 10 at center.	—	—	125,000.
3264	1256		Large printed. Green back. Face, Portrait of Washington at center with one "1"; bronze 10's in each corner. Back, Large outlined 10 at center.	35.00	75.00	175.

25 Cents

KL#	Fr#	Date	Description	Fine	XF	CU
3265	1291		3.3.1863. Red back. (No "a"). Face, Portrait of Fessenden at center. Back, Large outlined 25 at center.	45.00	120.	275.
3266	1292		Red back. Face, Portrait of Fessenden at center with small "a". Back, Large outlined 25 at center.	60.00	155.	300.
3268	1294		Green back. (No "a"). Face, Portrait of Fessenden at center. Back, Large outlined 25 at center.	35.00	70.00	150.
3269	1295		Green back. Face, Portrait of Fessenden at center with small "a". Back, Large outlined 25 at center.	40.00	100.	200.
3270	1296		Green back. "a" is 7mm to the right and down from normal location. (Very large "a"). Face, Portrait of Fessenden at center with large "a". Back, Large outlined 25 at center.	1000.	2000.	3500.
3271	1297		Fiber paper. Face, Portrait of Fessenden at center. Back, Large outlined 25 at center with overprint: "M—2—6—5".	55.00	125.	450.
3272	1298		Fiber paper. Face, Portrait of Fessenden at center with "a". Back, Large outlined 25 at center with overprint: "M—2—6—5".	70.00	150.	650.
3273	1299		Fiber paper. Face, Portrait of Fessenden at center with solid bronze ornamental overprint. Back, Large outlined 25 at center.	700.	1400.	2100.
3274	1300		Fiber paper. Face, Portrait of Fessenden at center with solid bronze ornamental overprint and "a". Back, Large outlined 25 at center.	2000.	3500.	5900.

50 Cents

KL#	Fr#	Date Description	Fine	XF	CU
3275	1324	3.3.1863. Small printed signature. Red back. Face, Portrait of General Spinner at center. Back, Large 50 at ends with overprint: "A—2—6—5" and 50.	75.00	170.	400.
3276	1325	Printed signature. Red back. Face, Portrait of General Spinner at center with "1" and "a". Back, Large 50 at ends.	250.	500.	950.
3277	1326	Printed signature. Red back. Face, Portrait of General Spinner at center with "1". Back, Large 50 at ends.	85.00	200.	325.
3278	1327	Printed signature. Red back. Face, Portrait of General Spinner at center with "a". Back, Large 50 at ends.	85.00	200.	400.
3279	1328	Large autograph signature. Red back. Face, Portrait of General Spinner at center. Back, Large 50 at ends.	90.00	200.	500.
3281	1329	Autograph signature. Red back. Face, Portrait of General Spinner at center. Back, Large 50 at ends.	125.	300.	700.
3282	1330	Autograph signature. Red back. Face, Portrait of General Spinner at center. Back, Large 50 at ends.	1250.	2500.	4500.
3283	1331	Green back. Face, Portrait of General Spinner at center. Back, Multiple 50's.	65.00	125.	275.
3284	1332	Green back. Face, Portrait of General Spinner at center with "1" and "a". Back, Multiple 50's.	70.00	175.	425.
3285	1333	Green back. Face, Portrait of General Spinner at center with "1". Back, Multiple 50's.	60.00	140.	300.
3286	1334	Green back. Face, Portrait of General Spinner at center with "a". Back, Multiple 50's.	55.00	110.	375.
3287	1335	Green back. Face, Portrait of General Spinner at center. Back, Multiple 50's with overprint: "A—2—6—5".	55.00	125.	400.
3288	1336	Green back. Face, Portrait of General Spinner at center with "1" and "a". Back, Multiple 50's.	750.	2500.	3500.
3289	1337	Green back. Face, Portrait of General Spinner at center with "1". Back, Multiple 50's.	100.	250.	650.
3290	1338	Green back. Face, Portrait of General Spinner at center with "a". Back, Multiple 50's.	80.00	200.	550.
3291	1339	Redesigned green back. Face, Portrait of General Spinner at center.	70.00	155.	325.
3292	1340	Redesigned green back. Face, Portrait of General Spinner at center with "1" and "a".	125.	300.	900.

KL#	Fr#	Date	Description	Fine	XF	CU
3293	1341		Redesigned green back. Face, Portrait of General Spinner at center with "1".	70.00	175.	375.
3294	1342		Redesigned green back. Face, Portrait of General Spinner at center with "a".	80.00	225.	450.
3295	1343	3.3.1863.	Red back. Small printed signature. Face, Justice seated at center.	100.	200.	450.
3296	1344		Printed signature. Red back. Face, Justice seated at center with "1" and "a".	700.	1200.	3500.
3297	1345		Printed signature. Red back. Face, Justice seated at center with "1".	100.	200.	450.
3298	1346		Printed signature. Red back. Face, Justice seated at center with "a".	100.	200.	500.

KL#	Fr#	Date	Description	Fine	XF	CU
3299	1347		Red back. Face, Justice seated at center. Back, Overprint: "A—2—6—5".	100.	200.	475.
3300	1348		Red back. Face, Justice seated at center with "1" and "a".	700.	1500.	2750.
3301	1349		Red back. Face, Justice seated at center with "1".	150.	400.	600.
3302	1350		Red back. Face, Justice seated at center with "a".	175.	400.	700.
3303	1351		Red back. Fiber paper. Small printed signature. Face, Justice seated at center. Back, Overprint: "S—2—6—4".	5000.	10,000.	19,000.
3304	1352		Red back. Fiber paper. Only 3 known. CAA 5/7/05 Fine $32,000. Stack's 5/04 AU $115,000. Face, Justice seated at center with "1" and "a".	30,000	70,000.	100,000.
3305	1353		Red back. Fiber paper. CAA 5/7/05 O'Mara Sale AU $15,000. Face, Justice seated at center with "1".	6000.	12,900.	21,000.
3306	1354		Red back. Fiber paper. CAA 5/7/05 O'Mara Sale AU $20,000. Face, Justice seated at center with "a".	8000.	16,000.	28,500.
3307	1355		Red back. Large autographed signature. Face, Justice seated at center.	125.	250.	450.
3308	1356		Large autographed signature. Red back. Face, Justice seated at center. Back, Overprint: "A—2—6—5".	150.	300.	575.
3309	1357		Large autographed signature. Fiber paper. Red back. Face, Justice seated at center. Back, Overprint: "S—2—6—4".	400.	800.	2000.
3310	1358		Green back. Face, Justice seated at center.	100.	200.	400.
3311	1359		Green back. Face, Justice seated at center with "1" and "a".	650.	1400.	2300.
3312	1360		Green back. Face, Justice seated at center with "1".	85.00	200.	475.
3313	1361		Green back. Face, Justice seated at center with "a".	95.00	225.	525.
3314	1362		Green back. Face, Justice seated at center. Back, Overprint: "A—2—6—5" compactly spaced. (92mm x 30mm).	95.00	225.	450.

KL#	Fr#	Date	Description	Fine	XF	CU
3315	1363		Green back. Face, Justice seated at center with "1" and "a". Back, Overprint: "A—2—6—5" compactly spaced. (92mm x 30mm).	200.	425.	750.
3316	1364		Green back. Face, Justice seated at center with "1". Back, Overprint: "A—2—6—5" compactly spaced. (92mm x 30mm).	90.00	175.	500.
3317	1365		Green back. Face, Justice seated at center with "a". Back, Overprint: "A—2—6—5" compactly spaced. (92mm x 30mm).	100.	200.	525.
3318	1366		Green back. Face, Justice seated at center. Back, Overprint: "A—2—6—5" widely spaced (98mm x 34mm).	150.	300.	550.
3319	1367		Green back. Face, Justice seated at center with "1" and "a". Back, Overprint: "A—2—6—5" widely spaced (98mm x 34mm).	1200.	2000.	5000.
3320	1368		Green back. Face, Justice seated at center with "1". Back, Overprint: "A—2—6—5" widely spaced (98mm x 34mm).	250.	500.	900.
3321	1369		Green back. Face, Justice seated at center with "a". Back, Overprint: "A—2—6—5" widely spaced (98mm x 34mm)	300.	650.	900.
3322	1370		Fiber paper. Green back. Face, Justice seated at center. Back, Overprint: "A—2—6—5".	175.	375.	750.
3323	1371		Fiber paper. Green back. Face, Justice seated at center with "1" and "a". Back, Overprint: "A—2—6—5".	1200.	2000.	4500.
3324	1372		Fiber paper. Green back. Face, Justice seated at center with "1". Back, Overprint: "A—2—6—5".	185.	400.	900.
3325	1373		Fiber paper. Green back. Face, Justice seated at center with "a". Back, Overprint: "A—2—6—5".	190.	425.	925.
3326	1373A		Fiber paper. Green back. CAA O'Mara Sale 5/7/05 AU $46,000. Face, Justice seated at center. Back, Overprint: "S—2—6—4".	—	46,000.	

FOURTH ISSUE

10 Cents

KL#	Fr#	Date	Description	Fine	XF	CU
3327	1257	3.3.1863.	Watermarked paper with pink silk fibers Face, Bust of Liberty at left; 40mm red seal. Back, Large 10 at left and right.	30.00	75.00	150.
3328	1258		Unwatermarked paper with pink silk fibers. Face, Bust of Liberty at left. Back, Large 10 at left and right.	35.00	100.	175.
3329	1259		Paper with violet silk fibers. Face, Bust of Liberty at left with bluish right side of face. Back, Large 10 at left and right.	30.00	75.00	145.
3331	1261		Face, Bust of Liberty at left; 38mm red seal; bluish right side of face. Back, Large 10 at left and right.	40.00	100.	175.

15 Cents

KL#	Fr#	Date	Description	Fine	XF	CU
3332	1267	3.3.1863. Watermarked paper with pink silk fibers. Face, Bust of Columbia at left; 40mm red seal. Back, Large 15 at left and right.	60.00	125.	250.
3333	1268	Unwatermarked paper with pink silk fibers. Face, Bust of Columbia at left. Back, Large 15 at left and right.	350.	700.	1200.
3334	1269	Paper with violet silk fibers. Face, Bust of Columbia with bluish right side of face. Back, Large 15 at left and right.	65.00	100.	250.
3336	1271	Face, Bust of Columbia at left. 38mm red seal; bluish right side of face. Back, Large 15 at left and right.	70.00	125.	250.

25 Cents

KL#	Fr#	Date	Description	Fine	XF	CU
3337	1301	3.3.1863. Watermarked paper with pink silk fibers. Face, Portrait of Washington at left; 40mm red seal.	35.00	75.00	175.
3338	1302	Unwatermarked paper with pink silk fibers. Face, Portrait of Washington at left; 40 mm seal.	40.00	100.	225.
3340	1303	Paper with violet silk fibers. Face, Portrait of Washington at left. Bluish right side of face.	40.00	125.	300.
3342	1307	Face, Portrait of Washington at left. 38mm red seal; bluish right side of face.	40.00	100.	275.

50 Cents

KL#	Fr#	Date	Description	Fine	XF	CU
3343	1374	3.3.1863. Watermarked paper with silk fibers. Face, Portrait of Lincoln at right.		150.	400.	550.

KL#	Fr#	Date	Description	Fine	XF	CU
3345	1376	3.3.1863. Face, Portrait of Stanton at left; red seal.		60.00	150.	225.

KL#	Fr#	Date	Description	Fine	XF	CU

KL#	Fr#	Date	Description	Fine	XF	CU
3347	1379	3.3.1863.	Face, Portrait of Dexter at left; green seal.	50.00	100.	200.

FIFTH ISSUE, SERIES OF 1874/1875

Shield Varieties

10 Cents

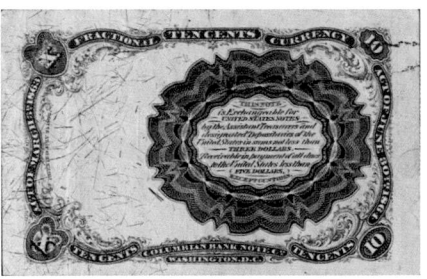

KL#	Fr#	Date	Description	Fine	XF	CU
3348	1264		Face, Portrait of Meredith at left. Green seal with long key. Back, Small 10 at top right and bottom right.	40.00	75.00	125.
3349	1265		Face, Portrait of Meredith at left. Red seal with long key. Back, Small 10 at top right and bottom right.	25.00	50.00	90.00
3350	1266		Face, Portrait of Meredith at left. Red seal with short key. Back, Small 10 at top right and bottom right.	25.00	50.00	100.

25 Cents

KL#	Fr#	Date	Description	Fine	XF	CU
3351	1308	1874. Face, Portrait of Walker at left. Red seal with long key. Back, Large 25 cents at right.	25.00	45.00	85.00
3352	1309	Face, Portrait of Walker at left. Red seal with short key. Back, Large 25 cents at right.	30.00	75.00	100.

Long key   *Short key*

FIFTH ISSUE, SERIES OF 1874/1875

Shield Varieties

50 Cents

KL#	Fr#	Date	Description	Fine	XF	CU
3357	1381	White paper. Face, Portrait of Crawford at left.	25.00	75.00	125.

Fractional Currency Shield

KL#	Fr#	Description	Fine	XF	CU
3354	1382	Grey background	—	—	4000.
3355	1383	Pink background	—	—	10,000.
3356	1383A	Green background	—	Rare	18,000.

Specimens

3 CENTS

THIRD ISSUE

KL#	Fr#	Date	Description	Fine	XF	CU
3252SP a	1226		Face with narrow margins, light background. Fr.#1226NF.	—	—	125.
3252SP b	1226		Face with wide margins, light background. Fr.#1226WF. Rare.	—	—	7000.
3252SP c	1226		Back with narrow margins. Fr.#1226NB.	—	—	195.
3252SP d	1226		Back with wide margins. Fr.1226WB.	—	—	350.
3253SP a	1227		Face with narrow margins, dark background. Fr.#1227NF.	—	—	125.
3253SP b	1227		Face with wide margins, dark background. Fr.#1227WF.	—	—	450.

5 CENTS

FIRST ISSUE "POSTAGE CURRENCY"

KL#	Fr#	Date	Description	Fine	XF	CU
3212SP a	1231		Face with narrow margins. Fr.#1231NF.	—	—	125.
3212SP b	1231		Face with wide margins. Fr.#1231WF.	—	—	300.
3212SP c	1231		Back with narrow margins. Fr.#1231NB.	—	—	125.
3212SP d	1231		Back with wide margins. Fr.#1231WB.	—	—	600.

SECOND ISSUE

KL#	Fr#	Date	Description	Finc	XF	CU
3226SP a	1232		Face with narrow margins. Fr.#1232NF.	—	—	175.
3226SP b	1232		Face with wide margins. Fr.#1232WF.	—	—	300.
3226SP c	1232		Back with narrow margins. Fr.#1232NB.	—	—	175.
3226SP d	1232		Back with wide margins. Fr.#1232WB.	—	—	300.

THIRD ISSUE

KL#	Fr#	Date	Description	Fine	XF	CU
3254SP a	1236		Face with narrow margins. Fr.#1236NF.	—	—	200.
3254SP b	1236		Face with wide margins. Fr.#1236WF.	—	—	350.
3254SP c	1236		Red back with narrow margins. Fr.#1236NB.	—	—	195.
3254SP d	1236		Red back with wide margins. Fr.#1236WB.	—	—	400.
3256SP c	1238		Green back with narrow margins. Fr.#1238NB.	—	—	125.
3256SP d	1238		Green back with wide margins. Fr.#1238WB.	—	—	300.

10 CENTS

FIRST ISSUE "POSTAGE CURRENCY"

KL#	Fr#	Date	Description	Fine	XF	CU
3216SP a	1243		Face with narrow margins. Fr.#1243NF.	—	—	125.
3216SP b	1243		Face with wide margins. Fr.#1243WF.	—	—	300.
3216SP c	1243		Back with narrow margins. Fr.#1243NB.	—	—	125.
3216SP d	1243		Back with wide margins. Fr.#1243WF.	—	—	300.

SECOND ISSUE

KL#	Fr#	Date	Description	Fine	XF	CU
3230SP a	1244		Face with narrow margins. Fr.#1244NF.	—	—	125.
3230SP b	1244		Face with wide margins. Fr.#1244WF.	—	—	300.
3230SP c	1244		Back with narrow margins. Fr.#1244NB.	—	—	125.
3230SP d	1244		Back with wide margins. Fr.1244WF.	—	—	300.

THIRD ISSUE

KL#	Fr#	Date	Description	Fine	XF	CU
3258SP a	1251		Face with narrow margins. Engraved Colby/Spinner.	—	—	125.
3258SP b	1251		Face with wide margins. Engraved Colby/Spinner.	—	—	325.
3258SP c	1251		Red back with narrow margins.	—	—	150.
3258SP d	1251		Red back with wide margins.	—	—	400.
3260SP a	1253		Face with narrow margins. Autograph Colby/Spinner.	—	—	190.
3260SP b	1253		Face with wide margins. Autograph Colby/Spinner.	—	—	500.
3261SP a	1254		Face with narrow margins. Autograph Jeffries/Spinner.	—	—	395.
3261SP b	1254		Face with wide margins. Autograph Jeffries/Spinner.	—	—	3900.
3262SP c	1255		Green back ith narrow margins.	—	—	150.
3262SP d	1255		Green back with wide margins.	—	—	325.

15 CENTS

KL#		Fr#	Date	Description	Fine	XF	CU
3453SP	a	1272		Face with narrow margins. Engraved Colby/Spinner.	—	—	750.
3453SP	b	1272		Face with wide margins. Engraved Colby/Spinner.	—	—	900.
3453SP	c	1272		Green back with narrow margins.	—	—	300.
3453SP	d	1272		Green back wih wide margins.	—	—	425.
3454SP	a	1273		Face with narrow margins. Autographed Colby/Spinner.	—	—	2500.
3455SP	a	1274		Face with narrow margins. Autographed Jeffries/Spinner.	—	—	750.
3455SP	b	1274		Face with wide margins. Autographed Jeffries/Spinner.	—	—	900.
3455SP	c	1274		Red back with narrow margins.	—	—	400.
3455SP	d	1274		Red back with wide margins.	—	—	1000.
3456SP	a	1275		Face with narrow margins. Autographed Allison/Spinner.	—	—	750.
3456SP	b	1275		Face with wide margins. Autographed Allison/Spinner.	—	—	1000.
3457SP	a	—		Face with narrow margins. Without signatures. Rare.	—	—	—

25 CENTS

FIRST ISSUE "POSTAGE CURRENCY"

KL#		Fr#	Date	Description	Fine	XF	CU
3220SP	a	1282		Face with narrow margins. Fr.#1282NF.	—	—	125.
3220SP	b	1282		Face with wide margins. Fr.#1282WF.	—	—	300.
3220SP	c	1282		Back with narrow margins. Fr.#1282NB.	—	—	125.
3220SP	d	1282		Back with wide margins. Fr.#1282WB.	—	—	300.

SECOND ISSUE

KL#	Fr#	Date	Description	Fine	XF	CU
3236SP a	1283		Face with narrow margins. Fr.#1283NF.	—	—	125.
3236SP b	1283		Face with wide margins. Fr.#1283WF.	—	—	300.
3236SP c	1283		Back with narrow margins. Fr.#1283NB.	—	—	125.
3236SP d	1283		Back with wide margins. Fr.#1283WB.	—	—	300.

THIRD ISSUE

KL#	Fr#	Date	Description	Fine	XF	CU
3265SP a	1291		Face with narrow margins.	—	—	125.
3265SP b	1291		Face with wide margins.	—	—	350.
3265SP c	1291		Red back with narrow margins.	—	—	150.
3265SP d	1291		Red back with wide margins.	—	—	350.
3268SP c	1294		Green back with narrow margins.	—	—	125.
3268SP d	1294		Green back with wide margins.	—	—	325.

50 CENTS

FIRST ISSUE "POSTAGE CURRENCY"

KL#	Fr#	Date	Description	Fine	XF	CU
3225SP a	1313		Face with narrow margins. Fr.#1313NF.	—	—	125.
3225SP b	1313		Face with wide margins. Fr.#1313WF.	—	—	425.
3225SP c	1313		Back with narrow margins. Fr.#1313NB.	—	—	125.
3225SP d	1313		Back with wide margins. Fr.#1313WB.	—	—	300.

SECOND ISSUE

KL#	Fr#	Date	Description	Fine	XF	CU
3245SP a	1316		Face with narrow margins. Fr.#1316NF.	—	—	125.
3245SP b	1316		Face with wide margins. Fr.#1316WF.	—	—	350.
3245SP c	1316		Back with narrow margins. Fr.#1316NB.	—	—	125.
3245SP d	1316		Back with wide margins. Fr.#1316WB.	—	—	500.

THIRD ISSUE

KL#	Fr#	Date	Description	Fine	XF	CU
3275SP a	1324		Face with narrow margins. Engraved Colby/Spinner.	—	—	200.
3275SP b	1324		Face with wide margins. Engraved Colby/Spinner.	—	—	350.
3275SP c	1324		Red back with narrow margins.	—	—	250.
3275SP d	1324		Red back with wide margin.	—	—	450.
3279SP a	1328		Face with narrow margins. Autograph Colby/Spinner.	—	—	300.
3279SP b	1328		Face with wide margins. Autograph Colby/Spinner.	—	—	700.
3281SP a	1329		Face with narrow margins. Allison/Spinner. Rare.	—	—	4500.
3281SP b	1329		Face with wide margins. Allison/Spinner. Rare.	—	—	14,500.
3282SP a	1330		Face with narrow margins. Allison/New.	—	—	395.
3282SP b	1330		Face with wide margins. Allison/New. Rare.	—	—	7000.
3283SP c	1331		Green back with narrow margins.	—	—	125.
3283SP d	1331		Green back with wide margins.	—	—	350.
3291SP c	1339		Green back with narrow margins.	—	—	4500.
3291SP d	1339		Green back with wide margins.	—	—	5500.
3295SP a	1343		Face with narrow margins. Engraved Colby/Spinner.	—	—	350.
3295SP b	1343		Face with wide margins. Engraved Colby/Spinner.	—	—	700.
3307SP a	1355		Face with narrow margins. Autographed Colby/Spinner.	—	—	300.
3307SP b	1355		Face with wide margins. Autographed Colby/Spinner.	—	—	700.
3309SP a	1357A		Face with narrow margins. Autographed Jeffries/Spinner.	—	—	500.
3309SP b	1357A		Face with wide margins. Autographed Jeffries/Spinner. Rare.	—	—	9000.

Military Payment Certificates

Military Payment Certificates (MPC) were special currency issued by the U.S. Armed Forces between the end of World War II and 1973.

Their issue to and use by the military and certain civilian personnel in lieu of regular U.S. currency was designed to minimize black market trafficking in occupied areas and around U.S. military installations. The various series of MPC replaced each other with no advanced warning, and the scrip, exchangeable only by those to whom its issue was authorized, could become worthless overnight. This discouraged its acceptance by unauthorized local civilians.

Given the low rate of military pay during most of this period and the fact that no MPC retains any redemption value, it is no wonder that high denomination notes in uncirculated condition are rare in many of the series.

MPC replacement notes, analogous to star notes in regular U.S. currency, are designated by the lack of a suffix letter in the serial number. They are especially sought-after by collectors.

SERIES 461

Issued: European Theater, Sept. 16, 1946; Pacific Theater, Sept. 30, 1946
Withdrawn: March 10, 1947 **Areas of Use:** Austria, Belgium, England, France, Germany, Greece, Hungary, Iceland, Italy, Japan, Korea, Morocco, Philippines, Ryukyus, Scotland, Trieste, Yugoslavia.

KL#	Denomination	Fine	VF	XF	Unc
M1	5 Cents	4.00	7.50	20.00	65.00
M1r	5 Cents Replacement A-	150.	400.	750.	1000.
M2	10 Cents	4.00	7.50	20.00	65.00
M2r	10 Cents Replacement A-	150.	400.	750.	1000.
M3	25 Cents	13.00	25.00	45.00	250.
M3r	25 Cents Replacement A-	950.	1100.	—	—
M4	50 Cents	14.00	25.00	70.00	250.
M4r	50 Cents Replacement A-	950.	1100.	—	—

KL#	Denomination	Fine	VF	XF	Unc
M5	1 Dollar	5.50	10.00	30.00	185.
M5r	One Dollar Replacement A-	200.	500.	900.	1300.
M6	5 Dollars	30.00	85.00	125.	325.
M6r	Five Dollars Replacement A-	1100.	1750.	—	—
M7	10 Dollars	25.00	45.00	75.00	300.
M7r	Ten Dollars Replacement A-	350.	1000.	1600.	—

SERIES 471

Issued: March 10, 1947

Withdrawn: March 22, 1948 **Areas of Use:** Austria, Belgium, England, France, Germany, Greece, Hungary, Iceland, Italy, Japan, Korea, Morocco, Philippines, Ryukyus, Scotland, Trieste, Yugoslavia

KL#	Denomination	Fine	VF	XF	Unc
M8	5 Cents	7.50	15.00	30.00	90.00
M8r	5 Cents Replacement B-	750.	950.	2000.	—
M9	10 Cents	6.00	12.00	30.00	90.00
M9r	10 Cents Replacement B-	800.	1000.	1800.	—
M10	25 Cents	15.00	25.00	75.00	300.
M10r	25 Cents Replacement B-	750.	1250.	—	—
M11	50 Cents	20.00	50.00	110.	325.
M11r	50 Cents Replacement B-	—	Rare	—	—

KL#	Denomination	Fine	VF	XF	Unc
M12	1 Dollar	15.00	35.00	85.00	275.
M12r	1 Dollar Replacement B-	700.	1000.	1500.	—
M13	5 Dollars	775.	1000.	2375.	20,000.
M13r	5 Dollars Replacement B-	—	Rare	—	—

KL#	Denomination	Fine	VF	XF	Unc
M14	10 Dollars	200.	350.	600.	2400.
M14r	10 Dollars Replacement B-	—	Rare	—	—

SERIES 472

Issued: March 22, 1948 **Withdrawn:** June 20, 1951 **Areas of Use:** Austria, Belgium, England, France, Germany, Greece, Hungary, Iceland, Italy, Japan, Korea, Morocco, Philippines, Ryukyus, Scotland, Trieste, Yugoslavia

KL#	Denomination	Fine	VF	XF	Unc
M15	5 Cents	1.00	2.00	4.00	12.50
M15r	5 Cents Replacement C-	50.00	75.00	300.	750.
M16	10 Cents	2.25	6.50	18.00	70.00
M16r	10 Cents Replacement C-	110.	175.	375.	675.

KL#	Denomination	Fine	VF	XF	Unc
M17	25 Cents	8.00	17.50	65.00	225.
M17r	25 Cents Replacement C-	—	Rare	—	—
M18	50 Cents	10.00	28.00	75.00	275.
M18r	50 Cents Replacement C-	600.	900.	—	—
M19	1 Dollar	12.00	18.00	85.00	250.
M19r	1 Dollar Replacement C-	225.	400.	750.	2400.
M20	5 Dollars	125.	250.	900.	2750.
M20r	5 Dollars Replacement C-	—	Rare	—	—
M21	10 Dollars	50.00	130.	275.	2000.
M21r	10 Dollars Replacement C-	—	Rare	—	—

SERIES 481

Issued: June 20, 1951 **Withdrawn:** May 25, 1954 **Areas of Use:** Austria, Belgium, England, France, Germany, Greece, Hungary, Iceland, Italy, Japan, Korea, Morocco, Philippines, Ryukyus, Scotland, Trieste, Yugoslavia

KL#	Denomination	Fine	VF	XF	Unc
M22	5 Cents	2.00	4.00	9.00	27.50
M22r	5 Cents Replacement D-	75.00	125.	300.	600.

KL#	Denomination	Fine	VF	XF	Unc
M23	10 Cents	2.50	4.50	15.00	35.00
M23r	10 Cents Replacement D-	85.00	150.	300.	450.
M24	25 Cents	10.00	18.50	25.00	60.00
M24r	25 Cents Replacement D-	225.	400.	450.	800.
M25	50 Cents	10.00	25.00	55.00	275.
M25r	50 Cents Replacement D-	—	Rare	—	—

KL#	Denomination	Fine	VF	XF	Unc
M26	1 Dollar	20.00	45.00	95.00	295.
M26r	1 Dollar Replacement D-	450.	475.	600.	1000.

KL#	Denomination	Fine	VF	XF	Unc
M27	5 Dollars	80.00	175.	550.	3000.
M27r	5 Dollars Replacement D-	—	Rare	—	—
M28	10 Dollars	35.00	85.00	300,	1750
M28r	10 Dollars Replacement D-	900.	Rare	—	—

SERIES 521

Issued: May 25, 1954 **Withdrawn:** May 27, 1958 **Areas of Use:** Austria, Belgium, England, France, Germany, Greece, Hungary, Iceland, Italy, Japan, Korea, Morocco, Philippines, Ryukyus, Scotland, Trieste, Yugoslavia

KL#	Denomination	Fine	VF	XF	Unc
M29	5 Cents	2.00	5.00	9.00	30.00
M29r	5 Cents Replacement E-	300.	500.	900.	1500.
M30	10 Cents	3.00	6.00	12.50	32.50
M30r	10 Cents Replacement E-	300.	500.	1000.	2000.

KL#	Denomination	Fine	VF	XF	Unc
M31	25 Cents	8.00	15.00	27.50	85.00
M31r	25 Cents Replacement E-	500.	1000.	1500.	2250.
M32	50 Cents	10.00	25.00	75.00	150.
M32r	50 Cents Replacement E-	600.	800.	1600.	2500.
M33	1 Dollar	9.50	20.00	50.00	175.
M33r	1 Dollar Replacement E-	300.	500.	1000.	2250.

KL#	Denomination	Fine	VF	XF	Unc
M34	5 Dollars	300.	550.	1300.	3000.
M34r	5 Dollars Replacement E-	1600.	2250.	—	—

KL#	Denomination	Fine	VF	XF	Unc
M35	10 Dollars	100.	165.	650.	1800.
M35r	10 Dollars Replacement E-	1900.	3000.	3600.	—

SERIES 541

Issued: May 27, 1958 **Withdrawn:** May 26, 1961 **Areas of Use:** Cyprus, England, France, Germany, Iceland, Northern Ireland, Italy, Japan, Korea, Morocco, Philippines, Ryukyus, Scotland

KL#	Denomination	Fine	VF	XF	Unc
M36	5 Cents	1.50	3.00	6.00	17.50
M36r	5 Cents Replacement E-	50.00	75.00	175.	350.

KL#	Denomination	Fine	VF	XF	Unc
M37	10 Cents	5.00	10.00	20.00	50.00
M37r	10 Cents Replacement F-	50.00	75.00	175.	350.
M38	25 Cents	9.00	15.00	30.00	80.00
M38r	25 Cents Replacement F-	75.00	125.	225.	600.
M39	50 Cents	30.00	55.00	100.	325.
M39r	50 Cents Replacement F-	40.00	50.00	150.	300.

KL#	Denomination	Fine	VF	XF	Unc
M40	1 Dollar	30.00	50.00	100.	400.
M40r	1 Dollar Replacement F-	250.	375.	1000.	1500.
M41	5 Dollars	1250.	2250.	3750.	15,000.
M41r	5 Dollars Replacement F-	—	Rare	—	—

KL#	Denomination	Fine	VF	XF	Unc
M42	10 Dollars	300.	500.	1500.	3500.
M42r	10 Dollars Replacement F-	2375.	3750.	—	—

SERIES 591

Issued: May 26, 1961 **Withdrawn:** Pacific, Jan. 6, 1964; Europe, Jan. 14, 1946
Areas of Use: Cyprus, Iceland, Japan, Korea, Philippines

KL#	Denomination	Fine	VF	XF	Unc
M43	5 Cents	3.50	7.00	12.50	55.00
M43r	5 Cents Replacement G-	225.	400.	800.	1250.
M44	10 Cents	4.00	10.00	15.00	65.00
M44r	10 Cents Replacement G-	1200.	1400.	1600.	2500.
M45	25 Cents	17.50	35.00	55.00	140.
M45r	25 Cents Replacement G-	—	Rare	—	—

KL#	Denomination	Fine	VF	XF	Unc
M46	50 Cents	35.00	60.00	85.00	240.
M46r	50 Cents Replacement G-	600.	700.	800.	1200.

KL#	Denomination	Fine	VF	XF	Unc
M47	1 Dollar	25.00	40.00	90.00	275.
M47r	1 Dollar Replacement G-	800.	1000.	1600.	2500.

KL#	Denomination	Fine	VF	XF	Unc
M48	5 Dollars	550.	850.	1750.	4500.
M48r	5 Dollars Replacement G-	—	Rare	—	—
M49	10 Dollars	200.	300.	350.	2000.
M49r	10 Dollars Replacement G-	1250.	2500.	3500.	—

SERIES 611

Issued: Jan. 6, 1964 **Withdrawn:** April 28, 1969
Areas of Use: Cyprus, Japan, Korea, Libya

KL#	Denomination	Fine	VF	XF	Unc
M50	5 Cents	5.00	7.50	19.00	40.00
M50r	5 Cents Replacement H-	45.00	60.00	90.00	125.

KL#	Denomination	Fine	VF	XF	Unc
M51	10 Cents	5.00	8.00	20.00	45.00
M51r	10 Cents Replacement H-	45.00	60.00	90.00	125.
M52	25 Cents	30.00	75.00	110.	275.
M52r	25 Cents Replacement H-	1000.	1250.	—	—
M53	50 Cents	30.00	75.00	100.	275.
M53r	50 Cents Replacement H-	—	Rare	—	—

KL#	Denomination	Fine	VF	XF	Unc
M54	1 Dollar	5.00	10.00	17.50	100.
M54r	1 Dollar Replacement H-	60.00	90.00	120.	250.
M55	5 Dollars	125.	175.	375.	2000.
M55r	5 Dollars Replacement H-	900.	1200.	1875.	3000.

KL#	Denomination	Fine	VF	XF	Unc
M56	10 Dollars	130.	225.	375.	1400.
M56r	10 Dollars Replacement H-	750.	1100.	1275.	2100.

SERIES 641

Issued: Aug. 31, 1965 **Withdrawn:** Oct. 21, 1968 **Areas of Use:** Vietnam

KL#	Denomination	Fine	VF	XF	Unc
M57	5 Cents	1.00	2.00	3.50	13.50
M57r	5 Cents Replacement J-	75.00	125.	200.	300.
M58	10 Cents	1.00	2.00	4.00	18.50
M58r	10 Cents Replacement J-	75.00	120.	200.	450.
M59	25 Cents	2.50	4.00	10.00	23.00
M59r	25 Cents Replacemetn J-	75.00	120.	200.	450.
M60	50 Cents	3.50	7.00	15.00	35.00
M60r	50 Cents Replacement J-	120.	200.	450.	750.
M61	1 Dollar	4.00	9.00	17.50	45.00
M61r	1 Dollar Replacement J-	450.	750.	1000.	1250.

KL#	Denomination	Fine	VF	XF	Unc
M62	5 Dollars	17.50	30.00	75.00	250.
M62r	5 Dollars Replacemetn J-	900.	1100.	2750.	3750.

KL#	Denomination	Fine	VF	XF	Unc
M63	10 Dollars	10.00	17.50	30.00	250.
M63r	10 Dollars Replacement J-	325.	425.	600.	1500.

SERIES 651

Issued: April 28, 1969 **Withdrawn:** Japan, May 19, 1969; Libya, June 11, 1969; Korea, Nov. 19, 1973 **Areas of Use:** Japan, Korea, Libya

KL#	Denomination	Fine	VF	XF	Unc
M72A	5 Cents	—	—	—	700.
M72B	10 Cents	—	—	—	700.
M72C	25 Cents	—	—	—	700.

KL#	Denomination	Fine	VF	XF	Unc
M72D	50 Cents	—	—	—	275.

KL#	Denomination	Fine	VF	XF	Unc
M72E	1 Dollar	6.00	15.00	25.00	45.00
M72Er	One Dollar Replacement A-	—	Rare	—	—
M73	5 Dollars	50.00	85.00	150.	275.
M73r	5 Dollars Replacement A-	—	Rare	—	—
M74	10 Dollars	50.00	85.00	150.	275.
M74r	Ten Dollars Replacement A-	2000.	2500.	—	—

SERIES 661

Issued: Oct. 21, 1968 **Withdrawn:** Aug. 11, 1969 **Areas of Use:** Vietnam

KL#	Denomination	Fine	VF	XF	Unc
M64	5 Cents	—	1.50	3.00	10.00
M64r	5 Cents Replacement B-	400.	500.	600.	800.

KL#	Denomination	Fine	VF	XF	Unc
M65	10 Cents	—	1.50	3.00	10.00
M65r	10 Cents Replacement B-	75.00	120.	200.	375.
M66	25 Cents	2.00	5.00	12.50	27.50
M66r	50 Cents Replacement B-	100.	150.	250.	600.
M67	50 Cents	2.00	5.00	10.00	23.00
M67r	50 Cents Replacement B-	—	Rare	—	—

KL#	Denomination	Fine	VF	XF	Unc
M68	1 Dollar	5.00	8.00	12.50	24.00
M68r	1 Dollar Replacement B-	125.	225.	450.	750.
M69	5 Dollars	5.00	8.00	15.00	30.00
M69r	5 Dollars Replacement B-	300.	500.	600.	800.

KL#	Denomination	Fine	VF	XF	Unc
M70	10 Dollars	200.	325.	750.	1850.
M70r	10 Dollars Replacement B-	800.	1200.	3500.	5000.

KL#	Denomination	Fine	VF	XF	Unc
M71	20 Dollars	125.	200.	350.	1450.
M71r	20 Dollars Replacement B-	700.	1000.	1600.	3000.

SERIES 681

Issued: Aug. 11, 1969 Withdrawn: Oct. 7, 1970 Areas of Use: Vietnam

KL#	Denomination	Fine	VF	XF	Unc
M75	5 Cents	—	2.00	5.00	12.00
M75r	5 Cents Replacement C-	75.00	100.	150.	250.
M76	10 Cents	—	2.00	5.00	16.00
M76r	10 Cents Replacement C-	60.00	90.00	125.	250.
M77	25 Cents	2.00	5.00	10.00	27.50
M77r	25 Cents Replacement C-	—	Rare	—	—

KL#	Denomination	Fine	VF	XF	Unc
M78	50 Cents	3.00	10.00	15.00	24.00
M78r	50 Cents Replacement C-	90.00	150.	300.	450.
M79	1 Dollar	3.00	10.00	15.00	25.00
M79r	1 Dollar Replacement C-	75.00	125.	275.	400.

KL#	Denomination	Fine	VF	XF	Unc
M80	5 Dollars	10.00	20.00	50.00	125.
M80r	5 Dollars Replacement C-	475.	750.	1250.	2250.

KL#	Denomination	Fine	VF	XF	Unc
M81	10 Dollars	30.00	60.00	125.	300.
M81r	5 Dollars Replacement C-	—	Rare	—	—

KL#	Denomination	Fine	VF	XF	Unc
M82	20 Dollars	30.00	70.00	100.	1100.
M82r	20 Dollars Replacement C-	—	Rare	—	—

SERIES 691

Printed but not released.

KL#	Denomination	Fine	VF	XF	Unc
M87	1 Dollar	—	—	—	250.

KL#	Denomination	Fine	VF	XF	Unc
M88	5 Dollars	—	—	—	—
M93	10 Dollars	—	—	—	—
M94	20 Dollars	—	—	—	300.

SERIES 692

Issued: Oct. 7, 1970
Withdrawn: Fractional denominations, June 1, 1971; dollar denominations, March 15, 1973
Areas of Use: Vietnam

KL#	Denomination	Fine	VF	XF	Unc
M83	5 Cents	1.00	3.00	8.00	16.50
M83r	5 Cents Replacement E-	50.00	75.00	125.	200.
M84	10 Cents	1.00	3.00	8.00	17.50
M84r	10 Cents Replacement E-	60.00	90.00	125.	250.
M85	25 Cents	3.00	7.00	15.00	29.50
M85r	25 Cents Replacement E-	225.	300.	450.	750.
M86	50 Cents	4.00	8.00	16.50	40.00
M86r	50 Cents Replacement E-	225.	300.	450.	750.
M87	1 Dollar	8.00	20.00	35.00	95.00
M87r	1 Dollar Replacement E-	80.00	120.	200.	450.
M88	5 Dollars	50.00	95.00	200.	1000.

KL#	Denomination	Fine	VF	XF	Unc
M89	10 Dollars	75.00	150.	275.	1150.

KL#	Denomination	Fine	VF	XF	Unc
M90	20 Dollars	30.00	75.00	200.	1200.
M92r	5 Dollars Replacement E-	—	Rare	—	—
M93r	10 Dollars Replacement E-	—	Rare	—	—
M94r	20 Dollars Replacement E-	325.	600.	1000.	1800.

SERIES 701

Printed but not released.

KL#	Denomination	Fine	VF	XF	Unc
M103	1 Dollar	—	—	—	750.
M104	5 Dollars	—	—	—	750.
M105	10 Dollars	—	—	—	750.
M106	20 Dollars	—	—	—	750.

Philippines

The catalog numbers shown here are those from the
Standard Catalog of World Paper Money, Volume 2, General Issues.

BANCO ESPAÑOL FILIPINO

1904 Issue

#A31-A36 Denominations w/o *FUERTES*.

		Good	Fine	XF
A31	**5 Pesos**	—	—	—
	1.1.1904. Black. Bank arms at upper center. Pink. Printer: BFL. Rare.			
A32	**10 Pesos**	—	—	—
	1.1.1904. Black. Bank arms at upper center. Green. Printer: BFL. Rare.			
A33	**25 Pesos**	—	—	—
	1.1.1904. Black. Bank arms at upper center. Light purple. Printer: BFL. Rare.			
A34	**50 Pesos**	—	—	—
	1.1.1904. Black. Bank arms at upper center. Green. Printer: BFL. Rare.			
A35	**100 Pesos**	—	—	—
	1.1.1904. Black. Bank arms at upper center. Yellowish brown. Printer: BFL. Rare.			
A36	**200 Pesos**	—	—	—
	1.1.1904. Black. Bank arms at upper center. Back: Multicolor. Yellowish brown. Printer: BFL. Rare.			

1908 Issue

#1 and 2 with 1 stamped signature (at left) and 2 printed signatures. #4-6 with only 2 printed signatures.

		Good	Fine	XF
1	**5 Pesos**	200.	500.	900.
	1.1.1908. Black on red underprint. Woman seated at left. Signature *J. Serrano* at left. Back: Red. Printer: USBEP (without imprint).			

		Good	Fine	XF
2	**10 Pesos**			
	1.1.1908. Black on brown underprint. Woman with flowers at center. Back: Brown. Printer: USBEP (without imprint).			
	a. Signature *Julian Serrano* at left. Rare.	—	9000.	—
	b. Signature *J. Serrano* at left.	400.	900.	—

3	**20 Pesos**	Good	Fine	XF
	1.1.1908. Black on lilac underprint. Woman at left. Back: Tan. Printer: USBEP (without imprint).			
	a. Signature Julian Serrano at left. Rare.	—	—	—
	b. Signature J. Serrano at left.	750.	2000.	—
4	**50 Pesos**			
	1.1.1908. Black on blue underprint. Woman standing with flower at left. Back: Red. Printer: USBEP (without imprint).	750.	2000.	4500.
5	**100 Pesos**			
	1.1.1908. Black on green underprint. Woman seated with scroll and globe at left. Back: Olive. Printer: USBEP (without imprint).	600.	1000.	—
6	**200 Pesos**			
	1.1.1908. Black on tan underprint. Justice seated with scales and shield at center. Back: Orange. Printer: USBEP (without imprint). Rare.	—	15,000	—

BANK OF THE PHILIPPINE ISLANDS

1912 Issue

#7-12 Replacement notes of b. varieties: Star prefix.

7	**5 Pesos**	Good	Fine	XF
	1.1.1912. Black on red underprint. Woman seated at left. Similar to #1. Back: Light red. Printer: USBEP (without imprint).			
	a. Signature D. Garcia and Jno. S. Hord.	50.00	150.	300.
	b. Signature D. Garcia and E. Sendres.	50.00	150.	300.
8	**10 Pesos**			
	1.1.1912. Black on brown underprint. Woman with flowers at center. Similar to #2. Printer: USBEP (without imprint).			
	a. Signature D. Garcia and Jno. S. Hord.	75.00	175.	350.
	b. Signature D. Garcia and E. Sendres.	75.00	175.	350.

9	**20 Pesos**	Good	Fine	XF
	1.1.1912. Black on lilac underprint. Woman at left. Similar to #3. Printer: USBEP (without imprint).			
	a. Signature D. Garcia and Jno. S. Hord.	250.	700.	1500.
	b. Signature D. Garcia and E. Sendres.	250.	500.	1200.

10	50 Pesos		Good	Fine	XF
	1.1.1912. Black on blue underprint. Woman standing with flower at left. Similar to #4. Printer: USBEP (without imprint).				
	a. Signature D. Garcia and Jno. S. Hord.		400.	2000.	4000.
	b. Signature D. Garcia and E. Sendres.		26.00	900.	3000.

11	100 Pesos		Good	Fine	XF
	1.1.1912. Black on green underprint. Woman seated with scroll and globe at left. Similar to #5. Printer: USBEP (without imprint).				
	a. Signature D. Garcia and Jno. S. Hord.		500.	1200.	2000.
	b. Signature D. Garcia and E. Sendres.		500.	1500.	3000.
12	200 Pesos				
	1.1.1912. Black on tan underprint. Justice with scales and shield at center. Similar to #6. Signature D. Garcia and Jno. S. Hord. Printer: USBEP (without imprint).		1000.	2600.	—

1920 Issue

#13-15 like #7b-9b except for date and serial # prefix-suffix. Replacement notes: Star prefix.

			Good	Fine	XF
13	**5 Pesos**				
	1.1.1920. Black on red underprint. Woman seated at left. Like #7b. Signature D. Garcia and E. Sendres. Back: Orange. Printer: USBEP (without imprint).		50.00	250.	400.
14	**10 Pesos**				
	1.1.1920. Black on brown underprint. Woman with flowers at center. Like #8b. Signature D. Garcia and E. Sendres. Printer: USBEP (without imprint).				
	a. Issued note.		75.00	250.	500.
	r. Replacement. * at end of serial #.		—	2600.	—
15	**20 Pesos**				
	1.1.1920. Black on lilac underprint. Woman at left. Like #9b. Signature D. Garcia and E. Sendres. Printer: USBEP (without imprint).				
	a. Issued note.		5.00	30.00	85.00
	r. Replacement. * at end of serial #.		—	3200.	—

1928 Issue

#16-21 designs like #7-12 but without underprint. Replacement notes: Star prefix.

			Good	Fine	XF
16	**5 Pesos**				
	1.1.1928. Black. Woman seated at left. Like #7. Signature D. Garcia and Fulg. Borromeo. Back: Orange. Printer: USBEP (without imprint).		40.00	150.	300.

17	10 Pesos	Good	Fine	XF
	1.1.1928. Black. Woman with flowers at center. Like #8. Signature D. Garcia and Fulg. Borromeo. Printer: USBEP (without imprint).	40.00	250.	500.
18	20 Pesos			
	1.1.1928. Black. Woman at left. Like #9. Signature D. Garcia and Fulg. Borromeo. Printer: USBEP (without imprint).			
	a. Issued note.	100.	400.	800.
	r. Replacement. * at end of serial #.	—	1600.	—
19	50 Pesos			
	1.1.1928. Black. Woman standing with flower at left. Like #10. Signature D. Garcia and Fulg. Borromeo. Printer: USBEP (without imprint).	100.	350.	1000.
20	100 Pesos			
	1.1.1928. Black. Woman seated with scroll and globe at left. Like #11. Signature D. Garcia and Fulg. Borromeo. Printer: USBEP (without imprint).	100.	300.	500.
21	200 Pesos			
	1.1.1928. Black. Justice with scales and shield at center. Like #12. Signature D. Garcia and Fulg. Borromeo. Printer: USBEP (without imprint).	500.	3500.	7500.

1933 Issue

#22-24 like #16-18 except for date and serial # prefix-suffix. Replacement notes: Star prefix.

22	5 Pesos	Good	Fine	XF
	1.1.1933. Black. Woman seated at left. Like #16. Signature D. Garcia and P.J. Campos. Printer: USBEP (without imprint).	15.00	100.	250.
23	10 Pesos			
	1.1.1933. Black. Woman with flowers at center. Like #17. Signature D. Garcia and P.J. Campos. Printer: USBEP (without imprint).	15.00	100.	275.
24	20 Pesos			
	1.1.1933. Black. Woman at left. Like #18. Signature D. Garcia and P.J. Campos. Printer: USBEP (without imprint).			
	a. Issued note.	100.	300.	600.
	r. Replacement note. * at end of serial #.	—	2000.	—

PHILIPPINE ISLANDS
1903 Issue

25	2 Pesos		Good	Fine	XF
	1903. Black on blue underprint. Portrait José Rizal at upper left. Back: Blue. Printer: USBEP (without imprint).				
	a. Signature William H. Taft and Frank A. Branagan.		250.	450.	650.
	b. Signature Luke E. Wright and Frank A. Branagan.		400.	900.	1500.
	p. Uniface proofs. Face and back pair.		—	—	12,000.

26	5 Pesos		Good	Fine	XF
	1903. Black on red underprint. Portrait President William McKinley at left. Back: Red. Printer: USBEP (without imprint).				
	a. Signature William H. Taft and Frank A. Branagan.		350.	900.	2000.
	b. Signature Luke E. Wright and Frank A. Branagan.		500.	2500.	3250.
	p. Uniface proofs. Face and Back pari.		—	—12,000.	
27	10 Pesos				
	1903. Black on brown underprint. Portrait George Washington at lower center. Back: Brown. Printer: USBEP (without imprint).				
	a. Signature William H. Taft and Frank A. Branagan.		400.	900.	2000.
	b. Signature Luke E. Wright and Frank A. Branagan.		300.	900.	3000.
	p. Uniface proofs. Face and back pair.		—	—12,000.	
27A	10 Pesos				
	1903. Black on brown underprint. Portrait George Washington at lower center. Like #27. Signature Henry C. Ide with title: *Governor General* and Frank A. Branagan. Back: Brown. Overprint: Black vertical text: *Subject to the provisions of the/Act of Congress approved/ June 23, 1906* Printer: USBEP (without imprint).		2000.	4000.	—

Note: The chief executive's title before 1905 was: Civil Governor.

1905 Issue

#28-31 issued with overprint like #27A. Sign. Luke E. Wright with title: *Governor General* **and Frank A. Branagan.**

		Good	Fine	XF
28	**20 Pesos**	—	4750.	—
	1905. Black on yellow underprint. Mt. Mayon at center. Signature Luke E. Wright and Frank A. Branagan. Back: Tan. Overprint: Black vertical text: *Subject to the provisions of the/Act of Congress approved/ June 23, 1906* Rare.			
29	**50 Pesos**	—	—	—
	1905. Black on red underprint. Portrait Gen. Henry W. Lawton at left. Signature Luke E. Wright and Frank A. Branagan. Back: Red. Overprint: Black vertical text: *Subject to the provisions of the/Act of Congress approved/ June 23, 1906* Rare.			
30	**100 Pesos**	—	—	—
	1905. Black on green underprint. Portrait Ferdinand Magellan at center. Signature Luke E. Wright and Frank A. Branagan. Back: Olive. Overprint: Black vertical text: *Subject to the provisions of the/Act of Congress approved/ June 23, 1906* Rare.			
31	**500 Pesos**	—	—	—
	1905. Black. Portrait Miguel Lopez de Legazpi at center. Signature Luke E. Wright and Frank A. Branagan. Back: Purple. Overprint: Black vertical text: *Subject to the provisions of the/Act of Congress approved/ June 23, 1906* Rare.			

1906 Issue

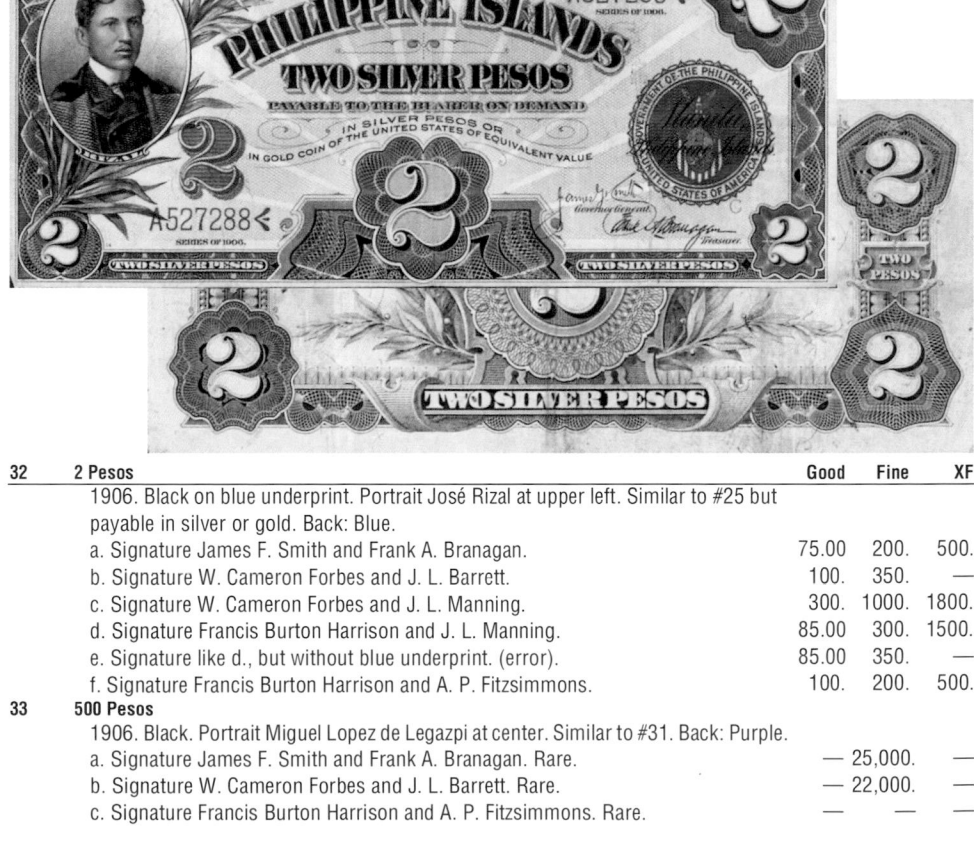

		Good	Fine	XF
32	**2 Pesos**			
	1906. Black on blue underprint. Portrait José Rizal at upper left. Similar to #25 but payable in silver or gold. Back: Blue.			
	a. Signature James F. Smith and Frank A. Branagan.	75.00	200.	500.
	b. Signature W. Cameron Forbes and J. L. Barrett.	100.	350.	—
	c. Signature W. Cameron Forbes and J. L. Manning.	300.	1000.	1800.
	d. Signature Francis Burton Harrison and J. L. Manning.	85.00	300.	1500.
	e. Signature like d., but without blue underprint. (error).	85.00	350.	—
	f. Signature Francis Burton Harrison and A. P. Fitzsimmons.	100.	200.	500.
33	**500 Pesos**			
	1906. Black. Portrait Miguel Lopez de Legazpi at center. Similar to #31. Back: Purple.			
	a. Signature James F. Smith and Frank A. Branagan. Rare.	—	25,000.	—
	b. Signature W. Cameron Forbes and J. L. Barrett. Rare.	—	22,000.	—
	c. Signature Francis Burton Harrison and A. P. Fitzsimmons. Rare.	—	—	—

1908 Issue

34	20 Pesos	Good	Fine	XF
	1908. Black on yellow underprint. Mt. Mayon at center. Similar to #28. Back: Tan.			
	a. Signature James F. Smith and Frank A. Branagan.	250.	750.	3000.
	b. Signature W. Cameron Forbes and J. L. Barrett.	250.	750.	2000.
	c. Signature W. Cameron Forbes and J. L. Manning.	175.	600.	1000.
	d. Signature Francis Burton Harrison and J. L. Manning.	200.	600.	2500.
	e. Signature Francis Burton Harrison and A. P. Fitzsimmons.	125.	450.	—

1910 Issue

35	5 Pesos	Good	Fine	XF
	1910. Black on red underprint. Portrait President William McKinley at left. Similar to #26. Back: Red.			
	a. Signature W. Cameron Forbes and J. L. Barrett.	150.	500.	1200.
	b. Signature W. Cameron Forbes and J. L. Manning.	200.	1000.	2000.
	c. Signature Francis Burton Harrison and J. L. Manning.	200.	1000.	—
	d. Signature Francis Burton Harrison and A. P. Fitzsimmons.	100.	350.	1000.

1912 Issue

		Good	Fine	XF
36	**10 Pesos**			
	1912. Black on brown underprint. Portrait George Washington at lower center. Similar to #27. Back: Brown.			
	a. Signature W. Cameron Forbes and J. L. Barrett.	250.	1400.	—
	b. Signature W. Cameron Forbes and J. L. Manning.	250.	1400.	—
	c. Signature Francis Burton Harrison and J. L. Manning.	250.	1300.	—
	d. Signature Francis Burton Harrison and A. P. Fitzsimmons.	250.	300.	1600.

1916 Issue

		Good	Fine	XF
37	**50 Pesos**			
	1916. Black on red underprint. Portrait Gen. Henry W. Lawton at left. Similar to #29. Back: Red. Rare.	—	8000.	—
38	**100 Pesos**			
	1916. Black on green underprint. Portrait Ferdinand Magellan at center. Similar to #30. Back: Olive. Rare.	—	40,000	—

PHILIPPINE NATIONAL BANK

1917 Emergency WW I Issue

		VG	VF	UNC
39	**10 Centavos**			
	20.11.1917. Gold on yellow underprint. Back: Yellow. American bald eagle. Printer: Local.	—	20.00	50.00
40	**20 Centavos**			
	20.11.1917. Blue on yellow underprint. Back: Blue. American bald eagle. Printer: Local.	—	20.00	50.00

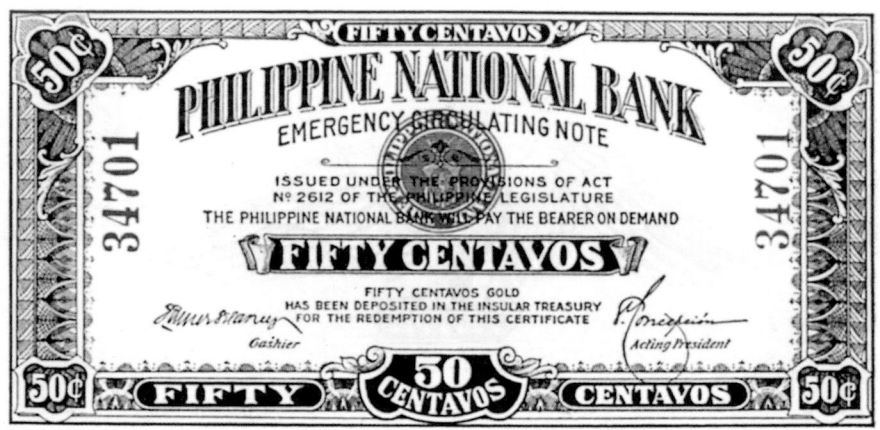

		VG	VF	UNC
41	**50 Centavos**			
	22.9.1917. Black on green underprint. Back: Green. American bald eagle. Printer: Local.	5.00	25.00	65.00
42	**1 Peso**			
	22.9.1917. Black on red underprint. Back: Red. American bald eagle. Printer: Local.	10.00	40.00	125.

1919 ND Emergency Issue

#43-43B new bank name, seal, signignature overprint on Bank of the Philippine Islands notes.

			VG	VF	UNC
43	5 Pesos				
	ND (1919 - old date 1912). Black on red underprint. Woman seated at left. Back: Light red. Overprint: New bank name, seal and signature on #7. Rare.		2100.	6000.	—
43A	10 Pesos				
	ND (1919 - old date 1912). Black on brown underprint. Woman with flowers at center. Back: Brown. Overprint: New bank name, seal and signature on #8. Rare.		—	8500.	—
43B	20 Pesos				
	ND (1919 - old date 1912). Black on lilac underprint. Woman at left. Back: Tan. Overprint: New bank name, seal and signature on #9. Rare.		5500.	—	—

1916-20 Regular Issue

#44-50 Replacement notes: Star prefix.

			Good	Fine	XF
44	1 Peso				
	1918. Black on orange underprint. Portrait Charles A. Conant at left. Back: Green. Printer: USBEP (without imprint).		100.	400.	1000.
45	2 Pesos				
	1916. Black on blue underprint. Portrait José Rizal at left (similar to Silver and Treasury Certificates). Back: Blue. Printer: USBEP (without imprint).		100.	400.	1000.
46	5 Pesos				
	1916. Black on red underprint. Portrait Pres. William McKinley at left (similar to Silver and Treasury Certificates). Back: Red-orange. Printer: USBEP (without imprint).				
	a. Signature S. Ferguson and H. Parker Willis.		250.	750.	—
	b. Signature S. Mercado and V. Concepcion.		10.00	40.00	90.00
	r. As b. Replacement note. * at end of serial #.		—	—	600.

47	10 Pesos	Good	Fine	XF

1916. Black on brown underprint. Portrait George Washington at center (similar to Silver and Treasury Certificates). Back: Brown. Printer: USBEP (without imprint).

		Good	Fine	XF
a.	Signature S. Ferguson and H. Parker Willis.	250.	750.	1500.
b.	Signature S. Mercado and V. Concepcion.	30.00	100.	350.
r.	As b. Replacement note. * at end of serial #.	—	800.	—

48	20 Pesos	Good	Fine	XF
	1919. Black on yellow underprint. Portrait Congressman William A. Jones at lower center. Back: Tan. Printer: USBEP (without imprint).	200.	650.	1250.

49	50 Pesos	Good	Fine	XF
	1920. Black on green underprint. Portrait Gen. Henry W. Lawton at left. Back: Red. Printer: USBEP (without imprint).	35.00	75.00	350.

Note: #49 was never officially issued. 10,000 pieces were captured and issued during WWII by the Japanese (serial #90001-100000). The others were looted by

Moros in the province of Mindanao who sold them at one-tenth of their face value.
This accounts for their relative availability.

		Good	Fine	XF
50	**100 Pesos**			
	1920. Green on red underprint. Portrait Ferdinand Magellan at center. Back: Olive. Printer: USBEP (without imprint). Rare.	—	3400.	—

1921 Issue

#51-55 designs like previous issue but notes without underprint. Replacemnet notes: Star prefix.

		Good	Fine	XF
51	**1 Peso**			
	1921. Black on orange underprint. Portrait Charles A. Conant at left. Like #44. Back: Green. Printer: USBEP (without imprint).	50.00	200.	550.
52	**2 Pesos**			
	1921. Black on blue underprint. Portrait José Rizal at left. Like #45. Back: Blue. Printer: USBEP (without imprint).	100.	300.	600.

		Good	Fine	XF
53	**5 Pesos**			
	1921. Black on red underprint. Portrait Pres. William McKinley at left. Like #46. Back: Red-orange. Printer: USBEP (without imprint).	40.00	75.00	150.
54	**10 Pesos**			
	1921. Black on brown underprint. Portrait George Washington at center. Like #47. Back: Brown. Printer: USBEP (without imprint).	25.00	100.	300.
55	**20 Pesos**			
	1921. Black on yellow underprint. Portrait Congressman William A. Jones at lower center. Like #48. Back: Tan. Printer: USBEP (without imprint).	20.00	75.00	800.

1924 Issue

#56, Replacement notes: Star prefix.

56	1 Peso	Good	Fine	XF
	1924. Black on orange underprint. Portrait Charles A. Conant at left. Like #51. Back: Green.	25.00	100.	500.

1937 Issue

#57-59 Replacement notes: Star prefix.

57	5 Pesos	VG	VF	UNC
	1937. Black on red underprint. Portrait Pres. McKinley at left. Similar to #53. Text reads: *PHILIPPINES.* Back: Red-orange. Printer: USBEP.	5.00	20.00	60.00

58	10 Pesos	VG	VF	UNC
	1937. Black on brown underprint. Portrait George Washington at center. Similar to #54. Text reads: *PHILIPPINES.* Back: Brown. Printer: USBEP.	50.00	150.	350.
59	20 Pesos			
	1937. Black on yellow underprint. Portrait Congressman William A. Jones at lower center. Similar to #55. Text reads: *PHILIPPINES.* Back: Tan. Printer: USBEP.	100.	225.	750.

PHILIPPINE ISLANDS

1918 Issue

#60-67 Replacement notes: Star prefix.

60	1 Peso	Good	Fine	XF
	1918. Black on green underprint. Portrait A. Mabini at left. Back: Green. Printer: USBEP (without imprint).			
	a. Signature Francis Burton Harrison and A. P. Fitzsimmons.	25.00	100.	325.
	b. Signature Francis Burton Harrison and V. Carmona.	50.00	100.	300.
61	2 Pesos			
	1918. Black on blue underprint. Portrait J. Rizal at left. Back: Blue. Printer: USBEP (without imprint).	100.	500.	1000.
62	5 Pesos			
	1918. Black on light red underprint. Portrait President William McKinley at left. Back: Red-orange. Printer: USBEP (without imprint).			
	a. Issued note.	250.	750.	7500.
	r. Replacement note. * at end of serial #.	—	—	10,000.

63	**10 Pesos**	Good	Fine	XF
	1918. Black on brown underprint. Portrait George Washington at center. Back: Brown. Printer: USBEP (without imprint).	400.	1000.	1500.

63A	**20 Pesos**	Good	Fine	XF
	1918. Black on yellow underprint. Mayon volcano at center. Ornate blue *XX* at upper left. Signature Francis Burton Harrison and A. P. Fitzsimmons. Back: Tan. Printer: USBEP (without imprint).	125.	1000.	2500.
64	**20 Pesos**			
	1918. Black on yellow underprint. Mayon volcano at center. Like #63A. Signature Francis Burton Harrison and V. Carmona. Back: Tan. Printer: USBEP (without imprint).	200.	650.	2750.
65	**50 Pesos**			
	1918. Black on green underprint. Portrait Gen. Lawton at left. Back: Red. Printer: USBEP (without imprint).			
	a. Signature Francis Burton Harrison and A. P. Fitzsimmons.	2500.	7500.	—
	b. Signature Francis Burton Harrison and V. Carmona.	2500.	14,000.	—
66	**100 Pesos**			
	1918. Black on green underprint. Portrait Ferdinand Magellan at center. Back: Olive. Printer: USBEP (without imprint).			
	a. Signature Francis Burton Harrison and A. P. Fitzsimmons. Rare.	—	—	—
	b. Signature Francis Burton Harrison and V. Carmona. Rare.	3000.	4250.	—
67	**500 Pesos**			
	1918. Black on orange underprint. Portrait Legazpi at center. Back: Purple. Printer: USBEP (without imprint). Rare.	—	750.	—

1924 Issue

#68-72 without underprint, otherwise designs like previous issue. Replacement notes: Star prefix.

68	1 Peso	Good	Fine	XF
	1924. Black. Portrait A. Mabini at left. Like #60. Back: Green. Printer: USBEP (without imprint).			
	a. Signature Leonard Wood and Salv. Lagdameo with title: *Acting Treasurer*.	15.00	75.00	200.
	b. Signature Leonard Wood and Salv. Lagdameo with title: *Treasurer*.	20.00	90.00	225.
	c. Signature H. L. Stimson and Salv. Lagdameo.	30.00	100.	200.
	r. As a or c. Remainder. * at end of serial #.	—	1800.	—
69	2 Pesos			
	1924. Black. Portrait J. Rizal at left. Like #61, but large denomination numeral added in red at lower left center. Back: Blue. Printer: USBEP (without imprint).			
	a. Signature Leonard Wood and Salv. Lagdameo with title: *Acting Treasurer*.	50.00	250.	550.
	b. Signature Leonard Wood and Salv. Lagdameo with title: *Treasurer*.	60.00	300.	600.
	c. Signature Henry L. Stimson and Salv. Lagdameo.	75.00	350.	500.

70	5 Pesos	Good	Fine	XF
	1924. Black. Portrait President William McKinley at left. Like #62. Printer: USBEP (without imprint).	75.00	250.	800.

71	**10 Pesos**	Good	Fine	XF
	1924. Black. Portrait George Washington at center. Like #63. Back: Brown. Printer: USBEP (without imprint).	60.00	200.	600.
72	**500 Pesos**			
	1924. Black on blue underprint. Portrait Legazpi at center. Blue numeral. Like #67. Printer: USBEP (without imprint).			
	a. Back light green.	2500.	6000.	10,000.
	p. Back purple. Proof.	—	—	—

Note: Though official records indicate that the backs of #72 were printed in purple, the only issued notes seen in collections have lt. green backs. Further reports are needed.

1929 Issue

#73-80 Replacement notes: Star prefix.

Many changes were effected on US-Philippine currency with the 1929 Issue, as the United States changed from the large to small size formats. Significant design alterations were introduced as well as some color changes.

73	**1 Peso**	Good	Fine	XF
	1929. Black on orange underprint. Portrait A. Mabini at left. Similar to #60 with minor alterations in plate. Back: Orange. Printer: USBEP (without imprint).			
	a. Signature Dwight F. Davis and Salv. Lagdameo.	50.00	250.	350.
	b. Signature Theodore Roosevelt and Salv. Lagdameo.	55.00	275.	300.
	c. Signature Frank Murphy and Salv. Lagdameo.	10.00	25.00	125.
74	**2 Pesos**			
	1929. Black on blue underprint. Portrait J. Rizal at left. Similar to #61 with minor alterations in plate. Back: Blue. Printer: USBEP (without imprint).			
	a. Signature Theodore Roosevelt and Salv. Lagdameo.	15.00	200.	250.
	b. Signature Frank Murphy and Salv. Lagdameo.	10.00	175.	325.
	r. As b. Replacement note. * at end of serial #.	—	900.	—
	s. Specimen. Pin perforated.	—	Unc	2000.
75	**5 Pesos**			
	1929. Black on yellow underprint. Portrait William McKinley at left, Adm. Dewey at right. Back: Yellow. Printer: USBEP (without imprint).	120.	500.	1300.

76	10 Pesos	Good	Fine	XF
	1929. Black on brown underprint. Portrait George Washington at left. Back: Brown. Printer: USBEP (without imprint).			
	a. Issued note.	75.00	400.	1250.
	p. Proof. Uniface front.	—	Unc	550.
77	20 Pesos			
	1929. Black on yellow underprint. Mayon volcano at center. Similar to #64 with minor alterations in plate. Back: Tan. Printer: USBEP (without imprint).	150.	500.	1250.
78	50 Pesos			
	1929. Black on pink underprint. Portrait Gen. Lawton at left. Back: Dark red. Printer: USBEP (without imprint).	500.	3500.	—
79	100 Pesos			
	1929. Black on green underprint. Portrait Ferdinand Magellan at left. Back: Green. Printer: USBEP (without imprint). Rare.	—	2500.	—
80	500 Pesos			
	1929. Black on orange underprint. Portrait Legazpi at left. Back: Purple. Printer: USBEP (without imprint). Rare.	—	—	—

COMMONWEALTH

1936 Issue

#81-88 new red Commonwealth seal. Signature Manuel Quezon and Antonio Ramos. Title reads: *PHILIPPINES*. Replacement notes: Star prefix.

81	1 Peso	VG	VF	UNC
	1936. Black on orange underprint. Portrait A. Mabini at left. Similar to #73. New red Commonwealth seal. Signature Manuel Quezon and Antonio Ramos. Back: Orange. Printer: USBEP (without imprint).			
	a. Issued note.	7.50	25.00	75.00
	r. Replacement note. * at end of serial #.	300.	—	—

82	2 Pesos		VG	VF	UNC

1936. Black on blue underprint. Portrait J. Rizal at left. Similar to #74. New red Commonwealth seal. Signature Manuel Quezon and Antonio Ramos. Back: Blue. Printer: USBEP (without imprint). — 40.00 — 250. — 400.

83 5 Pesos

1936. Black on yellow underprint. Portrait William McKinley at left, Adm. Dewey at right. Similar to #75. New red Commonwealth seal. Signature Manuel Quezon and Antonio Ramos. Back: Yellow. Printer: USBEP (without imprint).

a. Regular issue. Serial # D1D to D3 244 000D. — 40.00 — 250. — 400.

b. U.S.A. War Department Issue (1944). D3 244 001D to D3 544 000D. — 50.00 — 400. — 750.

84 10 Pesos

1936. Black on brown underprint. Portrait George Washington at left. Similar to #76. New red Commonwealth seal. Signature Manuel Quezon and Antonio Ramos. Printer: USBEP (without imprint).

a. Regular issue. Serial # D1D to D2 024 000D. — 75.00 — 650. — 1200.

b. U.S.A. War Department issue (1944). D2 024 001D to D2 174 000D. — 150. — 750. — 1500.

85 20 Pesos

1936. Black on yellow underprint. Mayon volcano at center. Similar to #77. New red Commonwealth seal. Signature Manuel Quezon and Antonio Ramos. Back: Tan. Printer: USBEP (without imprint).

a. Regular issue. D1D to D1 664 000D. — 75.00 — 800. — 1500.

b. U.S.A. War Department issue (1944). D1 664 001D to D1 739 000D. — 500. — 2750. — 5000.

86 50 Pesos

1936. Black on pink underprint. Portrait Gen. Lawton at left. Similar to #78. New red Commonwealth seal. Signature Manuel Quezon and Antonio Ramos. Back: Dark red. Printer: USBEP (without imprint). — 550. — 2750. — 5500.

87 100 Pesos

1936. Black on green underprint. Portrait Ferdinand Magellan at left. Similar to #79. New red Commonwealth seal. Signature Manuel Quezon and Antonio Ramos. Back: Green. Printer: USBEP (without imprint).

a. Regular issue. Serial # D1D to D41 000D. — 500. — 1500. — —

b. U.S.A. War Department issue (1944). D41 001D to D56 000D. Rare. — 1750. — — — —

88	500 Pesos	VG	VF	UNC
	1936. Black on orange underprint. Portrait Legazpi at left. Similar to #80. New red Commonwealth seal. Signature Manuel Quezon and Antonio Ramos. Back: Purple. Printer: USBEP (without imprint). Rare.	2500.	13,000.	—

Note: #83b, 84b, 85b and 87b were made at the request of Army Headquarters, Brisbane, Australia in 1944 for use in military operations.

1941 Issue

#89-93 like previous issue. Replacement notes: Star prefix.

89	1 Peso	VG	VF	UNC
	1941. Black on orange underprint. Portrait A. Mabini at left. Like #81. Signature Manuel Quezon and A.S. de Leon. Back: Orange. Printer: USBEP (without imprint).			
	a. Regular issue. Serial # E1E to E6 000 000E.	2.50	10.00	20.00
	b. Processed to simulate used currency at Bureau of Standards (1943). #E6 008 001E to E6 056 000E; E6 064 001E to E6 072 000E; E6 080 001E to E6 324 000E. Total 300,000 notes.	125.	450.	—
	c. Naval Aviators' Emergency Money Packet notes (1944). E6 324 001E to E6 524 000E.	25.00	125.	250.
	r. Replacement note. * at end of serial #.	—	—	300.
90	2 Pesos			
	1941. Black on blue underprint. Portrait J. Rizal at left. Like #82. Signature Manuel Quezon and A.S. de Leon. Back: Blue. Printer: USBEP (without imprint).	35.00	100.	375.
91	5 Pesos			
	1941. Black on yellow underprint. Portrait William McKinley at left, Adm. Dewey at right. Like #83. Signature Manuel Quezon and A.S. de Leon. Back: Yellow. Printer: USBEP (without imprint).			
	a. Regular issue. Serial #E1E to E1 188 000E.	40.00	200.	400.
	b. Processed like #89b (1943). #E1 208 001E to E1 328 000E.	650.	—	—
	c. Packet notes like #89c (1944). #E1 328 001E to E1 348 000E.	100.	500.	950.
	r. As a. Replacement note. * at end of serial #.	—	1000.	—

92	10 Pesos	VG	VF	UNC
	1941. Black on brown underprint. Portrait George Washington at left. Like #84. Signature Manuel Quezon and A.S. de Leon. Back: Brown. Printer: USBEP (without imprint).			
	a. Regular issue. Serial #E1E to E800 000E.	75.00	350.	750.
	b. Processed like #89b (1943). E810 001E to E870 000E.	10,000.	—	—
	c. Packet notes like #89c (1944). #E870 001E to E890 000E.	125.	450.	1000.
93	20 Pesos			
	1941. Black on yellow underprint. Mayon volcano at center. Like #85. Signature Manuel Quezon and A.S. de Leon. Back: Tan. Printer: USBEP (without imprint).	75.00	325.	—

Note: 50, 100 and 500 Pesos notes Series of 1941 were printed but never shipped because of the outbreak of World War II. All were destroyed in 1949, leaving extant only proof impressions and specimen sheets.

1944 ND Victory Issue

#94-101 with overpritn text: *VICTORY Series No. 66* **twice on face instead of date, blue seal. Replacement notes: Star suffix.**

94	1 Peso	VG	VF	UNC
	ND (1944). Black on orange underprint. Portrait A. Mabini at left. Like #89. Text: *VICTORY*. Series No. 66 twice instead of date, with blue seal. Signature Sergio Osmeña and J. Hernandez. Back: Orange. Overprint: Black VICTORY in large letters on back. Printer: USBEP (without imprint).			
	a. Issued note.	.75	3.00	11.00
	r. Replacement note. * at end of serial #.	—	75.00	—
	s. Specimen.	—	—	800.

95	2 Pesos	VG	VF	UNC
	ND (1944). Black on blue underprint. Portrait J. Rizal at left. Like #90. Text: *VICTORY*. Series No. 66 twice instead of date, with blue seal. Back: Blue. Overprint: Black VICTORY in large letters on back. Printer: USBEP (without imprint).			
	a. Signature Sergio Osmeña and J. Hernandez with title: *Auditor General*.	1.00	4.00	20.00
	b. Signature Manuel Roxas and M. Guevara with title: *Treasurer*.	5.00	20.00	70.00
	r. Replacement note. * at start of serial #.	—	75.00	—
	s. Specimen. Pin perforated.	—	—	1000.
96	5 Pesos			
	ND (1944). Black on yellow underprint. Portrait William McKinley at left, Adm. Dewey at right. Like #91. Text: *VICTORY*. Series No. 66 twice instead of date, with blue seal. Signature Sergio Osmeña and J. Hernandez. Back: Yellow. Overprint: Black VICTORY in large letters on back. Printer: USBEP (without imprint).			
	a. Issued note.	2.50	10.00	65.00
	r. Replacement note. * at start of serial #.	—	1500.	—
	s. Specimen. Pin perforated.	—	—	1500.
97	10 Pesos			
	ND (1944). Black on brown underprint. Portrait George Washington at left. Like #92. Text: *VICTORY*. Series No. 66 twice instead of date, with blue seal. Signature Sergio Osmeña and J. Hernandez. Back: Brown. Overprint: Black VICTORY in large letters on back. Printer: USBEP (without imprint).			
	a. Issued note.	5.00	20.00	130.
	s. Specimen. Pin perforated.	—	—	1500.
98	20 Pesos			
	ND (1944). Black on yellow underprint. Mayon volcano at center. Like #93. Text: *VICTORY*. Series No. 66 twice instead of date, with blue seal. Back: Tan. Overprint: Black VICTORY in large letters on back. Printer: USBEP (without imprint).			
	a. Signature Sergio Osmeña and J. Hernandez with title: *Auditor General*.	15.00	150.	325.
	b. Signature Manuel Roxas and M. Guevara with title: *Treasurer*.	50.00	250.	500.
	s. Specimen. Pin perforated.	—	—	2000.

99	50 Pesos	VG	VF	UNC

ND (1944). Black on pink underprint. Portrait Gen. Lawton at left. Like #86. Text:
VICTORY. Series No. 66 twice instead of date, with blue seal. Back: Dark red.
Overprint: Black VICTORY in large letters on back. Printer: USBEP (without
imprint).

	VG	VF	UNC
a. Signature Sergio Osmeña and J. Hernandez with title: *Auditor General.*	75.00	750.	1750.
b. Signature Manuel Roxas and M. Guevara with title: *Treasurer.*	40.00	375.	1000.
s. Specimen. Pin perforated.	—	—	2000.

100	100 Pesos	VG	VF	UNC

ND (1944). Black on green underprint. Portrait Ferdinand Magellan at left. Like
#87. Text: VICTORY Series No. 66 twice instead of date, with blue seal. Back:
Green. Overprint: Black VICTORY in large letters on back. Printer: USBEP (without
imprint).

	VG	VF	UNC
a. 1944. Sergio Osmeña and J. Hernandez with title: *Auditor General.*	75.00	325.	850.
b. Signature Sergio Osmeña and M. Guevara with title: *Treasurer.*	100.	350.	1000.
c. Signature Manuel Roxas and M. Guevara.	250.	1000.	2000.
r. As a. Replacement note. * at start of serial #.	—	2600.	—

101	500 Pesos			

ND (1944). Black on orange underprint. Portrait Legazpi at left. Like #88. Text:
VICTORY. Series No. 66 twice instead of date, with blue seal. Back: Purple.
Overprint: Black VICTORY in large letters on back. Printer: USBEP (without
imprint).

	VG	VF	UNC
a. Signature Sergio Osmeña and J. Hernandez with title: *Auditor General.*	6000.	15,000.	2200.
b. Signature Sergio Osmeña and M. Guevara with title: *Treasurer.*	2500.	10,000.	1200.
c. Signature Manuel Roxas and M. Guevara.	1250.	5000.	2400.

ERROR NOTES

by Frederick J. Bart and Doris A. Bart

United States Paper Money Production

Paper money is produced at Bureau of Engraving and Printing (BEP) in Washington, D.C. with a satellite facility in Fort Worth Texas. Federal Reserve Notes are printed via the dry intaglio method and finished on the currency overprinting and processing equipment (COPE).

First Printing (back). Back designs are produced on a 32 subject printing plate. Each plate has the back design along with the same back plate check number. The sheet passes between the engraved plate and the impression cylinder under tremendous pressure. The sheet is then allowed to dry before advancing to the next stage of printing.

Second Printing (face). The second printing consists of the portrait, outer borders, series, and engraved signatures of the Treasurer of the United States and the Secretary of the Treasury. The second printing is accomplished in black ink. After the printing, the sheets are cut vertically into sixteen subject panes and then piled into stacks of 10,000 half sheets to advance to the third stage of printing

Third Printing (overprint). The last stage includes the serial numbers and seals. However, in some cases the treasury seal may be applied independently of the serial numbers. The currency overprinting and processing equipment contains built in electronic and photoelectric sensors that interrupt the operation when a mistake is found. Otherwise, the sheets are stacked into piles of one hundred consecutively numbered bills, strapped together and sealed into a "brick" with plastic shrink-wrap. The bricks are then sent to 12 Federal Reserve banks or one of the 24 Federal Reserve Bank branches.

With literally billions of notes produced on an annual basis, it becomes impossible for even experienced inspectors within the BEP to catch every mistake. This chapter presents a smattering of errors that have escaped the watchful eyes of government personnel. This format is based upon the book,

United States Paper Money: A Comprehensive Catalog & Price Guide, 2nd Edition, Frederick J. Bart, Krause Publications, 2003.

Numerous factors influence the price of error currency. These include: the state of preservation or grade, the type of paper money, the series, the denomination, the rarity, and eye-appeal.

DOUBLE DENOMINATIONS

The dual denomination oddity is aptly titled "The King of Errors". It reigns supreme among paper money mistakes. The double denomination note has the face of one value and the back of another. Large size double denominations are found in more different varieties than those on small size notes. The authors speculate that as many as two hundred double-denomination notes exist. The value of both large and small size double denomination notes are about the same.

Fine $17,500   EF $25,000   CU $27,500

FAULTY ALIGNMENTS

Faulty alignments are caused by from improper relationship between the printed designs on one side of the note relative to the other side. One side of the note is well centered while the other side appears "shifted". Faulty alignments are a common error and range from just a small "shift" to a major mis-position showing portions of the adjacent note. Collectors of all levels seek examples of faulty alignments.

Minor faulty alignments value;

Fine $75
EF $150
CU $250

More dramatic faulty alignments value;

Fine $500
EF $1000
CU $2000

INSUFFICIENT INKINGS

Insufficient inking occurs when the ink fountain fails to fully charge or fill the printing plate. This causes the image to be faint or incomplete. The insufficient inking error may involve all or part of the design, depending on the amount of the plate which is affected. Most insufficient inking occurs on the 1st or 2nd printings.

Minor insufficient ink value;

Fine $50
EF $100
CU $200

More dramatic insufficient ink;

Fine $100
EF $200
CU $400

INVERTED BACKS

The inverted back error is caused when a stack of currency sheets, after receiving the first printing, is rotated 180 degrees and enters the printing press. In actuality, because the back is printed first the error should be called an "inverted face". One might anticipate that the inverted back error would be rather common, as there is no visible error for the BEP inspectors to notice; however, this is one of the most difficult errors to find.

Small size inverted backs value;

Fine $500
EF $1000
CU $2000

Large size inverted back value;

Fine $1500
EF $3000
CU $7500

BLANK BACKS

Missing printing errors are readily identified because the back of the note is entirely missing. There are other types of missing printing that occur during the 2nd and 3rd printing which will be covered in this chapter. Most common cause of this error is due to two uncut sheets being fed into the press at the same time, with one sheet accepting an impression and the other sheet passing through protected and leaving the press blank.

Fine $150   EF $250   CU $350

MULTIPLE ERRORS

The scarcity of multiple errors cannot be overstated. Multiple errors arise independently of each other either during the printing or cutting process. The value of these errors remains a matter of negotiation and agreement between the seller and the buyer. Therefore it is impractical to attempt to provide any guide to values of these elusive multiple mistakes.

MULTIPLE PRINTINGS

Multiple printing errors go through the normal three printing stages. There are several causes for this error: a loose impression cylinders or the press operator stops the machinery, keeps the sheet in position, and then re-starts the press. However, the most common cause of the multiple printing error is a sheet which is re-run through the same printing press for a second or subsequent time. If the note is re-fed thru the 1st or 2nd printing stages, one often finds different plate check numbers on the finished product. Value varies depending on the eye-appeal of the error.

Fine $750
EF $1250
CU $2000

OBSTRUCTED PRINTINGS

Whenever stray material comes between the currency paper and the printing plate an obstruction error occurs. The intervening material causes a portion of the note to be left blank. Several causes are paper, cellophane, fiber threads, adhesive bandage backing, masking tape and cardboard, to mention a few. If the obstructing item is recovered along with the affected note, the value of the error increases significantly.

Obstructed print without fragment value;

Fine $100
EF $250
CU $500

Obstructed print with fragment value;

Fine $2500
EF $5000
CU $7500

OFFSET PRINTINGS

Offset errors look like one side of the note "bled through" to the other. However, the offset is a mirror image of the note's opposite side. This error occurs when a sheet of currency fails to enter the press. As such, the plate contacts the impression cylinder. When the next currency sheet is inserted it receives not only the intended printing on the correct side, but a transfer or offset printing on the opposite side as well. The ink lightens with each sheet that is fed. Not surprisingly, the amount of the design imprinted onto the impression cylinder dictates the size and shape of the offset. Offsets occur front to back or back to front. The rich, bold offsets demand the highest price; with the first and second impressions being desirable.

Minor partial offset value
Fine $15   EF $25   CU $35

Complete offset value
Fine $100   EF $200   CU $400

OVERPRINTS (3rd print) ON BACK

The serial number, Treasury seal and, if applicable, the Federal Reserve bank or universal seal and district numbers appear on the wrong side of the bill. Overprint on back errors occur when the sheet is fed into the press with the back side towards the overprinting press instead of the front. Inverted overprinted errors on back occur the same way, except the sheet is not only fed on the wrong side but rotated 180 degrees causing the 3rd printing to be inverted as well. Mistakes appear on both sides of the note. There is a lack of information on the face while the back appears quite crowded.

Overprint on back;
Fine $100   EF $175   CU $350

Overprint on back inverted value;
Fine $750   EF $1500   CU $3500

INVERTED OVERPRINTS

Inverted overprints demonstrate the seal and serial numbers upside down relative to the face printing. These errors occur when the ½ sheet is fed into the press 180 degrees from the proper alignment before and during the 3rd printing.

Inverted Overprint value;
Fine $150   EF $355   CU $750

MISALIGNED OVERPRINTS

Misaligned overprint errors are easily spotted by the shift in the 3rd printing causing the serial numbers and seals to be off center. This occurs when the paper is improperly fed either at a angle or with unequal amounts of paper on the right and left sides. For a misalignment to qualify as an error, a portion of the overprint must rest atop a portion of the design it was not intended to cover. These errors can range from hardly noticeable—and, therefore only minimally desirable-- to incredibly dramatic and the object of great desire.

Minor Misaligned Overprint value;

Fine $30
EF $45
CU $65

Major Misaligned Overprint value;

Fine $250
EF $500
CU $800

MISSING OVERPRINTS

Missing overprint error lacks the application of the 3rd printing. An example of this mistake is missing the serial numbers and seals. The error occurs from any of several different causes. The most frequent occurrence involves two sheets being fed through the overprinting press at the same time. This results in the top sheet accept a normal imprint while the bottom sheet misses the 3rd printing. Another cause of the missing overprint error develops when the sheet is fed properly, but the press fails to engage and does not make contact with the sheet. Alternatively, there may be a large obstruction blocking the sheet.

Fine $200
EF $500
CU $1000

MISSING 2ND PRINTINGS

This error occurs again when 2 sheets are fed at the same time, with the top sheet receiving the second printing and the bottom sheet missing all of the second printing. Another explanation for this visually dramatic mistake is the accidental advancement of a stack of sheets from the 1st printing presses to the overprinting presses without the intervening stop for the face printing. These are among the most dramatic of mistakes encountered.

L 17930132 A

12   12

L 17930132 A
12   12

Fine $250
EF $500
CU $850

MISMATCHED SERIAL NUMBERS

Mismatched serial numbers occur when a press operator fails to set the same sequence of numbers on the two different numbering wheels prior to initiating the printing. Mismatched errors will also occur when the numbering machine sticks at a particular serial number, while the other continues to advance normally. Prefix and suffix letters also are subject to be mismatched. Mismatched prefix or suffix letters result from human error during the press set-up. Mismatched characters are actually scarcer than mismatched numbers.

Single Digit Mismatch value
Fine $250   EF $500   CU $1000

Mismatch Prefix value
Fine $250   EF $500   CU $750

STUCK DIGITS

Stuck digit errors and partially turned digits occur from a clogging of the numbering wheel on the cylinder that imprints the serial numbers. If the wheel freezes in place it will print a partially turned digit. Once it advances a stuck digit may result

Stuck Digit value;
Fine $40   EF $75   CU $125

CUTTING ERRORS

Cutting errors occur during the terminal stage of production. The 16-subject half-sheets are separated into 2-subject blocks and then into individual notes. A cutting error is generated by misalignment of the uncut sheet upon meeting the knives. Unlike faulty alignments, which occur on only one side of the note. The cutting error shows a shift or misalignment on both sides from being cut incorrectly. There are various types of cutting errors from minor to dramatic.

Minor Cutting Error
Fine $5   EF $15   CU $45

Major Cutting Error value;

Fine $750   EF $3000   CU $5500

GUTTER OR INTERIOR FOLDS

Gutter fold or interior folds occur when a wrinkle occurs in the currency paper as it receives a printed image. The appearance is an unprinted, blank, white channel interrupting the back, face, or over printing.

Occasionally, the paper will wrinkle several times causing multiple gutters. Gutters are the second most common type of errors found on United States paper money.

Single Gutter Fold value;

Fine $30   EF $40   CU $50

Multiple Gutter Fold value;
Fine $75   EF $150   CU $300

PRINTED OR EXTERIOR FOLDS

Printed folds may occur prior to or during any stage of the production process. As the name implies, the currency sheet folds over and remains folded during the printing. The ultimate shape of the note depends upon whether the sheet unfolds before cutting. The fold may be minor with just a corner tip being folded or more dramatic with a large portion of the note being folded. Occasionally a tear occurs in the paper with a similar effect in the final product.

Printed Fold value;

Fine $500
EF $1500
CU $2500

Printed Tear value
Fine $500   EF $1500   CU $2500

INK SMEARS

Ink smears occur from the printing plates being cleaned inadequately. The amount of residual ink left on the surface of the plate determines the size and shape of the smear. This can range from a small spot or fine line to a large portion of the note covered with ink. The term "solvent smear" is solvent, which smears. This occurs when the ink is heavily diluted with a solvent solution. The excessive amount of solvent reaches the printing plate causing the ink to be blurry and watery.

Minor Ink Smear value;
Fine $10   EF $25   CU $40

Major Ink Smear value;
Fine $150   EF $300   CU $500

Solvent Smear value;
Fine $150   EF $300   CU $500

FAKE ERRORS

Collectors need to be aware of the existence of fake errors. Trickery and greed are everywhere. Unscrupulous sellers go to great lengths to fool collectors. Internet auction sites are overrun with bogus mistakes. Some of the most frequently encountered alterations include: the backs of notes which are yellow or orange, seals or serial numbers which have been erased, removed, or changed color, spurious addition of a design, and cutting errors created from uncut sheets sold directly to the public. numbers and seals. And one of the most dramatic is the cutting error. On Federal Reserve notes from 1981 or later with the serial numbers beginning with 96000000, most of these notes were released in uncut sheet form and are especially subject to alteration.

AT PMG, EVERY DAY IS
INDEPENDENCE DAY